A Global History A Global History A Global History A Global History A Global History A Global History

The World since 1500

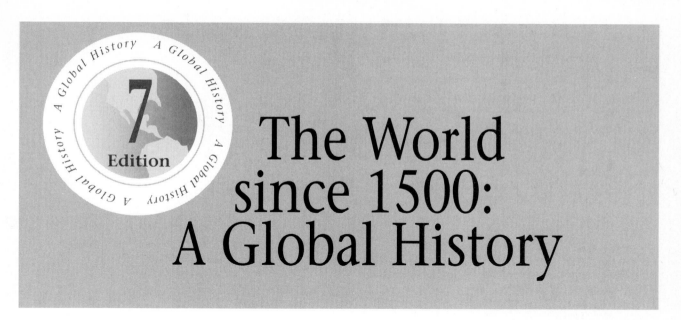

7 Edition

A Global History A Global History A Global History A Global History A Global History

The World since 1500: A Global History

L.S. Stavrianos

PRENTICE HALL, Englewood Cliffs, NJ 07632

Library of Congress Cataloging-in-Publication Data
Stavrianos, Leften Stavros.
    The World since 1500: a global history/L.S. Stavrianos.—7th
ed.
        p.   cm.
    Includes bibliographical references and index.
    ISBN 0–13–250912–1
    1. History, Modern.   I. title.
D208.S7   1995
909.08—dc20 94-25899

                                        CIP

Editorial/production supervision: *Mary Kathryn Bsales*
Acquisitions editor: *Sally Constable*
Editorial assistant: *Tamara Mann*
Buyer: *Nick Sklitsis*
Interior and cover design: *Amy Rosen*
Page layout: *Mike Bertrand, Yvette Raven, Joh Lisa*
Editor-in-chief: *Charlyce Jones Owen*
Marketing manager: *Alison Pendergast*
Copy editor: *Eleanor Ode Walter*
Photo editor: *Lorinda Morris-Nantz*
Photo researchers: *Teri Stratford and Page Poore Kidder*
Cover art: *Nova Universi Orbis Descripto*, Paris, 1602. Map engraved for
Le Clerc by Jodocus Hondius. Hand-colored copper plate engraving.
Courtesy of W. Graham Arader III, New York.

© 1995, 1991, 1988, 1982, 1975, 1971, 1966 by Prentice-Hall, Inc.
A Simon & Schuster Company
Englewood Cliffs, New Jersey 07632

Printed in the United States of America
10 9 8 7 6 5 4 3 2

ISBN   0-13-250912-1

Prentice-Hall International (UK) Limited, *London*
Prentice-Hall of Australia Pty. Limited, *Sydney*
Prentice-Hall Canada Inc., *Toronto*
Prentice-Hall Hispanoamericana, S.A., *Mexico*
Prentice-Hall of India Private Limited, *New Delhi*
Prentice-Hall of Japan, Inc., *Tokyo*
Simon & Schuster Asia Pte. Ltd., *Singapore*
Editora Prentice-Hall do Brasil, Ltda., *Rio de Janeiro*

This book is for
Marjorie, Peter,
and in Memory of Bertha

Contents

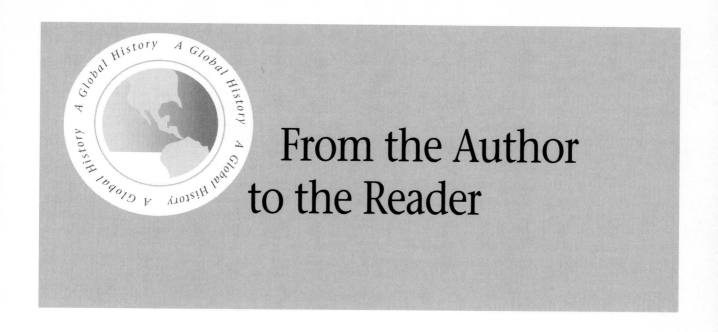

From the Author to the Reader

The use of history is to give value to the present hour.

Ralph Waldo Emerson

The old term "Western civilization" no longer holds. World events and the common needs of all humanity are joining the culture of Asia with the culture of Europe and the Americas, to form for the first time a world civilization.

Franklin Delano Roosevelt

This book is distinctive in three ways.

First, it connects the past to the present. History is something more than "one damned thing after another," as a famous historian once complained. That type of history is more likely to give intellectual indigestion than intellectual understanding. This does not mean that only the study of current affairs is useful and worthwhile. Rather it means that the past should be analyzed in a manner that is meaningful for the present, and that the relationship between past and present should be noted and emphasized. This is why each of the four parts of this volume ends with an essay entitled "What It Means for Us Today."

The second distinctive feature of this book is that it connects not only the past and the present but also the present and the future. Many argue that history cannot be used to foresee the future because it is not an exact science like chemistry or physics. They argue that history deals with human beings whose actions cannot be predicted with the precision and certainty with which a chemist can predict what will happen when element A is combined with element B. Therefore, it is argued that the historian cannot use the past with the confidence that a scientist can use predictable experiments in the laboratory.

On first thought this argument seems correct, but if we think again we find that it is false. Its error becomes clear if we compare meteorologist with historians. Meteorologists are very successful in predicting that tornados will strike in this region or that, and therefore they are considered scientists. But meteorologists cannot predict which house in a given region will be struck and which house will not. This does not mean that meteorology is not a science. It only means that different sciences provide different levels of predictability. Therefore the chemist with his flasks can predict more precisely than the meteorologist with his gauges. Yet meteorology remains a valid science with useful predictive purposes, and it is becoming steadily more precise with the use of computers and satellites.

So it is with history. It cannot be used like a

crystal ball to predict which political party will win or what national leader will be assassinated or which country will have a revolution or where a war will break out. But history, properly studied, shows what combination of conditions and policies have resulted in the past in assassinations and revolutions and wars. If we understand such past patterns, then we have some guide to the present and to the future. But if we have not studied the past, the present will seem mysterious and the future terrifying.

The last chapter in the second volume of this history (*The World since 1500)* is entitled "Second Industrial Revolution: Global Repercussions." It shows that all societies today—developed and underdeveloped, capitalist and socialist—are experiencing profound internal disruptions as well as the external threat of "nuclear winter." If we end our history with that chapter, the future will indeed seem hopeless. The reader might well ask, "Why bother studying the history of the past since none of us may survive to enjoy the future?" For this reason that final chapter is followed by a concluding essay entitled "Human Prospects," in which we try to find some guidelines from our study of the past and present so that we can have some idea what to expect in the future.

This brings us to the third distinctive feature of this book, which is that it is a *world* history. It deals with the entire globe rather than with one country or region. It is concerned with *all* peoples. It is as though you, the reader, were perched on the moon looking down on our whole vast planet. From there your viewpoint would be different from that of an observer living in Washington, D.C., London, or Paris—or for that matter, in Peking, Delhi, or Cairo.

This global approach is a departure from traditional modern history. Since the days of the Enlightenment in the eighteenth century, historical emphasis has been on nations rather than on peoples. But in recent years, interest in world history has been growing, in response to present-day events that are sweeping our globe. With astronauts and cosmonauts encircling the entire planet in a few hours and venturing out in space exploration and with headlines concerned just as much with Asia and Africa as with Europe and the Americas, we must have a wider angle of vision. World history is essential for the understanding of a world that has become "one" in reality as well as in rhetoric.

The need for world understanding is not the only reason for turning to world history. Equally important is the fact that the story of humankind from its very beginnings has a basic unity that must be recognized and respected.

We cannot truly understand either Western or non-Western history unless we have a global overview that encompasses both. Then we can see how much interaction there is between all peoples in all times, and how important that interaction is in determining the course of human history.

At first the interaction was fitful and rather slight. But then the Europeans Columbus and da Gama set forth on their overseas explorations. In the following decades they and their successors brought all parts of the world into direct contact, and the intimacy of the contact has grown steadily to the present day. By contrast, the many human communities prior to 1500 had existed in varying degrees of isolation. Yet this isolation was never absolute. During the long millennia before the European discoveries, the various branches of the human race had interacted one with the other—though the precise degree to which they did differed enormously according to time and location. The details of this interaction, from early human history to roughly the year 1500, are the subject of this book. Following that date, the earth, in relation to humankind's growing communication and transportation facilities, has been steadily shrinking faster and faster, so that today it has become a "spaceship earth," a "global village."

If we accept the fact that all people share a common world history, how can we possibly learn about the whole world by taking a single course or reading a single book? Some historians say that world history, by definition, encompasses all civilizations, and thus it is a subject far too broad for classroom purposes. Western civilization, they say, is barely manageable by itself; how can all the other civilizations—including the Chinese, the Indian , and the Middle Eastern—all be encompassed? The answer, of course, is that they cannot, and that world history, *thus defined,* is obviously impractical. But such a definition is inaccurate and misleading. World history is not the sum of histories of the civilizations of the world, just as Western history is not the sum of the histories of the countries of the West.

If the study of Western civilization were simply a series of surveys of British history, of German history, of French, Italian, Spanish, Balkan, and the rest, Western civilization would not be a feasible subject of study. Yet, in fact, it is feasible, and the reason is that the approach is not agglomerative. Rather it focuses on those historical forces or movements that affected the West as a whole, such as Christianity, Islam, the Crusades, the Renaissance, the Reformation, the French Revolution, the scientific and industrial revolutions, and so forth. So it is with world history, though the stage in this case is global rather than regional, and the emphasis consequently is on movements of worldwide influence.

In Paleolithic times, for example, humans emerged in Africa and gradually spread through Eurasia, Australia, and the Americas. The fateful breakthrough to agriculture occurred during the neolithic period, followed by metalworking and assorted other crafts and leading to urban life and civilization. This in turn led to the development of the great Eurasian civilizations—the Chinese, Indian, Middle Eastern, and European—which for millennia developed autonomously along parallel lines. The amount of interaction among Eurasian civilizations varied as a result of powerful interregional historical forces such as Hellenism, Christianity, Buddhism, and the recurring invasions from the central Eurasian steppes. After 1500 this Eurasian balance gradually gave way to a global unity imposed by an emerging West and culminating in the nineteenth century in an unprecedented worldwide domination. Finally in the twentieth century, world history becomes the story of the growing reaction against this domination and the perilous groping toward a new world balance that was made necessary by the rapid diffusion of Western technology and ideology. This, in a nutshell, is the rationale and structure of world history. It is a structure that is no more complex than that of Western history. The difference is merely that the stage is our planet rather than the continent of Europe.

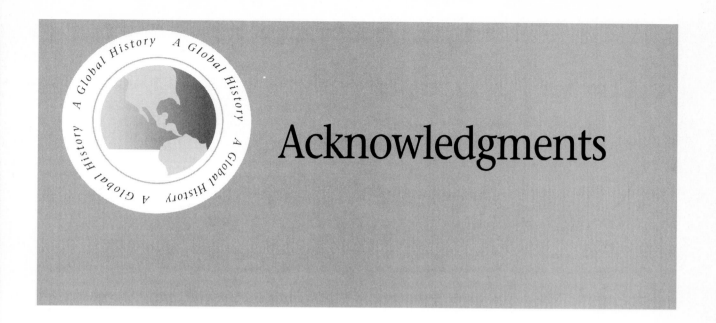

Acknowledgments

In the preparation of this edition, the author was generously assisted by his colleague, Edward Reynolds, particularly with materials relating to Africa.

Grateful acknowledgment is made to the following authors and publishers for permission for quotation of the chapter opening epigraphs:

Chapter 18, Étienne Gilson, *Les Métamorphoses de la Cité de Dieu* (Paris: Publications Universitaires de Louvain, 1942); Chapter 23, Lynn White, Jr., "Technology and Invention in the Middle Ages," *Speculum,* XV (1940), 156; Chapter 26, B. H. Sumner, *A Short History of Russia* (New York: Harcourt Brace Jovanovich, 1943), p.1; Chapter 28, Herbert Butterfield, *Origins of Modern Science* (London: G. Bell & Sons, Ltd., 1957), p. 179; Chapter 30, Peter Chaadayev, *Apology of a Madman,* cited in H. Kohn's *The Mind of Modern Russia* (New Brunswick, N.J.: Rutgers University Press, 1955), p. 50; Chapter 31, H.A.R. Gibb, "Social Change in the Near East," in P.W. Ireland, ed., *The Near East* (Chicago: The University of Chicago Press, 1942), p. 43; Chapter 32, Arnold J. Toynbee, *The World and the West* (London: Oxford University Press, 1953); Chapter 33, J.K. Fairbank, "The Influence of Modern Western Science and Technology on Japan and China," from *Explorations in Entrepreneurial History,* VII, No. 4; Chapter 37, K.M. Panikkar, *Asia and Western Dominance* (London: Geroge Allen & Unwin, Ltd., 1969); Chapter 40, Arnold J. Toynbee, *Survey of International Affairs, 1931,* (London: Oxford University Press, 1932) under the auspices of the Royal Institute of International Affairs, p. 1; and Chaper 45, René Grousset, *A History of Asia* (New York: Walker & Co., 1963).

Maps

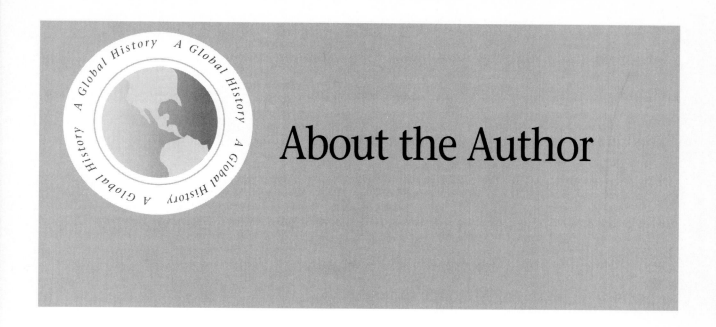

About the Author

L.S. Stavrianos has been engaged in the study of world history for over fifty years. After learning his Ph.D. from Clark University, Stavrianos began his eminent teaching career at Queens University in Canada before going on to Smith College in Massachusetts. In 1946, he embarked on a long and distinguished career at Northwestern University. During this time he was awarded with, among others, a Guggenheim Fellowship, a Ford Faculty Fellowship, a Rockefeller Foundation Fellowship, and several grants from the Carnegie Corporation of New York. He has written about a dozen books (some listed below) and almost four dozen articles. He is currently Emeritus Professor at Northwestern University and Adjunct Professor with the University of California, San Diego.

SOME OTHER BOOKS BY L. S. STAVRIANOS

The Balkans, 1815–1914

Balkan Federation: A History of the Movement toward Balkan Unity in Modern Times

The Balkans since 1453

A Global History, Sixth Edition

Greece: American Dilemma and Opportunity

The Ottoman Empire: Was It the Sick Man of Europe?

The World to 1500: A Global History, Sixth Edition

The Promise of the Coming Dark Age

Global Rift: the Third World Comes of Age

Lifelines from Our Past: A New World History

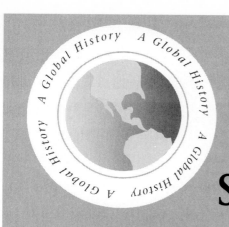

The World
since 1500

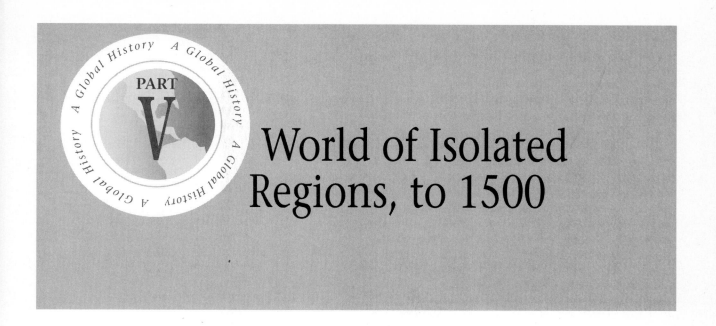

World of Isolated Regions, to 1500

Part V is concerned with two basic questions: Why should a study of world history begin with the year 1500, and why was it that Westerners took a primary role in carrying out the fantastic discoveries and explorations of the late fifteenth and early sixteenth centuries? The first question will be answered in Chapter 18; the second will be the subject of the remaining chapters of Part V.

We usually take it for granted that only Westerners could have made the historic discoveries that would change the course of humanity and begin a new era in world history. This assumption is quite unjustified, particularly in view of the great seafaring traditions of the Moslems in the Middle East and the Chinese in East Asia. Why then did the West take the initiative in overseas enterprise with repercussions that are still felt today? Chapters 19, 20, and 21 will analyze the traditional societies in the Moslem, Confucian, and non-Eurasian worlds, and chapters 22 and 23 will offer an examination of the contrasting dynamism of Western society.

18 Introduction: From Regional to Global History

The throes of the contemporary world are those of a birth. And what is being born with such great pain is a universal human society. . . . What characterizes the events we witness, what distinguishes them from all preceding events back to the origins of history is . . . their global character.

Étienne Gilson

Why should a world history begin with the year 1500? Human beings and their *hominid* ancestors have existed on this globe for over 4 million years. Why then should this small fraction of 1 percent of humanity's total history be selected for special attention?

The answer is that until 1500, humans had lived largely in regional isolation. The various racial groups had been scattered about in a pattern of virtual global segregation. Not until about 1500 was there for the first time direct contact among them all. Not until approximately that date were they finally all brought together, whether they were Australian aborigines or cultivated Chinese Mandarins or primitive Patagonians.

The year 1500, therefore, represents a major turning point in human history. A parallel may be drawn between Columbus, who broke the bonds of regional isolation by landing on San Salvador, and the astronauts, who likewise broke the bonds of planetary isolation by landing on the moon.

Indeed, world history in the strict global sense did not begin until the voyages of Columbus and da Gama and Magellan. Prior to their exploits, there were relatively parallel histories of separate peoples rather than one unified history of humankind. During the long millennia of the Paleolithic period, *Homo sapiens* gradually scattered from their birthplace in Africa to all the

291

A symbolic hand shake between two workmen with the two countries's flags in
the Channel Tunnel near Calais, Northern France, a few hours before the
French and British teams of diggers make their breakthrough October 30, 1990.

continents except Antarctica. Then the ending of
the Ice Age raised the level of the oceans, thereby
splitting Africa from Europe, the Americas from
Northeast Asia, and Australia from Southeast
Asia, to mention only the major separations.

Henceforth humankind lived in varying degrees of regional isolation. Some people were
completely cut off, like the Australian aborigines;
they had no contact with the outside world for
more than 50,000 years, a period spanning from
the last migrations from Southeast Asia to the appearance of Captain James Cook. Almost as isolated were the inhabitants of North and South
America, because for tens of thousands of years
before Columbus, they had no direct contact with
the rest of the world. The end of the Ice Age about
10,000 years ago released huge quantities of water
that had been frozen in the vast ice sheets that
covered much of the globe. The released water
raised the sea levels of all oceans, submerging existing land bridges between northeast Siberia and
North America and also between Southeast Asia
and Australia. In this way the human race found
itself divided into several blocs that had little or
no contact with each other. Most isolated were
the inhabitants of Australia and of North and

South America. Almost as isolated, though not as
completely, were the Africans, who were partly
cut off from Europe and Asia by the harsh and expanding Sahara Desert as well as by the Indian
Ocean and the Mediterranean Sea.

The remaining branches of the human family occupied the landmass stretching from Morocco to Kamchatka, and from Norway to Malaya.
This landmass, commonly referred to as Eurasia,
constitutes the "heartland" of world history. It
spreads over two-fifths of the land area of the
globe and includes nine-tenths of the world's people. It is the place of origin of the earliest and
most advanced *civilizations* of humankind. Prior
to 1500, world history was essentially the history
of Eurasia as here defined. Only in Eurasia was
there continuous and substantial interaction of
peoples and civilizations. While the Australian
aborigines and the American Indians lived for *millennia* in virtually complete isolation, the Eurasians by contrast were exchanging technologies,
ideas, institutions, and material goods (See map of
Culture Areas of the World About 1500, p. 293.)

Interaction within Eurasia was much less intensive before 1500 than after, when direct sea
contact was established among all regions. Dur-

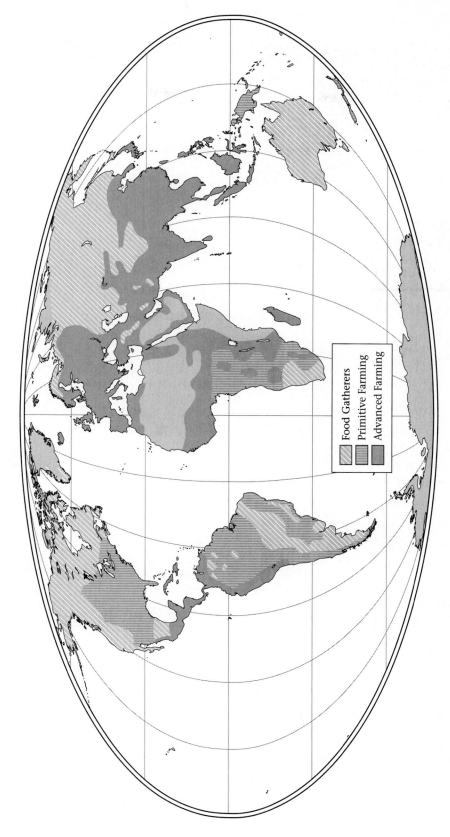

Culture Areas of the World About 1500

Food Gatherers

Primitive Farming

Advanced Farming

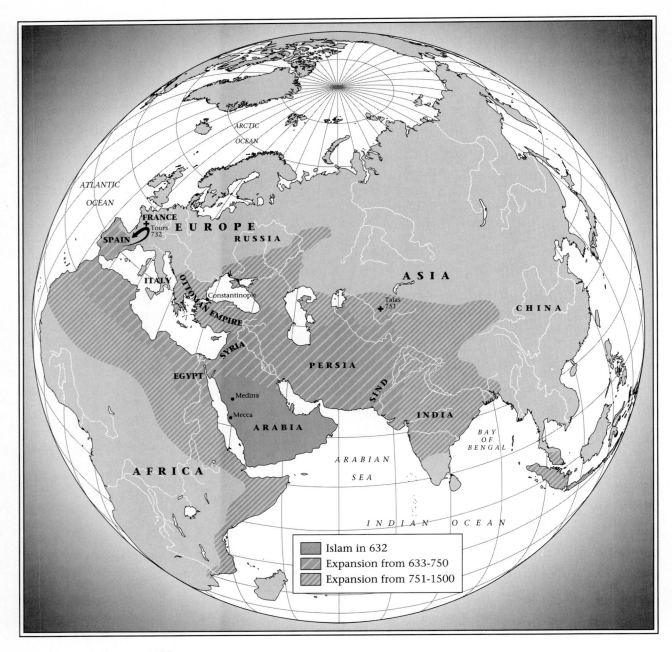

Expansion of Islam to 1500

ing the pre-1500 period, interaction varied greatly from era to era. In general, it was most limited in the early millennia and then gradually increased in scope and tempo. The ancient civilizations that flourished in the Nile, Tigris-Euphrates, Indus, and Yellow River valleys during the pre-Christian millennia were confined mostly to their restricted localities. There was, of course, some give and take. Yet the fact remains that these early civilizations were tightly circumscribed oases surrounded by vast stretches of less developed territories, across which there was relatively little communication.

The pattern changed radically during the centuries of the classical civilizations. By A.D. 100, when the Classical Age was at its height, the Ro-

man Empire extended around the entire Mediterranean basin, the Parthian Empire stretched
across the Middle East, the Kushan Empire covered northeastern India, and the Chinese Han
Empire included all the remaining territory eastward to the Pacific Ocean. Thus the political
units of the period encompassed entire regions
rather than single river valleys, and the civilized
world extended in a continuous band from the
Scottish highlands to Southeast Asia. As a result,
there came to be interregional contacts of a new
magnitude and of all varieties. This was the period when religions such as Christianity and Buddhism began to spread over large areas of Eurasia,
with far-reaching political and cultural as well as
religious repercussions. At this time also the
mixed Greek–Middle Eastern culture known as
Hellenism spread from the eastern Mediterranean
in all directions—to Western Europe, North Africa,
India, and, to a certain degree, China and Japan.
This was also a period of greatly increased interregional trade. Both by land and by sea there was
an exchange of linen, copper, tin, and glass from
the Roman Empire; cotton textiles, aromatics,
and precious stones from India; spices from
Southeast Asia; and, above all, silk from China.

Later, in the Middle Ages, there was even
more interaction among Eurasian peoples, with
the establishment for the first time of great interregional empires. Between 632 and 750 the
Moslems conquered an empire stretching from
the Pyrenees to the Indian Ocean and from Morocco to the borders of China. In later centuries
Islam expanded much further into central Asia,
India, Southeast Asia, and Africa's interior. Even
more impressive was the thirteenth-century
Mongol Empire, which included Korea, China,
all of central Asia, Russia, and most of the Middle
East (see map of Expansion of Islam to 1500, p.
294.)

Indicative of the new horizons opening up
were the exploits of famous travelers who now
took advantage of the peace and security prevailing in the Moslem and Mongol empires to journey back and forth across the breadth of Eurasia.
Best known in the West is the Venetian Marco
Polo (1254–1324), who entered the service of the
Mongol ruler Kublai Khan, functioned as governor of a Chinese city of a million inhabitants,
and after twenty-five years returned home to as-

tound his fellow citizens with tales of his adventures. Even more extensive were the travels of the
Moslem Ibn Battuta (1304–1378). Starting from
his native Morocco, he made the pilgrimage to
Mecca and journeyed on through Samarkand to
India, where he served as judge and also as ambassador to China. Returning later to Morocco,
he resumed his travels, crossing north to Spain
and then south to central Africa, where he
reached Timbuktu. Less well known is Rabban
Bar Sauma, a Nestorian monk who was born in
Peking and who traveled across Eurasia from east
to west. In 1287 he reached Mesopotamia and
then went through Constantinople to Naples,
Rome, Paris, and London, meeting en route both
Philip IV of France and Edward I of England.

Integration and interaction within Eurasia
did not proceed without interruptions. Empires
rose and fell; channels of communication opened
and closed. The flourishing silk trade between
China and the West dwindled to a trickle with the
collapse of the Roman and Han empires. Likewise,
European merchants could not follow in Marco
Polo's footsteps for very long because of the early
disintegration of the Mongol Empire. Yet the fact
remains that during this entire pre-1500 period,
Eurasia was a dynamic and self-renewing unit in
comparison with the scattered and isolated lands
of the non-Eurasian world.

The basic difference in the degree of isolation prevailing within Eurasia as compared to the
rest of the globe is of primary importance for
world history. Its significance is indicated by the
following observation of the distinguished anthropologist Franz Boas:

The history of mankind proves that advances of culture depend upon the opportunities presented to a social group to learn from the experience of their neighbors. The discoveries of the group spread to others,
and the more varied the contacts, the greater the opportunities to learn. The tribes of simplest culture are
on the whole those that have been isolated for very
long periods and hence could not profit from the cultural achievements of their neighbors.[1]

In other words, *if other geographic factors are
equal,* the key to human progress is accessibility
and interaction. Those people who are the most
accessible and who have the most opportunity to
interact with other people are the most likely to

forge ahead. Those who are isolated and receive no stimulus from the outside are likely to stand still.

If this hypothesis is applied on a global scale, the remote Australian aborigines should have been the most retarded of all major groups; next, the American Indians in the New World; then the Negroes of sub-Saharan Africa; and finally, the least retarded, or the most advanced, the various peoples of Eurasia who were in constant and generally increasing contact with each other. This, of course, is precisely the gradation of culture levels found by the European discoverers after 1500 (See map of Culture Areas of the World About 1500, p. 293.) The Australian aborigines were still at the Paleolithic *food-gathering* stage; the American Indians varied from the Paleolithic tribes of California to the impressive civilizations of Mexico, Central America, and Peru; the African Negroes presented comparable diversity, though their overall level of development was higher; and finally, at quite another level, there were the highly advanced and sophisticated civilizations found in Eurasia—the Moslem in the Middle East, the Hindu in south Asia, and the Confucian in east Asia.

If the Boas hypothesis is applied to Eurasia alone, it helps to explain the traditional primacy of the Middle East. Centrally located at the crossroads of three continents, the Middle East was in fact the region that pioneered in human progress during most of history. It was here that agriculture, urban life, and civilization originated, as well as the Christian, Jewish, and Islamic religions. It is significant also that after civilization got under way in the Middle East about 3500 B.C., it then took root in India about 2500 B.C., and finally, about 1500 B.C., in China, on the isolated eastern tip of Eurasia, and in western Europe, on the isolated western tip. The degree to which these individual regional civilizations were the products of diffusion or of autonomous development remains in dispute. Recent archeological discoveries and improved dating techniques tend to favor the autonomists against the diffusionists.

During most of the pre-1500 period, northwest Europe was what today would be termed an underdeveloped area. Its peoples were looked down on as backward "natives." Greeks, Romans, Byzantines, and Moslems all assumed that the Europeans living to the north of the Mediterranean were stupid and uneducable. Yet it was the descendants of those Europeans who discovered continents unknown to the Greeks and Romans and eventually became the masters of the entire globe.

This surprising outcome raises a fundamental question: Why was it the western Europeans who became the leaders of the world in recent centuries? In view of their previous backwardness, why was it they, rather than the Chinese or Arabs, who brought together the continents of the world and thus began the global phase of world history? If Columbus had been an Arab or Chinese, the world today would be very different from what it is. Why was he a European?

SUGGESTED READINGS

Two essential aids for the study of world history are *The Times Atlas of World History,* rev. ed. (Times Books, 1991); and W. L. Langer, *An Encyclopedia of World History* (Houghton Mifflin, 1972). For ongoing research in world history, see the *Journal of World History,* the official journal of the World History Association, published twice yearly by the University of Hawaii Press. Noteworthy also are the following: R. Lewin, *In the Age of Mankind* (Smithsonian Books, 1988); and G. Clark, *Space, Time and Man* (Cambridge University Press, 1992), which present the latest findings about prehistory, and which conclude with thoughtful speculation on current human prospects. The most recent survey of pre-1500 world history is by L. S. Stavrianos, *The World to 1500: A Global History,* 6th ed. (Prentice Hall, 1995).

19 Moslem World at the Time of the West's Expansion

He who would behold these times in their greatest glory, could not find a better scene than in Turkey.

H. Blount, 1634

To answer the question posed in Chapter 18 of why Columbus was not Chinese or Arabic, it is necessary to see what was going on in the Confucian and Moslem worlds at that time. In this chapter, and the following one, we shall analyze why China and the Middle East lacked the expansionism of western Europe, even though they were highly developed and wealthy regions. We shall see that paradoxically, it was their wealth and high level of development that left them smug and self-satisfied, and therefore unable to adapt to their changing world.

I. RISE OF MODERN MOSLEM EMPIRES

An observer on the moon looking at this globe about 1500 would have been more impressed by the Moslem than by the Christian world. The mythical observer would have been impressed first by the extent of the Moslem world and then by its unceasing expansion. The earliest Moslems were the Arabs of the Arabian peninsula who were united for the first time under their religious leader, Mohammed. Believing that he had received a divine call, Mohammed warned his peo-

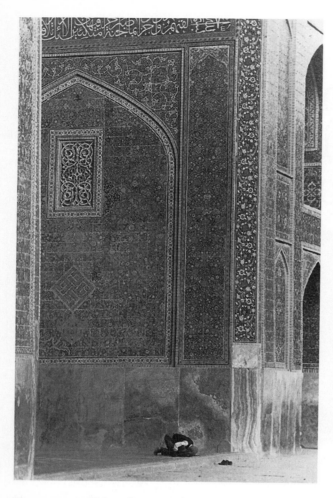

The success of Islam lies mainly in the devotion of its members. Here, a worshipper is seen in prayer in the Shah Mosque, Iran.

ple of the Day of Judgment and told them of the rewards for the faithful in Paradise and the punishment of the wicked in Hell. He called on his followers to perform certain rituals known as the Five Pillars of Islam (including daily prayers, alms giving, fasting, and a pilgrimage to Mecca.) These rituals, together with the precepts in the Koran, provided not only a religion but also a social code and a political system. The converts felt a sense of brotherhood and common mission, which served to unite the hitherto scattered Arab peoples.

After the death of Mohammed in A.D. 632, the Arabs burst out of their peninsula and quickly overran the Byzantine and Sassanian empires in the Middle East. Then they expanded eastward

toward China and westward across North Africa and into Spain. By 750, the end of this first phase of Islamic expansion, there existed a huge Moslem Empire that stretched from the Pyrenees to India and from Morocco to China (see map of Expansion of Islam to 1500, p. 294.) The Moslems carried out the second phase of their expansion between 750 and 1500, during which time they penetrated westward to central Europe, northward to central Asia, eastward to India and Southeast Asia, and southward into the interior of Africa. Thus, the Moslem world doubled in size. It far surpassed in area both the Christian world on the western tip of Eurasia and the Confucian world on the eastern tip.

Not only was the Moslem world the most extensive about 1500, but it also continued to expand vigorously after that date. Contrary to common assumption, western Europe was not the only part of the world that was extending its frontiers at that time. The Moslem world was still expanding, but by overland routes, whereas the Christian world was reaching out overseas. The Portuguese in the early sixteenth century were gaining footholds in India and the East Indies, and the Spaniards were conquering an empire in the New World. But at the same time, the Ottoman Turks, a central Asian people that had converted to *Islam,* were pushing into central Europe. They overran Hungary, and in 1529 they besieged Vienna, the Hapsburg capital in the heart of Europe. Likewise, in India the great Mogul emperors were steadily extending their empire southward until they became the masters of almost the entire peninsula. Elsewhere the Moslem faith continued to spread into Africa, central Asia, and Southeast Asia.

The steady expansion of Islam was due partly to the forceful conversion of nonbelievers, though compulsion was not employed so commonly by Moslems as by Christians. But much more effective than these measures was the quiet missionary work of Moslem traders and preachers, who were particularly successful among the less civilized peoples. Frequently, the trader appeared first, combing proselytism with the sale of merchandise. His profession gave the trader close and constant contact with the people he wanted to convert. Also, there was no color bar, for if the trader were not of the same race as the villagers, he probably would marry a native woman. Such a marriage often led to the adoption of Islam by members of the woman's family. Soon religious instruction was needed for the children, so schools were established and frequented by pagan as well as Moslem children. The children were taught to read the *Koran* and were instructed in the doctrines and ceremonies of Islam. This explains why Islam, from the time of its appearance, was far more successful in gaining converts than any other religion. Even today, Islam is more than holding its own against Christianity in Africa, thanks to its unique adaptability to indigenous cultures as well as to the popular identification of Christianity with the foreign white master.

Apart from this ceaseless extension of frontiers, the Moslem world about 1500 was distinguished by its three great empires: the Ottoman in the Middle East, North Africa, and the Balkans; the Safavid in Persia; and the Mogul in India. These empires had all risen to prominence at this time and now dominated the heartland of Islam.

Their appearance was due in part to the invention of gunpowder and its use in firearms and cannon. The new weapons strengthened central power in the Moslem world, as they did at the same time in Christian Europe. Firearms, however, were by no means the only factor explaining the rise of the three Moslem empires. Equally significant were the appearance of capable leaders who founded *dynasties* and the existence of especially advantageous circumstances that enabled these leaders to conquer their empires. Let us consider now the particular combination of factors that made possible the growth of each of the three Moslem empires.

Ottoman Empire

The Ottoman Turks, who founded the empire named after them, were a branch of widely scattered Turkish people who came originally from central Asia (in contrast to the Semitic Arabs, who came originally from the Arabian peninsula). Over the centuries, successive waves of Turkish tribespeople had penetrated into the rich lands of the Middle East. They had appeared as early as the eighth century and infiltrated into the Islamic Empire, where they were employed first as mercenaries. In the tenth century, Mongol pressure from the rear forced more Turkish tribes, including a group known as the Seljuk Turks, to move into the Middle East. These newcomers broke the

traditional frontier of Asia Minor along the Taurus Mountains—the frontier that had sheltered Rome and Byzantium for 1,400 years—by defeating the Byzantine army in the fateful battle of Manzikert in 1071. The victory made most of Asia Minor a part of the Seljuk Empire, leaving only the northwest corner to the Byzantines.

The Seljuk Empire, however, experienced a decline, disintegrating into a patchwork of independent principalities, or sultanates. In the late thirteenth century, the disorder was heightened by new bands of Turkish immigrants. One of these bands settled down on the extreme northwestern fringe of Seljuk territory, fewer than fifty miles from the strategic straits separating Asia from Europe. In 1299 the leader of this band, a certain Uthman, declared his independence from his Seljuk overlord. From these humble beginnings grew the great Ottoman Empire, named after the obscure Uthman.

The first step in this dazzling success story was the conquest of the remaining Byzantine portion of Asia minor. By 1340 all of Asia Minor had fallen to the star and crescent. In 1354 the Turks crossed the straits and won their first foothold in Europe by building a fortress at Gallipoli. They hardly could have selected a more advantageous moment for their assault on Europe. The whole of Christendom in that century was weakened and divided. The terrible plague, the Black Death, had carried off whole sections of the populations of many Christian nations. The ruinous Hundred Year's War immobilized England and France. (The dates of this conflict are significant. It began in 1338, when the Turks were rounding out their conquest of Asia Minor, and it ended in 1453, when they captured Constantinople.) The Italian states also could do little against the Turks because of the long feud between Venice and Genoa. And the Balkan peninsula was hopelessly divided by the religious strife of Catholic and *Orthodox Christians* and heretic Bogomils, as well as by the rivalries of the Byzantine, Serbian, and Bulgarian empires, all long past their prime. And in the Balkans, as in Asia Minor, the Christian peasants frequently were so discontented that they offered little or no resistance to the Turkish onslaught.

These circumstances explain the extraordinary success of the Ottomans as they spread out from their base in Asia Minor. In 1384 they captured Sofia, and soon after they had control of all Bulgaria.

Five years later they destroyed a south Slav army at the historic battle of Kossovo, which spelled the end of the Serbian Empire. These victories left Constantinople surrounded on all sides by Turkish territory. In 1453 the beleaguered capital was taken by assault, ending a thousand years of imperial history.

The Turks next turned southward against the rich Moslem states of Syria and Egypt. In a whirlwind campaign, they overran Syria in 1516 and Egypt the following year. The final phase of Ottoman conquest took place in central Europe. Under their famous Sultan Suleiman the Magnificent, the Turks crossed the Danube River and in one stroke crushed the Hungarian state in the Mohacs Battle in 1526. Three years later, Suleiman laid siege to Vienna but was repulsed, partly because of torrential rains that prevented him from bringing up his heavy artillery. Despite this setback, the Turks continued to make minor gains: Cyprus in 1570, Crete in 1669, and the Polish Ukraine in the following decade.

At its height, the Ottoman Empire was indeed a great imperial structure. Its heartland was Turkish Asia Minor, but the majority of the population consisted of Moslem Arabs to the south and Balkan Christians to the west. The empire sprawled over three continents and comprised some 50 million people, compared to the 5 million of contemporary England. Little wonder that Christians of the time looked on the ever-expanding Ottoman Empire with awe and described it as "a daily increasing flame, catching hold of whatsoever comes next, still to proceed further."[1]

Safavid Empire

The second great Moslem empire of this period was the Safavid in Persia. That country had fallen under the Seljuk Turks, as had Asia Minor. But whereas Asia Minor had become Turkified, Persia remained Persian—or Iranian—in race and culture. Probably the explanation for this different outcome is that Persia had already become Moslem during the first stage of Islamic expansion in the seventh century, in contrast to Asia Minor, which had formerly been a part of the Christian Byzantine Empire. For this reason, Persia was not swamped by Moslem warriors as Asia Minor had been, and Persian society was left basically unchanged by the comparatively small ruling class of Turkish administrators and soldiers.

Persia remained under the Seljuk Turks from approximately A.D. 1000 to the Mongol invasion in 1258. The new Mongol rulers, known as the Il-Khans, were at first *Buddhists* or Christians, but about 1300 they became Moslems. Persia suffered considerable permanent damage from the Mongols, who destroyed many cities and irrigation systems, but this setback was overcome when the Il-Khan dynasty was replaced by the Safavid in 1500.

Shah Ismail I founded the new dynasty of Safavid monarchs, the first native Persian rulers in several centuries. In the twenty-four years of Ismail's reign, his military abilities and religious policy enabled him to unite the country. By his proclamation, the *Shiite sect* of Islam became the state religion; and through his ruthlessness, the rival *Sunnite sect* was crushed. (The Sunnites, or traditionalists, accept as authoritative certain traditions, or *Sunna,* of Mohammed and also approve the historic order of succession of the first four heirs to Mohammed. The Shiites maintain that the fourth of these successors, Ali, should have been the first. This repudiation of the first three caliphs as usurpers is regarded by Sunnites as the chief, though not the only, wrong of the Shiites.) The significance of this doctrinal dispute for Persia in 1500 was that it provided a basis for the unification of the country and for the development of a certain national sentiment. Persians identified themselves with Shiism, differentiating them from the Turks and other surrounding Moslem peoples who were mostly Sunnites. In fact, Ottomans and Persians fought a long series of wars caused as much by religious differences as by the inevitable political rivalries between two powerful neighboring dynasties.

The greatest of the Safavid rulers was Abbas I, the shah from 1587 to 1629. It was he who modernized the Persian army by building up its artillery units. Under his rule, Persia became an internationally recognized great power, as seen by the constant stream of envoys from European countries who sought an alliance with Persia against the Ottoman Empire. In fact, both these Moslem states figured prominently in European diplomacy during these years. Francis I of France, for example, cooperated with Suleiman the Magnificent in fighting against the Hapsburg Emperor Charles V. And the Hapsburgs, in turn, cooperated with the Persians against their two common foes. These relationships between Christian and

Moslem states were denounced at the time as "impious" and "sacrilegious," but the fact was that the Ottoman and Safavid empires had become world powers that no European diplomat could afford to overlook.

Mogul Empire

Just as two outstanding Safavid rulers founded a "national" dynasty in Persia, so two outstanding Mogul rulers—Babur and Akbar—founded a "national" dynasty in India, a very remarkable achievement for Moslem rulers in a predominantly Hindu country.

The Moslems came to India in three waves, widely separated in time. The first consisted of Arab Moslems who invaded the Sind region near the mouth of the Indus in A.D. 712. These Arabs were unable to push far inland, so their influence on India was limited.

The second wave came in about 1000, when Turkish Moslems began raiding India from bases in Afghanistan. These raids continued intermittently for four centuries, with much loss of life and property. The net result was that numerous Moslem kingdoms were established in northern India, whereas southern India remained a conglomeration of Hindu states. But even in northern India the mass of the people continued to be Indians in race and Hindu in religion. They did not become Islamicized and Turkified, as did the people of Asia Minor. The explanation again is that Turks who came down from the north were an insignificant minority compared to India's teeming millions. They could fill only the top positions in the government and the armed forces. Their Hindu subjects were the ones who tilled the land, worked in the bazaars, and comprised most of the *bureaucracy*. In certain regions, it is true, large sections of the population did turn to Islam, especially some depressed *castes* who sought relief from their exploitation in the new religion. Yet the fact remains that India was an overwhelmingly Hindu country when the third Moslem wave struck in 1500 with the appearance of the Moguls.

The newcomers again were Turks, their leader being the colorful Babur, a direct descendent of the great Turkish conqueror Timur, or Tamerlane. In 1524 Babur, with a small force of 12,000 men armed with matchlock muskets and artillery, defeated an Indian army of 100,000. After his victory, Babur occupied Delhi, his new capital. Four years later he died, but his sons followed his path, and the empire grew rapidly. It reached its height during the reign of Babur's grandson, the famous Akbar, who ruled from 1556 to 1605.

Akbar was by far the most outstanding of the Mogul emperors. He rounded out his Indian possessions by conquering Rajputana and Gujarat in the west, Bengal in the east, and several small states in the Deccan peninsula in the south. Mogul rule now extended from Kabul and Kashmir to the Deccan, and later under Aurangzeb (1658–1707) it extended still further—almost to the southern tip of the peninsula. In addition to his military exploits, Akbar was a remarkable personality of great versatility and a wide range of interests. Although illiterate, he had a keen and inquiring mind that won the grudging admiration of Jesuits who knew him well. The astonishing range of his activities is reminiscent of Peter the Great. Like his Russian counterpart, Akbar had a strong mechanical bent, as evidenced in his metallurgical work and in his designs for a gun with increased firepower. He learned to draw, loved music, was an expert polo player, and played various instruments, the kettledrum being his favorite. Akbar even evolved an entirely new religion of his own, the *Din Ilahi*, or "Divine Faith." It was eclectic, with borrowings from many sources, especially from the Parsees, the Jains, and the Hindus. Akbar hoped that a common faith would unite his Hindu and Moslem subjects. But in practice, it had little impact on the country. It was too intellectual to appeal to the masses, and even at court there were few converts.

What Akbar failed to achieve by his synthetic faith, he did by ending discriminatory practices against Hindus and establishing their equality with Moslems. He abolished the pilgrim tax that Hindus had been required to pay when traveling to their sacred shrines. He ended the poll tax on Hindus, a standard levy on nonbelievers in all Moslem countries. Akbar also opened the top state positions to Hindus, who now ceased to look on the Mogul Empire as an enemy organization. A new India was beginning to emerge, as Akbar had dreamed—a national state rather than a divided land of Moslem masters and a Hindu subject majority.

II. SPLENDOR OF MOSLEM EMPIRES

Military Strength

All three of the Moslem empires were first-class military powers. Eloquent proof is to be found in the appeal sent in December 1525 by the king of France, Francis I, to the Ottoman sultan, Suleiman the Magnificent. The appeal was for a Turkish attack on the Holy Roman emperor and head of the House of Hapsburg, Charles V. Suleiman responded in 1526 by crossing the Danube, overrunning Hungary, and easing the pressure on Francis. This was only one of many Ottoman expeditions that not only aided the French—and incidentally provided the Turks with additional territories and booty—but also saved the Lutheran heretics by distracting Hapsburg attention from Germany to the threatened Danubian frontiers. It is paradoxical that Moslem military power should have contributed substantially to the cause of Protestantism in its critical formative stage.

Moslem military forces generally lagged behind those of Europe in artillery equipment. They depended on the Europeans for the most advanced weapons and for the most experienced gunners. The discrepancy, however, was one of degree only. It was not a case of the Moslem empires being defenseless because of lack of artillery. Plenty of equipment was available, though it was not as efficient and as well-manned as were the best contemporary European armies. The Moslems, and especially the Turks, were shrewd enough to pay for both Western artillery and artillerymen, but they lacked the technology and the industries to keep up with the rapid progress of Western armaments.

On the other hand, European observers were impressed by the vast military manpower of the Moslem world. It is estimated that the permanent regular forces of the whole of India at the time of Akbar totaled well over 1 million men, or more than double the size of the Indian armies in 1914. Furthermore, these huge military establishments were well trained and disciplined when the Moslem empires were at their height. For obvious geographic reasons, Europeans were most familiar with the Ottoman armed forces, with whom they had a good deal of firsthand experience. After this experience the Europeans were very impressed and respectful. Typical were the reports of Ogier Ghis-

elin de Busbecq, Hapsburg ambassador to Constantinople during the reign of Suleiman the Magnificent. After Busbecq inspected an Ottoman army camp in 1555, he wrote home as follows:

It makes me shudder to think of what the result of a struggle between such different systems [as the Hapsburg and the Ottoman] must be. . . . On their side is the vast wealth of their empire, unimpaired resources, experience and practice in arms, a veteran soldiery, an uninterrupted series of victories, readiness to endure hardships, union, order, discipline, thrift, and watchfulness. On ours are found an empty exchequer, luxurious habits, exhausted resources, broken spirits, a raw and insubordinate soldiery, and greedy generals; there is no regard for discipline, license runs riot, the men indulge in drunkenness and debauchery, and, worst of all, the enemy are accustomed to victory, we, to defeat. Can we doubt what the result must be? The only

The Sultan, Suleiman the Magnificent, battling the Hungarians.

obstacle is Persia, whose position on his rear forces the invader to take precautions. The fear of Persia gives a respite, but it is only for a time.[2]

Administrative Efficiency

All heads of Moslem states had absolute power over their subjects. Accordingly, the quality of the administration depended on the quality of the imperial heads. In the sixteenth century, they were men of extraordinary abilities. Certainly Suleiman and Abbas and Akbar were the equals of any monarchs anywhere in the world. Akbar had a well-organized bureaucracy whose ranks were expressed in terms of cavalry commands. Excellent pay and the promise of rapid advance in the Mogul service attracted the best men in India and from abroad. It is estimated that 70 percent of the bureaucracy consisted of foreigners such as Persians and Afghans. The rest were Indian Moslems and Hindus. Upon the death of an official, his wealth was inherited by the emperor, and his rank became vacant. This practice lessened the evils of corruption and hereditary tenure that plagued Western countries at the time.

Since Akbar opened his bureaucracy to all his subjects, ability rather than religion became the criterion for appointment and advancement. Busbecq in Constantinople made precisely the same point about the Ottoman administrative system:

In making his appointments the Sultan pays no regard to any pretensions on the score of wealth or rank. . . . He considers each case on its own merits, and examines carefully into the character, ability, and disposition of the man whose promotion is in question. It is by merit than men rise in the service, a system which ensures that posts should only be assigned to the competent. . . . Among the Turks, therefore, honours, high posts, and judgeships are the rewards of great ability and good service. If a man be dishonest, or lazy, or careless, he remains at the bottom of the ladder, an object of contempt. . . . These are not our ideas, with us there is no opening left for merit; birth is the standard for everything; the prestige of birth is the sole key to advancement in the public service.[3]

Economic Development

As far as economic standards were concerned, the Moslem states in early modern times were, in current phraseology, developed lands. Certainly they were so regarded by western Europeans, who were ready to face any hardships or perils to reach fabled India and the Spice Islands beyond. Closer to home, the Ottoman Empire was an impressive economic unit. Its vast extent assured it of virtual self-sufficiency. The fertile plains of Hungary, Wallachia, Asia Minor, and Egypt produced an abundant supply of foodstuffs and raw materials. The skilled artisans of Constantinople, Saloniki, Damascus, Baghdad, Cairo, and other ancient cities turned out a multitude of handicraft products. The empire also possessed large timber resources and important mineral deposits, particularly iron, copper, and lead. All these goods were bought and sold without hindrance in the vast freetrade area provided by the far-flung Ottoman frontiers. The empire's strategic position at the junction of seas and continents also promoted a substantial foreign and transit trade.

For most Europeans, more dazzling than the Ottoman Empire was far-off, exotic India, the weaver of fabulous textiles, especially fine cotton fabrics unequaled anywhere in the world. India was the country that, since the early days of the Roman Empire, had drained gold and silver away from Europe—a fact that made a big impression on the bullion-minded Europeans of the time. It is true that when the Europeans were able to observe firsthand the Indian countryside, they could not help noticing the wretched condition of the peasant masses that lived virtually at subsistence level. But it did not make as deep an impression as it does today, for Europe then had its own peasantry living close to subsistence.

As significant as the wealth of the Moslem empires was the control of south Asian commerce by Moslem merchants. Particularly important was the trade in spices, which were eagerly sought after in a world that knew so little of the art of conserving foodstuffs apart from salting. For centuries the spices, together with many other goods such as silk from China and cotton fabrics from India, were transported back and forth along two sets of trade routes. The northern land routes extended from the Far East through central Asia to ports on the Black Sea and Asia Minor; the southern sea routes, from the East Indies and India along the Indian Ocean and up the Persian Gulf or the Red Sea to ports in Syria and Egypt. With the collapse of the Mongol Empire, conditions in central Asia became so anarchical that the north-

The wealth of the Moslem empires is perfectly exemlified by this structure—Humayun's Tomb, Delhi.

ern routes were virtually closed after 1340. Henceforth, most of the products were funneled along the southern sea routes, which by that time were dominated by Moslem merchants.

This commerce contributed substantially to the prosperity of the Moslem world. It provided not only government revenue in the form of customs duties but also a source of livelihood for thousands of merchants, clerks, sailors, shipbuilders, camel drivers, and stevedores, who were connected directly or indirectly with the trade. The extent of the profits is indicated by the fact that articles from India were sold to Italian middlemen in Alexandria at a markup of over 2,000 percent.

When the Portuguese broke into the Indian Ocean in 1498, they quickly gained control of much of this lucrative commerce. But they did so because their ships and guns, rather than their goods or business techniques, were superior. In fact, we shall find that the Portuguese at first were embarrassed because they had little to offer in return for the commodities they coveted. They were rescued from this predicament only by the flood of bullion that soon was to pour in from the mines of Mexico and Peru.

III. DECLINE OF MOSLEM EMPIRES

The Moslem world of the sixteenth century was most impressive. Suleiman, Akbar, and Abbas ruled empires that were at least the equals of those in other parts of the globe, and yet these empires began to go downhill during the seventeenth century. By the following century they were far behind western Europe, and they have remained behind to the present day.

One explanation is the deterioration of the ruling dynasties. Suleiman the Magnificent was succeeded in 1566 by Selim II, who was lazy, fat, dissipated, and so addicted to wine that he was known to his subjects as Selim the Sot. His successors proved to be even more degenerate. The same thing happened in Persia after Abbas, and in India after Akbar. Dynastic decline, however, was not the only factor responsible for the blight of the Moslem lands. All the European royal families had their share of incapable and irresponsible rulers, yet their countries did not go down with them.

A more basic explanation for the misfortunes of the Moslem world was that it lacked the dynamism of Europe. It did not have those far-reaching changes that were revolutionizing European society during these centuries (as we shall see in chapters 23 and 24). In the Moslem economic field, for example, there were no basic changes in agriculture, in industry, in financial methods, or in commercial organization. A traveler in the Moslem lands in the seventeenth or eighteenth centuries would have observed essentially the same economic practices and institutions as the *Crusaders* saw five hundred years earlier. As long as the rulers were strong and enlightened, the autocratic empires functioned smoothly and effectively, as Busbecq reported. But when central authority weakened, the courtiers, bureaucratic

OTTOMAN EMPIRE IN DECLINE

The British consul and merchant William Eton lived in the Ottoman Empire for many years at the end of the eighteenth century. His colorful report on Ottoman conditions and institutions reflects how far the empire had declined since its days of glory. *

General knowledge is, from these causes, little if at all cultivated; every man is supposed to know his own business or profession, with which it is esteemed foolish and improper for any other person to interfere. The man of general science, a character so frequent and so useful in Christian Europe, is unknown; and any one, but a mere artificer, who should concern himself with the founding of cannon, the building of ships, or the like, would be esteemed little better than a madman. The natural consequence of these narrow views is, that the professors of any art or science are themselves profoundly ignorant, and that the greatest absurdities are mixed with all their speculations. . . .

From the mufti to the peasant it is generally believed, that there are seven heavens, from which the earth is immovably suspended by a large chain; that the sun is an immense ball of fire, at least as big as the whole Ottoman province, formed for the sole purpose of giving light and heat to the earth; that eclipses of the moon are occasioned by a great dragon attempting to devour that luminary; that the fixed stars hang by chains from the highest heaven &c. &c. . . .

They distinguish different Christian states by different appellations of contempt.

Epithets which the Turks apply to those who are not Osmanlis, and which they often use to denominate their nation:

Albanians	gut-sellers
Armenians	t-rd-eaters, dirt-eaters, also pack-carriers
Bosniaks and Bulgarians	vagabonds
Christians	idolaters
Dutch	cheese-mongers
English	atheists
Flemmings	panders
French	faithless
Georgians	louse-eaters
Germans	infidel blasphemers
Greeks of the islands	hares
Italians or Franks	many-coloured
Jews	mangy dogs
Moldavians	drones
Poles	insolent infidels
Russians	mad infidels
Spaniards	lazy
Tatars	carrion-eaters
Walachians	gypsies

It is a certain fact, that a few years ago a learned man of the law having lost an eye, and being informed that there was then at Constantinople an European who made false eyes, not to be distinguished from the natural, he immediately procured one; but when it was placed in the socket, he flew into a violent passion with the eye-maker, abusing him as an impostor, because he could not see with it. The man, fearing he should lose his pay, assured him that in time he would see as well with that eye as with the other. The effendi was appeased, and the artist liberally rewarded, who having soon disposed of the remainder of his eyes, left the Turks in expectation of seeing with them. . . .

* W. Eton, *A Survey of the Turkish Empire*, 4th ed. (London: 1809), pp. 190–93.

officials, and army officers all combined to fleece the productive classes of society, whether peasants or artisans or merchants. Their uncontrollable extortions stifled private enterprise and incentive. Any subject who showed signs of wealth was fair game for arbitrary confiscation. Consequently, merchants hid their wealth rather than openly investing it to expand their operations.

Another cause and symptom of decline was the blind superiority complex of the Moslems, with their attitude of invincibility vis-à-vis the West. It never occurred to them at this time that they might conceivably learn anything from *giaours,* or nonbelievers. Their attitude stemmed partly from religious prejudice and partly from the spectacular successes of Islam in the past. Islam had grown from an obscure sect to the world's largest and most rapidly growing religion. Consequently, Moslem officials and scholars looked down with arrogance on anything relating to Christian Europe. As late as 1756, when the French ambassador in Constantinople announced the alliance between France and Austria that marked a turning point in the diplomatic history of Europe, he was curtly informed that the Ottoman government did not concern itself "about the union of one hog with another."[4] This attitude was perhaps understandable in the sixteenth century; in the eighteenth it was suicidal.

One of the most damaging results of this self-centeredness was that it let down an intellectual iron curtain between the Moslem world and the West, especially in the increasingly important field of science. Moslem scholars knew virtually nothing of the epoch-making achievements of Paracelsus in medicine; Vesalius and Harvey in anatomy; and Copernicus, Kepler, and Galileo in astronomy. Not only were they ignorant of these scientific advances, but also Moslem science itself had stagnated, with little impetus for new discoveries in the future.

A final factor explaining Moslem decline is that the three great Moslem empires were all land empires. They were built by the Turks, the Persians, and the Moguls, all peoples with no seafaring traditions. Their empires faced inward toward central Asia rather than outward toward the oceans. The rulers of these empires were not vitally interested in overseas trade. Therefore they responded feebly, if at all, when Portugal seized control of the Indian Ocean trade routes.

This situation was significant, because it allowed the Europeans to become the masters of the world trade routes with little opposition from the Moslems, who hitherto had controlled most of the trade between Asia and Europe. The repercussions were far-reaching. The control of world trade enriched the Europeans tremendously and further stimulated their economic, social, and political development. Thus a vicious circle developed, with worldwide trade making western Europe increasingly wealthy, productive, dynamic, and expansionist, while the once-formidable Moslem empires, taking little part in the new world economy, remained static and fell further and further behind.

SUGGESTED READINGS

Directly relevant to this chapter is the excellent collection of sources by J. J. Saunders, ed., *The Moslem World on the Eve of Europe's Expansion* (Prentice Hall, 1966). The spread of Islam from the time of Mohammed to the end of the nineteenth century is well described by T. W. Arnold, *The Preaching of Islam,* rev. ed. (Constable, 1913).

For the various Islam empires, see H. A. R. Gibb and H. Bowen, *Islamic Society and the West,* Parts 1 and 2 (Oxford University, 1950, 1957); H. Inalcik, *The Ottoman Empire: The Classical Age, 1300–1600* (Weidenfeld and Nicolson, 1972); the multivolume *Cambridge History of Iran* (Cambridge, 1968ff.); N. Itkowitz, *Ottoman Empire and Islamic Tradition* (University of Chicago, 1980); the sprightly written S. Wolpert, *A New History of India* (Oxford University, 1977); and R. Dunn, *The Adventures of Ibn Battuta: A Muslim Traveller of the Fourteenth Century* (University of California, 1986), which presents a revealing overview of the Moslem world.

Finally, on the decline of the Moslem Empires, see J. J. Saunders, "The Problem of Islamic Decadence," *Journal of World History,* 7 (1963), 701–720; T. Stoianovich, "Factors in the Decline of Ottoman Society in the Balkans," *Slavic Review,* 21 (December 1962), 623–632; and B. Lewis, "Some Reflections on the Decline of the Ottoman Empire," in C. M. Cipolla, ed., *The Economic Decline of Empires* (Methuen, 1970), pp. 215–234.

20

Confucian World at the Time of the West's Expansion

One need not be obsessed with the merits of the Chinese to recognize that the organization of their empire is in truth the best that the world has ever seen.

Voltaire, 1764

Corresponding to the Moslem world in the Middle East and south Asia was the Confucian world in east Asia. Just as the Moslem world was dominated by the Ottoman, Safavid, and Mogul empires, so the Confucian world was dominated by China, with Korea and Japan on the periphery. The two worlds were similar in one fundamental respect: They were both agrarian-based and inward-looking societies. Their tempo of change was slow and within the framework inherited from earlier times. On the other hand, the Confucian world differed substantially from the Moslem because of its much greater unity. China had no indigestible minority blocs comparable to the various Balkan Christians in the Ottoman Empire, and no religious divisions comparable to the Hindus and Moslems in the Mogul Empire. This cohesiveness of China was not a recent phenome-

non. It dated back for millennia to the beginnings of Chinese civilization and has persisted to the present day. Indeed, the Chinese civilization is the oldest continuous civilization in the world.

I. CONTINUITY OF CHINESE CIVILIZATION

One reason for the longevity of the Chinese civilization is geographic, for China is isolated from the world's other great civilizations to an unprecedented degree. China has nothing comparable to the Mediterranean, which linked Mesopotamia, Egypt, Greece, and Rome, or the Indian Ocean, which allowed India to interact with the Middle East, Africa, and south Asia. Instead, during most of its history, China was effectively cut off on all sides by mountains, deserts, and the vast Pacific Ocean. The significance of this isolation is that it allowed the Chinese to develop their civilization with fewer intrusions from the outside than the peoples of the Middle East or India had to face. Consequently, their civilization was both more continuous and also more distinctive. It has more fundamental differences from the other great Eurasian civilizations than any of them have from each other.

The unique size of China's population has also contributed to the continuity of civilization. From the beginning China has been able to support a huge population because of a favorable combination of soil and climate. The monsoon rains come during the warm months of the year, so that two crops per year are possible in some areas south of the Yangtze River, in contrast to the average one-crop yields of the Middle East and Europe. Furthermore, rice produces a much larger yield per acre than the wheat or barley grown in most parts of Eurasia. Thus the census of A.D. 2 showed that Han China had a population of 59.5 million—more than that of the Roman Empire at its greatest extent. By the early sixteenth century, when the Portuguese first arrived, China's population was over 100 million, more than that of all Europe. By the mid-nineteenth century, when China was being forced open by Western gunboats, its population had spurted upward to over 400 million, partly because of the introduction of such New World food crops as peanuts, maize, and sweet potatoes.

Such an unequalled population made it possible for the Chinese to retain their identity regardless of the course of events. They had been conquered and ruled by the Mongols and Manchus, as well as battered and undermined by the West. But in the end their superiority in numbers together with their superiority in civilization always enabled them to assimilate or expel the intruders and to adapt selected aspects of foreign cultures to their traditional civilization. Never has wholesale transformation been imposed from the outside, as it was in Europe with the Germanic invasions, or in the Middle East and in India with the Moslem ones.

Another important factor in China's cohesiveness is the existence of a single written language that goes back several millennia to the earliest Shang dynasty. This written language is of special significance because it is understood by Chinese from all regions, speaking dialects as different from each other as Italian is from Spanish or Swedish from German. The reason it is understandable to all is that it consists of characters representing ideas or objects. These characters are pronounced in different ways in different parts of China, but the meaning of any character is the same no matter how it is pronounced. A Western parallel would be the arabic number system: For example, the word for the number 8 is pronounced differently in Italian, in Swedish, or in English, but the meaning of the symbol 8 remains the same in all three tongues. This common written language has been an important force in providing unity and historic continuity to China. In fact, it has done so to all of east Asia, for the Chinese method of writing has been adopted in whole or in part by most of the surrounding peoples, including the Japanese, Koreans, and some of the Southeast Asians.

Related to the common written language is the extraordinary system of public examinations which formed the basis of the merit system by which for nearly two millennia China staffed its civil service. "When the right men are available, government flourishes. When the right men are not available, government declines." This Confucian maxim expresses the fundamental Chinese doctrine that problems of state are better met by recruiting people of talent than by depending on laws and institutions, as was done in the West. When fully evolved, the Chinese system consisted of a series of examinations held, in ascending order, in district and prefectural cities, provincial capitals, and finally the imperial capital.

At first the examinations were fairly comprehensive, emphasizing the Confucian classics but including also subjects like law, mathematics, and political affairs. Gradually, however, they came to concentrate on literary style and Confucian orthodoxy. The net result was a system that theoretically opened offices to all males of talent but that in practice favored the classes with sufficient wealth to afford the years of study and preparation. This did not mean that a hereditary aristocracy ruled China; rather, it was a hierarchy of the learned, a *literocracy,* providing China with an efficient and stable administration that won the respect and admiration of Europeans. On the other hand, it was a system that stifled originality and bred conformity. As long as China remained relatively isolated in east Asia, it provided stability and continuity. But with the intrusion of the dynamic West the system prevented effective reaction and adjustment. It was finally abolished altogether in 1905.

Perhaps the most important factor contributing to the cohesiveness of Chinese civilization was the moral code and the literary and intellectual heritage known as *Confucianism*. This was made up of the teachings of Confucius (551–479 B.C.), the name being a Latinized form of K'ung-fu-tzu, or "Master Kung." Like most Chinese thinkers, Confucius was concerned primarily with the establishment of a happy and well-organized society in this world. His first principle was "every man in his place": "Let the ruler be a ruler and the subject a subject; let the father be a father and the son be a son." Confucius defined the proper social relationships between people of different stations of life. If each individual acted in accordance with his or her station, the family would be orderly, and when the family was orderly, the state would be peaceful and all would be harmonious under Heaven.

Confucius also provided China with a philosophy of government. His innovation was the concept that government is basically an ethical problem. He made no distinction between politics and ethics, since social harmony depended on virtuous rulers providing for the welfare and happiness of their subjects. Just as the individual should be subordinate to the family, so the family should be subordinate to the emperor. But the emperor in turn should set an example of benevolent fatherhood, and this was to be done by following the ethics of Confucianism rather than a system of law. Confucius thus was the founder of a great ethical tradition in a civilization that, more than any other, came to concentrate on ethical values. Confucianism's moral justification for authority and social inequality appealed to rulers and to the wealthy. Yet at the same time, its high ethical principles gave the status quo a stronger foundation than mere hereditary right and served as a constant stimulus to improve government and social relationships.

Confucius instructing his disciples in the precepts of living in a happy and organized society.

All these factors are necessary to explain the continuity of Chinese civilization since its beginnings about 1500 B.C. The history of the Middle East presents a sharp contrast: Alexander's conquests spread the new Hellenistic culture; the Moslem conquests brought radical changes in race, language, and culture, as well as religion. India, likewise, was transformed fundamentally with the Aryan invasions about 1500 B.C. and the Moslem invasions after A.D. 1000. The historical evolution of China was never jarred by such violent upheavals. There were many invasions, and on two occasions foreign dynasties ruled the entire country, but these intrusions disturbed rather than transformed. Instead of massive breaks and new beginnings, China throughout its history experienced merely the rise and fall of dynasties within the traditional framework.

II. DYNASTIC CYCLES

The cyclical rise and fall of dynasties can be explained by certain recurring trends in Chinese history. Each new dynasty normally began by ruling the country efficiently and starting a period of comparative peace and prosperity. It stimulated intellectual and cultural life and protected the country by sending military expeditions against the nomads and extending the imperial frontiers. But gradually the dynasty was weakened by the personal degeneration of individual rulers and by court struggles between cliques of gentry and palace eunuchs. This deterioration and factionalism undermined central authority and promoted corruption in the bureaucracy. Together with the increasing luxuriousness of court life, the corruption meant heavier taxes on the peasantry, who ultimately had to produce the surplus that supported the entire imperial structure. Taxes tended to increase also because of the costly foreign wars and the practice of the emperors of granting tax exemption to many of the gentry and to Buddhist temples and monasteries. As the government became lax, the irrigation systems and other public works essential for agriculture tended to be neglected.

Thus an increasingly impoverished peasantry had to bear the burden of a mounting tax load. When the inevitable crop failures and famines were added to the burden, the explosion came, and revolts broke out against the government tax collectors and landlord rent agents. In time, local uprisings broadened into general insurrections. These in turn were an invitation to the nomads to invade, especially since the imperial armies by this stage were poorly maintained. The combination of internal rebellion and external invasion usually heralded the beginning of a new cycle—the approaching end of the old dynasty and the coming of a new one.

The first dynasty, the Shang (1523–1028 B.C.), arose in the north in the Yellow River valley. Already the Chinese had learned to make silk, had devised their distinctive writing system, had mastered the art of creating beautiful earthenware and bronze vessels, and had begun to make a clear distinction between "Chinese" and "barbarians" based on a sense of cultural rather than racial superiority.

The succeeding Zhou dynasty (1028–221 B.C.), although long lived, was unable to establish a stable central government. The Zhou political structure was somewhat similar to that of medieval Europe, with a large number of warring feudal states that disregarded the nominal Zhou overlord. But this troubled political scene led to anxious soul searching among Chinese intellectuals. Their speculations on the nature of humanity and society culminated in the great philosophical systems and literary classics of Chi-

nese civilization. Both Confucianism and *Taoism* evolved, so that the Zhou centuries, spanning a period as long as the entire European Middle Ages, stand out as the era when the cultural foundations of China were laid.

The following Ch'in dynasty (221–206 B.C.), despite its short duration, was responsible for replacing Zhou feudalism with a tightly organized imperial structure that lasted, with occasional lapses, until the fall of the last dynasty in 1912. This structure included an all-powerful emperor, an efficient and disciplined bureaucracy, a network of military roads and the Great Wall in the north, all of which gave China the most stable and lasting government in the world.

The Ch'in dynasty was succeeded by the Han (206 B.C.–A.D. 220), which is noted for its expansion of China's frontiers in all directions—west into Central Asia, north into Manchuria, and south into Indochina. The Han Empire was at least the equal of the contemporary Roman Empire in size, population, wealth, and cultural achievement. And like the Roman, it collapsed because of internal decay and invasions from the north. But in the West the fall of Rome led to several centuries of disorder and convulsion until a radically different type of society emerged. The Europe of A.D. 1000, when the various invasions finally petered out, was very different from the Europe of Roman days. The new Europe was a combination of German and Christian as well as Roman elements. It was a Europe with a new religion, new ethnic strains, new Germanic and Romance languages, and new nation-states arising from the imperial ruins. In China, by contrast, the Han dynasty was followed, after an intervening period of disorder, by the T'ang and Sung dynasties (618–907 and 960–1279), which represented a continuation of the traditional civilization, although with certain refinements and modifications.

The Yüan dynasty that followed (1279–1368) was unique in that it was Mongol rather than Chinese. The Mongols, in fact, had overrun most of Eurasia, so that China was now part of a huge empire extending from the Pacific to the Black Sea. But these Mongol rulers were few in number compared to their millions of Chinese subjects, and they failed to win the support of the Chinese gentry and peasants. They ruled as conquerors, making few concessions to Chinese institutions or to the Chinese way of life. When their military power declined, their regime was swept away by rebellious peasants and hostile scholar-bureaucrats.

Following the expulsion of the Mongols, China was ruled by two more dynasties, the Chinese Ming (1368–1644) and Manchu Ch'ing (1644–1911). Although the Manchus were foreigners like the Mongols, they were successful in ruling China because they gave prestige and opportunity to Chinese scholar-bureaucrats while maintaining administrative control. They respected and utilized Chinese institutions but created a system of checks to protect their own position. A substantial minority of Chinese were included in the top imperial councils, although local government remained largely in Chinese hands. Consequently, the transition from the Ming to the Ch'ing was relatively easy. This entire period, from the mid-fourteenth century to the nineteenth, when the European intrusion in China began in earnest, is one of the great eras of orderly government and social stability in human history. The traditional institutions and practices continued smoothly and satisfyingly— the agricultural economy, the Confucian way of life, the examination system for the selection of public officials, and the revered rule of the Son of Heaven in Peking.

In ordinary times such order and permanence would be considered a blessing. But these were the centuries that witnessed the rise of a new and dynamic Europe—the centuries of the Renaissance, the Reformation, the commercial and industrial revolutions, the French Revolution, and the rise of powerful national states that quickly extended their domination over the entire globe. In such a period, stability became a curse rather than a blessing. China appeared, and in fact was, relatively static and backward. The idea of continual change and "progress," which now was taken for granted in the West, remained alien to the Chinese mind. The basic difference between Chinese and European attitudes toward the world about them was manifested in the Chinese decision to discontinue the spectacular overseas expeditions of the Ming dynasty (see Chapter 23, Section V).

III.   EARLY RELATIONS WITH THE WEST

Relations between China and the West did not become continuous until the expansion of Europe following the voyages of Columbus and the Portuguese navigators. Prior to that time the interaction between the extreme east and west ends of the Eurasian landmass had been sporadic and usually indirect. The earliest was the silk trade with Rome. Carried on through Middle Eastern merchants, this trade reached such proportions that the Roman economy was affected by the resulting drain of gold and silver, since the Chinese were not interested in importing Roman or any other foreign goods. Much greater interaction with the lands to the west occurred during the Mongol period. Thanks to the continent-wide Mongol conquests, safe travel between China and Europe became possible for the first time during the century after 1240. A considerable number of Europeans now journeyed eastward. Some were missionaries who hoped to convert the Mongols to Christianity. Others, like the Polos, were merchants who were attracted by the dazzling new trade opportunities. But with the disintegration of the Mongol Empire, the Moslems once again blocked the routes between East and West, and direct relations ceased.

China began to feel the direct impact of the dynamic new Europe when Portuguese merchants opened trade with Canton in 1514 and established a permanent commercial base at Macao in 1557. The Portuguese purchased Chinese silks, wood carvings, porcelain, lacquerware, and gold, and in return they sold nutmeg, cloves, and mace from the East Indies; sandalwood from Timor; drugs and dyes from Java; and cinnamon, pepper, and ginger from India. No European goods were involved for the simple reason that there was no market for them in China. The Portuguese were functioning as carriers and middlemen for a purely intra-Asian trade.

The Dutch and the British arrived in the early seventeenth century to challenge Portugal's monopoly in the China trade. Neither was given official permission to trade, so for decades the Dutch and English preyed on Portuguese shipping and conducted an irregular trade along the south China coast. By the mid-eighteenth cen-

Russians travelled through Siberia and set up forts along the Amur River, attempting to open trade relations with China. With Jesuit priests acting as interpreters and advisers, the treaty of Nerchinsk was signed in 1689.

tury the Chinese opened up the trade to all countries, though confining it to Canton and Macao. The English soon won the lion's share of this trade, partly because of their growing commercial and industrial superiority and also because of their convenient base of operations in India.

Meanwhile, the Russians in Siberia had been trying to open trade relations with China, and the Chinese had reacted by restricting and regulating the commerce closely. The treaties of Nerchinsk (1689) and Kiakhta (1727) allowed the Russians to trade at three border points and to send commercial caravans every three years to Peking. There they were permitted to build a church and maintain a priest and three curates, though their community in the Chinese capital was limited in numbers to 300. Under these terms a few goods were exchanged—Russian furs, leather goods, textiles, cattle, horses, and glassware for Chinese silks, tea, lacquerware, and porcelain.

Cultural interaction between China and the West during these early centuries was confined to the efforts of the Jesuits to propagate their faith. In 1582 Matteo Ricci was allowed to reside in Canton, and twenty years later, to resettle in Peking, where his knowledge of mathematics and astronomy impressed Chinese officials and intellectuals. When at last he ventured to discuss religious matters, he sought to show that Christian doctrine was compatible with Confucianism. Later Jesuit priests continued with this approach, but they were challenged by other Catholic orders (Dominicans and Franciscans) who argued that Confucianism was a heathen religious doctrine. When the pope finally ruled against the Jesuits in 1742, the emperor retaliated by banning all Christian missionary activities. From then on Christianity declined rapidly in China.

The net result of centuries of Jesuit enterprise was negligible. Indeed, Europe had been much more impressed by China's examination system and Confucian ethics than China had been by Europe's science and mathematics. During the century following the papal decision, there was no intellectual contact between China and the West. The Chinese remained supremely self-confident and self-contained following their first encounter with Europe. They had kept Western merchants confined to few seaports and frontier trading posts; they had accepted with a few exceptions only tributary relations in their conduct of international affairs; and they had shown only a passing interest in Jesuit teachings about science and theology. Rarely in history had a people faced the future with so much self-assurance and with so little understanding of the storms that awaited them.

IV.   JAPAN ABSORBS CHINESE CIVILIZATION

Compared to China, Japan was on the periphery in the sixteenth century when the Europeans first appeared. This does not mean that the Japanese were primitive; indeed, they had evolved a complex and dynamic society. Although their first reaction to the appearance of the Europeans was positive—many of them embraced Christianity—soon they reacted against the "insolent barbarians" and severed virtually all ties with them. But the Japanese eventually came to realize that a policy of withdrawal was not realistic. They proceeded to study the ways of the West and adapt elements of Western culture to their needs. Thanks to their unique historical and cultural

JESUIT REPORT ON SIXTEENTH-CENTURY CHINA

The Jesuit missionary Matteo Ricci labored in China from 1583 to 1610.
The following excerpts from his diary show how impressed the Europeans were
at that time by the Chinese civilization. *

He whose authority extends over this immense kingdom is called Lord of the Universe, because the Chinese are of the opinion that the extent of their vast dominion is to all intents and purposes coterminous with the borders of the universe. . . .

Relative to the extent of China, it is not without good reason that the writers of all times have added the prefix great to its name. Considering its vast stretches and the boundaries of its land, it would at present surpass all the kingdoms of the earth, taken as one, and as far as I am aware, it has surpassed them during all previous ages. . . .

Due to the great extent of this country north and south as well as east and west, it can be safely asserted that nowhere else in the world is found such a variety of plant and animal life within the confines of a single kingdom. The wide range of climatic conditions in China gives rise to a great diversity of vegetable products, some of which are most readily grown in tropical countries, others in arctic, and others again in the temperate zone. . . .

All of the known metals without exception are to be found in China. Besides brass and ordinary copper alloys, the Chinese manufacture another metal which is an imitation silver but which costs no more than yellow brass. From molten iron they fashion many more articles than we do, for example, cauldrons, pots, bells, gongs, mortars, gratings, furnaces, martial weapons, instruments of torture, and a great number of other things, all but equal in workmanship to our own metalcraft. . . .

. . . It seems to be quite remarkable when we stop to consider it, that in a kingdom of almost limitless expanse and innumerable population, and abounding in copious supplies of every description, though they have a well-equipped army and navy that could easily conquer the neighboring nations, neither the King nor his people ever think of waging a war of aggression. They are quite content with what they have and are not ambitious of conquest. In this respect they are much different from the people of Europe, who are frequently discontent with their own governments and covetous of what others enjoy. While the nations of the West seem to be entirely consumed with the idea of supreme domination, they cannot even preserve what their ancestors have bequeathed them, as the Chinese have done through a period of some thousands of years. . . .

Another remarkable fact and quite worthy of note as marking a difference from the West, is that the entire kingdom is administered by the Order of the Learned, commonly known as The Philosophers. The responsibility for orderly management of the entire realm is wholly and completely committed to their charge and care.

* From *China in the Sixteenth Century: The Journal of Matthew Ricci: 1583–1610,* translated by Louis J. Gallagher, S. J. Copyright 1942 and renewed 1970 by Louis J. Gallagher, S. J. Reprinted by permission of Random House, Inc.

Yoritomo (1147–1198), first Minamoto Shogun of Japan and founder of the Kamakura Shogunate. He was the first founder of a long line of actual rulers of Japan.

background, the Japanese were extraordinarily successful and quickly outdistanced the Chinese, who for so long had been their teachers.

The importance of geographic location is particularly apparent in the case of Japanese history. In this respect there is a close parallel with the British Isles at the other end of the Eurasian landmass. The Japanese islands, however, are more isolated than the British. One hundred and fifteen miles separate them from the mainland, compared to the twenty-one miles of the English Channel. Thus until their World War II defeat by the United States, the Japanese had only once before been seriously threatened by foreign invasion, and that was in the thirteenth century by the Mongols. The Japanese, therefore, have been close enough to the mainland to benefit from the great Chinese civilization, but distant enough to be able to select and reject as they wished.

The Japanese are basically a Mongoloid people who migrated from northeast Asia. But the hairy Caucasoid *Ainu* who originally inhabited the Japanese islands contributed to their racial composition, and Malayan and Polynesian migrants from the south probably did also. Early Japan was organized in a large number of clans, each ruled by a hereditary priest-chieftain. Toward the end of the first century A.D., the Yamato clan established a loose political and religious control over the others. Its chief was the emperor, and its clan goddess, the Sun Goddess, was made the national deity.

This clan organization was undermined by the importation of Chinese civilization, which began on a large scale in the sixth century. Buddhism, introduced from Korea, was the medium for cultural change, fulfilling the same function here as Christianity did among the Germans and Slavs in Europe. Students, teachers, craftsmen, and monks crossed over from the mainland, bringing with them a new way of life as well as a new religion. The impetus for change culminated in the Taika Reform, which began in 645 and sought to transform Japan into a centralized state on the model of the T'ang dynasty in China. In accordance with the Chinese model, the country was divided into provinces and districts ruled by governors and magistrates who derived their power from the emperor and his council of state.

These and other changes were designed to strengthen imperial authority, and they did so in comparison with the preceding clan structure. But in practice, the Japanese changed and adapted everything they borrowed from China. They limited the power of their emperor by allowing the hereditary aristocracy to keep their large landholdings. They borrowed Chinese ideographs but developed their own system of writing. They borrowed Confucianism, but modified its ethics and adjusted its political doctrines to satisfy their own spiritual needs, while retaining their native Shintoism. They built new imperial capitals, first at Nara and then at Kyoto, that were modeled after the T'ang capital, Ch'ang-an. But there was no mistaking the Japanese quality of the temples, pavilions, shrines, and gardens.

V.   TOKUGAWA SHOGUNATE

The Chinese system of imperial organization introduced by the Taika Reform of 645 worked effectively for a long period. By the twelfth century, however, it had been undermined and replaced by a Japanese variety of *feudalism.* One reason for this was the tendency of provincial governors, who were too fond of the pleasures of Kyoto, to delegate their powers and responsibilities to local subordinates. Another was that powerful local families and Buddhist communities were always hungry for land and often able to seize it by force. These trends reduced the amount of taxpaying land, which meant an increased tax load for the peasant owner-cultivators. The latter in turn either fled to the northern frontier areas where the Ainu were being pushed back by force of arms, or else they commended themselves and their lands to lords of manors. This relieved them of taxes and provided them with protection, but at the cost of becoming serfs. The net result of this process was that by the end of the twelfth century, tax-paying land amounted to 10 percent or less of the total cultivated area, and local power had been taken over by the new rural aristocracy.

At the same time, this aristocracy had become the dominant military force because of the disintegration of the imperial armed forces. The Taika Reform had made all males between the ages of twenty and sixty subject to military service. But the conscripts were required to furnish their own weapons and food and were given no relief from the regular tax burden. This arrangement proved unworkable and was abandoned in 739. Government military posts became sinecures generally filled by effeminate court aristocrats. As a result, the campaigns against the Ainu were conducted by the rural aristocrats. They became mounted warriors and gradually increased their military effectiveness until they completely overshadowed the imperial forces. A feudal relationship now developed between these rural lords and their retainers, or samurai (literally, "one who serves"). This relationship was based on an idealized ethic, known as bushido, or "way of the warrior." The samurai enjoyed special legal and ceremonial rights, and in return they were expected to give unquestioning service to their lords.

By the twelfth century, Japan was controlled by the competing groups of feudal lords. In the end, one of these lords emerged victorious, and he was appointed by the emperor to the position of *Seii-Tai-Shogun* (Barbarian-Subduing-Generalissimo), with the right to nominate his own successor. Henceforth Japan was controlled by a succession of *shogun* families, or shogunates. They commanded the military forces while the emperor lived in seclusion in Kyoto. The most important of these families was the Tokugawa Shogunate, founded by Tokugawa Ieyasu in 1603. It ruled the country until the restoration of imperial rule and the beginning of modernization in 1868. Ieyasu and his immediate successors formulated policies designed to perpetuate their family dominance. The material basis of their power lay in the Shogunal domain, which comprised between a fourth and a third of the total arable land and consisted of estates scattered strategically throughout the country. These estates provided control points against potentially hostile *daimyo,* or local landholding families. Top government posts were filled by members of the Tokugawa family or personal retainers. The emperor was provided with revenues for his own support as well as that of a small group of court nobles, but he had no political function or authority.

As part of their effort to prevent any change that might undermine their rule, the Tokugawa perpetuated a rigid, hereditary class structure. At the top was the aristocracy, comprising about 6 percent of the population. This included the court nobles, who had social priority but no power or property and were therefore dependent on the shogun for support. Much more important was the feudal aristocracy headed by the shogun and including the daimyo as well as the samurai retainers.

The vast majority of Japanese were farmers, the second-ranking class, which included landless tenants as well as landholders with plots ranging from an acre and a quarter to as many as eighty-five acres. Whatever their status, these peasants produced the rice that, in the final analysis, supported the aristocracy. The latter, in fact, measured their income in terms of rice.

The last two classes recognized by the Tokugawa were, in order of rank, the artisans and the merchants. The long period of peace and security during this shogunate allowed these townspeople to grow enormously in numbers and wealth. Money became increasingly the medium of payment, and the rice brokers and money exchangers became the most important merchants. They disposed of the surplus produce of the feudal aristocracy and provided credit at high interest, usually on the security of next year's income. Many of the daimyo, and sometimes the shogun himself, became indebted to these merchant-financiers. Thus, the wealth of the country flowed increasingly into the coffers of the merchants. In large cities such as Edo and Osaka, they lived on a lavish scale and generated their own cultural forms, such as the Kabuki drama, the woodblock print, and the novel of high life.

The Tokugawa created an ideological basis for their regime by sponsoring the Chu Hsi school of Confucianism, which stressed the virtues of filial piety and of loyalty to one's superior in any social grouping. Paternal power was absolute and unquestioned in the ideal Japanese family, and even more specifically spelled out than in China. Particularly appealing to the Tokugawa was the Confucian emphasis on the moral basis of political legitimacy and on all the conservative virtues. Ieyasu himself, in his *Laws for the Military Houses,* prescribed a code of conduct for his samurai that stressed personal loyalty, sobriety, frugality, and the acceptance of class distinctions. One effect of this ideology was

that the Japanese family system, especially that of the samurai, was closely integrated into Tokugawan society because of its subordination to the interests of the shogun or the daimyo. This harmony between the family and the state, much stronger than in China, facilitated the modernization of Japan in the nineteenth century by providing a grassroots basis for national unity and action.

VI.   EARLY RELATIONS WITH THE WEST

For a while the Tokugawa policy of preserving the status quo was threatened by the intrusion of western Europeans. The first to appear were Portuguese traders in the mid-sixteenth century, who discovered that rich profits could be made in commerce between China and Japan. Because of raids by Japanese pirates, the Ming emperors had banned all trade with Japan. The Portuguese quickly stepped into the void and prospered handsomely, exchanging Chinese gold and silk for Japanese silver and copper. These merchants combined missionary enterprise with their commercial activities. Francis Xavier and other Jesuit fathers landed in 1549 and were allowed to preach among the masses of the people. They were unusually successful, apparently because their revivalist methods of proselytism satisfied the emotional needs of the downtrodden peasantry.

With the advent of the Tokugawa in 1603, Dutch traders, and a few British, were active in Japan alongside the Portuguese. The intense rivalry among these Europeans gave the Japanese a new freedom of action. They could now move against the missionaries without fear of losing the commerce. And they did want to curb the missionaries, whose success they feared was undermining the traditional Japanese society. Accordingly, Ieyasu decreed in 1614 that all missionaries must leave, and their converts, who by now numbered 300,000, must renounce their faith. This order was ruthlessly enforced. As a control measure, converts were forced to belong to a Buddhist temple, and many were executed for refusing. Missionaries also were martyred, but it was often difficult to distinguish between commercial and religious activities. The Japanese therefore went a step further and in 1624 banned all Spaniards, since they had been the most aggressive and defiant. In 1637 all Portuguese also were forced to depart, leaving only the Dutch, who had never shown any interest in propagating Christianity. Henceforth the Dutch were the only Europeans allowed to carry on trade, but only under severely restricted conditions on the Deshima islet in Nagasaki harbor. The isolationist policy was extended in 1636 to Japanese subjects, who were prohibited from going abroad on penalty of death. Over two centuries of seclusion had begun for Japan.

The policy of excluding all foreign influences and freezing the internal status quo was designed to perpetuate the Tokugawa dominance. In practice it proved extraordinarily effective. Japan was reunified and subjected to a centralized political control as thorough and as efficient as in any European state before the French Revolution. But a heavy price was paid for this security and stability. Japan did not have the transformation and rejuvenation of historical movements that western Europe did during this period. There was no ending of feudalism, no Renaissance or Reformation—or Counter-Reformation—and no overseas expansion. For the Japanese, as for the Chinese, the price of two centuries of comforting seclusion was institutional and technological backwardness. This became apparent, more quickly to the Japanese than to the Chinese, when the Europeans forcibly broke into the hermit world of east Asia in the mid-nineteenth century.

SUGGESTED READINGS

Useful annotated bibliographies are provided by the Service Center for Teachers of History of the American Historical Association: J. W. Hall, *Japanese History* (1961); C. O. Hucker, *Some Approaches to China's Past* (1973); and J. K. Fairbank, *New Views of China's Tradition and Modernization* (1968). Source materials on the culture of east Asia are available in W. T. de Bary et al., *Source of Chinese Tradition* (Columbia University, 1960); and R. Tsunoda et al., *Sources of the Japanese Tradition* (Columbia University, 1958).

An authoritative study of all east Asia is by E. O. Reischauer and J. K. Fairbank, *East Asia: Tradition and Civilization*, rev. ed. (Houghton Mifflin, 1978). Standard general histories of China are by W. Rodzinski, *The Walled Kingdom: A History of China from Antiquity to the Present* (Free Press, 1984); and C. O. Hucker, *China's Imperial Past: An Introduction to Chinese History and Culture* (Stanford University, 1975). Noteworthy is M. Elvin, *The Pattern of the Chinese Past* (Stanford University, 1973), which analyzes why medieval China's flair for technology did not lead to an industrial revolution. Comparable histories of Japan are by E. O. Reischauer, *Japan: The Story of a Nation*, rev. ed. (Knopf, 1970); G. B. Sansom, *Japan, A Short Cultural History*, rev. ed. (Prentice Hall, 1944), and the same author's definitive *A History of Japan*, 3 vols. (Stanford University, 1958–1964).

Finally, for the initial contact between east Asia and the West, see the multivolume work by D. F. Lach, *Asia in the Making of Europe* (University of Chicago, 1965 ff.); W. Franke, *China and the West* (Blackwell, 1967); G. F. Hudson, *Europe and China: A Study of Their Relations from Earliest Times to 1800* (Beacon, 1961); C. R. Boxer, *Fidalgos in the Far East, 1550–1770* (Martinus Nijhoff, 1948); C. R. Boxer, *The Christian Century in Japan, 1549–1650* (University of California, 1951); and J. D. Spence, *The Memory Palace of Matteo Ricci* (Viking, 1984), which provides a fascinating juxtaposition of two cultures, through the experiences of Ricci.

21

Non-Eurasian World at the Time of the West's Expansion

To the nations, however, both of the East and West Indies, all the commercial benefits which can have resulted from these events [the expansion of Europe] have been sunk and lost in the dreadful misfortunes which they have occasioned.

Adam Smith

When the Europeans penetrated the Moslem and Confucian worlds by sea, their first reaction was generally one of respect and admiration. In nearly every way they found the peoples of the Middle East and of south and east Asia to be at the least their equals. Actually, the only real superiority the Westerners enjoyed was in naval warfare. This explains why three centuries passed before the Europeans were able to impose any control over India and China.

In the non-Eurasian world, however, the situation was quite different. The peoples of sub-Saharan Africa, the Americas, and Australia had not reached comparable levels of political organization, economic development, and military effectiveness. Consequently, most succumbed eventually to European domination, though in quite different degrees and time spans. This chapter will deal with the conditions and institutions prevailing in the non-Eurasian world at the time of the West's intrusion. Three questions will receive special emphasis: (1) why sub-Saharan Africa remained relatively impervious, apart from its coasts, to outsiders until the nineteenth century; (2) why the Americas were relatively accessible; and (3) why Australia was wide open to Western intrusion from the very beginning.

I. SUB-SAHARAN AFRICA

Geography

Sub-Saharan Africa (hereafter referred to as Africa) presents a curious paradox so far as its relations with Eurasia are concerned. Africa, in contrast to the Americas and Australia, has maintained an unbroken, though at times tenuous, contact with Eurasia. Yet the Europeans were much slower in penetrating into Africa than into either the Americas or Australia. Africa remained the "Dark Continent" centuries after the other newly discovered continents had been opened up and colonized. As late as 1865, when the Civil War was ending in the United States, only the coastal fringe of Africa was known, together with a few isolated sections of the interior. Even by 1900 about a fourth of the interior of Africa remained unexplored.

What is the explanation for Africa's successful resistance to Europe's dynamism? The answer is to be found in part, though by no means entirely, in certain geographic factors. One of these is the hot, humid climate and, closely associated with it, the many tropical diseases that are particularly prevalent in the low-lying coastal areas. Not all of Africa is unhealthful: Along the northern, southern, and eastern fringes of the continent are small but important areas of Mediterranean and subtropical climates where the majority of the European settlers live today. But large portions of the continent's coasts have an inhospitable climate, and it was usually these portions that the Europeans first encountered.

The continent is also extraordinarily inaccessible. One reason is that the coastline, unbroken by bays, gulfs, or inland seas, is even shorter than Europe's though Africa has three times the area. And the lack of a sea such as the Mediterranean, Baltic, or Black Sea means that Africa's interior is not open to the outside world. Africa's inaccessibility was increased by a formidable barrier in the north made up of the great Sahara Desert and the Nile marshes. Effective barriers were to be found also in the form of thousand-mile-long sand bars along both the east and west coasts. And if these bars were penetrated, then still another obstacle remained—the rapids and waterfalls created by the rivers tumbling down a succession of escarpments from the interior plateau to the low coastlands.

The early Europeans were further discouraged by the lack of readily available sources of wealth in the interior of Africa, for there was nothing comparable to the gold and silver of the Americas or the spices of the East Indies. We shall see later (Chapter 24, Section I) that the Portuguese became pioneers of European overseas exploration in order to tap the profitable gold and slave trade in the interior of Africa, which had formerly been controlled by Moslem merchants. But after the Portuguese discovered the Cape route to the Spice Islands of the East Indies, and after the Spaniards stumbled on the treasures of Mexico and Peru, the African trade seemed unimportant. The Europeans continued to hold their posts on the west coast of Africa in order to obtain slaves for the plantations of the New World. But the coastal footholds were sufficient for that purpose, so no serious effort was made by Europeans to penetrate the interior until the establishment of the African Association in London in 1788.

Geography, however, was not the only factor that hindered European penetration. At least as important was the fact that the African peoples' general level of social, political, and economic organization was high enough for them to effectively resist the Europeans for centuries.

Cultures

The cultures of Africa were the outcome of a much greater degree of interaction with the outside world than had been possible in the Americas or Australia (see map of African Empires and Trade Routes, p. 320.) Agriculture, for example, which originated in Mesopotamia and then took root in Egypt in the fifth millennium B.C., may have spread from there to the Sudan. This is the *savanna* zone, or grassland, located between the Sahara and the tropical rain forests and stretching from the Ethiopian highlands to the Atlantic coast. Some authorities believe that agriculture was invented independently in this zone, along the upper reaches of the Niger River. Whether or not this is so, the fact remains that the great majority of the plants that eventually were cultivated in sub-Saharan Africa were importations. The most important were these: from Mesopo-

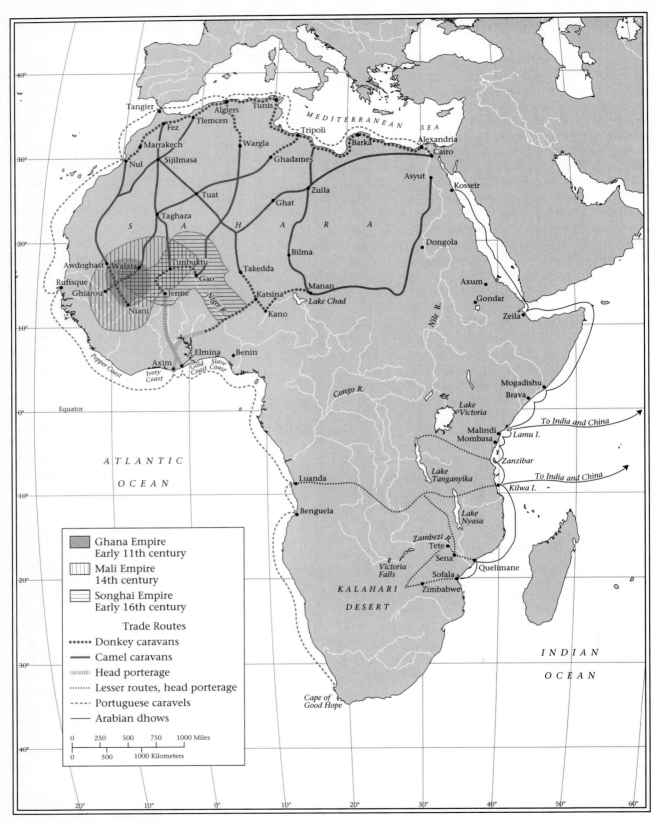

Legend:

Ghana Empire
Early 11th century

Mali Empire
14th century

Songhai Empire
Early 16th century

Trade Routes
• • • • Donkey caravans
━━━ Camel caravans
|||||| Head porterage
• • • • • • Lesser routes, head porterage
– – – Portuguese caravels
━━━ Arabian dhows

0   250   500   750   1000 Miles
0   500   1000 Kilometers

African Empires and Trade Routes

Map labels: Tangier, Fez, Algiers, Tlemcen, Tunis, Tripoli, Barka, Alexandria, Cairo, Marrakech, Sijilmasa, Nul, Wargla, Ghadames, Asyut, Kosseir, Tuat, Zuila, Ghat, Taghaza, Bilma, Dongola, Awdoghast, Walata, Timbuktu, Gao, Takedda, Manan, Axum, Rufisque, Ghiarou, Jenne, Niani, Katsina, Kano, Lake Chad, Gondar, Zeila, Elmina, Benin, Axim, Dongola, Congo R., Lake Victoria, Mogadishu, Brava, Malindi, Mombasa, Lamu I., Zanzibar, Luanda, Lake Tanganyika, Kilwa I., Benguela, Lake Nyasa, Zambezi R., Tete, Sena, Victoria Falls, Sofala, Quelimane, Zimbabwe, KALAHARI DESERT, Cape of Good Hope, Niger R., Nile R., Pepper Coast, Ivory Coast, Gold Coast, Slave Coast, MEDITERRANEAN SEA, ATLANTIC OCEAN, INDIAN OCEAN, To India and China, S A H A R A, Equator tamia and Egypt via the Nile—barley, wheat, peas, and lentils; from Southeast Asia—bananas, sugar cane, the Asian yam, and new forms of rice; from the New World via the Portuguese and later slave traders—tobacco, corn, lima and string beans, pumpkins, and tomatoes.

As basic for Africa as the introduction of agriculture was that of iron metallurgy. Some archeologists believe that it came across the Sahara from Carthage or up the Nile valley from the Assyrians. Others maintain that West African communities learned independently to smelt iron. There is also a third possibility: that both diffusion and independent development occurred, depending on whether the people concerned where located close to or far from the routes of Eurasian diffusion.

Regardless of the origins of agriculture and iron metallurgy, both had profound repercussions in Africa. Population increased spectacularly, thanks to the new food plants and also the new iron tools that made it possible to extend agriculture into the rain forest. Another important effect was the radical change in the ethnic composition of the continent. It was the accessible Negroes of the Sudan, rather than the inaccessible Pygmies and Bushmen of the rain forests and the southern regions, who adopted and profited from agriculture and iron metallurgy. Consequently, it was also they who increased disproportionately in number and who were able, with their iron tools and weapons, to push southward at the expense of the Bushmen and Pygmies.

This expansionism was particularly marked in the case of the *Bantu,* a predominantly Negroid linguistic group. Starting from their original center in the Cameroon Highlands, they infiltrated in the early Christian era into the Congo basin, where they developed a symbiotic relationship with the sparse Pygmy hunters. From there some pushed southeast to the fertile, open Great Lakes country, between A.D. 600 and 900. Then they continued southward across the savanna at the expense of the Bushmen. These migrations explain why the Negroes were the predominant ethnic group by the time the Europeans arrived, whereas a millennium earlier they had shared sub-Saharan Africa fairly evenly with the Bushmen and Pygmies. (See map of Global Race Distribution, p. 18.)

The development of Africa was affected basically not only by the coming of agriculture and iron but also by the manifold contributions of Islam. These came partly from the Moslem colonies along the East African coast but much more from Moslem North Africa. Contacts with North Africa increased greatly when the Moslem Arabs overran the entire region in the seventh century A.D. Later the Moslems also extended their influence down Africa's east coast, first as merchants, and from the thirteenth century onward, as colonists. Their settlements dominated the coast as far south as Zanzibar, and their influence was felt much beyond to the mouth of the Zambezi.

From their bases on the northern and eastern coasts of the continent, the Moslem Arabs exerted a profound influence on Africa. They used the camel, much more than did the Romans, and correspondingly expanded the trans-Saharan trade. Likewise on the east coast they traded with the Negro interior for ivory, gold, slaves, and, later, iron ore. The ore was shipped to southern India, made into steel, reshipped to Persia and Asia Minor and worked into the so-called Damascus blades. Among the products imported in return for these African commodities were Chinese and Indian cloth and Chinese porcelain, remains of which can be found along the entire coast.

Commercial contacts led to Moslem cultural penetration. Islam spread down the east coast as far as Zanzibar, and sometimes beyond. From the Mediterranean coast it spread south across the Sahara into the Sudan. As is usually the case with the diffusion of a new faith, Islam was adopted first by the Negro ruling class and then seeped through to the people. In this manner an important part of the Negro Africa was Islamized and became part of the vast Moslem world. This is why Ibn Battuta, the enterprising fourteenth-century Arab traveler, included the Sudan in his journeys, which extended as far east as China.

The Islamization of the Sudan had repercussions extending far beyond religious matters. This was most obvious in the externals of life—names, dress, household equipment, architectural styles, festivals, and the like. Islam also greatly stimulated the intellectual life of the Sudan. Literacy was spread with the establishment of Koranic schools. Scholars could continue their

In Senegal, the Ker Moussa Monastery. The chapel is decorated with African frescoes and musical instruments that are used during services.

studies at various Sudanese universities, of which the University of Sankore at Timbuktu was the most outstanding. This institution was modeled after other Moslem universities at Fez, Tunis, and Cairo. It was the custom for scholars to move about freely among these and other universities in the Moslem world, in order to study at the feet of particular masters.

The adoption of Islam also enhanced the political cohesion of the Sudanic kingdoms. Traditionally, Sudanic rulers could claim the allegiance only of their own kinship units or clans and of any other related kinship units that claimed descent from a great founding ancestor. But when the kingdoms were enlarged into great empires, this kinship relationship became inadequate as the basis for imperial organization. The larger the empire, the more alien its emperor appeared to a large proportion of the subjects. Local chiefs could not be depended on to serve as faithful vassals. They tended instead to lead their own people in resistance to imperial rule. Islam helped to meet this institutional problem by strengthening

the imperial administration. Moslem schools and colleges turned out a class of educated males who could organize an effective imperial bureaucracy. These men were not dominated by their kinship alliances; their own interests were tied to imperial authority, and they normally could be counted on to serve the authority loyally.

It was the combination of agricultural and metallurgical progress, along with the corresponding growth in economic productivity, flourishing interregional trade, and the stimulus from Islam, that explains the process of state building that went on in Africa from the eighth century onward. As we might expect, the most complex political structures appeared in the Sudan, where long-distance trade was most highly developed and where Islamic influence was the strongest. Three great empires emerged in that region: Ghana (700–1200), Mali (1200–1500), and Songhai (1350–1600). The Songhai Empire stretched almost 1,500 miles from east to west, and in this expanse the rule of law and a common administrative system were given to many diverse subjects. Songhai's outstanding ruler Askia the Great (1493–1528) was one of the foremost monarchs of his time—the equal of the contemporary European kings and superior to many in humaneness, religious tolerance, and devotion to learning.

We must emphasize that in contrast to what is often assumed, Islam was not the only, or even the leading, force behind these empires. In fact, the Ghana Empire largely preceded Islamic influence, which did not affect the Sudan until the eleventh century. Furthermore, the Islamic world played a destructive as well as constructive role in Africa. The disintegration of the Sudanic empires was in part the result of devastating Arab invasions across the Sahara. These marauding expeditions decimated the local populations, ruined prosperous agricultural areas, and disrupted lucrative trade patterns. Indeed, there is a striking parallel here between African and European history. Western Europe was able to forge ahead of eastern Europe in the late Middle Ages because the eastern region suffered continual invasions from further east, whereas western Europe was immune after the tenth century. Likewise, the Sudanese empires, which at one point boasted civilizations comparable to those of their European

A tribe of Hottentots—the woman returning from the water and men around a dead harte-beest.

contemporaries, fell far behind in modern times partly because of the invasions from the north. These corresponded to the Mongol and Turkish invasions of eastern Europe, and were in fact more cataclysmic in their consequences.

Largely because sub-Saharan Africa was broken up into many parts, the level of general development varied strikingly from region to region. Uniform growth was impossible because of natural obstacles obstructing communication and movement among savanna grasslands, rain forests, and deserts. Political units included individual village communities that recognized only local chieftains, as well as the great empires of the Sudan. Economically, the range was as great: from the food-gathering Bushmen-Hottentot-Pygmies to the West Africans with their flourishing agriculture and extensive trade. When the western Europeans first came to Africa, they traded with the West Africans, who, being advanced, had the most to trade. And because they were advanced, the West Africans were able to hold their own against the Europeans much better than had the American Indians.

During centuries of trans-Saharan trade with the Arabs, the Africans had learned about firearms, and therefore were not frightened by their flash and loud noise. The Africans also had developed immunity to European diseases, whereas the Europeans had none against the tropical diseases of the African coasts. Thus for centuries the Africans were able to control the terms under which they traded with the Europeans. Whereas the Europeans had been able to penetrate into the interior of the Americas wherever they wished, in Africa it was the opposite. There, the coastal chieftains refused to allow the Europeans to go inland because they wanted to monopolize their profitable position as middlemen between European buyers on the coasts and the producers in the interiors. A British official wrote in 1793 that Africa remained an unknown continent "from the jealousy of the inhabitants of the sea coasts in permitting white men to travel through their country. . . ." The reason for this jealousy, he explained, was their fear "that the advantages of their trade with Europe should be lessened [and] transferred from them to their neighbours; or that the inland kingdoms by obtaining European arms" would become dangerous rivals.[1]

II.   AMERICAS

Geography

The Europeans were easily able to penetrate the Americas despite the fact that an ocean separated the old and the new worlds. One reason, as we have seen, is that the Americas, in contrast to Africa, were easily accessible. No sand bars obstructed the approaches to the coasts. Harbors were much more frequently available along the indented coastline of the Americas than along the unbroken coastline of Africa. Also the Americas had a well-developed pattern of interior waterways that were relatively free of impediments and offered easy access to the interior. There was no counterpart in Africa to the majestic and smooth-flowing Amazon, Mississippi, or St. Lawrence. The explorers soon learned the use of the native birch-bark canoe, and they discovered that with comparatively few portages they could paddle from the Atlantic up the St. Lawrence, along the Great Lakes, and thence south down the Mississippi to the Gulf of Mexico, or north down the Mackenzie to the Arctic Ocean, or west down the Columbia or the Fraser to the Pacific Ocean.

The climate of the Americas, too, is generally more attractive than that of Africa. The Amazon basin, it is true, is hot and humid, and the polar extremities of both continents are bitterly cold. But the British and the French settlers flourished in the lands they colonized north of the Rio Grande, and the Spaniards likewise felt at home in Mexico and Peru, which became their two principal centers. The climate there is not much different from that of Spain, and certainly a welcome contrast to the sweltering Gold and Ivory coasts.

Peoples

The Indians whom the Europeans found in the Americas were descended from the stock that had crossed the Bering Sea. Recent archeological findings indicate that the first crossing occurred at least 20,000 years ago, and probably twice that long ago or more. The last migration, that of the Eskimos, took place about 4000 B.C. The actual crossing to the New World was not difficult for the early Indians. The level of the sea was then considerably lower because much of the earth's water was frozen in the ice sheets. Accordingly, the first immigrants crossed a 130-mile-wide land bridge connecting northeast Asia and northwest North America. After the sea level rose, the narrow straits could have been easily crossed in primitive boats without ever being out of sight of land. Most of those who crossed to Alaska moved on into the heart of North America through a gap in the ice sheet in the central Yukon plateau. They pressed forward because of the same forces that initially led them to migrate to America—the search for new hunting grounds and the con-

tinual pressure of tribes from the rear. In this manner both American continents were soon peopled by scattered tribes of hunters.

Regardless of their origin, all Indians may be classified as Mongoloids. They have the characteristic high cheekbones and straight black hair, sparse on the face and body. Not all Indians, however, look alike. Those on the northwest coast of North America have flatter faces and noses and narrower eyes (Mongolian fold) than do those of the southwest. The explanation of this difference is twofold. One is the date of the arrival in the Americas. The earliest immigrants are much less Mongoloid in appearance because they left Asia before the Mongoloids, as we know them today, had fully evolved. The other reason is that the immigrants at once spread out and settled in small inbred groups in a variety of climates. This led to the evolution of a great variety of physical types, even though they are all of the same Mongoloid family.

The American Indians differed much more in the languages they spoke than in their physical appearance. Indeed, it is quite impossible to generalize about their languages, since virtually every kind of phonetic and grammatical structure can be found. This linguistic diversity, like the physiological, developed because the Indians migrated to the Americas in small groups over a long period of time, and continued wandering and splitting up after their arrival. Thus, dialect variations rapidly became emphasized and developed into separate languages. Closely related languages may be found in widely separated parts of America, reflecting the degree to which tribes moved about. The net result is that some 2,000 distinct Indian languages have been classified. This represents almost as much variation in speech as in the entire Old World, where about 3,000 languages are known to have existed in A.D. 1500.

Cultures

Anthropologists have defined some twenty-two culture areas in the New World—the Great Plains area, the Eastern Woodlands, the Northwest Coast area, and so forth. A simpler classification, on the basis of how food was obtained, involves three categories: hunting, gathering, and fishing cultures; intermediate farming cultures; and ad-

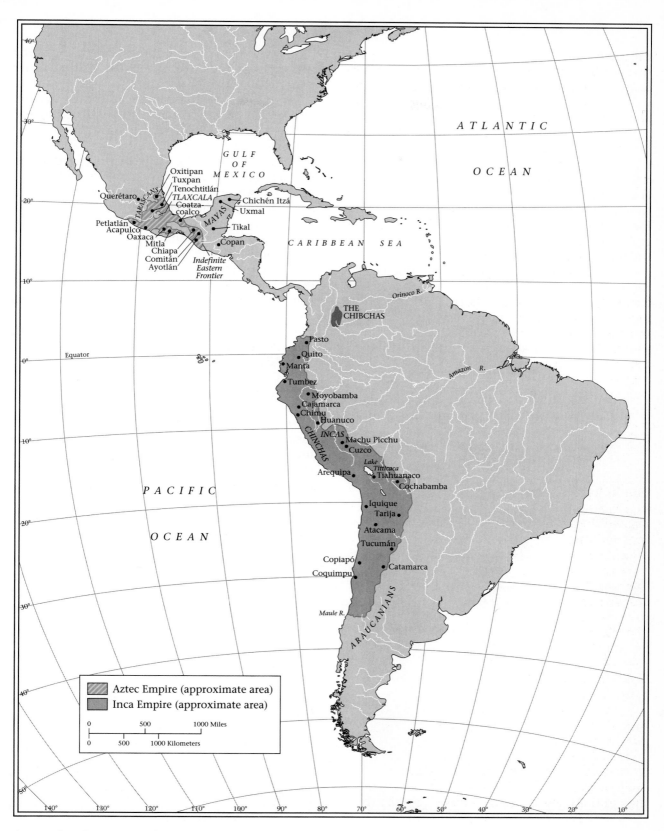

Amerindian Empires on the Eve of The Spanish Conquest

325

vanced farming cultures. This scheme is not only simpler but is also meaningful from the viewpoint of world history, for it helps to explain the varied responses of the Indians to the European invaders.

The advanced farming cultures were located in *Mesoamerica* (today, central and southern Mexico, Guatemala, and Honduras) and the Andean highland area (Ecuador, Peru, Bolivia, and northern Chile). The intermediate farming cultures were generally in the adjacent regions, while the food-gathering cultures were in the more remote regions—the southern part of South America and the western and northern part of North America.

In approximately 7000 B.C. the domestication of maize began in the semidesert valleys of the central highlands of Mexico. During the following millennia two major varieties of maize were developed by hybridization, one adapted to the semiarid Mexican plateau and the other to the humid tropical coastal lands. At the same

Mayan Art. Polychrome vase depicting an elite figure in ceremonial dress.

time other plants were domesticated, including two species of squash, the bottle gourd, tepary bean, chili peppers, amaranths, and avocados. From this original Mesoamerican center, agriculture spread both north and south. Maize arrived in the American Southwest about 3000 B.C. but did not have much effect until A.D. 750 because the primitive nature of maize before that date left food collecting a more productive activity. Likewise, in eastern North America the Indians did not shift to predominant dependence on agriculture until about A.D. 800, when they developed field cropping based on several varieties of maize, beans, and squash. Meanwhile, agriculture had spread southward from Mesoamerica, reaching Peru about 750 B.C. On the other hand, the presence in Peru of non-Mesoamerican maize and bean varieties of considerable antiquity suggests the possibility of original plant domestication in the Andean as well as the Mexican plateaus.

All in all, the Indians domesticated over 100 plants, or as many as were domesticated in all Eurasia—a truly extraordinary achievement. About 50 percent of the crop tonnage of the world is from plants domesticated by Indians, which means that the world population today would be much smaller were it not for Indian agriculturists. Also the fact that none of the plants grown in America was cultivated in the Old World before the discoveries proves conclusively that the origins of agriculture in the two hemispheres were independent.

The regions where the Indians started agriculture were also the regions where they first developed it further and gradually evolved advanced farming cultures. These cultures in turn profoundly changed the Indians' way of life. In general, the result was, as in Eurasia, a greatly increased sedentary population and the development of those cultural activities not directly connected with bare subsistence. In other words, it was in these advanced farming cultures that it was possible to build large empires and sophisticated civilizations comparable in certain respects to those of West Africa. Unfortunately, these indigenous American civilizations were suddenly overwhelmed by the Spaniards and thus left little behind them except their precious domesticated plants (see map of Amerindian Empires on the Eve of the Spanish Conquest, p. 325.)

The three major American civilizations were the Mayan (in present-day Yucatan, Guatemala, and Belize), the Aztec (in present-day Mexico), and the Inca (stretching for 3,000 miles from mid-Ecuador to mid-Chile). The Mayan civilization was outstanding for its extraordinary development of the arts and sciences. Its accomplishments included a unique stone architecture; a sculpture that ranks among the great art of all times; an *ideographic writing* in which characters or signs were used as conventional symbols for ideas; and a knowledge of the movements of heavenly bodies, which showed the Mayas to be better astronomers than any in contemporary Europe and as competent mathematicians. The Aztecs were brusque and warlike compared to the artistic and intellectual Mayas—a contrast reminiscent of that between the Romans and the Greeks in the Old World. The Aztecs paid more attention to the army, training all able-bodied men for war and holding them liable for military service. Their state also was better organized, including a well-developed judiciary and arrangements for the care of the needy.

The Incas were even more advanced than the Aztecs in their material accomplishments. Their remarkable roads, fortresses, and temples were built of great blocks of stone so perfectly joined that even now, nearly 500 years later, a knife cannot be inserted between them. An extensive irrigation system, parts of which are still in use, made the Inca Empire a flourishing agricultural area. Above all the Incas organized the only integrated and dynamic state in the Americas—a state geared for indefinite expansion outside and for regimentation and paternalism inside. The instruments of control included state ownership of land, mineral wealth, and herds; obligatory adherence to the official Sun religion; careful census compilations for tax and military purposes; deposition of local hereditary chieftains; forced population resettlement for the assimilation of conquered peoples; and mass marriages under state auspices. The Inca Empire probably was the most successful totalitarian state the world has ever seen.

Impressive as these attainments are, the fact remains that a comparative handful of Spanish adventurers were able to overthrow and ruthlessly destroy all three of these civilizations, and this despite the fact that these civilizations had dense populations numbering tens of millions. The explanation is to be found ultimately in the isolation of the Americas, which left the Indians too far behind in *technology*. By A.D. 1500 the New World had reached the stage of civilization that western Europe had attained in 1500 B.C. and the Middle East in 3500 B.C.

Precisely what did this mean when the clash occurred with the arrival of the Spaniards? It meant, in the first place, that the Indians found themselves economically and technologically far behind the civilizations of the invaders. Their cultivation techniques never advanced beyond the bare minimum necessary for feeding populations that rarely reached the density of those of the Old World. Their tools were made only of stone, wood, or bone. They were incapable of smelting ores. They did work with metal, but it was almost exclusively for ornamental purposes. The only ships they constructed were canoes and seagoing rafts. For land transportation they made no use of the wheel, which they knew but used only as a toy. With the exception of the llama and the alpaca, which were used in the Andes but could not carry heavy loads, only the human back was available for transportation.

The immediate significance of this technological lag should not be exaggerated. The Indians obviously were at a grave disadvantage with their spears and arrows against the Spaniards' horses and guns. But after the initial shock the Indians became accustomed to firearms and cavalry. Furthermore, the Spaniards soon discovered that the Indian weapons were sharp and durable, and they came to prefer the Indian armor of quilted cotton to their own.

This suggests that factors in addition to technological disparity lay behind the Spanish victories. One was the extreme centralization of the Aztec and the Inca empires, which made them fatally vulnerable. Once the Indian kings Montezuma and Atahualpa had fallen into Spanish hands, the Aztec and Inca empires became bodies without heads, and resistance was paralyzed. Furthermore, the Spaniards were able everywhere to take advantage of dissension among the Indians and to play one group against the other. Cortes, for example, could not have won his victories without the active assistance of discontented native tribes that had been subjugated or antagonized by the Aztecs.

Probably the most important single factor behind the conquest of the Amerindians was their lack of immunity against the diseases brought by the Europeans and their African slaves. Because the Indians had no contacts with peoples of other continents after crossing the Bering Sea tens of thousands of years earlier, they became biologically vulnerable to the diseases of the newcomers—diseases such as smallpox, measles, typhus, and yellow fever. A total of 43 million to 72 million Indians are believed to have lived in North and South America in 1491. Within a few years their numbers had shrunk tragically. Mexico's population fell from about 25 million in 1492 to about one million in 1608. The decline was worse in other regions. The island of Hispaniola (today Haiti and the Dominican Republic) had 60,000 Amerindians in 1508, 30,000 in 1554, and 500 in 1570.

This demographic holocaust explains why early European colonists often found abandoned fields and deserted village sites, which they could take over without any resistance. Later, when the full flood of immigration from Europe got under way, the Indians were hopelessly overwhelmed. First came the traders, who penetrated throughout the Americas with little competition or resistance, for the Americas, unlike Africa, had no rival native merchant class. Then appeared the settlers, who, attracted by the combination of healthy climate and fertile land, came in ever-increasing numbers and inundated the hapless Indians. When the latter occasionally took up arms in desperation, they were foredoomed to failure because they lacked both unity and the basic human and material resources. Thus, the unequal contest ended relatively quickly with the victorious white man in possession of the choice lands and the Indians relegated to reservations or to the less desirable regions that did not interest the new masters. The only exception was in the lands of the Aztecs, Incas, and Mayas, which had been more densely populated, and where a larger number survived the European flood. Gradually these survivors staged a comeback until today they comprise the majority of the total population in countries such as Bolivia and Guatemala.

It is apparent that the balance of forces was quite different in America than in Africa. Geography, and a comparatively low level of economic, political, and social organization all worked against the Indians to make it possible for the Europeans to take over the Americas at a time when they were still confined to a few toeholds on the coasts of Africa.

III.   AUSTRALIA

Australia is the most isolated large landmass in the world. It is more extreme in this respect than the southern tips of South America and of Africa. This isolation made it possible for archaic forms of life to survive to modern times, including plants such as the eucalyptus family and mammals such as the monotremes and the marsupials. In Australia also survived archaic human types that were still in the Paleolithic stage when the first British settlers arrived in the late eighteenth century. These aborigines were descended from three different ethnic groups that had ferried to Australia perhaps over 30,000 years ago when narrow straits separated the continent from the Indonesian archipelago. These three strains are discernible in the present-day aboriginal population. The majority are slender, long-limbed people with brown skins, little body hair, and wavy to curly head hair and beards. They have survived in substantial numbers because they live in desert areas that are of little use to the white man. In the cool and fertile southeastern corner of the continent are a few survivors of a very different native stock—thickset with light-brown skin, heavy body hair, and luxuriant beards. Along the northeastern coast, in the only part of Australia covered with dense tropical rain forest, lives the third ethnic group, part of the Negroid family. They are small, of slight build, and with woolly hair and black skins.

The culture of these peoples was by no means uniform. The most advanced were those in the southeast, where rainfall was adequate for permanent settlements. But throughout the continent the aborigines, thanks to their complete isolation, had remained Paleolithic food gatherers. Their retardation was particularly evident in their technology and in their political organiza-

AUSTRALIAN ABORIGINES

When the Europeans expanded overseas, the most technologically backward people they encountered were the food-gathering Australian aborigines. The following description of the Arunta tribe is by two white Australians who lived with the aborigines for twenty years and became initiated members of the tribe. *

If, now, the reader can imagine himself transported to the side of some waterhole in the centre of Australia, he would probably find amongst the scrub and gumtrees surrounding it a small camp of natives. Each family, consisting of a man and one or more wives and children, accompanied always by dogs, occupies a *mia-mia*, which is merely a lean-to of shrubs so placed as to shield the occupants from the prevailing wind, which, if it be during the winter months, is sure to be from the southeast. In front of this, or inside if the weather be cold, will be a small fire of twigs, for the black fellow never makes a large fire as the white man does. In this respect he certainly regards the latter as a strange being, who makes a big fire and then finds it so hot that he cannot go anywhere near to it. The black fellow's idea is to make a small fire such that he can lie coiled round it and, during the night, supply it with small twigs so that he can keep it alight without making it so hot that he must go further away.

Early in the morning, if it be summer, and not until the sun be well up if it be winter, the occupants of the camp are astir. Time is no object to them, and, if there be no lack of food, the men and women all lounge about while the children laugh and play. If food be required, then the women will go out accompanied by the children and armed with digging sticks and *pitchis* [wooden troughs], and the day will be spent out in the bush in search of small burrowing animals such as lizards and small marsupials. The men will perhaps set off armed with spears, spearthrowers, boomerangs and shields in search of larger game such as emus and kangaroos. The latter are secured by stalking, when the native gradually approaches his prey with perfectly noiseless footsteps. Keeping a sharp watch on the animal, he remains absolutely still, if it should turn its head, until once more it resumes its feeding. Gradually, availing himself of the shelter of any bush or large tussock of grass, he approaches near enough to throw his spear. The end is fixed into the point of the spearthrower, and, aided by the leverage thus gained, he throws it forward with all his strength. Different men vary much in their skill in spearthrowing, but it takes an exceptionally good man to kill or disable at more than twenty yards. Sometimes two or three men will hunt in company, and then, while one remains in ambush, the others combine to drive the animals as close as possible to him. . . .

It may be said that with certain restrictions which apply partly to groups of individuals and partly to individuals at certain times of their lives, everything which is edible is used for food. . . .

As a general rule the natives are kindly disposed to one another, that is of course within the limits of their own tribe, and, where two tribes come into contact with one another on the border land of their respective territories, there the same amicable feelings are maintained between the members of the two. There is no such thing as one tribe being in a constant state of enmity with another so far as these Central tribes are concerned.

* B. S. Spencer and F. J. Gillen, *The Native Tribes of Central Australia* (Macmillan, 1899), pp. 1–54.

tion. They wore no clothing except for decorative purposes. Their housing consisted, in dry country, of simple, open windbreaks, and in wet country, of low, domed huts thrown together of any available material. Their principal weapons were spears, spearthrowers, and boomerangs, all made of wood. They were ignorant of pottery, their utensils consisting merely of a few twined bags and baskets and occasional bowls of bark or wood. As food gatherers and hunters they were highly skilled and ingenious. They had a wide range of vegetable as well as animal foods and an intimate knowledge of the varieties, habits, and properties of these foods.

The poverty of Australian technology was matched by an almost equal poverty of political organization. Like most food-gathering peoples, the aborigines lived in bands, groups of families who normally camped together and roamed over a well-defined territory. They had no real tribes but only territorial divisions characterized by differences in language and culture. Consequently they did not have chiefs, courts, or other formal agencies of government. Yet these same aborigines had an extraordinarily complex social organization and ceremonial life. The hunter who brought in game or the woman who returned from a day of root digging was required to divide his or her take with all the kin according to strict regulations. Among the northern Queensland natives, when a man sneezed, all those within hearing slapped themselves on their bodies, the place varying according to their precise relationship to the sneezer.

So involved were these nonmaterial aspects of Australian society that they have been a delight to students of primitive institutions. But precociousness in these matters was of little help to the aborigines when the Europeans appeared in the late eighteenth century. If the American Indians with their flowering civilizations and widespread agricultural communities were unable to stand up to the white man, the Paleolithic Australians obviously had no chance. They were few in numbers, totaling about 300,000 when the Europeans arrived. They lacked both the arms and the organization necessary for effective resistance. And unlike the American Indians and the African Negroes, they showed little inclination to secure and use the white man's "fire stick." Thus

the unfortunate aborigines were brutally decimated by the British immigrants, many of whom were lawless convicts shipped out from overcrowded jails. The combination of disease, alcoholism, outright slaughter, and wholesale land confiscation reduced the native population to about 45,000 today, together with some 80,000 mixed breeds. The treatment accorded to the Australians is suggested by the following typical observation of a Victorian settler in 1853: "The Australian aboriginal race seems doomed by Providence, like the Mohican and many other well known tribes, to disappear from their native soil before the progress of civilization."[2]

SUGGESTED READINGS

A useful introduction to Africa is provided by J. F. A. Ajayi and M. Crowder, eds., *Historical Atlas of Africa* (Longman, 1985). On African geography, see W. A. Hance, *The Geography of Modern Africa,* 2nd ed. (Columbia University, 1975); and R. Stock, *Africa South of the Sahara: A Geographical Interpretation* (Guilford, 1994). Collections of source materials are provided by B. Davidson, *The African Past: Chronicles from Antiquity to Modern Times* (Little, Brown, 1964); and P. J. M. McEwan, ed., *Africa from Early Times to 1800* (Oxford University, 1968). The pre-Western history of Africa is presented as authoritatively as current knowledge permits by P. D. Curtin et al., *African History* (Little, Brown, 1978); J. D. Fage, *A History of Africa* (Knopf, 1978); and in more detail in R. Oliver and J. D. Fage, eds., *The Cambridge History of Africa,* 8 vols. (Cambridge University, 1975ff.); and in the UNESCO *General History of Africa* (University of California, 1981ff.).

The most recent information on the peopling of the Americas is given in R. Shutler, Jr., ed., *Early Man in the New World* (Sage, 1973), which also contains a selection on the parallel peopling of Australia. A stimulating analysis of the European impact on the American Indians is given by F. Jennings, *The Invasion of America: Indians, Colonialism, and the Cant of Conquest* (University of North Carolina, 1975). The latest estimates on the numbers of American Indians are given in M. Denevan, ed., *The Native Population of the Americas in 1492* (University of Wisconsin,

1976). A lavishly illustrated volume on the American Indians from their early migrations to the present day is *America's Fascinating Indian Heritage* (Reader's Digest Press, 1978). A stimulating interpretation is by P. Farb, *Man's Rise to Civilization as Shown by the Indians of North America . . .* (Dutton, 1968), which includes an analysis of the significance for modern people of the experiences of the Indians. Other noteworthy studies are by A. M. Josephy, Jr., *The Indian Heritage of America* (Knopf, 1968); C. Beals, *Nomads and Empire Builders: Native Peoples and Cultures of South America* (Chilton, 1961); and the excellent collection of readings by H. E. Driver, ed., *The Americas on the Eve of Discovery* (Prentice Hall, 1964). V. W. Von Hagen has readable accounts of all three of the leading American civilizations: *The Aztec: Man and Tribe* (New American Library, 1958), *The Incas: People of the Sun* (World, 1961), and *World of the Maya* (New American Library, 1960). The best general study of the Eskimos is by K. Birket-Smith, *The Eskimos* (Crown, 1971).

For the Australian aborigines the standard works are A. P. Elkins, *The Australian Aborigines,* 3rd ed. (Angus, 1954); W. E. Harney, *Life Among the Aborigines* (Hale, 1957); R. M. and C. H. Berndt, *The World of the First Australians: An Introduction to the Traditional Life of the Australian Aborigines* (University of Chicago, 1964); A. A. Abbie, *The Original Australians* (Muller, 1969); G. Blainey, *Triumph of the Nomads: A History of Aboriginal Australia* (Overlook Press, 1976); and R. Broome, *Aboriginal Australians* (Allen and Unwin, 1982).

22

Expanding Civilization of the West: Renaissance and Reformation

Men can do all things if they will.

Leon Battista Alberti

For the work of God cannot be received and honored by any works, but by faith alone.

Martin Luther

. . . by an eternal and immutable counsel God has once and for all determined both whom He would admit to salvation, and whom He would condemn to destruction.

John Calvin

In the late Middle Ages, a curious and fateful development occurred in the Eurasian world. On the one hand, Islamic and Confucian empires were becoming increasingly ossified and were withdrawing into themselves. On the other hand, the western tip of Eurasia was experiencing an unprecedented and thoroughgoing transformation. Far-reaching changes were taking place in almost all phases of west European life. The end result was the emergence of a new type of dynamic, expansionist civilization—modern civilization, which was qualitatively different from the traditional agrarian-based civilizations of the rest of Eurasia and, for that matter, of the rest of the globe. Thus began what is now termed the process of modernization, which has persisted at an accelerating tempo to the present day and which has determined the course of modern world history.

I.   MODERNIZATION

Economists define *modernization* as the process by which humans have increased their control over their physical environment as a means to increasing per capita output. Sociologists and anthropologists point out other features of modernization, including the awakening and activation of the masses, more interest in the present and the future than in the past, a tendency to view human affairs as understandable rather than as manipulated by supernatural forces, and, until recent years, a faith in the beneficence of science and technology.

From the viewpoint of world history the significance of this modernization process is that it led inexorably to European domination of the globe. The reason is that modernization provided the Europeans not only with superior economic and military power but also with superior sociopolitical cohesion and dynamism. For example, a handful of British merchants and soldiers were able to conquer and rule the great Indian subcontinent more because of its sociopolitical fragility than because of British military technology. Conversely, it is significant that there never has been any speculation about the possibility of a reverse course of events—the landing in England of Indian soldiers and merchants with the designs for trade and booty that had motivated the English nabobs. The notion that Indians might have been able to do in England what Robert Clive and Warren Hastings did in India seems so preposterous as never to be considered even as a remote possibility. But it is preposterous precisely because of the difference between English and Indian societies—the latter hopelessly fragmented, with an infinitely greater gulf between rulers and ruled than in the former. Whereas Clive and Hastings had been able to play off Moslems against Hindus, prince against prince, and local potentates against imperial officials, while the peasant masses remained inert in their villages, any Indian counterpart of Clive and Hastings doubtless would have encountered a united front of Protestants and Catholics and of government and citizens, including the gentry, the townspeople, and the peasants.

Such was the chasm, so fateful for world history, separating traditional societies from those that had undergone modernization. Furthermore, this modernization was not a one-shot affair. It continues to the present day and at an ever faster pace. In late medieval and early modern times, as we shall note in this chapter and the following one, modernization comprised the *Renaissance* and *Reformation,* economic expansion, emerging capitalism, state building, and overseas enterprise. These developments set off a chain reaction in the form of the great scientific, industrial, and successive political revolutions (chapters 28 and 29) that have molded human history from the seventeenth century to the present.

II.   RENAISSANCE

The term *Renaissance* is polemical. It means new birth or revival, and was coined by fifteenth-century intellectuals who believed that their age represented the rebirth of classical culture following an intervening "age of darkness," as they termed the medieval period. This interpretation was accepted through the nineteenth century, but historians today no longer consider it to have been a case of medieval pitch darkness against Renaissance dazzling light. The fact is that interest in the classics was by no means completely absent during the Middles Ages, and conversely, certain characteristics associated with medievalism were very much in evidence during the Renaissance. So modern historians, although not discarding the familiar term, now define the Renaissance as connoting not a sharp break or turning point but rather an age of transition from medieval to modern civilization—roughly from 1350 to 1600.

The Renaissance began first in Italy, and hence reflected the conditions and values of contemporary Italian society. This was a bustling urban society based on flourishing industries and on the profitable commerce between western Europe and the wealthy Byzantine and Islamic empires. The Italians were the middlemen in this commerce and prospered accordingly. By about 1400 the Venetian merchant fleet was made up of 300 "large ships," 3,000 ships of less than 100 tons, and 45 galleys, manned in all by some 28,000 men. Venetian shipyards employed an additional 6,000 carpenters and other workers. Comparable activity was to be found in other

The true "Renaissance man"—Leonardo da Vinci. Painter, sculptor, inventor, Leonardo demonstrated how far ahead of his time he truly was with his *Study of the Human Body*, 1492.

Italian cities such as Florence, Genoa, Pisa, and Rome. These cities were dominated by the great merchant families that controlled politics as well as trade and crafts. These families were the patrons of Renaissance artists and writers. Their needs, interests, and tastes colored the Renaissance cultural revival even though the patrons also included ducal families such as the Sforza of Milan, as well as popes such as Nicholas V, Pius II, Julius II, and Leo X. This explains the secularism and humanism of the Renaissance—its concern with this world rather than the hereafter and its focus on pagan classics rather than Christian theology.

At the center of most Renaissance art and literature was the person—the new Renaissance person who was the molder of his or her own destiny rather than the plaything of supernatural forces. People did not need to be preoccupied with supernatural forces; rather, the purpose of life was to develop one's innate potentialities. "Men can do all things if they will," wrote Leon Battista Alberti (1404–1472), and his own attainments abundantly validated this maxim. This Florentine patrician was an architect, mathematician, and archeologist, as well as playwright; poet; art critic; organist; singer; and, in his youth, a well-known runner, wrestler, and mountain climber.

The secularism and individualism of the Renaissance were reflected in its scholarship and education. The so-called father of Renaissance literature, Francesco Petrarca, or Petrarch (1304–1374), stressed the value of the classics as a means for self-improvement and a guide to social action. Likewise, the new boarding schools of the Re-

Raphael's masterpiece—*School of Athens.*

naissance trained not priests but the sons of merchants. The curriculum emphasized classical studies and physical exercise and was designed to educate the students to live well and happily and to function as responsible citizens.

The Renaissance spirit is most strikingly expressed in its art. Since the church no longer was the sole patron, artists were encouraged to turn to subjects other than the traditional biblical themes. Giotto (1276—1337) marked the transition in painting to naturalism. This trend was carried much further by Masaccio (1401–1428), who mastered the distinctive Renaissance invention of perspective. In contrast to medieval painting, that of the Renaissance projected light and shadow and gave the appearance of depth to figures and scenes.

By the mid-fifteenth century Italian Renaissance painting attained its maturity. In Florence, Masaccio was followed by Sandro Botticelli (1444–1510) and by the versatile genius Leonardo da Vinci (1452–1519), who was a sculptor, musician, architect, and engineer as well as painter. As such, Da Vinci was the personification of the "new Renaissance person." His 72-page notebook, known as the Codex Hammer, was sold in London on November 15, 1994 for $30.8 million. In this manuscript he speculated on why the sky is blue and why fossils are found on mountaintops. He also predicted the invention of the submarine and the steam engine.

About 1550, after two centuries of sparkling achievement, the Italian Renaissance began to wane. One reason for the decline was the French invasion of 1494, which precipitated decades of war that involved the various European powers and left the Italian peninsula devastated. More basic in the long run was the economic blow suffered when Vasco da Gama sailed into Calicut Harbor, India, on May 22, 1498. This ended the profitable monopoly that the Italians had enjoyed as the middlemen in the trade between western Europe and the East. In four years (1502–1505), the Venetians were able to obtain an average of only 1 million English pounds of spices a year at Alexandria, whereas in the last years of the fifteenth century they had averaged 3.5 million pounds. Conversely, Portuguese spice imports rose from 224,000 pounds in 1501 to an average of 2,300,000 in the four years from 1503 to 1506.

More serious than this commercial decline was the industrial. For centuries Italy had exported manufactured goods, especially textiles, to northern Europe and the Near East, and also had derived substantial revenues from banking and shipping services. But by the late sixteenth century the British, French, and Dutch had surpassed the Italians, who were hampered by restricting guild regulations, high taxes and labor costs, and failure to adapt goods to changing tastes. Thus the average annual production of woolens in Florence was 30,000 cloths between 1560 and 1580, but only 13,000 between 1590 and 1600, and 6,000 by 1650. Likewise, Venice was producing an average of 20,000 to 30,000 cloths about 1600, but only 2,000 by 1700. This gap between Italy and the northern European countries was further widened by the growing importance of colonial trade, from which the Italian cities, lacking overseas possessions, were excluded.

To use modern terminology, Italy, which had been the developed part of Europe during the Middle Ages, now became the underdeveloped. It was Italy that henceforth exported raw materials (oil, wine, grain, wool, and raw silk) to northern Europe in return for manufactured goods. This meant that cities and their grandi no longer were dominant in Italy, their primacy being replaced by that of landed proprietors of a feudal character. Thus the economic foundations of the Renaissance crumbled.

III.   RENAISSANCE LEGACY

The Renaissance was not an exclusively Italian phenomenon. Its innovations spread to northern Europe in the sixteenth century. The instruments of diffusion were Italian diplomats and generals employed by northern monarchs and the printing press, which speeded up the circulation of books and ideas. In the process of transmission northward the Renaissance changed somewhat in character. Whereas in Italy it had manifested itself primarily in art and literature, in the north it found expression more in religion and morals. But this was by no means exclusively so, as evident in the works of German painters such as Albrecht Dürer (1471–1528) and Hans Holbein the Younger (1497–1543), and of Flemish painters such as the Van Eycks and Peter Breughel. Breughel was the most unorthodox and socially conscious of the northern artists. Turning away from the traditional themes of his predecessors—religious subjects and portraits of merchant families amid their luxurious surroundings—he focused on scenes from everyday peasant life. He also used his art to combat Spanish rule in the Netherlands, as in his painting *The Massacre of the Innocents,* depicting Spanish soldiers slaughtering women and children.

Printing was particularly influential in northern Europe because literacy was more widespread there than in the southern and eastern regions of Europe. The flood of printed matter certainly fomented popular agitation concerning political and religious issues, thereby contributing substantially to the Reformation and the ensuing religious and dynastic wars. Printing also stimulated the development of national schools of literature during this early modern period. Luther's translation of the Bible provided the basis for modern literary German. Likewise, the King James Bible and the plays of Shakespeare (1564–1616) laid the foundation for modern English literature. In Spain, Miguel de Cervantes (1547–1616) made the same contribution to the national language with his novel *Don Quixote.* And in France, this was the role of François Rabelais (c. 1490–1553) and Michel de Montaigne (1533–1592). The significance of such literary endeavors was implicitly recognized in 1635 when the *Académie Française* was established for the purpose of officially defining the vocabulary and grammar of the national language.

In conclusion, what is the significance of the Renaissance in the perspective of world history? It is apparent that new emphasis on persons and on what they could accomplish obviously was more conducive to overseas expansion than the preceding medieval outlook. On the other hand, this point can easily be exaggerated and needs serious modification. The fact is that Renaissance Europe was not science-oriented. The leading figures tended to be more aesthetic and philosophical than objective and skeptical. They retained in various degrees certain medieval patterns of thought. They persisted in admiring and believing the incredible and the fantastic. They continued to seek the philosopher's stone that would convert other metals into gold. They still believed in astrology and confused it with astronomy.

The Iberian pioneers of overseas expansion definitely were not "Renaissance men." Prince Henry the Navigator, for example, was described by his contemporaries as a rigid, pious, and chivalrous ascetic rather than as a humanist. Although a generous patron of sailors and cartographers, he was not interested in learning and the arts. The story of a school of astronomy and mathematics that he allegedly supported at Sagres is a myth. Thus the stimulation of rapidly widening "new intellectual horizons" explains less about the origins of European expansion before 1500 than it does about the impetus and irresistible power that that explosion of knowledge provided after 1600. Indeed, European expansion was vastly important in its own right. The fact remains that there was an intellectual ferment in western Europe and that it had no counterpart in the rest of Eurasia. This is a fundamental difference of enormous significance.

In the Ottoman Empire, for example, the Moslem *medressehs*, or colleges, emphasized theology, jurisprudence, and rhetoric at the expense of astronomy, mathematics, and medicine. The graduates of these schools were uninformed about what was being done in the West and quite uninterested in finding out. No Moslem Turk could believe that a Christian infidel could teach him anything of value. Now and then, a rare, farsighted individual warned of the dangers of the intellectual iron curtain that separated the Ottoman Empire from neighboring Christendom. One of the voices was Katib Chelebi, the famous Turkish bibliographer, encyclopedist, and historian who lived in the first half of the seventeenth century. Coming from a poor family, he was unable to obtain a formal higher education. This was to be a blessing in disguise. He was spared the superficial, hairsplitting specialization on Moslem

sacred studies that characterized Ottoman education at this time. The fact that he was self-taught explains in large part his open-mindedness toward Western learning.

One of Chelebi's works was a short naval handbook that he compiled following a disastrous defeat of the Ottoman fleet in 1656. In the preface of this work, Chelebi emphasized the need for mastering the science of geography and map making.

For men who are in charge of affairs of state, the science of geography is a matter of which knowledge is necessary. They may not be familiar with what the entire globe is like, but they ought at least to know the map of the Ottoman State and of those states adjoining it. Then, when they have to send forces on campaign, they can proceed on the basis of knowledge, and so the invasion of the enemy's land and also the protection and defense of the frontiers becomes an easier task. Taking counsel with individuals who are ignorant of that science is no satisfactory substitute, not even when such men are local veterans. Most such veterans are entirely unable to sketch the map of their own home regions.

Sufficient and convincing proof of the necessity for learning this science is the fact that the heathen, by their application to and their esteem for those branches of learning, have discovered the New World and have over-run the markets of India.[1]

Chelebi grasped the connection between Europe's intellectual advance and its overseas expansion. In his last work before his death in 1657, Chelebi warned his fellow citizens that if they did not abandon their dogmatism they would soon "be looking at the universe with the eyes of oxen." His prediction proved prophetic. The Turks remained steeped in their religious obscurantism, and like other non-Western peoples, they paid a high price. The Christian infidels with their new learning eventually became the masters not only of the New World but also of the ancient empires of Islam and Confucianism.

IV.   REFORMATION IN GERMANY

The term *Reformation* is as misleading as the term *Renaissance*. Luther began as a reformer but ended as a revolutionary, driven by the logic of his basic convictions to challenge and reject the foundations of the Roman Church. Superficially, the Reformation can be interpreted as the reaction to certain abuses within the Church, including the illiteracy of many of the priests; the dissolute lives of some of the clergy, including popes; and the sale of religious offices, of dispensations (exemptions from church laws), and of indulgences (pardons for sins). Provocative as these abuses were, the fact is that they were more the pretext than the root cause of the Protestant Reformation. Indeed, at the time when the Reformation was getting under way, pious Catholics within the Church were beginning their own reform efforts to correct these conditions. To explain a basic upheaval that shattered the age-old unity of Western Christendom, it is necessary to go beyond abuses and to consider certain background historical forces that had been building up for centuries.

One was the undermining of the prestige of the papacy during the fourteenth-century "Babylonian Captivity," when soldiers of King Philip IV of France arrested Pope Boniface VIII. The arrest was followed by the transference of the papal capital to Avignon, where the popes perforce were subservient to French interests. Even more ruinous to papal prestige was the Great Schism at the end of the fourteenth century. Two popes, one in Rome and one in Avignon, each claimed to be the legitimate successor of St. Peter and excommunicated each other. Another factor behind the Reformation was the legacy of earlier heresies such as those of John Wyclif in England and John Hus in Bohemia. The latter was burned at the stake at the Council of Constance in 1415, but his followers were still alive when Luther began preaching essentially similar doctrines a century later.

Political factors also were involved in the Reformation, namely the growth of national feeling in northern Europe and the related rise of the "New Monarchs" in various states. Both monarchs and subjects increasingly viewed the popes as foreigners with no right to meddle in national affairs or to raise revenues within national frontiers. This led to the final force behind the Reformation—the popular resentment against the taxes collected by the Church and against its great landed properties scattered throughout Western Europe. The economic dispute, together with the preceding political factor, will be considered in more detail in the following chapter.

Here it should be noted that the interests of the growing middle class and of the national monarchs led both to eye greedily the vast landholdings of the Church and its enormous movable wealth in the form of jewels, bullion, art objects, and luxurious furnishings. Equally coveted were the revenues flowing from the states to Rome in the form of the tithe; the funds from the sale of offices; and the innumerable fees for appeals, dispensations, and indulgences.

This combination of historical forces reached the explosion point first in Germany because that land was then a collection of over a hundred principalities—fiefs, ecclesiastical city-states, free cities, counties, and duchies—whose rulers were too weak to resist the powerful Church in cases of excessive exactions. One of these cases was the decision of the pope in 1517 to sell a large number of indulgences throughout Europe to pay for the repair of St. Peter's Church in Rome. The indulgence in Germany that triggered the Reformation promised absolution "from all thy sins, transgressions, and excesses, how enormous soever they may be . . . so that when you die the gates of punishment shall be shut, and the gates of the paradise of delight shall be opened. . . ." It was in protest against this "unbridled preaching of pardons" that Luther, then a priest at the University of Wittenburg, posted his ninety-five theses on the church door. Most of his propositions were not revolutionary, but he did argue that the "word of God" lay not in the doctrine of the Church but in the Bible, thereby undercutting Church authority.

Pope Leo X dismissed the incident as a "squabble among monks," but the theses were quickly translated into German and widely circulated in print. The enthusiastic popular response demonstrated that Luther had given voice to deeply felt national grievances. The ensuing public debate led Luther to spell out the revolutionary implications of his basic doctrine of justification by faith—that is, that the priestly offices and ministrations of the Church were unnecessary intermediaries between the individual and God. By the end of 1520 Luther had broken irrevocably with the Church and embraced the earlier heresies of Wyclif and Hus as "most Christian." In October 1520 Luther burned a papal bull of excommunication, and the following year he was summoned to appear before the Imperial Diet meeting at Worms. Called on to recant, Luther refused "unless I am convinced by the testimony of the Scriptures or by clear reason." The emperor secured passage of an edict condemning the obstinate friar as a heretic, but the sympathetic Elector Fredrick of Saxony provided refuge in his castle and saved Luther from the fate of Hus.

In this place of exile Luther busied himself in the following years translating the Bible into German and building an independent German church. Emperor Charles V was unable to move decisively against the spreading heresy because he was involved in wars with the French and the Turks. By 1546 he was free of these distractions so he set out to crush the Lutheran princes and restore the unity of the church. He was encouraged in this by the pope, who provided money and troops. But the Lutherans banded together in the Schmalkaldic League and won support from the Catholic French king, who was more concerned with dynastic than religious considerations. The fighting dragged on inconclusively until the signing of the Peace of Augsburg (1555), which granted each German prince the right to select either the Catholic or Lutheran faith and to impose it on his subjects. Thus the end result of the Reformation in Germany was the roughly equal division of the country into Lutheran and Catholic states.

V. REFORMATION BEYOND GERMANY

The Peace of Augsburg opened the gates to the rising flood of heresy, or rather heresies. The settlement at Augsburg had recognized only Lutheranism as a possible alternative to the Catholic faith. But Protestantism by its very nature lent itself to a continual proliferation of new sects. Luther's fundamental doctrine of individual interpretation of the Scriptures led inevitably to different interpretations and hence to new varieties of Protestantism. In Switzerland, for example, John Calvin joined Luther in rejecting salvation by "works" but also rejected his doctrine of salvation by "faith." Instead Calvin preached predestination—each individual's fate was decreed by God before birth. "In conformity, therefore, to the clear doctrine of Scripture, we assert that by

an eternal and immutable counsel God has once for all determined both whom He would admit to salvation, and whom He would condemn to destruction." Calvin differed from Luther also in requiring that the Church should actively intervene in community affairs to ensure the elimination of heresy, blasphemy, and wickedness. During his ascendancy in Geneva (1541–1564), his Consistory of Elders transformed that city into a Christian community whose austerity and holiness astonished visitors. Furthermore, the availability of printing presses enabled Calvin to make Geneva the headquarters of a proselytizing drive that profoundly affected such countries as Bohemia, Hungary, the Netherlands, Scotland, England, and the thirteen American colonies overseas.

An entirely different form of Protestantism was that of the *Anabaptists,* whose religious and social radicalism earned them persecution by Catholics, Lutherans, and Calvinists alike. Carrying to its logical conclusion Luther's doctrine that every man should follow the dictates of his conscience, they demanded full religious liberty, including separation of church and state. Equally radical were their social teachings—their opposition to individual accumulation of wealth, to class or status differentiation, to military service, and to payment of taxes for war-making purposes. It is not surprising that these tenets, undermining the authority of all religious and political establishments, led to the persecution and wholesale massacre of Anabaptists throughout Europe. The Hutterites and Mennonites are their survivors who have managed to hold out to the present day.

The prevailing factor determining the religion of a state almost invariably was the decision of its prince. If he favored a break with Rome, the Reformation triumphed; if he opposed a break, the Reformation was doomed. Very substantial benefits awaited the prince who opted in favor of Protestantism. His political power increased for he became the head of his national church rather than having to accept the ecclesiastical suzerainty of the international papacy. His economic position also improved because he could confiscate Church lands and movable wealth, and also check the flow of revenue to Rome. Despite these advantages of turning against the pope, as many princes remained loyal as chose to break away. One reason was the threat of attack by the imperial forces of Charles V supported by the pope. Also many princes found they could extract as many political and economic concessions from the papacy by remaining Catholic as they were likely to obtain as Protestant princes—hence the hodge-podge religious map of Europe that evolved after Luther's death.

This religious map eventually showed almost half the German states Lutheran, along with the Baltic lands of the Teutonic order and the Scandinavian kingdoms of Denmark-Norway and Sweden-Finland. In England, Henry VIII was a good Catholic in doctrinal matters and enjoyed as much control over the Catholic clergy as did the French king across the Channel. Yet Henry eventually established the independent Church of England (1534) because he was determined to divorce his wife, Catherine of Aragon. The pope could not oblige him because Catherine was the aunt of Emperor Charles V, whose army had sacked Rome a few years earlier. So Henry now became the head of the new Anglican church, and to ensure the support of his gentry, he gave them the expropriated monastery lands. But as long as he was alive, the new church remained staunchly Catholic in doctrine and ritual, the only innovation being the translation of the Bible into English. Henry's successors introduced changes in accord with their individual inclinations—Edward VI (1547–1553) moving far toward Protestantism, Mary (1553–1558) reverting to Catholicism, and Elizabeth (1558–1603) settling on a moderate Protestantism.

In the Netherlands (present-day Holland and Belgium), a combination of religious and political issues led to protracted war. The majority of the population in the northern Dutch provinces had become Calvinistic, which caused friction with the devout Catholic sovereign, Philip II of Spain. Political differences also were involved, the Netherlands challenging Philip's interference in what they considered to be their domestic affairs, and resenting also his heavy taxes and commercial restrictions. In 1566 Dutch resistance flared into what became the first modern revolution for national independence. The revolution in turn became an international war when Queen Elizabeth of England went to the aid of the Dutch rebels. Philip responded by sending his Invincible Armada of 132 ships northward in 1588. But the more maneuverable English ships forced the armada northward around Scotland and southward back to Spain—a defeated and battered remnant of the original expedition. The war continued its bloody course until a compromise settlement in 1609 recognized the independence of the northern provinces as the Dutch Republic, whereas the southern Belgian provinces remained under Spanish rule.

Meanwhile Calvinism had been spreading in France, where its adherents were known as Huguenots. The dynasty was not tempted to join its Protestant subjects because Francis I had obtained, by the Concordat of Bologna (1516), almost complete control over the Church offices and revenues in his realm. His successor, Henry II (1547–1559), severely persecuted the Huguenots. Mere ownership of a Bible was enough to condemn a subject as a heretic. Henry's death gave the Huguenots an opportunity, as neither the Queen Mother, Catherine de Medici, nor her weak sons enjoyed the popular support that Elizabeth did in England. Despite Catherine's efforts for a compromise, the country was polarized between the growing, dynamic Huguenots and the large Catholic majority. The ensuing religious war culminated in the St. Bartholomew's Day Massacre (August 24, 1572), when thousands of Huguenots were massacred throughout the country. Even this slaughter did not subdue the new faith, the struggle dragging on with the Huguenots receiving help from Protestant groups in England, Holland, and Germany, whereas the Catholics received men and money from King Philip of Spain. Peace was not restored until 1598, when Henry IV issued the Edict of Nantes guaranteeing freedom of conscience to the Huguenots. By granting legal recognition and status to two religions in the same state, this settlement represented a turning point in European religious history comparable to the Augsburg Treaty that allowed a prince to choose between two religions.

VI.   CATHOLIC REFORMATION

The Catholic Reformation formerly was known as the Counter-Reformation, but historians now recognize it as being more than simply an anti-Protestant movement. Its roots go back to pre-Luther times, so that the Catholic Reformation was a religious reform movement similar to the

RELIGION AND THE EXPANSION OF EUROPE

The expansion of Europe may be explained in part by the militancy of the Christian Church. Christianity asserted itself as a universal religion. Missionary spirit was especially active in the sixteenth century because of the centuries of armed conflict with Islam and the experiences during the Reformation. In the following selection, one of the conquistadors describes how the Indians in Spanish America were taught the "true" faith.*

After we had abolished idolatry and other abominations from among the Indians, the Almighty blessed our endeavors and we baptized the men, women, and all the children born after the conquest, whose souls would otherwise have gone to the infernal regions. With the assistance of God, and by a good regulation of our most Christian Monarch, of glorious memory, Don Carlos, and of his excellent son Don Philip, our most happy and invincible king, to whom may God grant a long life and an increase of territory, several pious monks of different orders arrived in New Spain, who travelled from place to place, preached the gospel to the inhabitants, and baptized new-born infants. By their unremitted exertions Christianity became planted in their hearts, so that the inhabitants came to the confessional once every year; and those who were better instructed in our Christian faith received the holy communion. Their churches are very richly ornamented with altars, crucifixes, candelabras, different-sized chalices, censers, and everything else required in our religious ceremonies, all of pure silver. The more wealthy townships have the vestments of choristers, the chasuble and the full canonicals of a priest, mostly of velvet damask or silk, and of various colours and manufacture. The flags which hang to the crosses are of silk, and richly ornamented with gold and pearls. The funeral crosses are covered with satin, and bear the figure of a death's head and cross bones; the funeral palls, in some townships, are also more or less splendid. The churches are likewise provided with a set of bells, have a regular band of choristers, besides flutes, dulcimers, clarions, and sacbuts, and some have even organs. I do believe there are more large and small trumpets in the province of Guatimala, where I am writing this, than in my native country Old Castile. It is indeed wonderful, and we cannot thank God too much for it, to behold the Indians assisting in the celebration of the holy mass, which they particularly do in those places where the Franciscan friars or the Brothers of Charity officiate at the altar.

It was also a great blessing for the Indians that the monks taught them to say their prayers in their own language, and frequently to repeat them. The monks have altogether so accustomed them to reverence everything relating to religion, that they never pass by any altar or cross without falling down on their knees and repeating a Pater Noster or an Ave Maria. We also taught the Indians to make wax lights for the holy services, for, previous to our arrival, they made no manner of use of their wax. We taught them to be so obedient and respectful to the monks and priests, that whenever one of these religious men approach a township the bells are rung, and the inhabitants go out to meet him with wax-lights in their hands; and they always give him a hospitable reception. On the day of Corpus Christi, the birth of Mary, and on other saint-days, when we are accustomed to form processions, the inhabitants of the districts surrounding Guatimala likewise march out in procession with crucifixes, light candles, and carry about their tutelar saint splendidly dressed up, all the time chanting hymns, accompanied by the sound of flutes and trumpets.

---

* *The Memoirs of the Conquistador Bernal Diaz Del Castillo . . .* (Hatchard, 1844), II, 390–391.

Protestant Reformation. In the late fifteenth and early sixteenth centuries, Catholic leaders in various countries had sought to correct abuses and regenerate spiritual values. In the process they organized new religious orders, such as the Capuchins, to revive Catholic piety and promote social service. But these early reformers, who tended to be contemplative and aristocratic, failed to arouse the masses or to win support in high Church circles in Rome. The Catholic Reformation did not become a dynamic and effective movement until the seriousness of Luther's challenge in Germany became clear. The reformers within the Church had hesitated to launch a counter movement against the Protestants for fear of irrevocably splitting Western Christendom. And the popes for long ignored Luther, viewing him as another of the long line of critics and heretics who in the past had always been suppressed or won back to the fold. Not until Pope Paul III (1534–1549) and his three successors who presided in Rome until the end of the sixteenth century did the papacy appreciate the significance of Protestantism and take appropriate steps.

The two measures of Paul III that proved the most significant in shaping the course and character of the Catholic Reformation were his summoning of the Council of Trent, which met intermittently from 1545 to 1563, and his approval of the founding of the Jesuit order, the Society of Jesus, in 1540. The main achievements of the Council of Trent were the reaffirmation of traditional Catholic doctrine in firmly anti-Protestant terms and the adoption of practical measures to eliminate abuses and restore Church discipline. These measures included a ban on the sale of indulgences, the prohibition of any bishop from holding more than one benefice, the stipulation that every diocese should establish a seminary to train priests, and the publication of an *Index* of books that Catholics would be forbidden to read.

The Jesuit order was the creation of the Spanish Basque nobleman Ignatius Loyola (1491–1556). While convalescing from a serious war wound he read various religious tracts that induced a profound spiritual crisis. He resolved to turn his back on his past life of philandering and brawling and to devote himself to serving the Lord. With a group of like-minded young men he organized the Society of Jesus along military lines. Its members did not lead the contemplative lives of earlier Catholic reformers. Rather, they viewed themselves as soldiers of Christ, and they strictly followed Loyola's first rule in his *Spiritual Exercises,* requiring unquestioning obedience to the "Hierarchical Church."

It was the discipline and militancy of these Jesuits that ensured implementation of the reforms of the Council of Trent. Many members served as agents of the Inquisition, which had been founded in 1542 to root out heresy wherever it was discovered. Others established schools that trained a new generation of priests and laymen with the theological certainty and confidence that had made the Protestant heretics so formidable. Jesuit schoolmen and diplomats were largely responsible for the stamping out of Protestantism in countries such as Austria, Bavaria, and Poland, where it had gained many converts. In addition to combatting Christian heretics in Europe, the Jesuits extended their operations all over the world to spread the gospel among the heathen in Asia, Africa, and the Americas. The nature and extent of their activities are indicated by the careers of such men as St. Francis Xavier in Japan, Matteo Ricci in China, Robert de Nobili in India, and Father Jacques Marquette in America.

VII. REFORMATION LEGACY

The legacy of the Reformation is ambiguous. It engendered doctrinal dissension and intolerance, which culminated in a succession of bloody religious wars. But the resulting fragmentation of Western Christendom compelled the contending sects to accept the fact that the hegemony of any universal church was not feasible—hence the gradual acceptance and implementation of religious toleration, a process so slow and contested that it is not yet fully complete. The Reformation was equally ambiguous concerning the status of the individual. Luther championed individual interpretation of the Scriptures, but when this led to the radicalism of the Anabaptists and to peasant revolts, he called on the civil authorities to destroy the "murdering, thieving hordes." Yet the emphasis on the reading of the Bible did lead to greater literacy, which opened doors to books and ideas other than religious.

The Reformation was ambiguous also in its effect on the status of women. In certain respects the Reformation enabled women to move forward. Protestant leaders rejected the medieval Catholic belief in the moral superiority of celibacy. Instead they considered married life desirable for three reasons: procreation of children, sexual satisfaction, and mutual help and comfort between partners. This attitude toward marriage and family encouraged the new idea of a single standard of morality for men and women, and also the equally novel idea of the right of a prospective bride or groom to veto a proposed marriage. Of course the transition from the old to the new was slow and erratic. Protestant theologians railed against adultery by men as well as women, but practice lagged far and long behind theory. Also young men were considered to be foolish "poor greenheads" if they did not select a wife who was not only compatible but "fit," a concept that encompassed the practical considerations usually emphasized by parents.

The principal Protestant leaders never considered or undertook a systematic reappraisal of the status of women. They stressed mutual love and respect between husband and wife, but they also took for granted the husband's primacy in the family. Luther made this quite clear: "Men have broad and large chests, and small narrow hips, and more understanding than the women, who have but small and narrow breasts, and broad hips, to the end they should remain at home, sit still, keep house, and bear and bring up children."[2]

Very different from mainline Protestantism were the radical sects such as the Lollards, Anabaptists, and Levellers. They favored free divorce and allowed women to participate in church government and to preach, and some even championed sexual freedom for both women and men. These sectarians were ahead of their time, not only for political reasons but also technological. The English Leveller leader, Gerrard Winstanley, conceded that sexual freedom outside the family left the mother and children vulnerable, "for the man will be gone and leave them, and regard them no more than other women . . . after he hath had his pleasure. Therefore you women beware. . . . By seeking their own freedom they embondage others."[3] Winstanley was acknowledging the fact that before the advent of effective birth control, sexual freedom amounted to freedom only for men.

Finally, as far as the immediate legacy of the Reformation was concerned, it shattered the universal medieval Church into a large number of local territorial churches—some national, some princely, some provincial, and some confined to a single city. The common feature of all these local churches was their control by secular rulers. Regardless of whether the church remained Catholic in doctrine or adhered to one of the Protestant faiths, it was the secular authority that controlled ecclesiastical appointments and church finances. The immediate and decisive legacy of the Reformation was the transfer of power from church to state. In this sense, the Reformation represents a stage in the evolution of the modern nation-state—the subject of the following chapter.

SUGGESTED READINGS

Standard general histories of this period are W. K. Ferguson, *Europe in Transition: 1300–1500* (Houghton Mifflin, 1962); E. F. Rice, Jr., *The Foundations of Early Modern Europe* (W. W. Norton & Co., 1970); E. P. Cheyney, *The Dawn of a New Era, 1250–1453* (Harper & Row, 1952); M. Gilmore, *The Age of Humanism, 1453–1517* (Harper & Row, 1952); and J. R. Major, *The Age of the Renaissance and Reformation* (Lippincott, 1970). An excellent general introduction to the Renaissance is by E. Breisach, *Renaissance Europe 1300–1517* (Macmillan, 1973). Also noteworthy is P. Kristeller, *Renaissance Thought,* 2 vols. (Torchbook, 1961–1965).

Interpretations of the Renaissance and Reformation from various viewpoints are provided by J. H. Plumb, *The Italian Renaissance* (Houghton Mifflin, 1987); F. H. New, *The Renaissance and Reformation: A Short History* (Wiley, 1977); and O. Chadwick, *The Reformation* (Penguin, 1972). Selections from contemporary sources are presented by R. H. Bainton, *The Age of the Reformation* (D. Van Nostrand, 1956); and by E. M. Burns, *The Counter Reformation* (D. Van Nostrand, 1964).

For the results of the cultural and religious upheavals, see R. L. De Molen, ed., *The Meaning of the Renaissance and Reformation* (Houghton Mifflin, 1974); R. H. Tawney, *Religion and the Rise of Capitalism* (Mentor, 1954); E. Troeltsch, *Protes-*

*tantism and Progress: A Historical Study of the Rela-
tion of Protestantism to the Modern World* (Beacon
Press, 1966); and E. I. Eisentein, *The Printing Press
as an Agent of Change: Communications and Cultural Transformations in Early Modern Europe,* 2
vols. (Columbia University, 1979).

The status of European women during these
centuries is summarized in S. M. Wyntjes, "Women in the Reformation Era," in R. Bridenthal
and C. Koonz, eds., *Becoming Visible: Women in
European History* (Houghton Mifflin, 1977), pp.
165–191; and analyzed in detail in the two studies by R. Bainton, *Women of the Reformation in
Germany and Italy* and *Women of the Reformation
in France and England* (Augsburg Publishing
House, 1971 and 1973).

23 Expanding Civilization of the West: Economic Growth and State Building

. . . the chief glory of the later Middle Ages was not its cathedrals or its epics or its scholasticism: it was the building for the first time in history of a complex civilization which rested not on the backs of sweating slaves or coolies but primarily on non-human power.

Lynn White, Jr.

Therefore it is necessary for a prince, who wishes to maintain himself, to learn how not to be good, and to use this knowledge and not use it, according to the necessity of the case.

Niccolo Machiavelli

The Renaissance and Reformation, as we saw in the preceding chapter, contributed to the modernizing of western European civilization. During these times literacy increased and there was much intellectual ferment. There was a mass awakening and a degree of participation unequaled in other regions of Eurasia. A more direct contribution to the modernizing process was made by the concurrent economic expansion and state building. These provided Europe with the resources and dynamism necessary for the fateful expansion overseas. This expansion, which has molded world history to the present day, did not occur simply because Columbus sailed westward and stumbled on the new world. The Vikings also had stumbled on North America in the eleventh century and for about a hundred years had unsuccessfully tried to maintain settlements there. By contrast, Columbus was followed by people from all countries of Europe in a massive and overwhelming penetration

The three-field system of farming improved efficiency and increased production from the eighth century onward.

of both North and South America. The difference in the reaction between the eleventh and fifteenth centuries suggests that certain developments had occurred in the intervening half-millennium that made Europe able and anxious to expand overseas. These developments included economic expansion and state building.

I. EXPANDING ECONOMY

Europe's economy did not grow uninterrupted during the medieval period. There was a steady rise from 900 to 1300, but then came the fourteenth-century slump, brought on by a combination of factors: a series of crop failures and famines, especially during 1315 and 1316; the Black Death, which carried off between one-third and two-thirds of the urban populations when it first struck in 1348 and 1349 and which recurred periodically thereafter for generations; and the Hundred Years' War between England and France and other conflicts in Germany and Italy. Shortly after 1400, however, a revival set in, and the trend from then on was generally upward.

Apart from the fourteenth-century decline, then, western Europe had fairly steady economic growth after the early medieval centuries. One reason for the advance was the cessation of invasions after 1000, with the ending of the Magyar and Viking attacks. Freedom from invasion was most significant, for it saved western Europe from the devastation suffered in eastern Europe from the series of onslaughts that lasted until the defeat of the Turks at the end of the seventeenth century. Many people do not realize that eastern Europe functioned as a shock absorber for the West during those centuries and so contributed substantially to the West's progress.

This also explains in part the marked increase of population in central and western Europe between the tenth and fourteenth centuries. Population in those regions grew about 50 percent, a rate of increase that seems insignificant today but that was unmatched at the time in any equivalent world area. The demographic spurt stimulated improvements in agriculture to support the growth of population, and the increased food supply in turn made possible further population increase.

Europe's rising agricultural output was obtained in two ways. One was through intensive development—through improved methods of cultivation. One outstanding improvement was the gradual adoption from the eighth century onward of the three-field system of farming. The three-field system raised productivity substantially, since only a third of the land was allowed to lie fallow instead of half. More effective use of horsepower also helped increase agricultural output. In antiquity the horse had been of little use on the farm because the yoke then used strangled the horse if it pulled too hard. Moreover, without nailed shoes the horse often injured its hoofs and became useless. By the tenth century, however, Europe had developed the horse collar, which

Expansionism of the Medieval West

Conquests and Reconquests by Christendom

Reconquest of Iberia from the Moors, 1000-1492

1029-1096	
1097-1186	
After 1200	

Norman Conquest of South Italy and Sicily, 1042-1147

Major routes of the Crusaders to The Holy Land, 1097-1250

Teutonic Order, 1100-1250

0 50 100 Miles
0 100 Kilometers

Swedes convert the Finns, c. 1150

Infidels defeated temporarily and the Latin States were created 1099-1244

SWEDES
Novgorod
Moscow
Astrakhan
Volga R.
RUSSIANS
Kiev
Dniester R.
BALTIC SEA
Danzig
Lübeck
Bremen
Oder R.
Elbe R.
Ratisbon
Vienna
HOLY ROMAN EMPIRE
Rhine R.
BLACK SEA
Danube R.
SULTANATE OF ROUM
Constantinople
BYZANTINE EMPIRE
Tigris R.
Euphrates R.
SARACENS
Edessa
THE HOLY LAND
Antioch
Tripoli
Acre
Jerusalem
CYPRUS
Alexandria
SARACENS
MEDITERRANEAN SEA
CRETE
NORTH SEA
ENGLAND
London
Bruges
NORMANDY
Metz
FRANCE
Loire R.
Clermont-Ferrand
Vézelay
Lyons
Toulouse
Rhône R.
Marseilles
Genoa
Milan
Pisa
Venice
Zara
ITALY
Rome
Naples
CORSICA
SARDINIA
Normans to Italy
Normans from Normandy
SICILY
Tunis
MALTA
SARACENS
IBERIA
Lisbon
Toledo
Granada
Ceuta
ATLANTIC OCEAN

347

NGRAVING BY THEODORE DE BRY, 1594, LIBRARY OF CONGRESS   N. Y. PUBLIC LIBRARY

Shipbuilding in 1500—an example of the technological advances that increased European expansion.

rests on the horse's shoulders and does not choke the neck. In addition, the horseshoe was invented and also the tandem harness, which allows more than one pair of horses to pull a load. The net result was that the horse, faster and more efficient compared to the ox, became an essential source of power in farming operations.

Europe's agricultural output was also raised through extensive development. Areas were opened up that had not been farmed before. It is startling but true that in the twelfth century only about half the land of France, a third of the land of Germany, and a fifth of the land of England was under cultivation. The rest was forest, swamp, waste. All around the edges of the small, tilled regions were larger, untilled areas open for settlement. Into these vacant spaces the European peasants streamed, preparing the way for the plow and hoe by clearing forests, burning brushwood, and draining swamps. The peasants not only cultivated the unused lands in their midst but also migrated eastward into the vast underpopulated areas of eastern and southern Europe. Just as the United Sates had its westward movement to the

Pacific Ocean, so Europe had its eastward movement to the Russian border (see map of Expansionism of the Medieval West, p. 347.)

The growth of population and of agriculture stimulated a corresponding growth of commerce and cities. From new farm lands, surplus food was shipped back to more densely populated western areas, which in return provided the tools and the manufactured goods needed by frontier regions. Thus commerce flourished and towns grew up, especially along the Baltic coast. This economic growth is very important. It represents the beginning of the rise of northwestern Europe, a trend that later helped the British and the Dutch to overshadow the Spaniards and the Portuguese throughout the world.

Commerce was growing not only within Europe but also between Europe and the outside world. Here, again, growth began when the Viking raids stopped, ending the terror that had dominated European coasts from the Arctic to Sicily in the ninth and tenth centuries. Another impetus from the eleventh century onward was provided by the Crusades. The tens of thousands of Europeans who had participated in the expeditions returned with an appetite for the strange and luxurious commodities they had seen and enjoyed abroad. Also, the Crusades enabled the Europeans to snatch the Mediterranean from the Moslems and to make it a great trade route between East and West, as it had been in ancient times. A third reason for the growth of international trade was the establishment in the thirteenth century of the Mongol Empire, which imposed unity on most of the vast Eurasian landmass. European traders, especially the Italians, took advantage of the peace, security, and well-serviced routes, and traded almost directly with the Orient.

The extension and intensification of commercial relations had important repercussions. Europe's economy became much more geared to international trade than did the economies of the more self-sufficient empires of the East. Both the consumer and the producer in Europe became accustomed to, and dependent on, foreign commodities and foreign markets. As populations increased, the scale of operations also increased. The demographic pressure, together with the spur of competition between nations and city-states, drove merchants to seek new sources, new routes, new markets. Their competitive attitude was very different from that of the contemporary Chinese, who voyaged several thousand miles for completely noneconomic reasons (see Section V, this chapter). Since the Chinese were quite uninterested in trade, they brought back to their self-contained homeland such curiosities as giraffes for the pleasure of their emperor. For obvious geographic reasons, Europe was far from self-contained. It had urgent need for spices and other foreign products, which, together with the burgeoning economic activity and vitality, eventually put European ships on every ocean and European merchants in every port.

II. DEVELOPMENT OF TECHNOLOGY

While its economy expanded, Europe's technology also developed and provided the materials and techniques necessary for expansion. It would have been physically impossible for Europeans to reach India or the Americas without adequate ships and navigational instruments. The basis for their technological success in these areas is the steady, unspectacular, but immensely significant progress in improving tools and techniques that was made during the medieval period.

As Lynn White, Jr., has observed, the "chief glory of the later Middle Ages" was its unprecedented development of "non-human power." Examples were the water mills and windmills that were developed and used for grinding cereal, cutting wood, and draining swamps and mines. Other useful inventions included the carpenter's plane, the crank, the wheelbarrow, the spinning wheel, and the canal lock. Indeed, the Greeks and the Romans, despite their lofty achievements in philosophy and art, did less in a thousand years to relieve human toil through machine power than the medieval Europeans did in a few centuries. Presumably this can be explained by the stimulus to invention caused by the relative lack of population in Europe and by the labor-demanding kinds of tasks that are typical of an underdeveloped, frontier-type community. The tendency of the medieval European to shift from a slave or serf economy to a machine-power economy injected a novel and dynamic element into Western culture.

An interesting illustration of the technological progress made by the western Europeans during the medieval period is found in a letter written in 1444 by a Greek scholar, Cardinal Bessarion. Bessarion, who had lived many years in Rome, was impressed by the advanced state of handicrafts in Italy. So he wrote to Constantine Paleologos, then ruler of the autonomous Byzantine province of Morea, and suggested that "four or eight young men" should be sent surreptitiously to Italy to learn Italian craft skills. They should also learn Italian "so as to be conversant with what is said." Bessarion was particularly impressed by the waterdriven sawmills that eliminated hand labor. He wrote about "wood cut by automatic saws, millwheels moved as quickly and as neatly as can be." He referred to water-driven bellows when he mentioned that "in the smelting and separation of metals they have leather bellows which are distended and relaxed untouched by any hand, and separate the metal from the useless and earthy matter that may be present." Bessarion also reported that in Italy "one may easily acquire knowledge of the making of iron, which is so useful and necessary to Man." The significance of this testimony is obvious. The technological advances made by medieval western Europe had been of such magnitude that now, for the first time, an Easterner was recommending that pupils should be sent to the West to learn the "practical arts."[1]

As far as the overseas expansion of Europe was concerned, the most significant technological advances were those in shipbuilding, in the instruments and techniques of navigation, and in naval armaments. Between 1200 and 1500 the tonnage of the average European ship doubled or tripled. Slender galleys with a burden of 150 to 200 tons gave way to round-hulled sailing ships of 600 to 800 tons. The stern rudder, adopted in the thirteenth century, rapidly displaced the older and less efficient lateral steering devices. Equally important was the Portuguese adaptation in the fourteenth century of the Arab lateen rig, which enabled vessels to sail more directly into the wind. Such advances in the construction and rigging of ships were a combination of features originally developed in northern Europe, in the Mediterranean, and in the Middle East. The net result was a ship that was larger, speedier, and more maneuverable. It was also more economical because, through elimination of the 100 to 200 oarsmen formerly necessary, plus their food and equipment, cargo space was greatly increased.

Hand in hand with these advances in shipbuilding went advances in the art of navigation. The most important contributions in this field came from the Mediterranean. The Chinese appear to have possessed a magnetic compass, but it is not certain that the Europeans acquired it from them or from Arab intermediaries. In any case, the compass was the most useful single instrument for navigators, but it was supplemented by several others. The astrolabe, a graduated brass circle for estimating the altitude of heavenly bodies, was known before 800 but was first used in Western navigation by the Portuguese about 1485. It was an expensive instrument and was soon replaced by the simpler and cheaper quadrant. The determination of longitude presented more of a problem. A rough estimate could be gained by means of an hourglass, but precise reckoning had to await Galileo's discovery of the principles of the pendulum in the seventeenth century. Navigators were also aided by compilations of nautical information and by maps. The *portolani* of the Mediterranean seamen were the first true maps, furnished with accurate compass bearings and explicit details concerning coastlines and harbors.

When the Europeans reached the highly developed and militarily powerful countries of south and east Asia, their one decisive advantage was the superiority of their naval armament. This was attained only about the time their overseas expansion began, for naval battles in the Middle Ages had consisted largely of boarding and hand-to-hand fighting on decks. During the fifteenth century, European ships were equipped with guns, but these were of small size, shooting stones weighing ounces rather than pounds. They could kill men but could not damage ships. Accordingly, they supplemented rather than supplanted the traditional boarding tactics of naval warfare. In the first two decades of the sixteenth century the metallurgists of Flanders and Germany, and later of England, developed techniques for casting guns that were light enough to mount on ships and yet had great firing power. These new pieces, five to twelve feet long, could shoot round stones—and later cast-iron balls—that weighted five to sixty pounds and could damage a hull at a range of 300 yards. Naval tactics now shifted from boarding to broadside gunfire, and warships were redesigned so that soon they were able to carry an average of forty guns.

These developments gave the Europeans a decisive advantage and enabled them to seize and retain control of the oceans of the world. Eastern rulers hastened to arm their own ships, but their vessels were neither designed nor built for mounting guns. Before they could redesign their vessels, European naval armaments developed so rapidly that the designs of the Easterners were already obsolete. Hence the gap increased rather than narrowed, and the Westerners remained the unchallenged masters of the seas until the epochal victory of the Japanese over the Russians at Tsushima in 1905.

As important as the European advances in marine technology was their discovery of the world wind systems. Thanks to Portuguese mariners, Columbus knew he could sail west with the trade winds, confident that further north he would find westerlies to bring him back home. Likewise, Vasco da Gama learned the basic pattern of Indian Ocean monsoons from local pilots. By 1522, when Magellan's ships returned to Spain after the first European voyage around the world, the wind system of the Pacific as well as of the Atlantic was known to the Europeans. Now they could sail all oceans with confidence.

Having made these advances in shipbuilding and in knowledge of world wind systems, the Europeans were able to exploit their advantages because of their favorable geographic location for crossing the Atlantic and reaching the treasures of the New World. Of course, West Africa also juts out into the Atlantic, as does the Iberian peninsula. But West African commerce for centuries had been directed northward across the Sahara to the Mediterranean. In East Africa the port of Sofala was engaged in overseas trade, but that trade naturally was conducted eastward across the adjacent Indian Ocean. Sofala is 3,000 miles farther away from the Americas than the Canary Islands (Columbus's jumping-off point), and China was still much more distant. So geographic location was an important factor, along with several others, in determining that Columbus should have been a European rather than an African or Asian.

III. EMERGENCE OF CAPITALISM

Because Columbus for various reasons turned out to be a European, it was Europe that experienced a powerful economic stimulus from the gold and silver that poured in from the Americas. The flow was so large that it tripled Europe's silver stock during the sixteenth century, and increased the gold stock by 20 percent. In addition to this bullion windfall from the New World, Europe was further enriched by numerous overseas enterprises, so that profits poured in from the slave trade, from the spice trade, from exports to the colonies and imports from the colonies, and even from piracy. This external economic boost, combined with the internal commercial revival and technological progress noted above, led to greatly increased use of money in Europe's economy.

This monetarization undermined the feudal order that had developed after the fall of Rome. The bonds of serfdom could not be preserved indefinitely when it became known that freedom could be gained by flight to the growing towns or to the frontier lands opening eastward. The lords had to modify their demands or risk the loss of their labor supply. Serfs in western Europe increasingly paid for their land with money rather than labor, so that feudal lords became landlords and serfs became free peasants. The weakening of serfdom was a prerequisite to the expansion of Europe. It created a more fluid society that could accumulate the capital; provide the organization; and free the population needed for the work of exploration, conquest, and settlement. It is not accidental that among the European nations the degree of success in overseas enterprise was in direct ratio to the degree of liberation from the bonds of feudalism.

Likewise, use of money undermined the feudal craft and merchant guilds in the towns. The guilds, with their strict regulation of workmanship and of pricing and trading practices, were geared not to making profit but to preserving a traditional way of life. Guild members were committed to the concept of a "just price," and profiteering at the expense of a neighbor was considered unethical and definitely un-Christian. But these concepts and practices broke down with the appearance of entrepreneurs. They avoided the guilds by purchasing raw material and taking it to underemployed artisans in the countryside, who labored on a piece-work basis. The rationale of this "putting-out" system was profit rather than "just price." The entrepreneurs paid as little as possible for the material and labor, and they sold the finished product as dearly as possible to secure the maximum return on their capital investment.

Europe's economy was changed not only by the growing use of money but also by the minting of standardized coins that were acceptable everywhere and by the development of banks and of credit instruments. Florence led the way in 1252 with the gold florin, and other cities and states soon followed. Simple bills of exchange also appeared in Italy as early as the twelfth century. Gradually, mighty banking families appeared, first in Italy and later in northern Europe.

RISE OF COMMERCE AND OF TOWNS

Medieval technological progress increased productivity and left a growing surplus for commerce, hence the rise of trading centers or towns. The following contemporary description of twelfth-century London reflects the vigorous life of that city and the pride of its citizens. *

Among the noble and celebrated cities of the world that of London, the capital of the kingdom of the English, is one which extends its glory farther than all the others and sends its wealth and merchandise more widely into distant lands. Higher than all the rest does it lift its head. It is happy in the healthiness of its air; in its observance of Christian practice; in the strength of its fortifications; in its natural situation; in the honour of its citizens; and in the modesty of its matrons. It is cheerful in its sports, and the fruitful mother of noble men. . . .

Everywhere outside the houses of those living in the suburbs, and adjacent to them, are the spacious and beautiful gardens of the citizens, and these are planted with trees. Also there are on the north side pastures and pleasant meadow lands through which flow streams wherein the turning of millwheels makes a cheerful sound. Very near lies a great forest with woodland pastures in which there are the lairs of wild animals: stags, fallow deer, wild boars and bulls. The tilled lands of the city are not of barren gravel, but fat Asian plains that yield luxuriant crops and fill the tillers' barns with the sheaves of Ceres. . . .

Immediately outside one of the gates there is a field which is smooth both in fact and in name. On every sixth day of the week, unless it be a major feast-day, there takes place there a famous exhibition of fine horses for sale. Earls, barons and knights, who are in the town, and many citizens come out to see or to buy. It is pleasant to see the high-stepping palfrey with their gleaming coats, as they go through their paces, putting down their feet alternately on one side together. Next, one can see the horses suitable for esquires, moving faster though less smoothly, lifting and setting down, as it were, the opposite fore and hind feet: here are colts of fine breed, but not yet accustomed to the bit, stepping high with jaunty tread; there are the sumpter-horses, powerful and spirited; and after them are the war-horses, costly, elegant of form, noble of stature, with ears quickly tremulous, necks raised and large haunches. . . .

By themselves in another part of the field stand the goods of the countryfolk: implements of husbandry, swine with long flanks, cows with full udders, oxen of immense size, and woolly sheep. There also stand the mares fit for plough, some big with foal, and others with brisk young colts closely following them.

To this city from every nation under heaven merchants delight to bring their trade by sea. The Arabian sends gold; the Sabaean spice and incense. The Scythian brings arms, and from the rich, fat lands of Babylon comes oil of palms. The Nile sends precious stones; the men of Norway and Russia, furs and sables; nor is China absent with purple silk. The Gauls come with their wines. . . .

I do not think there is a city with a better record for church-going, doing honour to God's ordinances, keeping feast-days, giving alms and hospitality to strangers, confirming betrothals, contracting marriages, celebrating weddings, providing feasts, entertaining guests, and also, it may be added, in care for funerals and for the burial of the dead. The only plagues of London are the immoderate drinking of fools and the frequency of fires.

* From *English Historical Documents, 1042–1189,* edited by D. C. Douglas and G. Greenaway, 1953. Reprinted by permission of Oxford University Press, Inc.

What was happening to Europe, then, was a historic shift to a fundamentally different type of economic system, the type known today as capitalism. Capitalism has been defined as ". . . [a] system in which the desire for profits is the driving motive and in which large accumulations of capital are employed to make profits by various elaborate and often indirect methods."[2]

The emergence of capitalism was epoch making. It affected not merely the economy but all aspects of life. Whereas in the early Middle Ages money had been peripheral and little used, by the late Middle Ages it provided energy that was responsible for Europe's future meteoric rise. No earlier societies or economic systems had been based on the notion of growth. Their aim had been only to maintain the material well-being of the past rather than to enhance it. But henceforth, with capitalism, the precise opposite was the case. Profits now were plowed back to increase the quantity of capital available for production. "Capitalizing" of profits, in the sense that surplus was converted into more capital, is the rationale behind the term *capitalism*. The new "capitalists" were not content with making a living but were driven by the urge to enlarge their assets. They did not cease their efforts when their needs for consumption were satisfied. The new "capitalist spirit" is epitomized by the statement of Jacob Fugger, the wealthiest banker of the sixteenth century, who said, "Let me earn as long as I am able."

In order to "earn," Fugger and his fellow bankers needed to be free to charge interest on money they loaned. But the medieval Church for long had denounced interest as constituting usury, a mortal sin and "a vice most odious and detestable in the sight of God." By 1548, however, some Church members were pleading for the acceptance of "moderate and acceptable usury." This modification soon gave way to the cynical attitude: "He who takes usury goes to hell; he who does not goes to the poorhouse." Given the choice of hell in afterlife, or poorhouse in the present, it is not surprising that usury won out. So it was the affluent European bankers who organized the numerous joint stock companies that won control of commerce on all oceans, garnering the ensuing profits.

These joint stock companies were the counterpart in early modern times of the multinational corporations of today. These new organizations were most effective instruments for economic mobilization and penetration. Anyone who wished to speculate with a little money could do so without risking one's whole future. The individual risked only the amount invested in company shares, and that person could not be held further liable for whatever losses the company might incur. Furthermore, there was no need for the individual investors to know or trust each other or to concern themselves with the specific conditions of the market and the policies of the company. These details of management were entrusted to directors selected for their responsibility and experience, and these directors in turn could choose dependable individuals to manage company affairs in the field. This arrangement made it attractive for all sorts of scattered individuals—a London wool merchant, a Paris storekeeper, a Harlem herring fisher, an Antwerp banker, or a Yorkshire landowner—to invest their savings in individual ventures. In this way it was possible to mobilize European capital easily and simply, and vast amounts were invested in various overseas undertakings. No Eastern merchants, limited to their own resources or those of their partners, and choosing their managers from their family or circle of acquaintances, could hope to compete with the powerful and impersonal joint stock company. It became the instrument for the operation of European capitalism on a global scale. World commerce fell under the control of the various East India and Levant companies, the Muscovy Company, and the still-operating Hudson's Bay Company.

Thus we can see why an American historian has concluded that the most important figures in Europe's overseas expansion were not Columbus and da Gama and Magellan. Rather, they were the new entrepreneurs with capital. They were the merchants who stayed in the home ports but who were "responsible for the foundation of many of the colonies . . . who kept the colonies supplied . . . who opened new markets, sought new lands, and enriched all of Europe. . . ."[3]

The new capitalist economic system not only dominated the world economy in early modern times but it continues to do so to the present day. The basic reason is to be found in its ruling principle: profit or perish. To avoid perishing, capitalist entrepreneurs through the centuries have maximized profit in two ways: by reducing the wages they pay their workers or by increasing their workers' productivity through improved technology. The first strategy has been much used but it can be carried only so far because workers obviously have to be paid a certain minimum amount if they are to be kept alive, healthy, and productive. The second strategy—improving technology—can be continued indefinitely. In fact, this is precisely what happened, as indicated by the constantly accelerating pace of technological innovation, strikingly evident in today's high technology. This built-in technological dynamism explains why Europe's capitalist entrepreneurs in early modern times won control of the global economy with their unceasing technological innovations and their joint stock companies, and also why today's capitalists continue to control the world economy with their biotechnology, their computers, and their multinational corporations. Just as Europe's joint stock companies a few centuries ago planted colonies in the Americas and penetrated irresistibly the markets of the Middle East and the Far East, so today the same inherent dynamism drives multinational corporations to move factories from continent to continent, to erect golden arches in scores of countries, and even to establish a 500-seat Kentucky Fried Chicken in Beijing's historic Tienanmen Square with a view of the Gate of Heavenly Peace and of Mao Tse-tung's mausoleum. The new enterprise retains its familiar slogan in Chinese—*Haodao shun shouzhi* ("So good you suck your fingers").

IV.   RISE OF THE NEW MONARCHS

The emergence of capitalists in Europe was paralleled by the concurrent emergence of the "New Monarchs" who were building cohesive political structures. The roots of this consolidation process goes back to the death of Charlemagne in 814, when Europe entered a period of disintegration and political anarchy. In very broad terms, the political evolution of western Europe after Charlemagne may be divided into three stages. Between the ninth and eleventh centuries, popes and emperors generally cooperated. The popes helped the

emperors against the German secular lords, and in return were supported against the Byzantine opponents to papal authority. In 1073, with the accession of Pope Gregory VII, began the second stage, a period of papal supremacy. The investiture dispute between the papacy and the emperors—the struggle to control the selection of German bishops—was won by Gregory. Thus imperial administration and power were undermined. For over two centuries, the papacy was generally recognized as the head of Latin Christendom, particularly because there was a succession of pious French and English kings in the mid-thirteenth century. The period of papal supremacy ended in 1296, when Philip IV of France won out over Pope Boniface VIII on the issue of taxation of clergy. In that year, the pope issued a bull asserting that the laity had no authority over the clergy and threatening to excommunicate anyone who attempted to tax the clergy. Philip rejected the pope's claims and was able to enforce his policies with complete success. He even forced the transfer of the papal seat from Rome to Avignon, and from there the papacy collaborated openly with the French monarchy.

By the end of the fifteenth century, this trend away from the universal Church and toward national monarchies was apparent in the powerful political structures presided over by Ferdinand and Isabella in Spain (1479–1516), by Henry VIII in England (1509–1547), and by Francis I in France (1515–1547). One reason for the success of these rulers was the revolution in military technology that came with the advent of artillery. Feudal lords no longer could defy royal authority from behind their castle walls. Only national monarchs possessed the financial resources and administrative organization necessary to purchase the guns, powder, and shot and to provide the required logistical support.

Another source of power for the new monarchs was their informal alliance with the growing merchant class. From this class the monarchs obtained essential financial support and also competent and subservient officials to staff the growing state bureaucracies. In return, the consolidation of royal power aided the burghers by ending the incessant feudal wars and doing away with the crazyquilt pattern of local feudal authorities, in which each had had its own customs, laws, weights, and currencies. As late as the

Niccolo Machiavelli

end of the fourteenth century there were thirty-five toll stations on the Elbe, over sixty on the Rhine, and so many on the Seine that the cost of shipping grain 200 miles down the river was half its selling price. The elimination of such domestic barriers obviously was a great boon to entrepreneurs. So was the patronage of the increasingly elaborate royal courts, which supported craftspeople and sometimes whole industries, as in the case of Gobelin tapestry and Sèvres porcelain in France.

The new monarchs naturally had their own defenders and rationalizers, as do all political establishments. The best known of these was Niccolo Machiavelli (1459–1527). A product of the ruthless struggle for survival among the competing city-states of Renaissance Italy, Machiavelli viewed politics as a struggle for power in which the end justifies the means. In his book, *The Prince,* he set forth guidelines for the ruler who aspired to unite the fragmented Italian peninsula and to rid it of the French and Spanish invaders. With cool and relentless realism he rejected moral restraints and spelled out the difference between politics and religion or philosophy.

National monarchs pursuing strategies based on the precepts of *The Prince* were bound to clash with the two universal institutions of Europe, the papacy and the empire. The conflict was sharpened by the sensational rise of the Spanish dynasty through marriage ties. Ferdinand and Isabella married their daughter Joanna to Philip of Hapsburg. Charles, the offspring of this union, inherited the united Spanish kingdom together with the Spanish possessions in the New World and in Italy (Sardinia, Sicily, Naples). He also held the hereditary Hapsburg lands in central Europe (the duchies of Austria, Styria, Carinthia, Carniola, and the county of Tirol). In addition, Charles's grandmother, Mary of Burgundy, left him Burgundian territories, Franche-Comté, Luxembourg, and the wealthy Netherlands. And to crown this imposing edifice, Charles was elected in 1519 Holy Roman Emperor in spite of the opposition of the French and English monarchs, Francis I and Henry VII, respectively. Thus Charles V, at the age of nineteen, became the ruler of a larger territory than had been collected under one monarch since the breakup of Charlemagne's empire seven centuries earlier.

For a time it appeared that western Europe would be united once more in a vast international organization. But the other European dynasties, and especially the Valois of France, were determined to prevent Hapsburg hegemony. The result was the long series of wars, partly religious, partly dynastic, noted in the preceding chapter—the campaigns in Germany, the Dutch war, the armada engagement, and the bloody religious strife in France. This prolonged violence was followed by the even more disastrous Thirty Years' War (1618–1648). Although the Thirty Years' War was precipitated by the question of the succession to the Bohemian throne, it soon became essentially a struggle between the Bourbon and Hapsburg dynasties for control of the continent of Europe. The principal victims of the three decades of fighting were the civilians who suffered at the hands of undisciplined mercenaries, especially when their pay was not forthcoming, as often happened. About a third of the population of Germany and Bohemia perished, and wholesale devastation ensued in the cities and the countryside.

The territorial provisions of the Treaty of Westphalia (1648) did not last, but their overall significance is clear. The princes of central Europe, backed by France, Sweden, and other countries, successfully resisted the centralizing efforts of the Hapsburgs. The empire now was a collection of small independent states, each with the right to conduct its foreign as well as domestic affairs. Henceforth the individual sovereign state was recognized as the basic unit in European politics, and relations between the states were conducted according to generally accepted tenets of diplomatic practice. Thus began the international anarchy of a world composed of states with unlimited sovereignty—a world that has persisted from the Westphalia conference to the present day.

V.   WESTERN EUROPE ON THE EVE OF EXPANSION

Modern world history had been dominated by European expansion overseas and then by the disintegration of European empires during the twentieth century. The fateful expansion of Europe was largely the product of the historical forces analyzed in this chapter: the technological progress, the population increase, the resulting growth in economic productivity and resources, the emergence of dynamic capitalism, and the rise of the new monarchs. It was the European monarchs who issued charters to joint stock companies and backed them up, if necessary, with their royal navies. The Spanish and Portuguese courts, for example, provided the backing necessary for the achievements of Columbus and da Gama. The British and French courts followed suit somewhat later, though with equal interest and support. In fact, there were closer relations between merchants and monarchs in northwestern Europe than in the Iberian peninsula. Particularly in Spain, the long struggle against the Moslems had brought together the crown and the feudal lords, whereas the few large towns tended to oppose both and to demand complete autonomy. In

northwestern Europe, by contrast, the merchant class gradually won social prestige and state backing that was unequaled elsewhere in Eurasia.

In China and India merchants were looked down on as inferior and undesirable; in northwestern Europe they had status and, as time passed, growing wealth and political power. In China, the merchants at various times suffered restrictions concerning clothing, carrying of weapons, riding in carts, and owning land. Their function of transporting commodities from place to place was regarded as nonproductive and parasitic, and they were placed at the bottom of the social scale. Likewise in India, the merchant could have no prestige in the face of Hinduism's emphasis on the renunciation of worldly goods. The ideal human in India was not the bustling merchant who made money and built mansions but the mystic who sat on mats, ate from plantain leaves, and had no material possessions. Consequently, none of the merchants in any of the oriental empires could rise to positions of authority. In China, government was carried on by scholars; in Japan, by soldiers; in the Malay lands and in the Rajput states of India, by the local nobility; but nowhere by merchants.

Nowhere, that is, except in northwestern Europe, where they were steadily gaining in political as well as economic power. There they were becoming lord mayors in London, senators in the German Imperial Free Cities, and grand pensioners in Holland. Such social status and political clout meant more consideration and more consistent state support for the merchants' interests and overseas ventures.

The significance of the unique western European complex of interests, institutions, and traditions is pointed up by the remarkable history of the famous maritime expeditions sent out from China during the Ming period (see map of Early Fifteenth-Century Chinese and Portuguese Voyages, p. 357). Between 1405 and 1433, seven ventures were made under the superintendency of the chief court eunuch, a certain Cheng Ho. The expeditions were startling in their magnitude and in their achievements. The first, comprised of 62 ships, carried 28,000 men. The average ship had a beam of 150 feet and a length of 370 feet, but the largest were 180 feet wide and 444 feet long. They were veritable floating palaces com-

Early fifteenth-century Chinese and Portuguese Voyages

357

pared to Columbus's little flagship, the *Santa Maria* which was 120 feet long and 25 feet wide. And the *Santa Maria* was twice as large as Columbus's two other ships, the *Pinta* and the *Niña*. The Chinese expeditions were impressive in performance as well as in size. They sailed around Southeast Asia to India; some went on to Aden and the head of the Persian Gulf; and individual ships entered ports on the east coast of Africa. During this time, it should be recalled, the Portuguese were only beginning to feel their way down the coast of Africa, and they did not reach Cape Verde until 1445.

Yet these remarkable Chinese expeditions were suddenly halted by imperial order in 1433. Why they were halted remains as much a mystery as why they were started in the first place. But the significant point here is that an order to stop would have been utterly inconceivable in Europe. There was no European counterpart to the Chinese emperor, who could and did issue orders binding on his entire realm. Instead, there were rival national monarchies that were competing in overseas ventures, and no imperial authority existed to prevent them from doing so. The political power and social prestige of the merchants in northwestern Europe, in contrast to the merchants' inferior position in China, made it quite impossible to enforce any decree banning overseas enterprise. Furthermore, Europe had a tradition of trade with the outside world. Its genuine need and strong demand for foreign products was altogether lacking in China.

In short, there was an impelling dynamism in Europe—a lust and an opportunity for profit. The uniqueness of western Europe is reflected in contemporary European and Chinese writings. "Coming into contact with barbarian peoples," wrote Chang Hsieh in 1618, "you have nothing more to fear than touching the left horn of a snail. The only things one should really be anxious about are the means to mastery of the waves of the seas—and, worst of all dangers, the minds of those avid for profit and greedy of gain."[4] By contrast, the Portuguese Captain João Ribeiro boasted in 1685, "From the Cape of Good Hope onwards we were unwilling to leave anything outside of our control; we were anxious to lay hands on everything in that huge stretch of over 5,000 leagues from Sofala to Japan . . . there was

not a corner which we did not occupy or desire to have subject to ourselves."[5]

During the Middle Ages, a combination of developments isolated and fenced in the western Europeans, and so further stimulated their natural tendency to look overseas. The loss of the Crusaders' outposts in the Levant, the breakup of the Mongol Empire, and the expansion of the Ottoman Turks into central Europe up to the walls of Vienna served to restrict the Europeans. European merchants could no longer penetrate into central Asia, because chaos reigned where once the Mongols had enforced order. The Black Sea also became closed to Christian merchants when the Turks transformed it into a Moslem preserve. The all-important spice trade was little affected. Italian merchants continued to meet Arab traders in various ports in the Levant to pick up the commodities demanded by the European public. But though this arrangement was satisfactory for the Italians and Arabs, who reaped the golden profits of the middleman, other Europeans were not so happy. They sought earnestly for some means to reach the Orient directly, in order to share the prize. This explains why there were numerous plans in late medieval times for breaking through or getting around the Moslem barrier that confined Europeans to the Mediterranean. Europe at this time, as one author has put it, was like a "giant fed through the chinks of a wall."[6] But the giant was growing in strength and in knowledge, and the prison walls were not to contain him for long.

SUGGESTED READINGS

General interpretations of why European society became expansionist are given by E. L. Jones, *The European Miracle* (Cambridge University, 1981); E. R. Wolf, *Europe and the People Without History* (University of California, 1982); M. Beaud, *A History of Capitalism, 1500–1980* (Monthly Review Press, 1983); L. S. Stavrianos, *Global Rift: The Third World Comes of Age* (William Morrow, 1981); J. Baechlev, J. A. Hall, and M. Mann, eds., *Europe and the Rise of Capitalism* (Basil Blackwell, 1987); and the important three-volume study of F. Braudel, *Civilization and Capitalism, 15th–18th Century* (Harper and Row, 1981–84).

The development of Europe's economy in early modern times is analyzed in the first three volumes of the *Cambridge Economic History* (Cambridge University, 1941–1963); B. H. S. van Bath, *The Agrarian History of Western Europe, 500–1850* (Edward Arnold, 1963); F. Braudel, *Capitalism and Material Life, 1400–1800* (Harper & Row, 1973); and H. I. Miskimin, *The Economy of Early Renaissance Europe, 1300–1460* (Prentice Hall, 1969). European technological progress of this period is analyzed in the studies by L. White, Jr., *Medieval Technology and Social Change* (Oxford University, 1962), and *Machina Ex Deo: Essays in the Dynamism of Western Culture* (MIT, 1968); and also in the works of C. M. Cipolla, *Literacy and Development in the West* (Pelican, 1969), and *European Culture and Overseas Expansion* (Pelican, 1970), the latter dealing with guns, sails, and clocks. Provocative interpretations of the economic and technological changes in Europe are presented in the classics by R. H. Tawney, *Religion and the Rise of Capitalism* (Mentor, 1926); M. Weber, *The Protestant Ethic and the Spirit of Capitalism* (Scribner's, 1948); and, more recently, A. O. Hirschman, *The Passions and the Interests: Political Arguments for Capitalism Before Its Triumph* (Princeton University, 1977).

The question of why the West rather than some other region of Eurasia took the lead in overseas expansion is considered by J. Needham, *Science and Civilization in China* (Cambridge University, 1956ff.), especially Vol. 4, Part 3, which deals with Chinese nautical technology, including the Ming voyages. Other works on this subject are by C. G. F. Simkin, *The Traditional Trade of Asia* (Oxford University, 1968); J. R. Levenson, ed., *European Expansion and the Counter-Example of Asia, 1300–1600* (Prentice Hall, 1967); and J. M. Blaut, *The Colonizer's Model of the World* (Guilford Press, 1993). The latter book is unique in challenging the concept of a "European miracle," and emphasizing the role of overseas lands in stimulating Europe to global primacy.

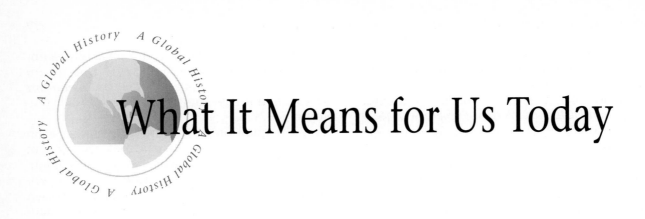

What It Means for Us Today

HISTORY AND FADS

Five centuries ago, Christopher Columbus set foot on San Salvador, a tiny island in the Bahamas. He assumed he had reached Southeast Asia, so he referred to the native islanders as Indians—a name that has stuck ever since. Soon after Columbus died, his assumption was proven wrong when Balboa reached the Pacific Ocean in 1513 and when Magellan's expedition sailed around the world from 1519 to 1522.

The realization that the Americas were a "new world" led to speculation about the origins of the Indians. Either they had originated in the New World, or they had arrived there from somewhere else. The idea of independent origin in the Americas was unthinkable heresy, for that would imply a dual creation—a duplicate Adam and Eve in a transatlantic Garden of Eden—a belief that clashed too much with the teachings of the Old Testament. So it was agreed that the Indians must be the descendants of Adam and Eve. A new question now arose: How did these descendants make their way from the Old World to the New? A great debate has raged over this question, with dozens of theories being advanced during the

past four centuries and new ones still popping up in the present day.

Most of the theories are false, based more on faith than on reason. Various fads have gone through popularity cycles, each reflecting the knowledge and prejudices of their times. One of the earliest was the Lost Tribes of Israel hypothesis, for in those days, ancient Hebrew ethnology as described in the Old Testament was almost the only known example of the "primitive" way of life. So the early theorists were convinced that the Indians were the descendants of the Hebrew tribes conquered and carried away from Samaria by the king of Assyria in 721 B.C. Some supporters of the Lost Tribes theory believed that the Hebrews reached the New World by crossing the mythical continent of Atlantis, but most preferred a route across Persia and China to the Bering Strait.

In the eighteenth century Europeans were impressed by the achievements of the ancient Mediterranean peoples, and especially the Phoenicians, who were famous for their seafaring skills. The Phoenicians were believed to have rounded Africa's Cape of Good Hope and also to have crossed the Atlantic to the Americas. However, with the advent of nineteenth-century archeological discoveries in Egypt, that country came to be considered the origin of American Indian civilizations. This theory was widely accepted as fact because of the existence of pyramids in Mesoamerica that seemed similar to those of Egypt. Many other fads about the origins of the American Indians have come and gone. Thus our "redskins" have been traced back to Greeks, Trojans, Romans, Etruscans, Scythians, Mongols, Chinese Buddhists, Mandingoes or other Africans, early Irish, Welsh, Norse, Basques, Portuguese, French, Spaniards, and even survivors of the "lost continents" of Mu and Atlantis, which allegedly sank 11,000 years ago beneath the Pacific and Atlantic oceans, respectively.

All of these claims have been disproven, or at least found to be questionable, with a single exception: A late tenth-century Norse settlement in Newfoundland has been scientifically confirmed. One reason why so many believed, and still believe, in so many groundless theories is that they wrongly assume that common customs mean a common origin. On the contrary, one can go to the human relations area files in any major university and ask for an inventory of all the peoples of the world who practice some particular custom—say, preferred-cousin marriage. One will quickly be given dozens of examples from peoples all over the world who could not possibly have borrowed that marriage practice from one common source. But early writers, unfamiliar with modern anthropological science, very naturally assumed historical connection between similar customs in the distant past.

Also, apparently similar institutions or structures have proven on close examination to be quite different. Pyramids have been found in both Egypt and Mesoamerica, but those of Mesoamerica were primarily centers of religious ritual, whereas those of Egypt were vast tombs. Equally important is the fact that recent excavations reveal the gradual evolution of Mesoamerican pyramids over thousands of years. This long development period demolishes the theory that the technique of pyramid building had been transplanted full-blown across the Atlantic. Likewise, in the native California language known as Yuki, the word *ko* means "go," and *kom* means "come," yet no one could conclude from this example that Yuki and English are historically related.

Even if small numbers of ancient Old World seafarers had reached the New World, the claim that their cultures would have instantly dominated New World customs is highly questionable. Those who assume that small groups of Hebrews, Greeks, Romans, Phoenicians, or others could have arrived in the New World and spread their culture among natives over vast areas should consider the experience of eighteen Spaniards (sixteen men and two women) who were shipwrecked on the coast of Yucatan six years before Cortes arrived. All were sacrificed and ritually eaten, except for two men who were enslaved by local chieftains. One of these survivors went so completely native that he wore the elaborate nose plug and earrings of his adopted tribe and refused to give up his new life to rejoin Cortes. Likewise, the Vikings, who we know did actually land in Newfoundland, were forced to give up their attempt to establish a colony because of the hostility of the local Indians. Thus until the appearance of modern repeating rifles and machine guns, small landing parties were either wiped out or assimilated into the local culture.

These are some of the reasons why a 1968 symposium held in Santa Fe, New Mexico, concluded that "there are to date—excluding the Viking contacts (that is, Newfoundland)—no verified archaeological finds of artifacts from one hemisphere in pre-Columbian context to the other." The symposium likewise agreed that "there is no hard and fast evidence for any pre-Columbian human introduction of any single plant or animal across the ocean from the Old World to the New World or vice-versa. This is emphatically *not* to say that it could not have occurred."[1]

What is the significance of this discussion for the student of history? In the first place, it points up the basic question of how human civilizations have developed—whether by diffusion from one or a few early centers or by independent inventions in various parts of the world. This question probes not only the origins of the American Indian civilizations but also the origins of civilizations throughout the globe. Did civilization spread from the Middle East to northwest Europe, North Africa, south Asia, and east Asia, or was it independently developed in these various regions? The controversy between the *diffusionists* and the *independent inventionists* has been long standing.

Increasingly we are realizing that it is not a case of either/or but rather of varying degrees of diffusion and independent invention. These varying degrees can be determined not by romantic speculations based on preconceived notions but rather by painstaking research and objective evaluation of the results. The more archeologists unearth human prehistory, the more they are realizing that all branches of the human race have been inventive in responding to their environments. The nature and the extent of their responses and achievements have varied greatly, depending on their historical and geographical backgrounds, especially the degree of accessibility to outside stimulation, as has been noted before.

Equally significant for students of history is the fact that many laypersons still cherish the vision of assorted Europeans, Asians, or Africans landing on the shores of the pre-Columbian New World, bearing aloft the torch of civilization. The fact is that humans today, as in earliest Paleolithic times, are mesmerized by the cult of the mysterious. They cling to romantic and simplistic explanations, even when they do not square with known facts. Our food-gathering ancestors depended on their totems and shamans or medicine men. Modern humans have similar faith in UFOs, numerology, tarot cards, intelligent plants, and astrology. Readers of this text will appreciate the significance of the following report by George Abell, professor of astronomy at the University of California, Los Angeles:

I have polled the general university students taking my survey astronomy courses and find that about a third have an interest and belief in astrology. From discussions with my colleagues in other parts of the country I gather that about the same ratio holds everywhere and that it probably fairly well represents the fraction of Americans who believe in astrology. It is estimated that there are more than 5,000 astrologers making a living in the subject in the United States. More than 1,200 daily newspapers carry astrology columns.[2]

Professor Abell's report was made in 1975. Polls since that date indicate that faith in astrology is steadily increasing. Between 1980 and 1985 the proportion of American teenagers who believe in astrology has grown from 40 to 55 percent.[3] This resurgence of astrology today is especially noteworthy in view of the fact that it largely disappeared when modern astronomy began in the sixteenth century.

SUGGESTED READINGS

An interesting analysis of science and irrationality is given by M. Gardner, *Fads and Fallacies in the Name of Science* (Dover, 1957). The best general surveys of pre-Columbian contacts with the New World are R. Wauchope, *Lost Tribes and Sunken Continents* (University of Chicago, 1962); N. Davies, *Voyagers to the New World* (William Morrow, 1979); A. S. Ingstad, *The Discovery of a Norse Settlement in America* (Columbia University, 1977); M. McKusick, *Atlantic Voyages to Prehistoric America* (Southern Illinois University, 1980); and C. L. Riley et al., *Man Across the Sea: Problems of Pre-Columbian Contacts* (University of Texas, 1971), the latter presenting the proceedings of the 1968 symposium mentioned in the text.

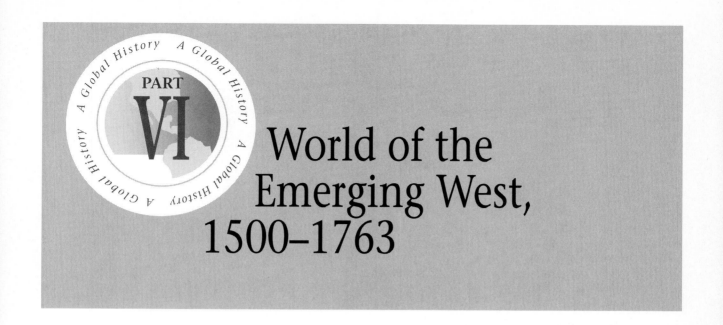

World of the Emerging West, 1500–1763

During much of the medieval period the western Europeans felt isolated and threatened on the western tip of Eurasia. Situated as they were at the terminal of the classic invasion route—the endless expanse of steppes stretching from north China across the length of Eurasia to the Danube valley in central Europe—they had been traditionally vulnerable to attack from the east. A long succession of nomadic invaders—Huns, Germans, Avars, Magyars, Mongols, and Turks—had used their unmatched mobility to break into the centers of civilization whenever imperial weakness gave them the opportunity.

The age-old pattern was reversed in early modern times by the emergence of a dynamic new West with superior technology, particularly in armaments and naval shipbuilding. This gave the western Europeans the same mobility and superiority on the oceans of the world that had been enjoyed hitherto by the nomads on the steppes of Eurasia. The result was a funda-mental alteration in the configuration of world affairs. All Eurasia now was enveloped by two gigantic European pincers. One arm was the Russian thrust overland across Siberia to the Pacific, and the other, the west European expansion around Africa to India, Southeast Asia, and China. At the same time other Westerners, beginning with Columbus, ventured westward across the Atlantic, discovering the New World and circumnavigating the globe.

It is true that during these same decades Turkish janissaries, like many of their Asian predecessors, were pressing up the Danube valley and besieging Vienna in the heart of Europe. But in the context of the new global historical stage, this was only a minor operation of local importance. What was truly significant in the perspective of world history was the initial Iberian expansion overseas, the later overseas activities of the northwest Europeans, and the simultaneous overland expansion of the Russians to the Pacific.

24 West European Expansion: Iberian Phase, 1500–1600

The discovery of America, and that of passage to the East Indies by the Cape of Good Hope, are the greatest and most important events recorded in the history of mankind.

Adam Smith

The two countries of the Iberian peninsula, Spain and Portugal, took the lead in the expansion of Europe in the sixteenth century. For several reasons this seems paradoxical on first thought: The Iberian peninsula for centuries had been a Moslem stronghold. A large number of Moors and Jews were left behind in the country, creating ethnic and religious divisions. And it is well known that after the sixteenth century the Iberian countries declined rapidly, and that throughout modern times they have been insignificant. What, then, is the explanation for the short-lived but brilliant expansion of Spain and Portugal during the sixteenth century? This chapter is concerned, first, with the roots of Iberian expansionism; second, with the process of empire building in the East and in the New World; and, finally, with the causes and results of Iberian decline at the end of the sixteenth century.

I. ROOTS OF IBERIAN EXPANSIONISM

Religion was an important factor in European overseas expansion, but nowhere was it so important as in the Iberian peninsula. Both the Spaniards and the Portuguese were urged on by memories of their long anti-Moslem crusade. To other peoples of Europe, Islam was a distant menace, but for the Iberians it represented a traditional and ever-present enemy. Most of the peninsula at one time had been under Moslem rule, and now, in the fifteenth century, Granada in the south was still a Moslem stronghold. Furthermore, the Moslems were in control of the nearby North African coast, and the growing Turkish seapower was making itself felt throughout the Mediterranean. Other Europeans were crusaders by fits and starts, but for the devout and patriotic Iberian, the struggle against Islam combined religious duty and patriotic necessity (see map of Expansionism of the Medieval West, p. 347.)

Prince Henry the Navigator first won fame in 1415 for his gallant role in the capture of the North African fortress and town of Ceuta, across the Straits of Gibraltar. Likewise, Queen Isabella, moved by intense religious conviction, was determined to wipe out Moslem Granada and also to carry the war into the enemy's territory in North Africa, as the Portuguese had done at Ceuta. Isabella began her crusade against Granada in 1482 and pressed on, village by village, until final victory in 1492. Immediately thereafter, the Spaniards crossed the straits and captured the city of Melilla. Again in 1492, a royal decree was promulgated requiring all Jews in Spain to accept the Catholic faith or leave the realm. Ten years later a similar decree was issued against the Moslems remaining in Castile. At the time of their oceanic discoveries, the Iberians took their crusading spirit with them across the oceans, where they found more Moslems to exterminate and new heathens to save from idolatry.

The Iberians were lured overseas also by four island groups—the Canaries, the Madeira, the Azores, and the Cape Verde—stretching westward across the Atlantic and southward down the coast of Africa. These were highly attractive, in part because they were fertile and productive, but also because they provided strategic bases and ports of call. After much local fighting and several appeals to the pope, the Canaries were recognized as Spanish and the other three island groups as Portuguese. Throughout the fifteenth century, progressively more adventurous Spanish and Portuguese sailors had been discovering these islands stretching a quarter of the way across the Atlantic. It was natural that they should assume there were more islands awaiting discovery and exploitation. The agreement that Columbus reached with Isabella in 1492 stated that he should head an expedition "to discover and acquire islands and mainland in the Ocean Sea."

It was Portugal, however, not Spain, that took the lead in overseas enterprise during the fifteenth century. Spain moved belatedly, and usually in reaction to Portuguese initiative. There were two reasons for Portugal's head start. One was its small size and its location on the Atlantic coast, where it was surrounded on three sides by Spanish territory. This position effectively saved the Portuguese from the temptation to squander their resources in European wars. Thanks to the leadership of Prince Henry, they turned instead to seafaring projects. The other advantage was Portugal's superior knowledge of navigation, gained primarily from the Italians. Lisbon was on the route of the Genoese and Venetian sea traffic with Flanders that sailed through the Straits of Gibraltar. The Portuguese took advantage of this to lure Italian captains and pilots into the royal navy. Prince Henry followed up by employing talented seamen, including Italians, Catalans, and even a Dane. Furthermore, Henry's work was continued by the crown following his death, so that the Portuguese became the most knowledgeable of all Europeans in seamanship and geography.

Portugal's interest in exploration quickened following the capture of Ceuta in 1415. Moslem prisoners gave information about the ancient and profitable trade across the Sahara with the Negro kingdoms of the Sudan. For centuries the Sudan had provided ivory, slaves, and gold in return for various manufactured goods and salt. Since western Europe in general and Portugal in particular were then suffering from a serious shortage of bullion, Prince Henry was intrigued by the possibility of sending his captains down the African coast and tapping the gold trade. In short, Henry's original objective was confined to Africa and did not extend to the East.

A major step forward in early Portuguese exploration was taken when Prince Henry's captains passed south of Africa's desert coast in 1445 and found below it a fertile, green land. By the time of Henry's death, the coast had been explored down to Sierra Leone and a number of coastal stations had been established, so that the Portuguese were able to exploit at least part of the African caravan trade that they had sought.

Meanwhile, even before Henry's death, Portuguese aspirations had come to include India as well as Africa. Europe at this time was blocked from access to the East by the Moslems, who controlled all of North Africa and the Middle East. The Mediterranean was for the Europeans a prison rather than a highway. Therefore, with the exception of the Venetians, who profited as middlemen, the Europeans eagerly sought a new route "to the Indies where the spices grow." Prince Henry had not thought of India when he first began his operations, but as his ships crept further and further down the African coast, it was natural that his horizon should expand from the African caravan trade to the Indies spice trade. From then on, the discovery and domination of the spice route was the prime objective of Portuguese policy.

II.   COLUMBUS DISCOVERS AMERICA

In view of Portugal's pioneering work in the theory and practice of maritime navigation, it is paradoxical that the first great discovery—that of the New World—was made under Spanish auspices. It is even more paradoxical that the reason for this outcome is that the Portuguese were more advanced in their geographical knowledge than the Spaniards and realized that Columbus was wrong in his calculations. By the fifteenth century, informed people knew that the world was round. The question was not the shape of the world but its size and what precise relationship its continents bore to the oceans. Columbus had based his calculations on several sources. By combining (1) Marco Polo's estimate of the east-west extent of Asia, which was an overestimate; (2) Polo's report of the distance of Japan from the Asian mainland—1,500 miles, an extreme overestimate; and (3) Ptolemy's estimate of the circumference of the globe, which was an underestimate, Columbus concluded that fewer than 3,000 miles of ocean separated Europe from Japan. Accordingly, he believed that the shortest and easiest route to Asia was by a short voyage across the Atlantic, and this was the project that he proposed before various courts. The Portuguese, thanks to Prince Henry, had more practical experience and were better informed of the most advanced knowledge of the day. They were convinced that the globe

Columbus departs from Palos.

COLUMBUS DISCOVERS THE NEW WORLD

On his return from his first voyage, Columbus described his discoveries in a letter to Gabriel Sanchez (March 1493). The letter shows how anxious Columbus was to convince people that he had discovered valuable lands, and that he was ready to strip those lands of their riches and to make their "honest" and affectionate people into slaves. *

As I know that it will afford you pleasure that I have brought my undertaking to a successful result, I have determined to write you this letter to inform you of everything that has been done and discovered in this voyage of mine.

On the thirty-third day after leaving Cadiz I came into the Indian Sea, where I discovered many islands inhabited by numerous people. I took possession of all of them for our most fortunate King by making public proclamation and unfurling his standard, no one making any resistance. . . . The inhabitants of both sexes of this and of all the other islands I have seen, or of which I have any knowledge, always go as naked as they came into the world, except that some of the women cover parts of their bodies with leaves or branches, or a veil of cotton, which they prepare themselves for this purpose. They are all, as I said before, unprovided with any sort of iron, and they are destitute of arms, which are entirely unknown to them, and for which they are not adapted; not on account of any bodily deformity, for they are well made, but because they are timid and full of terror. They carry, however, canes dried in the sun in place of weapons, upon whose roots they fix a wooden shaft, dried and sharpened to a point. But they never dare to make use of these, for it has often happened, when I have sent two or three of my men to some of their villages to speak with the inhabitants, that a crowd of Indians has sallied forth; but when they saw our men approaching, they speedily took to flight, parents abandoning their children, and children their parents. This happened not because any loss or injury had been inflicted upon any of them. On the contrary, I gave whatever I had, cloth and many other things, to whomsoever I approached, or with whom I could get speech, without any return being made to me; but they are by nature fearful and timid. But, when they see that they are safe, and all fear is banished, they are very guileless and honest, and very liberal of all they have. No one refuses the asker anything that he possesses; on the contrary, they themselves invite us to ask for it. They manifest the greatest affection toward all of us, exchanging valuable things for trifles, content with the very last thing or nothing at all. . . .

Finally, to sum up in a few words the chief results and advantages of our departure and speedy return, I make this promise to our most invincible Sovereigns, that, if I am supported by some little assistance from them, I will give them as much gold as they have need of, and in addition spices, cotton, and mastic, which is found only in Chios, and as much aloes-wood, and as many heathen slaves as their Majesties may choose to demand.
        . . .
As these things have been accomplished, so have they been briefly narrated. Farewell.

CHRISTOPHER COLOM,
Lisbon, March 14th.
Admiral of the Ocean Fleet.

* Reprinted from *Old South Pamphlets*, Vol. 2, No. 33 (Directors of the Old South Work, 1897).

was larger than Columbus held, that the oceans were wider, and that the shortest route to the Orient was around Africa rather than across the Atlantic. For this reason the Portuguese king turned Columbus down when he applied for financial assistance in 1484. Two years later Columbus was at the Spanish court, where, after a preliminary rejection, he finally won the support of Queen Isabella.

On August 2, 1492, Columbus set sail from Palos with three small ships manned by reliable crews with capable and seasoned officers. By mid-October he had landed at one of the Bahaman Islands, which Columbus named San Salvador. One of the supreme ironies of world history is that Columbus was convinced until the end of his life that he had reached Asia. He was certain that San Salvador was very near to where Japan ought to be, and the next step was to find Japan itself. When he sailed southwest to the mainland of the New World, he believed that he was somewhere near the Malacca Straits. The fact that Columbus persisted in his delusion had momentous consequences: It spurred on further exploration of the Americas until the great prizes in Mexico and Peru were discovered.

The Spanish monarchs loyally supported Columbus and invested large sums in outfitting him for three additional expeditions. But not until 1519 did the Spaniards stumble on the rich Aztec empire in Mexico. During the quarter-century between this windfall and Columbus's first expedition, disappointment followed disappointment as the Spaniards explored the innumerable and unpromising islands of the West Indies. Columbus's great discovery appeared to be a grand failure. Several thousand adventurers had flocked to the West Indies and found disappointingly small quantities of gold. But there was an immediate reaction to the discovery of the New World that was very important. It prodded the Portuguese to circumnavigate Africa and reach India directly by sea.

III. PORTUGAL IN ASIA

The Portuguese in the meantime had been making considerable profit from their trade along the African Guinea coast. Coarse pepper,

The credulity of the West regarding unexplored territories is illustrated by this engraving, *The Wondrous People to Be Found in Guinea.*

gold, ivory, cotton, sugar, and slaves now entered European commerce through Portugal. Prince Henry's successors continued his work of opening up the West African coast. A breakthrough occurred in 1487 when Bartholomeu Dias, while sailing along the coast, was caught by a gale that blew his ships south for thirteen days out of sight of land. When the wind moderated, Dias steered for the West African coast but discovered that he had already passed the Cape without knowing it. He landed at Mossel Bay on the Indian Ocean and wanted to explore further, but his weary and frightened men forced him to return. On the homeward passage he first sighted the great cape, and named it the Cape of Storms. It was the Portuguese king who, upon Dias's return, renamed it the Cape of Good Hope. But the king did not follow up on this rounding of the Cape because of political and financial complications. The result, as noted, was that Columbus was the first to reach the New World, which he insisted in claiming as the Orient.

The more knowledgeable Portuguese were dubious from the beginning, but they now hastened to open and secure the Cape route to

Vasco da Gama.

India. On July 8, 1497, Vasco da Gama sailed from Portugal with four ships, and at the end of May 1498, he entered Calicut harbor. Da Gama did not receive a warm welcome in Calicut. The resident Arab merchants were naturally alarmed by the threat to their traditional monopoly and did their best to throw obstacles in the way of the European intruders. Furthermore, the Portuguese trade goods—mostly trinkets and woolen cloth—were unsuitable for the Indian market. The fact is that the Portuguese had completely underestimated the level and sophistication of Indian civilization. Thus, da Gama had difficulty trading in Calicut not only because of the hostility of the resident Arab traders but also, and more important, because Portugal (and all Europe) produced little at this time that was of interest to the Eastern peoples. European manufactures were generally inferior in quality and higher in price than the goods produced in the East.

With much effort da Gama collected a cargo of pepper and cinnamon and cleared for home, arriving in September 1499. The cargo proved to be worth sixty times the cost of the entire expedition. Dazzling horizons opened up before the delighted Portuguese, and King Manuel assumed the titles "Lord of the Conquest, Navigation, and Commerce of Ethiopia, Arabia, Persia, and India." These titles were taken quite seriously. The Portuguese were determined to monopolize the trade along the new route and to exclude not only other Europeans, but also the Arabs and other Eastern peoples who had traded in the Indian Ocean for centuries. To enforce their claims, the Portuguese resorted to ruthless terrorism, particularly when they encountered the hated Moslems. Da Gama, on a later voyage, found some unarmed vessels returning from Mecca. He captured the vessels and, in the words of a fellow Portuguese, "after making the ships empty of goods, prohibited anyone from taking out of it any Moor and then ordered them to set fire to it."[1]

Such was the nature of the epoch-making meeting of two Eurasian cultures when they came face to face for the first time after millennia of regional isolation. The Europeans were the aggressive intruders. They were the ones who seized the initiative and retained it until gradually but inexorably they emerged the masters in every quarter of the globe. This unprecedented domination of the world is at first difficult to understand. Why was Portugal, with a population of approximately 2 million, able to encroach on highly civilized Asiatic countries with much greater human and natural resources?

First, the Portuguese had the great advantage of being ready to use the vast bullion supply that was soon to start pouring in from the New World. The flood of bullion from the treasures of the Aztec and Inca empires and from the Mexican and Peruvian silver mines came just in time to finance Portugal's trade with the East. Without this windfall the Portuguese would have been very seriously restricted, because they had neither natural resources nor manufactured goods that were of interest to the Eastern peoples.

Second, the Portuguese triumphed because of the disunity of the Indian subcontinent. When the Portuguese arrived on the scene, northern India was controlled by the new Mogul invaders, who were interested in conquest rather than trade, and southern India, and especially the Malabar coast, was under the control of petty Hindu rulers who were fighting one another. By contrast, the Portuguese and their European successors had a singleness and continuity of purpose that more than counterbalanced their inferiority in resources. The Europeans obviously were not united; they were riddled with political and religious dissension. But on one point they were all agreed—the need to expand eastward to reap profits and to outflank Islam. In pursuit of this objective the Europeans demonstrated a determination to succeed that was stronger than the will of the Asiatic peoples to resist. When da Gama returned from his historic voyage, the Portuguese court was prepared to follow up promptly. It had a detailed plan for organized trade, involving the establishment of trading posts in the Malabar ports and the sending of annual fleets under royal charter.

The Portuguese were successful also because of the superiority of their naval power. They had developed efficient new naval artillery that enabled them to use ships as floating batteries rather than as transports for boarding parties. The gun, not the foot soldier, was now the main instrument of naval warfare, and the guns were employed against the enemy's ships rather than against its men. It was these new developments that made it possible for the Portuguese to smash

Da Gama's flagship, the *São Gabriel.*

Moslem naval power in the Indian Ocean and to win a profitable Asiatic empire.

The architect of this empire was the great Alfonso de Alburquerque, governor general from 1509 to 1515. His policy was to smash the Arab trade network by capturing control of the narrow sea passage leading to and from the Indian Ocean. He seized the islands of Socotra and Hormuz, which were the keys to the Red Sea and the Persian Gulf, respectively. In India he took the city of Goa, located in the middle of the Malabar coast. He made Goa his main naval base and general headquarters, and it remained a Portuguese possession until 1961. Further to the east he captured Malacca, commanding the strait through which all commerce with the Far East had to pass. Two years later, in 1513, the first Portuguese ship to reach a Chinese port put into Canton. This was the first recorded European visit to China since Marco Polo's day. The

Portuguese obtained the right to establish a warehouse and a settlement in Macao, a little downstream from Canton, and from there they carried on their Far Eastern operations.

The Portuguese Empire in Asia was small in actual extent, made up of only a few islands and coastal posts. But these possessions were so strategically located that they gave the Portuguese command of trade routes spanning half the globe. Each year Portuguese fleets sailed down the African coast, which was dotted with stations for provisioning and refitting the ships. After they rounded the Cape, they put in at Mozambique in East Africa, another Portuguese possession. Then they sailed with the monsoon across to Cochin and Ceylon, where they loaded the spices that had been brought in from the surrounding territories. Further east was Malacca, which gave them access to the trade of east Asia and for which they served as middlemen and carriers. Thus, the Portuguese profited from purely Asian trade—between China and Japan and the Philippines, for example—as well as from the trade between Europe and the East.

With this network of trading stations and strong points, Albuquerque had broken the traditional monopoly of the Arab merchants in the Indian Ocean. In doing so he was competing with the Venetian merchants for the "spiceries" that they had customarily obtained in the ports of the Levant. The Venetians no longer found the spices they had bought for centuries in Alexandria and other Levant ports. Instead, the spices were now being shipped on the longer but cheaper ocean route to Lisbon. This explains why in 1508 the Egyptians, with full Venetian support, sent a naval expedition to help the Indian rajas drive the Portuguese interlopers out of the Indian Ocean. The effort failed, but the Turks, who conquered Egypt in 1517, continued the campaign against the Portuguese and sent several fleets during the following decades. They were all unsuccessful, and the spices continued to flow around the Cape to Europe.

Yet it should not be assumed that the old routes through the Middle East fell into complete disuse. In fact, after the initial dislocation, the old routes regained much of the lost trade for a variety of reasons. One reason was that there were some corrupt Portuguese officials who were willing, when bribed, to allow Arab shipping to enter the Red Sea and the Persian Gulf. The Arabs and Venetians thus were able to compete successfully with the Portuguese throughout the six-

Arabs and Turks battling the Portuguese.

teenth century. It was not until the following century, with the appearance in the Indian Ocean of the more efficient and economically powerful Dutch and English, that the old Italian and Arab middlemen were completely displaced. The tradition Middle Eastern trade routes then gave way to oceanic routes.

IV.   DIVISION OF THE WORLD

When the Europeans began to expand overseas, they adopted the convenient doctrine that they had the right to take the lands of non-Christians without regard for the native peoples concerned. Another doctrine, adopted at least by Portugal and Spain, was the right of the pope to give sovereignty to any lands not possessed by a Christian ruler. As early as 1454, Pope Nicholas V issued a decision granting to the Portuguese title over territories they were discovering along the African coast toward India. When Columbus returned from his voyage convinced that he had reached the Indies, the Spanish court feared Portuguese counterclaims and therefore pressed Pope Alexander VI for recognition of Spanish sovereignty. On May 4, 1493, Pope Alexander defined a dividing line running 100 leagues west of the Azores and Cape Verde Islands; to the west of this line he granted all lands to Spain, and to the east all lands went to Portugal. On June 7, 1494, Spain and Portugal negotiated an agreement, the Treaty of Tordesillas, moving the line 270 leagues further west. This change gave Portugal a claim to Brazil in the New World.

The riches that Portugal reaped from the spice trade after da Gama's voyage goaded the other European countries into a frantic search for another route to the Indies. The successive failures of Columbus to find Cathay did not kill the hope of reaching Asia by sailing west. It might still be possible to thread a way between the various masses of inhospitable land so far discovered. This was the aim of a new class of professional explorers that appeared in the early sixteenth century. Mostly Italians and Portuguese—the best-informed and the most experienced explorers at that time—they were ready to carry on explorations for any monarch

willing to finance them. The Italians included Amerigo Vespucci, who sailed for Portugal and Spain; John Verrazano, who sailed for France; and the two Cabots, father and son, who sailed for England. The Portuguese included Juan Diaz de Solis, Juan Fernandez, and Ferdinand Magellan, all of whom sailed for Spain.

Magellan was the only one who found the passage to Asia. Spain sent him to find it because, with regular spice cargoes arriving in Lisbon, the Spanish realized that they were being beaten in the race for the Spice Islands. Since they claimed that the line of demarcation defined by the Tordesillas Treaty ran around the globe, they sent Magellan west to find Asia, hoping that at least some of the Spice Islands were on the Spanish side of the line.

In one of the great epics of seafaring, Magellan set out from Seville on September 10, 1519, with a fleet of five ships, each about 100 tons. By October he reached the straits that bear his name, but the seas were so rough that it took well over a month to cross into the Pacific. Meanwhile one ship had been wrecked and another had deserted, so with the remaining three he sailed up the Chilean coast to the fiftieth latitude and then veered to the northwest.

During the next eighty days only two uninhabited islands were sighted. Magellan and his men ran short of food and water and suffered terribly from scurvy. On March 6 they reached an island, perhaps Guam, where they were able to obtain provisions. On the sixteenth of the same month they arrived at the Philippines, where Magellan and forty of his crew were killed in a local war. With the aid of native pilots, the surviving Spaniards sailed to Borneo and thence to their destination, the Moluccas or Spice Islands, which they finally reached in November 1520. The Portuguese, who were already there, did not hesitate to attack the two remaining Spanish ships (one had been abandoned in the Philippines). Despite all obstacles the Spaniards were able to obtain cargoes of cloves, and then set off on the journey home by different routes. The ship that tried to recross the Pacific was turned back by head winds and captured by the Portuguese. The other successfully completed a fantastic voyage through the Macassar Strait, across the Indian Ocean, around the Cape of

In Goa, Portuguese adopted Eastern dress.

Good Hope, and up the entire length of Africa. On September 3, 1522, this last surviving ship, the Victoria, leaking badly and with a decimated crew, limped into the harbor of Seville. Yet the single cargo of spices was valuable enough to pay the expense of the entire expedition.

The Spaniards sent out another expedition, which reached the Spice Islands in 1524. But it was a disastrous failure because the Portuguese were too firmly established to be challenged profitably. Furthermore, the Spanish king was desperately in need of money at this time to finance his war with France. So in 1529 he signed the Treaty of Saragossa with Portugal. In return for 350,000 ducats, he gave up all claims to the Spice Islands and accepted a demarcation line fifteen degrees east of them. This treaty marked the end of a chapter in the history of discovery (see map of Western Knowledge of the Globe, A.D. 1 to 1800, p. 375.) The Portuguese held on to the Spice Islands until they lost them to the Dutch in 1605, whereas the Spaniards continued to show interest in the Philippines and eventually conquered them in 1571, even though the islands were east of the line stipulated by the Saragossa Treaty. Long before this, however, Spain shifted her attention to the New World, where great treasures had been found equal in value to the spices of the East.

V.   CONQUISTADORS AND NEW SPAIN

The year 1519, in which Magellan left Seville on his famous voyage around the world, was also the year Hernando Cortes left Cuba on his equally famous expedition against the Aztec Empire. In doing so, Cortes began what might be termed the age of the *conquistadors*. The preceding decades, from 1500 to 1520, had been the age of the explorers, when numerous navigators under various flags probed the entire length of the Americas in search of a passageway. In the thirty years that followed, a few thousand Spanish adventurers won the first great European overseas empire.

One of these soldiers of fortune, a typical product of the Iberian crusading tradition, was Hernando Cortes, an unsuccessful law student and the son of a respectable family. In 1504 he arrived in Hispaniola, and six years later he participated in the conquest of Cuba. Distinguishing himself during this campaign, he was selected to head an expedition to Yucatan to investigate reports of civilized city dwellers living in the interior. In March 1519 Cortes landed on the mainland coast near present-day Veracruz. He had only 600 men, a few

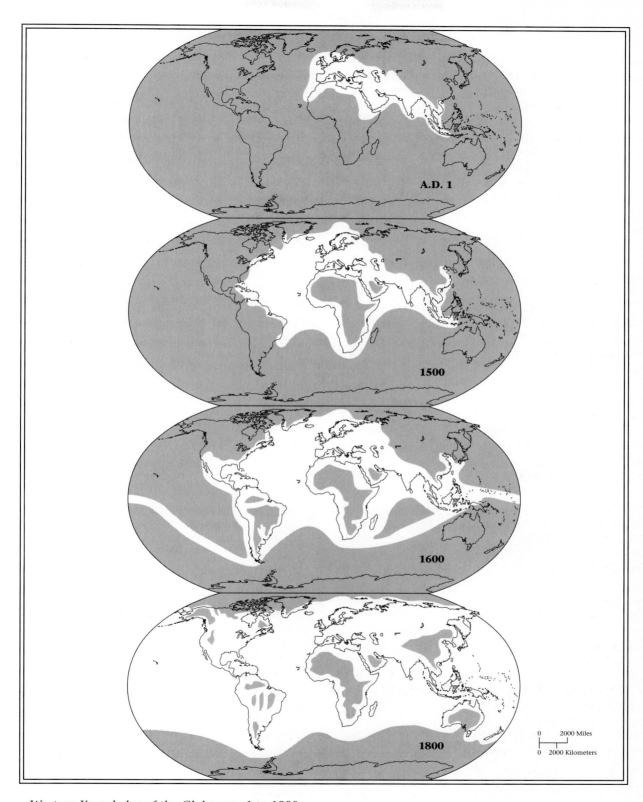

Western Knowledge of the Globe, A.D. 1 to 1800.

small cannon, thirteen muskets, and sixteen horses. Yet with this insignificant force he was to win fabulous riches and become master of an exotic, highly advanced empire.

Cortes began by scuttling his ships to show his men that they had no hope of returning to Cuba in case of setbacks. Then, after some fighting, he reached agreements with various tribes that were hostile to their Aztec overlords. Without the food, the porters, and the fighting men provided by these tribes, Cortes could not have won the victories he did. By playing on the superstitions of Montezuma, the Aztec war chief, Cortes was able to march peacefully into the capital, Tenochtitlan. He was graciously received by Montezuma, whom he treacherously took prisoner and kept as a hostage. But the Indians were vastly superior in numbers, and their priests stirred them to rebellion. The Spanish policy of destroying native temples provoked an uprising during which Montezuma was killed. Cortes fought his way out of the capital by night, losing a third of his men and most of his baggage in the process. He recovered from this setback because his Indian allies remained loyal and reinforcements arrived from Cuba. A few months later Cortes returned and laid siege to the capital with a force of 800 Spanish soldiers and at least 25,000

Indians. The fighting was bitter and dragged on for four months. Finally, in August 1521 the surviving defenders surrendered their city, which was almost entirely reduced to rubble. Today, Mexico City stands in its place, with hardly a trace left of the original Aztec capital.

Even more audacious was the conquest of the Inca Empire by a Spanish expedition comprising 180 men, twenty-seven horses, and two cannons. The leader was Francisco Pizarro, an illiterate drifter who was the illegitimate son of a Spanish officer. After preliminary explorations from which he learned the general location of the Incas, he set forth in 1531, with his four brothers, on his great adventure. After a long delay in crossing the Andes, Pizarro reached the deserted city of Cajamarca on November 15, 1532. The following day the Inca ruler, Atahualpa, who was curious about these strange "men with beards," paid a formal visit to Pizarro. In imitation of Cortes, Pizarro captured the unarmed and unsuspecting emperor and massacred many of his followers. The emperor paid an enormous ransom for his freedom—a room twenty-two feet by seventeen feet piled seven feet deep with gold and silver articles. Pizarro seized the booty, and with customary treachery and bigotry, executed Atahualpa. The Inca Empire now was left leader-

Conquistadors introducing Negro slaves to work in the gold and silver mines in Hispaniola.

Quauhtemoc, the last king of the
Aztecs, surrendering to Cortes.

less, and the Indian population, used to paternalistic regimentation, offered little resistance. A few weeks later Pizarro entered and looted the capital, Cuzco. The next year, 1535, he left for the coast, where he founded Lima, still the capital of Peru.

The triumphs of Cortes and Pizarro inspired other conquistadors to march through vast areas of both the American continents in search of more booty. They found nothing comparable to the Aztec and Inca treasures, but they did determine the major configuration of all of South America and of a large part of North America. By the middle of the sixteenth century they had followed the Amazon from Peru to its mouth. By the end of the century they were familiar with the entire coastline of South America, from the Gulf of California south to Tierra del Fuego and north to the West Indies. Likewise in North America, Francisco de Coronado, in his search for the fabled Seven Cities of Cibola, traversed thousands of miles and discovered the Grand Canyon and the Colorado River. Hernando de Soto, who had been prominent in the conquest of Peru, explored widely in the southeast of what was to become the United States. He landed in Florida in 1539, made his way north to the Carolinas and west to the Mississippi, and followed that river from its junction with the Arkansas River to its mouth. These men, and many others like them, opened the New World for the Spaniards in the same way

that La Salle and Lewis and Clark opened it for the French- and English-speaking peoples.

By 1550 the conquistadors had completed their work. The way was now clear for the Spaniards to proceed with the development of their overseas possessions. Since the native populations were not so dense or so highly organized as those of Africa and Asia, it was possible for the Iberians to settle in considerable numbers in the New World and to impose their cultures. Thus they built Europe's first true colonial empire—something quite different from the purely commercial empires in Africa and Asia.

The swashbuckling conquistadors were effective as empire builders but quite ineffective as empire administrators. Incapable of settling down, they fell into fighting among themselves, and their ranks were decimated by feuding and warfare. The Spanish crown replaced the conquistadors with bureaucrats who imposed royal authority and royal justice.

At the top of the imperial administrative structure was the Council of the Indies, located in Spain and closely supervised by the crown. It made all important appointments and exercised general jurisdiction over colonial affairs. Supreme authority in the New World was entrusted to two viceroys who sat in Mexico City and Lima. The official in Mexico City headed the viceroyalty of New Spain, which was made up of all the Spanish

Pizarro's attack on Cuzco.

territories in North America together with the West Indies, Venezuela, and the Philippines. The Lima official presided over the viceroyalty of Peru, which was made up of the remaining Spanish possessions in South America. These two vast viceroyalties were subdivided into smaller units ruled by *audiencias,* or courts. Audiencias were staffed by professional lawyers who usually had no excessive family pride or military ambition and therefore made ideal royal servants. In the sixteenth century there were ten such audiencias in the New World.

A basic problem of Spanish administration in the Americas was the treatment of the Indians. The crown granted to deserving conquistadors, known as "protectors," or *encomenderos,* the right to draw specified tribute from assigned Indian villages and also to levy forced labor. In return, the encomenderos were required to give military service and to pay the salaries of the parish clergy. The provision for forced labor obviously opened the door to abuse, so it was modified in the mid-sixteenth century. The natives still could be made to work, but by public officials rather than private encomenderos, and official wage

rates had to be paid to the laborers so recruited. Needless to say, these safeguards were not always enforced. The colonies were too far from Madrid and too isolated from each other. Yet the fact remains that the Spaniards discussed seriously and conscientiously the problem of exploitation, for which there were no precedents.

The all-important fact for the economy of the Spanish colonial empire is that with the work of native labor a great flood of gold and silver poured in from the mines of Mexico and Bolivia. The law required that all precious metals be taken to the royal offices to be stamped and taxed at the rate of one-fifth their value, the royal quinto. Between 1503 and 1660 Spain received from America a total of 18,600 registered tons of silver and 200 registered tons of gold. Unregistered bullion smuggled into Spain has been variously estimated at from 10 to 50 percent of the total.

Apart from mining, the principal occupations in Latin America were agriculture and stock raising in the haciendas and plantation monoculture in the tropical coastlands. The haciendas employed Indian labor and produced foodstuffs for their own use and for sale to nearby cities and mining settlements. The plantations were quite different, employing mostly imported African slaves and producing only one crop for the European market. The first plantations were evolved for the growing of sugar on the Atlantic islands— the Azores, Madeiras, Cape Verdes, and Canaries. Later this institution was further developed, first in the sugar plantations of Brazil and the West Indies, and later in the tobacco, cotton, and coffee plantations of North and South America.

VI.   IBERIAN DECLINE

During the sixteenth century the Iberian countries led Europe in overseas enterprise and won vast riches from the Eastern spice trade and from the New World silver mines. But by the end of the century they were rapidly slipping back from their respective positions of primacy. The French, Dutch, and English were poaching with increasing success in Portugal's Eastern empire and in Spain's American colonies. One reason for the Iberian decline was their involvement in the religious and dynastic wars of the sixteenth and seventeenth centuries. As noted previously (see Chapter 22, Sections IV and V, and Chapter 23, Section IV), Spanish manpower and treasure were squandered by Charles V and Philip II in fighting the religious wars against the Protestants; the recurring campaigns against the formidable Turks; and the dynastic struggles against rival royal houses, especially the French. In waging these campaigns the rulers of Spain fatally overextended themselves. They attempted to play the leading role on land as well as on sea. Their actions were in striking contrast to the successful strategy pursued later by England of remaining on the periphery of continental affairs and intervening only in case the balance of power was seriously threatened. British strategy enabled them to concentrate their efforts on the defense and development of their colonies. But Spain, like France, focused on the European continent and was continually involved in its wars. The end result was that the British were able to build a great worldwide empire, whereas the Spaniards lost economic, and then political, control of their empire.

Although the Iberian states definitely were weakened by foreign entanglements, a more important cause for their continued decline was the fact that they had become economic dependencies of northwest Europe. They had been so before they began their overseas expansion and they remained so afterward. As a result they were unable to exploit the economic opportunities offered by their newly won empires, and their empires, like the mother countries, fell under the domination of the northwest European states and became their colonies or semicolonies.

The economic dependence of the Iberian countries was a part of the general shift of the economic center of Europe in the late Middle Ages from the Mediterranean basin to the north. The reason for the shift was the accelerating productivity of northern Europe (see Chapter 23, Sections I-III), which enabled the new mass trade of the Baltic–North Sea area (grain, lumber, fish, and coarse cloth) to surpass the traditional luxury trade of the Mediterranean (spices, silks, perfumes, and jewelry). As the European economy grew and living standards rose, the mass trade catering to the general population increased much more rapidly than the luxury trade for the wealthy few.

Northern commerce was controlled by the Hanseatic League, which played the same role in the Baltic and North seas as Venice and Genoa did in the Mediterranean. In the sixteenth century the Hansa was dislodged by the Dutch, who built such a large and efficient merchant marine that they soon dominated the Atlantic seaboard. Formerly the Atlantic trade had been controlled by the Venetians and Genoese sailing northward with luxury commodities. But now it was controlled by the Dutch sailing southward with bulk cargoes. In this new trade pattern, the dependent economic status of the Iberian states was evident in their exports, which were almost exclusively raw materials—wine, wool, and iron ore from Spain, and African gold and salt from Portugal. In return the Iberians received back their own wool, which had been manufactured abroad into cloth, as well as metallurgical products, salt, and fish. Thus the Iberian states, like the Italian, were declining at this time from the status of developed to underdeveloped societies relative to the burgeoning capitalist economies of northern Europe (see Chapter 22, Section II, for the similar decline of Italy).

The economically backward Iberian states were able to take the lead in overseas expansion only because of a fortunate combination of favorable geographic location, maritime technology, and religious drive. But their expansion was not based on economic strength and dynamism, which explains why the Iberian states could not exploit their new empires effectively. They lacked the shipping necessary for imperial trade and also the industries to supply the manufactured goods needed in the Spanish American colonies. It is true that Spanish industry for a few decades was stimulated by the expanding overseas market for manufacturers. But the industrial growth stopped about 1560, and chronic decline then set in.

Paradoxically enough, one reason for the decline was the great inflow of treasure, which produced a sharp inflation. Prices rose approximately twice as high in Spain as in northern Europe, and Spanish wages lagged only slightly behind the soaring prices, whereas wages in the rest of Europe were much lower. The inflation penalized Spanish industry, making its products too expensive to compete in the international market.

At least as important as the price and wage inflation was the ruinous influence of the Spanish aristocrat, or *hidalgo,* on the national economy and on national values. Although the aristocrats, together with the higher churchmen, comprised less than 2 percent of the population, they owned 95 to 97 percent of the land. It follows that the peasants, about 95 percent of all Spaniards, were almost all landless. The remaining 3 percent—clerics, merchants, and professional people, many of whom were Jews—were not a middle class in any economic or social sense. They were completely overshadowed by the nobility who had social status and prestige. And because the nobility looked down on careers in commerce or industry as demeaning, this prejudice became the national norm. Nor was this mere empty vanity, for the hidalgo had all the advantages—honors, exemption from taxation, and territorial wealth, which was more secure than commercial or industrial riches. Consequently, the ambition of successful merchants was to acquire estates; buy titles, which were sold by the impoverished crown; and thus abandon their class and become hidalgos. The blighting influence of this hidalgo spirit was felt in all branches of the economy—in the favoritism shown toward sheep farming as opposed to agriculture, in the expulsion of the industrious Jews and Moslems, and in the negative attitude of the Cortes assembly toward commercial and industrial interests. As a result of these attitudes, the economic spurt that occurred in Spain in the first half of the sixteenth century ended in failure.

This failure made it impossible to overcome the traditional Iberian economic backwardness and subservience to northwest Europe. It also doomed the Iberian colonial possessions to a corresponding backwardness and subservience. First the Dutch and then the British controlled most of the carrying trade with the Spanish and Portuguese colonies. The northwest Europeans also were soon supplying up to 90 percent of the manufactured goods imported by Brazil and Spanish America, as well as a high proportion of similar goods consumed in the Iberian peninsula itself. The merchant guild of Seville enjoyed a monopoly of all trade with the colonies, in which foreigners were forbidden by law to participate. But it was the foreigners who possessed the shipping and the manufactured goods needed in the colonies. Inevitably the Spanish merchants exported under their own name goods that belonged to foreign firms and were of foreign manufacture. Also through an elaborate set of pretenses, foreign merchants and financiers became members by proxy of the Seville guild. Thus the legal members conducted a vast commission business for foreigners that soon surpassed their own legitimate trade. The end result is apparent in the following complaint of a contemporary Spaniard: "All that the Spaniards bring from the Indies after long, prolix, and hazardous navigations, and all that they harvest with blood and labour, foreigners carry off to their homelands with ease and comfort."[2]

It is ironic that the net effect of Spanish overseas enterprise was to fuel the booming capitalist economy of northwest Europe, whereas in the Iberian peninsula it provided just enough wealth to forestall the basic institutional reforms that were long overdue. This is the root cause for the sudden and irreversible decline that followed so soon after the few decades of imperial glory.

Today's parallel to the boomerang effect of New World bullion on the Iberian peninsula is to be found in the Gulf oil states, where huge oil revenues are being squandered for foreign luxuries and consequently are ending up in foreign industrialized countries. When the Persian Gulf oil fields are exhausted, the flow of oil revenues will cease, as did the earlier flow of American bullion. The Gulf states then will find themselves in an even worse position than the Iberian states because after the oil is gone, the Gulf region will be left with little more than sand and dry holes.

SUGGESTED READINGS

The best overall survey of Europe expansion is provided by J. H. Parry, *The Age of Reconnaissance: Discovery, Exploration and Settlement 1450–1650* (New American Library, 1963), and his *European Reconnaissance: Selected Documents* (Harper & Row, 1968). See also G. V. Scammell, *The World Encompassed: The First European Maritime Empires, c. 800–1650* (University of California, 1981). The following interpretations of European expansion reflect an Indian viewpoint: K. M. Panikkar, *Asia and Western Dominance* (Harper & Row, 1954); and K. N. Chaudhuri, *Trade and Civilization in the Indian Ocean* (Cambridge University, 1985). The lethal biological repercussions of European expansion are analyzed by A. W. Crosby, *Ecological Imperialism: The Biological Expansion of Europe, 900–1900* (Cambridge University, 1986). The religious factor in European expansion is presented by C. R. Boxer, *The Church Militant and Iberian Expansion 1440–1770* (Johns Hopkins University, 1978).

For Portuguese maritime and colonial enterprise, see B. W. Diffie, *Prelude to Empire: Portugal Overseas Before Henry the Navigator* (University of Nebraska, 1963); E. Bradford, *Southward the Caravels: The Story of Henry the Navigator* (Hutchinson, 1961); C. R. Boxer, *The Portuguese Seaborne Empire, 1415–1825* (Knopf, 1969); and G. R. Crone, *The Discovery of the East* (St. Martin's, 1972). The best general analyses of the Spanish colonial system are C. H. Haring, *The Spanish Empire in America* (Oxford University, 1947); and J. Lockhart and S. B. Schwartz, *Early Latin America* (Cambridge University, 1983). See also C. Gibson, *The Aztecs Under Spanish Rule: A History of the Indians of the Valley of Mexico, 1519–1810* (Stanford University, 1964); J. Descola, *Daily Life in Colonial Peru 1710–1820* (George Allen & Unwin, 1968); and J. H. Parry, *The Spanish Seaborne Empire* (Knopf, 1966). For the Portuguese efforts in America there are G. Freyre, *Brazil, an Interpretation* (Knopf, 1945); and C. R. Boxer, *The Golden Age of Brazil, 1695–1750: Growing Pains of a Colonial Society* (University of California, 1963).

Finally, the roots and course of Iberian decline are presented in J. Lynch, *Spain Under the Hapsburgs,* Vol. I, *Empire and Absolutism, 1516–1598* (Oxford University, 1964); in J. H. Elliott, *Imperial Spain 1469–1716* (New American Library, 1966); in the two excellent studies by R. T. Davies, *The Golden Century of Spain, 1501–1621* (Macmillan, 1954), and *Spain in Decline, 1621–1700* (Macmillan, 1957); and in the stimulating analysis by S. J. and B. H. Stein, *The Colonial Heritage of Latin America* (Oxford University, 1970).

25

West European Expansion: Dutch, French, British Phase, 1600–1763

I should like to see Adam's will, wherein he divided the earth between Spain and Portugal.

King Francis I

In the period between 1600 and 1763 Spain and Portugal were overtaken and surpassed by the powers of northwestern Europe—Holland, France, and Britain. This development was of great significance for the entire world. It made northwestern Europe the most influential and dynamic region of the globe. And the countries of northwestern Europe were to dominate the world—politically, militarily, economically, and, to a certain degree, culturally—until 1914. Their practices and institutions became the models for peoples everywhere.

The domination of the world by northwestern Europe did not actually materialize until after 1763. But it was between 1600 and 1763 that the basis for domination was laid. These were the years when the British gained their first foothold in India, when the Dutch drove the Portuguese out of the East Indies, when all the northwestern powers set up stations on the coasts of Africa, and when the British and the French became the masters of North America above the Rio Grande and came to control much of the commerce of the Iberian colonies south of it.

This chapter will analyze the roots of northwest European primacy, and the struggles of Holland, France, and Britain for leadership, culminating in 1763 with the emergence of Britain as the dominant colonial power of the world.

I. EARLY NORTHWEST EUROPEAN EXPANSION

Northwestern Europe did not rise from utter obscurity to the leading position in continental commerce and overseas enterprise. As noted in the preceding chapter, the foundation was laid during the late Middle Ages when the economic center of Europe shifted from the Mediterranean basin northward, and when the principal trade routes likewise shifted from the Mediterranean to the Atlantic. In addition to economic superiority, northwestern Europe possessed a social structure and a cultural climate that were particularly responsive to economic interests. Far from regarding business enterprise with disdain, the patricians of Holland and the nobility of England, and even of France, were always ready to participate in any business venture that promised profit. Not only did the gentry take part in commerce, but there was also much greater class mobility in the north, where merchants and financiers often entered the ranks of the nobility. This favored a positive attitude toward economic enterprise, in contrast to the short-sighted hidalgo spirit that contributed so much to Iberian decadence.

Finally, northwestern Europe was aided by a price-wage-rent differential. Prices rose 256 percent in England during the sixteenth and seventeenth centuries, whereas wages rose only 145 percent. Rents also lagged badly behind prices in northwestern Europe. This meant that of the three main elements of society—the laborers, landlords, and entrepreneurs—the entrepreneurs were the ones who reaped golden profits during these centuries of inflation. Profits were plowed back into mining ventures, industrial establishments, and commercial enterprises, with the result that the economy of northwestern Europe boomed ahead at an unprecedented rate. The famous British economist John Maynard Keynes has described the period from 1550 to 1650 as follows: "Never in the annals of the modern world has there existed so prolonged and so rich an opportunity for the business man, the speculator, and the profiteer. In these golden years modern capitalism was born."[1] That it was born in northwestern Europe explains why the northwestern countries forged ahead of Spain and Portugal and attained a predominant position in world affairs, a position they were to retain until the outbreak of World War I.

The countries of northwestern Europe were naturally envious of the lucrative empires of Spain and Portugal. But for a long time they refrained from poaching on these imperial preserves for fear of Iberian power. Accordingly, the English, the Dutch, and the French turned to the North Atlantic, which was beyond the limits of Iberian activity. Henry VII of England sent John Cabot out into the North Atlantic in 1496, the year of Columbus's second return. And Cabot discovered a resource that turned out in the long run to be even more valuable than the silver mines of the Spaniards: He found fish. The sea off Newfoundland was teeming with fish—probably the most important article of trade in fifteenth- and sixteenth-century Europe. Fish was the winter staple of the people and their diet on fast days throughout the year. The regular supply of immense quantities of cod was a great windfall for a continent where many people at that time lived near starvation level for part of every year. And the Newfoundland fisheries bred successive generations of mariners who were trained and fitted for ocean navigation. The ships that later probed the Arctic for a northeast or a northwest passage, the expeditions that began the settlement of North America, the English and the Dutch fleets that fought the armadas of Spain and Portugal—all these were largely manned by seamen trained in the hard school of the Banks fisheries.

The maritime states of northwestern Europe were by no means satisfied with cod. They still hankered after spices, but they were not yet prepared to challenge Portugal's mastery of the Cape route. So they began their long and fruitless series of expeditions in search of a northeast or northwest passage to the Orient. They rea-

Leaves and berries of canella or "wild cinnamon" (*Ravensara aromatica*).

Leaves and berries of the pepper plant.

The clove tree.

These drawings are by Cristobal de Acosta. They are reproduced here from Sir Clements Markham (ed. and trans.), *Colloquies on the Simples, and Drugs of India, by Garcia da Orta* ... (London, 1913).

One of the causes of western Europe's expansionism was a demand for foreign products, among them spices. Here, in three drawings by Cristobal de Acosta, are shown (from left to right) three of those spices—leaves and berries of wild cinnamon, a clove tree, and the leaves and berries of the pepper plant.

soned that since the tropics had proved passable, contrary to all expectations, the Arctic should be passable too. Hence the 1553 English expedition under Sir Hugh Willoughby and Richard Chancellor sought a northeast passage to China, only to be blocked by a wall of ice. This expedition, however, did succeed in making a landing on the shores of the White Sea, where it established contact with the court of Tsar Ivan IV. This contact led to the founding of the Muscovy Company (1555) for the purpose of direct trade between England and Russia. Other attempts to find a northeast passage proved futile. Several expeditions seeking a northwest passage (John Davis, 1585–1587; Henry Hudson, 1607–1611; William Baffin, 1615–1616) had no better luck. But just as the efforts in the northeast brought about trade with Russia, so the northwest ventures discovered the Hudson Strait and Hudson Bay. Together they provided a back entrance to

the richest fur-producing region of the New World.

The failure of the northern Europeans to find new routes to the East drove them to encroach on the preserves of the Iberian powers. Since Portugal's eastern possessions were still too strongly guarded, the northerners struck first at the more vulnerable Spanish colonies in the Americas. English interlopers showing up in Spanish America at this time tried to carry on trade on a peaceful, commercial basis. They wanted not to plunder but to take advantage of the opportunities offered by the inability of the weak Spanish industry to meet the needs of the colonies. Of the two commodities most in demand in the Spanish colonies—cloth and slaves—the English produced the first and could purchase the second in West Africa. Because he was shrewd enough to see the possibilities of the situation and bold enough to act without regard

Landing of Richard Chancellor at Holmogory in the White Sea, 1553.

for legal niceties, Sir John Hawkins won fame and fortune as the founder of the English slave trade. In 1562 he made his first voyage. He picked up slaves in Sierra Leone and exchanged them in Hispaniola (Haiti) for hides and sugar. The profits were so spectacular that Queen Elizabeth and several of her Privy Councilors secretly invested in his second voyage. He followed the same procedure as before and returned with a cargo of silver that made him the richest man in England.

The Spanish ambassador in London made strong protests against this contraband trade. Even though Hawkins had peacefully exchanged slaves for colonial commodities, the fact remained that it was illegal for foreigners to trade with the Spanish colonies. Although not piracy, it definitely was poaching. Hawkins nevertheless sailed out for a

third time in 1567. This venture ended in disaster, with three of Hawkins's five ships sunk or captured. The other two, one commanded by Hawkins and the other by his cousin Francis Drake, reached England in 1569 in disabled condition.

If the commerce could not be conducted peacefully and legally, it was bound to be carried on by other means. The opportunities for profit were too great for the English and the other northerners to refrain and forget. During the following decades, the Protestant sea captains visited the Spanish Indies as pirates and privateers rather than as peaceful, though illegal, traders. When King Philip of Spain sent his armada against England in 1588, two of its most formidable adversaries were John Hawkins and Francis Drake. The defeat they inflicted on the armada was, for them, sweet revenge for what they had suffered in the West Indies.

Formal war with Spain (which at this time had absorbed Portugal) removed any inhibitions that may have restrained the Protestant powers. They broke boldly and openly into the Iberian imperial preserves—into the Portuguese East as well as into Spanish America. And the more they penetrated, the more they were encouraged to go further as they found out how weak the Iberians were. The Dutch were the first to exploit the opportunity afforded by Iberian decline. The seventeenth century was to be for Holland *Het Gouden Eeuw*— "the Golden Century."

II. HOLLAND'S GOLDEN CENTURY

The remarkable rise of Holland to power and prosperity in the seventeenth century was in part a result of its favorable geographic location. Backed by the great hinterland of Germany, Holland was strategically located along the ancient trade routes of Europe running north-south from Bergen to Gibraltar, and east-west from the Gulf of Finland to Britain. Basic trade commodities were transported along these routes: herring and salt from Biscay; wine from the Mediterranean; cloth from Britain and Flanders; copper and iron from Sweden; and cereals, flax, hemp, timber, and wood products from the Baltic.

The Imperial Court of Peking receiving Pieter Van Hoorn's Dutch Trade Delegation (1668).

The Dutch began their rise to greatness by serving as the carriers of these commodities. Their merchant marine owed its start to the local coastal fisheries. The Dutch devised new methods of preserving, salting, and smoking, and they exported their catch to all parts of Europe in return for corn, timber, and salt. With the building of the Spanish and Portuguese overseas empire, the Dutch picked up cargoes of the new colonial products in Seville and Lisbon and dis-tributed them throughout Europe. In return, they supplied the Iberian countries with Baltic grain and naval stores. The Dutch transported these commodities in their *fluyt,* or flyboat, an inexpensive general carrier with enormous capacity. Hitherto the typical merchantman had been built with heavy timbering and galleried transom so that it could mount cannon and serve, when necessary, as a man-of-war. The Dutch were the first to take the risk of building a

By the 1600s, the Dutch were seriously challenging Spain's superiority on the seas. Here the Dutch are shown capturing Spanish ships.

merchant packet deliberately designed to carry only goods and no guns. The fluyt's broad beam, flattened bottom, and restricted cabin accommodations gave it maximum hold space and unusual economy of building material. This slow and ugly but cheap and capacious boat was the mainstay of the Dutch merchant marine that came to dominate the seas of the world.

At the end of the sixteenth century the Dutch began to challenge Portugal's empire in the East. The first task was to collect reliable data to guide the navigators around the long Cape route. The Portuguese had taken the greatest precautions to keep such information from their rivals, but their navigation secrets gradually leaked out. The most important source of information for the northerners was the *Itinerario,* a geographical description of the world published in 1595 by the Dutchman Jan Huhghen van Linschoten. He had lived in India for seven years as a servant of the Portuguese archbishop of Goa, so that he was able to include in his book detailed sailing instructions for the Cape route.

The very year it was published Linschoten's *Itinerario* was used to guide the first Dutch fleet to the East Indies. The losses were heavy during the two-and-a-half-year expedition. Only 89 of the original 289 men returned. But the trade was so lucrative that there were substantial profits despite the losses in manpower and equipment. The next expedition was more fortunate and cleared a profit of 400 percent. The Dutch now swarmed into the Eastern waters. No fewer than five fleets made up of twenty-two ships sailed in the year 1598 alone. From the beginning they outmatched the Portuguese. They were better sailors, they could transport spices more cheaply in their fluyten, and their trade goods were cheaper and better constructed because their home industry was superior to that of the Iberian states.

By 1602 the Dutch amalgamated their various private trading companies into one great national concern, the Dutch East India Company. The English had organized their own East India Company two years earlier, in 1600, but they were no match for the Dutch. The subscribed capital of the English company was small, and the Dutch had the services of a governor-general of genius, Jan Pieterszoon Coen. He did

Bengali entertainers performing before Europeans, as seen by a Dutch visitor in the seventeenth century.

for his country what Albuquerque had done for Portugal. During his term of office (1618–1629) he drove the Portuguese from the East Indies and made it possible for his successors to expel them from Malacca (1641) and from Ceylon (1658). Coen also harassed the English, chased them out of the archipelago, and compelled them to retreat to their posts in India. Equally important was Coen's development of inter-Asiatic trade, much greater in volume than the traffic that rounded the cape to Europe. The Portuguese had participated in this trade, but Coen went much further, establishing a base on Formosa (Taiwan) and from there controlling the commerce routes to China, Japan, and the Indies.

In later years, the Dutch East India Company established a network of fortified posts to enforce its trade monopoly. The posts made it necessary to have treaties with local rulers. Treaties led to alliances, and alliances, to protectorates. By the end of the seventeenth century the Dutch were actually administering only a small area, but numerous states making up a much greater area had become protectorates. Then during the eighteenth and nineteenth centuries the Dutch annexed these protectorates outright and built up a great territorial empire.

The export of spices to Europe diminished in value after about 1700, but the inter-Asiatic trade that Coen had developed made up for the shrinkage. Moreover, the Dutch developed a new economic resource at about that time when they introduced coffee bushes into the East Indies. Modestly beginning in 1711 with a harvest of 100 pounds of coffee, by 1723 they were marketing 12 million pounds. Thus, as Europe acquired a taste for coffee, the Dutch became the principal suppliers of this exotic beverage. Through these various means the Dutch East India Company managed to average annual dividends of 18 percent throughout the seventeenth and eighteenth centuries.

Dutch overseas activities were not confined to the East Indies, however. In the Arctic waters around Spitzbergen the Dutch virtually monopolized the whaling industry. In Russia they badly outdistanced the English Muscovy Company. They also dominated the rich Baltic trade so that they became the chief provisioners in western Europe of all-important naval stores—timber, pitch, tar, hemp for rope, and flax for canvas sailcloth.

Their merchant marine was by far the largest of the world, numbering 10,000 ships as early as 1600. Dutch shipyards were highly mechanized and could produce almost a vessel a day. Furthermore, the ships were economical to build and to operate, so that Dutch shipowners undercut their competitors. Thus, they served as the carriers among Spain, France, England, and the Baltic. Not until the eighteenth century were the English able to compete with the Dutch in merchant shipping.

In the New World, the Dutch founded the profitable but short-lived colony of New Amsterdam on Manhattan Island in 1612 and also briefly held various islands and coastal strips in the West Indies. But the Dutch colony that proved to be the most durable of all was the small settlement established in 1652 on the Cape of Good Hope in South Africa. This was not a trading station but a true colony founded to provide fuel, water, and fresh provisions for the ships en route to the East. The colony soon proved its value. The fresh meat and vegetables it provided to Dutch and other ships helped keep down scurvy and saved the lives of thousands of seamen. Today the descendants of these Dutch peasants, or Boers, comprise three-fifths of the 3 million Europeans residing in South Africa.

During the eighteenth century Holland fell behind Britain and France in economic development and overseas activity. One reason for this decline was the persistent efforts of the French and British governments to build up their merchant marines with the help of discriminatory decrees against the Dutch. Examples of this legislation were the several British Navigation Acts passed from 1651 onward. These provided that no goods could be imported into or exported from any English colony except in English ships—that is, ships built in England or an English colony and owned and at least three-quarters manned by British citizens or colonials. The Dutch were weakened also by a series of exhausting wars—with Britain from 1652 to 1674 over mercantile disputes, and with France from 1667 to 1713 over the territorial ambitions of Louis XIV.

Perhaps the chief reason for the decline of the Dutch was that they lacked the resources of their rivals. The French had a large population, a flourishing agriculture, and a rich homeland with outlets on both the Atlantic and the Mediterranean. The English also had much greater natural resources than the Dutch and enjoyed the great boon of an insular location, which spared them the cost of periodic invasions. Furthermore, the English had behind them the rapidly growing wealth and strength of their overseas colonies, whereas the Dutch were backed by only one small and isolated settlement on the tip of South Africa. Thus the value of British exports rose from £8 million in 1720 to £19 million in 1763, and the French exports increased from 120 million livres in 1716 to 500 million in 1789. The Dutch, who has already reached their peak, were simply incapable of matching such growth. In the final analysis, Holland gave way to Britain and France in the eighteenth century for the same reason that Britain and France were to give way to the United States and the Soviet Union in the twentieth.

III.   ANGLO-FRENCH RIVALRY

The eighteenth century was marked by a struggle between Britain and France for colonial supremacy. The two countries were in face-to-face rivalry throughout the globe—in North America, in Africa, and in India.

In North America, the British and French possessions had many characteristics in common. They were settled at about the same time. They were located on the Atlantic seaboard and in the West Indian islands. The native populations were relatively sparse and primitive so that the British and the French, unlike the Spanish, could not hope to live off native labor, although they did depend on Negro slave labor in the sugar islands. Since the British and French found no precious metals, they had to support themselves by agriculture, fishing, lumbering, commerce, and fur trading.

The English colonies fell roughly into three groups: Virginia and its immediate neighbors, which produced mostly tobacco; New England with its little groups of nonconformist settlements, which engaged in fishing, lumbering, commerce, and the fur trade; and the British West Indies, by far the most highly prized because of their extremely profitable sugar plantations. One characteristic of the English colonies, taken as a whole, was their large populations, which were much greater than those of the French. Their other chief characteristic was their political independence. Every colony had a governor, an executive council, and a judiciary, all appointed from England. Nearly every colony also had an elective legislative assembly, and as a rule it was at loggerheads with the appointed officials. Its most common quarrel with the London government was the insistence of the latter that all colonial products be sent to England in English ships. This seemed to the royal officers a reasonable requirement, since they in turn gave the colonies a monopoly of the home market for their products. But the colonial merchants and planters protested bitterly when they were prohibited from using the cheaper Dutch shipping and from exporting their products to more profitable non-English markets.

John Smith's map of Virginia, 1612.

The French settlements in North America were outstanding because of their strategic location. The first French posts were established in Acadia, or Nova Scotia, in 1605; in Quebec in 1608; and in Montreal in 1642. Using the St. Lawrence River valley as their main base of colonization, the French took advantage of the incomparable inland water system to push westward to Lake Superior and southward to the Ohio River. In 1682 a French nobleman, La Salle, paddled down the Mississippi and laid claim to the whole basin, which he named Louisiana in honor of Louis XIV. This raised complications, for most of the colonial charters issued by the English crown in the seventeenth century included clauses granting lands "from sea to sea"—that is, from the Atlantic to the Pacific. It was clear that whenever the English colonists reached and crossed the Appalachian Mountains, the rival French and English claims would clash head-on. At the outset, however, the French had the great advantage of possession. Their explorers had been the first to open up these regions, after which their officials had planted numerous forts along the route from the St. Lawrence to Louisiana. The English colonies along the Atlantic seaboard were effectively encircled by a great arc running from the Gulf of St. Lawrence to the Gulf of Mexico.

The French not only possessed the commanding positions in North America, but they also had the great advantage of discipline and cohesion. There were no uncontrollable elective bodies in the French colonies. Paris appointed the governors, who were responsible for the defense of each colony, and the intendants, who handled financial and economic affairs. This arrangement was quicker and more efficient than the creaking English representative system. The governors of the English colonies could only request and urge their assemblies to take a certain course of action. They could scarcely command, especially since the assemblies voted the funds for their salaries. In the French colonies the governors and intendants gave the orders, and their subordinates carried them out.

The French and English were neighbors also in the West Indies. The chief French possessions in this region were Martinique and Guadeloupe; the English were Jamaica, Barbados, and the Bahamas. These colonies were valuable as stations for trade with the Spanish and Portuguese colonies to the south, but their greatest asset was their tropical produce—sugar, tobacco, and indigo—which supplemented the economies of France and Britain.

India also was the scene of sharp Anglo-French conflicts, paralleling those in North America. The British had fallen back on the Indian subcontinent when they were driven out of the East Indies by the Dutch in the early seventeenth century. By the end of the century they had four major footholds in India: Calcutta and Madras on the eastern coast, and Surat and Bombay on the western. The French had organized an East India Company of their own in 1604, but it soon became inactive. It was revived in 1664, and by the end of the century the French were ensconced in two major posts—Chandarnagar, near Calcutta, and Pondichéry, near Madras.

During the seventeenth century all Europeans who resided and traded in India did so on the sufferance of the powerful Mogul emperors. The Moguls could easily have driven the Europeans into the sea had they not behaved themselves and humbly submitted petitions for the privilege of carrying on their commercial operations. During the eighteenth century the situation was completely reversed because of the disintegration of the Mogul empire. Emperor Akbar's successors persecuted the Hindu majority, which led to disaffection and turmoil. Provincial governors began to assert their independence and to establish hereditary local dynasties. The Marathas, who represented Hindu nationalism in a vague and incipient sense, expanded from their capital of Satara, about a hundred miles south of Bombay on the west coast to within two hundred miles of Calcutta on the east. This disintegration of central authority gave the British and the French East India companies the opportunity to transform themselves from mere commercial organizations to territorial overlords and tribute collectors. They built forts, maintained soldiers, coined money, and entered into treaties with surrounding Indian potentates. No central authority in India was able to stop this spread of British and French influence.

IV.   ENGLAND'S TRIUMPH

Such, then, was the lineup of the rival British and French empires in India and the Americas. The duel between the two empires during the seventeenth and eighteenth centuries ended in an overwhelming British triumph. One reason was that France was less interested in overseas possessions than in European hegemony. Since the sixteenth century, the French Bourbons had concentrated primarily on gaining ground in Italy and on combating the Hapsburgs in Austria and Spain.

Another reason for Britain's triumph was that many more Englishmen than Frenchmen emigrated to the colonies. By 1688 there were 300,000 English settlers concentrated in the narrow region along the Atlantic coast compared to a mere 20,000 French scattered over the vast areas of Canada and the Mississippi valley. The disparity arose in part from the refusal of Paris to allow the French Protestants, or Huguenots, to emigrate to the colonies, whereas Massachusetts was populated in large part by nonconformists who left England because they could not accept Anglicanism. Another significant factor was the richness of the French soil compared to that of England. The peasant masses of France were deeply attached to their holdings and were able to earn enough so that they did not have to resort to emigration. In England, on the other hand, large-scale land enclosures had been taking place for some time in order to produce more wool for the growing textile industry and more foodstuffs for the growing towns. Both these commodities could be produced more efficiently on consolidated, scientifically operated holdings than on the small, separate field strips inherited from the Middle Ages. Enclosures meant more productivity, but they also meant dispossessed peasants, and it was the peasants who provided the mass basis of the emigration from England to the colonies. At the time of the American Revolution the population of the English colonies amounted to no fewer than 2 million. The mass transplantation explains in large part why Britain was victorious over France in 1763 and why the American Republic defeated Britain two decades later.

The remarkable development of Britain's industry also contributed to its success in overseas competition. Britain's industrial growth during the century between 1550 and 1650 was to be surpassed only by its growth during the industrial revolution after 1760. England's growth advanced its overseas enterprises in various ways. More capital became available for colonial development, an important consideration because both the English and the French colonies required heavy initial expenditures. Unlike the Spanish colonies, they had no bullion and no native labor force that could be exploited. The English and French promoters of colonization therefore had to transplant whole communities with a complete labor force of Europeans. They had to provide transportation, tools, seed, and equipment for all these people. This involved a heavy capital outlay, and generally it was more often forthcoming from London than from Paris. England's industries also provided cheaper and more durable goods, which gave English colonists and traders an advantage over their French rivals. In North America, for example, the English fur traders were able to offer the Indians cheaper and better blankets, kettles, and firearms in return for their pelts. English industry, besides, was well equipped for naval construction. This fact, together with the greater awareness in English ruling circles of the importance of sea power, explains in large part the superiority of the British navy during the long series of Anglo-French wars.

The colonial and commercial rivalry between Britain and France was fought out in a series of four wars that dragged on for almost a century until England's great victory in 1763. All these wars had two phases, one European and the other overseas. The European revolved about dynastic ambitions, especially those of Louis XIV of France and Frederick the Great of Prussia. The overseas operations were fought over diverse issues—the balance of power in India, conflicting territorial claims in America, terms of trade in the Spanish colonies, and control of the world trade routes. The dichotomy between the European and overseas aspects of these wars was sufficiently marked so that each one was known by one name in Europe and another in America. Hence the wars have come down in history as the War of the League of Augsburg, or King William's War (1689–1697); the War of the Spanish Succession, or Queen Anne's War (1701–1713); the War of the Austrian Succession, or King George's War (1740–1748); and the Seven Years' War, or the French and Indian War (1756–1763).

The first three wars were not decisive overseas. In Europe they did settle important matters: Louis XIV was effectively checkmated, and Frederick the Great successfully seized the province of Silesia and catapulted Prussia into the first rank of European powers. But in America, where most of the overseas engagements were fought, there were only isolated and inconclusive campaigns. The French enjoyed the support of most of the Indian tribes, partly because their missionaries were far more active than the English, and also because the few French settlers did not represent so great a threat to the Indians as did the steadily advancing tide of English settlement that had begun to spill over the Appalachians. With their Indian allies, the French repeatedly harried and burned the English frontier villages. The English, on the other hand, used their superior manpower and naval strength to attack French possessions in present-day Nova Scotia and Cape Breton Island that were vulnerable by sea.

The net result of these first three wars were that the British acquired Nova Scotia, Newfoundland, and the Hudson Bay territories. But these conquests did not settle the basic question of whether the French would retain Canada and the Mississippi Valley, and thereby restrict the English to the Atlantic seaboard. This question was finally answered conclusively by the fourth war, which also settled the future of India.

This fateful struggle is known as the Seven Years' War because it was waged for seven years—between 1756 and 1763—in Europe. But in America it began two years earlier because of the growing rivalry for the possession of the Ohio valley. British colonials had already begun to stream westward through the mountains into the valley when in 1749 the British government chartered the Ohio Company, organized by Virginia and London capitalists for the colonization of the valley. But at the same time the French were constructing a line of forts in west-

ern Pennsylvania—Fort Presqu'Isle (Erie), Fort Le Boeuf (Waterford), and Fort Venango (Franklin). The Ohio Company countered the French by building a fort in 1754 at the strategic junction of the Monongahela and Allegheny rivers. The French promptly captured it, enlarged it, and christened it Fort Duquesne in honor of the governor of Canada. In the following year the British General Braddock arrived in America with a regular army to retake Fort Duquesne. But he refused to take the advice of his colonial officers on how to wage frontier warfare. His forces were badly defeated and he himself killed. The British reverses continued through 1756.

The turning point of the war came in 1757, largely because of William Pitt (the Elder), who then entered the British cabinet. Pitt concentrated his resources on the navy and the colonies, while subsidizing his ally, Frederick of Prussia, to fight on in Europe. His strategy was, as he put it, to win an empire on the plains of Germany, and he succeeded brilliantly. His reinforced navies swept the French off the seas, and the American colonists, stirred by his leadership, joined the British regulars to form a force of about 50,000 men. This huge army overwhelmed one French fort after another. The climax came with the siege of Quebec, the heart of French Canada and a great natural stronghold on the banks of the St. Lawrence. In the ensuing battle, the British and the French commanders, General James Wolfe and the Marquis de Montcalm, were killed. But the British veterans prevailed, and Quebec surrendered in September 1759. The fall of Montreal the following year spelled the end of the French colonial empire in America.

In India the success of the English was no less complete. The situation was quite different than in America, for neither the British nor the French government had territorial ambitions in India. This was true also of the directors of the English and French East India Companies, who insisted that their agents in India attend strictly to business. They were interested only in profits, and they resented every penny or sou spent on noncommercial objectives. But because it took a year or more to communicate between London and India, agents frequently took advantage of this fact to act independently and involve their companies in Indian affairs. The disintegration of

A view of the taking of Quebec by the English forces commanded by General Wolfe, September 13, 1759.

the Mogul Empire was taking place at this time, a situation that offered dazzling opportunities for personal financial profit and for empire building, and agents of the India companies could not resist the temptation to interfere.

The first European to intervene on a large scale in Indian affairs was the French governor Joseph Dupleix, who drilled native Indians along European military lines. The trained Indian troops, or *sepoys,* enabled him to back claimants to various Indian thrones. He could then build up a clientele of native rulers who were under obligation to him. But Dupleix was recalled to France in 1754 because the company feared that his aggressive tactics would lead to war with Britain. Yet war did come to India in 1756 with the outbreak of full-scale hostilities between Britain and France.

At the outset the French, thanks to Dupleix's activities, were in the stronger position. But in the end the British won a crushing victory. Again naval superiority was the deciding factor. Britain was able to transport troops, money, and supplies from Europe while preventing France from doing likewise. The British, too, had the inspired leader-

ship of Robert Clive, a company official who had come out years before as a clerk. Clive possessed both outstanding military talents and an ability to understand Indian politics. In 1756, on hearing of the war in Europe, he marched on Bengal. With the support of Indian merchants who had become wealthy in the trade with Europe, Clive defeated the pro-French Moslem ruler at the Battle of Plassey in 1757. He put his own puppet on the throne and extorted huge reparations both for himself and for his company. During the rest of the war, thanks to the strong British navy, Clive was able to shift his forces at will from one part of India to another. At the same time he severed the communications of the French posts with each other and with France. The end came with the surrender in 1761 of the main French base at Pondichéry.

The overseas phase of the Seven Years' War was decided by the fall of Quebec in America and of Pondichéry in India. But the war dragged on in Europe until 1763, when the belligerents concluded the Peace of Paris. Of its American possessions, France retained only Guiana in South America; the insignificant

GENERAL WOLFE CONQUERS NEW FRANCE

Captain John Knox, one of General Wolfe's officers, describes in the following selection the victory of General Wolfe over the French General Montcalm. This battle, fought on the Plains of Abraham at Quebec, made New France, or Canada, a British colony. *

We . . . clambered up one of the steepest precipices that can be conceived, being almost a perpendicular, and of an incredible height. As soon as we gained the summit, all was quiet, and not a shot was heard. . . . We then faced to the right, and marched towards the town by files, till we came to the plains of Abraham; an even piece of ground which Mr. Wolfe had made choice of. . . . Weather showery; about six o'clock the enemy first made their appearance upon the heights, between us and the town; whereupon we halted, and wheeled to the right, thereby forming the line of battle. . . . The enemy had now likewise formed the line of battle, and got some cannon to play on us, with round and canister-shot; but what galled us most was a body of Indians and other marksmen they had concealed in the corn opposite to the front of our right wing. . . . About ten o'clock the enemy began to advance briskly in three columns, with loud shouts and recovered arms, two of them inclining to the left of our army, and the third towards our right, firing obliquely at the two extremities of our line, from the distance of one hundred and thirty—until they came within forty yards, which our

troops withstood with the greatest intrepidity and firmness, still reserving their fire, and paying the strictest obedience to their Officers: this uncommon steadiness, together with the havoc which the grape-shot from our field-pieces made among them, threw them into some disorder, and was most critically maintained by a well-timed, regular, and heavy discharge of our small arms, such as they could no longer oppose; hereupon they gave way, and fled with precipitation, so that, by the time the cloud of smoke was vanished, our men were again loaded, and, profiting by the advantage we had over them, pursued them almost to the gates of the town. . . . Our joy at this success is inexpressibly damped by the loss we sustained of one of the greatest heroes which this or any other age can boast of—General James Wolfe, who received his mortal wound, as he was exerting himself at the head of the grenadiers of Louisbourg. . . . Thus has our late renowned Commander . . . made a conquest of this fertile, healthy, and hitherto formidable country, with a handful of troops only, in spite of the political schemes, and most vigorous efforts, of the famous Montcalm. . . .

* Captain John Knox, *An Historical Account of the Campaigns in North America for the Years 1757, 1758, 1759, and 1760.* A. G. Doughty, ed. (Champlain Society, 1914), II, 94–103.

islands of St. Pierre and Miquelon on the Newfoundland coast; and a few islands in the West Indies, including Guadeloupe and Martinique. Britain therefore received from France the whole of the St. Lawrence valley and all the territory east of the Mississippi. Spain had entered the war late on the side of France and was, therefore, compelled to cede Florida to

Britain. As compensation, France gave Spain western Louisiana; that is, the territory west of the Mississippi River. In India the French retained possession of their commercial installations—offices, warehouses, and docks—at Pondichéry and other towns. But they were forbidden to build fortifications or make political alliances with the Indian princes. In other words, the

French returned to India as traders and not as empire builders.

When the Treaty of Paris was signed, the British political leader Horace Walpole remarked, "Burn your Greek and Roman books, histories of little people." This far-seeing observation points up the long-range, worldwide implications of the peace settlements. As far as Europe was concerned, the treaty allowed Prussia to keep Silesia and to become Austria's rival for the leadership of the Germanies. But of much more significance for world history was France's loss of North America and India, which meant that America north of the Rio Grande was to develop in the future as a part of the English-speaking world.

France's expulsion from India was also a historical event of global significance, for it meant that the British were to take the place of the Moguls there. Once installed in Delhi, the British were well on their way to world empire and world primacy. It was the incomparable base offered by the vast and populous subcontinent of India that enabled the British in the nineteenth century to expand into the rest of south Asia and then beyond to east Asia. For these reasons the 1763 settlement has profoundly affected the course of world history to the present day.

SUGGESTED READINGS

For works on general European overseas expansion, see the bibliography for Chapter 24. On the eighteenth-century period, see J. H. Parry, *Trade and Dominion: The Overseas European Empires in the Eighteenth Century* (Praeger, 1971); and W. L. Dorn, *Competition for Empire, 1740–1763* (Harper & Row, 1940). For Holland's overseas activities, see C. R. Boxer, *The Dutch Seaborne Empire, 1600–1800* (Knopf, 1965); D. W. Davies, *A Primer of Dutch Seventeenth Century Overseas Trade* (Nijhoff, 1961); and G. Musselman, *The Cradle of Colonialism* (Yale University, 1963). The reasons why the Dutch displaced the Portuguese in Asia are analyzed in N. Steensgaard, *The Asian Trade Revolution of the Seventeenth Century* (University of Chicago, 1974); and H. Furber, *Rival Empires of Trade in the Orient 1600–1800* (University of Minnesota, 1976).

A general survey of French overseas activity is available in H. I. Priestly, *France Overseas Through the Old Regime: A Study of European Expansion* (Prentice Hall, 1939). More specialized studies are the two works of N. M. Crouse, *French Pioneers in the West Indies, 1624–1664* (Columbia University, 1940), and *The French Struggle for the West Indies, 1665–1713* (Columbia University, 1943); G. M. Wrong, *The Rise and Fall of New France*, 2 vols. (Macmillan, 1928); and S. P. Sen, *The French in India* (Mukhopadhyay, 1958).

Two excellent general surveys of Britain overseas are C. E. Carrington's *The British Overseas: Exploits of a Nation of Shopkeepers* (Cambridge University, 1950); and W. B. Willcox's *Star of Empire: A Study of Britain as a World Power, 1485–1945* (Knopf, 1950). The colonial wars are described by E. P. Hamilton, *The French and Indian Wars: The Story of Battles and Forts in the Wilderness* (Doubleday, 1962). The classic history of the most dramatic phase of the Seven Years' War in America is by F. Parkman, *Montcalm and Wolfe*, 2 vols. (Boston, 1884).

26 Russian Expansion in Asia

Throughout Russian history one dominating theme has been the frontier; the theme of the struggle for the mastering of the natural resources of an untamed country, expanded into a continent by the ever-shifting movement of the Russian people and their conquest of and intermingling with other peoples.

B. H. Sumner,
A Short History of Russia

At the same time that western Europeans were expanding overseas to all corners of the globe, the Russians were expanding overland across the entire length of Eurasia. The mastering of the continental expanses of Siberia is an epic story comparable to that of westward expansion across the United States to the Pacific. In fact, the ever-advancing frontier has left as indelible a stamp on the Russian character and Russian institutions as it has on the American. The Russians were not the only European peoples who were affected by a frontier. During the medieval period, large parts of central and eastern Europe were lightly populated (see Chapter 23, Section I). For centuries, various European peoples, and particularly the Germans, pressed a line of settlement eastward along the Baltic coast and down the Danube valley. But by the end of the Middle Ages, internal colonization no longer was a dominant movement. Overseas colonization took its place, and the peoples of western Europe concentrated their energies on opening and exploring new frontiers in new worlds. The Russian people, by contrast, continued to expand overland into the vast Eurasian plain stretching out from their doorstep. This was a stupendous undertaking, which continued for several centuries until the last of the Moslem khanates in central Asia was subdued in 1895. It is not surprising, then, that the frontier has been a major factor throughout the course of Russian history, as it has been throughout American history. In this chapter we shall examine the nature and the course of Russian expansion into Siberia and the Ukraine.

I. GEOGRAPHY OF RUSSIAN EXPANSION

To understand the remarkable Russian expansion across the plains of Eurasia we must first understand the geography of those plains. A glance at the map shows their staggering proportions (see map of Russian Expansion in Europe and Asia, p. 388.) Russia encompasses a sixth of the land surface of the globe and is larger than the United States, Canada, and Central America combined. Another prominent characteristic of the Russian landmass is its remarkable topographical uniformity. It is in very large part a flat plains area. The Ural Mountains do run across the plains in a north-south direction, and they are commonly thought of as dividing the country into two separate parts—European Russia and Asiatic Russia. But the fact is that the Urals are a single, narrow, worn-down chain of mountains with an average altitude of only 2,000 feet. Furthermore, they do not extend further south than the fifty-first parallel, leaving a wide gap of flat desert country stretching down to the Caspian Sea. This topographic uniformity helps to explain why the Russians were able to spread so rapidly from the Baltic to the Pacific.

The Eurasian plains that make up most of present-day Russia are surrounded by a natural southern boundary stretching from the Black Sea to the Pacific Ocean. This boundary consists of an uninterrupted chain of mountains, deserts, and inland seas; beginning in the west and moving eastward, they are the Caucasus Mountains; the Caspian Sea; the Ust Urt Desert; the Aral Sea; the Kizil-Kum Desert; the Hindu Kush, Pamir, and Tien Shan ranges; the Gobi Desert; and the Great Khingan Mountains, which extend east to the Pacific Ocean. The ring of mountains surrounding the Eurasian plains keeps out the moisture-laden winds from the Pacific and the warm monsoons from the Indian Ocean, and explains both the desert climate of central Asia and the cold, dry climate of Siberia. The whole expanse of Siberia, from the Baltic to the Pacific, has essentially the same continental type of climate, with short, hot summers and long, cold winters. The uniformity of climate, like that of topography, facilitated Russia's eastward expansion, for the frontierspeople felt equally at home throughout the 5,000-mile expanse of plains. The central Asian deserts, on the other hand, seemed strange and forbidding. Moreover, they were held by militarily powerful Moslem khanates in contrast to the weak tribes in Siberia. As a result, the Russians did not master the central Asian deserts until 250 years after they had reached the Pacific further north.

Russian expansion was affected by river systems as well as by topography and climate. Because of the flat terrain, Russian rivers are generally long, wide, and unencumbered by rapids. Consequently they are invaluable as routes for commerce, colonization, and conquest. West of the Urals there are a number of outstanding rivers: the Western Dvina flowing into the Baltic; the Dniester, the Dnieper, and the Don flowing south to the Black Sea; and the Volga flowing first east and then south to the Caspian. East of the Urals the Siberian plains are watered by four vast river systems: the Ob in the west, the Yenisei in the center, the Lena in the northeast, and the Amur in the southeast. Since the whole of Siberia tilts downward from the massive Tibetan ranges, the first three of these rivers flow northward into the Arctic, whereas the fourth makes its way eastward to the Pacific. These rivers, together with their numerous tributaries, provide a natural network of highways across the plains. Thus the Russian fur traders were able to make their way eastward with few portages to the Pacific Ocean, just as French and English fur traders in the New World made their way westward along similar riverways to the same ocean.

A final geographic factor in the pace and course of Russian expansion is the combination of soil and vegetation prevailing in various parts of the country. Four major soil-vegetation zones run in east-west layers across Russia. (See map of Soil and Vegetation Zones of Eurasia, p. 389.) In the far north, along the Arctic coast, is the barren *tundra,* frozen the year round except for a six- to eight-week growing period in the summer. To the south of the tundra is the *taiga,* or forest belt. The

Russian Expansion in Europe and Asia

Soil and Vegetation Zones of Eurasia

399

largest of the four zones, it is 600 to 1,300 miles wide and 4,600 miles long. It includes a fifth of the total forest area of the world. The Russians felt at home in the forests, and they were able to cross the whole of Eurasia without ever losing the familiar protective covering.

On their southern edges the forests thin out, and the trees grow smaller until they give way completely to the open, treeless *steppe*. Here there is fertile black earth formed by millennia of decayed grass. Today it is the breadbasket of Russia, but for centuries it was a source of misery and woe. The steppe was the home of the marauding horse nomads of central Eurasia. When these nomads were sufficiently strong, they struck out along the line of least resistance—sometimes westward into central Europe or eastward into China. More frequently they attacked the vulnerable Russians in eastern Europe. A major theme of Russian history is this continued conflict between the Slavic peasants of the forest zone and the Asiatic nomads of the steppe. At first the nomads prevailed, and the result was two centuries of Mongol rule over Russia. But in the end the Slavic woodspeople became stronger, and they were able not only to win their independence but also to expand over the Eurasian plains.

The fourth zone, the desert, is the smallest in area, starting in China but extending westward only to the Caspian Sea. We have seen that for various reasons—inaccessibility, severe climate, and the military power of the native peoples—the desert zone was not engulfed by the Russian tidal wave until the late nineteenth century.

II.   EARLY RUSSIAN EXPANSION

About 1,500 years ago, the Russians began their advance eastward from their place of origin in the upper reaches of the Dniester, Dnieper, Neman, and Dvina rivers. From there they fanned out in a great arc. The broad plains beckoned them on to the Arctic shores in the north, to the Black Sea in the south, and to the Urals and beyond in the east. Their subsistence type of agriculture could not support a dense population, so they lived in scattered homesteads and small hamlets rather than in compact villages or towns. The few towns

that did appear grew up as trade centers along main river routes. This was the case with Kiev on the Dnieper River, which carried the north-south traffic, and with Novgorod on Lake Ilmen, which commanded the east-west commerce. This long-distance trade provided the basis for the first Russian state, which developed in the ninth century A.D. The center was Kiev, but the state remained a loose federation of principalities strung out along the river routes. Kiev itself was extremely vulnerable to invasion because it was located at the point where the forest zone gave way to the steppe. Consequently, it was forced to wage a continual struggle for existence against the nomad peoples. Russian colonists were unable to settle more than 150 miles south and east of Kiev, for the threat of invasion by the nomads hung over their heads like the sword of Damocles.

The sword descended in 1237 when the Mongols swept over the Russian lands as they did over most of Eurasia. The Mongols continued their devastating inroads into central Europe, to the gates of Italy and France. Then they withdrew voluntarily, retaining only the Russian lands in Europe. Their sprawling empire did not survive long as an entity. It broke up into regional fragments. One fragment, the so-called Golden Horde, included the Russian territories. The capital of the Golden Horde, and of Russia also for the next two centuries, was Sarai, near present-day Volgograd. The age-old struggle between the forest and the steppe had been settled decisively with the victory of the steppe and its nomad peoples.

The Russians now surrendered their small enclaves on the steppe and withdrew into their forest fastnesses. There they were left alone as long as they recognized the suzerainty of the khan and paid him annual tribute. Gradually the Russians recovered their strength and developed a new national center—the principality of Moscow, located deep in the forest zone away from the dangerous steppe. Moscow had advantages other than its relative inaccessibility to the nomads. A number of rivers flowing in various directions came closest to each other in the Moscow region, so Moscow could profit from an inland water system. The principality also enjoyed the advantage of a line of rulers who were peaceful, frugal, and calculating. The rulers added to their possessions patiently and ruth-

Ivan the Terrible
(Nationalmuseum, Copenhagen)

lessly, until Moscow became the new national nucleus. Whereas at the opening of the fourteenth century the principality was made up of only about 500 square miles, by the mid-fifteenth century it had grown to 15,000 square miles. And a century later, during the reign of Ivan the Terrible (1533–1584), all the Russian principalities were brought together under Moscow's rule.

This "gathering of the Russian lands" reversed the balance of power between the Russians and the Mongols or Tatars, as they were now more commonly known. Originally the Tatars had triumphed because they were united, in contrast to the strife-ridden Kievan state, and also because they were militarily more advanced with their fast-moving cavalries. But by the sixteenth century it was the Russians who were united under Moscow, whereas the Golden Horde had split into the three rival khanates of Kazan, Astrakhan, and the Crimea, as well as the khanate of the Siberian Tatars to the east of the Urals. Furthermore, the Russians were also pulling ahead in military techniques, because they were able to profit from the great advances being

made in western Europe, especially in firearms and artillery. Thanks to this military advantage, the Russians were able to overrun the whole Kazan Khanate. They swept down the Volga valley and in 1556 captured Astrakhan. To consolidate their gains, the Russians built a series of fortified posts along the banks of the Volga to its mouth at Astrakhan. Thus the Russians became the masters of the great Volga basin and reached the Caspian Sea in the south and the Urals in the east. The way now was open for limitless Russian expansion beyond the Volga and the Urals (see map of Russian Expansion in Europe and Asia, p. 388.)

III.   CONQUEST OF SIBERIA

The Russian victories had eliminated the Kazan and Astrakhan khanates. But the Tatars in the Crimea and across the Urals remained independent and continued to harass the Russian colonists with frequent raids. For various reasons discussed later in this chapter, the Russians had to suffer the attacks of the Crimean Tatars until the late eighteenth century. But they were able to destroy the Siberian Khanate with little difficulty, and in doing so they began their epic march to the Pacific.

The crossing of the Urals and the conquest of Siberia were largely the work of the rough-and-ready frontierspeople known as the *Cossacks*. In many respects they resembled the frontierspeople of the American West. Most of them were former peasants who had fled from Russia or Poland to escape the bonds of serfdom. Their refuge was the wild steppe country to the south, where they became hunters, fishers, and pastoralists. Just as their counterparts in America became half-Indian, so they became half-Tatar. They were a liberty-loving and equalitarian, but unruly and marauding, element, ever ready to turn bandit or freebooter if it seemed profitable to do so.

A typical product of this frontier environment was Yermak Timofeevich. At the age of twenty-one he was condemned to death for stealing horses, so he fled to the Volga where he became the leader of a band of river pirates. He preyed indiscriminately on Russian shipping and Persian caravans until government troops began to close in. Then he fled with his band up the Volga valley to the Kama tributary, where a wealthy merchant, Grigori Stroganov, had been given vast land concessions. Stroganov's efforts to colonize his domain were being frustrated by nomad raids from across the Urals. The organizer of these raids was the militant Moslem leader of the Siberian Tatars, the blind Khan Kuchum. Faced with this predicament, Stroganov welcomed Yermak and his men and hired them to guard the settlements.

Yermak the robber now showed that he had in him the stuff of a great empire builder. He did for Russia in Siberia what Pizarro and Cortes had done for Spain in America. With the audacity of the conquistador, Yermak decided that the best defense was the offense. On September 1, 1581, he set out at the head of 840 men to attack Khan Kuchum on his own territory. Yermak, like his Spanish counterparts, had the great advantage of superior weapons. He was well equipped with firearms and cannon, and after stiff fighting, he captured Kuchum's capital, Sibir. The Russians now gave the name of the city to the entire trans-Ural area,

which became known as Sibir, or, in its Anglicized form, Siberia. The road to the Pacific lay open.

The Russian conquest of Siberia was a remarkable achievement. Like the Spaniards in America, the Russians in Siberia won a great empire in a few years with incredibly small forces. Kuchum's Khanate in the Irtysh basin proved to be only a thin crust without solid substance below. Once the crust was pierced, no serious opposition was encountered for thousands of miles. The pace of the Russian advance was staggering. Yermak campaigned between 1581 and 1584, at the same time (1584) that Sir Walter Raleigh landed on Roanoke Island in North Carolina. Within half a century, by 1637, the Russians reached Okhotsk on the Pacific Ocean, covering a distance half as much again as that between the Atlantic and the Pacific coasts of the United States. During that same period the English colonists had not crossed to the other side of the Allegheny Mountains.

Various factors explain the rapidity of the

The type of Russian horseman who conquered Russia's eastern lands.

Yermak's conquest of Siberia.

Russian advance. The climate, the terrain, the vegetation, and the river systems were, as we have seen, all favorable to the invaders. The native peoples were handicapped by small numbers, inferior armaments, and lack of unity and organization. We must give credit also to the stamina and courage of the Cossacks, who—like the *coureurs des bois,* or fur traders, of French Canada—endured fantastic hardships and dangers in the wilderness. And the reason they did so may be summed up with one word—fur. The sable lured them ever eastward, from river to portage and on to new rivers.

As the Cossacks advanced, they secured their communications by building fortified posts, or *ostrogs,* which were like the blockhouses of the American frontier. Thus they advanced from Sibir to the Ob River, to the Yenisei, and to the Lena, which they followed down to the Arctic coast in 1645. Two years later they reached the shores of the Pacific, where they built Okhotsk.

Up to this point the Russians had not encountered any power capable of stopping them. But when they pushed down into the Amur valley they more than met their match. There they came up against the outposts of the mighty Chinese Empire, which then was at the height of its strength (see Chapter 20, Section III). It was hunger that drove the Russians to the Amur basin. The frozen north yielded furs but no food, and the distant granaries of European Russia might as well have been on another planet. So the Russians hopefully turned southward where, according to native lore, there existed a fabulous country with fertile soil and golden grain.

The Cossack Vasily Poyarkov led the way down the Amur valley in 1643–1644. He was followed by a series of adventurers who captured the town of Albazin, built a string of ostrogs, and killed and pillaged in typical Cossack fashion. The Chinese emperor finally was sufficiently exasperated by these outrages on the fringe of his empire to send an expedition northward in 1658. The Chinese recaptured Albazin and cleared the Russians out of the whole Amur basin. After

Siberian tribesmen, traveling by reindeer and skis. In the background is a Russian fort.

more skirmishes the two governments negotiated the Treaty of Nerchinsk (August 27, 1689). The frontier was fixed along the Stanovoi mountain range north of the Amur River, so that the Russians were forced to withdraw completely from the disputed river valley. In return, the Russians were given commercial privileges allowing subjects of both empires to travel freely across the frontier and buy and sell without hindrance. The trade that grew up in the following years, carried on by caravan, consisted of gold and furs which the Russians exchanged for tea. It was from the Chinese that the Russians obtained what was to become their national drink. The Russians soon became greater tea drinkers than even the English.

With the signing of the Nerchinsk Treaty, the first stage of the Russian expansion in Asia came to a halt. For the next 170 years the Russians observed the provisions of the treaty and stayed out of the Amur basin. They did not resume their advance southward until the mid-nineteenth century, when they were much

stronger than in the days of Vasily Poyarkov, and the Chinese were relatively weaker.

IV.   ADMINISTRATION AND DEVELOPMENT OF SIBERIA

The fur trade dominated Siberia throughout the seventeenth century. The government was the chief fur trader; indeed, fur was one of its most important sources of revenue. The government acquired furs by various means: It collected tribute, or tax, from the natives in furs, and it took a 10 percent tax in the best furs from the Russian trappers and traders. In addition, it reserved the right to buy the best furs obtained by both the natives and the Russians. By 1586, the state treasury was receiving annually from these various sources 200,000 sables, 10,000 black foxes, and 50,000 squirrels, besides beavers and ermines. Furthermore, the government had a lucrative monopoly of the foreign trade in furs. Estimates of the revenue derived from Siberian furs in the

One of the few remaining Siberian trappers after the effects of Russian expansion were felt, 1706.

mid-seventeenth century vary from 7 to 30 percent of the total income of the state. A leading student of this subject has concluded that "The government paid the administrative expenses in Siberia out of the fur trade, retained a large surplus, and added an immense region to the state."[1]

The impact of the Russian expansion on the Siberian tribes was as disastrous as the effect of the American expansion on the American Indians. On the one hand, the Moscow government repeatedly instructed its officials to treat the natives with "clemency and kindness." On the other hand, it ordered the same officials to "seek profit for the sovereign with zeal."[2] Since the number of furs collected definitely affected official advancement, it is understandable that the welfare of the natives did not receive primary consideration. One effect of this fur-tribute system was that it checked the missionary activities of the Russian Orthodox Church. Converts were not required to pay tribute, so missionary work was discontinued for a long time; it was a luxury that the state treasury could not afford. As a result, Islam spread widely among the Tatar peoples on the southern fringes of the forest zone, and Buddhist Lamaism spread among the Mongol Buriat. Thus we see that a basic difference between the Russian expansion in Siberia and the Spanish in the Americas was the great difference in the intensity of Catholic and Orthodox proselytizing zeal. The Catholic Church never would have allowed another creed to be propagated among the Indians of New Spain.

In the eighteenth century, the traders and trappers began to give way to permanent colonists in the area of the Yenisei. Some colonists were prisoners shipped off to Siberia in the same manner that prisoners from the western European countries were shipped to America, Australia, and the French West Indies. Most of these prisoners were hardened criminals, but a considerable proportion were political offenders, who were the most enlightened and cultivated strata of society. Other colonists were forced to go by official summons. Each region of European Russia was required to provide a certain number of peasants each year for the colonization of Siberia. These people were granted certain exemptions and state assistance so that they could get started in their new surroundings.

Most of the permanent settlers in Siberia were neither prisoners nor compulsory colonists but peasants who emigrated voluntarily to escape creditors, military service, religious persecution, and, above all else, the bonds of serfdom. Whereas serfdom had developed and spread through European Russia in the sixteenth and seventeenth centuries, it did not take root in Siberia at any time. The explanation seems to be that serfdom existed primarily to satisfy the needs of the nobility, who were essential for the functioning of the state. But the nobles did not migrate to Siberia, which offered no attractions comparable to those of Moscow and St. Petersburg. Consequently, Siberia escaped the nobility and thus also escaped serfdom. The growth of population in Siberia to 1763 is given in Table 26.1.

It is significant that whereas only 420,000 Russians were living in Siberia by 1763, the population of the thirteen colonies in North America had risen by the same date to between 1,500,000 and 2 million, or about four times as many. In other words, the Russians, who had been much faster in exploring and conquering, were now much slower in colonizing. One reason was that Siberia could draw only on Russia for immigrants, whereas the American colonies were receiving immigrants from several European countries. Even more important was the greater attractiveness of America for would-be colonists. Climatic conditions in Siberia were akin to those prevailing in Canada. It is no accident that by 1914 the populations of Canada and Siberia were about the same—8 million for Canada and 9 million for Siberia. By that same year the United States, smaller in area than either Canada or Siberia, had grown to a population of 100 million.

V. CONQUEST OF THE UKRAINE

We noted earlier that Ivan the Terrible's conquest of Kazan and Astrakhan in the mid-sixteenth century left two independent khanates—that of the Crimean Tatars in the south and of Kuchum's Tatars across the Urals. The latter were subdued in a few years by Yermak and his successors, but the Crimean Tatars held out until the end of the eigh-

REFLECTIONS ON CROSSING SIBERIA

In 1908 a young Russian diplomat crossed Siberia by railway en route to the embassy in Peking. His thoughts are revealing of Siberia as a country and as a class-divided society. *

On my way to Peking I had to cross the whole of Siberia, Manchuria, and North China. No one can fail to be impressed by the journey through Siberia, especially the first time. The dimensions of Russia are staggering. You travel a day, you travel a week, you travel ten days, and you are still in Russia. Except for the Ural Mountains and a stretch near Lake Baikal, the country is absolutely flat. After you leave European Russia the population becomes very scarce; you pass hours and hours without seeing any village or habitation. Near the stations there are a few houses. Usually, when the express train arrives at the station, the entire local population comes to stare at the travelers. Especially in the evenings, when the train is brilliantly illuminated by electricity and the elegant figures of some inhabitants of Shanghai or other Far Eastern ports are visible inside, the travelers must appear to the local residents like men from another planet. What envy and dissatisfaction the exotic creatures in furs must provoke in the hearts of those doomed to spend their entire life in some miserable station!

I imagine a young girl who has not yet lost the capacity to dream waiting on the station platform. She hears the express approaching and sees it all illuminated. The train stops for five minutes. The passengers, looking like people from a fairy land, jump on the platform; they laugh and joke. There is a whistle, the train with its passengers disappears, and darkness, emptiness, and dullness reign again.

It is unjust that some should move from place to place in luxury, while others must remain in some forsaken place in misery. Small wonder that this should cause irritation and discontent. I am convinced that the Siberian express played an important part in the awakening of the population of Siberia and thereby hastened the coming of the revolution.

The sight of unlimited space and the absence of life begins to affect you, and the passengers prefer to pass their time in the diner, drinking endless glasses of tea and playing cards. . . .

The Memoirs of Dmitrii Ivanovich Abrikossow, MS, 1, 191–194, as edited and translated by G. A. Lensen. Published with permission of the Archive of Russian and East European History and Culture, Columbia University.

Table 26.1	Siberian Population Growth to 1763[*]		
	Natives	**Russians and Foreigners**	**Total**
1622	173,000	23,000	196,000
1662	288,000	105,000	393,000
1709	200,000	229,227	429,227
1763	260,000	420,000	680,000

[*]*The Great Siberian Migration: Government and Peasant in Resettlement from Emancipation to the First World War*, by Donald W. Treadgold (copyright © 1957, 1985 renewed by Princeton University Press): part of Table 1, p. 32. Reprinted with permission of Princeton University Press.

teenth century. One reason for their survival is that they enjoyed the powerful support of the Ottoman Empire. The khan at Bakhchisarai, the capital of the Crimean Horde, recognized the suzereignty of the Ottoman sultan in Constantinople and supplied him with cavalry forces in time of war. In return the sultan went to the assistance of the khan whenever he was threatened by the Christian infidels. Furthermore, the khan usually could play off against each other the various infidels who had conflicting claims to the Ukrainian steppes—that is, the Russians, the Poles, and the Cossacks. The khan was also greatly aided by the inaccessibility of his domain. The Perekop Isthmus guarding the approaches to the Crimean peninsula was 700 miles direct from Moscow, and far more in actual riding miles. The last 300 miles were across a particularly arid type of steppe country in which it was extremely difficult to find water and provisions for an invading army. Thus, the Russians were not able to undertake serious campaigning against the Crimean Tatars until their line of settlement had advanced sufficiently far south to provide them with a base for striking across the steppes.

These various factors explain why the Crimean Khanate survived until the time of Catherine the Great in the late eighteenth century. The 250 years between Ivan the Terrible and Catherine the Great were years of bloodshed and anarchy on the Ukrainian steppes north of the Black Sea. The Ukraine was a wild no man's land in which Russians, Poles, Cossacks, and Tatars fought intermittently and in constantly changing combinations. Particularly devastating were the incessant Tatar raids that were, in effect, slave-hunting expeditions. In 1571 the Tatars burned Moscow itself. But after 1591 they never succeeded in crossing the Oka River in front of Moscow, and gradually their raids penetrated less and less far northward. Nevertheless, small bands of a few hundred men continued to harass the Russian peasantry, slipping through where they perceived an opportunity and retiring swiftly with their human booty.

Finally Catherine the Great was able to remove the Tatar thorn from the side of Russia. She succeeded where so many of her predecessors had failed because several factors were operating in her favor. One was the rapid decline of both Poland and Turkey, the two powers that hitherto had contested Russia's claims to the Ukraine. Russia, by contrast, was growing steadily stronger, partly because of its spectacular territorial expansion and also because of its strongly centralized government. Russia's power was particularly effective during Catherine's reign because the empress was a superb diplomat and skillfully took advantage of every opportunity afforded by the international situation. She concluded agreements with Joseph II of Austria and Frederick the Great of Prussia that enabled her to wage war against Turkey without becoming embroiled with any major European power. Furthermore, Catherine had the gift of selecting first-class advisers and generals. The most outstanding was General Aleksandr Suvorov, a military genius comparable to Napoleon and a matchless instrument for Catherine's policies. Moreover, in the eighty years since Peter the Great's campaigns, the Russian peasantry had been unobtrusively and patiently advancing its line of settlement southward, so that Suvorov had a stronger base for operations than his predecessors.

Catherine fought two wars against the Tatars and the Turks. The first, between 1768 and 1774, gave Russia effective control of the Crimean peninsula. The Treaty of Kuchuk-Kainarji in 1774 severed the ties between Bakhchisarai and Constantinople and gave Russia several strategic strongholds in the Crimea. The second war, from 1787 to 1792, was marked, like the first, by spectacular victories won by Suvorov. In fact, his great triumphs created difficulties because both Prussia and Austria became alarmed at the sweeping Russian advances toward the Mediterranean. Catherine, however, shrewdly took advantage of the outbreak of the French Revolution by pointing out to the Austrian and Prussian rulers that the revolutionary movement in Paris represented a far greater peril than Russian expansion in the Near East. Thus Catherine was able to press her war against the Turks until, in 1792, they accepted the Treaty of Jassy. This settlement gave to Russia the entire north shore of the Black Sea from the Kuban River in the east to the Dniester River in the west.

The whole of the Ukraine now was under Russian rule. The forest at last had triumphed over the steppe. The desert zone of central Asia still held out, but it also was destined to fall under Muscovy's sway during the following century. In this manner a small duchy in eastern Europe expanded through the centuries to become the world's largest state with dozens of

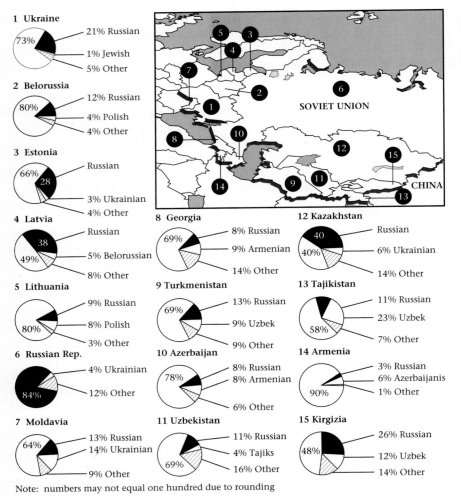

ETHNIC COMPOSITION OF SOVIET REPUBLICS.
This chart of the fifteen constituent republics that comprised the USSR shows how ethnic groups retained their numerical predominance within each republic. Consequently they were able to demand and win independent statehood when the USSR was replaced by the Commonwealth of Independent States.

1 Ukraine
73% — 21% Russian
— 1% Jewish
— 5% Other

2 Belorussia
80% — 12% Russian
— 4% Polish
— 4% Other

3 Estonia
66% / 28 — Russian
— 3% Ukrainian
— 4% Other

4 Latvia
38 — Russian
49% — 5% Belorussian
— 8% Other

5 Lithuania
80% — 9% Russian
— 8% Polish
— 3% Other

6 Russian Rep.
84% — 4% Ukrainian
— 12% Other

7 Moldavia
64% — 13% Russian
— 14% Ukrainian
— 9% Other

8 Georgia
69% — 8% Russian
— 9% Armenian
— 14% Other

9 Turkmenistan
69% — 13% Russian
— 9% Uzbek
— 9% Other

10 Azerbaijan
78% — 8% Russian
— 8% Armenian
— 6% Other

11 Uzbekistan
69% — 11% Russian
— 4% Tajiks
— 16% Other

12 Kazakhstan
40 — Russian
40% — 6% Ukrainian
— 14% Other

13 Tajikistan
58% — 11% Russian
— 23% Uzbek
— 7% Other

14 Armenia
90% — 3% Russian
— 6% Azerbaijanis
— 1% Other

15 Kirgizia
48% — 26% Russian
— 12% Uzbek
— 14% Other

SOVIET UNION

CHINA

Note: numbers may not equal one hundred due to rounding

minority peoples in addition to the original Slavs. Until 1917, this state was known as the Tsarist Empire; after the 1917 Bolshevik Revolution it became the Union of Soviet Socialist Republics (USSR). This existed until its disintegration in 1991, when it was replaced by the Commonwealth of Independent States, as we shall see in Chapter 45, Section III.

The dozens of minority peoples in the USSR preserved their sense of identity, despite the centuries they spent under Tsarist and then Soviet rule. Therefore they were able to establish independent states when the USSR fell apart in 1991. By contrast, the equally large number of ethnic elements comprising the United States have not demanded an independent existence. Why the basically different situation in the two countries?

One explanation is that the USSR was a mosaic of nationalities, while the United States is a melting pot of nationalities. The USSR was a mosaic because centuries ago, as we noted above, the Russians began conquering their neighbors all the way to the Pacific Ocean and then combined them into one empire, like a mosaic holding together many different-colored pieces of glass. Just as each piece of glass in a mosaic retains its color, so the various nationalities in the Tsarist-Soviet mosaic retained their identity. In 1991 those broke off and became independent states.

The Americans also conquered the various Indian tribes all the way to the Pacific Ocean, just as the Russians conquered the Eurasian peoples all the way to the Pacific Ocean. But the number of Indians between the Atlantic and Pacific oceans was much smaller than the number of Eurasians between the Ural Mountains and the Pacific Ocean. So the Americans were able to push all the Indians into a few reservations. That cleared the ground for the immigration of millions of people from all over the world into the relatively empty lands of the United States. In those lands the immigrants "mixed up" so that today descendants of many different peoples often live side by side as neighbors in one American city block or in one apartment building, instead of a whole republic consisting entirely, or largely, of one people or another, as is the case with the fifteen Soviet Socialist Republics (SSRs) that comprised the USSR. That is one reason why the many elements in the melting pot (Mexicans, Koreans, Chinese, Germans, African-Americans, and so on) are not demanding autonomy or independence in the United States, as did the Baltics, Armenians, Ukrainians, and various Moslem ethnic groups in the USSR. The accompanying illustration, "Ethnic Composition of Soviet Republics," provides statistics that demonstrate why the USSR disintegrated as a mosaic, in contrast to the melting pot that has survived as the United States.

SUGGESTED READINGS

The best general surveys of the Russian expansion into Siberia are by F. A. Golder, *Russian Expansion on the Pacific, 1641–1850* (Clark, 1914); R. J. Kerner, *The Urge to the Sea: The Course of Russian History* (University of California, 1942); the volume of readings by G. A. Lensen, ed., *Russia's Eastward Expansion* (Prentice Hall, 1964); T. Armstrong, *Russian Expansion in the North* (Cambridge University, 1965); and L. H. Neatby, *Discovery in Russian and Siberian Waters* (Ohio University, 1973).

Special phases of Siberian history are treated in D. W. Treadgold, *The Great Siberian Migration* (Princeton University, 1957); R. H. Fisher, *The Russian Fur Trade, 1550–1700* (University of California, 1943); G. V. Lantzeff, *Siberia in the Seventeenth Century* (University of California, 1943); V. Chen, *Sino-Russian Relations in the Seventeenth Century* (Nijhoff, 1966); A. S. Donnelly, *The Conquest of Bashkiria, 1552–1740* (Yale University, 1968); and J. R. Gibson, *Feeding the Russian Fur Trade: Provisionment of the Okhotsk Seaboard and the Kamchatka Peninsula* (University of Wisconsin, 1969).

27

Beginning of Global Unity

The discovery of America . . . certainly made a most essential [change]. By opening a new and inexhaustible market to all the commodities of Europe, it gave occasion to new divisions of labour and improvements of art, which in the narrow sphere of ancient commerce, could never have taken place. . . . The silver of the new continent seems in this manner to be one of the principal commodities by which the commerce between the two extremities of the old one is carried on, and it is by means of it, in great measure, that those distant parts of the world are connected with one another.

Adam Smith

The early modern period from 1500 to 1763 was one of the more critical periods in human history. It was at this time that European explorers made the great discoveries that disclosed new continents and thereby heralded the global phase of world history. During this period also the Europeans began their rise to world primacy because of their leadership in overseas activities. Certain global interrelationships that developed during these centuries naturally became stronger with the passage of time. Hence the years from 1500 to 1763 are the period when global unity got under way—the period of transition from the regional isolationism of the pre-1500 era to the

European global hegemony of the nineteenth century. The purpose of this chapter is to analyze the precise nature and extent of the global ties that developed in various fields (see map of World of the Emerging West, 1763, p. 411.)

I. NEW GLOBAL HORIZONS

The first and most obvious result of Europe's expansion overseas and overland was an unprecedented widening of horizons. No longer was geographic knowledge limited to one region or continent or hemisphere. For the first time, the shape

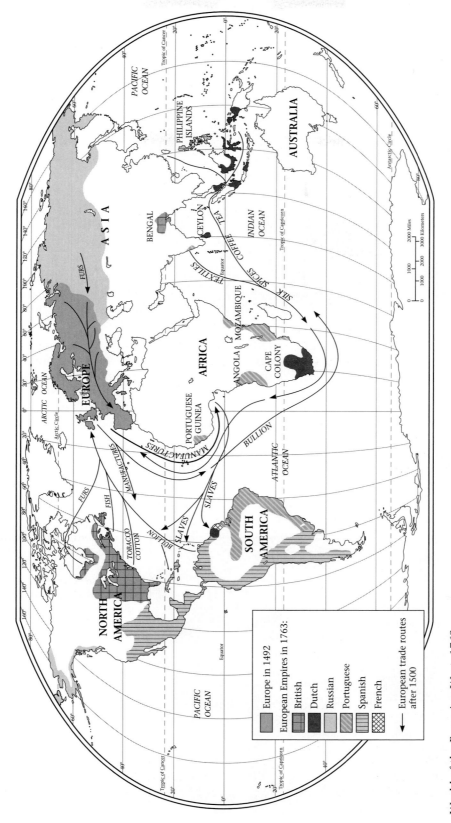

World of the Emerging West, 1763.

A depiction of the inhabitants of the Andaman Islands, based on a report given Marco Polo that these people had heads, eyes, and teeth "like those of dogs."

of the globe as a whole was known and charted (see map of Western Knowledge of the Globe, A.D. 1 to 1800, p. 375.) This was largely the work of the western Europeans, who had taken the lead in transoceanic exploration. Before the Portuguese began feeling their way down the coast of Africa in the early fifteenth century, Europeans had accurate information only of North Africa and the Middle East. Their knowledge concerning India was vague. It was still vaguer regarding central Asia, east Asia, and sub-Saharan Africa. The very existence of the Americas and of Australia—let alone Antarctica—was, of course, unsuspected.

By 1763 the picture was altogether different. The main coastlines of most of the world had become known in varying degrees of detail, including the Atlantic coast of the Americas, the Pacific coast of South America, the whole outline of Africa, and the coasts of south and east Asia. In certain areas European knowledge went beyond the coastlines. The Russians were reasonably familiar with Siberia, and the Spaniards and Por-

In the century following the European intrusion, millions of Indians died. One of the causes was the spread of European diseases, such as smallpox, depicted in this sixteenth-century drawing.

tuguese with Mexico, Central America, and parts of South America. North of the Rio Grande the Spaniards had explored considerable areas in their futile search for gold and fabled cities, and further north the French and English ranged widely, using the canoes and the river-lake routes known to the Indians.

On the other hand, the Pacific coast of North America was largely unknown, and Australia, though sighted on its west coast by Dutch navigators, was almost wholly uncharted. Likewise, the interior of sub-Saharan Africa was almost completely blank, and so was central Asia, about which the main source of information still was the thirteenth-century account of Marco Polo. In general, then, the Europeans had gained knowledge of most of the coastlines of the world during the period to 1763. In the following period they were to penetrate into the interior of continents and also to explore the polar regions.

II.   GLOBAL DIFFUSION OF HUMANS, ANIMALS, AND PLANTS

The European discoveries led not only to new global horizons but also to a new global distribution of races. Prior to 1500 there existed, in effect, worldwide racial segregation. The Negroids were concentrated in sub-Saharan Africa and a few Pacific islands; the Mongoloids in central Asia, Siberia, east Asia, and the Americas; and the Caucasoids in Europe, North Africa, the Middle East, and India. Today this pattern has been fundamentally altered to the point where half the people of African descent live outside of Africa. By 1763 this radically different race distribution was clearly discernible. The Russians had begun their slow migration across the Urals into Siberia. Much more substantial was the mass migration to the Americas—voluntary in the case of the Europeans, involuntary for the Africans.

The influx changed the Americas from purely Mongoloid continents to the most racially mixed regions of the globe. Immigration of Africans continued to the mid-nineteenth century, reaching a total of 10 million slaves. European immigration also steadily increased, reaching a high point at the beginning of the twentieth century when nearly 1 million arrived each year. The net result is that the New World today is peopled by a majority of whites, with substantial minorities of blacks, Indians, mestizos, and mulattoes, in that order (see Chapter 36, Section I, and map of Racial Distribution in the World, p. 414.)

The new global pattern that resulted from these depopulations and migrations has become so familiar that it is now taken for granted and its extraordinary significance generally overlooked. What happened in the period to 1763 is that the Europeans staked out claims to vast new regions, and in the following century they peopled those territories—not only the Americas but also Siberia and, eventually, Australia. We can see the vital importance of the redrawing of the world racial map if we imagined that the Chinese rather

Russian trading settlement on Norfolk Sound. The fort is on a hill, with the Russian flag flying over it. Outside the fort are baths and craftspeople's living quarters.

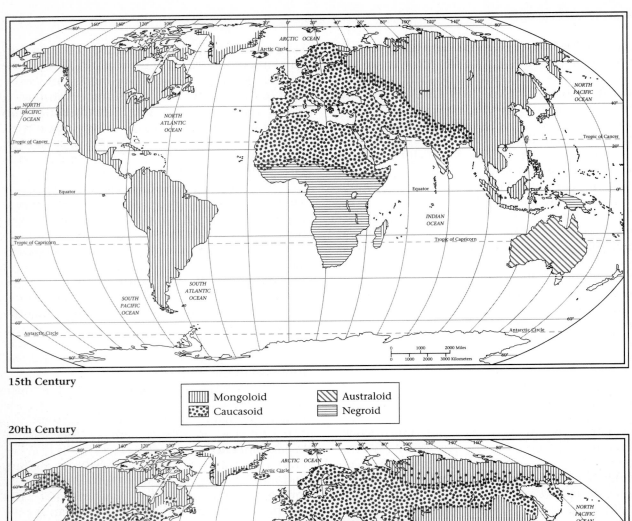

15th Century

‖‖‖ Mongoloid	⧄ Australoid
⣿ Caucasoid	☰ Negroid

20th Century

Racial Distribution in the World.

than the Europeans first reached and settled the underpopulated continents. In that case the proportion of Chinese to the total world population would probably be closer to three out of five rather than one out of five, as it is now.

The intermixture of human races was accompanied inevitably by a corresponding intermixture of plants and animals. With a few insignificant exceptions, all plants and animals being utilized today were domesticated by prehistoric humans in various parts of the world. Their diffusion from their places of origin had proceeded slowly until 1500, when globe-spanning Homo sapiens began transplanting them back and forth among continents. An important contribution of the Old World were the various domesticated animals, especially horses, cattle, and sheep. The New World had nothing comparable. The llama and alpaca were of relatively little value. Old World grains also were important, especially wheat, rye, oats, and barley. The Spaniards, who loved their orchards, brought with them a large variety of fruits, as well as the olive and the European vine.

The American Indians in return contributed their remarkable store of food plants, particularly corn and potatoes, but also cassava, tomatoes, avocados, sweet potatoes, peanuts, and certain varieties of beans, pumpkins, and squashes. So important are these Indian plants that today they are responsible for about one-half of the world's total plant-food production. In addition to these food plants, the American Indians were responsible for two major cash crops: tobacco and cotton, as well as several native American drugs that are prominent in modern pharmacology. They contributed coca for cocaine and novocaine, curare used in anesthet-

William Penn's treaty with the American Indians when he founded the province of Pennsylvania, 1681.

ics, cinchona bark (the source of quinine), datura used in pain relievers, and cascara for laxatives.

The interchange of animals and plants was not, of course, confined to Eurasia and the Americas. The entire globe was involved, as is illustrated strikingly in the case of Australia. Australia is now a leading world exporter of primary products such as wool, mutton, beef, and wheat, all commodities derived from species that were transplanted from elsewhere. The same is true of Indonesia with its great rubber, coffee, tea, and tobacco production, and of Hawaii with its sugar and pineapples.

Today the global intermixture of humans, plants, and animals continues, though at an accelerating pace as steamships and jet planes replace canoes and sailboats. Frequently the mixing occurs accidentally, and with repercussions that sometimes are disastrous. For example, marine creatures of all types are being transferred routinely every day from one end of the world to another in the ballast tanks of ships. Dumped into new habitats when the ships make port, billions of organisms spread out, sometimes replacing native species. Scientists sampling the ballast tanks of 159 Japanese cargo ships arriving at Coos Bay, Oregon, discovered in their ballast waters 367 different types of plants and animals, mostly in larval form. "We found shrimps, crabs, fish, barnacles, sea urchins, starfish, worms, jellyfish, clams, snails, really the complete spectrum of marine life. . . . Perhaps 5 to 10 percent of species

introduced to a new environment become established there."[1]

Even when the mixing is planned rather than accidental, the results sometimes are unexpected and injurious. An example of this is the deliberate importation of the tropical American toad to Australia to combat the sugar-cane beetle. Belatedly it was discovered that the toads are nocturnal feeders and the beetles are abroad by day, while the toads sleep under rocks and boards. By night the toads flourish, reproducing exuberantly and eating everything around them. Today they are thriving so well that some reach the size of dinner plates. Nobody knows what to do about them. An Australian naturalist had warned of the dangers of introducing the American toad to his country, but had been ignored. The ongoing ballast problem could be met, according to one proposal, by dumping the ballast on the high seas and reballasting with mid-ocean water. The assumption is that mid-ocean species would not survive in shallow coastal waters—an assumption requiring careful study and testing.

Ballasts are by no means the only problem in controlling species diffusion. The rapidly increasing volume of global trade and travel probably is the most important diffusion force today. Species are spreading everywhere along with live animals, plants, and seeds, and also with the ships, planes, and trucks on which they are transported. The diffusion, of course, is a two-way process—outward

Cuban sugar industry—cutting and loading the cane on the plantation of Las Canas.

The Indian village of Secota (North Carolina) in the late sixteenth century.

from the United States as well as the reverse. The slipper limpet was inadvertently exported from the United States to Europe in the 1880s with a shipment of oysters; a North American moth currently is defoliating trees in a large area in central China; and a pinewood nematode from the southeastern United States is killing black pines in Japan.

III. GLOBAL ECONOMIC RELATIONS

By the latter part of the eighteenth century a large intercontinental trade had developed for the first time in history. Before 1500, Arab and Italian merchants transported mostly luxuries from one part of Eurasia to another—goods such as spices, silk, precious stones, and perfumes. By the late eighteenth century the limited luxury

trade had been transformed into a mass trade based on the exchange of new, bulky necessities. Atlantic commerce especially became enormous since the New World plantations produced huge quantities of tobacco, sugar, and, later, coffee, cotton, and other commodities that were sold in Europe. Because the plantations practiced *monoculture,* they had to import all necessities such as grain, fish, cloth, and metal products. They also had to import their labor. This led to the flourishing triangle trade: rum, cloth, guns, and other metal products from Europe to Africa; slaves from Africa to the New World; and sugar, tobacco, and bullion from the New World to Europe.

Another important aspect of the new mass global trade of this era was the exchange of products between western and eastern Europe. Here again western Europe received raw materials, especially bread grains, which were in great demand because of population increase and because much arable land had been converted into pasture. At Danzig, chief port for the Baltic grain trade, rye prices between 1550 and 1600 rose 247 percent, barley 187 percent, and oats 185 percent. This stimulated a great increase in the export of grains and other raw materials, so that the value of Polish and Hungarian exports to the West during these decades usually was double that of imports. Poland, Hungary, Russia, and ultimately the Balkans received textiles, arms, metal products, and colonial goods, and in return provided grain, cattle, hides, ship stores, and flax. They also provided furs, which were obtained by the Russians in Siberia in the same way that the Spaniards obtained bullion in the New World; namely, by exploiting native labor.

Europe's trade with Asia was not equal to the trade with the Americas or eastern Europe for two principal reasons. The first was that the European textile industries opposed the importation of cotton goods from various Asiatic countries. Foreign cottons were immensely popular in Europe because they were light, bright, inexpensive, and above all, washable, and they began to be imported in large quantities. Soon objections were raised by native textile interests and by those who feared that national security was endangered by the loss of the bullion that was drained away to pay for the textiles. These interests brought sufficient pressure to bear on their respective governments to secure the passage of laws forbidding or reducing the importation of Indian cottons.

The Indians of South Carolina were said to kill alligators by driving long sticks down their gullets, turning them over, shooting them with arrows, and then beating them to death.

The second factor limiting European commerce with Asia was the difficulty of finding something that would sell in the Asiatic market. This problem dated back to classical times, when the Roman Empire was drained of its gold to pay for Chinese silk and Indian textiles. Likewise in the sixteenth, seventeenth, and eighteenth centuries, Asia remained uninterested in European goods, and Europe was reluctant to send bullion to pay for the Asiatic produce it wanted. Europe did not solve this problem of trade with Asia until it developed power machinery at the end of the eighteenth century. Then the situation was reversed, for it was Europe that was able to flood Asia with cheap, machine-made textiles. But until that time, East-West trade was hampered by the fact that Asia was willing to accept little else but bullion from Europe.

What was the significance of the new worldwide economic ties? First and foremost, international division of labor for the first time had been achieved on a significant scale. The world was on the way to becoming an economic unit. The Americas and eastern Europe (with Siberia) produced raw materials, Africa provided labor, Asia an assortment of luxury commodities, and western Europe directed these global operations and concentrated more and more on industrial output.

The requirements of the new global economy raised the question of how to get a big enough labor supply in the regions producing raw materials. The New World plantations met this need by importing African slaves on a large scale. Hence African populations are most numerous today in precisely those areas that had formerly been devoted to plantation agriculture—northern Brazil, the West Indies, and the southern United States. The early Europeans' solution to their labor needs was to leave a bitter legacy. These areas to the present day are wracked by basic problems dating back to the colonial period—the problems of race discrimination and of underdevelopment. The current racial conflict in American ghettos and on Caribbean islands is the end result of over four centuries of transatlantic slave trade. Likewise, the underdevelopment of all Latin America is simply a continuation of the economic dependency on northwestern Europe of the Spanish and Portuguese colonies (and of Spain and Portugal themselves).

Whereas the price for the participation of the Americas in the new global economy was slavery, the price for eastern Europe was serfdom. The basic reason was the same—namely, the need for a plentiful and reliable supply of cheap labor to produce goods for the lucrative west European market. Heretofore the nobles in Poland and Hungary had required minimal labor from the peasants—three to six days a year—for there was no incentive to increase output. But when production for market became profitable, the nobles responded by drastically raising the labor obligations to one day a week, and by the end of the sixteenth century to six days a week. To make sure that the peasants would remain to perform this labor, laws were passed limiting their freedom of movement more and more strictly. Eventually they were completely bound to the soil, thereby becoming serfs, denied freedom of movement and subject to the exactions of the nobles.

Africa also was vitally affected by the new global economy, serving as the source of slave labor for the American plantations. Slavery existed in Africa before the transatlantic trade, with slaves being used as soldiers and farmers. Slaves also were exported, along with gold, over ancient trade routes across the Sahara to the Mediterranean coast, whence they were shipped mostly to the Middle East. An estimated 3.5 million to 10 million Africans were sold in this fashion prior to the Atlantic slave trade.

The Portuguese, who were the pioneers in the transatlantic trade, began by selling Africans in Spain, Italy, and Portugal, where they were used for domestic and farm labor. Their numbers were small, however, compared to the multitudes that soon were being shipped to work on New World plantations. Local Indians could not be used for that purpose because they were disappearing—victims of European diseases. The plantation owners at first tried to get along with the indentured European workers, but they proved to be too expensive and undisciplined. So African slaves were substituted, the first ones being shipped soon after Columbus's first voyage. Their numbers rose sharply after the discovery of silver in Peru in the 1520s and the establishment of sugar plantations in Brazil in the 1540s, and soared still more as new plantations were established in Mexico and the Caribbean islands for other crops such as tobacco, rice, and coffee. Estimates of the total number of slaves vary widely; the most recent studies indicate between 12 million and 20 million being forcibly shipped from Africa between 1500 and 1867. Consequently, by 1850 there were three or four enslaved Africans in the Americas for every white person.

The effect of the slave trade varied greatly from one part of Africa to the other. Angola and East Africa suffered severely because their populations were relatively sparse to begin with and their economies were often close to the subsistence level. For them, even a small population loss was devastating. By contrast, West Africa was more advanced economically and hence more populous, so that the devastations of the slavers were not so ruinous. Considering the continent as a whole, the effect on the population was not as great as might be expected, because the slaves were taken over a period stretching from 1450 to 1870 and from a total sub-Saharan population estimated at 70 million to 80 million. Nevertheless, the slave trade had a corrosive and unsettling effect on the entire African coast from Senegal to Angola and for 400 to 500 miles inland. The appearance of the European slavers with their cargoes of rum, guns, and hardware set off a chain reaction of slave-hunting raids into the interior. Wars broke out among various groups for control of the lucrative and militarily decisive trade. Some, like the Ashanti Confederacy and the Dahomey Kingdom, rose to ascendancy, whereas others, like the Yoruba and Benin civilizations and the Congo Kingdom, declined. The overall effect was definitely disruptive.

And yet the slave trade did involve trade as well as slavery. In return for their fellow native people, whom the Africans themselves sold to the Europeans, they received not only alcohol and firearms but also certain useful and economically productive commodities, including textiles, tools, and raw materials for local smithies and workshops. A more important positive influence in the long run was the introduction of new food plants from the Americas. Corn, cassava, sweet potatoes, peppers, pineapples, and tobacco were brought in by the Portuguese and spread very rapidly from tribe to tribe. Therefore it has been argued that the substantially larger number of people that could be supported with these new foods probably outweighed the population lost to the slave trade. On the other hand, the slave trade was not essential for the introduction of the new food plants. They were spreading rapidly during these centuries all over the globe. Slavery or no slavery, they doubtless would have reached the interior of Africa as they did the interior of China.

Of the various continents, Asia was the least affected, because it was sufficiently strong militarily, politically, and economically to avoid direct or indirect subjugation. Most of Asia was quite unaware of the persistent and annoying European merchants who were appearing in the coastal

ADAM SMITH ON THE EXPANSION OF EUROPE

In his world-famous Wealth of Nations *(1776), Adam Smith paid considerable attention to the effect of colonies. He noted that they added to the wealth of the European countries except Spain and Portugal, which owned the colonies.*

The discovery of America, and that of a passage to the East Indies by the Cape of Good Hope, are the two greatest and most important events recorded in the history of mankind. Their consequences have already been very great: but, in the short period of between two and three centuries which has elapsed since these discoveries were made, it is impossible that the whole extent of their consequences can have been seen. What benefits or what misfortunes to mankind may hereafter result from those great events, no human wisdom can foresee. By uniting, in some measure, the most distant parts of the world, by enabling them to relieve one another's wants, to increase one another's enjoyments, and to encourage one another's industry, their general tendency would seem to be beneficial.

In the meantime, one of the principal effects of those discoveries has been to raise the mercantile system to a degree of splendour and glory which it could never otherwise have attained to. It is the object of that system to enrich a great nation rather by trade and manufactures than by the improvement and cultivation of land, rather by the industry of the towns than by that of the country. But, in consequence of those discoveries, the commercial towns of Europe, instead of being the manufacturers and carriers for but a very small part of the world (that part of Europe which is washed by the Atlantic ocean, and the countries which lie round the Baltic and Mediterranean seas), have now become the manufacturers for the numerous and thriving cultivators of America, and the carriers, and in some respects the manufacturers too, for almost all the different nations of Asia, Africa, and America. Two new worlds have been opened to their industry, each of them much greater and more extensive than the old one, and the market of one of them growing still greater and greater every day.

The countries which possess the colonies of America, and which trade directly to the East Indies, enjoy, indeed, the whole show and splendour of this great commerce. Other countries, however, notwithstanding all the invidious restraints by which it is meant to exclude them, frequently enjoy a greater share of the real benefit of it. The colonies of Spain and Portugal, for example, give more real encouragement to the industry of other countries than to that of Spain and Portugal. In the single article of linen alone the consumption of those colonies amounts, it is said, but I do not pretend to warrant the quantity, to more than three millions sterling a year. But this great consumption is almost entirely supplied by France, Flanders, Holland, and Germany. Spain and Portugal furnish but a small part of it. The capital which supplies the colonies with this great quantity of linen is annually distributed among, and furnishes a revenue to, the inhabitants of those other countries.

*Adam Smith, *Wealth of Nations* (Edinburgh, 1838), p. 282.

regions. Only a few coastal areas in India, and some of the islands in the East Indies, felt the impact of Europe's early economic expansion. As far as Asia as a whole was concerned, its attitude was best expressed by the emperor of China, Ch'ien-lung. He replied as follows to a 1793 message from King George III of Britain asking for the establishment of diplomatic and commercial relations:

Swaying the wide world, I have but one aim in view, namely, to maintain a perfect governance and to fulfill the duties of the State: strange and costly objects

Slave fort on Goree Island, near modern Dakar.

do not interest me. . . . As your Ambassador can see for himself, we possess all things. I set no value on objects strange or ingenious, and have no use for your country's manufactures.[2]

Europe also was affected by the new global economy, but the effects in this case were all positive. The Europeans were the pioneer middlemen of world trade. They had opened the new oceanic routes and supplied the necessary capital, shipping, and technical skills. So it was natural that they should have profited most from the slave trade, the sugar and tobacco plantations, and the Eastern commerce. Some of the benefits trickled down to the European masses, as is indicated by the fact that tea cost about £10 a pound when introduced in England about 1650 but had become an article of common consumption a century later. More important than the effect on living standards was the effect the new global commerce had in stimulating Europe's economy. As we will see later, the industrial revolution that got under way in the late eighteenth century owed much to the capital earned from overseas enterprises and to the growing demand for European manufacturers in overseas markets.

It was during this period, then, that Europe forged ahead in the great ascent to global economic primacy. The overall results were positive because global division of labor led to increased global productivity. The world of 1763 was richer than that of 1500, and the economic growth has continued to the present day. But from the beginning, northwestern Europe, as the world's entrepreneur, received most of the benefits at the expense of the other regions. What this expense involved is apparent in the current conflict of races, in the discrepancy between rich and poor nations, and in the scars left by serfdom throughout eastern Europe and by slavery throughout the world.

IV. GLOBAL POLITICAL RELATIONS

Global political relations changed as fundamentally during the period to 1763 as did economic ones. The western Europeans were no longer fenced in on the western tip of Eurasia by an expanding Islam. Instead, they had outflanked the Moslem world in the south by winning control of the Indian Ocean. Meanwhile, the Russians had outflanked the Moslems in the north by their conquest of Siberia. At the same time, western Europeans by their discovery of the New World had opened up vast territories for economic exploitation and colonization. In doing so, they built up a tremendous reservoir of resources and power.

All this represented a basic and fateful change in the global balance of power—a change comparable to that which had occurred in the demographic balance. Hitherto the Moslem world had been the center of initiative, probing and pushing in all directions—into southeast Europe, into sub-Saharan Africa, into central and Southeast Asia. Now a new center had arisen that was able to operate on a global, rather than merely Eurasian, scale. From this new center, first in the Iberian peninsula and later in northwest Europe, the routes of trade and of political influence radiated outward to envelop the entire world—westward to the Americas, south around Africa, and east to India and around Southeast Asia.

All these territories were not actually controlled by 1763. But there was effective domination of the underpopulated lands—the Americas, Siberia, and later Australia—even though their actual peopling on a continental scale had to wait until the nineteenth century. In Africa and Asia the western Europeans obtained only coastal footholds during this period, but with one exception: The Dutch penetrated the Cape and the East Indies. Elsewhere the native peoples were too strong and highly organized to allow a repetition of what happened in the Americas and Siberia.

In West Africa, for example, the Europeans could not penetrate inland because of climatic difficulties. They were prevented also by the coastal chiefs, who jealously guarded their profitable position as middlemen between the interior tribes and the Europeans. In India the Europeans were kept at arm's length for 250 years following the arrival of Vasco da Gama in 1498. During those centuries they were allowed to trade in a few ports, but clearly and explicitly only on the sufferance of the native rulers. In China and Japan there was no chance at all of European territorial encroachment, as the Russians discovered when they entered the Amur valley.

We may conclude that in the political field, as in the economic, Europe in 1763 was at a halfway point. It was no longer a relatively isolated and unimportant peninsula of the Eurasian landmass. It had expanded overseas and overland, establishing its control over the relatively empty and militarily weak Americas and Siberia. But in Africa, the Middle East, and south and east Asia, the Europeans had to wait until the nineteenth century to assert their dominance.

Australian aborigines' war dance.

Abduction of wives in
Southern Australia.

Western ship arriving in Tientsin.

V. GLOBAL CULTURAL RELATIONS

The imposition of European culture, like that of European political rule, depended on the state of the native societies. In the Americas, for example, European culture was transported bodily because the native peoples were either wiped out or pushed aside. Yet even the casual traveler in Latin America cannot fail to notice evidence of Indian cultural survivals. There is, for example, the use of adobe for building purposes and of unmilled pine logs as beams, or *vigas*. Likewise, the blanket, or serape, that is draped over the shoulders is of Indian origin, as is also the pon-cho, consisting of two blankets sewn together with a slit for the head. The Roman Catholicism currently practiced in much of Latin America is a blend of Christian and Indian beliefs and practices. Although the names of native gods have been dropped, the Indians assign the attributes of these gods to the Virgin Mary and to the saints, expecting the images of the Catholic gods to cure disease, control the weather, and keep them from harm, as they believed their former gods had done. Perhaps the most conspicuous evidence of Indian influence is to be found in the Latin American cuisine. Tamales, tortillas, and the various chili dishes are based on the two great Indian staples, beans and corn.

Janissaries of the Ottoman Empire. The scourge of Europe, they twice besieged Vienna.

European influence on the native cultures of Africa and Eurasia was slight in the period prior to 1763, except for the diffusion of new food plants, which, as noted, was of primary importance. In West Africa the native chiefs confined the European traders largely to their coastal posts. In the old Middle Eastern, Indian, and Chinese centers of civilization, the native peoples, as might be expected, were not at all impressed by the culture of the European intruders. The Moslem Turks, who had the closest ties with the Christian Europeans, looked down on them with the utmost contempt. Even in the seventeenth and eighteenth centuries, when the Turks were themselves on the downgrade, they did not hesitate to express their disdain for the Christian infidels. "Do I not know you," burst out the grand vizier to the French ambassador in 1666, "that you are a Giaour [nonbeliever], that you are a hogge, a dogge, a turde eater?"[3]

Likewise, the native peoples on the mainland of India reacted very negatively when the Portuguese, who were ensconced at Goa, introduced the Inquisition in 1560. Between 1600 and 1773, seventy-three victims were consigned to the flames because of their heretical views. The Indian population could not fail to see the inconsistency in a religion that imprisoned, tortured, and condemned to the flames people whose only crime was unorthodoxy. But at the same time it prevented widows from being burnt of their own free will, a sublimely virtuous act by Hindu standards of the period. Furthermore, the lawless and boisterous behavior of European adventurers in India further lowered the Indian people's opinion of the Western Christians. An English, clergyman, Mr. Terry, was told in 1616, "Christian religion devil religion; Christian much drink; Christian much do wrong; Christian much beat; Christian much abuse others."[4]

The Chinese reaction to the Europeans was relatively favorable at the outset (as noted in Chapter 20, Section III) because of the exceptional ability and intellectual attainments of the Jesuit missionaries. The Jesuits succeeded in winning some converts, including a few scholars and some members of the imperial family. But even the capable Jesuits, with their knowledge of astronomy, mathematics, and geography, did not make much of an impression on most Chinese scholars, who rejected both Western science and religion. As far as the popular Chinese attitude to the Europeans at that time is concerned, it probably was reflected accurately in the proverb that Chinese alone possessed two eyes, the Europeans were one-eyed, and all the other inhabitants of the earth were blind. Given this attitude, it is not surprising that with the exception of certain specialized fields of learning such as astronomy, European influence on Chinese civilization before 1763 was very slight.

Although the Chinese, the Indians, and the Turks were unimpressed by European culture during this period, the Europeans, by contrast, were very much impressed by what they saw in Constantinople, in Delhi, and in Peking. They became familiar first with the Ottoman Empire, and their reaction was one of respect, admiration, and apprehension. As late as 1634, after the decline of the empire had set in, a thoughtful English traveler concluded that the Turks were "the only modern people great in action" and that "he who would behold these times in their greatest glory, could not find a better scene than Turkey."[5] During the seventeenth century the Ottoman Empire lost prestige among Europeans. But at the same time European intellectuals were becoming fascinated with numerous detailed accounts of the fabulous civilization of far-off Cathay. They were entranced as they learned of China's history, art, philosophy, and government. China came to be held up as a model civilization because of its Confucian system of morals; its examination system for government service; its respect for learning rather than for military prowess; and its exquisite handicrafts, including porcelain, silk, and lacquer work. Voltaire (1694–1778), for example, adorned the wall of his library with a portrait of Confucius, and the German philosopher Leibniz (1646–1716) extolled the Chinese emperor K'ang-hsi as "the monarch . . . who almost exceeds human heights of greatness, being a god-like mortal, ruling all by a nod of his head, who, however, is educated to virtue and wisdom . . . thereby earning the right to rule."[6]

In the late eighteenth century European admiration for China began to wane, partly because the Catholic missionaries were now being persecuted and also because the Europeans were beginning to be more interested in China's natural resources than in its culture. The shift in attitude is reflected in the sixteen volumes of the *Memoirs on the History, Sciences, Arts, etc., of the Chinese,* published in Paris between 1776 and 1814. The eleventh volume, which appeared in 1786, contained little but reports on resources that might interest traders—borax, lignite, quicksilver, ammoniac, horses, bamboo, and wool-bearing animals.

Just as European interest had shifted in the seventeenth century from the Ottoman Empire to China, so now in the late eighteenth century it shifted to Greece and, to a lesser extent, India. The classical Greeks became the great favorites among educated Europeans. "How can you believe," wrote a German scholar in 1778, "that uncultivated Oriental peoples produced annals and poetry and possessed a complete religion and morality, before the Greeks, who were the teachers of Europe, were able to read?"[7] A few European intellectuals became engrossed in Indian culture. The Hindu pandits, or learned men, were unwilling to impart their sacred lore to foreigners, but a few Europeans, mostly Jesuit fathers, acquired a knowledge of Sanskrit language, literature, and philosophy. The German philosopher Schopenhauer (1788–1860) fell as much under the spell of Hindu philosophy as Leibniz had under the Chinese. An English scholar, Sir William Jones, proclaimed before the Asiatic Society of Bengal in 1786 that "the

Sanskrit Language, whatever be its antiquity, is of wonderful structure; more perfect than the Greek, more copious than the Latin, and more exquisitely refined than either."[8]

VI. EARLY MODERN PERIOD IN HISTORICAL PERSPECTIVE

The early modern period from 1500 to 1763 represents a halfway point between the regional isolationism of the preceding ages and the European world domination of the nineteenth century. Economically, it was a time when the Europeans extended their trading operations to virtually all corners of the globe, though they were not yet able to exploit the interiors of the great landmasses. Intercontinental trade reached unprecedented proportions, though still far below the volume it was to reach in the following centuries.

Politically, the world was still far from being a single unit. The great Seven Years' War, which convulsed Europe, did not affect the Americas west of the Mississippi nor the interior of Africa nor most of the Middle East nor any of East Asia. The Europeans had secured a firm grip on Siberia, South America, and the eastern portion of North America, but they had as yet only a few territorial enclaves in Africa, India, and the East Indies. In the Far East they could venture only as merchants, and even in

A Jesuit attempt to reproduce ancient Chinese characters.

that capacity they had to submit to the most restrictive and arbitrary regulations.

Culturally, it was a period of widening horizons. Throughout the globe peoples were becoming aware of other peoples and other cultures. By and large, the Europeans were more impressed and affected by the ancient civilizations of Eurasia than vice versa. They felt a sense of wide-eyed wonder as they discovered new oceans and continents and civilizations. At the same time they were scrambling greedily for booty and for trade, they exhibited a certain humility. They even underwent an occasional anxious searching of conscience, as in the case of the treatment of the Indians in Spanish America. But before this period had passed, Europe's attitude toward the rest of the world was noticeably changing. It was becoming coarser and harder and more intolerant. In the mid-nineteenth century the French sinologist Guillaume Pauthier complained that the Chinese civilization, which in the time of Leibniz had keenly interested European intellectuals, "now scarcely attracted the attention of a select few.... These people, whom we daily treat as barbarians, and who, nevertheless, had attained to a very high state of culture several centuries before our ancestors inhabited the forests of Gaul and Germany, now inspire in us only a deep contempt."[9] The following chapters will be concerned with why the Europeans came to feel themselves superior to the "lesser breeds" and how they were able to impose their rule on them.

SUGGESTED READINGS

The general effect of Europe's expansion during the early modern period is analyzed in the multivolume work of I. Wallerstein, *The Modern World System* (Academic Press, 1974ff.); W. P. Webb, *The Great Frontier* (Houghton Mifflin, 1952); P. D. Curtin, *Cross-Cultural Trade in World History* (Cambridge University, 1984); E. F. Frazier, *Race and Culture Contacts in the Modern World* (Knopf, 1957); and L. S. Stavrianos, *Global Rift: The Third World Comes of Age* (William Morrow, 1981).

More specialized studies of Europe's impact are by E. Reynolds, *Stand the Storm: A History of the Atlantic Slave Trade* (Schocken, 1985); S. J. and B. H. Stein, *The Colonial Heritage of Latin America* (Oxford University, 1970); S. W. Mintz, *Sweetness and Power: The Place of Sugar in Modern History* (Viking, 1985); A. W. Crosby, Jr., *The Columbian Exchange: Biological and Cultural Consequences of 1492* (Greenwood Publishing Co., 1972); and A. G. Price, *the Western Invasion of the Pacific and Its Continents: A Study of Moving Frontiers and Changing Landscapes 1513–1958* (Clarendon, 1963).

The opposite process— the effect of overseas expansion on Europe—is analyzed in the multivolume study by F. D. Lach, *Asia in the Making of Europe* (University of Chicago, 1965ff.); J. E. Gillespie, *The Influence of Overseas Expansion on England to 1700* (Vol. 91 in Columbia University Studies in History, Economics and Public Law, 1920); A. I. Hallowell, "The Impact of the American Indian on American Culture," *American Anthropologist,* LIX (1957), 210–217; L. S. S. O'Malley, ed., *Modern India and the West* (Oxford University, 1941); A. Reichwein, *China and Europe: Intellectual and Artistic Contacts in the Eighteenth Century* (Knopf, 1925); and P. J. Marshall and G. Williams, *The Great Map of Mankind: Perceptions of New Worlds in the Age of Enlightenment* (Harvard University, 1982).

What It Means for Us Today

REGIONAL AUTONOMY VERSUS GLOBAL UNITY

The period after 1500 is significant because it marked the beginning of the clash between regional autonomy and global unity. Before that date there was no conflict because there were for global contacts, let alone global unity. For tens of thousands of years, human beings had lived in regional isolation. When the first humans fanned out from their ancestral birthplace, presumably in Africa, they lost contact with their original neighbors. They repeated this endlessly as they spread in all directions, until they inhabited all continents except Antarctica. For example, when the first Mongoloids crossed from northeast Siberia to Alaska, they pressed on throughout North and South America. They settled down in new communities in relative isolation. Over thousands of years they developed distinctive local languages and cultures and even physical types. This process went on all over the globe, so that until 1500, racial segregation existed on a global scale. All blacks, or Negroids, lived in Africa; all whites, or Caucasoids, lived in Europe and the Middle East; all Mongoloids, in east Asia and the Americas; and all Australoids, in Australia.

This traditional regional autonomy began to yield to global unity when Western overseas expansion began about 1500. Races no longer were isolated because millions of people moved, willingly or unwillingly, to new continents. Since the Europeans took the lead in this global activity, it was they who dominated the newly united world. By the nineteenth century they controlled the globe politically with their great empires and economically with their joint-stock companies and corporations. They also enjoyed cultural domination, so that Western culture became the global model. It was equated with civilization, and non-Western cultures came to be regarded as inherently inferior. This Western hegemony was taken for granted in the nineteenth century, not only by Europeans but also by non-Europeans. It was assumed to be almost divinely ordained—a part of the natural order of things.

Now in the twentieth century, the pendulum has begun to swing once more toward regional autonomy. Europe needed four centuries

(1500–1900) to build up its worldwide dominance. It has only taken five decades for that dominance to disintegrate. The disintegration began after World War I and picked up speed after World War II. Political disintegration took the form of the end of empires. Cultural disintegration is even more widespread. Western culture no longer is regarded as synonymous with civilization, nor are non-Western cultures equated with barbarism.

Western culture today is being directly challenged, and even rejected, throughout the world. In November 1979, when American embassy personnel in Teheran were taken hostage, Western reporters submitted a number of written questions to the youthful captors. The latter replied as a group, and their answer included the following: "Western culture is a splendid means for the colonialists, a tool that alienates the nation from itself. By making a nation accept Western and American values, they make it submit to their domination." The captors also expressed distrust of Western-trained or -influenced Iranian intellectuals. "What need do we have for these decaying brains. Let them go where they want. These decaying brains are those intellectuals molded on Western models and they have no role in our movement and our revolution."[1]

Such views are not limited to young radicals. They are now shared by many non-Westerners of all political beliefs. In his influential work *Beyond Marxism: Towards an Alternative Perspective,* Indian political theorist Vrajenda Raj Mehta argues that neither Western democracy nor Soviet communism offers appropriate guidelines for India's development. He rejects liberal democracy because he believes it reduces humans to producers and consumers, and results in a selfish, atomistic society. Likewise, he rejects communism because it emphasizes economic concerns and state activities, so that it leaves little to individual choice and destroys life's richness and diversity. Mehta therefore concludes that "Each national community has its own law of development, its own way to fulfill itself. . . . The broken mosaic of Indian society cannot be re-created in the image of the West. India must find its own strategy of development and nation-building suited to its own peculiar conditions."[2]

Rejection of Western global domination is not surprising. Such domination was a historical aberration, produced by a peculiar combination of circumstances, and therefore bound to be temporary. But what is surprising is that the forces of regional autonomy are also awakening today *within* the leading Western states. National groups or subgroups, which have been asleep for decades or for centuries, are now stirring and demanding autonomy. In the United States, there are the minority groups: blacks, Hispanics, and Native Americans. In neighboring Canada, the unity of the dominion is threatened by the separatist demands of the French Quebecois. Britain likewise is coping with would-be secessionists in Scotland, Ireland, and Wales. France is facing the same challenge from Corsican, Breton, and Basque liberation fronts.

The demand for regional autonomy is not directed only against central authority in the West. In Iran, the popular revolt against Western influences is paralleled by regional uprisings against Teheran—uprisings by minorities such as the Kurds, Arabs, Baluchis, and Turkomen. Since these minorities comprise almost half of the total population of that country, Iran is far more threatened by regional autonomy demands than is any Western country. The same was true of the USSR, where dozens of ethnic groups demanded self-rule as soon as Gorbachev loosened controls with his *glasnost* or openness—hence the unexpected end of the USSR in the 1990s and its replacement by the Commonwealth of Independent States.

Much of the turmoil of our age arises from the clash of two great contradictory forces. On the one hand, modern technology is uniting the globe as never before, thanks to modern communication media, *multinational corporations,* and world-encircling spaceships. On the other hand, the globe is being torn apart by the awakening of hitherto dormant masses who are determined to create their own futures. The roots of this historic modern conflict go back to the centuries after 1500 when Western explorers and merchants for the first time brought together all the peoples of the world. The fateful repercussions, both positive and negative, confront us to the present day. "Encircled nationalisms," writes the Egyptian journalist Mohammed Heikel, "have fortified themselves for a last ditch stand in the battle for their future, not their past."[3]

The outcome of this ongoing battle is becoming more uncertain with the passage of time. Issues no longer are as simple and clearcut as they seemed to be only a few decades ago. It cannot be merely a case of East versus West at a time when the Japanese are adopting and applying Western science and technology more successfully than the Westerners themselves. Likewise, it cannot be merely a case of socialism versus capitalism when the socialist countries are abandoning their planned economies and their one-party political systems. In the Third World, there is growing disillusionment with all foreign models, but the disillusionment has left a vacuum with no agreed-upon goals and no agreed-upon strategies. China's Premier Chou En-lai best described our times as an age of "great disorder under heaven."

SUGGESTED READINGS

The revolt against Western domination is best summarized by E. Fischer, *The Passing of the European Age,* rev. ed. (Harvard University, 1948). Various aspects of the worldwide challenge to central authority are analyzed in L. Kohr, *The Breakdown of Nations* (Routledge & Kegan Paul, 1957); D. Morris and K. Hess, *Neighborhood Power: The New Localism* (Beacon, 1975); C. Bezold, ed., *Anticipatory Democracy* (Random House, 1978); A. Amalrik, *Will the Soviet Union Survive Until 1984?* (Harper & Row, 1979); H. C. d'Encausse, *Decline of an Empire: The Soviet Socialist Republics in Revolt* (Newsweek, 1979); and T. G. Verhelst, *No Life Without Roots: Culture and Development* (Zed Books, 1990), which summarizes global alternatives to the Western development model. The most recent survey of the "great disorder under heaven" is by Z. Brzezinski, *Out of Control: Global Turmoil on the Eve of the 21st Century* (Scribner's, 1993). The turmoil in the vast area of Central Asia is analyzed in A. Rashid, *The Resurgence of Central Asia. Islam or Nationalism?* (Zed Books, 1994).

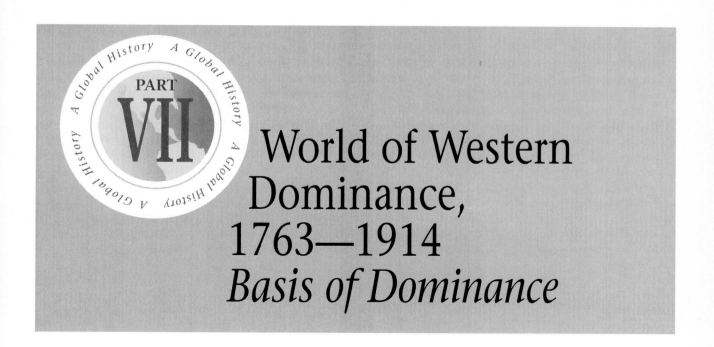

PART VII
World of Western Dominance, 1763—1914
Basis of Dominance

The century and a half between 1763 and 1914 stands out in the course of world history as the period of European domination over a large part of the globe. In 1763 Europe was still far from being the master of the world. It had only coastal footholds in Africa and in Asia. But by 1914 the European powers had annexed the whole of Africa, and they had effectively established their control over Asia: either directly, as in India and Southeast Asia, or indirectly, as in the Chinese and Ottoman empires. The unprecedented expansion of Europe was made possible by the continuation and acceleration of the modernization process. This process was set in motion earlier by the Renaissance, Reformation, technological development, capitalist enterprise, state building, and overseas expansion (see Chapter 22, Section I). These triggered a chain reaction in the form of the three great revolutions—scientific, industrial, and political—which gave Europe irresistible dynamism and power.

Two features of these revolutions might be noted at this point. One is that they were well under way before 1763. The English Civil War, a major phase of the political revolution, occurred in the 1640s. The scientific revolution took place primarily during the century and a half between the publication of Copernicus's *De revolutionibus*

orbium coelestium (1543) and of Newton's *Principia* (1687). Likewise, the roots of the industrial revolution were planted in the sixteenth and seventeenth centuries, when the countries of northwestern Europe "were seething with such genuinely capitalistic phenomena as systematic mechanical invention, company formation, and speculation in the shares of financial and trading concerns."[1] But the worldwide impact of none of these revolutions was fully felt until the nineteenth century. That is why we are considering them here rather than earlier in this text.

The other point to note about the three great revolutions is that they did not run in parallel or independent lines. Scientific, industrial, and technological events were interdependent and reacted continuously upon each other. Newton's discovery of the laws governing the movements of heavenly bodies and Darwin's theories of biological evolution both had profound effects on political ideas. Likewise, we could not conceive of modern nationalism without technological innovations such as printing and the telegraph. Conversely, politics affected science, as in the case of the French Revolution, which provided a powerful stimulus to scientific advancement. Politics also affected economics, as was made clear by the English manufacturer John

Wilkinson, who stated bluntly, "manufacture and commerce will always flourish most where Church and King interfere least."[2]

After analyzing the nature and the unfolding of these three European revolutions, we shall then, in the following chapters of Part VII of this volume, trace their effect on various parts of the globe. We shall see how they made possible the Europeanization of the Americas and of Australia, the partitioning of Africa, and the domination of Asia.

28 Europe's Scientific and Industrial Revolutions

The so-called scientific revolution . . . outshines everything since the rise of Christianity and reduces the Renaissance and Reformation to the rank of mere episodes, mere internal displacements within the system of medieval Christendom. . . . It looms so large as the real origin both of the modern world and of the modern mentality that our customary periodisation of European history has become an anachronism and an encumbrance.

Herbert Butterfield

The manufacturing system as it exists in Great Britain, and the inconceivably rapid creation of immense towns under it, are without previous parallel in the history of the world.

Manchester Guardian
November 17, 1832

The material culture of the human race has changed more in the past two hundred years than it did in the preceding five thousand. In the eighteenth century people were living essentially in the same way as the ancient Egyptians and Mesopotamians. They were still using the same materials to erect their buildings, the same animals to transport themselves and their belongings, the same sails and oars to propel their ships, the same textiles to make their clothes, and the same candles and torches to provide light. But today metals and plastics supplement stone and wood; the railroad, the automobile, and the airplane have replaced the oxen, the horse, and the donkey; steam, diesel, and atomic power drive ships in place of wind and labor; many synthetic fabrics compete with the traditional cottons, woolens, and linens; and electricity has replaced the candle and become a source of power for many tasks at the flick of a switch.

The origins of this great transformation are to be found in the scientific and industrial revolutions, the outstanding contributions of Western civilization to human development. In the light of historical retrospect it appears that these two revolutions are of even greater significance than the agricultural revolution of Neolithic times. The agricultural revolution made civilization possible, but once this great step forward was taken, agriculture had no further contribution to make. Scientific technology, on the other hand, is cumulative by its very methodology. It contains within itself the possibilities of infinite advance. If we bear in minds its achievements in the past few centuries and its present accelerating pace of development, we may appreciate, if not comprehend, its staggering potential and significance. Scientific technology, furthermore, is universal. Based as it is on an objective methodology, it has obtained general assent to its propositions. It is the one product of Western civilization that non-Western peoples generally respect and seek. In fact, it was science and its related technology that made it possible for Europe to dominate the world in the nineteenth century. And today the formerly subject peoples are striving to redress the imbalance by learning the mysteries of the West's great and unique contribution to humanity.

It is easy to see why the scientific and industrial revolutions are of basic significance for the study of world history. This chapter will trace the unfolding of these revolutions from their beginnings in early modern times until World War I.

I. ROOTS OF THE SCIENTIFIC REVOLUTION

The roots of science may be traced to ancient Mesopotamia, Egypt, and China; to classical Greece; and to the medieval Moslem world. Yet the scientific revolution is a unique product of Western civilization. The reason seems to be that only in the West did science become part and parcel of general society. Or, to put it another way, only in the West were the philosopher-

scientist and the artisan united so that they stimulated each other. And it was this union of science and society, of scientist and artisan, that contributed greatly to the unprecedented blossoming of science in the Western world.

In all human societies the artisans developed certain skills in hunting, fishing, and farming and in working with wood, stone, metal, grasses, fibers, roots, and hides. Through their observations and experiments they gradually improved their techniques and sometimes reached very high levels, as in the case of the Eskimos. Yet the degree of progress achieved by all premodern societies was sharply restricted because the artisans were interested only in making pots or building houses or constructing boats; they did not bother with underlying chemical or mechanical principles. They did not ask about the relationship between causes and their effects. In short, the artisans by definition concerned themselves with technological know-*how* rather than with scientific know-*why*.

The philosophers and the artisans undoubtedly did work together at certain times to produce the elaborate calendars, the navigation aids, and the everyday rituals of antiquity. But the fact remains that until recent times the tendency was toward compartmentalization—toward the isolation of the thinker from the worker. The great achievement of the West was to bring the two together. This fusion of know-how and know-why gave science the grounding and the impetus that was to make it the dominant force that it is today.

Why did this epochal development take place in the West? One reason was the humanistic scholarship of the Renaissance. Scholars and artists had access not only to Plato and Aristotle but also to Euclid and Archimedes, who stimulated the study of physics and mathematics. Even more important was the impetus for the biological sciences. Medical students studied the complete works of Hippocrates and Galen, and naturalists those of Aristotle, Dioscorides, and Theophrastus. However, the fruits of human scholarship could not have brought about the scientific revolution without the favorable social atmosphere in western Europe. In this atmosphere the gulf between artisans and scholars was narrowed. Artisans were not so despised during the Renaissance as they had been in classical and medieval times. Respect was given to the practical arts of spinning, weaving, ceramics, glass making, and, most of all, the increasingly important arts of mining and metallurgy. All these crafts in Renaissance Europe were in the hands of free people rather than of slaves, as in classical times. And the people were not so far removed, socially and economically, from the ruling circles as were the artisans of the Middle Ages. The higher status of the Renaissance craftsman allowed him to strengthen his ties with the scholar. Each had an important contribution to make. The craftsman had the old techniques of antiquity, and added the new devices evolving during the Middle Ages. The scholars likewise provided the facts, speculations, and procedures of rediscovered antiquity and of medieval science. The two approaches fused slowly, but in the end they produced an explosive combination.

Closely connected with this union of the craftsperson and scholar was the corresponding union of labor and thought that was brought about by individual scholars or scientists. A strong prejudice existed in ancient times against combining creative learning and manual work. This prejudice, which presumably arose out of the ancient association of manual labor with slavery, persisted in medieval Europe even after slavery had almost disappeared. Medieval scholastic philosophers drew a distinction between the *liberal* and the *servile* arts, between work done with the mind alone and work that involved a change in matter. Poets, logicians and mathematicians, for example belonged to the first category, and sculptors, glaziers, and ironworkers to the second. This attitude held back progress, as was clearly evident in the field of medicine. Because the work of a physician did not change matter, it was regarded as "liberal," whereas that of a surgeon, by the same criterion, was considered "servile." Accordingly, experimentation was looked down on, and vivisection was deemed illegal and repulsive.

When William Harvey (1578–1657) made his great discovery concerning the movements of the heart and blood, he did so because he resolutely turned his back on this scorn for manual work. Instead, for decades he carried on painstaking experiments of all types. He cut the arteries and veins of living things, from large animals to tiny insects, observing and recording with care and patience the flow of the blood and the motions of the heart. He also utilized the new magnifying glass to observe wasps, hornets, and flies. Today this procedure seems sensible and obvious, but in Harvey's time it definitely was not. It took much courage for Harvey to use in his time what is considered today to be normal scientific method.

Science was stimulated also by the discoveries of explorers and the opening up of overseas lands. New plants, new animals, new stars, even new human beings and new human societies were found, and all these challenged traditional ideas and assumptions. Similarly, the growth of commerce and industry led to technological advances, which in turn stimulated, and were stimulated by, science. Oceanic commerce created an enormous demand for shipbuilding and navigation. A new class of mathematically trained craftsmen made compasses, maps, and instruments. Navigation schools were founded in Portugal, Spain, Holland, and France, and astronomy was studied seriously because of its obvious utilitarian value. Likewise, the needs of the mining industry brought about advances in power transmission and pumps. This was the beginning of a new interest in mechanical and hydraulic principles. In the same way, metallurgy was responsible for notable progress in chemistry. As mining operations expanded, new ores and even new metals, like bismuth, zinc, and cobalt, were discovered. Techniques for separating and handling these had to be found and refined by painful experience. But in doing so, a general theory of chemistry began to take form, involving oxidations and reductions, distillations and amalgamations. Finally, the new knowledge in all these fields was both stimulated and circulated by the universities and the printing press. The latter was especially important in promoting literacy and spreading new ideas.

These achievements gave the scientists, or philosophers, a self-assurance and a confidence that they were the signs of a new age. In 1662 Charles II of England granted a charter for the establishment of "The Royal Society of London for Promoting Natural Knowledge." Its members, seeing the advantage of cooperation between technicians and scientists, coordinated the efforts in every occupation throughout the country to gather data that might advance scientific knowledge.

All Places and Corners are now busy and warm about this Work: and we find many noble Rarities to be every Day given in [to the Society] not only by the Hands of learned and professed Philosophers; but from the Shops of Mechanicks; from the Voyages of Merchants; from the Ploughs of Husbandmen, from the Sports, The Fishponds, The Parks, The Gardens of Gentlemen. . . .[1]

At first, science received much more from the mine and the workshop than science itself could give back. During this early period science was not an integral part of economic life and was used sparingly and sporadically. This was true even in the early phase of the industrial revolution in the late eighteenth and early nineteenth centuries. But by the end of the nineteenth century the situation changed. Science no longer was in a subordinate position: It had begun to transform old industries and even to create entirely new ones.

II.   COURSE OF THE SCIENTIFIC REVOLUTION

As we might expect, the first major advance of modern science occurred in the field of astronomy, which was closely related to geography and to navigation. This advance was achieved in the sixteenth and seventeenth centuries, and the great names were Minolaj Kopernik, or Copernicus (1473–1543); Galileo Galilei (1564–1642); and Isaac Newton (1642–1727). Copernicus took up the idea of some ancient philosophers that the sun, rather than the earth, was the center of the universe, and the he demonstrated that this provided a simpler explanation of the movement of the heavenly bodies than did the traditional Ptolemaic system. Galileo supported Copernicus empirically by using the recently discovered telescope to see what actually was in the heavens. "By the aid of a telescope," he reported, "anyone may behold that . . . the Galaxy is nothing else but a mass of innumerable stars planted together in clusters. Upon whatever part of it you direct

the telescope straightaway a vast crowd of stars presents itself to view. . . ."[2]

By far the most outstanding figure of early science was Newton, a towering genius comparable to Euclid and Einstein. In addition to his pioneering work in optics, hydrodynamics, and mathematics, he discovered the law of gravitation: "Every particle of matter in the universe attracts every other particle with a force varying inversely as the square of the distance between them and directly proportional to the product of their masses."

Here was a sensational and revolutionary explanation that tore the veils from the heavens. Newton had discovered a fundamental, cosmic law that could be proved mathematically and applied to all matter, from the minutest object to the universe at large. Nature indeed appeared to be a gigantic mechanical object operating according to certain natural laws that could be found by observation, experiment, and calculation. All branches of human knowledge could be broken down into a few, simple, uniform laws that rational persons could discover. People began to apply the analytical method of Newtonian physics to the entire field of thought and knowledge, to human society as well as to the physical universe.

As the industrial revolution got under way in the late eighteenth century, it affected, and in return was affected by, the scientific revolution. An example is the development of the steam engine. It provided sorely needed power to operate machines and locomotives and, at the outset, to pump water out of mines. James Watt combined technical ingenuity and scientific knowledge to improve the steam engines to a reasonable level of efficiency. In 1769 Watt began to use a separate condensing cylinder, and soon after he converted linear into rotary motion by means of a crankshaft. If the relatively unlimited power of the steam engine had not been available, the industrial revolution might well have petered out. It might have amounted to a mere speed-up in textile manufacturing, as happened in China, where analogous technical advances had been made centuries earlier.

The science that made the most progress during the first half of the nineteenth century was chemistry—partly because of its close association with the textile industry, which experienced such rapid growth during those decades. The Newton of chemistry was Antoine Lavoisier (1743–1794), whose law of the conservation of matter is comparable to the law of gravitation: ". . . although matter may alter its state in a series of chemical actions, it does not change in amount; the quantity of matter is the same at the end as at the beginning of every operation, and can be traced by its weight." Lavoisier's successors in the nineteenth century made discovery after discovery that had important practical applications: Justus von Liebeg for chemical fertilizers; W. H. Perkin for synthetic dyes; and Louis Pasteur for his germ theory of disease, which led to the adoption of sanitary precautions and so brought under control old scourges like typhoid, diphtheria, cholera, and malaria.

As Newton dominated seventeenth-century science with his discovery of the laws governing the bodies of the universe, so Darwin dominated nineteenth-century science, for he discovered the laws governing the *evolution* of humanity itself. His doctrine of evolution holds that animal and vegetable species in their present diverse forms are not the fixed and unchangeable results of separate special acts of creation. They are different. They are capable of change. And they are the natural outcomes of a common original source. Darwin believed that the chief manner in which variation took place was by *natural selection.* He defined this process as follows:

As many more individuals of each species are born than can possibly survive, and as, consequently, there is a frequently recurring struggle for existence, it follows that any being, if it vary however slightly in any manner profitable to itself, under the complex and sometimes varying conditions of life, will have a better chance of surviving, and thus be naturally selected. From the strong principle of inheritance, any selected variety will tend to propagate its new and modified form.[3]

It may be hard to conceive of all the variety in nature as being the product of such an apparently slow process of change as that afforded by natural selection. Yet statistical calculations show that even if a mutation resulted in only a 1 percent better chance of survival, the change would establish itself in half the individuals of a species in a hundred generations. In other words, if 101 individuals with a particular mutation survived for every 100 without it, it would spread through the species in what is, biologically speaking, a short time. The details of Darwin's theories have been modified by later research, but virtually all scientists now accept the essentials of the doctrine. There was bitter opposition in certain quarters, particularly among the clergy. This was understandable, because Darwin was denying the act of divine creation. Just as the Copernican system of astronomy had deposed the earth from its central place in the universe, so Darwinism seemed to dethrone human beings from their central place in the history of the earth.

Despite the hostile reception in religious and other circles, Darwinism had profound repercussions on Western society. Its emphasis on survival of the fittest and struggle for survival fitted in admirably with the temper of the times. In politics, during this period, Bismarck was unifying Germany by blood and iron. Nationalistic admirers in all countries believed that Darwinism offered them support and justification. They held that in politics, as in nature, the strongest are victorious and that warlike qualities decide who will win in the international "struggle for survival." In economic life this was the period of free enterprise and rugged individualism. The upper and middle classes, comfortable and contented, stoutly opposed any state intervention for the promotion of greater social equality. They argued that they deserved their blessings and prosperity because they had proven themselves "fitter" than the shiftless poor. Furthermore, the absorption of smaller concerns by big business was a part of the "struggle for survival." The late nineteenth century was also the golden age of colonial expansion, and Darwinism was used to justify *imperialism.* The argument was that colonies were necessary for the prosperity and survival of a great power. Moreover, native peoples, judged in terms of worldly success, were weak, inferior, and in need of the protection and guidance of the superior and stronger Europeans.

The application of Darwin's theories to the social scene is known as Social Darwinism. Darwin himself had never dreamed, let alone intended, that his findings would be exploited in this fashion. But the fact remains that they were, for the simple reason that they seemed to offer scientific support for the materialism that was spreading over Europe at this time. Darwinism, in short, fitted in conveniently with Kipling's dictum:

That they should take who have the power
And they should keep who can.

III. SIGNIFICANCE OF THE SCIENTIFIC REVOLUTION

As the nineteenth century passed, science became an increasingly important part of Western society. At the beginning of the century science was still on the periphery of economic and social life. But by the end it was making basic contributions to the old, established industries; it was creating entirely new industries; and it was profoundly affecting the way of thinking as well as the way of living of Western society. Furthermore, the metamorphosis wrought by the scientific revolution affected the entire world in many ways, direct and indirect. It made Europe's domination of the globe technologically possible, and it determined to a large extent the nature and effects of this domination. Also it provided the basis for the West's intellectual predominance in the nineteenth century. European art or religion or philosophy did not affect non-Western peoples very much because they had made comparable contributions in these fields. But there was no such equality in science and technology. Only the West had mastered the secrets of nature and had exploited them for material advancement. This was an undeniable and persuasive fact. Non-Westerners no longer looked down on Europeans as uncouth barbarians who happened to have a certain superiority in sailing ships and firearms. Reluctantly they recognized the importance of Europe's scientific revolution. And today the primary aim of former colonial peoples is to experience this unique revolution themselves. For all these reasons, the distinguished British historian Herbert Butterfield concludes that the scientific revolution:

. . . proved to be so capable of growth, and so many-sided in its operations, that it consciously assumed a directing role from the very first, and, so to speak, be-

gan to take control of the other factors—just as Christianity in the middle ages had come to preside over everything else, percolating into every corner of life and thought. And when we speak of Western civilization being carried to an oriental country, like Japan in recent generations, we do not mean Graeco-Roman philosophy and humanist ideals, we do not mean the Christianising of Japan, we mean the science, the modes of thought and all that apparatus of civilization which were beginning to change the face of the West in the latter half of the seventeenth century.[4]

IV. ROOTS OF THE INDUSTRIAL REVOLUTION

The term *industrial revolution* is frequently challenged because it is used to describe, not a rapid overnight change, but a "revolution" that began before the eighteenth century and, for all practical purposes, has continued to the present day. Obviously, then, this was not a revolution in the sense of a spectacular change that began and ended suddenly.

Yet the fact remains that during the 1780s a breakthrough did occur in productivity, or as economists now put it, there was "a takeoff into self-sustained growth." More specifically, a mechanized factory system was created that produced goods in vast quantities and at rapidly diminishing costs, so it was no longer dependent on existing demand but could create its own demand. An example of this now common but hitherto unknown phenomenon is the automobile industry. It was not the demand for automobiles that existed at the turn of the century that created the giant automobile industry of today. Rather, the capacity to build the cheap Model-T Ford, in large quantities, stimulated the modern mass demand for them.

The first question that arises in considering the industrial revolution has to do with its timing. Why did it occur in the late eighteenth century rather than a hundred or a thousand years earlier? The answer in large part lies in the remarkable economic growth of Europe following the great expansion overseas. This growth was so pronounced that it is commonly referred to as the "commercial revolution."

One of the first innovations of the industrial revoluton—the assembly line used to build the Model-T Ford.

The commercial revolution was characterized in the first place by a change in the articles of world trade. Before the sixteenth century the most important items were spices traded from East to West and bullion traded in the opposite direction. But gradually new overseas products became staples of consumption in Europe and grew in commercial importance. These included new beverages (cocoa, tea, and coffee), new dyes (indigo, cochineal, and brazilwood), new flavors (allspice and vanilla), and new foodstuffs (guinea fowl and turkeys and a greatly increased supply of Newfoundland cod). The other main feature of the commercial revolution was the marked increase in the volume of trade. Between 1715 and 1787 French imports from overseas territories increased tenfold, and exports increased between seven- and eightfold. England's trade grew almost as spectacularly—in the period from 1698 to 1775 both imports and exports rose between 500 and 600 percent. Europe's general trade was growing, but colonial trade was accounting for a larger and larger portion of it. In 1698, for example, about 15 percent of England's seaborne trade was with its colonies, but by 1775 this figure had risen to 33 percent. Furthermore, the reexport of colonial goods was responsible for much of the increase of France's and England's trade with other European countries.

The commercial revolution contributed to the industrial revolution in several important respects. First, it provided large and expanding markets for European industries, particularly those producing textiles; firearms; hardware; ships; and ship accessories, including lumber, rope, sails, anchors, pulleys, and nautical instruments. To meet the demands of these new markets, industries had to improve their organization and technology. The commercial revolution also contributed the large amounts of capital necessary to finance the construction of factories and machines for the industrial revolution. The capital, in the form of profits, poured into Europe from all parts of the world—from the fur trade in Siberia and North America; from the silver mines of Mexico and Peru; from the African slave trade; and from the profits of the several East India companies, West India companies, Levant companies, Africa companies, and assorted others, including the Muscovy Company, the Hudson Bay Company, and the various land settlement companies in the Americas. It is estimated that the amount of capital extracted from India and from the West Indian sugar colonies during the eighteenth century was about equal to the amount of capital invested in British industry in 1800.

Profitable commercial enterprise, together with the accompanying technological growth and institutional change, explains why the industrial revolution reached the "takeoff" stage in the late eighteenth century. This raises the question of why the "takeoff" occurred first in England. One important advantage Britain enjoyed is that it had taken an early lead in the basic coal and iron industries. Because its forest reserves were being depleted, Britain early began using coal for fuel and for smelting iron. By the time of the French Revolution (1789), Britain was producing about 10 millions tons of coal per year, whereas France was producing 700,000 tons. England also pioneered in the development of the blast furnace, which, in contrast to the old forges, could mass-produce iron. In 1780 Britain's iron output had been a third that of France; by 1840, it was three times more. All this meant that Britain was pushing ahead in the production of goods for mass consumption. And there was a large and steady demand for these goods. France, on the other hand, specialized more in luxury commodities of limited and fluctuating demand.

England also had more fluid capital available for the financing of the industrial revolution. More profits from commerce poured into England than into any other country. English court and military expenditures were less than the French costs, so that English taxation was lighter and Eng-

lish government finances were in better condition. Furthermore, banking developed earlier and more efficiently in England, providing pooled funds for individual and corporate enterprise.

Noteworthy also is the impressive concentration of managerial talent in England. This is to be explained in part by the outstanding contributions of Nonconformists like the Darbys in the iron industry, Cookworthy in pottery, the Brights in cotton milling and in politics, and Dalton and Eddington in science. Freedom from convention and stress on personal responsibility produced a disproportionate quota of experiments and inventors among the Nonconformists, and their frugality led them to plow profits back into business rather than to squander them in luxurious living. The influence of the Nonconformists in England was enhanced by the influx of coreligionists from the continent. With the revocation of the Edict of Nantes in 1685, for example, France lost considerable managerial talent to England, especially in the textile industry.

Britain also had the advantage of a mobile and plentiful supply of labor. The great supply was made available by the earlier disintegration of the guilds and by the enclosing of the traditional strips of farmland. The end of the guilds, with their manifold restrictions, made it easier to introduce the putting-out system and to equip the factories with power machinery. The land *enclosures* began in the 1500s and continued for three centuries, reaching their height in the late eighteenth and early nineteenth centuries. The yeomen frequently were forced to sell out, because the enclosing of common and of waste lands left them no land for grazing and for fuel. The earlier enclosures were caused by the rising price of wool, so that the land was used mostly for grazing. In the later period the need to grow foodstuffs for the burgeoning cities was more important, so the enclosed land was cultivated according to the most up-to-date and efficient methods. Crop rotation replaced the wasteful old system of allowing fields to like fallow. Superior seeds were developed and cattle were improved by scientific breeding. Some agricultural machinery, such as a horse-driven hoeing machine and an automatic drill for planting seeds, was developed.

Between 1714 and 1820, over 6 million acres of land were enclosed in England. This meant serious dislocation and distress. The poor peasants lost part or all of their land and were forced to become tenants or day laborers or else seek employment in the cities. Socially minded people were appalled by this wholesale uprooting of England's yeomanry and spoke up against it. The process of enclosing the land was unsettling and unpleasant, but as far as the industrial revolution was concerned, it fulfilled two essential functions—it provided labor for the factories and food for the cities. For this reason the enclosures may be considered a prerequisite to England's industrial supremacy in the nineteenth century. Enclosures did occur in certain other European countries, but to a much lesser extent. In France, for example, the French Revolution provided the peasants with more land, and thereby increased their attachment to their birthplaces and their unwillingness to pack up and move.

V.   COURSE OF THE INDUSTRIAL REVOLUTION

Inventors seldom invent except under the stimulus of strong demand. Many of the principles that the new inventions of the industrial revolution were based on were known long before the eight-

eenth century but were not applied to industry because the incentive was lacking. This was the case, for example, with steam power. Although known in Hellenistic Egypt, it was used merely to open and close temple doors. In England, however, a new source of power was urgently needed to pump water out of mines and to turn the wheels of the new machinery. This need stimulated a series of inventions and improvements that finally resulted in the development of a commercially practical steam engine.

The pattern of demand leading to invention is plainly evident in the course of the industrial revolution. Inventions in one field created an imbalance and stimulated counterinventions in other fields to redress the balance. For example, the cotton industry was the first to be mechanized because cotton goods, which were originally imported from India, had become exceedingly popular with the British public. In fact, cotton was used so widely that the old and powerful woolen interests secured the passage of a law in 1700 prohibiting the importation of cotton cloth or goods. The law, however, did not ban the manufacture of cotton cloth. This created a unique opportunity for local industry, and enterprising middlemen soon were exploiting it. The problem was how to speed up the spinning

The spinning jenny.

and weaving enough to meet the demand of the large and protected home market. Prizes were offered for inventions that would increase output, and by 1830 a series of such inventions had completely mechanized the cotton industry.

Outstanding were John Kay's flying shuttle (1733), which speeded up weaving; Richard Arkwright's water frame (1769), which spun fine, strong yarn between rollers; James Hargreave's spinning jenny (1770), on which one person could spin eight, then sixteen, then finally over a hundred threads of yarn at once; and Samuel Crompton's spinning mule (1779) so called because it combined features of the water frame and the jenny. All these new spinning machines soon were producing far more thread than could be handled by the weavers. A clergyman, Edmund Cartwright, sought to redress the balance by patenting in 1785 a power loom operated first by horses and after 1789 by steam. At first the contraption was clumsy and commercially

unprofitable, but after two decades of improvement the most serious defects were remedied. By the 1820's the power loom had largely supplanted the handweavers in the cotton industry.

Just as inventions in spinning led to related inventions in weaving, so inventions in one industry encouraged people to invent machinery so that other industries could keep up. For example, the new cotton machines created a demand for more plentiful and reliable power than that provided by the traditional waterwheels and horses. The response was James Watt's multiple improvements on a primitive engine built by Thomas Newcomen about 1702. By 1800 some 500 Watt engines were in service, 38 percent being engaged in pumping water and the remainder in supplying rotary power for textile mills, iron furnaces, flour mills, and other industries.

The historical significance of the steam engine can scarcely be exaggerated. It provided a

English power-loom weaving in the early nineteeth century.

means for harnessing and utilizing heat energy to furnish driving power for machines. Thus, it ended the age-old dependence on animal, wind, and water power. A vast new source of energy now was available. Before long it was possible to tap the fossil fuels locked up in the earth—namely, oil and gas. In this way began the trend that has led to the enormous energy sources available to modern-day industrialized nations. For example, in 1975 western Europe had 11.5 times and North America had 29 times as much energy available per capita as did less industrialized Asia. The meaning of these figures is obvious in a world where economic and military strength depends directly on the energy resources available. Indeed, it may be said that Europe's domination of the globe in the nineteenth century was based more on the steam engine than on any other single device or force.

The new cotton machines and steam engines required an increased supply of iron, steel, and coal. The need was met by a series of improvements in mining and metallurgy—Abraham Darby's substitution of coal for coke in smelting iron ore, Henry Cort's "puddling" process for removing impurities in smelted iron, and the use of the Watt steam engine for operating the bellows and hammers and for rolling and splitting. As a result of these various developments, by 1800 Britain was producing more coal and iron than the rest of the world combined. Britain's coal output rose from 6 million tons in 1770 to 12 million tons in 1800 to 57 million tons in 1861. Likewise, its iron output increased from 50,000 tons in 1770 to 130,000 tons in 1800 to 3,800,000 tons in 1861. Iron had become plentiful and cheap enough to be used for general construction, and human society had entered the Age of Iron as well as the Age of Steam.

The expansion of the textile, mining, and metallurgical industries created a need for improved transportation facilities to move the bulky shipments of coal and ore. This started a canal-building boom that gave England 2,500 miles of canals by 1830. The canal era was paralleled by a great period of road building. After 1750 a group of road engineers—John Metcalf, Thomas Telford, and John McAdam—developed methods of building hard-surfaced roads that would bear traffic all through the year. Travel by coach increased from four miles an hour to six,

Cotton weaving in India in the early nineteenth century.

eight, or even ten. After 1830 both roads and waterways were challenged by the railroad. The chief figure here was a mining engineer, George Stephenson. In 1830 his steam engine *Rocket* pulled a train thirty-one miles from Liverpool to Manchester at an average speed of fourteen miles per hour. Within a few years the railroad dominated long-distance traffic, for it could move passengers and freight faster and more cheaply than was possible by road or canal. By 1838 Britain had 500 miles of railroad; by 1850, 6,600; and by 1870, 15,500.

The steam engine was also applied to water transportation. The pioneer was Robert Fulton, who in 1807 launched his *Clermont* on America's Hudson River. By 1833 the *Royal William* steamed from Nova Scotia to England, and five years later the *Sirius* and the *Great Western* crossed the Atlantic in the opposite direction. They took sixteen and one-half and thirteen and one-half days, respectively, or about half the time required

A RIDE ON AN EARLY RAILWAY

*The world's first railway was opened in 1825 and the second in 1830
between Liverpool and Manchester. A description of the second railway has been
left by the actress Frances (Fanny) Kimble, who rode on it as a young girl
in the year of its opening.* *

My father knew several of the gentlemen most deeply interested in the undertaking [the Liverpool-Manchester railway], and Stephenson having proposed a trial trip as far as the fifteen mile viaduct, they, with infinite kindness, invited him and permitted me to accompany them; allowing me, moreover, the place which I felt to be one of supreme honour, by the side of Stephenson. . . . He was a rather stern-featured man, with a dark and deeply marked countenance. . . .

We were introduced to the little engine which was to drag us along the rails. . . . This snorting little animal, which I felt rather inclined to pat, was then harnessed to our carriage, and, Mr. Stephenson having taken me on the bench of the engine with him, we started at about ten miles an hour. The steam-horse being ill-adapted for going up and down hill, the road was kept at a certain level, and appeared sometimes to sink below the surface of the earth, and sometimes to rise above it. Almost at starting it was cut through the solid rock, which formed a wall on either side of it, about sixty feet high. You can't imagine how strange it seemed to be journeying on thus, without any visible cause of progress other than the magical machine, with its flying white breath and rhythmical, unvarying pace. . . . We were to go only fifteen miles, that distance being sufficient to show the speed of the engine. . . . After proceeding through this rocky defile, we presently found ourselves raised upon embankments ten or twelve feet high; we then came to a moss, or swamp, of considerable extent, on which no human foot could tread without sinking, and yet it bore the road which bore us. . . .

We had now come fifteen miles, and stopped where the road traversed a wide and deep valley. Stephenson made me alight and led me down to the bottom of this ravine, over which, in order to keep his road level, he has thrown a magnificent viaduct of nine arches, the middle one of which is seventy feet high, through which we saw the whole of this beautiful little valley. . . . We then rejoined the rest of the party, and the engine having received its supply of water, the carriage was placed behind it, for it cannot turn, and was set off at its utmost speed, thirty-five miles an hour, swifter than a bird flies (for they tried the experiment with a snipe). You cannot conceive what that sensation of cutting the air was; the motion is as smooth as possible, too.

* F. A. Kimble, *Record of a Girlhood,* 3rd ed. (Richard Bentley, 1879), pp. 158–160.

by the fastest sailships. In 1840 Samuel Cunard established a regular transatlantic service, announcing beforehand dates of arrival and departure.

The industrial revolution was a revolution in communication as well as transportation. Hitherto a message could be sent to a distant place only by wagon, postrider, or boat. But in the middle of the nineteenth century the electric telegraph was invented. In 1866 a transatlantic cable was laid, establishing instant communication between the old and new worlds.

The industrial revolution did not end with the rise of railroads or transatlantic steamships or

THE WONDER of the AGE ! !

INSTANTANEOUS COMMUNICATION.

Under the special Patronage of Her Majesty & H.R.H. Prince Albert.

THE GALVANIC AND ELECTRO-MAGNETIC

TELEGRAPHS,

ON THE

GT. WESTERN RAILWAY.

May be seen in constant operation, daily, (Sundays excepted) from 9 till 8, at the

TELEGRAPH OFFICE, LONDON TERMINUS, PADDINGTON
AND TELEGRAPH COTTAGE, SLOUGH STATION.

An Exhibition admitted by its numerous Visitors to be the most interesting and ATTRACTIVE of any in this great Metropolis. In the list of visitors are the illustrious names of several of the Crowned Heads of Europe, and nearly the whole of the Nobility of England.

"This Exhibition, which has so much excited Public attention of late, is well worthy a visit from all who love to see the wonders of science."—MORNING POST.

The Electric Telegraph is unlimited in the nature and extent of its communications; by its extraordinary agency a person in London could converse with another at New York, or at any other place however distant, as easily and nearly as rapidly as if both parties were in the same room. Questions proposed by Visitors will be asked by means of this Apparatus, and answers thereto will instantaneously be returned by a person 20 Miles off, who will also, at their request, ring a bell or fire a cannon, in an incredibly short space of time, after the signal for his doing so has been given.

The Electric Fluid travels at the rate of 280,000 Miles per Second.

By its powerful agency Murderers have been apprehended, (as in the late case of Tawell,)—Thieves detected; and lastly, which is of no little importance, the timely assistance of Medical aid has been procured in cases which otherwise would have proved fatal.

The great national importance of this wonderful invention is so well known that any further allusion here to its merits would be superfluous.

N.B. Despatches sent to and fro with the most confiding secrecy. Messengers in constant attendance, so that communications received by Telegraph, would be forwarded, if required, to any part of London, Windsor, Eton, &c.

ADMISSION ONE SHILLING.

T HOME, *Licensee.*

Nurton, Printer. 48, Church St. Portman Market.

An English handbill, 1845.

telegraphic communication. It continues to the present day, with certain stages discernible in its evolution. The first stage lasted to the mid-nineteenth century and included, as noted, the mechanization of the cotton industry, of mining, and of metallurgy and the development of the steam engine and its application to industry and transportation. The second stage lasted through the latter part of the nineteenth century and was characterized by the more direct application of science to industry and by the development of mass-production techniques. Whereas science at the outset had little effect on industry, it gradually became an integral part of all large industrial enterprises. A spectacular example of the practical applications of industrial research laboratories are the many coal derivatives that have been developed. Coal not only yielded coke and a valuable gas that was used for illumination. It also gave a liquid, or coal tar. Chemists discovered a veritable treasure trove in coal tar: hundreds of dyes, aspirin, saccharin, wintergreen, disinfectants, laxatives, perfumes, photographic chemicals, high explosives, and essence of orange blossom.

Whereas Germany led the world in the nineteenth century in applying science to industry, the United States was the pioneer in developing mass-production techniques. These were of two varieties. One was the making of standard interchangeable parts and the assembling of these parts into the completed unit with a minimum of handicraft labor. The classic example is Henry Ford's endless conveyor belt. Car parts traveled along the belt and were assembled into the Model T by workers who were transformed into cogs of the machines. The other production technique was the manipulation of large masses of material by means of advanced mechanical devices. The prime example of this method is the steel industry, whose productivity was described in justifiably boastful terms by the industrial tycoon Andrew Carnegie:

Two pounds of ironstone mined upon Lake Superior and transported nine-hundred miles to Pittsburgh; one pound and one-half of coal, mined and manufactured into coke, and transported to Pittsburgh; one-half pound of lime, mined and transported to Pittsburgh; a small amount of manganese ore mined in Virginia and brought to Pittsburgh—and these four pounds of materials manufactured into one pound of steel, for which the consumer pays one cent.[5]

VI. EFFECT OF THE INDUSTRIAL REVOLUTION ON EUROPE

Diffusion of Industrialization

During the nineteenth century the industrial revolution spread gradually from England to the continent of Europe. The pattern of diffusion depended on various factors, such as supply of natural resources and the existence of a free and mobile working population, unencumbered by guild restrictions or feudal obligations. Belgium was the first country to be industrialized, so that by 1870 the majority of its population lived in cities and were directly dependent on trade or industry. After Belgium followed France, Germany, Austria-Hungary, Italy, and Russia. Meanwhile, non-European countries were being industrialized—first the United States and then the British dominions and Japan. Latecomers enjoyed the advantage of new and more efficient factories, so that Britain lost its original status as the "industrial workshop of the world."

T.28.1, listing the powers in the order of their industrial production, demonstrates the changes that have occurred in the world's industrial balance.

TABLE 28.1   Changing World Industrial Balance, 1860–1980

1860	1880	1900	1980
Great Britain	United States	United States	United States
France	Great Britain	Germany	Japan
United States	Germany	Great Britain	Soviet Union
Germany	France	France	Germany

Increase of Population

Another effect of the industrial revolution on Europe was further increase in population, which had started earlier with the increased productivity in agriculture. In spite of the emigration overseas of millions of Europeans during the nineteenth century, the population of the continent in 1914 was well over three times that of 1750. The reasons for this population explosion were, first, economic and, second, medical. Most mortality in earlier centuries had been due to infectious diseases, and the incidence of infection had depended mostly on the level of living standards. With the increased cultivation of the potato during the nineteenth century, nutritional levels rose, natural resistance to disease rose correspondingly, and mortality rates dropped correspondingly. Famine in most parts of Europe west of Russia became a memory of the past. Even if

crops failed, the new railway networks ensured adequate supplies from the outside. At the same time the industrial revolution made possible improved sewage systems and safer water supplies, which further lowered mortality rates. Thus mortality statistics reveal that deaths from major infectious diseases declined about thirty years before the major chemotherapy discoveries.

Then the application of new medical science through vaccination and segregation of infected persons further reduced death rates in western Europe. By 1914 they had fallen from at least thirty per 1,000 persons in 1800 to about fifteen in 1914. Thus Europe's population climbed steeply from 140 million in 1750 to 188 million in 1800, 266 million in 1850, 401 million in 1900, and 463 million in 1914. This rate of increase in Europe was so much higher than in the other regions of the world that it altered the global population balance (see T.28.2).

TABLE 28.2   Estimated Population of the World*

	1650	1750	1850	1900	1950	1990
Millions						
Europe	100	140	266	401	572	787
United States and Canada	1	1	26	81	166	276
Latin America	12	11	33	63	164	448
Oceania	2	2	2	6	13	27
Africa	100	95	95	120	219	642
Asia	330	479	749	937	1,368	3,113
TOTAL	545	728	1,171	1,608	2,502	5,293
Percentages						
Europe	18.3	19.2	22.7	24.9	23.0	15.0
United States and Canada	0.2	0.1	2.3	5.1	6.7	5.0
Latin America	2.2	1.5	2.8	3.9	6.3	8.5
Oceania	0.4	0.3	0.2	0.4	0.5	0.5
Africa	18.3	13.1	8.1	7.4	8.8	12.0
Asia	60.6	65.8	63.9	58.3	54.7	59.0
TOTAL	100.0	100.0	100.0	100.0	100.0	100.0

* These figures show that Europe's percentage of the total world population rose from 18.3 percent in 1650 to a high of 24.9 percent in 1900 to 18 percent in 1977. But by the twentieth century most of the population of the United States, Canada, and Oceania was of European origin, and at least half the population of Latin America was also. Accordingly, it is more meaningful to say that through the twentieth century the percentage of Europeans and people of European origin had risen to about one-third of the world total. Adapted from A. M. Carr-Saunders, *World Population* (Clarendon, 1936), p. 42, and *United Nations Demographic Yearbooks*.

Urbanization

The industrial revolution led also to an unprecedented urbanization of world society. The size of cities traditionally had depended on the amount of food that the surrounding land could produce. Thus the most populous cities were in the valleys and flood plains, like the Nile, the Fertile Crescent, the Indus, and the Hwang Ho. With the industrial revolution and the factory system, a mass influx flooded the new centers of industry. The large new urban populations could be fed because food supplies were available from all parts of the world. Technological and medical advances eliminated the plagues that previously had decimated cities and even made city living relatively endurable and pleasant. The most important of these advances were plenty of pure water, the perfecting of centralized sewerage and waste-disposal systems, insurance of an adequate food supply, and prevention and control of contagious diseases. Cities all over the world grew at such a rate that by 1930 they included 415 million people, or one-fifth of the human race. This represents one of the great social transformations in human history, for city dwelling meant an entirely new way of life. By 1914 many Western countries, such as Britain, Belgium, Germany, and the United States, had a substantial majority of their people living in cities.

✳Increase of Wealth

The industrial revolution, with its efficient exploitation of human and natural resources on a worldwide scale, brought about an increase in productivity that is without precedent in all history. Great Britain, which was the first affected, increased its capital from 500 million pounds sterling in 1750 to 1,500 million pounds in 1800, to 2,500 million pounds in 1833, and to 6,000 million in 1865. In the latter part of the nineteenth century the entire world felt the impact of the increasing productivity. The wool of New Zealand, the wheat of Canada, the rice of Burma, the rubber of Malaya, the jute of Bengal, and the humming factories of western Europe and the eastern United States—all these resources were enmeshed in a dynamic and constantly expanding global economy. The figures in T.28.3 indicate the rate at which industrial production rose, both in Europe and throughout the world, in the second half of the nineteenth century.

There has been much difference of opinion among authorities in recent years concerning the distribution of the wealth created during the industrial revolution. One group holds that all classes benefited to a greater or lesser extent, whereas the other maintains that a few made huge fortunes while the many were ruthlessly exploited and suffered declining standards of living.

There is no doubt that there was much exploitation and social disruption in the early days of industrialization. The tenant farmers were dispossessed, and the weavers and other craftspeople were wiped out by the irresistible competition of the new machine-made goods. These people, and others like them, faced the strain of moving to the city, finding employment, and adjusting to an unfamiliar environment and to strange ways of living and working. They were completely depen-

TABLE 28.3	Rise of Industrial Production (1913 = 100)*						
	1860	1870	1880	1890	1900	1910	1913
Germany	14	18	25	40	65	89	100
Great Britain	34	44	53	62	79	85	100
France	26	34	43	56	66	89	100
Russia	8	13	17	27	61	84	100
Italy	—	17	23	40	56	99	100
United States	8	11	17	39	54	89	100
World	14	19	26	43	60	88	100

* *F. Sternberg,* Capitalism and Socialism on Trial *(Day, 1951), p. 21.*

dent on their employers, for they had no land, no cottage, no tools, and no capital. In short, they had become mere wage earners and had nothing to offer but their labor.

When they found employment, they discovered that the hours were long. A sixteen-hour day was by no means rare. When the workers finally won the right to divide their work into two twelve-hour shifts, they looked on the change as a blessing. The long hours alone would have been tolerable, since they were no worse than the hours worked at home under the putting-out system. But the real hardship came in getting used to the discipline and monotony of tending machines in a factory. The workers came and went at the sound of the factory whistle. They had to keep pace with the movements of the machine, always under the strict supervision of an ever-present overseer. The work was monotonous—pulling a lever, brushing away dirt, mending broken threads. Employers naturally regarded their wage bill as an expense that should be kept as low as possible. Consequently, many of them, particularly in the textile industries, preferred to employ women and children, who were willing to accept lower wages and were more willing to follow orders. Exploitation of female and child labor reached such proportions that a number of parliamentary committees who conducted investigations found shocking conditions.

There is, however, another side to this question of the effect of the industrial revolution on the working class. In the first place, the parliamentary committees investigated only industries such as mining and textiles where conditions were worst. The shocking testimony of the witnesses who appeared before the committees were based on facts, but those facts were by no means applicable to English industry as a whole. Furthermore, the plight of the worker in early nineteenth-century England must be viewed in the light of contemporary rather than present-day standards. The fact is that the villages from which these workers came were in many respects as squalid as the cities. In the typical rural dwelling, rats and vermin infested the straw bedding, and the wind whistled through the thinly thatched roof and the poorly plastered walls. Day laborers in the countryside were so poorly paid that they kept crowding into the new industrial cities. Thousands of Irish also crossed over to fill the jobs opening up in the new factories. Furthermore, the population of England soared during these early days of the industrial revolution, a fact that does not jibe with the usual picture of the unrelieved and debilitating misery. It is quite possible that most of the workers in these early factories enjoyed higher real incomes than their forebears.

Although we cannot be sure of the effect of the industrial revolution on working-class living standards in the late eighteenth and early nineteenth centuries, we are quite certain that the standards rose substantially in the second half of the nineteenth century. The great increases in productivity together with the profits made from the huge overseas investments gradually benefited even the lower classes in western Europe. After the "Hungry Forties," when there was much suffering from unemployment, the workers of western Europe enjoyed general prosperity and rising living standards until World War I. The figures in T.28.4 show that between 1850 and 1913, *real* wages in Britain and France almost doubled.

TABLE 28.4	Rise in Real Wages, 1850–1913 (1913 = 100)*	
	Great Britain	**France**
1850	57	59.5
1860	64	63
1870	70	69
1880	81	74.5
1890	90	89.5
1900	100	100

* *F. Sternberg,* Capitalism and Socialism on Trial *(Day, 1951), p. 27.*

Cotton factories in Manchester.

New Consumerism

The increased income for the many at the bottom as well as for the few at the top made possible the emergence in England for the first time in human history of a consumer society. The desire to consume was not unique, for Shakespeare had noted in *Much Ado About Nothing* that "fashion wears out more apparel than the man." So what was unique in eighteenth-century England was not the desire to consume but the ability of many to do so. In all past human societies the income of the masses had been so meager that half to three-quarters of it was needed for food alone. The little that was left had to be spent on other necessities, so nothing remained for passing whims or fashions. This explains why fashions did not come and go with each season as they do today. It explains why for centuries the kimono remained unchanged in Japan, the dhoti in India, the pyjama in some Moslem countries, and the poncho in Latin America.

Eighteenth-century England was the first country to break with this traditional pattern. The break occurred because of the increase in national income, thanks to the agricultural revolution after the enclosures, the profits flowing in from overseas enterprises, and the productivity jump with the industrial revolution. Some of the swollen national income trickled down to the masses, so that a domestic market developed that was much greater than any in the past, when only the tiny elite at the top had any purchasing power.

Businesspersons soon developed techniques for tapping the rich, new domestic market. As early as the eighteenth century they were using the full range of what are now considered modern selling techniques, including market research, credit, discount schemes, handbills, catalogues, newspaper and magazine advertising, and money-back-if-not-satisfied sale offers. A pioneer in this mass merchandising was the potter Josiah Wedgwood, who states candidly that "Fashion is superior to merit." Accordingly he conducted sales campaigns that made his pottery the best known and most desired in the world, even though it often was neither the best nor the cheapest.

A student of this new consumerism has concluded that it "brought goods within the reach of classes never before offered such opportunities for buying, and made available a greater range of goods than ever before . . . the manipulation of social emulation made men pursue 'luxuries' where they had previously bought 'decencies,' and 'decencies' where they had previously bought only 'necessities' . . . in fact, fashion and its exploiters raised men's levels of 'pecuniary decency.' "[6] In this manner appeared in eighteenth-century England the mass consumerism that has become the hallmark of twentieth-century societies throughout the globe.

New Roles for Women

Led to having women choices

The industrial revolution was responsible not only for the new consumerism but also for new roles for women. The revolution had as profound an impact on women as did the agricultural revolution several millennia earlier. The general effect was to force women out of the family economy in which they had lived and worked into a new wage economy outside the household.

The family economy that existed in preindustrial times was based on the home, where the wife, husband, and even very small children worked together. This suggests pleasant and wholesome family activity, but usually it was far from that. Women had plenty of monotonous and repetitive work, such as spinning, tatting, and setting up looms. Their work often was auxiliary or preparatory to that of their fathers or husbands, so they normally worked long hours along with the men. Moreover, women had to combine this labor with other onerous tasks, namely, housekeeping and child care.

With the industrial revolution, the primary work place shifted from the home to factories and workshops, and female workers became a part of the money economy as wage earners. This had certain advantages, such as more steady work, since the industrialists had much capital

Women were the most harshly exploited adult workers during the early twentieth century. In the garment industry, mostly located in New York City, these "sweatshops" were common.

invested in their plant and machinery, and therefore closed down operations as little as possible. In addition to higher yearly incomes from year-round employment, factory women received substantially higher wages than they previously had earned with piecework in their family quarters. In the Manchester cotton factories, for example, working wives in 1914 were earning weekly sums more than twice as high as the wives who hemmed handkerchiefs at home.

The new factory jobs, on the other hand, did have certain negative features, which both male and female workers intensely disliked. As noted, these features included long hours; unhealthy working conditions; and myriad rules, regulations, and penalties. Women were especially vulnerable to abuse and exploitation because they tended to be docile and less likely to be organized into unions. The male leaders of the unions did little to encourage and much to discourage female membership. Also women usually lacked both the time and the money needed for participation in unions. Thus the average wage for women at the end of the nineteenth century was less than half of that for their male counterparts.

Most women workers gave up their factory jobs after marriage and the birth of children. But their husbands' wages usually were inadequate to cover all family expenses so the mothers took on as much home work as they could handle. This type of temporary work included taking in boarders, sewing clothes, making artificial flowers, washing laundry, and taking care of the children of working mothers.

In the late nineteenth century the status of middle-class women changed because infant mortality was declining sharply in western Europe. The birthrate dropped correspondingly, so wives were relieved of the burden of interminable pregnancies. Also new labor-saving devices now appeared, which eased the burden of household chores. This combination of circumstances theoretically should have lightened substantially the responsibilities and workloads of housewives. In practice the outcome was quite different. The labor-saving gadgets did not actually relieve the housewives as much as expected because the supply of cheap servants was drying up. So mothers discovered that in operating the new washing machines and electric irons, they were working more than in the old days when laundresses were in charge.

Equally important was the growing expectation that the primary responsibility of the middle-class wife was not housework but mothering. Books, magazines, and sermons all promoted the concept that mothers should be concerned with the emotional as well as the physical well-being of their families. Experts expounded new "scientific" techniques for successful modern mothers. At the same time these mothers were expected to uphold traditional values and to preserve their femininity. Little wonder that many middle-class women felt anxious and inadequate. Some began to question the assumption that marriage required their subordination to husband and children—hence the emergence of the feminist movement demanding equality and more opportunities for women, both inside the home and out.

Meanwhile, working-class women lacked the time, money, and energy to fret over middle-class concerns about housework versus motherhood. They could not realistically aspire to the role of perfect wife, perfect mother, and perfect housekeeper. Rather, they had to cope with the immediate daily crises precipitated by unemployment, desertion, sickness, and the chronic gap between wages and family expenses. For such hard-pressed working-class women, who always comprised a substantial percentage of the total, life boiled down to a never-ending struggle to keep the family afloat.

VII.   EFFECT OF THE INDUSTRIAL REVOLUTION ON THE NON-EUROPEAN WORLD

Europeanization of the Earlier Empires

In the period before 1763 the European powers had only a few footholds in Asia and Africa. Their major holdings were in the Americas. After 1763 they established their political control over large parts of Asia and almost all of Africa. In the Americas and the British dominions, they were able to do much more. Taking advantage of the sparse populations in those regions, millions of Europeans emigrated and filled up those relatively empty spaces.

The industrial revolution was largely responsible for the mass migrations. We have seen that increased productivity together with the advances of medical science led to a sharp increase in Europe's population in the nineteenth century. This created a population pressure that found an outlet in overseas migration. Railways and steamships were available to transport masses of people across oceans and continents, and persecution of one sort or another stimulated further emigration, as did disasters such as Ireland's potato famine. These various factors combined to produce a mass migration unequaled in human history to that date. With every decade the tide of population movement increased in volume. In the 1820s a total of 145,000 left Europe; in the 1850s about 2.6 million; and between 1900 and 1910 the crest was reached with 9 million emigrants, or almost 1 million per year (see map of Racial Distribution in the World, p. 414).

Before 1885 most of the emigrants came from northern and western Europe; after that date the majority were from southern and eastern Europe. By and large, the British emigrants went to the dominions and the United States; the Italians, to the United States and Latin America; the Spaniards and Portuguese, to Latin America; and the Germans, to the United States and, in smaller numbers, to Argentina and Brazil. From the perspective of world history, this extraordinary migration is significant because it was all directed to the New World and Oceania, with the exception of the large flow to Asiatic Russia and the trickle to South Africa. The result has been the almost complete ethnic *Europeanization* of Siberia, the British dominions excepting South Africa, and the Americas. The Indian population in Latin America managed to survive but was left a minority.

The ethnic Europeanization of overseas territories led inevitably also to political, economic, and cultural Europeanization. This process is described in Chapter 35.

New Imperialism Conquers New Empires

The industrial revolution was largely responsible not only for the Europeanization of overseas territories but also for the creation of huge European colonial structures in Asia and Africa. The great wave of empire building after 1870 was known as the *new imperialism*. It made a large part of the earth's surface into an appendage of a few European powers. The interrelationship of the new imperialism and the industrial revolution was manifested in a growing desire to obtain colonies that might serve as markets for the rising volume of manufactured goods. The several European and overseas countries that became industrialized during the nineteenth century were soon competing with each other for markets. In the process they raised tariffs to keep out each other's products. Soon it was being argued that each industrialized country must have colonies to provide "sheltered markets" for its manufactures.

The industrial revolution also produced surplus capital, which again led the great powers to seek colonies as investment outlets. The more capital piled up at home, the lower the profits fell and the greater the need to find better investment markets abroad. Vast amounts of capital were, in fact, invented in foreign countries, especially by Britain, France, and Germany. For example, Britain by 1914 had invested £4 billion abroad, a sum amounting to one-fourth of its total national wealth. Europe by 1914 had become the banker of the world. In the first half of the nineteenth century most overseas investments were made in the Americas and Australia—in the white man's world. But in the century's second half they were made mostly in the nonwhite and relatively unstable countries of Asia and Africa. The thousands of small private investors and the large banking combinations that provided the capital naturally were anxious about their investments' safety. They preferred "civilized" administration, preferably by their own respective governments, in the regions in which their investments were situated. This is how the need to invest surplus capital safely promoted the new imperialism.

The industrial revolution also created a demand for raw materials to feed the machines. Many of these materials—jute, rubber, petroleum, and various metals—came from the "uncivilized" portions of the globe. In most cases heavy capital outlays were needed to secure adequate production of these commodities. Such investments, as we have seen, usually led to the imposition of political control.

The new imperialism was not entirely economic in its origins; it was not related exclusively to the industrial revolution. A variety of other factors also were operative at this time. One was the desire to strengthen national security with strategic naval bases such as at Malta and Singapore. Another was the need to secure additional sources of labor, as the French did in North Africa. Still another factor was the influence of the missionaries, who were particularly active during the nineteenth century. Sometimes these missionaries were maltreated, or even killed, by the natives they were seeking to convert. Even though the missionaries themselves might be willing to tolerate such risks for the sake of their cause, public opinion frequently demanded action, and it was not unknown for governments to use such incidents as pretexts for military intervention. Finally, the vogue of Social Darwinism, with its doctrines of struggle for existence and survival of the fittest, led naturally to ideas of racial superiority. The white man's "burden" was to rule over the "inferior" colored peoples of the earth. The great empire builder Cecil Rhodes was quite outspoken on this matter. "I contend that we are the first race in the world, and that the more of the world we inhabit the better it is for the human race. . . . If there be a God, I think what He would like me to do is to paint as much of the map of Africa British red as possible."[7]

The net result of these economic, political, and intellectual-psychological factors was the greatest land-grab in the history of the world, unequaled even by the conquests of Genghis Khan. In the generation between 1871 and 1900 Britain added 4.25 million square miles and 66 million people to its empire; France added 3.5 million square miles and 26 million people; Russia in Asia added half and a million square miles and 6.5 million people; and Germany added 1 million square miles and 13 million people. Even little Belgium managed to acquire 900,000 square miles and 8.5 million inhabitants. These conquests, along with the existing colonial possessions, created a fantastic and unprecedented situation in which one small portion of the globe dominated all the rest.

The industrialized European powers not only owned these vast colonial territories outright. They also dominated those economically

and militarily weak areas that, for one reason or another, were not actually annexed. Examples are China, the Ottoman Empire, and Persia, all of which were nominally independent, but which, in fact, were constantly harried, humiliated, and controlled in various direct and indirect ways. Latin America also was an economic appendage of the great powers, though in this region military action by Europe was discouraged by the Monroe Doctrine. The Doctrine, however, did not preclude repeated armed intervention by the U.S. Marine Corps to "restore law and order." The great Russian Empire was also dominated economically to a very large extent by western Europe, but in this case the military strength of the tsarist regime was great enough to prevent foreign economic influence from extending into other areas. Thus we see that Europe's control extended not only over its farflung empires but also over the equally extensive dependent regions. In fact, more European capital was invested in the dependent countries than in the colonies.

Investments were safeguarded through various devices and pressures, such as military missions that trained the local armed forces, financial missions that supervised and usually controlled local finances, and extraterritorial and capitulatory arrangements that gave special privileges to European residing or doing business in these areas. If necessary as a last resort, there were always the Marines in the New World or the gunboats in the Old. In this manner most of the earth's surface and most of the world's population had by 1914 come under the direct or indirect domination of a few European countries, including Russia, and of the United States. This was a development without precedent in human history. Today, in the late twentieth century, much of the global turmoil represents the inevitable reaction to this European domination.

Impact of the New Imperialism

Why should we label the great European expansion of the late nineteenth century the *new imperialism?* Imperialism, after all, was not something new. If it is defined as "the rule or control, political or economic, direct or indirect, of one state, nation or people over similar groups," then imperialism is as old as human civilization.[8] Certainly the Romans were imperialistic, having conquered and for centuries ruled large parts of Europe and the Near East. And many other empires in all parts of the globe, both before and after the Romans, were conquered by all types of peoples.

Yet the term *new imperialism* is justified, because the late-nineteenth century European expansion was quite unique in its impact on the colonial and dependent territories. Rome exploited its possessions simply and directly by plundering and by collecting tribute, chiefly in the form of foodstuffs, but its exploitation did not particularly affect the economic life and structure of the colonies. They continued to produce pretty much the same foodstuffs and handicrafts in the same ways as in the past. To compare this imperialism with the later version that overran and remade entire continents is like comparing a spade to a steam shovel. The traditional imperialism involved exploitation but no basic economic and social change. The tribute merely went to one ruling clique rather than another. The new imperialism, by contrast, forced a thorough transformation of the conquered countries. This was not so much deliberate policy as it was the inevitable impact of the dynamic industrialism of western Europe on the static, self-contained agrarian regimes of Africa and Asia. In other words, Europe's industrial capitalism was far too complex and expansionistic to stop with a simple tribute relationship with the colonies.

At the outset, the European conquerors certainly did not hesitate to plunder and to levy tribute. The British did so in India, as the Spaniards had earlier in Mexico and Peru. But after this initial phase, Europe's dynamic economy began in various ways to enfold and refashion the colonial economic and social structures. This happened because, as we have seen, industrialized Europe needed sources of raw materials and markets for its surplus capital and manufactures. Thus the historic role of the new imperialism was to carry the industrial revolution to its logical conclusion—to enable the industrial nations, or industrial capitalism, to operate on a worldwide scale. The global operation of industrial capitalism resulted in much more extensive, coordinated, and efficient use of the material and human resources of the globe. Certainly world productivity rose greatly when European capital and skills were

combined with the raw materials and labor of the underdeveloped regions. The combination produced, for the first time, an integrated global economy. In fact, world industrial production increased threefold between 1860 and 1890 and sevenfold between 1860 and 1913. The value of world trade grew from £641 million in 1851, to £3,024 million in 1880, to £4,025 million in 1900, and to £7,840 million in 1913.

Everyone agrees that this increase in the size of the economic cake has been a great advantage. But there is much dispute over the question of how the cake has been sliced. Colonial peoples feel that in the past they have had less than their due share. The total amount that they have received obviously has increased; otherwise their rising populations could not have been supported. For example, a British economist has shown that in 1949 European companies engaged in mining in mineral-rich northern Rhodesia (Zimbabwe) sold their output for a total of £36.7 million. Of this, they spent only £12.5 million in northern Rhodesia, which meant that two-thirds of the money was transferred abroad. Moreover, of the £12.5 spent in northern Rhodesia, £4.1 million was paid to Europeans living and working there. Only £2 million out of the £36.7 million went to the Africans working in the mines. And yet these workers were receiving an average of £41 a year compared to an average income of £27 a year per adult African male in the colony.[9]

Under these circumstances it is understandable that colonial peoples are not very impressed by increased productivity or by the wages paid by foreign companies. They are more impressed by the wretched level at which they subsist, especially in comparison with Western levels. They also resent being cast in the role of hewers of wood and drawers of water, even in regions where there are human and material resources for industrial development.

There is an obvious parallel here between the reaction of Western workers to industrial capitalism and of colonial peoples to the new imperialism. Both have been dissatisfied with their lot, and both have supported movements designed to bring about radical change. But a basic difference is that the colonial peoples are ranged not against employers of their own nationality but rather against foreign rulers. Accordingly, their movement of protest, at least in the first stage, was not socialism but rather a range of Western political doctrines—liberalism, democracy, and, above all, nationalism.

We turn now to consider those "isms" that have made up Europe's political revolution. An understanding of that revolution is as essential for world history as an understanding of the industrial revolution. Because of Europe's political revolution, the world, as we shall see, was affected by Western political ideas, slogans, and institutions as well as by Western cottons, railways, and banks.

SUGGESTED READINGS

An excellent bibliography of the scientific revolution is provided by M. Boas, *History of Science* (Service Center for Teachers of History, 1958), No. 13. Excellent paperback surveys of the entire history of science are available, especially W. C. Dampier, *A Shorter History of Science* (Harcourt Brace Jovanovich, 1957); A. R. and M. B. Hall, *A Brief History of Science* (New American Library, 1964); and F. S. Taylor, *A Short History of Science and Scientific Thought* (W. W. Norton, 1949). See also the useful collection by W. C. Dampier Whetham and M. Dampier, *Cambridge Readings in the Literature of Science* (Cambridge University, 1928).

A convenient analysis of the interpretations and literature of the industrial revolution is provided by E. E. Lampard, *Industrial Revolution: Interpretations and Perspectives* (Service Center for Teachers of History, 1957), No. 4. The best overall survey is by D. S. Landes, *The Unbound Prometheus: Technological Change and Industrial Development in Western Europe from 1750 to the Present* (Cambridge University, 1969). See also the stimulating interpretation by A. Thompson, *The Dynamics of the Industrial Revolution* (Edward Arnold, 1973). For the diffusion of the industrial revolution from England, see W. D. Henderson, *The Industrial Revolution on the Continent* (Cass, 1961). For the social and political repercussions of the industrial revolution, see E. J. Hobshawn, *The Age of Revolution: Europe, 1789–1848* (Weidenfeld, 1962); E. P. Thompson, *The Making of the English Working Class* (Gollancz, 1963); T. McKeowan, *The Modern Rise of Population* (Academic Press, 1977); N. McKendrick et al., *The Birth of a Consumer Society: The Commercialization of Eighteenth-Century England* (Indiana University, 1982); L. Brockway, *Science and Colonial Expansion* (Academic Press, 1979); D. R. Headrick, *The Tools of Empire: Technology and European Imperialism in the 19th Century* (Oxford University, 1981); and H. Magdoff, *Imperialism from the Colonial Age to the Present* (Monthly Review Press, 1978).

The impact of the industrial revolution on women is summarized in R. Bridenthal and C. Koonz, eds., *Becoming Visible: Women in European History* (Houghton Mifflin, 1977), Chaps. 11–14. For more detailed works, see L. A. Tilly and J. W. Scott, *Women Work and Family* (Holt, Rinehart and Winston, 1978); E. S. Riemer and J. C. Fout, eds., *European Women: A Documentary History, 1789–1945* (Schocken, 1980); and J. Rendall, *The Origins of Modern Feminism: Women in Britain, France and the United States, 1780–1860* (Macmillan, 1985).

29 Europe's Political Revolutions

When individuals and nations have once got in their heads the abstract concept of full-blown liberty, there is nothing like it in its uncontrollable strength.

G. W. F. Hegel

Europe's domination of the world in the nineteenth century was based not only on its industrial and scientific revolutions but also on its political revolution. The essence of the political revolution was the end of the concept of a divinely ordained division of people into rulers and ruled. Government was no longer regarded as something above the people and the people as something below the government. Instead, the political revolution for the first time in history, at least on a scale larger than the city-state, called for the identification of government with people. The masses were awakened and activized so that they not only participated in government but also considered it their inherent right to do so. In this chapter we shall consider the general pattern of this political revolution, its origins in the English, American, and French revolutions, and its varied manifestations and worldwide impact during the nineteenth century.

I. PATTERN OF THE POLITICAL REVOLUTION

The political revolution, like the economic, developed in several stages. We noted that the economic revolution began in England, spread to the Continent and to the United States, and later to other parts of the globe. Likewise, the political revolution got under way with the English Revolution in the seventeenth century, developed much further with the American and French revolutions that followed, next affected the whole of Europe during the nineteenth century, and finally engulfed the entire globe during the twentieth.

The parallel course in the spread of the two revolutions was not accidental; indeed, the two were intimately related. The economic revolution was in large degree responsible for the political because it created new classes with new interests and with new ideologies that rationalized those interests. We will see this more clearly as we trace briefly the general course of the economic and political revolutions.

During the early medieval period, there were three well-defined social groups in western Europe: the nobility, who constituted a military aristocracy; the clergy, who formed an ecclesiastical and intellectual elite; and the peasants, who labored to support the two upper classes. With the development of commerce, the profile of the medieval social order began gradually to change with the appearance of a new element, the urban bourgeoisie. As this class grew in wealth and numbers, it became more and more discontented with the special privileges of the feudal orders and with the numerous restrictions that hampered the development of a free-market economy. Accordingly, the *bourgeoisie* made a mutually beneficial alliance with the national monarchies. The kings obtained financial support from the bourgeoisie and so were able to assert their authority over the feudal orders. The bourgeoisie in return profited from the establishment of law and order throughout the royal domains. The alliance lasted until it became irksome for the constantly growing middle class. Then the middle class turned against the kings to free itself from royal restrictions on commerce, from a growing burden of taxation, and from restraints on religious freedom. These objectives were important factors in the English, American, and French revolutions. The success of these revolutions also meant the success of *classical liberalism*—the new ideology that provided a rationalization for bourgeois interests and objectives. In this sense, liberalism may be defined as the particular program by which the growing middle class proposed to get for itself the benefits and control it was aiming for.

The middle class, with its creed of liberalism, was challenged in turn by the urban workers, or *proletariat*. With the industrial revolution of the late eighteenth century, the workers in the crowded cities became increasingly class conscious. More and more they felt that their interests were not identical to those of their employers, and that their situation could be improved only by combined action on their part. So the workers, or rather the intellectuals who led them, developed a new ideology, *socialism*. Socialism directly challenged the liberalism of the bourgeoisie, calling for social and economic change as well as for political reform. We shall see that socialism was to become a major force in European affairs in the late nineteenth century and in world affairs in the twentieth.

Europe's political revolution was powered not only by the dynamic creeds of liberalism and socialism but also by *nationalism*—an ideology that cut across classes and activated great masses of people. Traditionally the first allegiance of these people had been to region or to church. In early modern times it had extended to the new national monarchs. But beginning with the English Revolution, and particularly during the French Revolution, increasing numbers of Europeans gave their loyalty to the new cause of the nation. The rise of national churches, national dynasties, national armies, and national educational systems all combined to transform former ducal subjects, feudal serfs, and town *burghers* into all-inclusive nations. The new national ideology spread during the nineteenth century from western Europe, where it originated, to all parts of the Continent. Today, in the twentieth century, it is the driving force behind the awakening of formerly subject colonial peoples throughout the world.

These three creeds—liberalism, socialism, and nationalism—are the principal components of Europe's political revolution. Together they galvanized into action broader and broader strata of the peoples of Europe, giving them a dynamism and a cohesiveness unequaled in any other portion of the globe. In this way the political revolution, like the scientific and the economic revolutions, contributed vitally to Europe's world domination. When the Europeans began to expand overseas, they encountered societies where there was little rapport between rulers and ruled. The apathy of the masses—their lack of identification with their governments—explains why in region after region the Europeans were able to establish and to maintain their rule with little difficulty. India is perhaps the leading example of the extent to which lack of rapport between rulers and ruled made societies vulnerable. India was a society that had remained a disparate collection of peoples, religions, and conflicting provincial loyalties, and so it was easy prey. For over a century and a half, the great Indian subcontinent, with its teeming millions, its splendid civilization, and its ancient historical traditions, was ruled with little difficulty by a comparative handful of British officers and officials. When the mutiny against British rule broke out in 1857, it was put down not only by British troops but also by Indian troops. The correspondent of the London *Times* reported this fact with astonishment: "I looked with ever-growing wonder on the vast tributary of the tide of war which was running around and before me. All these men, women and children, with high delight were pouring towards Lucknow to aid the Feringhee [Europeans] to overcome their brethren."[1]

But European political and economic domination inevitably meant the diffusion of European political ideas. Just as the entire globe felt the impact of Stephenson's locomotive, of Fulton's steamship, and Gatling's machine gun, so it felt the impact of the Declaration of Independence, of the Declaration of the Rights of Man and Citizen, and the Communist Manifesto. The worldwide convulsions that are the hallmark of our present age are the direct outcome of these heady documents.

II. ENGLISH REVOLUTION

The first phase of Europe's political revolution was the English Revolution of the seventeenth century. The roots of the upheaval in England rest in the conflict between Parliament and the Stuart dynasty. The conflict degenerated into an open civil war from which Parliament emerged victorious. The Tudor dynasty, which preceded the Stuart, was generally popular, particularly with the middle class and the gentry. It brought the warring noble families under central control. It severed the ecclesiastical ties with Rome by es-

tablishing a national Anglican church, and in the process distributed extensive lands and other properties that had belonged to Catholic institutions. It also built up the navy and pursued an anti-Catholic foreign policy that met with popular approval.

The first Stuart king, James I (reigned 1603–1625), and his son and successor Charles I (1625–1649), soon dissipated this fund of goodwill. They tried to impose the doctrines and ritual of the Anglican church on all the people, thereby alienating their Nonconformist, or Puritan, subjects. They also tried to rule without Parliament but ran into difficulties, because Parliament controlled the national purse. They tried to get around this obstacle by selling monopolies in the export and import trades, in domestic commerce, and in many fields of manufacturing. This produced considerable revenue, but it also antagonized the bourgeoisie, which demanded that "all free subjects be inheritable to the free exercise of their industry."[2]

The crisis came when the Scots rose in rebellion against Charles's attempt to impose Anglican religion on them. To get funds to suppress the uprising, Charles was forced to call on Parliament, and this "Long Parliament," which met in 1640, ignored his requests for money and instead made a number of far-reaching demands. They called for the execution of the chief royal advisers and the complete reorganization of the Anglican church. Charles refused to submit, and in 1642 fighting broke out between the royalist Cavaliers and the Puritan Roundheads.

England did not settle down again for almost half a century, not until the so-called Glorious Revolution in 1688. The stirring events of those decades made up the English Revolution, which went through five stages. The first, from 1642 to 1645, was the civil war. The royalists were routed by the famous New Model Army that Oliver Cromwell had organized. During the second stage, from 1645 to 1649, a situation developed that was to be repeated with certain variations during the French Revolution in 1792 and the Russian Revolution in 1917. A split occurred between the moderate and radical elements among the victorious Puritans. The moderates led by Cromwell, prevailed over the radicals, led by John Lilburne. When Charles was executed in

1649, Cromwell emerged as the head of an English republic, which was known as the Commonwealth.

Cromwell and his Puritan followers ruled England with great efficiency and much godliness during the third stage, from 1649 to 1660. During this time, the various feudal rights were suppressed and the religious question settled. Cromwell died in 1658 and was succeeded as lord protector of the Commonwealth by his son Richard. The latter was a nonentity, and furthermore the country was weary of the restricted and austere life under the Puritans. Accordingly, the Stuarts were placed back on the throne, and from 1660 to 1668 England went through the fourth stage, which is known as the Restoration.

The restored Stuart kings, Charles II (1660–1685) and James II (1685–1688), did not and could not undo the reforms of the republic. But they did try to revive personal rule. This effort, together with their subservience to the French crown and their encouragement of Catholicism, made them increasingly unpopular. Finally, James II was overthrown in the Glorious Revolution of 1688, which marks the fifth and last stage of the English Revolution. The new ruler was William of Orange, son-in-law of James II. In 1689 William accepted a Bill of Rights, which expressed the essential principles of parliamentary supremacy. The bill provided that no law could be suspended by the king, no taxes raised or army maintained except by Parliament's consent, and no subject arrested and detained without legal process. Such provisions did not mean that England had become a democracy. It was not until the establishment of universal suffrage in the late nineteenth century that this goal was attained. But the settlement in 1689 did establish once and for all the supreme authority of Parliament, and in doing so it ended the English Revolution that had begun almost a half-century earlier.

From the viewpoint of world history, the major significance of the English Revolution is that it defined the principles of liberalism and put them to work. This was natural, because the English Revolution was essentially a middle-class affair. The merchants and the lesser gentry who supported Parliament had two principal ends in view—religious toleration and security of person and property. But there was no unanimity of opinion on the Puritan side concerning these matters. Many conflicting views were expressed and passionately debated. In the case of religion, for example, a veritable flood of new sects appeared, including the Congregationalists, the Baptists, and the Quakers. At the same time, the Presbyterians strove to establish their church as a national organization that could exercise its discipline on all citizens. These religious differences obviously had to be reconciled or else Parliament's victory would be undone and the state itself might founder. It was under these circumstances that the basic liberal doctrine of religious toleration was worked out and established. On grounds of principle as well as of expediency, it came to be generally agreed that it was both immoral and ineffective to coerce people into belief. It is true that the Anglican church remained the official, state-supported church and that its members were favored in the filling of government posts and in other respects. But by and large, the principle was established that liberty of conscience should be granted to all Christians who did not threaten public order or interfere with other people's worship.

The question of the rights of person and of property also aroused fierce controversy. This question divided the right- and left-wing elements among the Puritans even more sharply than did the religious issue. The split occurred gradually, as the common soldiers of the New Model Army came to feel that their interests were being ignored by their officers and by Parliament. Their feelings were articulated by the *Levellers,* a name of opprobrium given to a mass movement drawn chiefly from the lower-middle class and from agricultural tenants. It is true that legislation passed by the House of Commons for the establishment of the Commonwealth included basic Leveller doctrine: "The Peoples are, under God, the Original of all just Power," and the Commons "being chosen by, and representing the Peoples, have the supreme Power in this Nation."[3]

If Parliament was thus willing to accept the principle of the sovereignty of the people, what was the issue dividing Parliament and the Levellers? The answer is in the definition of the word *people*. Cromwell and his followers held that the "people" who should participate in the election of the Commons were those with a "real or permanent interest in the kingdom"—that is, property owners—whereas the Levellers maintained that "any man that is born in England ought . . . to have his voice in election of burgesses [members of Parliament]."[4] Thus, the issue was between constitutional parliamentary government and democratic government. Many of those who favored democratic government did so with the intention of using their votes to bring about social reform. And fear of such reform motivated Cromwell and his followers in their resolute opposition to the Levellers.

The fact is that there were two revolutions under way in seventeenth-century England. The first was the political revolution of the lesser gentry and the bourgeoisie, who were interested in winning the civil and religious freedom necessary to make their way in the world. The second was the social revolution of the lower-middle class and the tenant farmers, who had a vision of a community of small-property owners, with complete religious and political equality and with generous provisions for the poor. The social revolution failed in England in the seventeenth century, as it was to fail in France in the eighteenth. In both cases the protagonists lacked the numbers, the organization, and the maturity necessary for victory. Their time was to come in the late nineteenth century, when the industrial revolution had spawned a large and class-conscious urban proletariat. The proletariat was to evolve its own ideology—socialism—distinct from, and in opposition to, the liberalism of bourgeoisie.

III. ENLIGHTENMENT

The next stage in Europe's political revolution, following the upheaval in seventeenth-century England, was the so-called Enlightenment that manifested itself during the century before the French Revolution of 1789. The term *Enlightenment* owes its origin to the fact that the leaders of this movement believed that they lived in an enlightened age. They viewed the past largely as a time of superstition and ignorance, and they thought that only in their day were human beings at last emerging from darkness into sunlight. Thus, one basic characteristic of this Age of Enlightenment was the idea of progress, an idea that was to persist into the twentieth century. With the Enlightenment, it began to be generally assumed that the condition of humanity would steadily improve, so that each generation would be better off than that which came before.

How was this unceasing progress to be maintained? The answer was simple and confident: by the use of humankind's reasoning powers. Faith in reason was the other basic feature of the Enlightenment. Indeed, the two key concepts were progress and reason, and the exponents of these concepts were a highly articulate group known as the *philosophes*. Not to be confused with formal philosophers, the philosophes were not profound or systematic thinkers in any particular field. They were mostly literary men or popularizers—more journalists than philosophers. They were generally opposed to the existing order, and they wrote plays, novels, essays, and histories to popularize their ideas and to show the need for change.

Much influenced by the law of gravitation that Newton had demonstrated, the philosophes believed in the existence of natural laws that regulated, not only the physical universe, but also human society. Acting on this assumption, they proceeded to apply reason to all fields in order to discover the natural laws that operated in each. They subjected everything—all persons, all institutions, all traditions—to the test of reason. What would be a rigorous ordeal for any society in any period was particularly unsettling for France's *ancien régime,* past its prime and creaking in many joints. Thus the philosophes subjected the old regime in France, and throughout Europe, to a barrage of devastating criticism. More important, they evolved a set of revolutionary principles by which they proposed to effect a wholesale reorganization of society. Of particular interest to us are their specific proposals in three area—economics, religion, and government.

Their key slogan in economics was laissez-faire—let the people do what they will, let nature takes its course. The opposition to government intervention was a reaction to the rigid regulation of economic life generally known as *mercantilism.* In the early period of state building, mercantilism had been accepted as necessary for national security. But by the eighteenth century it seemed superfluous and damaging. The classic account of laissez-faire was made by the Scotsman Adam Smith in his famous work *An Inquiry into the Nature and Causes of the Wealth of Nations* (1776). He argued that individuals are motivated by self-interest as far as their economic activities are concerned, that the national welfare is simply the sum of the individual interests operating in a nation, and that each man knows his own interest better than does any statesman.

In religion the key slogan was *Écrasez l'infame!*—"crush the infamous thing," or stamp out religious fanaticism and intolerance. The philosophes rejected the traditional belief that God controls the universe and arbitrarily determines the fate of humanity. Instead, they sought a natural religion that followed the dictates of reason. The outcome was a variety of radical departures from religious orthodoxy. Some became outright atheists, denying the existence of God and denouncing religion as a tool of priests and politicians. Others became agnostics, who neither affirmed nor denied the existence of God. The majority were deists, willing to go along with the proposition that God existed and had created the universe but insisting that, after the act of creation, God allowed the universe to function according to certain natural laws and refrained from intervention. Thus the deists were able to have their cake and eat it too. They could accept God and the teaching of Christianity, and at the same time reject supernatural features such as the virgin birth, the resurrection, the divinity of Christ, and the divine inspiration of the Bible. The important point to note is that all these new dogmas—atheism, agnosticism, deism—reflected the unprecedented growth of skepticism regarding "revealed" or "supernatural" religion. For the first time since the triumph of Christianity in Europe, a definite break had occurred with the Christian tradition.

In government, also, the philosophes had a key phrase—"the social contract." The contract theory of government was not new. The English political theorist John Locke had formulated it in his *Essay on Civil Government* (1690), in which he defined government as a political contract between rulers and ruled. But the French philosopher Jean-Jacques Rousseau transformed it into a social rather than a political contract. For him it involved an agreement among the people themselves. In his major political work, *The Social Contract* (1762), Rousseau viewed government as simply a "commission," by which he justified revolution as a restoration to the sovereign people of its rightful power.

This brief survey suggests the significance of the Enlightenment for Europe's political revolution. The slogans "écrasez l'infame," "laissez-faire," and "social contract" were subversive of traditional institutions and practices. Furthermore, they represented a challenge to the status quo, not only in France but also throughout Europe and even in overseas lands. In fact, the philosophes thought of themselves not as Frenchmen or Europeans but as members of the human race. They thought and acted in global rather than Western terms. They sought to discover social laws that had universal application, like Newton's laws of the physical world.

If the philosophes did not discover fixed laws governing all humankind, their writings did influence thinking people in many parts of the world. Their greatest immediate success was in persuading a number of European monarchs to accept at least some of their doctrines. These monarchs still held to the theory that they ruled by divine right, but they changed their ideas about the purpose of their rule. Governmental authority was still to be the prerogative of the kings, but now it was to be used for the benefit of the people. Hence these rulers were known as *benevolent despots.*

The best known of these benevolent despots were Frederick the Great of Prussia (1740–1786), Catherine the Great of Russia (1762–1796), and Joseph II of the Hapsburg Empire (1765–1790). Catherine was perhaps the most articulate, frequently using typical slogans of the Enlightenment such as "All citizens ought to be equal before the law," "Sovereigns are made to serve their people," and "It is dangerous for a country to be divided into a few large estates." But Catherine and her fellow sovereigns did not merely talk about reform. Catherine improved the administrative and educational systems of her country substantially; Frederick did much to advance agriculture in Prussia; and Joseph II, the most sincere and conscientious of the *enlightened despots,* wore himself out during his reign trying to remold his empire in accord with the new principles. Yet in spite of their royal authority, these rulers had a very modest impact. Their successors frequently undid their work, and the clergy and the aristocrats were relentless in their fight against the reforms that menaced their vested interests.

IV. AMERICAN REVOLUTION

We should not overrate the role of the benevolent despots in putting the doctrines of the Enlightenment to work, for the Enlightenment did not have much effect on the masses of the people in Europe until the outbreak of the French Revolution in 1789. But before then a revolution had broken out in England's thirteen colonies, and this revolution was to offer a laboratory demonstration of the new doctrines in action.

We noted earlier (Chapter 25, Section III) that a leading characteristic of the colonies was their political independence. Their elective assemblies were continually at loggerheads with the governors and the other officials sent from London. We also noted that Britain decisively defeated France in the Seven Years' War and, by the Treaty of Paris of 1763, acquired France's colonies north to the Arctic and west to the Mississippi. Both the British and the Americans felt considerable pride in the magnitude of their joint victory. But at the same time that it settled old ones, the victory created new problems. One was the growing spirit of defiance in the colonies now that the danger of a French attack had been removed. Another was the decision of the British government, following its acquisition of vast new colonial territories, to tighten its imperial organization. This tightening might have been feasible at an earlier date, but now, after the elimination of the French danger, the colonists were convinced that they were able to take care of themselves and had every right to do so. Thus the American Revolution arose primarily out of the conflicting claims of British imperial authority and American colonial self-government.

Not all, or even most, of the American colonists favored violent revolution. In fact, they were split into two antagonistic camps. The conservatives wanted only to return to the loose relations between the mother country and the colonies that prevailed before 1763. The radicals, on the other hand, wanted a change in their relations with the British Empire that would give the colonies complete control of their own affairs. They also wanted a shift of political power inside the colonies in favor of the common people. On this point the conservatives were violently opposed. They had no desire for democracy. Rather, they wished to retain upper-class leadership after the fashion of the Glorious Revolution of 1688 in England. In the end the radicals had their way, thanks to the blunders of inept officials in Britain.

The steps leading to the revolution are well known and need not be related in detail. First there was the Proclamation of 1763 prohibiting settlement west of a line drawn along the crests of the Appalachians. This was intended as a temporary measure to preserve peace until an orderly land policy could be worked out, but the prospective settlers and speculators assumed that they were to be excluded forever for the benefit of a few British fur traders. Then there was a series of financial measures—the Sugar Act, Quartering Act, Stamp Act, and Townshend Duties—designed to shift a part of Britain's heavy tax load to the American colonists. These levies seemed reasonable to the British, especially since they had spent a great deal of money to defeat the French in the recent war, and since they estimated that they would have to spend even more to protect the American frontiers in the future. But the colonists were all affected by these imposts and unanimously opposed them. They called a continental congress, which organized a boycott of British goods to last until the financial measures were repealed. But then another series of ill-considered measures by the British government started a fresh storm that was to lead to revolution.

The sequence of the dramatic events is familiar—the East India Company's tea monopoly, the Boston Tea Party, and the Coercive, or Intolerable, Acts intended as punishment for the vandalism in Boston harbor. At the same time, in 1774, Parliament passed the Quebec Act, providing a governmental system for the conquered French Canadians and drawing the boundaries of Quebec to include all the territories north of the Ohio River—that is, the present states of Wisconsin, Michigan, Illinois, Indiana, and Ohio. Much

THE HORSE AMERICA, *throwing his Master.*

Cartoon from 1779 pictorializing the end result of the American Revolution.

can be said in defense of the Quebec Act, but the American colonists denounced it as another Intolerable Act that blocked their westward expansion for the benefit of the Catholic French Canadians. The First Continental Congress met in Philadelphia in September 1774 and organized another boycott against British goods. Fighting began the next year when British troops set out from Boston to seize unauthorized stores of weapons at Concord. It was during this operation that someone fired at Lexington Green the "shot heard round the world." The outcome was that the British troops found themselves besieged in Boston. When the Second Continental Congress met the following month, in May 1775, it had a full-fledged war on its hands and proceeded to raise an American army.

Congress was still reluctant to make the final break with the mother country, but sentiment for independence grew with the spread of

the fighting. In January 1776, Thomas Paine published his incendiary pamphlet, *Common Sense.* It was read everywhere in the colonies, and it contributed substantially to Congress's decision on July 4, 1776, to adopt the Declaration of Independence. Once military operations got fully under way, the decisive factor proved to be France's aid to the revolutionaries. During the first two years of the war, France, although not officially involved, poured large amounts of munitions into the colonies. Ninety percent of the arms used by the Americans in the crucial battle of Saratoga in 1777 were of French origin. The following year France signed an alliance with the insurgents and declared war on Britain. Holland and Spain joined France, and most of the other European powers formed an Armed Neutrality to protect their commerce from Britain's naval power. The help of the French navy and of a French expeditionary force of 6,000 men con-

THOMAS PAINE ON THE AMERICAN REVOLUTION

Thomas Paine's Rights of Man *(1791) is an eloquent appraisal of the American Revolution. It was written as a reply to Edmund Burke's negative* Reflections on the French Revolution. *Paine was typical of this time in looking forward to more revolutions that would open "a new era to the human race."**

What Archimedes said of the mechanical powers, may be applied to Reason and Liberty: "Had we," said he, "a place to stand upon, we might raise the world."

The revolution of America presented in politics what was only theory in mechanics. So deeply rooted were all the governments of the old world, and so effectually had the tyranny and the antiquity of habit established itself over the mind, that no beginning could be made in Asia, Africa, or Europe, to reform the political condition of man. Freedom had been hunted round the globe; reason was considered as rebellion; and the slavery of fear had made men afraid to think.

But such is the irresistible nature of truth, that all it asks, and all it wants, is the liberty of appearing. The sun needs no inscription to distinguish him from darkness; and no sooner did the American governments display themselves to the world, than despotism felt a shock, and man begin to contemplate redress.

The independence of America, considered merely as a separation from England, would have been a matter but of little importance, had it not been accompanied by a revolution in the principles and practices of governments. . . .

If universal peace, civilization, and commerce, are ever to be the happy lot of man, it cannot be accomplished but by a revolution in the system of governments. All the monarchical governments are military. War is their trade, plunder and revenue their objects. While such governments continue, peace has not the absolute security of a day. What is the history of all monarchical governments, but a disgustful picture of human wretchedness, and the accidental respite of a few years' repose? Wearied with war, and tired with human butchery, they sat down to rest, and called it peace. This certainly is not the condition that Heaven intended for man. . . .

The revolutions which formerly took place in the world, had nothing in them that interested the bulk of mankind. They extended only to a change of persons and measures, but not of principles, and rose or fell among the common transactions of the moment. What we now behold, may not improperly be called a "counter revolution." Conquest and tyranny, at some early period, dispossessed man of his rights, and he is now recovering them. And as the tide of all human affairs has its ebb and flow in directions contrary to each other, so also is it in this. Government founded in a moral theory, on a system of universal peace, on the indefeasible hereditary Rights of Man, is now revolving from west to east, by a stronger impulse than the government of the sword revolved from east to west. It interests not particular individuals, but nations, in its progress, and promises a new era to the human race.

*Thomas Paine, *Rights of Man* (London, 1792), pp. 1–5.

tributed substantially to the victories of George Washington's forces and to the final British surrender at Yorktown in 1781. The peace treaty signed at Paris in 1783 recognized the independence of the American republic, whose frontiers were to extend west to the Mississippi.

From the viewpoint of world history, the American Revolution is significant not because it created an independent state but because it created a new and different type of state. The Declaration of Independence proclaimed, "We hold these truths to be self-evident: that all men are created equal." Now the American people, both during and after the revolution, passed laws to make this declaration true in real life as well as on paper. They seized and distributed the large estates owned by the Tories. They extended the franchise until all men (but not women) had the right to vote. Many state governments passed laws forbidding the importation of slaves. Established churches were abolished, and freedom of religion became the law of the land. All thirteen states adopted constitutions that included bills of rights, which guaranteed the natural rights of citizens.

These changes were not so far-reaching and fundamental as those that were brought about later by the French and Russian revolutions. These later revolutions, and particularly the Russian, involved far more extensive social and economic reorganization. Nevertheless, the American Revolution had a profound impact in its time. The establishment of an independent republic in the New World was widely interpreted in Europe as meaning that the ideas of the Enlightenment were practicable—that it was possible for people to establish a state and a workable system of government based on the rights of the individual. Thus America became a symbol of freedom and of opportunity, envied as a new land, free from the burdens and chains of the past.

V.   FRENCH REVOLUTION

Roots of Revolution

The French Revolution looms much larger on the stage of world history than the English or the American revolutions. It brought about more economic and social change and influenced a larger portion of the globe than did the earlier upheavals. The French Revolution marked not only the triumph of the bourgeoisie but also the full awakening of the masses. Middle-class liberalism came to the fore, but so did nationalism with its appeal to the people in all sections of society. And indeed, "the people," long in the wings, now strode out to the front of the stage, to remain there ever since.

Why did this great change take place in France? The basic reason is that France, the home of the Enlightenment, was not ruled by an enlightened despot until the advent of Napoleon. Consequently, France was a country of such gross inefficiency and inequality that the machinery of government creaked to a standstill. The breakdown of government gave the ambitious and dissatisfied bourgeoisie a chance to make its successful bid for power.

The old regime in France was aristocratic in its organization. All French people belonged legally to an "estate," or order of society, and this membership determined their legal rights and privileges. The First Estate comprised the clergy, who numbered about 100,000 out of a total population of 24.5 million. The Second Estate was made up of the nobility, who totaled about 400,000. The Third Estate included everyone else—over 20 million peasants and about 4 million urban merchants and artisans. Thus, the first two estates made up only about 2 percent of the total population. Yet they owned about 35 percent of the land and enjoyed most of the benefits of government patronage. Despite these disproportionate advantages, they were exempted from almost all taxes, which indeed they thought were beneath their station.

The burden of taxation consequently fell on the Third Estate, and especially on the peasants. The peasants accounted for over 80 percent of the population but owned only 30 percent of the land. Furthermore, the peasants were required to pay a tithe to the church; an assortment of feudal dues to the nobles; and a land tax, an income tax, a poll tax, and various other imposts to the state. This tax load was particularly heavy because the across-the-board price level for general goods had risen 65 percent between 1720 and 1789, while the prices of farm goods (the source of peasant income) lagged far behind.

The artisans in the cities were also discontented, because their wages had risen only 22 percent during those same decades. The bourgeoisie, by contrast, were not so badly off in the matter of taxes because they could protect themselves better than the artisans and the peasants. Furthermore, most businessmen profited from the rising prices and from the fivefold increase in French trade between 1713 and 1789. Yet the bourgeoisie were thoroughly dissatisfied with the old regime. They resented being snubbed by the nobility; treated as second-class subjects by the crown; and excluded from the higher posts in the bureaucracy, church, and army. In short, the bourgeoisie wanted political power and social prestige to match their growing economic importance.

Aristocratic Revolution

Such was the nature of the old regime in France when the great upheaval began. The French Revolution, like others before and after, started moderately and became progressively more radical. In fact, it began, not in 1789 as a bourgeois revolution but in 1787 as an aristocratic revolution. Then it moved to the left through bourgeois and mass phases until a reaction occurred that brought Napoleon to power.

The aristocrats began the revolution because they wanted to regain the political power they had lost to the crown during the sixteenth and seventeenth centuries. The king's special commissioners, or intendants, had replaced the noble governors, and the king's bureaucracy controlled all levels of government throughout the country. The power of the monarchs was reflected in the fact that they had not bothered to call the Estates-General, or national parliament, since 1614. It is understandable then that when Louis XVI found himself in financial straits after the heavy expenses incurred in supporting the American Revolution, the nobles tried to seize the opportunity to regain power.

The nobility and the clergy forced the issue in 1787 when Louis attempted to levy a uniform tax on all landed property without regard to the social status of the holder. The privileged orders branded the new tax illegal and said that only the nation as a whole sitting in the Estates-General could institute so sweeping a change. The pinch

for money became so acute that the king finally gave way and summoned the Estates-General to meet in the spring of 1789. The nobility assumed that they would be able to control this body and thereby regain a dominant position in the government. But their assumption proved completely wrong. The meeting of the Estates-General led, not to the triumph of the nobility, but rather to the unleashing of an elemental revolutionary wave that was to sweep away established institutions and ruling classes in France and in much of Europe.

Bourgeois Revolution

The Estates-General that met in Versailles on May 5, 1789, did not represent the people of France. Rather, it represented the three estates into which they traditionally had been divided. From the beginning the Third Estate was the most dynamic and decisive. It had the advantage of numbers. There were 600 representatives in the Third Estate as against 300 each in the other two. Actually, the Third Estate outnumbered the other two combined because a certain number of clergy were ready to throw in their lot with the lower orders. There were also a few liberal-minded nobles, like the Marquis de Lafayette, who already had fought for the revolutionary cause in America and sided with the Third Estate. The middle-class representatives also had some reformist ideas. Knowing that they wanted to change the old regime, and— from their reading in the works of the philosophes—having at least a general idea of how they should bring about the change, the middle-class representatives also had the ready cash that the government needed so desperately, and they did not hesitate to use this potent weapon to get the concessions they wanted.

The commoners won their first victory by pressuring King Louis to transform the Estates-General into a National Assembly. This was a vital change because, as long as decisions were made on the basis of estates, the Third Estate would be in a perpetual minority of one among three. But as soon as the representatives of all three estates combined to form a National Assembly, the commoners, with their allies in the other two camps, would have a majority. King Louis, who was a rather stupid and unimaginative man, at first vacillated on this critical issue. But when the commoners boldly defied him and proclaimed themselves the National Assembly, Louis capitulated and, on June 23, instructed the three estates to merge.

The king's concession did not represent a change of heart. He continued to heed the counsels of the so-called "Queen's party"—the reactionary advisers of Marie Antoinette. The king's real intentions became apparent when, on July 11, he dismissed Jacques Necker, the minister who was regarded as most favorable to reform. At the same time several regiments of loyal troops were quietly transferred to Versailles. The rumor spread that the king was preparing to dissolve the National Assembly by force. Furthermore, it seemed that nothing could prevent him from doing so. He had the bayonets, whereas the commoners had only words and resolutions. But at this critical point the commoners in the National Assembly were saved by an uprising of the common people in Paris. The masses intervened decisively, initiating the third, or mass, phase of the revolution.

Mass Revolution

The masses that now saved the revolution in France were not the riffraff of the streets. In fact, they were the lesser bourgeoisie, made up of shopkeepers and heads of workshops. They were the ones who circulated news and organized demonstrations, and their illiterate journeymen and clerks followed their leadership. In the revolutionary outburst that followed the dismissal of Necker, mobs roamed the streets, demanding cheaper bread and parading busts of Necker draped in mourning. On July 14 they stormed and razed the Bastille, an ancient royal castle in Paris used as a prison. The event was of little practical significance since the Bastille by this time was little used. Nevertheless, it stood in the eyes of the populace as a symbol of oppression, and now this symbol was destroyed. That is why Bastille Day continues to be celebrated in France as Independence Day is in the United States.

The fall of the Bastille marks the appearance of the masses on the historical stage. Their intervention had saved the bourgeoisie, and the middle class was forced henceforth to rely on the street mobs to supply a "dose of revolution" at

crucial moments. There were to be a good many such moments in the years to come, as the bourgeoisie waged its struggle for power against the king, against the privileged orders, and, eventually, against the old order in all Europe.

Mass revolution occurred in the countryside as well as in Paris. The peasants took up arms, incited by their long-standing grievances and by the stirring news of the storming of the Bastille. In many parts of the countryside they tore down fences, seized lands, and burned manor houses. Faced with this revolutionary situation, the nobles and the clergy in the National Assembly made a virtue of necessity and voted with the commoners to abolish feudalism. During the famous "August Days" of 1789, legislation was passed that ended all feudal dues, the privilege of tax exemption, the right of the church to collect tithes, and the exclusive right of the nobility to hold office. Outstanding among the numerous other important measures decreed by the National Assembly were the confiscation of church lands, the reorganization of the judicial and administrative systems, and the adoption of the Declaration of the Rights of Man and Citizen.

The declaration set forth certain fundamental principles concerning liberty, property, and security—"Men are born, and always continue, free and equal, in respect of their rights. . . . The Nation is essentially the source of all sovereignty . . . law is an expression of the will of the community . . . liberty consists in the power of doing whatever does not injure another. . . ." The final clause showed that the bourgeoisie had not lost control of the direction of the revolution: "The right to property being inviolable and sacred, no one ought to be deprived of it, except in cases of evident public necessity, legally ascertained, and on condition of a previous just indemnity." This declaration was the essential message of the revolution. Printed in thousands of leaflets, pamphlets, and books, and translated into other languages, the declaration carried the revolutionary slogan of "Liberty, Equality, Fraternity" throughout Europe, and eventually to all the world.

King Louis was by no means willing to accept either the sweeping reforms of the Fourth of August or the revolutionary principles of the declaration. Once more it was the Paris mob that overcame the royal opposition. Early in October a hungry crowd, composed chiefly of women, raided bread stores in Paris and then marched on the royal palace in Versailles. Under the pressure of the mob, Louis agreed to move the court to Paris. The royal family took up residence in the Tuileries (a palace in Paris), where they became virtual prisoners, and the National Assembly settled down in a nearby riding school. These turbulent October days ensured the ratification of the decrees of August. They also increased the influence of the Paris mob tremendously. Both the royal family and the National Assembly were now vulnerable to mass action.

War and Terror

Although the king in Paris was virtually powerless, many of the clergy and nobles were determined to regain their lost estates and privileges. Some of them fled abroad, where they worked to enlist the aid of foreign powers in a war against the revolutionary regime in France. Their efforts were successful. The radical, or Girondist, group in the National Assembly also favored war because they believed that thereby a republic could be established in France and revolutionary doctrines disseminated throughout Europe. War began in April 1792, with Austria and Prussia ranged against France. At first the poorly prepared French were routed, but thousands of volunteers flocked to the colors in a wave of national patriotism. At the same time the Paris mob swung into action against the unpopular Louis and his hated Austrian queen, Marie Antoinette. Under pressure from the mob, the National Assembly suspended the king on August 10 and called for the election of a National Convention.

The convention, elected by universal male franchise, met on September 21, 1792, and was brilliantly successful in meeting its most pressing problem—the defense of the country against the Austrian-Prussian invaders. The combination of revolutionary élan and popular support proved irresistible. The Prussians and the Austrians were driven back across the frontier. In 1793 Britain, Holland, and Spain joined the coalition against France. The revolutionaries responded with their famous *levée en masse*. The people rose to the defense of their country. Fourteen armies were put into the field, under the command of young generals who had risen from the ranks. Inspired by the revolutionary slogan "Liberty, Equality, Fraternity," the French citizen armies swept everything before them. By 1795 the enemy coalition had been smashed.

Meanwhile, the National Convention was shifting more and more to the left, partly because it had been elected by universal franchise and also because of the revolutionary fervor engendered by the war effort. By June 1793, the Girondists had been displaced by the more radical Jacobins. The dominant organ of government now was the Committee of Public Safety. With revolutionary zeal and passionate patriotism, this committee appointed and discharged generals, spurred the masses to heroic action, conducted foreign policy, legislated on countless matters, and crushed the opposition by means of a ruthless Reign of Terror. Thousands were charged with treason, or merely with insufficient patriotism, and were subjected to the "national razor," as the guillotine was called.

But the terror got out of control, and the revolution began "devouring its own children." In the unceasing struggle for power, one after another of the revolutionary leaders followed Louis and Marie Antoinette to the guillotine. Equally disturbing for the bourgeoisie was the growing social radicalism of the revolution. The *sans-culottes* (literally, those who lacked the knee breeches of genteel society) were pressing hard for a more egalitarian state. Corresponding to the Levellers of the English Revolution, they demanded a more equitable division of the land, government regulation of prices and wages, and a social security system. Such measures were quite beyond the plans of the French bourgeoisie. So like their counterparts in England, they worked to halt the leftward course of the revolution. In England, the outcome was the defeat of the Levellers and rule by Cromwell. In France, the sansculottes were brought under control, first by a Directory of five in 1795, and then by Napoleon Bonaparte in 1799.

Napoleon

Napoleon won fame as a brilliantly successful general in Italy and used his reputation and popularity to overthrow the Directory. He governed

France as First Consul from 1799 to 1804 and as Emperor from 1804 to 1814. Two features of his fifteen-year rule of France are noteworthy for our purposes: his domestic reforms, which consolidated the gains of the revolution, and his military campaigns, which provoked a nationalist reaction in neighboring countries and eventually brought about his downfall.

As far as domestic policies are concerned, Napoleon may be compared to the enlightened despots. He was interested in technical efficiency rather than abstract ideas. He ruled the country autocratically but efficiently. He codified the laws, centralized the administration, organized a system of national education, established the Bank of France, and reached an agreement with the papacy concerning church-state relations in France. These solid achievements of Napoleon made him generally popular. There were diehards who hankered for the restoration of the old regime or who thought that Napoleon had betrayed the revolution. But the majority hailed him for ending the disturbance and instituting an honest and energetic government.

Napoleon squandered this goodwill by waging war unceasingly. Since he was a military genius, he was fabulously successful. By 1810 he reached the height of his fortunes. He had extended France's frontiers across the Rhine to Lubeck and across the Alps to Rome. The rest of Europe consisted of dependent satellites or allies. Britain alone remained independent and implacably hostile.

In all his conquered territories Napoleon put into practice some of the basic principles of the French Revolution. He abolished feudalism and serfdom, recognized the equality of all citizens, and instituted his famous law codes. These innovations disturbed and alienated vested interests everywhere, but there was also widespread support for them in many quarters. The bourgeoisie and many intellectuals responded favorably to them, but the facts remain that it was foreign rule and that, where necessary, it was imposed by force. Napoleon's non-French subjects eventually grew tired of the requisitioning, the taxes, the conscription, and the wars and rumors of wars. French rule usually meant a higher quality of administration, but the time came when people were more impressed by the Frenchness of the administration than by its quality.

In other words, people had become nationalistic, and their nationalism had developed as a movement of resistance against Napoleon's domination. This explains the unrest in Italy, the armed resistance in Spain, and the growing national unity in Germany. Most fatal for Napoleon was the bitter resistance of Russians of all classes when he invaded that country in 1812. Resistance, as much as ice and snow, was responsible for the catastrophic destruction of his Grand Army. From the frozen plains of Russia, the course of Napoleon's career ended precipitously and inevitably on the island of Elba. Thus the ideology of the French Revolution backfired on its originators. The people Napoleon had "offended" were people who had first been awakened and enthused by the slogan "Liberty, Equality, Fraternity." Then they had turned against their teacher when the very principles he had espoused were betrayed by him.

The Congress of Vienna, which met from September 1814 to June 1815 to redraw the map of Europe after Napoleon's downfall, was guided by three principles—legitimacy, containment, and compensation. By the principle of legitimacy, the monarchs of France, Spain, Holland, and the Italian states were restored to their thrones. By the principle of containment, the states bordering France were made as strong as possible. Holland was given Belgium; Austria received Lombardy and Venetia; and Prussia received lands along the Rhine as well as part of Saxony. The victorious allies compensated themselves by taking various territories—Norway went to Sweden; Malta, Ceylon, and the Cape of Good Hope to Britain; Finland, Bessarabia, and most of Poland to Russia; and Dalmatia and Galicia (as well as Lombardy and Venetia) to Austria. In anticipation of later events it should be noted that Germany and Italy remained disunited. Germany consisted of the loose Germanic Confederation of thirty-nine states. Italy was simply a "geographic expression." It was made up of nine states, all of them dominated by Austria because of its commanding position in Lombardy and Venetia.

Napoleon in Egypt: The Battle of the Pyramids, 1798.

VI. NATIONALISM

What is the significance for world history of the three great revolutions we have studied—the English, the American, and the French? The best answer to this question was given by an illiterate Greek guerrilla chieftain who led his fellow citizens in revolt against their Turkish overlord in 1821:

According to my judgment, the French Revolution and the doings of Napoleon opened the eyes of the world. The nations knew nothing before, and the people thought that kings were gods upon the earth and that they were bound to say that whatever they did was well done. Through this present change it is more difficult to rule the people.[5]

In this simple language the guerrilla leader summarized, too, the essence of the English and the American, as well as the French, revolutions. We have seen how the eyes of the world were opened by the Levellers and the Minutemen and the sans-culottes. This political awakening represented a profound social revolution. It marked the beginning for the first time in history of active and institutionalized mass participation in government. The revolution expressed itself in numerous "isms," which flourished during the nineteenth century. In the remainder of this chapter we shall concern ourselves with three of them—nationalism, liberalism, and socialism—the three that have since exerted the most influence on the course of European and world history.

Nationalism is a phenomenon of modern European history. It did not exist in recognizable form in the Middle Ages. At that time the universalism of the Roman Empire lived on in the Catholic Church, to which all Western Christians belonged; in the Latin language, which all educated people used; and in the Holy Roman Empire, ramshackle structure though it was. Consequently, mass allegiance to a nation was, during those centuries, unknown. Instead, most people considered themselves to be first of all Christians; second, residents of a certain region, such as Burgundy or Cornwall; and only last, if at all, French or English.

Three developments gradually modified this scale of allegiances. One was the rise of vernacular languages and the use of these languages for literary expression. Another was the breakaway from the Catholic Church of several national churches. Finally, the western European dynasties built and consolidated several large, homogeneous, independent states—England, France, Spain, Portugal, and Denmark. These developments laid the basis for the rise of nationalism, though until the late eighteenth century a nation was identified with the person of the sovereign. Luther, for example, regarded "the bishops and princes" as "Germany," and Louis XIV stated that the French nation "resided wholly in the person of the king."

Nationalism did not assume its modern form until the eighteenth century, when the western European bourgeoisie came to share or obtain full power. They did so in the name of the nation, so that the nation no longer was the king, his territory, and his subjects. Rather, it was now comprised of citizens (only propertied citizens until the late nineteenth century) "who inhabited a common territory, possessed a voice in their common government, and were conscious of their common (imagined or real) heritage and their common interests."[6]

This modern form of nationalism received its greatest boost during the French Revolution and the Napoleonic period. To survive the onslaught of the old regimes of Europe, the revolutionary leaders were forced to mobilize national armies—armies of politically conscious citizens ready and eager to fight for their fatherland. The French Revolution contributed to the development of nationalism in several other ways. It required all French citizens to speak French—"the central or national language"—in place of the numerous regional dialects. It established a network of public elementary schools for the purpose of teaching French and love of country. The French Revolution also stimulated the publication of newspapers, pamphlets, and periodicals that were cheap and popularly written, and therefore effective in leaving their imprint on the

whole nation. And it inaugurated such nationalist rites and symbols as the national flag, the national anthem, and national holidays. All these developments enabled nationalism to overcome the people's traditional commitments to religion and to region.

We noted earlier that this passionate identification with one's nation spread from France to neighboring countries. It did so by the natural diffusion of nationalist ideology. Its spread was also a reaction to French aggression and domination. Nationalism was further stimulated by the industrial revolution, which, with its new media (cheap newspapers, books, and leaflets) for mass communication, brought about a more effective and all-embracing indoctrination of citizens. Thus nationalism became a prime factor in European history in the nineteenth century and in world history in the twentieth. But nationalism changed in character as the nineteenth century passed. It began as a humane and tolerant creed, based on the concept of the brotherhood rather than the rivalry of the various nationalist movements. But in the latter part of the century it became increasingly chauvinistic and militaristic because of the influence of Social Darwinism and the success of Bismarck in uniting Germany by Machiavellian diplomacy and war, or, as he put it, by "blood and iron."

Nationalism manifested itself strongly immediately after 1815 because the territorial settlement of that year left millions of peoples either disunited or under foreign rule. This was the case with the Germans, the Italians, the Belgians, the Norwegians, and the numerous nationalities of the Hapsburg and Ottoman empires. The inevitable result was a series of nationalist revolts that broke out in all parts of Europe after 1815. The Greeks revolted successfully in 1821, winning their independence from Turkish rule. The Belgians did likewise in 1830, breaking away from Dutch domination. The Italians, after futile uprisings in 1820, 1830, and 1848, established an independent and united state between 1859 and 1871. The Germans, under the leadership of Prussia, built their German Empire after defeating Austria in 1866 and France in 1870–1871.

The principle of nationalism had triumphed in western Europe by 1871. But in central and eastern Europe the Hapsburg, tsarist, and Ottoman empires remained "prison of nationalities." The inmates of these prisons, however, were becoming increasingly ungovernable as nationalist movements succeeded all around them. The rulers of the three empires were aware of the consequences of nationalism for their multinational states, and they tried to check it by various restrictive measures and by deliberately playing one subject nationality against another. These measures were successful at first but could not prevail indefinitely. The first breaches in the imperial structures were made by the Balkan subjects of the Turks. By 1878 the Serbs, the Rumanians, and the Montenegrins had gained their independence, and in 1908 the Bulgarians did likewise. Much more significant was the assassination in June 1914 of the Hapsburg Archduke Francis Ferdinand by a young Serbian patriot, Gavrilo Princip. This was the fateful event that precipitated World War I, whose outcome was the destruction of all the empires of central and eastern Europe—the German, Austro-Hungarian, Russian, and Turkish. The peace treaties that terminated the war (discussed in Chapter 37, Section VII) were generally based on the principle of nationalism, so that several new states appeared—Poland, Czechoslovakia, Yugoslavia, and Albania—that expressed the independent existence of hitherto subject peoples. For better or for worse, nationalism had triumphed throughout Europe with the conclusion of World War I. And in the following decades, as we shall see in later chapters, the idea of nationalism began to awaken and spur to action the hundreds of millions of subject peoples in Europe's overseas possessions.

VII. LIBERALISM

Liberalism, whose central feature is the emancipation of the individual from class, corporate, or governmental restraint, was the second great European doctrine to affect the globe. Its rise was intimately related to the rise of the middle class, although in central and eastern Europe, where that class was weak, liberalism was espoused by enlightened members of the nobility. Still, liberalism developed in its classic form in western Europe, and it has remained essentially a middle-class movement in its theory and source of support.

Liberal doctrines were first clearly formulated and implemented during the English Revolution. At that time, these doctrines were primarily those of religious toleration and of security of person and of property against the arbitrariness of the crown. Specifically, carrying out these doctrines involved parliamentary control of government, the existence of independent political parties, and the recognition of the need for, and the rights of, opposition parties. On the other hand, the franchise was limited by property qualifications, so that the lower-middle class and the workers, who made up most of the population, were left voteless. Thus, liberalism in seventeenth-century England advanced middle-class interests.

Liberalism was further defined and applied as the American Revolution brought about substantial advances in restricting slavery, extending religious toleration, broadening the franchise, and establishing constitutional government. The federal Constitution adopted in 1791 was based on the principle of the separation of powers in order to prevent tyranny—by having the executive, legislative, and judicial powers check and balance each other. The Bill of Rights guaranteed freedom of religion, speech, press, and assembly. And the U.S. Constitution, like the English settlement, carefully safeguarded the interests of the propertied classes: by limiting the franchise and by providing for the indirect election of the president and the senators and for the election of the various branches of the government for different periods of time. These arrangements were designed to prevent a radical popular movement from getting control of the entire government at any one time and introducing dangerous changes.

Even more advanced in its liberal tenets than the American Revolution was the French. Its Declaration of the Rights of Man and Citizen is the classic statement of eighteenth-century liberalism, proclaiming in ringing phrases the liberties of the individual. But French liberalism, too, was primarily a bourgeois movement. The Declaration, like all the several constitutions adopted by the French revolutionaries, stressed the rights of property as "inviolable and sacred." And Napoleon's famous codes, which proved to be the most durable and influential, specifically forbade the organization of trade unions and the waging of strikes.

We may conclude that the liberalism that emerged from the English, American, and French revolutions took the institutional form of constitutional parliamentary government and was concerned about equal civil rights, though not equal political and social rights. As the nineteenth century passed, liberalism, like other historical movements, changed appreciably in character. It could not continue to concern itself mainly with bourgeois interests at a time when the masses were becoming more assertive as a result of increasing education and trade-union organization. Consequently, there was a shift from the early classical liberalism to a more democratic variety. Equality before the law was supplemented by equality before the ballot box. By the end of the nineteenth century male suffrage had been adopted in most of the western European countries. Even the hallowed principle of laissez-faire was gradually modified. Hitherto intervention by the government in economic and social matters had been regarded as mischievous and futile meddling with the operation of natural laws. This theoretical proposition, however, did not jibe with the facts of life as far as the workers were concerned. Civil liberties and the right to vote did not relieve them from the poverty and insecurity produced by unemployment, sickness, disability, and old age. So they used their voting power and union organization to press for social reforms. Under this pressure a new *democratic liberalism* developed that recognized the responsibility of the state for the welfare of all its citizens. Thus the western European countries, led by Germany, adopted social-reform programs, including old-age pensions; minimum-wage laws; sickness, accident, and unemployment insurance; and regulation of hours and conditions of work. These reforms of democratic liberalism were the prelude to the welfare state that has become the hallmark of our own age.

VIII. SOCIALISM

Socialism is the antithesis of the classical liberalism of the eighteenth and early nineteenth centuries. Liberalism emphasizes the individual and his or her rights; socialism, the community and its collective welfare. Liberalism represents society as the product of natural laws and is skeptical of advancing human welfare artificially by legislation. Socialism, by contrast, holds that people, by rational thought and action, can determine their own social system and social relationships. Furthermore, it maintains that human nature is primarily the product of social environment. Accordingly, contemporary evils may be eliminated by establishing a society specifically designed to promote collective well-being rather than individual profit and to instill cooperative social attitudes and patterns of behavior rather than competitive ones. In short, socialism stresses the collective society and planned social change rather than the individual and laissez-faire.

Plans for the reorganization of society are by no means peculiar to our modern age. Ever since the rise of civilization, political and economic power has been concentrated in the hands of a few. This has led prophets and reformers of all periods to advocate plans promoting social justice and equality. In the classical world, for example, Plato in his *Republic* called for an aristocratic communism, a dictatorship of communistic philosophers. In the medieval period the English peasant leader John Ball declared to his followers, "My good people,—things cannot go well in England, nor ever will, until all goods are held in common, and until there will be neither serfs nor gentlemen, and we shall all be equal."[7] The turmoil and the passions of the English and French revolutions naturally stimulated more schemes for the promotion of the common welfare, but the final outcome, as we have seen, was the triumph of the relatively conservative Cromwell and of Napoleon.

A vigorous new school of social reformers— the *Utopian Socialists*—appeared in the early nineteenth century. Outstanding were two Frenchmen, Henri de Saint-Simon (1760–1825) and Charles Fourier (1772–1837), and the English industrialist Robert Owen (1771–1858). Their proposals varied widely but had one basic characteristic in common. Although they paid much attention to the principles and to the precise workings of their projected model communities, they never seriously faced the problem of how these were to take the place of the existing society. Saint-Simon, for example, tried to enlist the support of the pope and of Louis XVIII. Fourier

Statue of Karl Marx in Karl Marx Park, Moscow.

sat in his room at noon every day for twelve years waiting in vain for responses to his newspaper appeals for support. These reformers definitely did not think in terms of revolution or of class warfare. In fact, they scarcely thought at all about how their elaborate blueprints might be put into practice. It is for this reason that they are known as "Utopian" Socialists.

Karl Marx (1818–1883), the father of modern socialism, differed fundamentally from the Utopian Socialists in almost every respect. He was as materialistic in his outlook as they were idealistic. He spent most of his life studying the historical evolution and the precise functioning of the existing capitalist society, whereas utopians prepared blueprints of model communities. Marx was convinced from his study of history that capitalism would be overthrown by *class struggle* and would be replaced by a new type of socialist society. He reached this conclusion because he believed that the wages paid to workers were insufficient for them to buy what they produced. This inadequate purchasing power eventually must lead to the closing of factories, unemployment, a further decline of purchasing power, and, at length, a full-scale depression. Furthermore, Marx believed that these depressions would become increasingly frequent and severe until finally the unemployed proletariat would be driven in desperation to revolution. In this way capitalism would be replaced by socialism, as feudalism earlier had been by capitalism. And the new socialistic society would be depression-proof because, with government ownership of the means of production, there could be no private employers, no profits, and hence no lack of purchasing power.

Marx did not limit himself to theorizing and writing. Throughout his life he combined intellectual activity with efforts to organize and activize workers. The last sentence of his 1848 *Communist Manifesto* reads, "Workers of the world, unite." Marx played an important role in the establishment in 1864 of the International Workingmen's Association or, as it is commonly called, the First International. This body was committed to Marx's program of the workers' seizure of power in order to reorganize society along socialistic lines. It attracted considerable attention with its propaganda and its participation in various strikes. But it disintegrated in 1873, largely because its membership included an undisciplined and constantly feuding assortment of romanticists, nationalists, and anarchists, as well as Socialists.

In 1884 the Socialist, or Second, International was established in Paris. This was a loosely knit organization affiliated with the numerous Socialist parties that had appeared by this time in various countries. The Second International grew rapidly, so that by 1914 it included the Socialist parties of twenty-seven countries with a total membership of 12 million workers. The Second International was much more moderate in its doctrines and its actions than the First. The reason for the shift in emphasis was that the major constituent parties were themselves turning away from simon-pure Marxism to what was termed *revisionism*. A number of factors explain this shift in emphasis. One was the gradual extension of the franchise in the western European countries, which meant workers could use ballots rather than bullets to attain their objectives. Another was the steady rise after 1850 in European living standards, which tended to make workers more willing to accept capitalism. The German revisionist leader Eduard Bernstein expressed the new viewpoint when he declared that Socialists should "work less for the better future and more for the better present." The new strategy, in other words, was to make immediate gains by gradual reform measures rather than to strive for a socialistic society by revolution. Not all Socialists were willing to go along with this revisionism.

Some of them remained true to what they considered to be the teachings of Marx, so that most Socialist parties split into "orthodox" and "revisionist" factions. The revisionists, however, were more in tune with the temper of the times and usually controlled their respective parties. Indeed, they were able to organize powerful trade union movements and to win millions of votes in electoral contests. In fact, the German, the French, and the Italian Socialist parties had by 1914 a larger number of seats in their respective national assemblies than any other political parties.

When World War I began in 1914, the Second International paid the price for its revisionism: The majority of its members proved to be nationalists first and socialists second. They responded to the exhortations of their respective national governments, with the result that millions of workers died fighting on both sides of the trenches. Thus the Second International was torn asunder, and although it was revived after the war, it never attained its former strength and prestige.

Socialism, however, did not peter out with the disintegration of the Second International. In fact, it was during World War I that the Russian Socialists, or Bolsheviks, as they were called, succeeded in seizing power and establishing the first proletarian government in history. Furthermore, the Bolsheviks organized the Third, or Communist, International to challenge the Second, or Socialist, International. Because peasants and workers in the underdeveloped countries have not enjoyed the prosperity and freedoms of workers in developed countries, Marxism won many followers in former colonial lands. This was especially true after the bloodshed and suffering of the two world wars. In recent years, Marxism has lost much of its appeal because, as we shall see below, the Marxist societies that have emerged in various parts of the world have proved to be very different from the shining ideals set forth by Marx in the nineteenth century.

IX. WOMEN IN POLITICAL REVOLUTIONS

Women played an active role in all the political revolutions, but with very mixed results. The basic reason is that women did not insist that their demands be formally accepted and incorporated in the revolutionary programs. Rather, they were content to serve as auxiliaries in male-controlled political movements. Their support naturally was welcomed during the struggle for power, but after victory was won, they were ignored and forced to return to their prerevolutionary subordinate status. This pattern is evident in all modern revolutions, from the English in the seventeenth century to the Russian and Chinese in the twentieth.

The various stages of the French Revolution show clearly how this pattern evolved. Before the revolution French women, like women throughout Europe, accepted the authority of father before marriage and of husband after. The Marquis de Condorcet was one of the very few leaders of the French Revolution who publicly urged that women be allowed to own property, to vote, to hold office, and to receive the same free public education as males. But the Marquis was far ahead of his time. Much more acceptable were the views of Rousseau, who expounded advanced political ideas in his *Social Contract* but in his novel *Emile* (1761) advised women to "Be simple in your dress, hard working in your homes, never go to the popular assemblies wanting to speak. . . . Is there a sight in this world so touching, so respectable as that of a mother surrounded by her children, directing the work of her domestics, procuring a happy life for her husband, and wisely governing the home?"

When the revolution began, middle-class women set forth their demands in their *cahiers* (notebooks) to the Estates General. They asked for safeguarding of women's dowries from profligate husbands, protection for wives against abuse, state jobs for women who were being forced to prostitution by economic necessity, and a public education system to widen employment opportunities for women. But the women did not press home their demands, so the Declaration of the Rights of Man adopted by the National Assembly on August 26, 1789, was silent on the rights of women. Working-class women were more forceful because there was no bread in Paris and they were hungry. In October 1789 they marched to the palace at Versailles and brought back with them the royal family, referring to them as "the baker, the baker's wife, and the baker's little boy."

By 1790 women were publishing their own newspapers in which they demanded the right to vote, to participate in assemblies, to serve on juries, and to obtain divorce. These demands were included in the Declaration of the Rights of Women, proclaimed by female leaders in 1791. Women became most active in the spring of 1793 when the king was executed for treason and France was invaded by five foreign armies. The hard-pressed Paris government called on French women to join in the defense of their country. They responded enthusiastically, rolling bandages in hospitals and making shirts, trousers, hats, stockings, and gloves for their soldiers. Some even volunteered and fought in the revolutionary armies.

The republican government showed its appreciation by passing laws legalizing divorce, making marriage a civil contract, granting wives a share of family property, and providing free and compulsory primary schools for both girls and boys. At the height of their activism, members of the Republican Revolutionary Women patrolled streets, wearing trousers with pistols in their belts and red caps on their heads.

A year later, when the danger of foreign invasion had passed, the reaction against female revolutionaries began. A specific issue was the ending of price controls and the reduction of the bread ration. Workers' families suffered while profiteers flaunted their new riches. When thousands of desperate men and women took up arms, the convention called out the regular army and surrounded the rebellious neighborhoods. The democratic constitution of 1793 was scrapped, as were most of the women's rights recently granted. Napoleon consolidated the reaction by including laws in his code that restored the absolute authority of father and husband.

The basic reason for the setback was that the cause of women's rights lacked mass support among the women themselves. During the revolution they had responded primarily to the needs of their class rather than of their sex. They had taken to the streets primarily for social reform and economic relief rather than for female rights. When the French Revolution, like the English before it, rejected social restructuring and turned conservative, the gains of the women as females were swept away along with their gains as workers. Apart from Condorcet, the top leaders of the revolution agreed wholeheartedly with Rousseau that women's place was in the home. They recognized and applauded the contributions that women had made during the revolution. But after the revolution the political leaders made speeches about the future contributions that women could make within the family, *not* outside it.

The feminist themes developed during the French Revolution were not forgotten in the postrevolution years. They were resurrected by middle- and upper-class European women throughout the nineteenth century. Feminist leaders published books and periodicals and established a network of national and international women's associations. These organizations promoted education for women, opposed state-regulated prostitution, supported aid for abandoned children and unwed mothers, agitated against alcoholism, and mounted peace movements that branded war as the ultimate expression of male politics. Progress was modest, and activist women concluded by the late nineteenth century that they could not gain their goals unless they shared political power with men on an equal basis. Henceforth the vote became the dominant issue for *suffragists* in all countries. Rapid progress was made in the twentieth century, so that the number of countries that enfranchised women rose from 1 in 1900 to 3 in 1910, 15 in 1920, 21 in 1930, 30 in 1940, 69 in 1950, 92 in 1960, 127 in 1970, and 129 in 1975.

The right to vote did not prove to be the cure-all for women's problems, as had been expected. Casting a ballot on election day did not automatically confer political power. Few women were elected to representative bodies, and still fewer ended up in positions with executive au-

Member of one of the earliest feminist movements—an early twentieth-century suffragette.

thority. In fact, the international women's movement lost much of its vigor after the franchise had been won. The doldrums persisted until World War II, when a combination of several new and decisive factors emerged to energize the feminist movement. The origins and nature of these new factors and their impact on women throughout the globe will be analyzed in the concluding chapter.

SUGGESTED READINGS

For a comparison and interpretation of the English, French, and Russian revolutions, see C. Brinton, *The Anatomy of Revolution* (Random House, 1958); and the collection of readings by R. W. Postgate, *Revolution from 1789 to 1906* (Harper & Row, 1962).

On the English Revolution, see P. Zagorin, *A History of Political Thought in the English Revolution* (Routledge & Kegan Paul, 1954); and the studies by C. Hill, *Intellectual Origins of the English Revolution* (Clarendon, 1962), and *The World Turned Upside Down: Radical Ideas During the English Revolution* (Viking, 1972). For the Enlightenment, see the surveys of R. B. Mowat, *The Age of Reason* (Houghton Mifflin, 1934); E. Cassirer, *The Philosophy of the Enlightenment* (Princeton University, 1951); and also the documentary collection of F. E. Manuel, ed., *The Enlightenment* (Prentice Hall, 1965).

Studies of the American Revolution are by P. Maier, *From Resistance to Revolution* (Routledge &

Kegan Paul, 1973); L. H. Gipson, *The Coming of the Revolution, 1763–1775,* and J. R. Alden, *The American Revolution, 1775–1783,* the latter two in the "New American Nation" series (Harper & Row, 1954). For the impact of the American Revolution on Europe, see M. Kraus, *The North Atlantic Civilization* (D. Van Nostrand, 1957); and G. D. Lillibridge, ed., *The American Image Past and Present* (D. C. Heath, 1968).

Of the thousands of books on the French Revolution, noteworthy is J. M. Thompson, 2nd ed., *The French Revolution* (Blackwell, 1966); and the collection of readings by J. H. Stewart, *A Documentary Survey of the French Revolution* (Macmillan, 1951). Of particular significance for the analysis of the revolutionary movement in the Western world between 1760 and 1800 is R. R. Palmer, *The Age of the Democratic Revolution: A Political History of Europe and America, 1760–1800,* 2 vols. (Princeton University, 1959, 1964). More recent studies are O. Connelly, *French Revolution–Napoleonic Era* (Holt, Rinehart & Winston, 1979); L. Hunt, *Politics, Culture and Class in the French Revolution* (University of California, 1986); and G. Rude, *The Crowd in History: Popular Disturbances in France and England* (Lawrence and Wishart, 1981).

A voluminous literature on nationalism now exists, some comprehensive surveys being B. C. Shafer, *Nationalism: Myth and Reality* (Harcourt Brace Jovanovich, 1955); and K. R. Minogue, *Nationalism* (Basic Books, 1967). The bibliography on liberalism also is tremendous, though there are few comprehensive studies. Outstanding among these are H. J. Laski, *The Rise of Liberalism* (Harper & Row, 1936); J. R. Pennock, *Liberal Democracy: Its Merits and Prospects* (Holt, Rinehart & Winston, 1950); J. Sigmann, *1848: The Romantic and Democratic Revolutions in Europe* (Harper & Row, 1973); and the brief survey, with appended readings, in J. S. Schapiro, *Liberalism: Its Meaning and History* (D. Van Nostrand, 1958).

On socialism, there is no end of literature, much of it controversial. Most recent is the appraisal of Marx's influence in D. McLellan, ed., *Marx: The First Hundred Years* (St. Martin's Press, 1983); A. S. Lindemann, *A History of European Socialism* (Yale University, 1983); the useful reference work by T. Bottomore, *A Dictionary of Marxist Thought* (Harvard University, 1983); and the paperback collection of relevant readings by C. Wright Mills, *The Marxists* (Dell, 1982).

Finally, for an overview of the role of women, see the relevant chapters in R. Bridenthal and C. Koonz, *Becoming Visible: Women in European History* (Houghton Mifflin, 1977). More detailed accounts are available in R. J. Evans, *The Feminists: Women's Emancipation Movements in Europe, America and Australia 1840–1920* (Barnes & Noble, 1978); P. Stock, *Better Than Rubies: A History of Women's Education* (Putnam's, 1978); C. Banks, *Faces of Feminism: A Study of Feminism as a Social Movement* (Oxford University, 1981); and J. Kelly, *Women, History and Theory* (University of Chicago, 1985).

30 Russia

PETER the GREAT

For three hundred years Russia has aspired to consort with Occidental Europe; for three hundred years she has taken her most serious ideas, her most fruitful teachings, and her most vivid delights from there.

Peter Y. Chaadayev

In a sense, it is paradoxical to consider Europe's impact on Russia; Russia, after all, is a part of Europe, and the Russian people are a European people. But Russia lies on the fringe of Europe and provides a great buffer zone between that continent and Asia. Because of this location the historical experience of the Russian people has been quite different from that of other Europeans, and the culture they have developed is correspondingly different. As a result, Russian thinkers have tormented themselves generation after generation with the basic issue of national orientation and national goals.

Russia's relationship with the West has generally been that of passive recipient. Only in the past century and a half has Russia been able to repay the West, at first with the creations of its great writers and composers, and later with the social stimuli generated by the Bolshevik Revolution. But until the twentieth century Europe's impact on Russia was much greater than was the reverse, and this influence has been a central factor in the development of the country.

I. RUSSIA AND EUROPE TO 1856

The first Russian state developed about the principality of Kiev in the ninth century after Christ (see Chapter 26, Section II). This early Russian state had numerous ties with the rest of Europe. It conducted a very considerable trade across the Black Sea with Byzantium and across the Baltic with northwest Europe. It is significant that Prince Yaroslav in the eleventh century had marriage connections with the leading dynasties of Europe. His sister was married to Casimir I of Poland, his son to a princess of Byzantium, and his two daughters to Henry I of France and to Harald II of Norway.

During the following centuries two crucial developments combined to isolate Russia. One

480

Tsar Peter the Great.

was Prince Vladimir's decision about A.D. 990 to adopt the Byzantine Orthodox form of Christianity rather than the Roman Catholic. Although the differences between the two religions were not very substantial at the time, during the following decades the development of the doctrine of papal supremacy and its increasing practice finally led in 1054 to a schism between the two churches. Russia inevitably became involved in this Catholic and Orthodox feuding. This was particularly so after the fall of Constantinople to the Turks (1453), which left Russia as the only independent citadel of Orthodoxy. These events made the Russians self-satisfied, self-righteous, and self-isolated, and they ignored and scorned the great changes that were transforming the rest of Europe.

The other development that cut Russia off from the West was the Mongol invasion in 1237. The Mongols did not interfere with the affairs of their Russian subjects as long as the latter accepted the domination of the khan and paid him

annual tribute. Nevertheless, Mongol domination severed most of the remaining ties between Russia and the rest of Europe. This rupture, which persisted during the two centuries of Mongol rule, came at a time when the West was experiencing the Renaissance, the Reformation, overseas expansion, and the commercial revolution. But isolated Russia remained largely unaffected by these profound economic and cultural movements. Furthermore, the Mongols left their own imprint on Russian society. Their ideas and administrative usages paved the way for the establishment of the semi-oriental absolutism of the later Muscovite tsars. And their ethnic contribution was also significant—for example, approximately 17 percent of the Moscow upper class at the end of the seventeenth century was of non-Russian, or Eastern, origin.

When the Russians rid themselves of Mongol rule in the fifteenth century, the Muscovite civilization that came to light was quite different from anything in western Europe. It was a homogeneous civilization in the sense that the Orthodox religion shaped and colored people's outlook and actions. But it was also a civilization largely devoid of the commerce, the industry, and the science that had made the West so dynamic and expansionist. More emancipated and far-seeing Russian leaders soon perceived that their economic and technological backwardness represented a threat to their national security. Thus it was that the Russians in the sixteenth century, like the Turks, the Japanese, and the Chinese in later centuries, began to borrow from the West as a measure of self-defense. And what they were primarily interested   owing was military technology.

There was n   tract about this policy.
death, for Russia
Swedes, Lithuan
by the Turks ar
is significant th
proposed a m
marriage to C
of Poland h
her to reje
wrote, "we
because h
not know

St. Petersburg—Tsar Peter's "Window to the West."

were deliberately trying to prevent that country from getting Western arms and techniques. The Russians, on their part, naturally tried to break the isolating encirclement, and they did so with increasing success. During the seventeenth century they hired many foreign military officers who were left unemployed when the Thirty Years' War ended.

The reign of Tsar Peter the Great (1682–1725) accelerated the process of westernization tremendously. With his iron will and herculean energy he issued over 3,000 decrees, many in his own hand, and almost all inspired by him. He reorganized his administration and armed forces along Western lines; established industries to support his armies; imported thousands of foreign experts of various types; sent droves of young Russians to study abroad; and set up a number of schools, all of them utilitarian in character. He founded schools of mathematics and navigation, ╌miralty schools, war-department schools, ci─ ╌g schools, and, at the summit, the Acad─ ╌ences. Peter also shattered all precedent ╌hrough western Europe to study for─ ╌nd practices at first hand. ╌ous ways Peter succeeded in ╌s goal of opening a "win─ ╌ore, he opened this

window in a literal sense by defeating Sweden and acquiring frontage on the Baltic Sea. Here he built his new capital, St. Petersburg—the symbol of the new Russia, as Moscow was of the old. These changes, however, were not brought about without bitter opposition from wide segments of the population. Peter had to fight against the overt and covert opposition of conservative *boyars* and churchmen, as well as against the apathy and suspicion of the masses. Even the changes that he did introduce were limited in two important respects: They were largely military, economic, and technical in character, and they affected only the sympathetic members of the thin upper crust of the population.

Peter's work was continued by the gifted and colorful Catherine the Great (1762–1796). Catherine regarded herself and her court as a medium for the Europeanization of Russia. She was much more intellectual than the pragmatic Peter and energetically patronized literature, art, theater, and the press. She was not an original thinker, but she readily absorbed the ideas of others, especially the philosophes. In fact, she prided herself on being an enlightened despot and often quoted the maxims of the Enlightenment. During her reign the higher Russian nobility became Europeanized. They had worn beards and flowing oriental robes during Peter's reign, but under Catherine they aped the court of Versailles in their speech, clothes, dwellings, and social functions. Their children were brought up by French governesses, learned French as their mother tongue, and then picked up only enough Russian to manage the servants. Thus the Europeanization of Russia was no longer confined to technical matters, yet it was also still limited to the upper class. Indeed, the gulf between the Europeanized upper crust and the peasant masses who were bound to the estates as serfs was becoming wider and more ominous.

This division between a favored ruling class and the exploited serfs who made up the great majority of the total population scarcely jibed with the principles of the Enlightenment that Catherine quoted so often. But Catherine was too much a realist to be unduly concerned about the discrepancy between theory and reality. Knowing that she depended on the nobles for her position, she never seriously challenged their interests and privileges. On the contrary, she turned violently against the teachings of the philosophes when the French Revolution broke out. She denounced the revolution as "an irreligious, immoral, anarchical, abominable, and diabolical plague, the enemy of God and of Thrones. . . . As for the people and its opinion, that is of no great consequence."[2]

Catherine could still afford in her time to so lightly dismiss the views of "the people," but it was to be different with her successors, especially after the great Russian victory over Napoleon's Grand Army. Between 1815 and 1818 a Russian army of occupation had been stationed in France. This naturally made a deep impression on Russian public opinion. For most, the Russian feeling of superiority and condescension toward the West had been reinforced, but many of the officers of the occupation army were much impressed by the relatively free Western society in which they had lived for four years. There they had absorbed the liberal and radical ideas in contemporary France and had been profoundly influenced by them. When they returned to Russia in 1818, they found the tsarist autocracy stifling.

Sentiments such as these explain the so-called Decembrist Revolt that broke out in December 1825, upon the death of Alexander I. The leaders were mostly army officers who wished to westernize Russia by abolishing serfdom and the autocracy. The revolt failed miserably because there was no mass support. The Russians at this time lived under conditions so utterly different from those prevailing in western Europe that they simply were not ready for Western political ideas and institutions. More specifically, Russia lacked the commerce, the industry, and the middle class that had played so decisive a role in the political evolution of the West. Instead, there were at the bottom the bound and inert serf masses—the "dark people," as they were called—and at the top the nobility and the court. Consequently, there was no mass support for the reforms and for the Western type of society desired by the Decembrists.

The meaning of these basic differences between Russia and the West divided Russian thinkers into two groups, the Westerners and the Slavophils. The Westerners deplored the differences, interpreting them as a product of Russia's slower rate of development. Accordingly, their hero was Peter the Great, and they urged that other rulers match Peter's heroic efforts to catch up with the West. The Slavophils, on the other hand, rejected the Westerner's basic assumption of the unity of human civilization. They maintained that every state embodies and expresses the peculiar national spirit of its people and that if an attempt is made to model one state after another, the inevitable result will be contradiction and discord. They held that the differences between Russia and the West were fundamental and inherent and reflected profound dissimilarities in national spirit rather than degrees of advance. Accordingly these Slavophils idealized the homogeneous Muscovite society of the period before Peter, and they regarded him as the arch-enemy of Russian civilization and national unity. Far from considering Western society superior, they rejected it as materialistic, irreligious, and torn by dissension and revolution.

II. RUSSIA AND EUROPE, 1856–1905

The issue between the Slavophils and the Westerners were settled, but not by persuasion of one side by the other, but by the irresistible pressure of the rapidly developing and expanding Western society. This pressure was dramatically illustrated by the Crimean War (1854–1856) between Russia and a number of Western powers, of which the most important were Britain and France. The war was fought on Russian soil—in the Crimean peninsula—and yet Russia was defeated and forced to accept the humiliating Treaty of Paris. This treaty required Russia to scrap its naval units in the Black Sea and its fortifications along the Black Sea coast. It also forced Russia to surrender certain small but strategic territories along the Danube.

The Crimean defeat was a severe shock for the Russian nationalists and Slavophils. Unlike many Westerners, who had warned of Russia's impending defeat because it had not kept up with the West, the Slavophils had predicted that the superiority of Russia's autocratic institutions would lead to a victory comparable to that of 1812 over Napoleon. Actually, the Crimean defeat unveiled the corruption and backwardness of the old regime. Russia's soldiers had fought as gallantly in 1855 as in 1812, but the odds were hopelessly against them. They had rifles that shot only a third as far as those of the Western armies. They had only sailing ships to use against the steamships of the British and the French. They had no medical or food-supply services that were worthy of the name. And the lack of railways in the Crimean peninsula forced them to haul military supplies in carts and to march on foot for hundreds of miles before reaching the front. In short, the war was lost because, as the Westerners had warned, "Europe has been steadily advancing on the road of progress while we have been standing still."

The revelation of the old regime's bankruptcy led to its modification. The first change was the emancipation of the serfs, who had been intensely restless even before the war. In fact, over five hundred peasant disturbances had broken out during the three decades of Nicholas I's reign between 1825 and 1855. With the disaster in the Crimea, the mounting pressure of the serfs became irresistible, and Nicholas's successor, Alexander II, accepted emancipation as the only alternative to revolution. His Emancipation Decree (March 1, 1861) freed the serfs and divided the land that they tilled between themselves and the noble proprietors. The proprietors were paid with government treasury bonds for the land that was distributed among the peasants. In return, the peasants were required to compensate the government by paying redemption dues for forty-nine years. This was a great turning point in Russian history, even greater than the 1863 Emancipation Proclamation in American history. Emancipation in the United States concerned only the Negro minority, whereas in Russia it involved the overwhelming majority of the population. The repercussions of the freeing of the serfs were so far reaching that a series of other reforms were unavoidable. These included the reorganization of the judiciary and of the local government.

During the decades following the Crimean War, western Europe further undermined the old regime in Russia by contributing decisively to the industrialization of the country. Of the total of £500 million invested in Russian industry in 1917, just over one-third was made up of foreign investments. Western capital controlled 50 percent of coal and oil output, 60 percent of copper and iron ore, and 80 percent of coke. The number of factory workers rose from 381,000 in 1865, to 1,620,000 in 1890, and to 3 million in 1898. By 1913, Russia was producing as much iron and three-fourths as much coal as France.

These developments meant that the Russia of 1914 was much more similar to Europe than the Russia of the Decembrists of 1825. But as the Slavophils had warned, the increasing similarity brought about certain divisions and conflicts within Russian society. One of these was the growing unrest and rising political consciousness among the peasants. The peasants had been far from satisfied with the terms of the Emancipation Decree, which they felt had left too large a proportion of the land to the nobles. During the following decades, as the peasants grew rapidly in numbers, their land hunger grew correspondingly, and they became increasingly dissatisfied. Another source of grievance for the peasants was the intolerably heavy tax load. They paid not only redemption dues for the land they had received in 1861 but also an assortment of local taxes. In addition, they bore much of the cost of Russia's industrialization, because high protective tariffs forced up the cost of the manufactured goods they bought. The extent and the intensity of peasant discontent were shown by the increasing frequency of violent peasant outbreaks against landlords and unpopular government officials.

Peasant disaffection found political expression in the Socialist Revolutionary party, which was organized in 1901. Since no political parties were allowed in Russia prior to the 1905 revolution, the Socialist Revolutionaries had to operate as an illegal underground group. The main plank of their platform was the distribution of state and noble lands among the peasantry. In two important respects they differed from the various types of Marxist socialists. In the first place, they regarded the peasantry rather than the urban proletariat as the main revolutionary force in Russia. In the second place, they advocated and practiced individual acts of terrorism, rather than relying on mass organization and pressure. Within the Socialist Revolutionary party was the highly secret Fighting Organization, which directed the terroristic activities. The success of the organization may be gauged from its long list of illustrious victims, including governors of provinces, ministers of state, and even the tsar's uncle, Grand Duke Sergei.

The unrest of the peasants was matched by that of the urban proletariat, who had appeared with the growth of industry. The early days of industrialization in Russia, as elsewhere in Europe, involved gross exploitation of labor: sixteen-hour working days, low wages, child labor, and abominable working and living conditions. Under these circumstances the Russian workers, like those of central and western Europe, came under the influence of Marxist doctrines. Thus a Social Democratic party was organized in 1898 just as similar Socialist parties had been established elsewhere in Europe. And like the other Socialist parties, the Russian party split into revisionist and orthodox factions—or, as they were called in this instance, the Mensheviks and the Bolsheviks.

The split occurred during the second party congress held in London in 1903. The issues concerned party membership and party discipline. Vladimir Lenin, the leader of the orthodox faction, maintained that because of the repressive tsarist autocracy, the Social Democratic party had to operate very differently from other Socialist parties. Membership should be open, not to each and every dues-paying sympathizer, but only to a small group of full-time professional revolutionaries. And this select membership was to function according to the principle of *democratic centralism.* Any major issue facing the party was to be discussed freely by the members until a decision was reached democratically by a vote. But then the "centralism" part of the principle became operative. Every party member, regardless of personal inclinations, was required on pain of expulsion to support undeviatingly what was now the "party line."

Only with such rigid discipline, Lenin maintained, could Russian Socialists carry on effectively their underground operations. Lenin won the support of most of the delegates to the 1903 congress, so that his followers henceforth were known as *Bolsheviks,* after the Russian word for "majority," and his opponents as Mensheviks, or "minority." It should be noted, however, that the Bolsheviks remained a small group until the outbreak of World War I. Then the chaos and misery produced by the Russian defeats at the front gave the Bolsheviks the opportunity to use their superior organization to mobilize and lead the disaffected masses.

In addition to the peasants and the urban workers, there was in Russia at the turn of the century a middle class that also was becoming increasingly discontented with the tsarist regime. The political organization reflecting the views of this group was the Constitutional Democratic party, commonly known under the abbreviated title of Cadets. The program of this party, founded in 1905, resembled that of the English Liberals: a constitutional monarchy balanced by a parliamentary body similar to Britain's House of Commons. The Cadets included many of Russia's outstanding intellectuals and businesspersons. When the tsar was forced to accept an elected assembly (Duma) following the 1905 revolution, the Cadets played a leading role in its deliberations because of their knowledge of parliamentary procedures. And yet the Cadets never won a mass following comparable to that of the Social Democrats or the Socialist Revolutionaries. One reason was that the middle class was relatively small in Russia because of the retarded development of commerce and industry. The middle class was further weakened because so much of the national economy was controlled by foreign interests. And the Cadets were peculiarly vulnerable to the pressures of the tsarist autocracy because, with their middle-class background, they were less willing to meet force with force.

Such, then, was the West's impact on Russia by the turn of the century. The intrusion of the West had undermined a distinctive and homogeneous society; and the repercussions of the resulting stresses and dissensions were to culminate in the great revolutions of 1905 and 1917. Before considering these upheavals, we shall survey Russian policies in Asia up to the time of the Russo-Japanese War, which set the stage for the 1905 revolution.

III.   RUSSIA AND ASIA TO 1905

Just as the relations between Russia and Europe were determined largely by the economic and technological superiority of Europe, so the relations between Russia and Asia were determined by the superiority of Russia. This superiority had enabled Russia between the sixteenth and eighteenth centuries to overcome the tribespeople of Siberia and to expand eastward to the Pacific. But in the southeast the Russians had been halted by the strong Chinese Empire and forced to accept the Nerchinsk Treaty (1689) confining them to the territory north of the Amur valley (see Chapter 26, Section III).

During the eighteenth and nineteenth centuries the Russians resumed their advance to the east and the south, rounding out their empire by acquiring Alaska, the Amur valley, and central Asia. The addition of Alaska involved simply a continuation of the earlier trans-Siberian push into relatively empty territories. But in the Amur valley the Russians prevailed over the Chinese Empire, and in central Asia they imposed their rule on ancient Moslem khanates. These successes were made possible by Russia's steady technological progress. Russia's technology, though inadequate vis-à-vis the West, and indeed, derived from the West, was nonetheless sufficient to give Russians a decisive advantage in their relations with the Chinese in east Asia and with the

Moslems in central Asia. Thus, the Russians continued to extend their imperial frontiers until they were stopped by powers that were technologically equal or superior—that is, by the Americans in Alaska, by the British in India and Persia, and by the Japanese in Manchuria.

Alaska

The Russian advance to Alaska began during the reign of Peter the Great. The westernizing tsar was as much interested in the Far East as in Europe, so he selected Captain Vitus Bering, a naval officer of Danish extraction, to lead expeditions to the American continent in 1728 and 1740. Bering sailed eastward across the sea that bears his name, explored the Aleutian Islands, and also landed on the coast of Alaska. Russian merchants followed on the heels of the explorers, attracted by the profitable trade in sea-otter skins. The merchants first exploited the Aleutian Islanders and then established posts along the Alaskan coast. In 1799 the various private trading companies combined to form the Russo-American Company. The outstanding Russian leader in Alaska was Alexander Baranov, who directed operations energetically and autocratically for a generation. His chief problem was transporting supplies from Siberia across one of the world's stormiest and foggiest seas. Accordingly, Baranov sent expeditions down the American coast to establish settlements where fresh supplies could be grown for the Alaskan posts. In November 1811, Fort Ross was established on the Russian River north of San Francisco, and by 1819 the Russians had a chain of nineteen settlements on the American coast.

This expansion led to friction with Spain and with the United States. In fact, the presence of the Russians in the northwest Pacific was partly responsible for the proclamation of the Monroe Doctrine in 1823. In the end, the Russians decided to give up their American holdings. The decline in the fur trade had brought the Russo-American Company to the point of bankruptcy, and the Russians feared that Alaska was too distant to be defended against American expansionism. Anticipating that they would lose the territory sooner or later, they sold it to the

A Russian church in Kodiak, Alaska.

United States in 1867 for $7.2 million, or less than two cents per acre.

Amur Valley

Meanwhile, the Russian activity in North America had reawakened Russian interest in the Amur valley. The Russians needed an outlet on the Pacific Ocean to serve as a base for supplying their American settlements. They had the port of Okhotsk, but this was altogether inadequate. It was frozen every year until June and almost continually fogbound. Consequently, the Russians once more looked longingly toward the broad and navigable Amur River, from which they had been ousted by the Nerchinsk Treaty in 1689.

Russian interest was further sharpened by the so-called Opium War of 1839–1842 between Britain and China (see Chapter 33, Section I). As a result of the war, Britain annexed Hong Kong and acquired a predominant influence in the Yangtze valley. The Russians now resolved to establish themselves in the Amur valley lest the British next gain control of the mouth of the river and block their natural outlet to the Pacific. In little more than a decade, the Russians gained all their objectives in this vital region. One reason for their success was the ambition and energy

of young Count Nikolai Muraviev, who was appointed governor general of eastern Siberia in 1847 at the age of thirty-eight. Another reason was the weakness of China, by that time a hollow shell compared to the powerful Chinese Empire that had expelled the Russians from the Amur valley in the seventeenth century.

Count Muraviev was given extensive vice-regal powers, but he went beyond them and sent out exploratory expeditions that planted the Russian flag on foreign soil. One of his officers, Captain (later Admiral) Nevelskoi, established the fortress of Petropavlovsk on the Kamchatka peninsula. He explored and occupied Sakhalin Island after ousting Japanese settlers, launched steamships on the Amur River, encouraged Russian colonists to settle in the Amur valley, and founded a number of posts along the coast between the mouth of the Amur and the Korean frontier. The Russians were able to expand so easily because the entire region was a no man's land over which the Chinese had only a vague suzerainty and no control whatsoever. In fact, the Chinese court was quite unaware of the Russian measures, and it was the Russian government itself that, in May 1851, informed the Chinese of what had taken place.

Five years later, in 1856, hostilities broke out once more between China and Britain. The

Chinese again were badly beaten and forced by the Tientsin Treaties (1858) to open more ports to Western merchants and to make other concessions. Muraviev seized the opportunity to warn the Chinese of the danger of British control of the Amur and to propose joint Russo-Chinese defense of the region. The outcome was the Aigun Treaty (1858) by which Russia obtained the left bank of the Amur to the Ussuri River. Beyond the Ussuri Russia and China were to exercise joint sovereignty over both banks of the river to the ocean.

Muraviev now explored carefully the newly won territories and discovered that the formation of ice on the lower Amur was such that control of both banks was essential for navigation. He also found a magnificent harbor on the coast near the Korean frontier. Despite the provisions of the Aigun Treaty, he founded a city there (1860), which he significantly named Vladivostok, or Lord of the East. Meanwhile, China had become embroiled in further trouble with the Western powers, and in 1860 Peking was occupied by Anglo-French forces. The Russian minister in Peking, Count Nikolai Ignatiev, offered his services as an intermediary and succeeded in getting the allies to evacuate the capital under conditions that were not too unfavorable for China. In return for this service the Chinese government negotiated the Treaty of Peking (1860), giving Russia both banks of the Amur from the Ussuri to the sea and the entire coastal area from the mouth of the Amur to the Korean border. With the winning of these new farflung frontiers (which exist to the present day), Russian expansion in the Far East came to a halt. It was not resumed again until the beginning of the twentieth century, when Tsar Nicholas II attempted to penetrate south into Korea and Manchuria, and thereby started a disastrous war with Japan.

Central Asia

In the meantime, the Russians had also been penetrating into central Asia, although their advance in this region did not begin until the second quarter of the nineteenth century. The delay was partly because of the lack of economic incentives comparable to the profitable fur trade in the north. But there were other reasons: The climate and vegetation of central Asia were quite different from that to which the Russians were accustomed. Immediately to the south of Siberia was the steppe country where the Kazakh nomads lived. Still further south began the great desert, dotted with rich oases that supported the ancient Moslem khanates of Bukhara, Khiva, and Kokand. Much stronger militarily than the scattered Siberian tribes, these khanates were able to keep the Russians at arm's length until the late nineteenth century.

During the three decades between 1827 and 1854 the Russians made their first advance into central Asia by conquering the Kazakh steppes to the Syr Darya River. They hoped that the river would serve as a permanent natural frontier, but this was not to be. The ambition of local commanders, far away from the capital and eager for glory and promotion, frequently forced the government's hand and presented it with a *fait accompli*. The constant harassment of marauding bands also led the Russians to press further in spite of misgivings in St. Petersburg and protests from Britain.

One after another, the legendary centers of central Asian Moslem civilization fell to the advancing Russians—Tashkent in 1865, Bukhara in 1868, Khiva in 1873, Geok-Tepe in 1881, and Merv in 1884. These thrusts greatly alarmed the British in India, and there were recurring crises and rumors of war. But the century passed without open conflict, primarily because the distances were so great and the means of transport so limited. Instead of going to war, the British and the Russians struggled to control intervening states, particularly Persia and Afghanistan.

Russian rule changed central Asia significantly. On the positive side the Russians abolished the widespread slavery and slave trade, freeing 10,000 slaves in Samarkand and its environs alone. The Russians also built railways—notably the Orenburg-Tashkent line—which helped them both to subjugate and to modernize the area. Thanks to the cheap transportation and the growing demands of the Russian textile industry, cotton cultivation increased spectacularly. In 1884, 300 desiatinas (1 desiatina = 2.7 acres) were planted in cotton on Russian initiative; by 1899, cotton acreage had jumped to 90,000 desiatinas. The Russians also introduced certain agrarian reforms, including a reduction of peasants' taxes and labor obligations to the state and to the landlords.

On the other hand, the Russians' systematic expropriation of Kazakh grazing lands led to a decrease in the size of herds and to widespread famine. The Russians did nothing for the education of the natives, leaving this task almost entirely to the Moslem mullahs. In other areas, such as the judiciary and local government, they were less active than the British were in India. The net result was that prior to the Bolshevik Revolution, which brought as many changes to central Asia as to other regions of the tsarist empire, the mass of Kazakhs, Kirghizes, Turkomans, Uzbeks, and Tajiks were little affected by the coming of the Russians. Despite the railway building and the spreading cotton cultivation, conquerors and conquered lived in different worlds, separated by barriers of language, religion, and customs.

Manchuria and the Russo-Japanese War

In the 1890s Russian interest was shifting from central Asia to the Far East. The Trans-Siberian railway, which was slowly nearing completion, presented new opportunities for Russian economic and political expansion. Count Sergei Witte, the newly appointed minister of finance, presented a report to Tsar Alexander III (November 6, 1892), in which he stated that the Trans-Siberian line would supersede the Suez Canal as the principal trade route to China. He foresaw Russia in the position of arbiter between Asia and the Western world and advocated a Russo-Chinese alliance as the best means for attaining that position.

The outbreak of the Sino-Japanese War in 1895 (see Chapter 33, Section I) paved the way for the alliance that Witte favored. China again was easily defeated, and it repeatedly requested Britain and the United States to mediate. Their refusal forced China to accept the Treaty of Shimonoseki (April 17, 1895), by which it ceded to Japan the Formosa and Pescadores Islands and the Liaotung Peninsula. But Russia, together with Germany and France, now intervened and compelled the Japanese to restore the peninsula.

This assistance impressed the Chinese, who, in the following year, signed a secret treaty with Russia. It provided for mutual assistance in case of Japanese aggression, and it also granted to a joint Russo-Chinese Bank a concession for the construction of the Chinese Eastern Railway across Manchuria to Vladivostok. The bank, nominally a private concern, was actually owned and operated by the Russian government. By the outbreak of the Russo-Japanese War in 1904, it had built a total of 1,596 miles of railway in Manchuria.

Russia's next advance in the Far East was in 1898, with the negotiation of a twenty-five-year lease of the Liaotung peninsula, including strategic Port Arthur. Two years later the Russians took advantage of the disturbances during the Boxer Rebellion to occupy the entire province of Manchuria. This steady Russian encroachment alarmed the Japanese, who had ambitions of their own on the mainland of Asia. Since they were in no position to stop the Russians singlehanded, they decided to strengthen themselves by securing an ally. On January 30, 1902, they concluded a military alliance with Britain (details in Chapter 33, Section VII), and, with this backing, they resolved to settle accounts with Russia. In July 1903, the Japanese proposed that Russia should recognize their "preponderant interests" in Korea, and in return they would recognize Russia's "special interests in railway enterprises in Manchuria."

The Russians were divided concerning the Japanese offer. The finance minister, Count Witte, favored acceptance because he was interested in economic penetration rather than in political annexation with its dangers of war. But influential Russian adventurers with vast timber concessions in northern Korea wished to involve their government to advance their personal fortunes. Russian military circles wanted to obtain a base along the Korean coast because of the great distance between their existing bases at Port Arthur and Vladivostok. And certain Russian politicians, concerned by the mounting revolutionary wave in the country, favored a "little victorious war" that would serve as a lightning rod for the popular unrest. There was no doubt in their minds, or in those of the military, that Russia would win in a war with Japan.

This group of adventurers, militarists, and politicians had its way. It secured the dismissal of Witte and virtually rejected the Japanese offer.

Assured by their alliance with the British, and apprehensive about the near completion of the Trans-Siberian railway, the Japanese struck promptly and decisively. On February 5, 1904, they broke off negotiations, and three days later they attacked the Russian fleet at Fort Arthur without a formal declaration of war.

In the campaigns that followed, the Japanese David consistently defeated the Russian Goliath. The single-track Trans-Siberian railway proved quite inadequate to supply Russian armies fighting several thousand miles from their industrial centers in European Russia. In the first stage of the war, the Japanese surrounded Port Arthur and, after a siege of 148 days, captured the fortress on December 19, 1904. The second stage consisted of a series of battles on the plains of Manchuria. The Japanese were victorious here also, driving the Russians north of Mukden. These campaigns, however, were not decisive because the Russian armies remained intact and were reinforced and strengthened as communications improved. But on the sea the Japanese won an overwhelming triumph that led to the beginning of peace negotiations. On May 27, 1905, the Russian Baltic fleet arrived at the Tsushima Straits between Japan and Korea after sailing a distance equivalent to more than two-thirds the circumference of the globe. It was attacked at once by a Japanese fleet that was superior both in numbers and in efficiency. Within a few hours virtually all the Russian units had been sunk or captured. The Japanese merely lost a few destroyers.

With this debacle the Russians were ready to discuss peace, especially since the war was very unpopular at home and the 1905 revolution had started. The Japanese also wanted peace negotiations because, although they had won the victories, their still meager resources had been strained by the burden of the war. On September 5, 1905, the Treaty of Portsmouth was signed, by which Russia acknowledged Japan's "paramount political, military, and economic interests" in Korea; surrendered all preferential or exclusive concessions in Manchuria; and ceded to Japan the southern half of Sakhalin Island and the lease of the Liaotung peninsula. In this way the Japanese halted Russia's expansion in the Far East. Not until four decades later, when the Japanese were disastrously defeated in World War II, was Russia able to recover the territories lost at Portsmouth.

IV. FIRST RUSSIAN REVOLUTION AND AFTERMATH, 1905–1914

While the Russo-Japanese War was being fought in the Far East, revolution was spreading behind the lines within Russia. The revolution had its roots in the chronic disaffection of the peasants, the urban workers, and the middle class. This disaffection was aggravated by the war with Japan, which was unpopular to begin with and became increasingly so after the string of defeats. Finally there occurred the so-called "Bloody Sunday" of January 22, 1905. The Imperial Guard fired on an unarmed crowd of several thousand persons who were peacefully carrying a petition to the Winter Palace in St. Petersburg. Between 75 and 1,000 were killed and 200 to 2,000 wounded. The discrepancy in the figures is due to the fact that some eyewitnesses reported only the Sunday casualties, whereas others included casualties that occurred in the next two days as the disturbance continued in the capital.

Bloody Sunday irreparably smashed the benevolent "Little Father" image of the tsar that so many Russians had traditionally cherished. Citizens throughout the empire turned against the regime, setting off the great Russian Revolution of 1905. This upheaval passed through three stages before the imperial government was able to reassert its authority. The first, between January and October 1905, was the rising wave of revolution. All classes and interests came out against the autocracy. The subject nationalities demanded autonomy, peasants pillaged houses and seized estates, city workers organized councils or "soviets" for revolutionary action, university students everywhere walked out of their classrooms, and the sailors of the Black Sea fleet mutinied and seized their ships. The tsar had no alternative but to yield, so he issued his famous October Manifesto (October 30). It promised freedom of speech, press, and assembly and also granted Russia a constitution and an elective national assembly, or *Duma*.

During the second stage of the revolution, between October 1905 and January 1906, the up-

A peasant revolt in Russia.

rising continued at high pitch, but the revolutionaries no longer were united. The moderates, consisting mostly of middle-class elements, accepted the October Manifesto, whereas the radicals, including the Social Democrats and the Socialist Revolutionaries, demanded that a constituent assembly, not the tsar's ministers, should prepare the new constitution. To gain their ends the radicals tried to prolong the revolution by organizing more strikes and disturbances. By this time, however, the government was getting stronger and was able to hit back. The signing of the Portsmouth Treaty with Japan on September 5, 1905, freed many troops, and they were sent home to restore order. A timely loan of $400 million from Paris and London greatly strengthened the faltering tsarist government. Consequently, it was able to crush a dangerous workers' revolt that raged in Moscow between December 22 and January 1. Meanwhile, the moderates, alienated by the prolonged violence, were swinging over to the government's side. Thus by the beginning of 1906 the crest of the revolutionary wave had passed.

The third stage of the revolution, from January to July 21, 1906, was that of tsarist consolidation of power. Government forces hunted down radicals and rebellious peasants, in some cases burning whole villages. On May 6 the government issued the so-called Fundamental Laws by which the tsar was proclaimed autocrat and retained complete control over the executive, the armed forces, and foreign policy. The elective Duma was to share legislative power with an upper chamber, and its budgetary power was closely restricted. When the Duma did meet on May 10, it refused to accept the Fundamental Laws and criticized the government violently. A deadlock ensued, and the tsar dissolved the Duma on July 21. The liberal Duma members retaliated by calling on the country to refuse to pay taxes. But the response was feeble. The fact is that by this time the revolutionary tide had ebbed and the First Russian Revolution had run its course.

Although the revolution failed, it left its imprint on the course of Russia's history. Russia now had a constitutional regime, even though the Duma had little power. A second Duma was elected in February 1907, but it proved to be even more defiant than the first. The government then restricted the franchise so drastically that the third and fourth Dumas elected in 1907 and 1912 were acceptably conservative and subservient. Nevertheless, the absolutist tsarist autocracy ended with the October Manifesto, and after World War I began, the Duma came increasingly into its own until it was swept away by the Bolshevik Revolution.

The events of 1905 are important also because of their contribution to Russian revolutionary experience and tradition. Soviets were organized in the cities and proved their value as organs for revolutionary action. It is true that after 1906 a lull seemed to set in, but it was only a brief respite. The number of workers on strike declined from 1 million in 1905 to 4,000 in 1910. But by 1912, the number had risen again to 1 million and it remained at that level during the next two years. Then all discord ceased abruptly with the outbreak of World War I. But with the catastrophic defeats at the front, new storm clouds gathered, and the tsarist regime entered a new time of troubles from which it never emerged.

Thus, the Russian Revolution of 1905 stands out as a dress rehearsal for the world-shaking revolution of 1917.

SUGGESTED READINGS

Aspects of the relations between Russia and the West are treated by D. W. Treadgold, *The West in Russia and China,* Vol. I, *Russia 1472–1917* (Cambridge University, 1973); W. L. Blackwell, *The Beginnings of Russian Industrialization, 1800–1860* (Princeton University, 1968); T. H. Von Laue, *Sergei Witte and the Industrialization of Russia* (Columbia University, 1963); and M. Malia, *Russia Under Western Eyes: From Peter the Great to Khrushchev* (Wiley, 1964).

For Russian expansion in central Asia, see G. V. Lantzeff and R. A Pierce, *Eastward to Empire: Exploration and Conquest on the Russian Open Frontier to 1750* (McGill University, 1973); E. E. Bacon, *Central Asia Under Russian Rule: A Study in Culture Change* (Cornell University, 1966); and S. Becker, *Russia's Protectorates in Central Asia: Bukhara and Khiva, 1865–1924* (Harvard University, 1968).

The Middle East

It is not open to question that all social changes in the Near East during the past century or so have arisen, directly or indirectly, from the impact of our Western society and the penetration of Western techniques and ideas.

H. A. R. Gibb

The West's influence on the Middle East was quite different from its influence on Russia, and the response of the Middle Eastern peoples was just as different. A new group of peoples, religions, and cultures was involved, to be sure, but there was also a different political and social organization. The Ottoman Empire, which embraced most of the Middle East during the nineteenth century, remained a hodgepodge of peoples, religions, and conflicting loyalties. We noted in Chapter 19 that the empire was organized as a theocracy on the basis of ecclesiastical communities rather than ethnic groups. These communities, the most important of which were the Greek Orthodox, Roman Catholic, and Jewish, were allowed considerable autonomy under their respective ecclesiastical leaders. Thus for centuries the various Moslem peoples (for example, Turks, Arabs, Albanians, and Kurds) and the various Christian peoples (for example, Serbs, Greeks, Bulgars, and Rumanians) lived side by side in semiautonomous and self-sufficient communities. Individual non-Moslems did suffer discrimination regarding dress, behavior, living areas, and higher taxes. Yet each community was allowed its own church, language, schools, and local government, as long as it accepted the sultan's authority and paid taxes to the imperial treasury.

The significance of this loose imperial organization is that Western ideas and pressures encountered a variety of cultures and conditions. Consequently, the West did not have a uniform impact on the Ottoman lands. Therefore, in analyzing the nature of that impact, it is essential to take into account the marked variations in regional conditions and responses. For this reason we shall now consider, not the Ottoman Empire as a whole, but rather its three main regions in turn—the Balkan peninsula, with its predominantly Christian population; Asia Minor, with its ruling Moslem Turkish population; and the provinces south of Asia Minor, with their Moslem Arab peoples.

I.   BALKAN CHRISTIANS

The Balkan peoples were under Turkish rule for four centuries or more. It is often assumed that these were centuries of unrelieved tyranny, that the oppressed Christians only yearned for freedom and waited impatiently for an opportunity to revolt. This interpretation does not fit the actual course of events. The various Balkan peoples greatly outnumbered the few Turks living in their midst. They lived in compact groups and retained their languages and religions. If they had been eager to revolt, they could have caused more trouble for the Turks than they actually did. Yet during the early centuries, the Turks had no more trouble ruling their Christian subjects in the Balkans than their Moslem subjects in Asia.

The explanation is that the Turkish conquerors were efficient and benevolent compared to the Byzantine emperors, Frankish nobles, Venetian signors, and Bulgarian and Serbian princes who formerly had ruled the Balkan lands. Ottoman administration was stern but just, taxation was light, and the non-Moslems enjoyed a degree of tolerance unparalleled in Christian Europe. During the eighteenth and nineteenth centuries, however, this situation changed drastically. The decline in Ottoman power and efficiency during this period led to widespread corruption and extortion, which in turn drove the now oppressed and embittered Balkan Christians to take up arms in self-defense. At the same time the Balkan peoples, for a number of reasons, were being affected and aroused by a variety of influences from the West.

The Balkan peoples were affected earlier and more profoundly by the West than any of the other ethnic groups of the Ottoman Empire. Mostly Christians, they were more receptive to the Christian West than were the Moslem Turks and Arabs. The territorial contiguity of the Balkan lands to the rest of Europe made it easier for persons and goods and ideas to converge on the Balkan peninsula from across the Danube and the Adriatic, Mediterranean, and Black seas. The increasing demand for food imports in western Europe stimulated agriculture in the Balkans, especially the cultivation of the new colonial products, cotton and maize. The export of these commodities in turn contributed to the growth of a class of native Balkan merchants and mariners. The expansion of trade also stimulated the demand and output of handicraft products. Important manufacturing centers appeared in various parts of the peninsula, frequently in isolated mountain areas where the artisans could practice their crafts with a minimum of Turkish interference. Finally, the rise of commerce and industry promoted the growth of a merchant marine along the Adriatic coast and among the

The Christianity of the Balkans is portrayed here as the garrison of Belgrade pledges its allegiance to King Milan I.

Aegean Islands. The new Balkan marine exported products such as cotton, maize, dyeing materials, wine, oil, and fruits, and it brought back mostly colonial products and manufactured goods—spices, sugar, woolens, glass, watches, guns, and gunpowder.

The significance of this economic renaissance is that it created a middle class of merchants, artisans, shipowners, and mariners that was particularly susceptible and sympathetic to Western ideas and institutions. These people, by their very nature, were dissatisfied with Ottoman rule, which by this time had become ineffective and corrupt. Merchants and seamen who journeyed to foreign lands, and who frequently resided there, could not help contrasting the security and enlightenment they witnessed abroad with the deplorable conditions at home. Very naturally, many concluded that their own future, and that of their fellow Balkan citizens, depended on the earliest possible removal of Turkish rule.

Serbian merchants in southern Hungary, Bulgarian merchants in southern Russia, and Greek merchants scattered widely in the main cities of Europe all contributed to the intellectual awakening of their fellow compatriots. They did so by publishing books and newspapers in their native languages, by establishing schools and libraries in their home towns and villages, and by financing the education of their young men in foreign universities. All this meant not only more education but a new type of education. It was no longer primarily religious. Instead, it was profoundly influenced by the current Enlightenment in western Europe.

Western influence in the Balkans became more directly political and inflammatory during the French revolutionary and Napoleonic era. Politically conscious elements were much impressed by the uprisings in Paris; by the slogan "Liberty, Equality, Fraternity"; and by the spectacle of Napoleon toppling over one dynasty after another. A contemporary Greek revolutionary testified, "The French Revolution in general awakened the minds of all men. . . . All the Christians of the Near East prayed to God that France should wage war against the Turks, and they believed that they would be freed. . . . But when Napoleon made no move, they began to take measures for freeing themselves."[1]

The tempo of national awakening varied greatly from one Balkan people to another. The Greeks came first because of certain favorable circumstances: the numerous contacts with the West; their glorious classical and Byzantine heritage, which stimulated national pride; and their Greek Orthodox Church, which embodied and preserved national consciousness. After the Greeks came the Serbs, who enjoyed a high degree of local self-government as well as the stimulating influence of the large Serbian settlements in southern Hungary. These advantages of the Greeks and the Serbs suggest the reasons for the slower rate of national revival among the other Balkan peoples. The Bulgars had no direct ties with the West and were located near the Ottoman capital and the solid Turkish settlements in Thrace and eastern Macedonia. The Rumanians suffered from a sharp social stratification that was unique in the Balkans and that produced a cultivated upper class and an inert peasant mass. The Albanians were the worst off, with their primitive tribal organization and their division among three creeds, Orthodoxy, Catholicism, and Islam.

These factors explain why in place of a common Balkan revolution against Ottoman rule, there were separate uprisings ranging from the early nineteenth century to the early twentieth. The Greeks won complete independence from the Turks following a protracted War of Independence between 1821 and 1829. The Serbs had revolted earlier in 1804 but only gained an autonomous status within the Ottoman Empire in 1815. It was not until 1878 that the Serbian Principality gained full independence and became the Kingdom of Serbia. The Rumanians came next, winning autonomy in 1859 and full independence in 1878. The Bulgarians followed later, gaining autonomy in 1878 and independence in 1908. Three of these Balkan peoples, the Serbs, Greeks, and Bulgarians, combined forces in 1912 to drive the Turks completely out of the peninsula. They were successful on the battlefield, and despite a fratricidal war amongst the victors, the Turks were compelled in 1913 to surrender all their remaining territories in the Balkans with the exception of an enclave stretching around the straits from Constantinople to Adrianople.

In this manner the imperial Ottoman frontiers shrank from the walls of Vienna in 1683 to

Russian officers lowering the Ottoman flag from a Turkish gunboat sunk in Rumania, 1877.

the Danube in 1815, to the mid-Balkans in 1878, and to the environs of Constantinople in 1913. As the empire receded, independent Balkan states took its place—Greece, Serbia, Rumania, Bulgaria, and, in 1912, Albania. The West contributed decisively to this resurgence of the Balkan peoples by providing a revolutionary nationalist ideology, by stimulating the growth of a middle class that was ready to act on the basis of that ideology, and by sporadically helping the Balkan revolutionaries in their struggle against Turkish rule.

II. TURKS

The West affected the Turks much less and much later than it did the Balkan Christians. Various factors explain this difference. The most important of these probably were the Turks' Moslem religion and their lack of a native middle class.

If the Christian faith of the Balkan peoples constituted a bond with the West, the Moslem faith of the Turks was a barrier—and a most formidable one because of the long history of antagonism and conflict between Christianity and Islam. The Turks also were little affected by the

West because they never developed their own middle class. They had no interest in or respect for commercial pursuits, so that the Ottoman bourgeoisie was largely Greek, Armenian, and Jewish. By contrast, the Turks were either peasants, who were generally apathetic, or teachers and judges in the Moslem ecclesiastical organization—which almost always meant that they were bitterly anti-Western—or else they were office-holders in the imperial bureaucracy—in which case they usually were interested only in retaining their posts and advancing in rank. When we think of the vital role played by Greek, Serbian, and Bulgarian merchants in their respective countries, the significance of the Turkish situation is obvious. With no comparable group of Turkish merchants, the rare advocates of reform among the Turks found themselves without any following. They found themselves, in other words, in the same plight as did the Decembrists in Russia in 1825, and for the same reason.

Yet during the course of the nineteenth century the Ottoman Empire, like the Russian, was penetrated, influenced, and controlled by the West in numerous direct and indirect ways. Of the several channels of penetration, the earliest, and in some respects the most effective, was the

THE SICK MAN OF EUROPE

*During the nineteenth century the Ottoman Empire was known as the "sick man of Europe." Why it was sick is evident in the following account by the British merchant and diplomat Sir Charles Eliot. He describes his efforts to interest the vali (governor) of Karakeui in development projects and the vali's negative response.**

I suppose I might be described as a concession hunter or a commission agent. The essence of my trade is to make Orientals buy what they don't want—anything from matches to railroads. I bribe them to purchase my wares and they bribe me to put down in the bill (which the Ottoman Government pays) a much larger sum than I have actually received. So we both make money. . . .

"If you would only develop," [I told him,] "the commercial and material resources of your Empire, Christians and Turks would have a common interest. The Christians would want to support your Empire as the source of their prosperity.

"We Turks [replied the Vali,] don't know how to make money; we only know how to take it. You want to introduce a system in which Christians will be able to squeeze all the money out of us and our country and keep it. Who profit by all these concessions for railways, harbours, and quays? Franks, Jews, Greeks, and Armenians, but never a Moslim. Do you remember that railway I helped you to build from Durograd to Moropolis? Franks travel by it, Greeks and Armenians sell the

tickets, and in the end all the money goes to the Jews. But what Turk wants the railway, and how much has any Turk made out of it?"

I might have said, "Exactly as much as passed into your Highness's pockets when the concession was arranged," but I forbore from this obvious retort and let the Vali go on. "This country is a dish of soup," he said, "and no one has any real intention except to eat it. We eat it in the good old-fashioned way with a big spoon. You bore little holes in the bottom of the soup-bowl and drain it off with pipes. Then you propose that the practice of eating soup with spoons should be abolished as uncivilised, because you know we have no gimlets and don't understand this trick of drinking through pipes."

"But surely your Highness has had experience yourself of the advantages which Osmanlis may obtain from commercial enterprises and—"

"Oh, I have had a suck at the pipe," said the Vali, "but, after all, I prefer eating with the spoon."

*Charles Eliot, *Turkey in Europe,* 2nd ed. (Edward Arnold, 1908), pp. 94–97.

military. Like the Russians, the Turks found it necessary to adopt European military techniques for self-preservation. During the latter half of the nineteenth century the Western powers actively encouraged the Turks to modernize their military forces in order to block Russian expansion into

the Middle East. But of the many young men who were sent abroad to study in foreign military academies, some inevitably learned about Western ideologies as well as Western military techniques. Thus it is not surprising that when the old Ottoman regime was finally overthrown in 1908,

The construction of the Suez Canal.

the coup was executed, not by a political party or a mass movement, but by an army clique.

In the field of religion, also, the West affected the Moslem Middle East. Missionaries were preaching and founding schools throughout the empire. By 1875 the American missionaries alone had 240 schools with 8,000 pupils. Most of the latter were Armenians and other Christians, since proselytism among Moslems was forbidden. But a fair number of Turkish students were to be found in the foreign colleges scattered throughout the empire—colleges such as the American-operated Constantinople Women's College and Robert College (also in Constantinople) and the French Jesuit University of St. Joseph at Beirut. The Turks themselves by this time had established several institutions of higher learning, including the School of Medicine (1867), the Imperial Lyceé (1868), the University of Constantinople (1869),

the School of Law (1870), and the School of Political Science (1878). The Turkish press, too, was developing rapidly during these years. In 1859 there were only one official and one semiofficial weekly in the empire. By 1882 there were three daily papers and several weeklies.

At least as significant as this cultural impact was the West's economic penetration of the Ottoman Empire. In 1869, after ten years of construction by a European syndicate headed by the French diplomat and promoter Ferdinand de Lesseps, the Suez Canal was opened. The effect of the canal was to place the Ottoman Empire once more on the main trade route between Europe and Asia. At the same time the Ottoman government was falling hopelessly into debt to European governments and to private financiers. They contracted their first loan in 1854, and by 1875 their debts totaled £200 million sterling.

Some £12 million sterling a year was required to meet annuities, interest, and sinking fund, a sum that amounted to a little more than half the total revenues of the empire. The load proved too heavy, and some of the interest payments were defaulted, whereupon in 1881 the European powers imposed the Ottoman Public Debt Administration. This body consisted mostly of foreign representatives and was entrusted with the revenues from various monopolies and customs duties for the service of the imperial debts.

In addition to this hold over Ottoman public finances, foreign interests had control over the Turkish banking and railway systems, irrigation works, mining enterprises, and municipal public utilities. The empire, besides, was still subject to the "capitulations," or extraterritorial privileges, that foreigners had enjoyed in the Ottoman Empire since the fifteenth century. These privileges included exemption from the jurisdiction of Ottoman courts and from certain taxes, including personal imposts and customs tariffs. The latter were set at a very low level and could not be raised by the Ottoman government without the consent of the European powers, which, needless to say, was not forthcoming. Thus we may conclude that the Ottoman Empire, much more than the Russian, was in a semicolonial economic relationship with Europe.

The effect of all these Western pressures and controls cannot be measured precisely, but there can be no doubt that they gradually cracked the hitherto impregnable and monolithic Islamic structure. Canals, railways, banks, missionaries, schools, and newspapers form the background and also provide the explanation for a literary and intellectual awakening that occurred among the Turks in the latter half of the nineteenth century.

The best-known leaders of this awakening were Ibrahim Shinassi, Namik Kemal, and Abdul Hamid Ziya. These men did not agree on all issues, but all had lived in western Europe, and all had been tremendously impressed by Western thought and literature, as well as by its material achievements. By 1865 a fairly well-defined group of young Western-minded writers had formed around the newspaper *Mushbir,* or *Herald of Glad Tidings.* The paper championed, among other things, the introduction of some form of constitutional representative government. This was too much for the imperial regime, which suppressed the paper in 1867. The editor and his colleagues were forced to flee to Paris and London, where they continued their journalistic attacks on the imperial regime.

Meanwhile, a few Turkish statesmen had realized that a comprehensive reform program along Western lines was essential for the survival of the empire. Outstanding were Reshid Pasha (1802–1858) and Midhat Pasha (1822–1884), both of whom served as grand vizirs and issued numerous reform decrees. In May 1876, Midhat took advantage of a financial crisis at home and a revolution in the Balkan provinces to force Sultan Abdul Aziz to abdicate. He then prepared a constitution providing for an elected parliament, a bill of rights, and an independent judiciary. The new sultan, Abdul Hamid II, was forced to accept the constitution, but he had no intention of abiding by it. In January 1877, he dismissed Midhat from office and banished him from Constantinople. The only signs of protest were a few placards on walls. Turkish reformers still were faced with a mass inertia comparable to that which had doomed the Russian Decembrists in 1825. Consequently, Abdul Hamid was able to rule as the unchallenged master of his empire for the rest of the century.

During those decades Abdul Hamid kept himself in power by relentlessly combating the disruptive forces of nationalism and constitutionalism. To this end he discouraged travel and study abroad, maintained a great host of informers, and enforced a strict censorship of the press. Periodically his agents flushed out small groups of disaffected elements, who usually fled to Paris for refuge. There they published periodicals and pamphlets criticizing the Hamidian autocracy, and thus they became popularly known in western Europe as the *Young Turks.* These Turkish exiles were joined by revolutionary leaders of the various subject peoples under Abdul Hamid, including Arabs, Greeks, Armenians, Albanians, Kurds, and Jews. Representatives of all these nationalities held a congress in Paris in February 1902, with the aim of organizing a common front against the autocracy. But they quickly discovered that their consensus was limited to their mutual dislike of the sultan. On all other matters there was disagreement. For example, one group wanted Turkish predominance and centralized rule, whereas another favored a decentralized empire with full autonomy for the subject peoples.

While the exiled intellectuals were quarreling in Paris, reform-minded Turkish army leaders were taking decisive measures to break the sultan's grip on the empire. Most of them had studied in the West or had contact with Western military missions within the empire. They had come to realize that the sultan's rigid policy was obsolete and dangerous. They organized the Ottoman Society of Liberty with headquarters in Saloniki. Army officers were the backbone of this body, though they were greatly aided by other groups, and particularly by the Jews, who were the most numerous and wealthy element in Saloniki. The Society of Liberty was organized into cells of five, so that no one knew more than four fellow members. A new recruit had to be sponsored by a regular member and was observed closely during a probationary period.

These conspirators openly revolted in July 1908. They telegraphed an ultimatum to the sultan, threatening to march on Constantinople unless the 1876 constitution was restored within twenty-four hours. Advised by his State Council to comply with the ultimatum, Abdul Hamid proclaimed the restoration of the constitution. The news of the sultan's capitulation was greeted with wild rejoicing, with Christians and Turks even embracing one another in the streets. But this euphoric atmosphere did not last long. The issue of centralization versus decentralization that had divided the exiles in Paris now had to be faced as an urgent matter of policy rather than of theory. There were also conservative elements who distrusted all Young Turks, as the new leaders were generally called. The dissension came to a head on April 2, 1909, when the conservatives staged a counterrevolution in Constantinople and seized control of the capital. The Young Turks gathered their forces in Macedonia, marched on Constantinople, captured the city after a few hours' fighting, and then compelled Abdul Hamid to abdicate. The new sultan, Mohammed V, who according to his own account had not read a newspaper in ten years, served as a compliant figurehead for the Young Turks, who now were the undisputed masters in Constantinople.

During the few years before the outbreak of World War I, they tried to strengthen and modernize their empire, but with little success. They attempted a policy of centralization and Turkification. They tried to promote loyalty to the Ottoman Empire and the Ottoman sultan rather than to the several minority nationalisms. But the more the Turks persisted, the more opposition they aroused. It was too late to deny the inexorable awakening of Albanians, Arabs, Greeks, Bulgarians, and other subject peoples. Thus the result was a vicious circle of repression and revolt. The Albanians took up arms in 1910, and two years later the Balkan states formed a league and turned on the Turks. Meanwhile, Italy had invaded the African province of Tripolitania in 1911. The Young Turks thus found themselves almost continually at war until 1914, when they decided to throw in their lot with the Central Powers.

It is apparent, then, that the efforts of the Turks to adjust to the West had proven ineffective. Because of religious and historical traditions, they had been more resistant to the West than the Russians, and for that very reason they had also become much more vulnerable. They did not develop their own industry, so that their armed forced remained dependent on Western arms as well as Western instructors. Indeed, the Ottoman Empire survived to World War I because of the conflicting interests and policies of the Great Powers rather than because of its own strength.

III.   ARABS

Like the Balkan Christians, the Arab peoples were under Ottoman rule for four centuries. But they were even less prone than the Balkan Christians to regard Ottoman rule as an onerous foreign yoke. In the first place, Ottoman administration in the early period was efficient and generally acceptable. The Arabs, who as Moslems thought in theocratic rather than secular (Western) terms, regarded the Turks more as fellow Moslems than as foreigners. Consequently they felt a genuine affinity with the Moslem Ottoman Empire of which they were a part. In modern times the aggressiveness of the Europeans, who conquered ancient Moslem kingdoms in North Africa and central and south Asia, enhanced this Arab tie with the Turks. Faced with such a formidable threat, the Arabs very naturally regarded the Turks as protectors, who, though they became increasingly corrupt and oppressive in the later period, were nevertheless still preferable to the infidels. These considerations explain why the Arabs lagged far behind the Balkan Christians in receptiveness to Western influences and in the development of nationalist aspirations.

The West's impact on the modern Arab world may be said to begin on the day in 1798 when Napoleon landed in Egypt with his army of invasion. Napoleon's real objective was to strike at Britain's position in the East, but after Admiral Nelson destroyed his fleet near Alexandria, Napoleon gave up his objective and returned home. Yet his expedition had a lasting effect on Egypt, for it was more than a military affair. It was also a cultural incursion by the West into the heart of the Arab world. Napoleon brought with him the first printing press to reach Egypt, and he was accompanied by scientists, who deciphered the ancient hieroglyphic writing, and by engineers, who prepared plans for joining the Mediterranean and Red seas.

Napoleon also smashed the power of the established ruling class in Egypt during his brief campaign in that country. This paved the way for the rise to power of an Albanian adventurer of genius, Mehemet Ali. Mehemet Ali is historically significant because he was the first Middle Eastern potentate who sensed the significance of Western technology and used it efficiently to serve his purposes. His achievements were numerous and revolutionary. He started Egypt's modern system of irrigation; introduced the cultivation of cotton, which quickly became the country's greatest resource; reopened the harbor of Alexandria; encouraged foreign trade; sent students to study abroad; opened schools of all varieties, though he himself was illiterate; and established a School of Translation, which translated into Arabic about two thousand European books between 1835 and 1848. Mehemet Ali also engaged foreign experts who helped him build the first modern army and navy in the Middle East. He even tried valiantly to build a modern industrial structure in Egypt, and he did erect a considerable number of factories in Cairo and Alexandria. These enterprises, however, eventually failed because of domestic deficiencies and the opposition of the European powers to Egyptian expansionism and industrialization.

Yet for a time these accomplishments transformed Egypt into a formidable power. Mehemet easily overran Arabia, the Sudan, the island of Crete, and the entire Levant coast that today includes Israel, Lebanon, and Syria. His plan was to create an Arab Empire out of the Ottoman provinces south of Asia Minor. But this was not acceptable to Britain, which preferred the weak Ottoman Empire rather than a strong Arab Empire dominating the routes to India. Mehemet was forcefully compelled to surrender all his possessions except Egypt, where he remained the hereditary and autonomous ruler. Great power interests had postponed the realization of Arab unity and independence and would continue to do so for over a century.

Thanks to Napoleon's expedition and to Mehemet Ali's herculean effort, Egypt became by far the most significant bridgehead for westernism in the Arab world. After 1870 Syria, which included the entire Levant coast at that time, rivaled Egypt as a center for Western influence. One reason was the flourishing commerce between Syria and Europe and the large number of Syrian merchants who engaged in business activities abroad. These merchants had the same catalytic effect on their fellow Syrians at home as the Balkan merchants had had for their peoples in earlier decades. Another reason was the extensive missionary-educational activity carried on mostly by the French Jesuits and the American Presbyterians. They established schools in Syria that trained Arab students and printed and distributed Arab books. In this manner the Syrian Arabs rediscovered their past and learned about Western literature, ideology, and technology.

This stimulus from the outside was responsible for the earliest manifestations of Arab nationalism. The leaders at the outset were mostly Christian Arabs, since the Moslems did not enroll in the missionary schools until a later date. In 1860 Butros el Bustani, a convert to Protestantism, began publication of his newspaper, *Nafir Suriya* (*Syrian Trumpet*). Ten years later he founded a political, literary, and scientific journal, *El Jenan* (*The Shield*). Its motto was "Love of our country is an article of faith"—a sentiment hitherto unknown in the Arab world.

Bustani and the other pioneer nationalists could not carry on political agitation openly because of the repressive measures of the Ottoman authorities. Consequently, the first avowedly political activity was the organization of a secret revolutionary society in 1875 by five students at the Protestant College. They drew up a national program that included demands for self-government, freedom of the press, and the adoption of Arabic as an official language. Turkish officials conducted an investigation and attempted to uncover the secret society's leadership. The society became alarmed and dissolved the organization in 1878. Then they made their way to Egypt, where the imperial agents had little control and where conditions were more promising for modern-minded Arabs.

The Western-educated Syrian intellectuals published newspapers and magazines that acquainted Egyptians with French and British currents of liberal and scientific thought. At the same time the deciphering of the hieroglyphs, the establishment of museums, and the development of Egyptology stimulated an awareness of Egypt's ancient history and a pride in its achievements. This budding nationalism was further aroused by the growing Western domination of the country. The domination was imposed because Khedive Ismail's (1863–1879) heavy borrowing on the European money markets had led to bankruptcy and ultimately to foreign military intervention and rule. During the sixteen years of Ismail's reign the funded debt rose from £3 million to £68 million. The Egyptians, like the Turks, were unaccustomed to the wiles of unscrupulous international financiers and were mercilessly fleeced. Loans that normally brought 6 or 7 percent were made to the Egyptians at anywhere between 12 and 27 percent.

By 1876 Ismail was bankrupt and was forced to accept the settling of the Egyptian debt by an international Public Debt Commission. This body saw to it that all obligations were promptly met, but the country was bled white in the process. The total revenue in 1877 amounted to £9.5 million, of which £7.5 million had to be paid out for the service of the debt, with other amounts paid for fixed obligations such as the annual tribute to the sultan. Only a little over £1 million was left for the administration of the country, a sum that was patently inadequate.

Under these circumstances a nationalist revolt broke out in 1882 under the leadership of an Egyptian army officer, Ahmed Arabi. It was directed partly against foreign intervention in Egyptian affairs and partly against the Khedive and the Turkish oligarchies that monopolized all the senior Egyptian posts in both the army and the bureaucracy. After some rioting and loss of life in Alexandria, a British fleet bombarded the fortifications of Alexandria in July 1882, and two months later an expeditionary force landed in Egypt and defeated Arabi. The expeditionary force remained to become an army of occupation. Egypt was still nominally a Turkish province, but Britain now controlled the country in every respect—economically, politically, and militarily.

These events naturally provoked strong antiforeign sentiment in Egypt, but it was directed more against the Westerners than against the Turks. At this time only a handful of Christian Arab leaders wished to break away from Constantinople. The Moslem masses were still largely apathetic, and the small minority of politically conscious Moslems simply wanted autonomy within the Ottoman imperial structure.

With the Young Turk revolt of 1908 it appeared that this desire would be satisfied. The Arabs, like the other peoples of the empire, welcomed the revolt with unrestrained enthusiasm. But the enthusiasm proved short lived, for the Young Turk leaders soon resorted to severe Turkification measures in a desperate attempt to hold the empire together against foreign military aggression and internal nationalist subversion. The Arabs resented this repression, as did the Balkan Christians. Yet the great majority of Arabs still aspired to autonomy under the Turks rather than full independence.

Such were the sentiments of the great majority of Arabs until the outbreak of World War I. Then the decision of the Young Turk leaders to throw in their lot with the Central Powers changed the situation overnight. It precipitated a chain reaction of events that culminated in the great Arab Revolt of 1916, and finally in the disappearance of the Ottoman Empire after World War I.

SUGGESTED READINGS

Bibliographical guides are available in R. H. Davison, *The Near and Middle East: An Introduction to History and Bibliography* (Service Center for Teachers of History, 1959); and B. Lewis and P. M. Holt, *Historians of the Middle East* (Oxford University, 1962).

General histories of the Balkans and the Near East include L. S. Stavrianos, *The Balkans Since 1453* (Holt, Rinehart and Winston, 1958); B. Jelavich, 2 vols., *History of the Balkans* (Cambridge University, 1983); S. N. Fisher, *The Middle East* (Knopf, 1959); and Y. Armajani, *Middle East: Past and Present* (Prentice Hall, 1969). For the West's cultural impact on the Middle East, see D. Lerner, *The Passing of Traditional Society: Modernizing the Middle East* (Free Press, 1958); B. Lewis, *The Middle East and the West* (University of Indiana, 1964), and his *Muslim Discovery of Europe* (Norton, 1982). For the West's economic impact, see C. Issawi, ed., *The Economic History of the Middle East, 1800–1914* (University of Chicago, 1966); and J. R. Lampe and M. R. Jackson, *Balkan Economic History: 1550–1950* (Indiana University, 1982).

Western influence on the Turks is analyzed in B. Lewis, *The Emergence of Modern Turkey* (Oxford University, 1961); B. Brande and B. Lewis, eds., *Christians and Jews in the Ottoman Empire: The Functioning of a Plural Society,* 2 vols. (Holmes and Meier, 1982); and F. Ahmad, *The Young Turks* (Oxford University, 1970). For Western influence on the Arab world, see A. Hourani, *Arabic Thought in the Liberal Age 1798–1839* (Oxford University, 1962); and B. Lewis, *The Arabs in History* (Hutchinson's University Library, 1950).

32

India

India is the one great non-Western society that has been, not merely attacked and hit, but overrun and conquered outright by Western arms, and not merely conquered by Western arms but ruled, after that, by Western administrators. . . . India's experience of the West has thus been more painful and more humiliating than China's or Turkey's, and much more so than Russia's or Japan's.

Arnold J. Toynbee

Prior to the appearance of the British, India had been invaded time and time again—by the Aryans, Greeks, Scythians, Turks, and Moguls. Each of these invaders left its mark on the great subcontinent, contributing in varying degrees to the evolution of India's traditional society. The historical role of the British was to disrupt and remold this traditional society. The other invaders wrought changes mostly at the top, but the British impact was felt down to the level of the village. The reason for this difference between the British and their predecessors is to be found in the dynamic and expansive nature of British society, which consequently undermined the comparatively static and self-sufficient society of India. To understand this process of penetration and transformation, it is necessary first to study the character of the traditional Indian society. Then we shall consider the nature of the British impact and the Indian reaction to it.

I. INDIA'S TRADITIONAL SOCIETY

The basic unit of traditional Indian society was the village, as it was in most of the rest of the world, including Europe, in the preindustrial period. Within the village it was not the individual that mattered but rather the joint family and the caste. This group form of organization was a source of social stability but also of national weakness. Loyalty to the family, to the caste, and to the village was the primary consideration, and this prevented the formation of a national spirit.

The land was regarded by immemorial custom as the property of the sovereign, who was entitled to a share of the gross produce or its equivalent. This constituted the land tax that was the main source of state revenue and the main burden of the cultivator. The share paid to the state varied from period to period, ranging from a sixth, to a third, or even to a half. Usually the responsibility for making this payment, whether in produce or in money, was collective, resting on the village as a unit. The peasant family had hereditary right to the use of the land as long as they paid their share of the taxes.

Transportation and communication facilities were primitive, so the villages tended to become economically and socially self-sufficient. Each village had its potter, who turned out on a wheel the simple utensils needed by the peasants; its carpenter, who constructed and repaired the buildings and plows; its blacksmith, who made axes and other necessary tools; its clerk, who attended to legal documents and wrote correspondence between people of different villages; its town herdsman, who looked after the cattle and returned them at night to the various owners; its priest and its teacher, who frequently were combined in the same person; and its astrologer, who indicated the auspicious time for planting, for harvesting, for marriages, and other important events. These artisans and professional men served their villages on something akin to a barter basis. They were paid for their services with grain from the cultivating households or with tax-free village land for their own use. These hereditary and traditional divisions of occupation and function were turned into obligations by the caste system.

The political structure of the village consisted of an annually elected council of five or more, known to this day as the *Panchayat* (*pancha* meaning "five"). The Panchayat, which normally consisted of caste leaders and village elders, met periodically to dispense local justice; to collect taxes; to keep in repair the village wells, roads, and irrigation systems; to see that the craftsworkers and other professionals were provided for; and to extend hospitality to travelers passing through the village and to furnish them with guides. The village had little contact with the outside world apart from the payment of the land tax and the irregular demand for forced labor. The combination of agriculture and hand industry made each village largely independent of the rest of the country except for a few indispensables like salt and iron. Consequently, the towns that existed in traditional India were not indus-

A group of men of the Banjara tribal community in India engaged in a discussion with village elders.

trial in character. Rather, they were religious centers such as Benares, Puri, and Allahabad; political centers such as Poona, Tanjore, and Delhi; or commercial centers such as Mirzapur on the trade route from central India to Bengal.

Some Indian writers have romanticized this traditional society, painting an idyllic picture of village life, continuing peacefully generation after generation in its slow and satisfying rhythm. It is true that the existence of group organizations such as the joint family, the caste, and the village council provided the peasants with both psychological and economic security. Each individual had recognized duties, rights, and status in his or her native village. If the central government was sufficiently strong to maintain order and to keep the land tax down to the customary sixth of the harvest, then the peasant masses did lead a peaceful and contented existence. But as often as not the central government was too weak to keep order, and the villagers were mercilessly fleeced by greedy tax collectors and by robber bands. This was the case in the seventeenth century when the Mogul imperial structure was disintegrating. Yet even in such trying periods the Indian village was not transformed in any basic respect. Individual regions were ravaged, but eventually the cultivators returned to resume their traditional institutions and their traditional ways of life.

II.   BRITISH CONQUEST

The Indian village, then, remained relatively unchanging and self-sufficient until the coming of the British. But before examining the impact of these Western intruders, we shall consider why they were able with comparatively little difficulty to conquer the whole of India during the late eighteenth and nineteenth centuries. This is a significant question because for 250 years after the Portuguese Albuquerque had captured Goa early in the sixteenth century, the Europeans had been able to cling only to a few stations along the coasts. Then within a few decades the balance of power shifted decisively, and the whole of the Indian subcontinent fell under British rule.

One reason for this outcome was the decline of Mogul power and authority (see Chapter 19, Section III). This enabled Moslem warlords and provincial governors to declare their independence and establish personal dynasties in various regions. At the same time the Hindus asserted themselves by organizing the powerful Maratha confederacy, with its center in the city of Poona. The Marathas won control of the entire Deccan peninsula and then, about 1740, began to invade northern India with the intention of displacing the declining Moguls. Thus India was in an anarchical state in the eighteenth century, with various officials seeking to convert their posts into hereditary princedoms and plotting with any power, whether Indian or foreign, if it would serve to realize their ambitions. The British consequently were able to play off one Indian prince against another until they became the masters of the entire peninsula. This was altogether different from China, where the Manchu imperial structure remained intact and compelled all foreigners to deal directly with the emperor in Peking.

Another important factor that contributed substantially to the vulnerability of India was the rise of a powerful merchant class whose economic interests were bound up with those of the Western companies. These companies were allowed to trade relatively freely in India (they were almost entirely excluded in China). During the sixteenth century India's economy was little affected by the trade because it was confined largely to spices and textiles. But in the seventeenth century various commercial crops such as indigo, mustard seed, and hemp, as well as saltpeter, were exported in large quantities. Bengal was the center of this trade, and in that province there now arose wealthy native merchants who dominated the local economy and who were becoming increasingly restless under the corrupt and inefficient rule of the Mogul officials. One of these merchants, Jagat Seth, bought the allegiance of the generals who supposedly were under the orders of the nawab, or governor, of Bengal. At the Battle of Plassey (1757) these generals refrained from fighting against the British, who lost only sixty-five men in that fateful encounter. As one Indian historian has put it, Plassey was "a transaction, not a battle."

The British now were the actual rulers of Bengal, though they continued to recognize puppet nawabs as a matter of form. In 1764, after defeating the Mogul's forces, the East India Com-

A spice market in the East Indies.

pany was granted the Diwani, or the right of tax collection, in the rich provinces of Bengal, Bihar, and Orissa. This opened up many opportunities for profit making and outright extortion, and the English agents exploited them to the full. By raising the taxes, controlling the trade, and accepting numerous "gifts" from native officials, they amassed fortunes for themselves and their superiors in London.

The foothold in Bengal gave the British the base and the resources necessary for further expansion in India. At that time there were four other contenders for the Mogul domains—the French, the Moslem rulers of Mysore and of Hyderabad, and the Maratha Confederacy. The French were eliminated during the course of the Seven Years' War, as they were forced to surrender virtually all their posts in India by the Treaty of Paris of 1763 (see Chapter 25, Section IV). Then during the American Revolution the British were challenged in India by a coalition of the three principal native powers. The governor-general, Warren Hastings, managed to hold out and later took the offensive. By 1800 only the British and the Marathas were left, and during the following years the British gradually prevailed be-

cause of dissension within the Maratha Confederacy. By 1818 the back of the Marathas had been broken, though some fighting continued with them, as well as with the Sikhs in the Punjab.

After they had established themselves in the heart of the subcontinent, the British began pushing northward in a search for natural frontiers. To the northeast, in Himalayan Nepal, they defeated the Gurkhas, who henceforth fought on the side of the British. Likewise to the northwest they finally defeated the proud Sikhs of the Punjab. Thus by the middle of the nineteenth century the British were the masters of all India, from the Indus to the Brahmaputra and from the Himalayas to Cape Comorin. A few major kingdoms still survived, including Kashmir, Hyderabad, Baroda, and Travancore, but these were now dependent territories, isolated from each other and powerless against the might of Britain.

III. BRITISH RULE

We have seen that the East India Company was at first very exploitive in its administration of the Indian territories it controlled. The excesses aroused public opinion in Britain and prompted Parliament to pass acts in 1773 and 1784 that placed the company under the supervision of the London government. The company continued to trade, and its servants and soldiers continued to govern and fight in India, but it functioned under the watchful eye of Parliament and the British government. This arrangement continued, with various modifications, until the Indian Mutiny of 1857.

The mutiny was not the national movement or war of independence that some Indian writers have called it. Rather, it was primarily a military outbreak that was exploited by certain discontented princes and landlords whose interests had been harmed by the British. Lord Dalhousie, the governor-general between 1848 and 1856, had dispossessed many princes and aroused uneasiness and suspicion among those who remained. Other groups, too, were dissatisfied: Conservative elements of the Indian population were deeply disturbed by the introduction of the railway and telegraph; the opening of Western-type schools; the aggressive activities of certain Christian missionaries; the legalization of remarriage by widows; and the abolition of practices such as infanticide and suttee, or the self-cremation of widows on their husband's funeral pyres. The Sepoys, as the Indian soldiers serving in the British forces were called, were disaffected because of prolonged campaigning in distant lands and the refusal of extra allowances for such service. The spark that set off the uprising was the introduction of cartridges that were greased with cow and pig fat, obnoxious to both the Hindus and the Moslems. All these factors combined to make the mutiny assume proportions of a popular uprising in certain scattered regions.

When the mutiny began on May 10, 1857, the British were caught by surprise and forced to go on the defensive. But the revolt did not spread throughout the country. It was confined largely to the north. Even there most of the important native states remained loyal to the British and gave invaluable assistance. Thus after about four months the British were able to counterattack, and by July 1858 the mutiny had been crushed. Both sides were guilty of brutality. The Indians murdered many captives, and the English burned down villages and indiscriminately killed the inhabitants.

A month after the suppression of the mutiny, Parliament passed the India Act, ending the rule of the East India Company and substituting that of the Crown. Henceforth India was ruled by a vast hierarchy with its base in India and its apex in London in the person of the secretary of state for India. This official was a member of the cabinet and generally was allowed a free hand by his colleagues. The top official in India was the governor-general, or viceroy, who acted as the direct representative of the Crown and was usually appointed for a five-year term. The viceroy was assisted by an executive council of five members, none of them Indian until 1909. Beneath these top officials was the famous Indian Civil Service, which collected the revenues, maintained law and order, and supervised the judicial system. Prior to 1919 almost all the members of this small but elite group consisted of British graduates of Oxford and Cambridge. The Civil Service in turn supervised a subordinate provincial service that was exclusively Indian in personnel. It was through these Indian officials in the lower ranks of the bureaucracy that the authority of the government penetrated to the masses.

The efficiency of British rule in India is reflected in the composition of the Indian bureaucracy; in 1900 there were a total of 4,000 British civilian administrators in the country compared to 500,000 Indians. And in 1910, the Indian army comprised 69,000 Britishers and 130,000 Indians. This small number of British soldiers and bureaucrats ruled a vast subcontinent with a population nearing 300 million at the beginning of the twentieth century. It should be noted that Britain's position in India was based not only on the army and the bureaucracy but also on the surviving Indian princes. Prior to the mutiny, the British often had no compunction about taking over principalities when it suited them to do so. But this policy was reversed following it, so that India remained thenceforth a crazy-quilt pattern of some 550 native states intermingled with British Indian provinces. The reason for this change of policy was made clear in 1860 by Lord Canning, the first viceroy following the mutiny: "If we could keep up a number of Native States without political power, but as royal instruments, we should exist in India as long as our naval supremacy was maintained."[1]

The storming of Delhi during the Indian Mutiny of 1857.

IV.   BRITISH IMPACT

The British impact on India was felt first in the economic field, and naturally so since the British arrived in India in search of markets and commodities. Particularly after they became masters of the country, the British affected its economy decisively, especially by their taxation and trade policies. Since they were unfamiliar with the Mogul revenue system and lacked experienced personnel, the British decided, with their Permanent Settlement of 1793, to recognize the former imperial tax farmers and district revenue officers as English-type landlords, or zamindars. The "permanent" feature of this arrangement was that the annual sum expected of the zamindars was frozen at £3 million, whereas they were free, as landlords, to raise the rents they collected from the peasants. This was easy to do as land values were rising and the peasants now were tenants-at-will rather than hereditary cultivators of village lands. By World War II the landlords were collecting £12 to £20 million annually, leaving them a huge surplus which, unlike their English counterparts, they did not use to improve their holdings. Nevertheless the British preserved this arrangement because, as Governor-General William Bentinck observed, it "created a vast body of rich landed proprietors deeply interested in the continuance of British Dominion and having complete command over the mass of the people."[2] This Permanent Settlement was confined to the Ganges basin. Elsewhere the British collected the land taxes either directly or from village communities. Their levies were not heavier than those of the Mogul period, but they had to be paid in cash, and there was less chance of evading payment.

There was a strong demand in the nineteenth century for Indian raw materials such as jute, oilseeds, wheat, and cotton. These commodities were transported to the seaports by a newly built railroad network totalling 4,000 miles by 1870 and 41,000 miles by 1939. The opening of the Suez Canal also facilitated the export of Indian raw materials by reducing the distance traversed by freighters between London and Karachi from 10,800 to 6,100 miles. Thus India became one of the world's important sources of raw materials. And because of the high prices commanded by these materials, India was left with a favorable balance of trade throughout the nineteenth century.

The resulting capital surplus could have been used to develop modern industry. The fact that this was not done doomed India to its present critical state of underdevelopment. Britain made no attempt to encourage manufacturing in India, and in certain crucial areas, such as textiles, actively discouraged it. Thus there was no chance to erect tariffs to protect Indian infant industries against the tidal wave of cheap machine-made products from British factories. Indian economic historians describe this as a case of "aborted modernization." India had entered the world market and earned large sums of capital with no structural change in its outmoded national economy. In place of the economic modernization that had occurred in Europe, the British and their associates "skimmed cash crops off the surface of an immobilized agrarian society."[3]

Meanwhile, thanks to Western medical science, health measures, and famine-relief arrangements, India's population rose from 255 million in 1872 to 305 million in 1921. Similar population growth had occurred earlier in Europe but had been absorbed by new factories in the cities. Since no such industrialization occurred in India, the new extra millions could only fall back on agriculture. They naturally put a terrible overpressure on the land. And this remains to the present day one of the most acute problems of the Indian economy—and indeed of most Third World economies since they also suffer from "aborted modernization," and for the same reasons.

British rule affected India profoundly in intellectual matters as well as economic. The impact began in 1823 when the British appointed a Committee on Public Instruction to determine educational policy. The committee split between the "Anglicists," who wished to encourage an English type of education, and the "Orientalists," who favored a traditional education based on Sanskrit, Arabic, and Persian. The deadlock was broken in 1835 when committee President Thomas Babington Macaulay issued his famous Minute on Education. This adopted the Anglicist position, concluding that "English is better worth knowing than Sanskrit or Arabic. . . ." Macaulay added,

It is impossible for us, with our limited means, to attempt to educate the body of the people. We must at present do our best to form a class who may be interpreters between us and the millions whom we govern; a class of persons, Indian in blood and color, but English in taste, in opinions, in morals, and in intellect.[4]

Macaulay worked hard to implement his recommendation as soon as it was officially adopted. During the following decades a national system of education was worked out. It was made up of universities, training colleges for teachers, high schools, and vernacular elementary schools designed for the masses. Between 1885 and 1900 the number of students in colleges and universities rose from 11,000 to 23,000, and those in secondary schools from 429,000 to 633,000. At the same time the introduction of the printing press greatly stimulated intellectual life in India. Sanskrit works because public property rather than the jealously guarded monopoly of *Brahmins*, and newspapers appeared in the various modern Indian languages as well as in English.

These developments affected the intellectual climate of India profoundly. They did not touch the masses, who remained completely illiterate. Nor, at first, did they reach the Moslems, who remained generally hostile to the new schools and books. Thus, English education became almost the exclusive possession of a small Hindu upper class. But this was enough to start off a chain reaction that has continued to the present day. English education created a new class of Indians familiar with foreign languages and cultures and committed to liberal and rational ideologies. This Western-educated class used European ideology to attack British domination and to organize a nationalist movement that eventually culminated in an independent India.

V. INDIAN NATIONALISM

Britain's intellectual impact stimulated an up-surge and a creativity in Indian thought and culture that is commonly known as the Indian Renaissance. To appreciate the significance of this movement, we should note that when the British arrived on the scene, *Hinduism* was in a rather depressed and demoralized state. During the preceding seven hundred years of Moslem domination, Hindusim had been looked down on as the idolatrous religion of a subject race. It lacked prestige, organization, and active leadership. But when the British overthrew Mogul rule, Hinduism for the first time in seven centuries was on a par with Islam. And when the British opened their schools, the Hindus, unlike the Moslems, flocked to them eagerly. By so doing, they benefited in two ways: They filled the posts in the new bureaucracy, and they experienced an intellectual revival because of their Western contacts.

The stimulus of the West provoked three types of reaction or three schools of thought among the Hindus, although the lines were by no means clear-cut, and there was much overlapping. The first was wholeheartedly and uncritically pro-Western and antitraditional: Everything Western was accepted as superior and preferable.

The second reaction was one of complete rejection. The West was admittedly stronger, but its ideas were subversive and its customs repugnant. No true Indians, Hindus, or Moslems should compromise with the evil West. Rather, they should withdraw as far as possible from contact with the foreigner and live their own lives in the traditional way. Proponents of this view regarded caste rule as unchangeable, accepted the authority of the Hindu classics without reservations, and opposed such reforms as the abolition of suttee or of infanticide.

The third and most common reaction to the West represented a compromise between worship and outright rejection. It accepted the essence of Western secularism and learning, but it also sought to reform Hinduism from within and to preserve its basic truths while ridding it of corruptions and grossly unhuman practices. The outstanding leader of this school of thought was Ram Mohan Roy, widely venerated as the "father of modern India." Born in 1772 in a devout Brah-man family of Bengal, he broke with his parents over the spectacle of his sister's torture on the funeral pyre of her husband. An insatiable student, he mastered Persian, Arabic, and Sanskrit and then learned English and entered the service of the government. He was fascinated by Western thought and religions, and he studied Greek and Hebrew in order to read the Scriptures in the original. Roy rejected formal doctrinal Christianity but accepted its humanitarian message. He also reinterpreted Hinduism in his Brahmo Samaj, or Society of God, a new reformed sect of Hinduism that he founded. The Samaj was a synthesis of the doctrines of the European Enlightenment with the philosophical views of the Upanishads. Roy was above all a rationalist who believed that Hinduism rested squarely on reason. This principle established, he proceeded both to prune current Hindu practices and to borrow freely from the West. Thus he left his followers a creed that enabled them to face the West without losing their identity or their self-respect.

Ram Mohan Roy was the pioneer leader not only of India's religious renaissance but also of its political awakening, or nationalist movement. This was a new phenomenon in India. Hitherto there had been cultural unity and regional loyalties but no all-Indian feeling of patriotism. Nationalism developed under British rule for several reasons. One was the "superiority complex" of the English—their conviction that they were a racial elite and divinely ordained to rule India permanently. This racism, which was particularly strong following the Indian mutiny, manifested itself in all fields—in the army and the bureaucracy, where Indians could not rise above certain ranks regardless of their qualifications, and in social life, where Indians were excluded from certain hotels, clubs, and parks. Under these circumstances it was inevitable that the Indians should counter with the gradual development of a sense of cultural and national consciousness.

The British also stimulated nationalism by imposing an unprecedented unity on the Indian peninsula. For the first time the whole of India was under one rule. The British also forged a physical unity with their railways and telegraph and postal services. Equally important was the linguistic unity that followed the adoption of English as the common speech of the educated.

"Reading room" of the Indian National Congress secretariat.

The British system of education introduced the whole body of Western literature and political thought into the country and thereby furthered Indian nationalism. The principles of liberalism and nationalism, of personal freedom and self-determination, inevitably were turned against the foreign British rule. The Indian leaders used not only Western political principles but also Western political techniques. Newspapers, platform oratory, pamphleteering, mass meetings, and monster petitions—all were used as grist for the nationalist mill.

Ram Mohan Roy laid the foundations of Indian nationalism with his agitation for political and social reform. It was largely his campaign against suttee that induced the British government to prohibit the practice. Roy also worked for administrative and judicial reforms and helped to establish English-language schools and newspapers. Many of the outstanding future leaders of Indian nationalism first came into contact with the new teachings at the famous Hindu College in Calcutta with which Roy was associated.

The graduates of Hindu College were "moderates," in the sense that they accepted British rule and sought merely to win certain concessions. Accordingly, they cooperated in supporting the Indian National Congress, founded in 1885. The expressed aim of this body was to provide "an unanswerable reply to the assertion that India is still wholly unfit for any form of representative institutions." But this aspiration for parliamentary government was completely compatible with a sincere loyalty to Britain. Dadabhai Naoroji, who served as president of the Congress on three occasions, declared in a presidential address,

Let us speak out like men and proclaim that we are loyal to the backbone (cheers); that we understand the benefits English rule has conferred upon us; that we thoroughly appreciate the education that has been given to us, the new light which has been poured upon us, turning us from darkness into light and teaching us the new lesson that kings are made for the people, not people for their kings; and this new lesson we have learned amidst the darkness of Asiatic despotism only by the light of free English civilization (loud cheers).[5]

The first generation of Indian nationalists, then, were admirers of Great Britain and apostles of cooperation. But after 1890 these "moderates" were challenged by the extremists led by Bal Gangadhar Tilak (1856–1920), the "father of Indian unrest." Tilak was a militant crusader who sought to transform the nationalist cause from an upperclass to a popular mass movement. This may explain his dogmatic support of many Hindu social customs. He even went so far as to organize a cow-protection society and to support child marriage. Yet at the same time he fought for a minimum wage for labor, freedom for trade union organization, creation of a citizen army, universal franchise, and free and compulsory education without distinction as to sex. Tilak won followers throughout the country with slogans such as "Educate, Agitate, and Organize"; "Militancy, not mendicancy"; and "Freedom is my birthright and I will have it."

Tilak was aided in his crusade by a series of famines and plagues in the 1890s that gave impetus to the growing sense of grievance. Indian militancy was also aroused by the revolution in Russia in 1905 and by Japan's defeat of Russia in the same year. The latter event was particularly excit-

INDIA FOR THE INDIANS

B. G. Tilak was an early Indian nationalist who demanded that the British get out and who raised the slogan "India for the Indians." This nationalist feeling is clear in the following selection from a speech by Tilak in 1906.*

One fact is that this alien government has ruined the country. In the beginning, all of us were taken by surprise. We were almost dazed. We thought that everything that the rulers did was for our good and that this English government has descended from the clouds to save us from the invasions of Tamerlane and Chingis Khan, and, as they say, not only from foreign invasions but from internecine [civil] warfare. We felt happy for a time, but it soon came to light that the peace which was established in this country did this . . . —that we were prevented from going at each other's throats, so that a foreigner might go at the throat of us all. *Pax Britannica* [British peace or rule] has been established in this country in order that a foreign government may exploit the country. That this is the effect of this *Pax Britannica* is being gradually realized in these days. It was an unhappy circumstance that it was not realized sooner. . . . English education, growing poverty, and better familiarity with our rulers, opened our eyes and our leaders. . . .

Your industries are ruined utterly, ruined by foreign rule; your wealth is going out of the country and you are reduced to the lowest level which no human being can occupy. In this state of things, is there any other remedy by which you can help yourself? The remedy is not petitioning but boycott. We say prepare your forces, organize your power, and then go to work so that they cannot refuse you what you demand. . . . Every Englishman knows that they are a mere handful in this country and it is the business of every one of them to befool you in believing that you are weak and they are strong. This is politics. We have been deceived by such policy so long. What the new party wants you to do is realize the fact that your future rests entirely in your own hands. . . . We shall not give them assistance to collect revenue and keep peace. We shall not assist them in fighting beyond the frontiers or outside India with Indian blood and money. We shall not assist them in carrying on the administration of justice. We shall have our own courts, and when time comes we shall not pay taxes. Can you do that by your united efforts? If you can, you are free from tomorrow. . . .

* B. G. Tilak, *His Writings and Speeches* (Ganesh and Co., 1923), pp. 55–67.

ing because it was taken as a refutation of the claim of Western superiority. At this point the Indian government passed in 1905 an act for the partition of Bengal into two provinces: the new East Bengal, with 18 million Moslems and 12 million Hindus, and the remaining Bengal, with 42 million Hindus and 12 million Moslems. The government's aim was to improve administration, for the original province had been too large and the area east of the Ganges had been neglected. But to the Indian nationalists it appeared that the splitting of Bengal into predominantly Moslem and predominantly Hindu sections represented a British policy of divide and rule. This issue united the nationalists throughout the country more than ever before. They fought the government very effectively with the slogans "Swaraj," or self-government within the British Empire, and "Swadeshi," or boycott of British goods. The strong feelings aroused by the Bengal issue enabled the extremists to control the 1906 meeting of the Indian Congress and to secure a majority vote in favor of Swaraj and Swadeshi. Some of the nationalists went further, and, following the example and methods of the underground in Ireland and Russia, resorted to acts of terrorism.

Widespread though it was, this nationalist movement was predominantly Hindu. Under the leadership of Sir Sayyid Ahmad Khan, the Moslems had for the most part stayed out of the Indian Congress. They foresaw that if the Congress's demand for representative government was satisfied, the Moslems would suffer as a permanent minority. The Moslems also were alarmed by the increasing strength and militancy of Hindu nationalism, particularly since some of the most ardent Hindu patriots referred to the Moslems as "foreigners." In self-protection the Moslems organized the Moslem League, which, like the Indian Congress, held annual meetings. The British naturally welcomed and supported the League as a counterweight to the Congress. The League's existence, however, did not result from British machinations but rather from the tactical errors of many Hindu nationalist leaders, such as Tilak, who based their campaigns on a revival of Hinduism. The formation of cow-protection societies, for example, undoubtedly aided

the nationalist movement. But it also alienated Moslem Indians who naturally felt apprehensive about their future in a Hindu-controlled India.

Meanwhile, the spread of terrorism and the growing dissatisfaction of even the "moderates" convinced the British government that some concession was necessary. Accordingly, in 1909 the secretary of state for India, Lord Morley, and the viceroy, Lord Minto, presented the so-called Morley-Minto Reforms. These provided that a very small group of Indian voters, selected on the basis of high property, income, or education, should elect a majority of the members in the provincial governors' legislative councils and a minority of members in the viceroy's Legislative Council. A specified proportion of the legislative seats were reserved for Hindus and Moslems, and Moslem representation was weighted very considerably. For example, to become an elector, the Moslem had to pay income tax on an income of 3,000 rupees a year, the non-Moslem, on an income of 300,000 rupees. Furthermore, even where an elective majority existed, as in the provincial councils, the British government could, and was prepared to, override any opposition. Thus the reforms were in no way designed to introduce responsible government. Rather, they were intended to split the opposition by apparently permitting representative government but leaving full power and final decisions in British hands.

The strategy succeeded quite well. The moderate nationalists, who had regained control of the Congress, passed a resolution expressing "deep and general satisfaction at the Reform proposals." They were further placated when the British made several more concessions in 1911. The British annulled the unpopular partition of Bengal, released certain political prisoners, and granted substantial sums for educational purposes. Thus although individual acts of terrorism continued sporadically, India was relatively tranquil between 1910 and 1914.

Throughout this period, the nationalist movement was confined largely to the intellectuals. True, the National Congress had grown remarkably during the quarter-century following its establishment in 1885. Its membership was now drawn from all parts of British India, not merely from Bengal and a few cities on the west coast, as was originally the case. Yet the fact remains that it was almost exclusively a middle-class movement of lawyers, journalists, teachers, and merchants. These people were more familiar with John Stuart Mill, Herbert Spencer, and Charles Darwin than with the misery, grievances, and aspirations of the masses of their own Indian people in the villages. Not unnaturally, there was little rapport between the nationalist leaders and the illiterate peasants. The gulf persisted until bridged by Mohandas Gandhi in the postwar period. And Gandhi succeeded because he sensed the essentially religious outlook of his people and preached, not political abstractions, but religious concepts to which he gave a political meaning (see Chapter 38, Section IV).

In conclusion, the impact of the West on India was quite different from its impact on Russia or the Middle East. In the case of Russia, the West exerted decisive cultural and economic influence, but Russia remained politically and militarily strong and independent. The Near East, on the other hand, was dominated economically and militarily by the West, yet because of strategic considerations, the Ottoman Empire managed to retain its independence until World War I. India, by contrast, was conquered outright by Britain during the late eighteenth and nineteenth centuries. British rule lasted for nearly two centuries in Bengal and for more than a century in the Punjab. Consequently India never had the privilege of picking and choosing those features of European civilization that were most appealing. It was subjected to the impact of Western power and culture more indiscriminately than any other major region of Asia.

SUGGESTED READINGS

A survey of the historical literature on India is provided in the pamphlet by R. I. Crane, *The History of India: Its Study and Interpretation* (Service Center for Teachers of History, 1958). A collection of primary materials is provided by W. T. de Bary, ed., *Sources of Indian Tradition* (Columbia University, 1950). An invaluable reference work is by J. E. Schwartzberg, ed., *A Historical Atlas of South Asia* (University of Chicago, 1978).

Good general histories of India are available in P. Spear, *A History of India* (Penguin, 1965); and the sprightly written S. Wolpert, *A New History of India* (Oxford University, 1982). General studies of British rule in India are provided by R. P. Masani, *Britain in India* (Oxford University, 1961); P. Woodruff, *The Men Who Ruled India,* 2 vols. (Jonathan Cape, 1954–1955); H. Furber, *John Company at Work* (Harvard University, 1951); and the collection of readings reflecting various viewpoints in M. D. Lewis, ed., *The British in India: Imperialism or Trusteeship* (Heath, 1962).

The most thorough study of Europe's impact on India is by L. S. S. O'Malley, *Modern India and the West* (Oxford University, 1941). For the intellectual and nationalist trends in India, see A. Seal, *The Emergence of Indian Nationalism* (Cambridge University, 1968); B. T. McCully, *English Education and the Origins of Indian Nationalism* (Columbia University, 1940); S. A. Wolpert, *Tilak and Gokhale: Revolution and Reform in the Making of Modern India* (University of California, 1962); J. R. McLane, *Indian Nationalism and Early Congress* (Princeton University, 1977); and the same author's collection of documents on *The Political Awakening in India* (Prentice Hall, 1970).

33

China and Japan

The historian who grasps the true secret of Japan's success in rapid Westernization has a key to modern Far Eastern history.

John K. Fairbank

The Far East was the last major region of Eurasia to feel the impact of expanding Europe. Various factors explain why China and Japan followed behind Russia, the Near East, and India in this respect. First, and most obvious, the Far East, by definition, is that portion of the Eurasian continent that is farthest removed from Europe. China and Japan do not touch upon Europe, as did the Russian and Ottoman empires, and they are much further to the east and north than India. Probably more significant than geographic isolation was the political unity of the two Far Eastern countries. In China and Japan the European intruders were not able to employ the divide-and-rule policy that had proven so effective in India. There were no independent local potentates who could be enlisted against the central governments in Peking and Tokyo. And because of the rigid seclusion policies of both these governments, there were no native merchants ready to collaborate with the Europeans.

Consequently, the Far Eastern countries were able to limit their contact with Europe to a mere trickle of closely supervised trade. But in the mid-

nineteenth century the situation changed suddenly and drastically. First China and then Japan were forced to open their doors and to accept Western merchants, missionaries, consuls, and gunboats. Both of the Far Eastern countries were fundamentally affected, though in very different ways. Japan adopted and used the instruments of Western power. It was able to exploit them for self-defense and, later, for aggrandizement. China, by contrast, was unable to reorganize itself to meet the Western challenge. Yet, being too large and cohesive to be conquered outright like India and the countries of Southeast Asia, China was never to succumb entirely. So China remained in an uncomfortable and unstable state until World War I, and even for some decades thereafter.

I. OPENING OF CHINA

Over a period of four thousand years the Chinese people developed a unique and self-contained society at the extreme eastern end of the Eurasian landmass. This society, like others in Asia, was based on agriculture rather than trade and was governed by landlords and bureaucrats rather than by merchants and politicians. A distinctly self-centered and self-assured society, it regarded the rest of the world as inferior and subordinate.

The Chinese first came into direct contact with the West when the Portuguese appeared off the southeast coast in 1514. After the Portuguese came the Dutch and the British, who also arrived by sea. The Russians came from the north overland to the Amur valley. The Chinese resolutely kept all these intruders at arm's length (see Chapter 20, Section III). They restricted commercial relations to a few ports and refused to establish diplomatic relations on a full and equal basis.

The Chinese were forcefully jarred out of their seclusion and complacency by three disastrous wars: the first with Britain in 1839–1842, the second with Britain and France in 1856–1858, and the third with Japan in 1895. The humiliating defeats suffered in these wars compelled the Chinese to throw open the gates, to end their condescending attitude toward the West, and to reappraise their own traditional civilization. The outcome was a chain reaction of intrusion and response that produced a new China, with repercussions that are still felt in the Far East and in the entire globe.

Britain was able to take the lead in opening up China because it had a powerful base in India as well as control of the seas. Britain's main objective was to remove the many obstacles that the Chinese had placed in the way of trading operations. Triggering the start of hostilities between Britain and China was the immediate issue of trade in opium. European sailors had introduced opium smoking in China in the seventeenth century, and the habit had spread rapidly from the ports. The demand for opium solved the British problem of paying for Chinese products. Hitherto the British had been forced to pay mostly in gold and silver, because the Chinese were little interested in Western goods. But now the market for opium reversed the balance of trade in favor of the British. The Peking government issued decrees in 1729 and 1799 prohibiting the importation of opium, but the trade was so profitable that Chinese officials could be bribed to permit smuggling.

The first Anglo-Chinese War, or the Opium War as it is frequently called, broke out when the Chinese attempted to enforce their prohibition of the opium traffic. The emperor appointed as special imperial commissioner a man of proven integrity and firmness, Lin Tse-hsu. Lin seized 20,000 chests of opium worth $6 million and destroyed them at a public ceremony. Complications following this action led to a clash between Chinese war junks and British frigates, and war began in November 1839. During the hostilities that followed the hopeless military inferiority of the Chinese became obvious. With a squadron of ships and a few thousand men, the British were able to seize port after port at will. The Chinese fought valiantly. Their garrisons often resisted to the last man. But the odds against the non-Europeans were even worse now than they had been between the conquistadors and the Aztecs. European warships and artillery had improved immeasurably between the sixteenth and nineteenth centuries, whereas Chinese military technology had stagnated at a level little above that of Aztec capabilities. In 1842, the Peking government capitulated and accepted the Treaty of Nanking, the first of a long series of unequal treaties that were to nibble away much of China's sovereignty.

By the Nanking Treaty China ceded the island of Hong Kong and opened five ports to foreign trade—Canton, Foochow, Ningpo, Amoy, and Shanghai. British consuls could be stationed at these ports and British merchants could lease land for residential and business uses. China also agreed to a uniform tariff fixed at 5 percent ad valorem, to be changed only by mutual agreement. This provision deprived China of tariff autonomy and hence of control over its national revenue. Furthermore, a supplementary treaty concluded the following year granted Britain extraterritoriality in criminal cases and also included a most-favored-nation clause assuring Britain any additional privileges that China might grant other powers in the future.

The Nanking Treaty did not end the friction between the Chinese and the Europeans. The later wanted more concessions in order to increase trade, whereas the Chinese felt that the treaties already had granted too many privileges to the Europeans. It is not surprising, then, that hostilities began again in 1856. The occasion this time was the imprisonment by Chinese officials of the Chinese crew on board a Chinese ship flying the British flag. When the Peking government refused to release the crew, the British bombarded Canton. The French also entered the war, using the murder of a French priest as a pretext. The Anglo-French forces proved irresistible, and in June 1858 the Chinese were compelled to sign the Tientsin Treaties. But they refused to carry out the provisions and the Anglo-French forces renewed the attack. They captured the capital and forced China to sign the Peking Conventions in 1860. The Tientsin and Peking agreements opened several

FIRESHIPS AND MONKEYS

*During the 1839 Opium War, the Chinese with their old-fashioned weapons had no chance against the British with their steam warships and artillery. This was proven when the Chinese tried to recapture the city of Ningpo. The resulting fiasco is described by the British historian Arthur Waley, who uses contemporary Chinese sources.**

There were a great many literary men on the [Chinese] General's staff, and ten days before the attack commenced (January 31st) he ordered them to compose announcements of victory. Thirty of these were sent in, and the General arranged them in order of merit. The first place went to Miu Chia-ku who had composed a detailed and vivid account of the exploits of the various heroes. Second on the list was Ho Shih-ch'i (a fairly well-known calligrapher) who sent in a vast composition, full of classical tropes and brilliant felicities.

The signal for the general attack was to be the setting alight of the fire-rafts which were to be let loose upon the English ships and, drifting against them, would set fire to them before they could weigh anchor. . . . The English ships' boats put out long before the blazing rafts arrived, took them in tow—a ticklish operation during which several sailors were badly burnt—and beached them. A second contingent of fire-rafts at a point some miles away was also prematurely ignited as soon as the flames were seen rising from the other rafts; but when less than half of this second contingent had been launched the Chinese irregulars in charge were attacked by boats put out from English warships, and fled.

Someone suggested that fire-crackers should be tied to the backs of a number of monkeys, who would then be flung on board the English ships. The flames would spread rapidly in every direction and might with luck reach the powder-magazine, in which case the whole ship would blow up. Nineteen monkeys were bought, and at the time of the advance were brought in litters to the advanced base. After the failure of the Chinese attack they accompanied the retreating armies to Tz'u-ch'i. "The fact is," says Pei, "that no one ever dared go near enough to the foreign ships to fling them on board, so that the plan was never put into effect." During the panic that ensued after the defeat of the remaining Chinese troops on the heights behind Tz'u-ch'i, the people fled from the town, including a Mr. Feng in whose charge the monkeys had been put. There was no one to care for them, and they eventually died of starvation in Mr. Feng's deserted front lodge.

*A. Waley, *The Opium War Through Chinese Eyes* (George Allen and Unwin, 1958), pp. 165, 169, 170.

more ports on the coast. In the interior, they redefined and extended extraterritoriality and permitted the establishment of foreign legations in Peking and of Christian missions throughout the country. We should recall that it was at this time that the Russians took advantage of China's difficulties and used diplomatic means to annex large areas in the Amur valley and along the Pacific coast (see Chapter 30, Section III).

The third defeat suffered by China was the most humiliating, for it was at the hands of the small neighboring kingdom of Japan. We shall see later in this chapter that the Japanese, in contrast to the Chinese, had been able to adapt Western technology to their needs and to build an efficient military establishment. Thus they accomplished what no other oriental state had been able to achieve thus far. Japan now pressed certain shadowy claims in Korea. Traditionally, the Koreans had recognized the suzerainty of China, but they had also periodically paid tribute to Japan. Thus when China sent a small force to Korea in 1894 in response to an appeal for aid in suppressing a revolt, the Japanese also landed a detachment of marines. The two forces clashed, and war was formally declared by China and Japan in August 1894. The Chinese armies again were easily routed, and, in April 1895, Peking was forced to accept the Treaty of Shimonoseki. Its terms required China to pay an indemnity; to recognize the independence of Korea; to cede to Japan the island of Formosa, the Pescadores Islands, and the Liaotung peninsula; and to open four more ports to foreign commerce. Some of the European powers were not at all pleased with the appearance of a new rival for concessions in China. Accordingly, Russia, France, and Germany joined in a demand that the strategic Liaotung peninsula be returned to China, a demand to which Japan yielded reluctantly.

The Japanese war was a shattering blow to the pride and complacency of China. The great empire had been shown to be completely helpless at the hands of a despised neighbor equipped with modern instruments of war. Furthermore, the European powers during the preceding years had been taking advantage of China's weakness and annexing outlying territories that traditionally had recognized Peking's suzerainty. Russia took the Amur valley and the Maritime Provinces and

for a while occupied the Ili River region in central Asia. France seized Indochina; Britain took Burma; and Japan, since it had established its predominance in Korea by defeating China, proceeded to annex the country outright in 1910. In addition to these territorial acquisitions, the Western states divided up China proper. They set up "spheres of influence" in which the political and economic primacy of each respective power was recognized. Thus Yunnan and the area bordering on Indochina became a French sphere, Canton and the Yangtze valley and the large area in between was a British sphere, Manchuria was Russian, Shantung was German, and Fukien Japanese.

China in the mid-nineteenth century was beset by domestic turmoil as well as foreign aggression. Many Chinese held the Manchu dynasty responsible for the national crisis, so several rebellions broke out. In the past, such a time of troubles would have been interpreted as indicating that the dynasty's "mandate from Heaven" had expired, so a new dynasty would have replaced the Manchu. For a while it seemed that the great Taiping Rebellion (1850–64) would effect such a change, but it was blocked from doing so by Great Power intervention.

At first the Powers were sympathetic to the Taiping Rebellion because its leader was a mystic who was much influenced by Christian missionaries and who opposed opium smoking, polygamy, prostitution, footbinding, and ancestor tablets. The rebels won control of the Yangtze valley, but the greater their victories, the more the Western powers shifted their support to the Manchu dynasty. The Taiping ban on opium threatened a major source of profit for Western companies, as did also the Taiping opposition to the opening of more Chinese ports to foreign trade. Therefore, the Great Powers propped up the Manchu dynasty in Peking with loans, with arms, and with mercenary soldiers who led the imperial armies against the rebels. Finally the Taipings were defeated, but only at the cost of tens of millions of casualties. Thus the Manchu dynasty survived but it was left weaker than ever because it obviously could not count on the support of its own people, and therefore it dared not resist demands by the Powers. These humiliations and disasters that China experienced in the latter half of the nineteenth century forced the traditionally self-centered Middle Kingdom to undertake a painful self-assessment and reorganization. We will now trace the course of this process, noting how the Chinese slowly and grudgingly tried to follow the Western model in a number of fields—first in the military, then in the economic, later in the social and intellectual, and finally in the political.

II.   MILITARY AND ECONOMIC IMPACT

Lin Tse-hsu, the Chinese commissioner who had tried to stem the flow of opium and who had borne the brunt of the first British attack, realized the superiority of foreign arms. In a letter to a friend he described the impossibility of coping with British warships and concluded that "ships, guns, and a water force are absolutely indispensable." But Lin was by no means willing to broadcast these views. "I only beg you to keep them confidential," he requested his friend. "By all means, please do not tell other persons."[1]

His aversion to publicity indicates that he feared a hostile reaction among his colleagues and superiors. This fear was fully justified. The scholar-officials who ruled China remained, with a few exceptions, profoundly hostile and scornful of everything Western. The shock of defeat compelled them to take certain measures toward imitating Western arms and techniques. But in actual practice they did little more than go through the motions. Even if they had sincerely wanted to imitate the West, which fundamentally they did not, the mandarins were hopelessly incompetent in mechanical matters. Thus China did little during the interwar years of 1842 to 1858 to face the challenge of European expansionism.

The second defeat at the hands of the Western powers forced a few forward-looking Chinese intellectuals to reconsider their traditional values and policies. Their response was what they called the "self-strengthening" movement. The phrase itself is from the Confucian classics and was used in the 1860s to mean the preservation of Chinese civilization by grafting on Western mechanisms. In this regard the leaders of China now were ready to go beyond purely military matters to in-

clude railroads, steamship lines, machine factories, and applied science generally. In the words of one of the reformers of this period, "China should acquire the West's superiority in arms and machinery, but retain China's superiority in Confucian virtue."[2] This "self-strengthening" movement was doomed to failure because the basic assumption on which it rested was false. Westernization could not be a halfway process; it was all or nothing. Westernization in tools led inevitably to westernization in ideas and institutions. So Western science could not be used to preserve a Confucian civilization; rather, it was bound to undermine that civilization.

For example, the China Merchants Steam Navigation Company was established in 1872 to build steamships for transporting rice from the Yangtze Delta to the capital in the north. The steamer fleet needed coal, so the Kaiping coal mines were opened north of Tientsin in 1878. To transport this coal, China's first permanent railroad began operations in 1881. This integrated complex of enterprises had a sound economic basis and should have prospered. But its directors were motivated, in the traditional Chinese fashion, more by family than by corporate considerations. They appointed needy relatives and greedy henchmen to the various posts, with the result that the entire undertaking fell heavily into debt and eventually passed to foreign control.

China's failure to build up its economy and its armed forces led inevitably to increasing Western penetration and control. Numerous loans were made to the Peking government, frequently under pressure and on conditions that gave the creditors control over segments of China's economy. Another means of economic influence were the concessions in various Chinese ports that were held by the European powers. Most important was the "international settlement" of Shanghai, which developed into a sovereign European city-state where Chinese laws did not apply and Chinese courts and police had no jurisdiction. These concessions profoundly affected China's economy, which traditionally had been self-sufficient and land based, but which was now becoming increasingly dependent on the foreign-controlled coastal cities, and particularly on Shanghai. The Western powers also dominated the great inland waterways as well as the coastal ports. They maintained fleets of gunboats that patrolled the Yangtze River between Shanghai and Chunking, a distance of 1,500 miles across the heart of China. In fact, Britain maintained an officer with the revealing title of "Rear-Admiral Yangtze"!

III. SOCIAL AND INTELLECTUAL IMPACT

In the late nineteenth and early twentieth centuries, the Chinese response to the West's challenge broadened from the military and economic spheres to the social and intellectual. One reason for the shift was that the extension of foreign business into the interior of the country stimulated the growth of a Chinese merchant class, which soon took over the distribution of Western goods. Later, Chinese manufacturers began to establish match factories, flour mills, cotton mills, and silk-spinning factories. These new economic leaders tended to be an independent political force. They disliked European domination because of the privileges it conferred on foreign business competitors. But they also had little use for the reactionary imperial court in Peking, which neither offered effective resistance to the foreigners nor showed any understanding of the nature and needs of a modern economy. Thus, these Chinese merchants felt no more loyalty toward the Manchu regime in Peking than the Indian merchants had felt earlier for the Mogul regime in Delhi. Consequently it was they who provided the dynamism behind the revolutionary nationalist movement that developed at the turn of the century. It was not accidental that the first antiforeign boycotts were organized in the coastal cities and that the 1911 revolution that overthrew the Manchu dynasty also broke out in those cities.

The perilous situation of China also affected the ruling scholar-bureaucrats, though they were pushed in the direction of reform rather than revolution. Because of their official positions and vested interests, they wanted only "change within tradition." They still held that China's Confucian civilization could be renovated to meet modern needs. An outstanding exponent of this view was the fiery Cantonese scholar K'ang Yu-wei (1858–1927), who startled his colleagues with his study *Confucius as a Reformer.* This iconoclastic work depicted Confucius as a champion of the rights of the people, rather than of imperial authority.

Advocacy of people's rights and of their participation in government was something new for China. Hitherto the Western concepts of democracy and nationalism had been conspicuously absent. Instead, the emphasis had been on the family, and as far as a broader allegiance was concerned, it took the form of "culturalism" rather than nationalism. By culturalism is meant identification with the native cultural tradition, which was viewed simply as the alternative to foreign barbarism. China's ruling scholar-bureaucracy was steeped in this tradition, and many of its members still avowed that it was "better to see the nation die than its way of life change."[3] But against the standpatism of this traditional culturalism, the reform leaders now accepted revolutionary Western concepts. "What does nationalism mean?" asked one of these reformers, who went on to answer his rhetorical question:

It is that in all places people of the same race, the same language, the same religion, and the same customs, regard each other as brothers and work for independence and self-government, and organize a more perfect government to work for the public welfare and to oppose the infringement of other races. . . . If we wish to promote nationalism in China, there is no other means of doing it except through the renovation of the people.[4]

IV. POLITICAL IMPACT

The new reformers in China were able to win a hearing following the defeat at the hands of the Japanese in 1895. They gained the ear of the young emperor, Kuang-hsü, who momentarily broke away from the influence of the empress dowager, Tz'u-hsi. The latter had determined China's policy since 1860, but now the reformers won the emperor over to their side. So impressed was he by their oral and written presentations that in the summer of 1898 he issued a series of sweeping reform decrees that are collectively called the Hundred Days Reform. Numerous sinecures were to be eliminated, the provincial

Boxers awaiting execution in Canton Prison, Canton, China.

governments were to be more centralized under Peking, new schools were to disseminate European learning, Western-style production methods were to be encouraged, and a national conscript army was to be organized along Western lines. These measures never got beyond the paper stage. The empress, with the support of the military, deposed the unfortunate emperor, declared herself regent, rescinded all the reform decrees, and executed six of the reform leaders.

The collapse of the Hundred Days Reform gave the reactionaries full power. In their zeal they actively channeled social and political discontent against the foreigners. Antiforeign secret societies, incited by court reactionaries and provincial governors, organized local militias to combat foreign aggression. Chief among these societies was the I Ho T'uan or "Righteous Harmony Fists," popularly termed *Boxers*. With official con-

nivance the Boxers began to attack foreigners, and by 1900 numerous Chinese Christians and foreigners had been killed in north China. When European naval detachments began to land at Tientsin, the Boxers declared war on all foreigners and besieged the foreign legations in Peking. Within a few months, international armies relieved the legations, and the imperial court fled from the capital. Once more China was forced to accept a peace with humiliating terms, including further commercial concessions and payment of an indemnity of $333 million.

The fiascos of the Hundred Days Reform and of the Boxer Rebellion dramatically demonstrated the futility of trying to modernize China by reform from above. The alternative was revolution from below, and this did take place in 1911, when the Manchu dynasty finally was overthrown and its place taken by a republic.

A Chinese Punch and Judy show used by the Boxers as antiforeign propaganda.

The leader and ideologist of the revolutionaries was Dr. Sun Yat-sen (1866–1925). Compared to the reform leaders who had hitherto been prominent, Sun was a strange and anomalous figure. He was not one of the upper-class literati; in fact, his training was as much Western as Chinese. He was born in the Canton Delta, which had been subject to foreign influence longer than any other area in China. At the age of thirteen he joined his brother in Honolulu, where he remained five years and completed a high school course in a Church of England boarding school. Then he went to Queen's College in Hong Kong, and after graduation he enrolled in the Hong Kong Medical College, where he received his medical degree in 1892. Thus Sun acquired an excellent scientific education that he could have used to win wealth and status. Instead he identified with the poor and always felt a passionate concern for their welfare. "I am a coolie and the son of a coolie," he declared on one occasion. "I was born with the poor and I am still poor. My sympathies have always been with the struggling mass."[5]

With such sentiments, he did not remain long in professional practice. The defeat by Japan in 1895 convinced him that the government of his country was rotten to the core and that nothing short of a revolution would provide the remedy. At a conference held in Tokyo in 1905 Sun founded the T'ung-meng-hui, or League of Common Alliance. Its program called for a republican government elected by "the people of the country" and also for the division of the land among the peasantry. It is significant that no one had earlier raised the issue of land distribution as a possible element in self-strengthening or reform. No one before Sun had proposed the notion that the peasant masses might be transformed into literate, property-owning, and politically active citizens.

Sun Yat-sen derived his main support from Chinese merchants overseas. Within the country only a few students and merchants were influenced by his ideas, and the mass of the population remained illiterate and apathetic. When the revolution came in 1911, it was partly the work of landlord gentry and commercial interests in the provinces that were opposed to the belated efforts of the Manchu regime to nationalize railway construction. The provincial leaders fomented strikes and riots, ostensibly on the ground that nationalization would lead to foreign control but actually because they feared they would lose the profits. In any case, the revolutionists exploited the discontent and worked effectively among students and soldiers. A small-scale republican uprising in Canton was suppressed, but on October 10, 1911, an accidental explosion in a revolutionist bomb factory at Hankow led to mutiny among nearby imperial troops. Despite lack of coordination, the revolutionary movement spread rapidly throughout the country. Sun Yat-sen, who was in the United States at the time, hurried back, and on December 30, 1911, a provisional revolutionary assembly elected him president of the United Provinces of China.

Sun was unable to control the country even though he was the nominal leader. Actual power was in the hands of an able and ambitious imperial official, Yuan Shih-k'ai (1859–1916), who commanded the most effective army in China. Rather than risk a civil war that would invite foreign intervention, Sun, in February 1912, yielded the presidency to Yuan, and the latter agreed to work with a parliament and a responsible cabinet. This arrangement, however, did not really settle the basic question of what form of government would replace the fallen Manchu regime. Yuan was all for Western military technology and administrative methods. But he regarded Western political institutions, including control of the executive by representatives of the people, as antithetical to China's traditions and certainly antithetical to his personal ambitions.

Sun Yat-sen founded a new political party, the *Kuomintang,* or National Peoples' party, which won a majority of seats in the National Assembly elected in April 1913. But this setback did not really restrict Yuan, for he had the backing of the army and the bureaucracy. Furthermore, the foreign powers preferred to back the strongman Yuan, just as they had backed the Manchu dynasty in earlier years. Yuan resorted to severe repression to consolidate his position, which led Sun to stage an armed uprising in the summer of 1913. The move was premature and Yuan suppressed the revolt with ease.

Sun fled to Japan with his principal followers, and Yuan made preparations to fulfill his ill-concealed ambition to establish himself as emperor. In October 1913, he had himself elected permanent president. Then he ordered the dissolution of both the Kuomintang and the Parliament. With the opposition out of the way, he engineered "spontaneous" requests that he fulfill his duty to his country and become emperor. In December 1915, Yuan announced that he would assume the imperial title on January 1, 1916.

His plans were upset by a revolt that broke out in Yunnan in December 1915 and quickly spread. Yuan found it necessary first to postpone and finally, in March 1916, to abandon the restoration of the monarchy. Humiliated and embittered, he died in June of the same year. After his death the army commanders who had served under him divided the country among themselves. These warlords paid little attention to the republican government that nominally ruled from Peking. Instead, they pillaged the countryside mercilessly and dragged China down to a brutalizing anarchy. These early years of the republic until 1926 marked one of the worst periods in the history of China.

Several factors account for this wretched outcome of several decades of response to the West. First there is the sheer size of China, which for many years left the interior of the country unaffected by Western contact. The interior functioned as a vast reservoir, out of which tradition-minded civil-service candidates continued to appear for several decades. The bureaucracy that they formed consisted of intellectuals who were steeped in the Confucian classics and who consequently placed much greater emphasis on ethical principles than on the manual arts or the technology of warfare. This ruling class was further inhibited by the fact that, apart from Buddhism, China had little or no tradition for borrowing from abroad. Thus it is not surprising that although China did change in the second half of the nineteenth century, the tempo of its change was far slower than that of the other countries responding to the West. Finally, the young Western-trained Chinese also were partly to blame. Some of them played leading roles in the early days of the republic, but they tried to set up in China carbon copies of the institutions they had observed abroad, especially in the United States. What they established naturally had no meaning for the Chinese people and quickly crumbled before the realities of Chinese politics.

V.   JAPAN IN SECLUSION

Historians have presented several explanations for the difference between the Chinese and the Japanese response to the challenge of the West. The physical compactness of the Japanese Islands facilitated both the forging of national unity and the spread of new values and new learning throughout the country. It also made the country vulnerable to, and aware of, foreign pressures, unlike the vast interior provinces of China, which for long were inaccessible to Western influences. Furthermore, Japan's long tradition of borrowing from the great Chinese cultural world made similar borrowing from the Western world in the nineteenth century less jarring and painful. Japan had adapted selected aspects of Chinese culture with the slogan "Japanese spirit and Chinese knowledge." Now it borrowed what it wished from the West with the slogan "Eastern morale and Western arts." Also, Japanese government and society were pluralistic in structure in comparison with the monolithic features of the Chinese Empire. The clan tradition and regional particularism of Japan were reinforced by geographic separation due to the broken mountainous terrain. The merchant class in Japan had more autonomy and economic strength, and, as we shall see, it was rapidly extending its power at the critical moment of the West's intrusion. The military elements in Japan were at the top of the social ladder, rather than at the bottom, as was the case in China. This meant that Japan had a ruling class that was much more sensitive and responsive to Western military technology than were the Chinese literati. In sum, geography, cultural traditions, and pluralistic organization combined to make Japan more vulnerable to Western intrusion than China, and quicker to respond to that intrusion.

Despite these basic differences, Japan, like China, remained in seclusion until the mid-nineteenth century. The Tokugawa shoguns severed one by one the ties between Japan and the Western world. By the mid-seventeenth century the sole remaining contact was the handful of Dutch traders who were confined to the islet of Deshima (see Chapter 20, Section VI). The aim of the Tokugawa leaders was to keep Japan isolated and unchanging in order to perpetuate their regime. But despite their efforts, certain developments did occur that gradually altered the balance of forces in the country and undermined the status quo. The long peace enforced by Tokugawa rule stimulated population growth, economic expansion, and the strengthening of the merchant class. The population jumped from 18 million in 1600 to 26 million in 1725. Cities grew disproportionately, Edo (later Tokyo) approaching the million mark by 1700, and Osaka and Kyoto each reaching 300,000. The population spurt increased the demand for commodities and encouraged merchants and rich peasants to invest surplus capital in new forms of production, including the domestic, or putting-out, system. They provided materials and equipment for peasants and craftspeople, and marketed the finished products. It appears that in certain areas this industrial development had reached the level of factory organization by the end of the Tokugawa period. Regional specialization based on available raw materials and local skills became widespread, so that particular areas were noted for their lacquerware, pottery, textiles, or rice wine.

Rising production led to wide-scale exchange of goods, which in turn led to the development of a money economy. At first money was imported from China and Korea, but in the seventeenth century a gold mint was established. The aristocrats became dependent on brokers to convert their rice into money and on merchants to satisfy their consumption needs. In these transactions the aristocrats lost out because the merchants manipulated the prices through monopolies and because the price of rice failed to keep up with the soaring costs of other commodities. The aristocrats, besides, had acquired a taste for luxuries and tended to compete with each other in ostentatious living. The net result was that they generally became indebted to the merchants, even though the merchants ranked far below in the social scale. In time the merchant families bought their way into the aristocracy by intermarriage or adoption. These families then dominated not only the economy but also the art and literature of the eighteenth and early nineteenth centuries.

We should note that these changes affected not only the top levels of the aristocracy but also the samurai, whose services were not so much in demand during this long period of peace. The mass of the peasants also suffered severely with the lag in the price of rice. Many of them migrated to the cities, but not all were able to find employment for the growth of the national economy was not keeping pace with the growth of population.

Thus Japanese society was in a state of transition. It was experiencing profound economic and social change, which gave rise to political tensions. These tensions were reaching the breaking point when Commodore Perry forced Japan's doors open to trade. One reason the Japanese proved so ready to reorganize their society under the impact of the West was precisely because many of them were all too aware that their society needed reorganizing.

On July 8, 1853, Commodore Matthew Perry cast anchor in Edo Bay and delivered a letter from President Fillmore asking for trading privileges, coaling stations, and protection for shipwrecked Americans. Within a week he sailed away after warning that he would be back for an answer the following spring. When he returned in February 1854, he made it clear that the alternative to a treaty was war. The Japanese yielded and on March 31 signed the Treaty of Kanagawa. Its terms opened the ports of Shimoda and Hakodate for the repair and provisioning of American ships, provided for proper treatment and repatriation of shipwrecked Americans, permitted the appointment of consular representatives if either nation considered it necessary, and promised most-favored-nation treatment for the United States.

In accordance with the provisions of this treaty, the United States sent Townsend Harris, an unusually able man, as the first consul to Japan. With his extraordinary tact and patience, Harris gradually won the confidence of the Japanese and secured the Commercial Treaty of 1858. This opened four more ports to trade, provided for mutual diplomatic representation, gave to Americans both civil and criminal extraterritoriality, prohibited the opium trade, and gave freedom of religion to foreigners. Soon after signing these two treaties with the United States, Japan concluded similar pacts with Holland, Russia, Britain, and France. Thus Japan, like China before it, now had to suffer the intrusion of the West. But its response to that intrusion was altogether different from that of the Middle Kingdom.

VI. MODERNIZATION OF JAPAN

The first effect of the Western encroachment was to produce a crisis that precipitated the downfall of the Tokugawa Shogunate. With the signing of the treaties the shogun was subject to conflicting pressures: on the one hand from the foreign powers, which were demanding implementation of all the provisions, and on the other from the Japanese population, which was strongly antiforeign. The popular sentiment was exploited by the anti-Tokugawa clans, especially the Satsuma, Choshu, Hizen, and Tosa, often referred to as the Satcho Hito group. Between 1858 and 1865 attacks were made on Europeans and their employees with the slogan "Honor the Emperor! Expel

the barbarians!" With the death in 1867 of both the emperor and the Tokugawa shogun, the way was clear for the so-called Meiji Restoration. The Tokugawa clanspeople were shorn of their power and fiefs, and their place was taken by the Satcho Hito clans, which henceforth controlled the government in the name of the new Meiji emperor. It was the young samurai in the service of these clans who now provided Japan with the extraordinary leadership that made possible successful modernization. In contrast to China's literati, Japan's new leaders realized that they were retarded in certain fields, and they were willing and able to do something about it.

This is not altogether surprising if we note that even during their centuries of seclusion the Japanese leaders had gone out of their way to keep informed of developments in Europe. In fact, the Dutch were allowed to continue trading primarily so that they could be questioned concerning the outside world. Both the shogunate and the clans promoted military industry and maintained schools for the study of foreign languages and foreign texts. The general level of knowledge rose to the point where, in the natural sciences, physics was separated from chemistry, and in medicine, students were trained in special fields such as surgery, pediatrics, obstetrics, and internal medicine. In the Nagasaki naval school, instruction was given in navigation and gunnery only after a solid base had been laid in mathematics, astronomy, and physics. In other words, the Japanese all along had been much more appreciative of and responsive to Western culture. In the light of this background, it is understandable why the Japanese acted quite differently from the Chinese once the Westerners forced their way in.

Japan's new leaders were interested only in those features of Western civilization that enhanced national power. In the field of religion, for example, the Meiji leaders supported Shinto as the state cult because it identified the national character with the emperor, who it held was descended from the Sun Goddess. In other words, Shinto stimulated national unity and patriotism, and these attributes were deemed necessary if Japan were to hold its own in the modern world. In education, it was explicitly stated that the objective was the furtherance of state interests rather than the development of the individual. Compulsory elementary education was required because the state needed a literate citizenry. Large numbers of foreign educators were brought to Japan to found schools and universities, and thousands of Japanese studied abroad and returned to teach in the new institutions. But the entire educational system was kept under close state supervision to ensure uniformity of thought as well as of administration.

In military affairs the Japanese abolished the old feudal levies and organized modern armed forces based on the latest European models. They built a conscript army with the aid of a German military mission and a small navy under the guidance of the British. The Meiji leaders foresaw that the new military forces required a modern economy to supply their needs. Accordingly, they secured the establishment of the needed industries by granting subsidies, purchasing stock, or forming government corporations. The government leaders were careful to support not only light industries such as textiles but also heavy industries such as mining, steel, and shipbuilding, which were necessary to fill military needs. Once these enterprises were founded, the government generally sold them to various favored private interests at extremely low prices. In this way a few wealthy families, collectively known as the Zaibatsu, gained a stranglehold on the national economy that has persisted to the present.

The Japanese also overhauled their legal system. This was in such a bad state when the Westerners appeared that their demand for extraterritoriality was understandable. The laws were chaotic and harsh, individual rights were disregarded, the police were arbitrary and all-powerful, and prison conditions were revolting. In 1871 a judicial department was organized, and in the following years new codes were adopted and a distinction was made between judicial and administrative powers.

At the same time various political innovations were made to provide Japan with at least the trappings of parliamentary government. A cabinet and a privy council were first established, and then, in 1889, a constitution was adopted. This document promised citizens freedom from arbitrary arrest; protection of property rights; and

freedom of religion, speech, and association. But in each instance the government was given authority to curb these rights when it so desired. The constitution provided Japan with a parliamentary facade while preserving oligarchic rule and emperor worship. Indeed, the first article of the constitution provided that "The Empire of Japan shall be reigned over and governed by a line of Emperors unbroken for ages eternal," and the third article likewise stipulated that "The Emperor is sacred and inviolable."

With the adoption of the constitution and of the legal reforms, the Japanese were in a position to press for the abolition of the unequal treaties. They could fairly argue that Japan now had taken its place in the ranks of civilized nations and that there was no longer any need for *extraterritoriality* and for the other infringements on their sovereignty. After prolonged diplomatic efforts they were able in 1894 to persuade Britain and the United States to end extraterritoriality and consular jurisdiction in five years. In the same year the Japanese won their unexpected and spectacular victory over the Chinese Empire. Henceforth there could be no more question of treating Japan as an inferior country, and the other powers soon followed Britain and the United States in yielding their special privileges. By 1899 Japan had gained legal jurisdiction over all foreigners on its soil, and in doing so, it became the first Asian nation to break the chains of Western control.

VII.   EXPANSION OF JAPAN

After its self-modernization, Japan embarked on a career of expansion on the mainland. This is not surprising in view of Japan's warlike tradition and the immense prestige that its military leaders enjoyed from earliest times. Furthermore, the Far East was then a hotbed of international rivalry, and the practical-minded leaders of Japan drew the obvious conclusion: Each people must grab for themselves. Their first expansionist move was in Korea where, as noted earlier in this chapter, the Japanese defeated the Chinese and then annexed Korea in 1910.

After their victory over China, the Japanese were faced by the much more powerful Russians, who were advancing southward into Manchuria and Korea. Described earlier (Chapter 30, Section III) was Japan's offer for a compromise settlement, Russia's refusal of the offer, Japan's attack and victory over Russia, and the Portsmouth Treaty (September 5, 1905) by which Japan won the southern half of Sakhalin Island and Russia's Liaotung leasehold, as well as recognition of Japan's special interests in Korea.

In retrospect this war stands out as a major turning point in the history of the Far East, and even of the world. Certainly it established Japan as a major power and altered the balance of forces in the Far East. But much more significant is the fact that for the first time an Asian state defeated a European state, and a great empire at that. This had an electrifying effect on all Asia. It demonstrated to millions of colonial peoples that European domination was not divinely ordained. For the first time since the days of the conquistadors, the white race had been beaten, and a thrill of hope ran through the non-white races of the globe. In this sense the Russo-Japanese War stands out as a landmark in modern history; it represents the prelude to the great awakening of the non-European peoples.

SUGGESTED READINGS

For background references, see the bibliography for Chapter 21. The best overall survey of the impact of the West on East Asia is by E. O. Reischauer, J. K. Fairbank, and A. M. Craig, *East Asia: Tradition and Civilization,* rev. ed. (Houghton Mifflin, 1978); and J. K. Fairbank, *China, a New History* (Harvard, 1992). See also the excellent study by G. M. Beckmann, *The Modernization of*
China and Japan* (Harper & Row, 1962); and J. K. Fairbank, *The Great Chinese Revolution, 1800–1985* (Harper & Row, 1986). The most important work on the West's impact on China is the following collection of documents with explanatory essays: Ssu-ye Teng and J. K. Fairbank, *China's Response to the West: A Documentary Survey, 1839–1923* (Harvard University, 1954). Also noteworthy are G. Rozman, ed., *The Modernization of China* (Free Press, 1981); H. Z. Schiffrin, *Sun Yat-sen and the Origins of the 1911 Revolution* (University of California, 1969); E. P. Young, *The Presidency of Yuan Shih-k'ai* (University of Michigan, 1977); and J. D. Spence, *The Gate of Heavenly Peace: The Chinese and Their Revolution, 1895–1980* (Viking, 1982).

The outstanding works on the West's impact on Japan are the documentary collection by R. Tsunoda, *Sources of the Japanese Tradition* (Columbia University, 1958); and the analysis by G. B. Sansom, *The Western World and Japan* (Knopf, 1950). Also noteworthy are E. O. Reischauer, *Japan: The Story of a Nation,* rev. ed. (Knopf, 1970); J. Halliday, *A Political History of Japanese Capitalism* (Pantheon, 1975); and W. W. Lockwood, *The Economic Development of Japan: Growth and Structural Change, 1868–1938* (Princeton University, 1954).

For Western diplomacy in the Far East, see W. L. Langer, *The Diplomacy of Imperialism, 1890–1902,* rev. ed. (Knopf, 1956). The problem of the contrasting response to China and Japan to the Western intrusion is considered in N. Jacobs, *The Origin of Modern Capitalism and Eastern Asia* (Hong Kong University, 1958); and in F. V. Maulder, *Japan, China and the Modern World Economy* (Cambridge University, 1977).

34

Africa

For better or for worse the old Africa is gone and the white races must face the new situation which they have themselves created.

Jan Christiaan Smuts

Europe's impact on sub-Saharan Africa was felt considerably later than that on Eurasia. The European powers fastened their rule on India, the East Indies, and much of North Africa before they expanded south of the Sahara. France acquired Algeria in 1830 and Tunisia in 1881, and England occupied Egypt in 1882. European penetration southward generally came later because of various reasons, including adverse climate, prevalence of disease, geographic inaccessibility, and the superior organization and resistance of the Africans compared to the American Indians or the Australian aborigines (see Chapter 21, Section I). Also, unlike the bullion of Mexico and Peru, there was a lack of exploitable riches to lure Europeans into the interior. Thus sub-Saharan Africa, apart from certain coastal regions, remained largely unaffected by Europe until the late nineteenth century. In the last two decades of that century, however, the European powers made up for lost time. They partitioned virtually the entire continent and exploited its material and human resources. By 1914 the African peoples had, in many respects, come under European influence even more than had the Asians, though many villagers in the interior regions continued to live as before and to be little influenced by the European intruder.

I. SLAVE TRADE

For centuries the most valuable of African resources for Europeans were the slaves, but these could be obtained at coastal ports, without any need for penetration inland. Slavery had been an established and accepted institution in Africa. Prisoners of war had been enslaved, as were also debtors and individuals guilty of serious crimes. But these slaves usually were treated as part of the family. They had clearly defined rights, and their slave status was not necessarily hereditary. Therefore it is commonly argued that Africa's traditional slavery was benign compared to the transatlantic slave trade organized by the Europeans. This argument, however, can be carried too far. Professor

Edward Reynolds warns against the illusion that "cruel and dehumanizing enslavement was a monopoly of the West. Slavery in its extreme forms, including the taking of life, was common to both Africa and the West . . . the fact that African slavery had different origins and consequences should not lead us to deny what it was—the exploitation and subjugation of human beings."[1] Neither can it be denied that the wholesale shipment of Africans to the slave plantations of the Americas was made possible by the participation of African chiefs who rounded up their fellow Africans and sold them at a handsome profit to European ship captains waiting along the coasts.

Granting all this, the fact remains that the transatlantic slave trade conducted by the Europeans was entirely different in quantity and quality from the traditional type of slavery that had existed within Africa. From the beginning the European variety was primarily an economic institution rather than social, as it had been in Africa. Western slave traders and slave owners were motivated by purely economic considerations, and were quite ready to work their slaves to death if it was more profitable to do so than to treat them more leniently. This impersonalism was reinforced by racism when the Europeans became involved in the African slave trade on a large scale. Perhaps as a subconscious rationalization they gradually came to look down on Negroes as inherently inferior, and therefore preordained to serve their white masters. Rationalization also may have been involved in the Europeans' use of religion to justify the traffic in human beings. Enslavement, it was argued, ensured the conversion of the African heathen to the true faith as well as to civilization.

In this self-satisfied spirit the Portuguese shipped thousands of African slaves to their homeland. This was but a petty prelude to the new and fateful phase of the slave trade that began in 1510 when the first shipload of African slaves was shipped to the New World. The venture was highly successful, for there was urgent need for labor in the Americas, especially on the sugar plantations. The market for slaves was almost limitless, and several other countries entered the slave trade to share in the rich profits. Portugal dominated the trade in the sixteenth century, Holland during most of the seventeenth, and Britain in the eighteenth. The West

African coast was dotted with about forty European forts that were used for defense against the rival trading nations and for storing the slaves while awaiting shipment across the Atlantic.

The typical voyage of the slave traders was triangular. The first leg was from the home port to Africa, with a cargo including salt, cloth, firearms, hardware, beads, and rum. These goods were bartered for slaves brought by fellow Africans from the interior to the coast. The unfortunate victims were packed under atrocious conditions in the vessels and shipped across the Atlantic on the so-called "middle passage." At their New World destinations the slaves were either sold at once or held in stockades to be retailed on demand. The final lap was the voyage home with plantation produce such as sugar, molasses, tobacco, or rice.

Thanks to the prevailing trade winds the "middle passage" was normally swift and brief, the average being sixty days. Nevertheless, the death rate during the trip ranged from 10 to 55 percent, depending on the length of the voyage, the chance occurrence of epidemics, and the treatment accorded the slaves. This treatment almost invariably involved inhuman crowding, stifling heat, and poor food. Even greater casualties were suffered earlier, during the overland march to the coast. Raiding parties plundered villages and broke up families in their search for strong young men and women. The captives were then driven from dawn to dusk in the blazing heat and pouring rain, through thick jungles or over dry plains. The survivors who reached the coast were driven naked into the market like cattle. Then they were branded with the name of the company or buyer and herded into the forts to await shipment across the ocean. It is not surprising that in supplying American plantations with between 12 and 20 million slaves, Africa suffered an estimated loss in casualties of about four times that number of people (see Chapter 27, Section III, for the overall effects on Africa).

Despite these horrors, Europeans continued to buy and sell Africans for over four centuries. The profits were so great that powerful vested interests strongly opposed any proposals for control or abolition. There were first of all the African chiefs, who received as much as £20 to £36 for a single able-bodied slave. These African leaders played a vital role in the slave-trade operations.

Lithograph depicting a slave ship plying between Africa and America before the Civil War.

Their participation was essential for the Europeans, who were confined to the coastal areas and who suffered mortality rates of 25 to 50 percent. Not only did the African middlemen reap handsome profits from the trade but they also were violently opposed to all abolition proposals. Indeed, riots against Europeans were organized on African soil in defiance of the abolition movement! It is true that a few chiefs did try to stop the abhorrent trade in their fellow Africans, but they had no chance because those who continued trading received firearms and threatened the existence of the few who tried to abstain. Thus the chiefs were caught in a trap from which the few dissenters could not escape.

The plantation owners in the Americas likewise supported the slave trade, especially the Barbados planters, who held an important bloc of seats in the eighteenth-century British Parliament. There were European vested interests also that championed the slave trade, both among the traders and the various merchants at home who provided the rum and the manufactured goods. According to one estimate, Britain shipped to Africa manufactures valued at 1 million pounds a year, and the other European countries sent an equal amount for the same purpose. The return on this outlay was so extraordinarily high that in the eighteenth century the prosperity of cities such as Liverpool and Bristol depended heavily on this traffic. The famous abolitionist leader William Wilberforce properly observed that "Interest can draw a film over the eyes so thick that blindness itself could do no more."[2]

Despite these formidable obstacles, a small group of reformers campaigned vigorously for

FORGING HOES.

MÁNGANJA AND MACHINGA WOMEN.

Iron tools were used in Africa long before the coming of the Europeans. This illustration taken from David Livingstone's *Last Journals* shows Africans forging hoes.

abolition. In 1787 they established in England the Society for the Abolition of the Slave Trade. In 1823 they founded the Anti-Slavery Society to end the institution of slavery as well as the slave trade. These abolitionists were aided by the progress of the industrial revolution, which was rendering slavery obsolete. Advancing technology called for overseas markets rather than for a cheap supply of human power. In fact, the abolitionists argued that the slave trade was inefficient

and insisted that a more profitable "legitimate" trade could be developed in Africa.

The first success of the abolitionists was a law in 1807 prohibiting British ships from participating in the slave trade and banning the landing of slaves in British colonies. Finally, in 1833 Parliament passed a decree that completely abolished slavery on British territory and provided 20 million pounds as compensation for the slaveholders. The British government went further and persuaded other European countries to follow its example in allowing British warships to seize slave ships flying other flags. At one period, a fourth of the whole British navy was patrolling the coasts of Africa, Cuba, and Brazil with a force of 56 vessels manned by 9,000 sailors. In twenty years these patrol ships captured over 1,000 slavers and set free their human cargoes. Needless to say, many traders continued to slip through the blockade, lured on by the fortunes awaiting them in the Americas. Complete success was not possible until the various countries in the New World gradually abolished slavery as an institution—as did Haiti in 1803, the United States in 1863, Brazil in 1888, Cuba at about the same time, and so forth.

While the slave trade was being stamped out on the west coast of Africa, it continued to be carried on by the Arabs in central and East Africa, though on a much smaller scale. The Arabs had been engaged in this trade long before the appearance of the Europeans, and they continued through the nineteenth century and even into the twentieth. The captives were marched across the Sahara to North African fairs, or they were taken to east coast ports and then shipped to Zanzibar, Madagascar, Arabia, Turkey, Persia, and even India. Many of these slaves worked in clove and sugar plantations on various Indian Ocean islands. This traffic was much more difficult to suppress than that on the west coast. Despite British naval patrols in the Red Sea and the Indian Ocean, it persisted until World War I and later.

II.   AGE OF EXPLORATION

The agitation for the abolition of slavery contributed directly to the exploration and opening up of the "Dark Continent." The abolitionists hoped to curtail the slave trade by pushing into the interior where the slaves were captured. There they hoped to develop "legitimate" or regular commerce that would replace the traffic in slaves. At the same time, a growing fad for geography made Europeans intensely curious about unexplored lands. These factors all combined to bring to Africa in the nineteenth century a number of remarkable and colorful explorers.

The systematic exploration of the continent began with the founding of the African Association in 1788. It was headed by the noted British scientist Joseph Banks, and its purpose was "to promote the cause of science and humanity, to explore the mysterious geography, to ascertain the resources, and to improve the conditions of that ill-fated continent." The association's attention was directed first to the problem of the Niger. As yet the river was only a name. Even before the beginning of the European slave trade rumors had circulated about fabulous cities on the banks of a great river called the Niger. No one knew where it rose or where it ended. To solve the mystery, the association in 1795 sent out a Scottish physician, Mungo Park. He and most of his companions fell victims to the dread African diseases. Not until 1830 did Richard Lander unlock the mystery of the Niger by following it to its mouth. In doing so, Lander proved that the so-called Oil Rivers, long known to Europeans as a source of palm oil and slaves, made up the delta of the Niger. The exploration of West Africa was most furthered during the 1850s by Dr. Heinrich Barth. This remarkable German visited the most important cities of the western Sudan and then crossed the Sahara and returned to England in 1855. His journey was one of the greatest feats in the history of African travel.

Interest shifted to East Africa after a disastrous trading expedition up the Niger proved that commercial opportunities were scanty there. The big question in East Africa was the whereabouts of the source of the Nile. Hostile natives, vast marshes, and innumerable rapids had defeated all attempts to follow the river upstream to its headwaters. In 1856 two Englishmen, John Speke and Richard Burton, started inland from the African east coast. They discovered Lake Tanganyika, and with Burton ill, Speke pushed on

another two hundred miles to discover Lake ~~toria~~. On a second trip (1860–1863), Speke sa~~w~~ the White Nile pouring from Lake Victoria at Ripon Falls and then followed the great river to Khartoum and on through Egypt to the Mediterranean.

Head and shoulders above all the other explorers stands the figure of the great David Livingstone. He had trained himself originally to become a medical missionary in China, but the outbreak of the Opium War diverted him to Africa, where he landed at Capetown and worked his way northward. In 1849 Livingstone crossed the Kalahari Desert to see what fields for missionary enterprise lay beyond. He discovered Lake Ngami, where he heard that the country ahead was populous and well watered, in contrast to the desert he had just crossed. In the following years he crossed the continent westward to the Atlantic and then back across to the Indian Ocean. In 1861 he disappeared in the African bush in search of the source of the Nile. No word from him was received by the outside world for five years, so the New York *Herald Tribune* sent its famous correspondent Henry M. Stanley to find the explorer. Stanley did find Livingstone in 1871 on Lake Tanganyika. Although Livingstone was weak and emaciated, "a mere ruckle of bones" in his own words, he refused to return home with Stanley. Instead he continued his explorations until May 1, 1873, when his followers found him dead in a praying position beside his cot.

Stanley was so inspired by Livingstone's character and career that he returned to Africa to solve some of the problems left by "the Good Doctor." He discovered that the Lualaba River, thought by Livingstone to flow into the Nile, instead became the Congo, which flowed westward to the Atlantic. Stanley arrived in Boma on the west coast on November 26, 1877, exactly 999 days after leaving Zanzibar. The last of the four great African rivers had at last been traced from source to mouth.

Two years later, in 1879, Stanley was again on the Congo River, but this time he was functioning as the agent for King Leopold of Belgium rather than as an explorer. The age of African exploration had given way to the age of African partition.

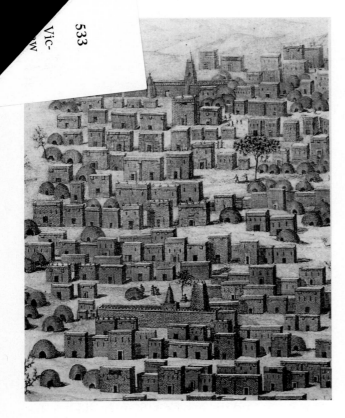

Timbuktu in 1828.

III. PARTITION OF AFRICA

Prior to 1870 the European powers had insignificant holdings in Africa. They consisted mostly of seaports and fortified trading stations, together with bits of adjacent territory acquired as adjuncts to trade rather than as bases for territorial expansion. With the termination of the European slave trade, most of these coastal footholds were virtually abandoned since the legitimate trade was not great enough to support them. European leaders during this early period repeatedly stated their opposition to the acquisition of colonies.

After 1870 a combination of factors (see Chapter 28, Section VII) produced a reversal of this anticolonial attitude. Colonies now were regarded as assets for the mother country, and the continent of Africa, being unoccupied and defenseless, became the focus of imperialist aspirations. The leader of the imperialist drive in Africa was King Leopold of Belgium. At the outset he was interested primarily in East Africa. But with Stanley's exploration of the Congo Basin from 1876 to 1877, Leopold at once saw the potential of this great central region. In fact, it had been Stanley himself who had seen the opportunity, but, unable to enlist support in England, in 1878 Stanley entered Leopold's service, returning in the following year to the Congo. Between 1879 and 1880 Stanley signed numerous treaties with chiefs, handing over no fewer than 900,000 square miles to the International Association of the Congo, a new organization set up under Leopold's direction. The chiefs had no way of knowing that signing the pieces of paper and accepting token payments meant permanent loss of their tribal lands. An African chief traditionally was entrusted with his people's land. His selling was like a mayor's selling "his" city hall. Yet this was the standard European procedure all over the continent, and repercussions are being felt to the present day.

The immediate effect of Leopold's machinations was to jolt the other European leaders to action. The French already had sent their famous explorer Count de Brazza to the lower Congo, and he was able to acquire for his country the lands to the north of the river. The Germans also entered the race, obtaining in 1884 Southwest Africa, Togoland, and the Cameroons. Now the Portuguese were eager to join in, especially since they claimed on the west coast both sides of the Congo mouth and inland indefinitely. Britain never had been willing to recognize these Portuguese claims, but now it changed its mind in hopes of checking the aggressive Belgians and French. So an Anglo-Portuguese Convention was signed on February 26, 1884, recognizing Portuguese sovereignty over the mouth of the Congo and providing for Anglo-Portuguese control of navigation on the river.

The treaty, furiously denounced by the other powers, led to the holding of an international conference in Berlin (1884–1885) to prepare rules for the further acquisition of African territories. It was agreed that no power should annex land or establish a protectorate without first giving notice of intent; that recognition of territorial claims must depend on effective occupation; and that disputes were to be settled by arbitration. The conference also recognized the rights of Leopold's International Association of the Congo to much of the Congo Basin, to be known as the Congo Free State. Finally, high-sounding declarations were made about uplifting the natives, spreading the Gospel, and stamping out slavery. All these were to be conspicuous by their absence in the so-called Free State.

Now that an international code for territorial aggrandizement was agreed on, the entire continent was partitioned in less than two decades. In the Congo, Leopold bought out in 1887 all non-Belgian interests in order to eliminate possible criticism of his enterprise. Then he reimbursed himself by reserving a Crown district of the richest rubber lands, ten times the size of Belgium. Here, as elsewhere in the Congo, special monopolies of the exploitation of natural products, including rights of native labor, were awarded to commercial concerns. Leopold was a heavy stockholder in most of these. His profits, therefore, were derived both from the stipends paid to the state by the concessionaries and from the dividends earned in the course of their immensely successful operations. In the final analysis, the fortunes that were made in the Congo were extracted by ruthless exploitation of the native peoples. So unbelievably brutal were the various methods of forced labor that the population of the Congo declined by one-half (from 20 million to 10 million) between 1885 and 1908 during its rule by Leopold.

If the Africans did not bring in the required amount of rubber and ivory, they were mutilated or shot. Mutilation meant chopping off a hand or a foot or both. To prove that they were doing their job properly, the bosses of the labor gangs brought to their superiors baskets full of human hands. And because the climate was hot and humid, the hands were sometimes smoked in order to preserve them. News of these atrocities leaked out, and Leopold was forced to turn over his Congo possessions to the Belgian government in 1908. What had been private property now became a Belgian colony. The government took measures to end the atrocities, though a modified form of forced labor did continue. Leopold, the mercenary promoter to the end, induced the Belgian parliament to compensate him handsomely for his "sacrifice" of the Congo.

In the rest of West Africa the French were the most active. Starting from their old trading posts on the Ivory Coast, in Dahomey, and on the north bank of the Congo, they conceived a grand plan for pushing inward and founding a French West African Empire that would stretch from Algeria to the Congo and from the Senegal to the Nile or even to the Red Sea. Since the Germans and the British also had footholds along the west coast, the French had to outflank their rivals in a race for the hinterland. By and large they were successful. Only the British in Nigeria and the Germans in the Cameroons were able to expand significantly into the interior. All the rest of West Africa, together with the vast Sahara, became a great French domain ruled from Paris.

In East Africa, the Portuguese had held Mozambique since the sixteenth century, and France had claims to Madagascar. The chief rivals for the remaining territory were the Germans and the British. At the end of 1884, while the Berlin conference was in session, a young German colonial enthusiast, Dr. Carl Peters, landed secretly in East Africa. Within ten days he had persuaded the local chiefs to sign away more than 60,000 square miles, an area almost one-third the size of his own homeland. The following year the German government proclaimed a protectorate over the region obtained by Carl Peters. The German activities aroused the British, who proceeded to sign treaties giving them the territory in the Kenya area. In 1886 and 1890 the British and the Germans signed agreements settling their claims in East Africa. The Germans retained the huge area known as the German East Africa Protectorate, to be named Tanganyika after 1919. The British kept their East Africa Protectorate, later to be known as Kenya Colony, together with a protectorate over Uganda.

Meanwhile, the Italians had belatedly joined the scramble for African territory. They managed to obtain two barren colonies on the Red Sea coast, Eritrea and Somaliland, and later, in 1896, they gambled for higher stakes by sending an army to conquer the kingdom of Ethiopia. The Christian Ethiopians were able to resist more effectively than the people in most other parts of Africa. Their Emperor Menelik had an army of 80,000 men trained by French officers and armed with French weapons. Able to defeat the small

Italian army of 10,000, his kingdom remained free from European rule. But except for the small republic of Liberia on the west coast, by 1914 Ethiopia was the only independent state on the whole continent. Even Liberia, set up in 1822 as a settlement for freed American Negroes (named from the Latin *liber,* meaning "free"), became a virtual U.S. protectorate in 1911 because of bankruptcy and internal disorders.

Meanwhile, on the southern tip of the continent the British were roused to action by the establishment of a German protectorate in Southwest Africa and by Portuguese plans for the linking of Angola on the west coast to Mozambique on the east. The British took control of three areas—Basutoland, Bechuanaland, and Swaziland—all of which were made into native reservations and placed under British commissioners. North of the Limpopo River the British were attracted by rich goldfields and healthy plateau lands that were suitable for white colonization. In 1889 the British government granted a charter to the British South Africa Company, whose field of operations was defined as "to the north and west of the South African Republic, and to the west of the Portuguese dominions." Settlers began to arrive, and in 1890 the town of Salisbury was laid out on the beautiful and salubrious plateau between the Limpopo and the Zambesi. After World War I the British company gave up its charter, and its lands were organized as the two colonies of Northern and Southern Rhodesia.

The British also had difficulties in South Africa proper, where a long, smoldering feud with the Boer settlers flared up into full-scale war in 1899. After the war the British granted self-government to the Boers in the Orange Free State and the Transvaal, and in 1907 these two colonies joined with Natal and Cape Colony to form the Dominion of the Union of South Africa.

The net result of this unprecedented territorial aggrandizement was the partitioning of the entire continent of Africa among the European powers. The only exceptions, as noted, were the fragile states of Liberia and Ethiopia. The partitioning was carried out with surprisingly little fighting. And where that was necessary, the conquering forces in each region usually consisted of only one to two thousand men. These "European" forces were mostly Africans, trained and led by European officers.

One reason why the Europeans carved up Africa so easily was that they were able to pit Africans against Africans (just as they had used Indians against Indians in conquering the Americas). Another reason was that the Africans waged frontal, head-on warfare, which left them sitting ducks to the murderous European firepower. After being defeated in the field, they usually retreated to walled cities where they were vulnerable to European artillery. If they had waged guerrilla warfare, their knowledge of the terrain and their assurance of mass support might have enabled them to hold out long enough to make conquest prohibitively expensive. As it was, they could not stand up to river gunboats, coastal warships, and Gatling and Maxim machine guns firing over ten shots per second.

Despite the overwhelming odds, the Africans were by no means passive pawns. In certain regions they put up enough resistance to slow down the "European" forces seriously. The conquest of West Africa took twenty-five years, and parts of the Ivory Coast, Mali, Niger, Eastern and Northern Nigeria, and Mauritania were not pacified till the second decade of the twentieth century. The leaders of this African resistance today serve as national heroes for the newly independent states of Africa.

IV.   EUROPE'S IMPACT

Economic

Since economic motives were prominent in the partitioning of Africa, it is not surprising that drastic economic changes followed in its wake. Europe no longer was content with boatloads of slaves at the coastal ports. The industrialized West no longer needed human slaves; technology had replaced them with an abundance of machines. Instead the West had need for the raw materials found in the interior of Africa, and it now had the technological means to extract these materials.

The first important step in the exploitation of Africa's resources came with the discovery of diamonds in Kimberly (1867) and gold in the

Witwatersrand (1884). Equally great mineral wealth was discovered in the Rhodesias (gold and copper) and in the Congo (gold, copper, and diamonds). Many portions of the west coast yielded rich supplies of such tropical forest products as palm oil, rubber, and ivory. European and American companies bought vast plantations in such regions as the Congo, the Cameroons, and French Equatorial Africa. One example was the Firestone Corporation, which in 1926 was given a ninety-year lease on 100,000 acres of land in Liberia.

Not only did foreign companies lease large tracts of land, but also foreign settlers took over much of the good agricultural land. From explorers' reports it was known that some of the interior plateaus had fertile soil as well as a pleasant climate. Consequently, European settlers flocked in, particularly to Southern Rhodesia and East Africa. Before long they had gained possession of the most desirable agricultural properties in these regions.

To transport the minerals and the agricultural commodities now being produced, the Europeans proceeded to build a network of railways in Africa, as they already had done in Asia. These railways were designed to facilitate the export of produce rather than to stimulate general economic development. The expansion of production and the construction of transportation facilities stimulated trade to the point where the traditional barter gave way to a monetary system. No longer did the Africans exchange slaves, gold dust, feathers, and ivory for the Europeans' salt, glassware, cloth, rum, and gin. By the end of the nineteenth century there was fairly widespread use of English silver coins and of Austrian and American dollars.

All of these economic developments naturally had profound effects on the native peoples. The inhabitants of the temperate plateau areas were affected most by the loss of the lands taken by white settlers. In some cases whole districts were reserved for exclusive white use, and the land could not be tilled by the Africans, even though it sometimes lay fallow. Consequently, the Africans were forced to work for wages on the white man's plantations, and some even "squatted" on the land of the white farmers for whom they worked to gain the privilege of tilling a small plot for themselves. In other regions the Africans found it necessary to leave their families and go to work in the mines. If the Africans refused to provide the labor needed for the plantations and mines, various types of forced labor were used. The most common was the levying of a head tax compelling the African to work in order to earn the money to pay the tax. These various developments reduced the traditional economic self-sufficiency of the African. No longer did he or she work simply to feed self and family. Africans were involved more and more in a money economy and so were affected by world economic conditions. Thus the effect of Europe's economic impact was twofold: to entangle the Africans in a worldwide money economy and to subordinate them, directly or indirectly, to the whites who were everywhere the "boss."

Cultural

Together with the European traders, investors, and settlers came the European missionaries. They had a profound effect on African culture because they were the first Europeans who consciously sought to change it. The others affected it only indirectly and incidentally, as when they forced Africans to leave their ancestral villages to work in cities or mines. But missionaries came with the avowed purpose of changing the African way of life. They used three instruments to carry this out: education, medicine, and religion.

Schools offering a Western education and Western ideals were an integral part of every mission station. These schools were particularly influential since most colonial governments left the job of educating to the missionaries. In many respects the mission schools were constructive in their influence: Often they taught the pupils how to build better houses, improve their agricultural methods, and observe the rudiments of hygiene and sanitation. They also taught reading and writing in African as well as European languages. The missionaries converted the African languages to writing and so laid the foundations for native African literature. The great majority of those Africans who chose literary careers were educated in missionary schools.

On the other hand, these schools inevitably had a subversive influence on the African people;

MEDICAL DOCTOR AND RAIN DOCTOR

Western missionaries in Africa brought a new culture as well as a new religion. The clash between old and new is illustrated in the following argument between David Livingstone (medical doctor) and a native rain doctor.*

R. D. *You* ought not to despise our little knowledge, though you are ignorant of it.

M. D. I don't despise what I am ignorant of; I only think you are mistaken in saying that you have medicines which can influence the rain at all.

R. D. That's just the way people speak when they talk on a subject of which they have no knowledge. When we first opened our eyes, we found our forefathers making rain, and we follow in their footsteps. You, who send to Kuruman for corn, and irrigate your garden, may do without rain; *we* cannot manage in that way. If we had no rain, the cattle would have no pasture, the cows give no milk, our children become lean and die, our wives run away to other tribes who do make rain, and have corn, and the whole tribe become dispersed and lost; our fire would go out.

M. D. I quite agree with you as to the value of the rain; but you cannot charm the clouds by medicines. You wait till you see the clouds come, then you use your medicines, and take the credit which belongs to God only.

R. D. I use my medicines, and you employ yours; we are both doctors, and doctors are not deceivers. You give a patient medicine. Sometimes God is pleased to heal him by means of your medicine; sometimes not—he dies. When he is cured, you take the credit of what God does. I do the same. Sometimes God grants us rain, sometimes not. When he does, we take the credit of the charm. When a patient dies, you don't give up trust in your medicine, neither do I when rain falls. If you wish me to leave off my medicines, why continue your own?

M. D. I give medicines to living creatures within my reach, and can see the effects though no cure follows; you pretend to charm the clouds which are so far above us that your medicines never reach them. The clouds usually lie in one direction, and your smoke goes in another. God alone can command the clouds. Only try and wait patiently; God will give us rain without your medicines.

R. D. Mahala-ma-kapa-a-a! ! Well, I always thought white men were wise till this morning. Who ever thought of making trial of starvation? Is death pleasant then?

M. D. Could you make it rain on one spot and not on another?

R. D. I wouldn't think of trying. I like to see the whole country green, and all the people glad; the women clapping their hands and giving me their ornaments for thankfulness, and lullilooing for joy.

M. D. I think you deceive both them and yourself.

R. D. Well, then, there is a pair of us (meaning both are rogues).

The above is only a specimen of their way of reasoning, in which, when the language is well understood, they are perceived to be remarkably acute. These arguments are generally known, and I never succeeded in convincing a single individual of their fallacy, though I tried to do so in every way I could think of. Their faith in medicines as charms is unbounded. The general effect of argument is to produce the impression that you are not anxious for rain at all; and it is very undesirable to allow the idea to spread that you do not take a generous interest in their welfare.

*D. Livingstone, *Missionary Travels and Researches in South Africa* (J. Murray, 1857), pp. 22– 25.

they often taught that the traditional way of life was primitive and wrong. In time the students listened less to their parents and elders and more to their European teachers, whom they learned to respect. In addition, the mission schools used European books that taught more about Europe than about Africa. In fact, the beginning lessons in early history textbooks used in the French colonies dealt with "our ancestors the Gauls." Missionary education encouraged individualism, which was contrary to the communal African way of life. It is not surprising that Africans subjected to several years of this type of education were usually loath to return to their villages. Instead they looked for jobs with the colonial governments, missions, or private business, and so moved further away from their traditional culture.

The missions also brought medical knowledge and facilities that saved the lives of many Africans. But besides saving lives, medicine also forced Africans to question their traditional ideas of what caused illness and death. Whites had the power to make people well even after the proper petitioning of spirits had not worked. So traditional religion no longer could be counted on to meet all emergencies and to provide all the answers. Even though the majority of Africans clung to their old faiths, traditional religion was no longer as effective as it previously had been in holding together the African's whole way of life.

Political

Europe's imprint was as marked in the political field as it was in the economic and cultural fields. When the boundaries of the various colonies were drawn, no attention was paid to the indigenous people concerned. Hence they often found themselves under the rule of two or even three European powers. Some of the Somali, for example, were ruled by the French, others by the British, still others by the Italians, and a number even found themselves within the boundaries of Ethiopia.

Once the boundaries had been settled, the problem of organizing some administrative system arose. The European governments lacked the population to rule all the peoples of the vast African continent directly. So they resorted to various forms of indirect rule; administration was conducted through tribal chiefs who were allowed to retain some of their authority. Usually the British allowed the chiefs more leeway than did the French, but even the French could not control everything because their African possessions were so vast and their supply of officials was so limited.

On the surface, then, the Africans retained their traditional political institutions. They still had their councils of elders, their laws, their courts, and their chiefs. But in practice this political structure was undermined. The chiefs could be appointed or removed by the local European administrators, and their decisions no longer had the force of law since tribespeople could go over their heads to the European officials whose word was final.

Perhaps the most important factors undermining the traditional political systems were the economic and cultural changes brought about by European rule. Since chiefs often were thought to get their authority from the tribal gods, their political power was backed up by their religious leadership. Obviously both their religious leadership and their political power were weakened when the people were converted to a new religion or when their faith was shaken in the old. Likewise, people who gained money wealth by working in cities or mines acquired a status and independence that would have been inconceivable had they remained in their villages. In some cases these newly rich people actually had more prestige and power than the old chiefs.

The most serious and direct challenge to the traditional tribal authorities came from the class of Western-educated Africans that gradually developed in almost all the colonies. They tended to challenge not only the native chiefs but also the European officials. They did so because they imbibed in Western schools certain political ideas such as individual liberty and political freedom, and they saw no reason why the principles of liberalism and nationalism should apply in Europe but not in Africa. They were also goaded into political agitation by the discrimination they frequently encountered in government and private employment. Usually they were not allowed to be more than poorly paid clerks in European firms or very minor officials in the colonial administration. Again they could not see why, when they had the required education and experience, they should be kept in subordinate positions simply because their skins were dark. The Christian religion, and especially Protestantism, stimulated nationalism because it emphasized individual judgment and initiative. This point was made by a writer in an Angolan journal who said, "To tell a person he is able to interpret the Bible freely is to insinuate in him an undue autonomy and turn him into a rebel. . . . A Protestant native is already disposed towards— not to say an active agent in—the revolt against civilized peoples."[3]

Conclusion

This survey indicates that in many basic respects Europe left a much deeper imprint on Africa than on Eurasia. There was no parallel in Eurasia to the draining of African labor through the slave trade. With the exception of Southeast Asia, there was also no parallel to the loss of agricultural lands, even though the loss was limited to East Africa and South Africa. Likewise, there was no parallel in Eurasia to the virtually total European domination of transport, finance, foreign trade, mining, and manufacturing. Finally, there was no parallel, with the exception of the Philippines, to the widespread diffusion of European Christianity and European languages and to the ever-growing cultural influence of the European missionaries with their schools and their medical facilities.

The basic reason for this contrast in degree of European influence is that there was a corresponding contrast in the level of general development attained in Africa and in Eurasia. This contrast of African underdevelopment prevailed in all fields—in the sophistication of cultures, in the development of economies and technologies, and, consequently, in the density of populations. It was this contrast that made sub-Saharan Africa infinitely more vulnerable to European missionaries, entrepreneurs, and settlers.

And yet this very underdevelopment of sub-Saharan Africa provided a natural resistance at the village level (as distinct from the European-influenced urban centers). In most parts of the continent prior to 1914, the interior villages retained their economic self-sufficiency and their integrated traditional cultures, which made them largely impervious to the West. Though we acknowledge the decisive impact of Europe in certain basic respects, we must still realize that many of the villages of sub-Saharan Africa remained relatively unchanged in their traditional patterns of life.

SUGGESTED READINGS

For general histories of Africa, see the bibliography for Chapter 22 and also the comprehensive survey of historical literature on this area by P. D. Curtin, *African History,* No. 56 (Service Center for Teachers of History, 1964). The most recent survey of the slave trade is the judicious study by E. Reynolds, *Stand the Storm: A History of the Atlantic Slave Trade* (Shocken, 1985), which provides a full annotated bibliography. A more recent study is the special section in the *Journal of African History,* 1989, Vol. 30, No. 1, devoted to the subject "Atlantic Slave Trade: Scale, Structure and Supply." How 10 million Africans left their homelands since 1500 and how they responded to their new environments are analyzed in M. L. Kilson and R. I. Rotberg, eds., *The African Diaspora: Interpretative Essays* (Harvard University, 1976); and also in G. W. Irwin, *Africans Abroad: A Documentary History of the Black Diaspora in Asia, Latin America, and the Caribbean During the Age of Slavery* (Columbia University, 1977). For the abolition movement, see E. Williams, *Capitalism and Slavery* (University of North Carolina, 1944); R. Anstey, *The Atlantic Slave Trade and British Abolition, 1760–1810* (Humanities Press, 1975); and S. Miers, *Britain and the Ending of the Slave Trade* (Longman, 1975).

The accounts of the explorers provide colorful material on the opening up of the continent. A convenient collection is provided by M. Perham and J. Simmons, *African Discovery: An Anthology of Exploration* (Faber & Faber, 1942). A readable survey of the history of African exploration is available in C. Hibbert, *Africa Explored: Europeans in the Dark Continent* (Penguin, 1985).

A survey of the partitioning of Africa is available in A. Boahen, *African Perspectives on Colonialism* (Johns Hopkins University, 1987); and T. Pakenham, *The Scramble for Africa* (Random House, 1991). Finally, for the impact of the West on Africa there are P. D. Curtin, ed., *Africa and the West: Intellectual Responses to European Culture* (University of Wisconsin, 1972); R. W. July, *The Origins of Modern African Thought* (Praeger, 1968); and A. D. Roberts, ed., *The Colonial Movement in Africa* (Cambridge University, 1986).

35

The Americas and the British Dominions

Afterwards the Spaniards resolved to go and hunt the Indians who were in the mountains [of Cuba], where they perpetrated marvellous massacres. Thus they ruined and depopulated all this island which we beheld not long ago; and it excites pity, and great anguish to see it deserted, and reduced to a solitude.

Bartolome De Las Casas, 1552

The disappearance of these people [Australian aborigines] before the white invaders is just as certain as the disappearance of wolves in a country becoming civilized and populous.

James Stephen, 1841

Even more far reaching than Europe's impact on Asia and Africa during the nineteenth century were its effects on the Americas and the British Dominions. In fact, this "impact" was so extensive and dramatic that it is more appropriate to refer to it as outright Europeanization.

Europeanization involves more than just political domination or cultural penetration. It involves actual biological replacement, the physical substitution of one people by another—as happened in the relatively empty ter-ritories of the Western Hemisphere and the South Pacific. The scanty indigenous populations were either wiped out or pushed aside, and tens of millions of European emigrants swarmed in and occupied the lands of the native peoples. With them the Europeans brought their political institutions, their ways of earning a living, and their cultural traditions. Thus the ethnic Europeanization of overseas territories was followed inevitably by political, economic, and cultural Europeanization.

I.   ETHNIC EUROPEANIZATION

In Chapter 28, Section VII, we explained why Europe was able to supply so many emigrants, and why these millions of people were willing to leave their ancestral homes and brave unknown dangers in far-off continents. The thin ribbons of European settlement that existed in 1763 had stretched by 1914 to cover entire continents, including Australia and New Zealand, which had still been untouched at the earlier date.

Tables 35.1 through 35.3 demonstrate that the majority of European emigrants went to the Americas. This is natural, since the earliest European colonies were established in the Americas. Also, those continents offered much greater natural resources and economic opportunities. However, since the first European settlements were in Central and South America, it is surprising that so many more of these emigrants settled in North America.

The fundamentally different character of the Spanish and Portuguese colonies, compared to the English, explains the greater immigrant population in North America. The Spaniards and the Portuguese settled in territories with relatively dense Indian populations. Although estimates of the number of Indians in the Americas before the coming of the Europeans vary tremendously, it is agreed that the Indian populations were concentrated in what came to be Latin America. These native peoples supplied all the labor that was needed, so European settlers were not required for that purpose. Accordingly emigrants to the Spanish and Portuguese colonies in the Americas were mostly soldiers, members of the clergy, government officials, and a few necessary craftspeople.

North of the Rio Grande, by contrast, the Indian population was relatively sparse and provided no reservoir of labor. The English along the Atlantic seaboard and the French on the banks of the St. Lawrence had to do their own work, whether it was cutting the forests, plowing the cleared land, or fishing the coastal waters. Under these circumstances North America wanted all the settlers it could get, and so the British North American colonies were opened to immigrants of all races, languages, and faiths. By 1835 there were 4.8 million European settlers in all of Central and South America as against 13.8 million in North America.

In the second half of the nineteenth century European emigration steadily increased, reaching its height between 1900 and 1910 when almost 1 million people left each year. This unprecedented flood poured into every continent, so that Australia, South Africa, and South America now were peopled by substantial numbers of Europeans, although North America continued to be the main beneficiary.

The migration of millions to the Americas resulted in the displacement of corresponding millions of native Amerindians. The extent of this displacement is being realized only now, when demographers and historians are discovering how wrong was the long-held assumption that the New World was largely empty, available for colonists from other continents. Recent research discloses that the old and new worlds were "roughly similar in density of inhabitants."[1] Nevertheless, the millions of newcomers had no difficulty finding lands for settlement, and the reason was not that they were empty lands. Rather, they were becoming empty because of the disappearance of the Indians. And the Indians were disappearing because they were dying; the estimated 5 million Amerindians who lived in the present-day United States in 1492 had declined to 600,000 by 1809.

TABLE 35.1	Racial Distribution in the Americas (in millions)*				
	White		Negro		Indian
	1835	1935	1835	1935	1935
North America	13.8	124.3	2.6	12.4	1.8
Central America	1.9	6.9	2.7	8.4	21.4
South America	2.9	40.9	4.5	18.7	29.2
Total	18.6	172.1	9.8	39.5	52.4

*See Table 35.3

TABLE 35.2 Racial Distribution in Africa*

	Whites		Africans
	1835	*1935*	*1935*
Mediterranean countries[a]	20,000	1,660,000[b]	30,000,000
Union of South Africa	66,000	1,950,000	6,600,000
Rest of South Africa[c]	3,000	190,000	12,200,000
Rest of continent	1,000	100,000	87,700,000
Islands	45,000	100,000	4,500,000
Total	135,000	4,000,000	141,000,000

*See Table 35.3
[a]Egypt, Libya, Tunis, Algeria, Moroccos, Spanish North Africa, Tangier.
[b]Includes only the settlers of European origin.
[c]Angola, S. W. Africa, Rhodesias, Nyasaland, Bechuanaland, Basutoland, Swaziland, Mozambique.

Some of the deaths were due to violence and overwork, but the chief cause was the combination of Eurasian and African diseases that the immigrants unwittingly introduced to the New World. Scientists have assembled lists of these diseases, which proved as lethal for the vulnerable Amerindians as the fourteenth-century Black Death had been for Eurasians. The lists comprise an intimidating array of afflictions that were largely, though not exclusively, responsible for the most devastating holocaust in human history. The lists include smallpox, measles, diphtheria, trachoma, whooping cough, chicken pox, bubonic plague, malaria, typhoid fever, cholera, yellow fever, dengue fever, scarlet fever, amoebic dysentery, influenza, and certain varieties of tuberculosis.

Because of this gruesome combination of diseases, one historian has concluded, "The Americans were not conquered: they were infected."[2] It may well be asked why the Amerindians, who originally also were immigrants from Eurasia, did not arrive in the Americas already immunized against those diseases. The offered explanation is that in those distant times the early immigrants were still in the food gathering stage, when those diseases had not yet appeared. Moreover, they had come from Siberia, where the scanty population and frigid climate was not conducive to epidemics. So the immigrants arrived without a built-in immunity, which they could not acquire after reaching the empty lands of the New World—hence their genocidal vulner-

TABLE 35.3 Racial Distribution in Oceania*

	Date	Whites	Natives
Australia	June 1935	6,674,000	81,000
New Zealand	Dec. 1935	1,486,000	76,000
Papua (Australia)	June 1933	1,000	275,000
Fiji Islands (Br.)	Dec. 1934	5,000	107,000
New Guinea (Austr.)	June 1935	4,000	679,000
Other islands (15)	1930s	109,756	464,525
Total (of 19 areas)		8,279,756	1,682,525

*R. R. Kuczynski, Population Movements (Clarendon, 1936), pp. 91, 95, 102–3, 118, by permission of The Clarendon Press, Oxford.

ability when the Europeans arrived with their native diseases and those of their African slaves.

As far as the specific sources of immigration were concerned, the Latin American countries were peopled, as might be expected, mostly by emigrants from the Iberian peninsula, although considerable numbers also came in the late nineteenth century from Italy and Germany. The great majority of the emigrants to North America were, until 1890, from northwestern Europe. After that date, approximately one-third came from northwestern Europe, and the remaining two-thirds came from eastern and southern Europe. In the case of the British dominions, immigration restrictions limited the supply largely to the British Isles. After World War I, and especially after World War II, the dominions liberalized their immigration policies in order to attract more people to fill their wide open spaces.

The net result of these migrations has been the ethnic Europeanization of the Americas and the British dominions. These areas have become largely European in population, although there are certain important exceptions such as the native Indian strain remaining predominant in Central America (58 percent of the total population) and highly significant in South America (33 percent). The substantial Negro element introduced into the Americas as a result of the slave trade is another exception to ethnic Europeanization. As observed earlier, it is estimated that between 12 million and 20 million slaves survived the transatlantic passage and reached the New World. Their descendants today comprise about 10 percent of the total population in North America, 30 percent in Central America, and 21 percent in South America. South Africa represents another exception to ethnic Europeanization; there the native Africans outnumber the whites (whether of Boer or British origin) by more than three to one.

II. POLITICAL EUROPEANIZATION

Ethnic Europeanization was accompanied by political Europeanization. The Americas and the British dominions adopted constitutional governments of various forms. They also had European-derived law codes—Anglo-Saxon law in the United States and the British dominions, Roman law in Latin America and Quebec.

Political Europeanization took many forms, reflecting original differences in the European mother countries, as well as different conditions existing in the overseas lands. For example, Latin America and Britain's thirteen colonies won their political independence through armed revolution in the late eighteenth and early nineteenth centuries. By contrast, the

A French settlement in the St. Lawrence Valley.

On May 10, 1869, the last rails of the Union Pacific and Central pacific (now the Southern Pacific) were joined at Promontory, Utah. A memorable scene was enacted as a spike of pure California gold was driven, signaling the completion of the first chain of railroads to span the American continent.

British dominions gained self-government in the late nineteenth century by acts of the British Parliament. Therefore, they have remained with the British Commonwealth of Nations to the present day, recognizing the sovereignty of the British Crown, and at the same time enjoying full self-rule.

Another example of diversity within political Europeanization is the successful unification of the thirteen colonies and their eventual expansion from the Atlantic to the Pacific as the United States of America. Latin America, by contrast, experienced political fragmentation. One reason was that mountain and jungle barriers separated one region from another. Also, the lack of communication facilities left some parts of Latin America in closer contact with Europe than with each other. In addition, Spain had discouraged contacts among its American colonies during the centuries of its rule. And after independence, ambitious political leaders preferred prominence in a small state to obscurity in a large union. For all these reasons, the original eight Spanish colonies in Latin America ended up as eighteen separate countries.

A final example of the variety of political Europeanization is the political stability of the United States and the British dominions as against the never-ending coups in Latin America. Whereas the United States has kept its 1787 Constitution to the present day, the Latin American states have adopted an average of ten different constitutions each. Almost all the "revolutions" responsible for these constitutions have been revolutions in name only. A true revolution is one that produces a fundamental change in a system, a basic reorganization of the social and political order. Most of the so-called "revolutions" in Latin America simply involve the replacement of one military dictator by another without fundamental changes in the existing order. A procession of military and civilian leaders have succeeded each other, with little attention being paid to the wishes of the people or to the needs of the countries involved.

In conclusion, political Europeanization involved the transplanting of European political institutions to overseas lands. But in the process of transplanting there was adaptation and change. A Canadian or Australian political leader would

OKLAHOMA LAND RUSH

A vivid example of how the Indian lands were flooded by Europeans is found in the opening for settlement of the Oklahoma Cherokee Strip in 1893. The following description is from one of the participants, Billy McGinty.*

I had already slipped over into the Strip and picked out the place I aimed to file on. A hundred and sixty acres on the bank of Camp Creek; land sloping down so pretty you could run furrows smooth and straight as ribbons. Dig up the brush and you could set out enough peach trees to keep a whole country in fruit. I'd sow seed and reap money. Then I'd find me a spry girl and raise myself a crop of kids on that stretch. . . .

Day of the Run, I beat the roosters up. . . . By eight o'clock, four hours till starting time, men and horses were packed in so close lightning couldn't have cut them loose.

Men cursed and snarled at each other like dogs, as they tried to cut in their wagons ahead of others. Fist fights broke out along with dog fights.

Eleven fifty. Ten minutes until hell would break, and every minute like a year of your life. Eleven fifty-five, but the soldiers on guard not noticing that my horse's front hoofs were already two inches across the line.

Eleven-fifty-nine. And now the talk was like the buzz of wild bees starting to swarm, as the official starter stepped on the line. He had his watch in one hand and his gun in the other. He looked at the watch and lifted the gun.

He fired one shot in the air. Wheels cracked! Whips popped! Hoofs thundered! The Run was on. . . .

All around me, wheel matched distance with saddle and man with man. Wagon was crashing against wagon. Horse's hides were raw red from being whipped to make them run faster. Drivers were standing up in wagons and buggies, lashing their own teams and those of other men when they crowded too close. . . .

Just before we reached the creek, I jumped off at the stretch I had picked out.

I grabbed rocks and sticks to mark off my hundred and sixty. . . . When I had put down the last marker, I cut a branch from a cottonwood and stuck my bandanna on it. For the law said you had to put up some kind of a banner when you had finished staking a place.

Then I stood up and looked out over that first piece of ground I had ever called my own. My heart was pounding as loud as the hoofs I had left behind.

"You're somebody now, Bill," I said to myself. "You got the finest horse, and you staked the finest claim. You outrode 'em all and, by thunder, you'll outfarm 'em all."

*Billy McGinty, "Plow Fever," in Harold Preece, *Living Pioneers* (Thomas Y. Crowell, 1952), pp. 190–201.

be quite lost today if he found himself at the head of an American political party with its precarious balance of sectional interests, nationality blocs, and big-city machines. He would have been even more bewildered by Latin American politics and their unceasing succession of constitutions and caudillos.

III.   ECONOMIC EUROPEANIZATION

Europeanization prevailed as much in the economic as the in the political field. As far as the European powers were concerned, their economic objectives and methods were basically the same at the outset. All believed in the mercantilist doctrine of subordinating colonial economies to those of the mother countries. Despite this common mercantilist background, the various European settlements soon developed distinctive economies that differed in many respects from each other.

The economic development of Latin America, as noted in Chapter 25, Section VI, has been influenced by several historical factors: (1) the availability of abundant bullion and native labor, both of which were lacking in British and French America; (2) the development of single-crop plantations based on African slave labor; and (3) the economic backwardness of the Iberian states, which was transmitted to their colonies. The end result has been that Latin America never achieved balanced economic growth. Instead there was chronic subservience to northwestern Europe and later to the United States.

The economic history of the thirteen colonies was fundamentally different. Strengthened by the fact that land was more plentiful than labor, the English colonists worked out their own economic institutions and practices. In the warm, rich southern colonies, settlers found their best crops were tobacco, rice, and indigo. In the middle colonies—Pennsylvania, New Jersey, Delaware—grain grew well, and this area quickly became the breadbasket of the colonies. Most of New England also turned to agriculture, but the long winters and rocky soil were a severe handicap. So they also resorted to other occupations, mainly fishing, shipping, and manufacturing.

We see, then, that the economy of the thirteen colonies was much more diversified than that of Latin America, and it was more dynamic because native laborers, held down to a level of bare subsistence, did not form its basis. In place of Indian serfs and African slaves who toiled century after century, using the same tools and techniques, there were in the thirteen colonies clipper ships sailing the seven seas; a string of factories along the river fall line; and individual frontiersmen, who, with rifle and ax, won homesteads in the wilderness and steadily pushed the line of settlement westward.

The same contrasting patterns of economic development continued after independence. After the mid-nineteenth century, there was a worldwide demand for Latin American foodstuffs and industrial raw materials—for Argentina's meat and grain, Chile's nitrate and copper, Mexico's gold and silver, Brazil's coffee and rubber, and Bolivia's tin. And so Latin America entered the world economy as it had never done before. On the other hand, this economic growth was in many respects one-sided and unhealthy. Most Latin American countries experienced booms in one or two commodities, whereas the rest of the economies remained static. The semifeudal hacienda system of land tenure and labor relations remained virtually unchanged, so the mass of people continued to exist as peons at subsistence level. And foreign economies penetrated and controlled most of the profitable enterprises, whether railways, public utilities, or mining properties. The benefits of this economic expansion, instead of being widely spread as they were in the United States, enriched only a small number of foreign and native landlords and merchants. This produced the social unrest that was responsible for the political instability already noted.

In the United States, by contrast, there was rapid and diversified economic growth, especially after the Civil War. The war itself stimulated a vast industrial expansion, and this continued in the following decades with the opening of the West and the building of transcontinental railroads. Great quantities of foodstuffs and various raw materials were hauled by railroads and steamships to the burgeoning urban centers of eastern United States and western Europe. At the same time, the millions of immigrants provided an abundant supply of cheap labor and further expanded the domestic market for American industrialists and farmers. The net result was that the U.S. economy spurted ahead in the second half of the nineteenth century at a rate unequaled in that time: In 1860 the United States was ranked fourth in the industrial nations of the world; by 1894 it was the first. Between 1860 and 1900 the number of U.S. industrial establishments increased three times, the number of industrial wage earners four times, the value of manufactured products seven times, and the amount of capital invested in industry nine times.

The striking contrast between the independent economic development of the United States and the dependent economic growth of Latin America was not merely the result of impersonal economic forces working toward a predetermined outcome. Equally important was the role played by protectionist leaders in the United States as opposed to the free-trade leaders in Latin

America. Champions of free trade preferred to integrate Latin America's economy into the world market rather than to set up tariff barriers behind which home industries could grow. They had their way, so the European countries flooded Latin America with their manufactures, and in return received coffee, cocoa, sugar, rubber, and minerals. But it was foreigners who gained most of the profits from all this exporting and importing because by 1914 they had investments in Latin America totaling $8.5 billion. They owned the mines, plantations, banks, railways, and shipping lines. Thus Latin America had won political independence in the nineteenth century but had remained economically dependent on Europe, and later on the United States.

Precisely the opposite was the outcome in the United States, where protectionists rather than free traders determined national policy. As soon as the American republic was established, Alexander Hamiltion urged that domestic indus-

Slaves working in the sugar cane fields of the West Indies during the mid-nineteenth century.

tries be encouraged to safeguard national security and prosperity. Hamilton's program was adopted, helping the United States from the beginning to develop an independent economy in contrast to that of Latin America. Likewise, after the Civil War, President Grant declared that the British had been protectionists until they became the greatest industrial power, and only then did they switch to free trade. So he urged that the United States also keep its protective tariffs; he forecast that when America has "gotten all that she can get from protection, she too will adopt free trade." The later course of events had proven Grant to have been a prophet. The United States did remain protectionist while rising to world economic leadership. After becoming the dominant economic power following World War II, the United States changed its policies and became a champion of free trade.

Like Latin America, the British dominions also lagged behind the United States in rate of economic growth. The cause in this case, however, was not the backwardness of a semifeudal society but rather inferior natural resources. The dominions do possess abundant resources, but it was not profitable to exploit them until the mid-twentieth century when air transportation made them accessible and when more readily available resources in other countries had been depleted. This happened after World War II, with the result that manufactures and extractive industries in the dominions have been booming in recent decades. But during the nineteenth century their economic development was modest, mainly based as it was on the export of foodstuffs and minerals, usually to the mother country.

In conclusion, Europe provided much of the labor, the capital, the technology, and the markets for the economic development of the overseas lands. Between 1820 and 1830, 36 percent of all American exports went to Britain, and 43 percent of all American imports came from Britain. European capital—mostly British, Dutch, and German—poured into the United States during the nineteenth century, especially in the building of railways. By 1914, foreign investments in the United States totaled $7.2 billion. And in the comparatively underdeveloped Latin American countries, European investments dominated the national economies to a much greater degree than they did the American.

IV. CULTURAL EUROPEANIZATION

Cultural Europeanization inevitably accompanied the ethnic, political, and economic Europeanization, and this was true almost as much of the regions that won independence as of those that remained with the British Commonwealth. In Latin America the predominant cultural pattern is Spanish, with the exception of Portuguese Brazil; this pattern is evident in the Spanish language spoken by the majority of the people and in the Roman Catholicism they profess. One sees it also in architectural forms such as the patio or courtyard, the barred window, and the house front that is flush with the sidewalk. Town planning, based on the central plaza rather than on the main street, is equally revealing. Much of the clothing is Spanish, including the men's broad-rimmed hats of felt or straw and the women's cloth head coverings—mantilla, head shawl, or decorative scarf. In family organization the typical Spanish pattern of male dominance and close supervision of young women has been followed, as has the tendency to regard physical labor as undignified and unsuitable for gentlemen.

Although Latin American culture is basically Spanish or Portuguese, a strong Indian influence prevails, especially in Mexico, Central America, and the northwestern part of South America, where the Indians make up a large percentage of the total population. This influence (see Chapter 27, Section V) is evident in cooking, clothing, building materials, and religious practices. Latin American culture also has a considerable African element, brought over by the millions of slaves imported to work on plantations. This African influence is strongest in the Caribbean area, where most of the slaves settled, although examples of their influence can be found in most parts of Latin America.

The culture that developed in the United States was less influenced by the native Indian population than was Latin American culture. The main reason is that the Indians were fewer in number and less advanced. Nevertheless, Indian influence was not altogether negligible: 25 states bear Indian names; at least 300 Indian words are now part of the English language; and many Indian inventions, such as moccasins, canoes, toboggans, and snowshoes, are in common use.

Early twentieth-century Shoshoni village in Wyoming.

Likewise, the United States has been less influenced by African culture than have certain Caribbean states. Still, the influence here has been considerable; blacks make up nearly 12 percent of the total U.S. population, compared to the one-half of 1 percent that is Indian.

Despite these Indian and African populations, American culture is overwhelmingly European in origin, even though its European characteristics were drastically modified during the process of transplantation and adaptation. As late as 1820, fully 80 percent of all books in the United States were imported from Britain, and by 1830 the figure remained as high as 70 percent. As far as European intellectuals were concerned, American culture was nonexistent. A typical attitude was that of the English critic Sydney Smith, who asked rhetorically in 1820: "In the four corners of the globe, who reads an American book? or goes to an American play? or looks at an American picture or statue?" This condescension was generally accepted by the Americans themselves. "All through life," wrote Henry Adams, "one had seen the American on his literary knees to the Europeans."[3]

Toward the end of the nineteenth century some change in this attitude began to be noticeable. Truly American writers like Walt Whitman and Mark Twain were read avidly throughout the world. Significant also was the publication in 1888 of British historian James Bryce's appreciative masterpiece, *The American Commonwealth*. As the century closed, European intellectuals were becoming increasingly aware of a growing galaxy of American stars: John Dewey, William James, Oliver Wendall Holmes, Thorstein Veblen, and William Dean Howells. Yet Europe's tutelage remained hard to shake. At the end of the century Henry Cabot Lodge still would write, "The first step of an American entering upon a literary career was to pretend to be an Englishman in order that he might win the approval, not of Englishmen, but of his own countrymen."[4]

Europe's cultural influence was stronger in the British dominions than in the United States or Latin America. One reason was the preservation of the imperial bonds, which caused more interaction with the mother country. Also, with the exception of South Africa, a much larger percentage of the peoples of the dominions were of European origin than were those of the United States and Latin America, with their substantial black and Indian elements. This does not mean, however, that the dominions all developed a uniform culture. Distinctive local environments created distinctive cultures.

An assembly of Indian chiefs at the Last Great Council in the Valley of the
Little Big Horn.

Canada's cultural development, for example, has been molded by two overriding factors. One is the French Canadian bloc that makes up one-third of the total population of the country. So determined are the French Canadians to preserve their identity in a predominantly Anglo-Saxon continent that by the 1980s, separatism became a threat to the unity of the Canadian Dominion.

The other major factor influencing Canadian culture is the American colossus to the south. This is evident in every aspect of national life, whether it be investments controlling jobs and national resources, or the magazines, novels, and radio and television programs that mold everyday life. The Canadian government has been concerned to the point of creating royal commissions and taking various measures to preserve national culture. This problem of American cultural intrusion exists also in Australia and New Zealand, though not so acutely as in Canada. Geographic isolation provides some cushion, as does also the greater ethnic homogeneity of those two dominions.

We may conclude, then, that the cultural Europeanization of the Americas and the British dominions has been both pervasive and enduring. A European need only visit New York, Mexico City, Montreal, or Melbourne, and then visit Cairo, Delhi, Tokyo, or Beijing, to sense the reality and the extent of the overseas diffusion of the European culture.

SUGGESTED READINGS

The overall picture of migrations in modern times is given by W. F. Willcox et al., *International Migrations,* 2 vols. (National Bureau of Economic Research, 1929, 1931); A. M. Carr-Saunders, *World Population* (Oxford University, 1936); W. S. and E. S. Woytinsky, *World Population and Production* (Twentieth Century Fund, 1953), Chap. 3; R. R. Kuczynski, *Population Movements* (Clarendon, 1936); F. D. Scott, ed., *World Migration in Modern Times* (Prentice Hall, 1968); and N. Sanchez-Albornoz, *The Population of Latin America* (University of California, 1974).

Studies of the American Revolution include R. Middlekauff, *The Glorious Cause: The American Revolution, 1763–1789* (Oxford University, 1982); and J. P. Greene, ed., *The Reinterpretation of the American Revolution* (Harper & Row, 1968). Corresponding studies of the Latin American revolutions are by J. Lynch, *The Spanish-American Revolutions, 1808–1826* (W. W. Norton, 1973); and the stimulating interpretation by E. B. Burns, *The Poverty of Progress: Latin America in the Nineteenth Century* (University of California, 1980).

General surveys of the process of Europeanization are E. Fischer, *The Passing of the European Age* (Harvard University, 1948); L. Hartz, *The Founding of New Societies* (Harcourt Brace Jovanovich, 1964); and W. B. Hamilton, ed., *The Transfer of Institutions* (Duke University, 1964). Much material has been published on this subject in numerous studies of the applicability of Frederick Jackson Turner's frontier hypothesis. Outstanding are the series of articles in W. D. Wyman and C. B. Kroeber, *The Frontier in Perspective* (University of Wisconsin, 1957); the bibliographical survey in R. A. Billington, *The American Frontier* (Service Center for Teachers of History, 1958); and the application of the frontier hypothesis to modern world history in W. P. Webb, *The Great Frontier* (Houghton Mifflin, 1952).

36

Consolidation of Global Unity

Above all I wish to urge upon you once again the immense vista of difficulty and possibility of danger opened up by the newly awakened ambitions and aspirations of the Eastern races. What may be the final outcome of the collision . . . it is impossible to foretell. This, however, is certain—that contact with Western thought and Western ideas has exercised a revivifying influence upon all the races of the East. Those that have come into sharpest contact with it have exhibited most markedly its effects.

Lord Ronaldshay, 1909

The period between 1763 and 1914 stands out in world history as the period when Europe became master of the entire globe, whether directly or indirectly. Europe's domination was evident not only in the political sphere—in the form of great colonial empires—but also in the economic and cultural spheres. On the other hand, the decade before 1914 also witnessed the first serious challenges to Europe's predominance. The most significant challenge was Japan's defeat of Russia. The contemporary revolutions in Turkey and Persia and the underground rumblings in various colonial or semicolonial regions were also noteworthy. Let us first consider Europe's political, economic, and cultural global predominance, to be followed by a look at the early challenges to this predominance.

I. EUROPE'S POLITICAL DOMINANCE

Between 1500 and 1763 Europe had emerged from its obscurity and gained control of the oceans and the relatively empty spaces of Siberia and the Americas. But as far as Asia and Africa were concerned, Europe's impact was still negligible at the end of the eighteenth century. In Africa there were only a string of slave-trading stations along the coasts and an insignificant settlement of Boers on the southern tip of the continent. Likewise, in India the Europeans were confined to their few coastal trading posts and had not yet begun to have a substantial effect on the vast hinterland. In East Asia the Westerners were rigidly restricted to Canton and Deshima despite their pleas for further contacts. If by some miracle the relations between Europe on the one hand and Africa and Asia on the other had been suddenly severed in the late eighteenth century, there would have been little left to show for the three centuries of interaction. A few ruined forts and churches would have been almost the only reminders of the intruders who had come across the sea. Everyday life would have continued along traditional lines as in the past millennia.

By 1914 this situation had changed fundamentally. Europe's impact had grown immeasurably, both in extent and in depth. Vast portions of the globe—the United States, Latin America, Siberia, and the British dominions—had been Europeanized. Europeans had migrated to those territories in droves, displacing to a greater or lesser degree the native peoples. It is true that by 1914 the United States and Latin America had won political independence, and the British dominions were self-governing. Nevertheless, as we have seen, the dominions had become Europeanized. They were intimately related to Europe as regards ethnic composition, economic ties, and cultural institutions.

Vast territories, including the entire continent of Africa, with the exception of Liberia and Ethiopia, and the greater part of Asia, had become outright colonial possessions of the European powers. Of the 16,819,000 square miles in Asia, no fewer than 9,443,000 square miles were under European rule. These included 6,496,000 square miles under Russia, 1,998,000 under Britain, 587,000 under Holland, 248,000 under France, 114,000 under the United States, and a paltry 193 for Germany. In contrast to these tremendous colonial territories, Japan, the only truly independent Asian nation in 1914, accounted for a mere 161,000 square miles.

The remaining portion of the globe, apart from these colonial possessions and the Europeanized territories, consisted of countries that were nominally independent but were actually semicolonial. These semicolonial countries included the great Chinese and Ottoman empires as well as such smaller states as Iran, Afghanistan, and Nepal. All these countries were dominated by European economic and military power. They were allowed to retain a nominal political independence simply because the European powers

Bronze musketeer reflects the image of the European slave trader in West Africa's Benin culture.

could not agree on the details of their dismemberment.

In this way the entire globe had come under Europe's domination by 1914. It was the extraordinary climax of the long process started a half-millennium earlier when Portuguese captains began to feel their way down the coast of Africa. One peninsula of the Eurasian landmass was now the center of the world, with a concentration of power altogether unprecedented in past history (see map of World of Western Dominance, 1914, p. 556).

II. EUROPE'S ECONOMIC DOMINANCE

The fact that by 1914 Europe's domination was unprecedented not only in extent but also in depth was evident in the economic control that

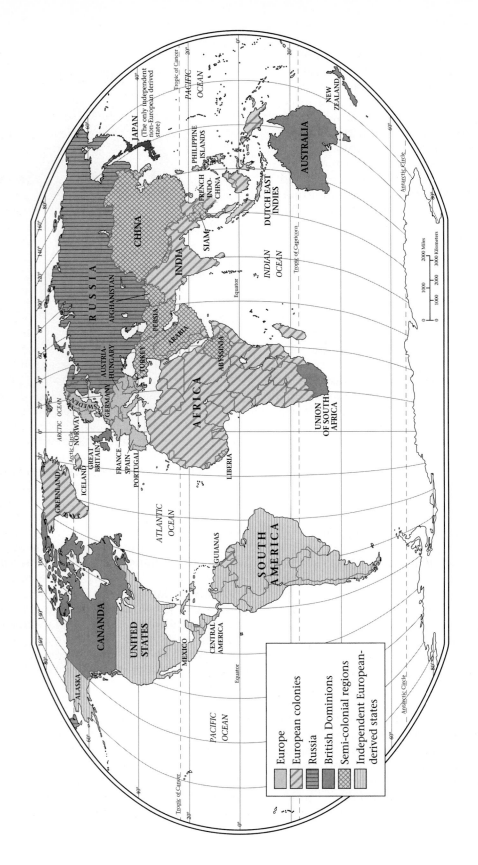

Legend:
- Europe
- European colonies
- Russia
- British Dominions
- Semi-colonial regions
- Independent European-derived states

World of Western Dominance, 1914.

Europe exercised. Europe had become the banker of the world, providing the capital needed for building transcontinental railroads, digging interoceanic canals, opening mines, and establishing plantations. Europe had become not only the banker but also the industrial workshop of the world. By 1870 Europe was responsible for 64.7 percent of the world's total industrial output. The only rival was the United States, with 23.3 percent. Even though the United States had forged ahead by 1913 to 35.8 percent, Europe's factories in that year still turned out 47.7 percent of the world's total production.

The effect of Europe's great outpouring of capital and technology was an unprecedented global economic unity. By 1914 over 516,000 kilometers of cables had been laid on ocean beds, as well as a vast network of telegraph and telephone lines on the land surface of the globe. By 1914 over 30,000 ships with a total tonnage of 50 million carried goods from one part of the world to another. Several canals were built to facilitate world commerce. The most important were the Suez (1869), which shortened the route between western Europe and India by 4,000 miles, and the Panama (1914), which reduced the distance between New York and San Francisco by almost 8,000 miles. Continents were opened for economic exploitation by the construction of several transcontinental railroads. The first in the United States was completed in 1869, the first in Canada in 1885, the trans-Siberian in 1905. The Berlin to Baghdad and the Cape to Cairo railroads were almost completed by 1914.

The economic integration of the continents led to a spectacular increase in overall global productivity. World industrial production multiplied no fewer than six times between 1860 and 1913, and the value of world trade increased twelve times between 1851 and 1913. Europe, as might be expected, benefited the most from this economic leap forward. Statistics are not available for conditions all over the globe, but it is estimated that the difference in per capita income between colonial or semicolonial regions and the European metropolitan countries was roughly three to one in 1800. By 1914 it had increased to about seven to one.

III. EUROPE'S CULTURAL DOMINANCE

The everyday life of the peasant masses in colonial territories had been drastically affected by the shift from a traditional natural economy to a money economy. Money had been used in the earlier period but only in a peripheral manner, and production had been carried on by the peasant households primarily to satisfy family needs. A few commodities might have been sold in the local market, but not for the purpose of making a profit. Rather, the aim was to get a little money to meet tax obligations and to buy a few essentials such as salt and a little iron. Frequently the transactions and obligations were met by simple barter, and no money changed hands. But a new market economy was introduced when the Europeans appeared with their railroads, their machine-made goods, and their insatiable demands for foodstuffs and industrial raw materials. Before long the peasants found themselves producing for an international market rather than for themselves and their neighbors, which in turn meant that they became subject to global economic fluctuations. And they were at the mercies of merchants and moneylenders, who now flourished in the new economy. The transition from a closed and static natural economy to a dynamic money and market economy was beneficial as far as productive capacity was concerned, but certainly its initial effects were disruptive and uncomfortable.

The way of thinking as well as the way of life was affected by Europe's intrusion. However, this intellectual change primarily involved the smaller upper class in the colonial world rather than the peasant masses. It was the few members of the thin upper crust who knew some Western language, who read Western newspapers and books, and who were familiar with European history and current politics. The initial response to this exposure to the alien culture was often an enthusiastic, uncritical admiration of everything Western. But it was usually followed by a reaction against the West and an attempt to preserve and foster at least some elements of the traditional culture. The ambivalent response to Western culture is clearly expressed in the following reminiscence written in 1925 by a prominent Indian:

Our fore fathers, the firstfruits of English education, were violently pro-British. They could see no flaw in the civilization or the culture of the West. They were charmed by its novelty and its strangeness. The enfranchisement of the individual, the substitution of the right of private judgement in the place of traditional authority, the exaltation of duty over custom, all came with a force and suddenness of a revelation to an Oriental people who knew no more binding obligation than the mandate of immemorial usage and of venerable tradition. . . . Everything English was good—even the drinking of brandy was a virtue; everything not English was to be viewed with suspicion. . . . In due time came the reaction, and with a sudden rush. And from the adoration of all things Western, we are now in a whirlpool that would recall us back to our ancient civilization and our time-honored ways and customs untempered by the impact of the ages that have rolled by and the forces of modern life.[1]

IV.   WHITE MAN'S BURDEN

The political, economic, and cultural dominance of Europe at the turn of the century naturally led Europeans to assume that their primacy arose from the superiority of their civilization and that this in turn reflected their superiority as a race. It was confidently believed that God had created people unequal. He had made the whites more intelligent so that they could direct the labor and guide the development of the inferior races, who had broad backs and weak minds. Hence arose the concept of the *white man's burden*—a preaching that cloaked the imperialism of the times with a mantle of idealistic devotion to duty. In the well-known lines of Rudyard Kipling, written appropriately at the end of the century (1899):

Take up the White Man's Burden—
Send forth the best ye breed—
Go bind your sons to exile
To serve your captives' need. . . .[2]

Whereas a British poet was writing in 1899 with complete self-assurance about the "white man's burden," a distinguished British historian wrote in 1992 a book entitled *Black Man's Burden.*[3] He was referring to certain institutions and practices that the Europeans had imposed on their colonial subjects, but that have since proven to be

unsuitable and unworkable—a "burden" for the "black man" rather than the "white."

In contrast to today's soul searching, Europeans in the time of Kipling were regarded almost as divinely ordained rulers. In India they were addressed respectfully as *sahib,* in the Middle East as *effendi,* in Africa as *bwana,* and in Latin America as *patron.* Under these circumstances it is scarcely surprising that Europeans came to view the world with a myopia and a self-centeredness that today seems incredible. Americans also shared this attitude. President Theodore Roosevelt in a message to Congress in 1904 warned Latin America that ". . . chronic wrongdoing, or an impotency which results in a general loosening of the ties of civilized society, may in America, as elsewhere, ultimately require intervention by some civilized nation."[4] Likewise, an American missionary, Henry W. Luce, father of the well-known publisher, reported from China in 1904 that conditions were favorable for their activities and that "We may work together for God, for China, and for Yale."[5] Most spectacular was the supreme self-confidence and aggressiveness of Cecil Rhodes, who was ahead of his time in dreaming of other planets to conquer:

The world is nearly parcelled out, and what there is left of it is being divided up, conquered, and colonized. To think of these stars that you see overhead at night, these vast worlds which we can never reach. I would annex the planets if I could; I often think of that. It makes me sad to see them so clear and yet so far.[6]

Cecil Rhodes may sound overconfident, but it was a confidence based solidly on the West's technological superiority. Since Western technology has continued to grow at an ever-accelerating pace, Rhodes's present-day successors in the business world are even more self-assured. Former Citicorp Chairman George Moore stated in 1987 that in twenty-five years the world would be dominated by a handful of large financial institutions that would have their headquarters on space platforms to avoid government regulations. Whereas Rhodes was saddened that the planets were inaccessible to him, his counterparts now assume those planets not only will become accessible, but will serve as their private launching pads.

PUNCH, OR THE LONDON CHARIVARI.—April 21, 1894.

THE BLACK BABY.

Mr. Bull. "WHAT, ANOTHER!—WELL, I SUPPOSE I MUST TAKE IT IN!!!"

A cartoon from *Punch,* April 21, 1894.

V.   FIRST CHALLENGES TO EUROPE'S DOMINANCE

In 1914 Europe's global domination seemed to be unassailable and eternal. But in the clearer light of retrospect one can easily perceive the lurking threat of a colonial world slowly awakening and striking the first blows against Western domination.

Throughout history, whenever a weaker society has been threatened by one more vigorous and aggressive, there have been two contradictory types of reactions: The first is to sever all contact with the intruding forces, withdraw into isolation, and seek refuge in traditional beliefs and practices. The second reaction is to try instead to adopt as many features of the alien society as are necessary to meet it on equal terms and thus to resist it effectively. The first reaction represents retreat and escapism; the other, adjustment and adaptation. The slogan of the first is "Back to the good old days"; that of the second, "Learn from the West in order to fight the West."

There were many examples during the nineteenth century of both types of reaction to the Western intrusion. Classic examples of the escapist variety were the Indian mutiny in 1857–1858 and the Boxer Rebellion in 1900 (see Chapter 32, Section III, and Chapter 33, Section IV, for details). Both the mutiny and the rebellion were bitter, bloody affairs, yet neither of them seriously challenged Europe's supremacy because they were essentially negative revolts, seeking to oust the hated Europeans by force in order to restore the good old days. But the power of Western arms and the dynamism of Western economic enterprise were irresistible. It was an entirely different matter, however, when native peoples began to adopt Western ideas and technology to use them against the West.

The Japanese were the first Asian people to succeed in carrying out the policy of resistance by adaptation. They defeated the weak Chinese Empire in 1894–1895 and then the mighty Russian Empire in 1904–1905 (see Chapter 33, Sections VI and VII, for details). The triumph of a small Asian kingdom over a giant European power marks a turning point in recent world history. It was an event that sent a tremor of hope and excitement throughout the colonial world. Just as influential as the outcome of the Russo-Japanese War was the great Russian Revolution, stimulated in part by the war (see Chapter 30, Section IV). The news that the tsarist autocracy was on the verge of downfall was as exciting to oppressed peoples everywhere as the reports from the battlefields of Manchuria. A Britisher who was in Persia at this time sensed an undercurrent of aroused emotions and expecta-tions in all the colonial lands. In a letter of August 1906 he reported:

It seems to me that a change must be coming over the East. The victory of Japan has, it would appear, had a remarkable influence all over the East. Even here in Persia it has not been without effect. . . . Moreover, the Russian Revolution has had a most astounding effect here. Events in Russia have been watched with great attention, and a new spirit would seem to have come over the people. They are tired of their rulers, and, taking example of Russia, have come to think that it is possible to have another and better form of government . . . it almost seems that the East is stirring in its sleep. In China there is a marked movement against the foreigners, and a tendency towards the ideal of "China for the Chinese." In Persia, owing to its proximity to Russia, the awakening would appear to take the form of a movement towards democratic reform. In Egypt and North Africa it is signalized by a remarkable increase in fanaticism, coupled with the spread of the Pan-Islamic movement. The simultaneousness of these symptoms of unrest is too remarkable to be attributed solely to coincidence. Who knows? Perhaps the East is really awakening from its secular slumber, and we are about to witness the rising of these patient millions against the exploitation of an unscrupulous West.[7]

Reception of Siamese ambassadors by Queen Victoria, 1857.

ASIANS CHEER JAPANESE VICTORY OVER RUSSIANS

*The spectacle of a small Asian kingdom defeating a great European power excited colonial peoples everywhere. The Chinese republican leader Dr. Sun Yat-sen described the excitement of those days in the following speech he delivered in 1924 in Tokyo.**

Thirty years ago . . . men thought and believed that European civilization was a progressive one—in science, industry, manufacture, and armament—and that Asia had nothing to compare with it. Consequently, they assumed that Asia could never resist Europe, that European oppression could never be shaken off. Such was the idea prevailing thirty years ago. It was a pessimistic idea. Even after Japan abolished the Unequal Treaties and attained the status of an independent country, Asia, with the exception of a few countries situated near Japan, was little influenced. Ten years later, however, the Russo-Japanese war broke out and Russia was defeated by Japan. For the first time in the history of the last several hundred years, an Asiatic country has defeated a European Power. The effect of this victory immediately spread over the whole Asia, and gave a new hope to all Asiatic peoples. In the year of the outbreak of the Russo-Japanese war I was in Europe. One day news came that Admiral Togo had defeated the Russian navy, annihilating in the Japan Sea the fleet newly despatched from Europe to Vladivostok. The population of the whole continent was taken aback. Britain was Japan's Ally, yet most of the British people were painfully surprised, for in their eyes Japan's victory over Russia was certainly not a blessing for the White peoples. "Blood," after all, "is thicker than water." Later on I sailed for Asia. When the steamer passed the Suez Canal a number of natives came to see me. All of them wore smiling faces, and asked me whether I was a Japanese. I replied that I was a Chinese, and inquired what was in their minds, and why they were so happy. They said they had just heard the news that Japan had completely destroyed the Russian fleet recently despatched from Europe, and were wondering how true the story was. Some of them, living on both banks of the Canal had witnessed Russian hospital ships, with wounded on board, passing through the Canal from time to time. That was surely a proof of the Russian defeat, they added.

In former days, the coloured races in Asia, suffering from the oppression of the Western peoples, thought that emancipation was impossible. We regarded the Russian defeat by Japan as the defeat of the West by the East. We regarded the Japanese victory as our own victory. It was indeed a happy event. Did not therefore this news of Russia's defeat by Japan affect the peoples of the whole of Asia? Was not its effect tremendous?

*Sun Yat-sen, *China and Japan* (China United Press, 1941), pp. 142–143.

This analysis proved prophetic. It was borne out by the 1905 Persian Revolution, the 1908 Young Turk Revolution, the 1911 Chinese Revolution, and the heightened unrest and terrorism in India. We may conclude that although Europe's global hegemony in 1914 seemed irresistible and everlasting, it was actually being challenged at many points and in many ways. In some cases the challenge was direct, as in India and in central Asia, where a few pioneer nationalists were beginning to demand independence from Britain and Russia. In other cases the challenge was made indirectly against the weak Ottoman and Manchu dynasties because they had failed to resist Western aggression. In the pre-1914 period the European powers were able to suppress the opposition, either by direct force or, as in China, by supporting the Manchu dynasty against the Taiping rebels, or by supporting the conservative Yuan Shih-kai against the radical Sun Yat-sen. Yet this early opposition did represent a beginning—the birth of the nationalist movements that after World War I, and especially after World War II, were to sweep everything before them.

SUGGESTED READINGS

The most important studies of the pre-1914 challenges to Europe's global hegemony are by E. R. Wolf, *Peasant Wars of the Twentieth Century* (Harper & Row, 1969); J. Romein, *The Watershed of Two Eras: Europe in 1900* (Wesleyan University, 1978); L. S. Stavrianos, *Global Rift: The Third World Comes of Age* (William Morrow, 1981); and R. Storry, *Japan and the Decline of the West in Asia* (St. Martin's Press, 1979).

MARX TURNED UPSIDE DOWN

Karl Marx assumed that revolution would occur in the industrialized countries before it did in the colonies. He noted that Western capitalists were investing their surplus money in the colonies where higher profits could be made. Like all the socialists of his time, Marx assumed that these investments would continue and that the colonies would become industrialized capitalist countries like their mother countries in western Europe. Marx wrote in his famous work *Das Kapital* (1867), "The industrialized developed country only shows the less-developed country the picture of its own future."

Marx also expected that as the colonies became industrialized and prosperous, the old manufacturing centers of the West would fall behind and suffer unemployment. This in turn would eventually force the suffering Western workers to rise in revolt and establish socialistic societies. Marx therefore concluded that revolution would come first in the West. In fact, in a letter to his friend Friedrich Engels (October 8, 1858), he expressed the fear that when Europe became socialist, the prosperous colonies would remain capitalist and would attack and "crush" the newly born Western socialistic societies. Today, more than a century later, we see that what has happened is the exact opposite of what Marx had feared. Revolution has come, not in the West, but in the former colonies, now known as the Third World. Thus history has turned Marx upside down. Why has it done so?

One reason is that Western workers won the right to vote and the right to organize in unions. They used these rights to increase their wages and to organize the welfare state, which provided help in case of accident, illness, or unemployment. Western workers therefore were relatively satisfied and became reformers rather than revolutionaries. A second reason is that he colonies, or the Third World, did not become industrialized. Western manufacturers did not want competition from overseas, so they actively opposed the establishment of industries in the colonies. As a result, the colonies remained producers of raw materials for Western factories and importers of manufactured goods made in Western factories. The trouble with this arrangement is that after 1880 world prices for raw materials fell steadily while the prices of manufactured goods rose steadily. Between 1880 and 1938, the amount of manufactured goods that Third World countries received for a set quantity of raw materials fell by over 40 percent.

This unfavorable trend in the "terms of trade," as the economists call it, is partly responsible for the serious economic problems of the Third World today. Other factors also have contributed to these problems (see Chapter 29, Section VIII). The end result has been the widening gap between rich countries and poor—between the developed First World and the underdeveloped Third World. The ratio of per capita income between these two worlds has increased as follows: from 3:1 in 1800, to 7:1 in 1914, to 12:1 in 1975.

These figures explain why history has turned out the exact opposite of what Marx had expected. Before Marx, all the great revolutions had occurred in the West—the English, American, and French revolutions. But in the twentieth century, all the great revolutions have been in the Third World: 1917—Russia; 1949—China; 1975—Indochina; 1976—Portuguese Africa; 1979—Iran and Nicaragua; 1980—Zimbabwe. In the 1990s still another surprise occurred, turning Marx upside down once more. The new revolutionary regimes established in the Third World since 1917 have been collapsing one after another because of the failure of their planned economies. So the Socialist regimes in the USSR, eastern Europe, and elsewhere have disintegrated, with ongoing frantic searching for alternative social systems, as we shall note in the concluding chapter.

SUGGESTED READINGS

Many studies of current global trends consider the unexpected interaction between the first and third worlds. Noteworthy are J. Hough, *The Struggle for the Third World* (Brookings Institution, 1985); L. S. Stavrianos, *Global Rift: The Third World Comes of Age* (William Morrow, 1981); P. Worsley, *The Three Worlds: Culture and World Development* (University of Chicago, 1984); and G. Chaliand, *Revolution in the Third World: Myths and Prospects* (Viking, 1977).

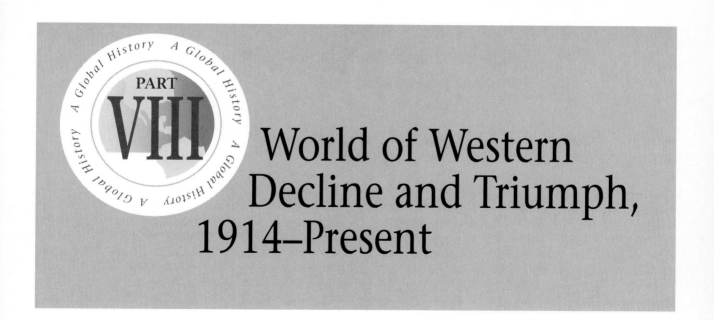

PART VIII

World of Western Decline and Triumph, 1914–Present

The decades since 1914 have witnessed at one and the same time both the decline and the triumph of the West. Indeed these two seemingly contradictory trends reinforced each other. The unprecedented integration of the globe led to the proliferation of Western technology, ideas, and institutions at an accelerating pace. But it was precisely this proliferation that undermined the global hegemony of the West that had appeared so invulnerable prior to 1914. Colonial peoples were selectively adopting Western civilization to better resist the West. For this reason, world history since 1914 is the history of the West's decline as well as of its triumph.

The combination of these two trends explains the turmoil of the world in which we live today. A glance at newspaper headlines or television screens shows that Beijing and Cairo and New Delhi are now as prominent in international affairs as Paris and London and Washington. And everywhere, the hitherto silent masses are taking over the historical stage and shouting demands that would have been inconceivable a few decades ago.

37

World War I: Global Repercussions

The Great War of 1914–1918 was from the Asian point of view a civil war within the European community of nations.

K. M. Panikkar
Indian diplomat and historian

In the autumn of 1914, as one European country after another was being dragged into the holocaust of World War I, the British foreign secretary, Earl Grey, remarked, "The lamps are going out all over Europe." His comment was indeed fully justified, and to a much greater degree than he could have foreseen. World War I was destined to bring down in ruins the Europe that Earl Grey was familiar with. It wiped out the centuries-old Hapsburg, Hohenzollern, Romanoff, and Ottoman dynasties. In their places there appeared new leaders, new institutions, and new ideologies that aristocrats such as Earl Grey only dimly understood. The Europe of 1918 was as different from that of 1914 as the Europe of 1815 had been different from that of 1789.

World War I also marked the end of the Europe that had dominated the globe so completely and abnormally during the nineteenth century. By the end of the war Europe's control had manifestly weakened and was everywhere being challenged. In one way or another the challenges were successfully resisted in most parts of the world. But the respite lasted only two decades, for the Second World War completed the undermining process begun by the first and left the European empires everywhere in shambles.

From the viewpoint of world history as well as European history, World War I stands out as a historic turning point. The purpose of this chapter is to analyze the roots, the course, and the global repercussions of this fateful event.

I.   ROOTS OF WAR

The Versailles Treaty terminating World War I included an article specifically stating that the war was provoked "by the aggression of Germany and her allies." This "war guilt" clause was of more than academic interest, for it was used by the Allies to justify their claim for reparation payments from the defeated Central Powers. Consequently, it stimulated a passionate and prolonged controversy that led to the publication of great collections of documents, totaling over 60,000, as well as thousands of articles and books, all of which championed one side or another in the continuing debate over who was responsible for the war. By the mid-1930s the polemics had quieted down, and relatively scholarly studies appeared that paid less attention to "war guilt" and more to historical conditions and forces that produced the war. Most historians now distinguish between background causes that had been operative for some decades and the immediate causes that came into play during the hectic weeks following the assassination of the Archduke Francis Ferdinand on June 28, 1914. The five most important background factors were economic rivalries, colonial disputes, conflicting alliance systems, irreconcilable nationalist aspirations, and irreversible military timetables.

Economic Rivalries

Considering first the economic rivalries, most of the major European powers became involved in tariff wars and in competition for foreign markets. For example, Italy and France waged a tariff war between 1888 and 1899, Russia and Germany between 1879 and 1894, and Austria and Serbia between 1906 and 1910. The most serious economic rivalry developed between Britain and Germany because of the latter's extraordinarily rapid rate of industrialization in the late nineteenth century. In 1870 Britain produced 31.8 percent of the world's total industrial output, compared to Germany's 13.2 percent. By 1914 Britain's share had dropped to 14 percent, whereas Germany's had risen slightly to 14.3 percent, or a shade greater than that of Britain. This German spurt meant stiff competition for Britain in overseas markets. It is impossible here to de-

Germany's upgraded naval strength at the start of World War I is typified by the battleship *Tann,* here shown in dock.

fine precisely all the political repercussions of this economic rivalry, but it did strain the relations between the two countries. It further contributed to international tension by stimulating competition in naval armaments. In both countries it was argued vociferously that building up naval strength was essential to safeguard trade routes and merchant shipping. Germany's new building program launched under Admiral von Tirpitz in 1897 embittered relations between Britain and Germany without basically changing the balance of power. The kaiser's determination to have a big navy, as well as the most powerful army, contributed significantly to the final outbreak of war.

In addition to the naval race, Europe had in the second decade of the twentieth century an economic slump that undermined the prevailing optimism and strengthened the political militants in each country. In Germany, the Social Democrats emerged as the strongest party after the 1912 Reichstag elections. In Britain, the Liberal government faced a military mutiny when it tried to grant home rule to Ireland. In Italy, the Socialists were turning sharply to the left and rioting in the streets.

☀ Colonial Disputes

Economic rivalries and domestic difficulties fomented colonial disputes, for additional colonies were eagerly sought after to ensure protected overseas markets for surplus capital and manufactures. Since the Germans did not enter the colonial race until after their national unification in 1871, they were particularly aggressive in their demands for an empire equal to their growing economic strength. The Pan-German League pointed to the substantial colonial possessions of small countries like Portugal, Holland, and Belgium, and insisted that Germany also must have its "place in the sun." But in almost every part of the globe the Germans found themselves blocked by the far-flung possessions of the British, whom they bitterly accused of "dog in the manger" selfishness.

The competition for colonies, however, was by no means restricted to Britain and Germany. Almost all the major powers were involved in the scramble for empire in the late nineteenth century, so they repeatedly clashed in one region or another: Britain and Germany clashed in East Africa and Southwest Africa; Britain and France, in Siam and the Nile valley; Britain and Russia, in Persia and Afghanistan; and Germany and France, in Morocco and West Africa. These colonial disputes created an atmosphere of rising tension during the three decades preceding World War I.

☀ Conflicting Alliance Systems

The colonial rivalries in turn contributed to the forging of conflicting alliance systems that were in large part responsible for the coming of war. These systems began in 1879 when the German chancellor, Otto von Bismarck, concluded the Dual Alliance with Austria-Hungary. This was a defensive pact designed to protect Germany against the French, who aspired to recover the Alsace-Lorraine provinces lost in 1871. It was also meant to protect Austria-Hungary against the Russians, with whom they continually clashed in the Balkans. In 1882 the Dual Alliance became the Triple Alliance with the addition of Italy. Again the objective was defensive: to protect Italy against France because of sharp conflict over Tunis. The Triple Alliance, then, was definitely not aggressive in intention or in its provisions. Germany and Austria-Hungary were both satisfied powers interested primarily in preserving the existing state of affairs on the Continent.

But from the other side of the fence the Triple Alliance seemed quite different. For France and Russia it was an overwhelming bloc that dominated Europe and left them isolated and vulnerable. Furthermore, France and Russia both had serious difficulties with Britain over colonial issues in several regions. The result was the Franco-Russian Alliance, concluded in 1894, with the double purpose of countering the Triple Alliance and resisting Britain in colonial disputes. The Franco-Russian Alliance became the Triple Entente with the signing of the Anglo-French Entente in 1904 and the Anglo-Russian Entente in 1907. Both of these arrangements were essentially colonial in nature. Britain and France, for example, agreed to recognize their respective interests in the Nile valley and Morocco, and Britain and Russia likewise agreed to divide Persia into spheres of influence. (See map of Europe, 1914, p. 571.)

Thus all the major powers now were aligned in rival alliance systems, with disastrous results for international relations. Whenever any dispute of consequence arose, the members of both blocs felt compelled to support their respective allies who were directly involved, even if they were doubtful about the issues. Otherwise they feared that their alliances would disintegrate, leaving them alone and exposed. Each dispute consequently was magnified into a major crisis involving, willy-nilly, all the members of both alliances.

Irreconcilable Nationalist Aspirations

Another background factor was the rising nationalist aspirations of Europe's subject minorities. This pressure was volatile enough in Alsace-Lorraine, where the ethnic French remained unreconciled to German rule. But it was a nightmare in central and eastern Europe, where the multinational empires were in danger of being literally torn to pieces by the growing demand for self-determination. In the Hapsburg Empire, for example, the ruling Austrians and Hungarians were confronted by the awakening Italians and Rumanians, as well as by the many Slavic peoples: Czechs, Slovaks, Ruthenians, Poles, Slovenes, Croats, and Serbs. Very understandably, the Hapsburg officials decided that firm measures were necessary if the empire was to survive. This was especially true regarding the militant Serbs, who were clamoring for unification with the independent Serbia across the Danube—hence the stiff terms sent to Belgrade when the archduke was murdered by a Serb patriot at Sarajevo. But behind Serbia was Russia, and behind Russia were France and Britain. Austria-Hungary, likewise, was backed by Germany and, theoretically, by Italy. Thus the combination of national self-determination and conflicting alliance systems drove the European powers to the holocaust.

Irreversible Military Timetables

The final background factor, irreversible military timetables, made it extremely difficult to reverse the drift to war following the Sarajevo assassinations. The late nineteenth century was a time when European military technology was making a great leap forward by integrating science and the military. Old weapons were being improved and new ones introduced, including submarines and airplanes. Private armament companies such as Armstrong in Britain, Krupp in Germany, and Schneider-Creusot in France, fomented a worldwide arms race by selling arms to one country, which aroused fears and stimulated sales to neighboring countries. The military leaders of the major powers played safe by ordering huge quantities of the latest weapons. Then they coordinated their bulging arsenals with their railway networks to prepare detailed mobilizations plans by which huge quantities of military supplies and millions of conscripted soldiers were to be moved to war fronts against any conceivable combination of enemies.

Once a button was pressed for activating Mobilization Plan A or B or C or whatever, men and supplies were programmed to move like clockwork and on a massive scale. No countermanding order could be tolerated because the flow of men and materials would be jammed, leaving the country defenseless in the resulting bedlam. Consequently, no major mobilization order could be reversed by any authority, whether emperor or prime minister. This "exigency of the military timetable," as historians have dubbed it, proved to be a major obstacle for those seeking a peaceful settlement following the Sarajevo assassinations on June 28, 1914. It is sobering to note that the diplomats of that era had a grace period of several weeks before guns actually began firing on August 4. Today the grace period has virtually vanished, with modern weapons-delivery technology able to span continents in minutes, and with thousands of autonomous combat systems, each with its own decision-making computers, leaving almost no time for human participation in the unleashing of nuclear Armageddon.

II. SARAJEVO

On June 28, 1914, Archduke Francis Ferdinand and his wife were assassinated in Sarajevo, the capital of the recently annexed province of Bosnia. The murder was committed by a young Bosnian Serb student named Gavrilo Princip. He was not alone in carrying out the murder. He was

Europe, 1914

backed by the secret Serbian organization *Ujedinjenje ili Smrt,* or "Union or Death," popularly known as the Black Hand. Founded in Belgrade in 1911, the Black Hand had as its avowed aim the realization of "the national ideal: the union of all Serbs." The Serbian government was not behind this society, which indeed was regarded as dangerously radical and militant. But this did not prevent the Black Hand from building an underground revolutionary organization that conducted an effective campaign of agitation and terrorism.

The unfortunate Francis Ferdinand played into the hands of these Serb revolutionaries by agreeing to pay an official visit to the Bosnian capital. When the archduke and his duchess began their procession on the radiant Sunday morning of June 28, no fewer than six assassins, armed with bombs and revolvers, were waiting along the designated route. As fate would have it, the procession stopped at the very corner where Princip was stationed. He drew his revolver and fired two shots, one at Francis Ferdinand and the other at General Potiorek, the governor of Bosnia. The second shot went wild and hit the duchess instead. Before medical aid arrived both the archduke and his wife were dead.

On July 23, Austria presented Serbia with a stiff ultimatum that included several demands. The Serbian reply on July 25 accepted nearly all of the terms but refused the demand that Hapsburg officials participate within Serbian territory in the investigation of the crime. Austria promptly broke off diplomatic relations and, on July 28, declared war on Serbia.

Russia now retaliated and ordered full mobilization on July 30. The next day Germany sent a twelve-hour ultimatum to Russia demanding that the mobilization be stopped. When no reply was received, Germany declared war against Russia on August 1 and against Russia's ally, France, on August 3. On the same day Germany began actual hostilities by invading Belgium. After Germany's involvement the British intervened, but not openly on the justification of their secret military commitment to France. Instead, they justified their entry as a reaction to the German invasion of Belgium, which was more palatable for the British public. Thus the great powers of Europe were at each other's throats five weeks after the murders at Sarajevo.

III.   EUROPEAN PHASE OF THE WAR, 1914–1917

1914: War of Attrition in the West

World War I began with peoples on both sides confidently expecting a brief and victorious war. Instead, they soon found themselves embroiled in a prolonged and brutalizing ordeal that took unprecedented toll of material wealth and human lives. The reason for the bloody deadlock was that from the beginning of the war defensive weapons proved superior over offensive. The traditional mode of attack was the massed infantry charge supported by a preliminary artillery barrage. But this was of no avail against the combination of deep trenches, barbed-wire entanglements, ingenious land mines, and machine-gun nests. Thus the casualties on the western front during the first four months were 700,000 Germans, 850,000 French, and 90,000 British. Contrary to the plans of all general staffs, the struggle in the west now became a war of position and attrition.

This was not the case on the Russian and Balkan fronts, where vast distances and scanty transportation facilities necessitated a fluid war of movement. The Russians led off with a surprisingly fast and powerful offensive into east Prussia, designed to relieve the pressure on the French in the west. The strategy worked, for the Germans transferred four divisions from Belgium to the east. Before they reached their destination, the issue had been decided by smashing victories over two Russian armies advancing into east Prussia. The German commanders, Hindenburg and Ludendorff, used their superior railway network to concentrate their forces against first one Russian army and then the other. By the middle of September, east Prussia was cleared of its invaders.

On the Balkan front the Austrians meanwhile were suffering humiliating setbacks. General Potiorek, who had barely escaped Princip's bullet in Sarajevo, was impatient to destroy "the viper's nest." On August 12 he crossed the Drina River into Serbia with 250,000 men. But he was met by a Serbian army of 350,000, of whom 90 percent were seasoned veterans of the Balkan Wars of 1912–1913. In less than two weeks the Serbs had forced the Austrians back across the river with a loss of one-third of their numbers. Potiorek returned to the attack in September and succeeded in taking Belgrade on December 2. But again the Serbians counterattacked, and by the end of the same month the Serb commander triumphantly announced, "On the territory of Serbia there remains not one free enemy soldier."[1]

1915: Russian Retreat in the East

The 1915 campaigns were dominated by the new German commander-in-chief, Erich von Falkenhayn. In view of the stalemate on the western front he concentrated his forces on the east in an effort to knock out the Russians. Combined German and Austrian armies attacked with stunning effect on May 1, advancing by the end of the summer an average of 200 miles. In addition to military casualties totalling 2,500,000 men, Russia lost 15 percent of its territories, 10 percent of its railways, 30 percent of its industries, and 20 percent of its civilian population. The tsarist regime suffered a blow from which it never was able to recover.

On the western front the war of attrition continued. The French General Joffre clung to his belief that intensive artillery bombardment plus massed frontal attack would bring victory. But repeated offensives left the lines unchanged and resulted only in appalling loss of life.

Turkey's entry into World War I on November 2, 1914, precipitated the famous Dardanelles campaign. When Turkey joined the Central Powers, the straits were automatically closed to the Allies, thus making it difficult to ship much-needed supplies to Russia. Accordingly, on March 18, 1915, a squadron of fourteen British and four French battleships steamed into the straits with guns blazing. Heavy losses from mines and coastal artillery forced the Allied ships to withdraw. An attempt then was made to take the straits by landings on the Gallipoli beaches, but only shallow footholds were secured in the face of withering machine-gun fire. The Turks held the heights above the beaches until the Allies finally faced facts and withdrew permanently in January 1916.

The failure at the straits together with the disaster on the Russian front persuaded Bulgaria to join the Central Powers on October 14, 1915. This intervention spelled the end for the Serbs. An overwhelming number of German, Austrian, and Bulgarian divisions attacked Serbia on October 6 from three sides. By the end of the year the entire country was occupied.

To counterbalance these setbacks in the Balkans, the Allies were strengthened by the decision of Italy to join their cause. Although the Italians technically had been allies of the Central Powers, they decided at the outset of the war to remain neutral. The bulk of the Italian people favored this course, especially since it was Austria that held the "unredeemed" lands across the Adriatic. The Allies now freely offered these lands to Italy, together with additional territories at the expense of Turkey. The bait was effective, and on April 29 Italy signed the Treaty of London, agreeing to enter the war in one month in return for these territorial promises. Actually, Italy's intervention scarcely affected the course of the war, apart from compelling the Austrians to divert a few divisions from the eastern front.

1916: Verdun and the Somme

By 1916 the Central Powers had reached the height of their military fortunes. They controlled the continent of Europe from Hamburg to the Persian Gulf, yet they were not able to force a peace settlement on the Allies. To secure such a settlement, the Germans in February 1916 launched an all-out attack on the key French fortress of Verdun. The British counterattacked with an offensive to the northwest at the Somme. But the defense again proved superior to the offense. The two 1916 drives cost about 850,000

The Americans in action on the Hindenburg Line during World War I.

German casualties and about 950,000 British and French. Yet neither side was able to advance more than seven miles.

Meanwhile the Russians, under General Brusilov, made a successful offensive on the eastern front. The failure of the Germans at Verdun and the unexpected success of the Brusilov offensive encouraged Rumania to intervene in the war on the side of the Allies on August 27, 1916. The Central Powers now decided to make an object lesson of Rumania as a warning to other neutrals who might be thinking of following its course. German, Austrian, Bulgarian, and Turkish forces descended in overwhelming force. By the end of the year the Rumanians had lost two-thirds of their country, including their capital.

The involvement of Rumania in the war left Greece as the only neutral in the Balkans. The Allies decided that Greek assistance was essential to succeed in Macedonia, where they had been fighting inconclusively against the Bulgars. Accordingly, the Allies resorted to various extralegal measures, such as seizing the Greek fleet, blockading Greek ports, and even landing troops at Piraeus. Finally, on June 27, 1917, Greece entered the war on the Allied side, and so paved the way for the 1918 offensives in Macedonia that knocked Bulgaria out of the war.

1917: Bloodletting and Defeatism

Meanwhile, the terrible bloodletting was continuing unabated on the western front. Whereas in 1916 the Germans had assumed the offensive at Verdun, now in 1917 the Allies took the lead. The cautious General Joffre was replaced by the audacious General Nivelle, who preached with persuasive fervor of a new type of lightning offensive that would bring victory with few casualties. Despite the opposition of many military leaders, both French and British, Nivelle's aggressive strategy was accepted.

The Germans at the same time had replaced Falkenhayn with their eastern front team of Hindenburg and Ludendorff. After the shattering experience of the previous year at Verdun and the Somme, they decided to go on the defensive on the western front and to open unrestricted submarine warfare at sea. They hoped thereby to starve England into submission, leaving France isolated on the Continent. They were all aware that submarine warfare involved the risk of American intervention, but they gambled that England would be broken before American aid could become effective.

We shall see shortly that this gamble came within an ace of being won, though in the end it brought disaster. But the defensive strategy on land paid off handsomely. To consolidate and strengthen his front lines, Hindenburg withdrew his forces to a new fortified position (the Hindenburg Line) that was straighter, shorter, and more heavily fortified. The withdrawal badly upset Nivelle's offensive plans, but he persisted in going through with them. French, British, and Canadian troops went over the top as scheduled, but they suffered one of the bloodiest defeats of the war. Hindenburg's defensive strategy had served the Germans well. They inflicted 400,000 casualties on the Allies, while incurring only 250,000 themselves.

By this time the peoples of Europe were enduring the fourth year of the most devastating and murderous war in history. Despite all the sacrifices and grief, no end was yet in sight. War weariness and defeatism appeared not only in the trenches but also among the civilians in both camps. One of the most spectacular manifestations was the passage of a Peace Resolution by the German Reichstag on July 19, 1917, by a vote of 212 to 126. In Austria-Hungary the death of the respected old Emperor Francis Joseph on November 21 brought to the throne the young Emperor Charles, who began secret peace overtures. Likewise in England, a former foreign secretary, Lord Lansdowne, wrote an open letter prophesying the collapse of Western civilization unless some way was found to end the conflict.

IV.   GLOBAL PHASE OF THE WAR: 1917 RUSSIAN REVOLUTION

Nineteen hundred seventeen proved to be the year of decision because of two fateful developments—the Russian Revolution and the intervention of the United States. These events changed the character of the war—from an essentially European affair fought over primarily European issues to a war of global proportions. It is true that Japan had entered the war on August 21, 1914, but it had done little more than help itself to scattered German colonial possessions in the Pacific. But now the entry of the United States involved a great non-European power that quickly decided the outcome of the war.

The American intervention and the Russian Revolution also introduced a new ideological element that immediately had worldwide effects. Wilson's Fourteen Points and Lenin's revolutionary slogans were universal and disruptive in their impact, unlike limited European issues such as the fate of Alsace-Lorraine or of the Hapsburg subject nationalities. It was in 1917, then, that the transition occurred from the European to the global phase of World War I.

Roots of Russian Revolution

Russians of all classes rallied behind their government when war with Germany began on August 1, 1914. In contrast to the Japanese War of 1904–1905, this conflict was popular with the masses, who were convinced it was a war of defense against the aggression of their traditional German enemies. The Russians not only were united against the Germans but also were confident that they would win the war in short order. Instead of quick victory, however, Russia suffered disastrous defeats. The most densely populated and highly industrialized provinces of the empire were lost to the Central Powers. The disasters of 1915 proved to be the beginning of the end of the tsarist regime.

One reason why Russia never recovered from the military setbacks is that it simply lacked the economic strength to wage modern warfare against first-class industrial powers. Russian factories were incapable of supplying the needed quantities of arms, munitions, and supplies. This economic weakness became much worse with the loss of the industrialized portions of the empire in 1915. The Russians were handicapped also by political quarrels on the home front. The Duma and the imperial bureaucracy were constantly feuding over their respective jurisdictions and prerogatives. Both of them, in turn, clashed with the military in assigning responsibility for the shortage of war supplies and, ultimately, for the defeats at the front. This discord might have been minimized and controlled if there had been strong leadership at the top. Unfortunately, Tsar Nicholas was a well-meaning but weak and vacillating ruler with limited intelligence and imagination.

March Revolution

Two revolutions occurred in Russia in 1917: The first, in March, ended tsarism and created a Provisional Government; the second, in November, toppled the Provisional Government and substituted Soviet rule. The first revolution was an unplanned affair that took everyone by surprise. Strikes and riots broke out in Petrograd on March 8 because of the desperate shortage of food and fuel due to poor transportation facilities. The authorities ordered the army to restore order, but instead the soldiers mutinied and sided with the demonstrators. The tsar, always distrustful of the Duma, suspected it of complicity and ordered its dissolution on March 11. The Duma leaders refused to obey the order, and the tsar discovered that he no longer could enforce obedience. The realization of powerlessness was to all intents and purposes the revolution itself. Russia no longer had a functioning government. This became the situation legally as well as factually when Tsar Nicholas abdicated on March 15 in favor of his brother Michael, and when Michael in turn gave up the throne the following day.

Some new structure had to be erected quickly lest the radical elements in the streets take over. On March 12 a Provisional Government was organized to administer the country until a Constituent Assembly could be elected. The new government was headed by the Liberal Prince Georgi Lvov and included the Cadet leader Professor Paul Miliukov, as minister for foreign affairs, and Alexander Kerensky, the only socialist, as minister of justice. This was a bourgeois, liberal, middle-of-the-road cabinet, which favored reform up to a certain point. In fact, it did proclaim freedom of speech, press, and assembly; it declared an amnesty for political and religious offenses; recognized the legal equality of all citizens without social, religious, or racial discrimination; and passed labor legislation, including the eight-hour day. However, despite its record of reform, the Provisional Government never sank roots in the country. For eight months it strove desperately but in vain to provide an adequate administration. At the end of that time the new government was not overthrown; rather, it collapsed as helplessly as the tsarist regime had in March.

General view of the flags on the burial day of the victims of the Russian Revolution—Petrograd, March 23, 1917.

Between Revolutions

The period between March and November 1917 was one of struggle for power between the Provisional Government and the *soviets*. In this struggle the Provisional Government was fatally handicapped because from the beginning it refused to consider the two things that most Russians wanted—peace and land. Prince Lvov and his ministers insisted that such a fundamental reform as redistribution of land must wait for a Constituent Assembly that would be truly representative of the people and would have the authority to decide on such a basic issue. Likewise, the government refused to end the war because Russia had certain commitments to its allies that could not be denied. These arguments were sensible and understandable, but politically they were suicidal. While the government was pleading for patience, the soviets were winning over the masses by demanding immediate peace and immediate distribution of land.

The origin of the soviets goes back to the 1905 Revolution, when the workers elected coun-

cils, or soviets, to coordinate their struggle against tsarism. Although suppressed at that time, the soviets had proven their value as organs for agitation and direct action. They had precisely that quality that the Provisional Government conspicuously lacked—intimate rapport with the masses.

Very naturally, soviets reappeared with the crisis precipitated by the war. Because of their origin and composition, they had none of the Provisional Government's squeamishness about waiting for elections before proceeding with peace negotiations and land distribution. Without hesitation or reservations they gave voice to popular needs, and in doing so they attracted more and more mass support. Soviets soon were appearing in the villages and in military units as well as in the cities. Thus the soviet movement mushroomed throughout the country, developing virtually into a grass-roots government that continually challenged that in Petrograd (formerly St. Petersburg, and soon to be known as Leningrad). Village soviets were organizing seizures of nobles' estates; city soviets were behind the unceasing demonstrations and riots in the streets; and the soldiers' soviets were gradually usurping the authority of the officers to the point where the soviets had control of all weapons and countersigned all orders before they could be executed.

At the beginning, the delegates elected to the soviets were predominantly Socialist Revolutionaries and Mensheviks. The Bolsheviks remained relatively insignificant until the return of their leaders from Switzerland. On April 16, Lenin arrived in Petrograd and issued his famous "April Theses" demanding immediate peace, land to the peasants, and all power to the soviets. In the light of what was to come, Lenin's demands may seem natural and logical. Actually they aroused much opposition within the soviets among the Socialist Revolutionaries and Mensheviks, and even some of the Bolsheviks. Especially controversial was the demand for "all power to the soviets." This seemed at the time preposterous and irresponsible. Time, however, was on Lenin's side, for the longer the war continued, the more the public discontent mounted, and the more popular his demands became. Slogans that seemed bizarre in April were to sound perfectly reasonable six months later. By late 1917 many were ready to fight for "all power to the soviets" if that would rid them of the Provisional Government, which stood in the way of the much-desired peace and land.

An early indication of shifting public opinion was the forced resignation of Foreign Minister Miliukov on May 17. His insistence that Russia remain in the war made him so unpopular that he was dropped, and a new Provisional Government was formed under Lvov and Kerensky. It remained in office until July 20, when Kerensky, who had been steadily emerging as the strongman, organized a new government with himself as premier. By this time the temper of the country had swung so far to the left that the new ministers were mostly Socialist Revolutionaries and Mensheviks. Gone were the days when the Cadets were regarded as the radicals of Russian politics. Now Kerensky was cooperating with the Mensheviks and the Socialist Revolutionaries in order to withstand Lenin and his Bolsheviks.

Bolshevik Revolution

Kerensky declared that his main objective was "to save the revolution from the extremists." In an effort to halt the growing seizure of estates he warned that the future Constituent Assembly would not recognize land transfers made after July 25. He also tried to restore some discipline in the armed forces by reintroducing the death penalty for certain offenses. These measures naturally made Kerensky very unpopular with the Bolsheviks and other radi-

Russian citizens line up in Red Square to view Lenin's Tomb.

cals. Furthermore, by this time the Bolsheviks were becoming increasingly influential within the soviets as public opinion veered more and more to the left. By October the Bolsheviks had a majority in both the Petrograd and Moscow soviets. Lenin now decided that the time had come to overthrow Kerensky and bring about the socialist revolution. But his own party still was not ready for the final plunge. It feared that it would not be able to retain power even

if it were able to topple the Provisional Government. Lenin replied that 240,000 Bolshevik party members could govern Russia in the interest of the poor against the rich as easily as 130,000 landlords previously had governed in the interest of the rich against the poor. Finally, after threatening to resign, Lenin persuaded the Central Committee of his party to vote for revolution, and the date was set for November 7.

LENIN PROCLAIMS THE NEW ORDER

*The day after the overthrow of the Provisional Government, Lenin delivered a speech before the Petrograd Soviet in which he set forth the general objectives of his new regime. The text of his speech reveals the basic difference between the former Provisional Government and the new Bolshevik leaders, with their aim for "socialist revolution" within Russia and throughout the world.**

Comrades, the workmen's and peasants' revolution, the need of which the Bolsheviks have emphasized many times, has come to pass.

What is the significance of this revolution? Its significance is, in the first place, that we shall have a soviet government, without the participation of bourgeoisie of any kind. The oppressed masses will of themselves form a government. The old state machinery will be smashed into bits and in its place will be created a new machinery of government by the soviet organizations. From now on there is a new page in the history of Russia, and the present, third Russian revolution shall in its final result lead to the victory of Socialism.

One of our immediate tasks is to put an end to the war at once. But in order to end the war, which is closely bound up with the present capitalistic system, it is necessary to overthrow capitalism itself. In this work we shall have the aid of the world labor movement, which has already begun to develop in Italy, England, and Germany.

A just and immediate offer of peace by us to the international democracy will find every-

where a warm response among the international proletariat masses. In order to secure the confidence of the proletariat, it is necessary to publish at once all secret treaties.

In the interior of Russia a very large part of the peasantry has said: Enough playing with the capitalists; we will go with the workers. We shall secure the confidence of the peasants by one decree, which will wipe out the private property of the landowners. The peasants will understand that their only salvation is in union with the workers.

We will establish a real labor control on production.

We have now learned to work together in a friendly manner, as is evident from this revolution. We have the force of mass organization which has conquered all and which will lead the proletariat to world revolution.

We should now occupy ourselves in Russia in building up a proletarian socialist state.

Long live the world-wide socialistic revolution.

*F. A. Golder, ed., *Documents of Russian History 1914–1917* (Appleton, 1927), pp. 618–619.

Russia in Revolution, 1917 –1921.

The actual revolution was anticlimactic. With almost no resistance the Bolshevik forces seized key positions in Petrograd—railway stations, bridges, banks, and government buildings. Blood was shed only at the Winter Palace, and casualties there totaled one Red soldier and five Red sailors. Kerensky managed to escape, and after a futile attempt to organize resistance, he fled to exile abroad. Thus the Provisional Government fell with a humiliating casualness much like the end of tsarism. There was no fighting because Kerensky had as few dedicated supporters in November as Nicholas had had in March.

The easy victory of the Bolsheviks did not mean that they commanded the support of all the Russian people, or even the majority. This was demonstrated by the composition of the Constituent Assembly, which was finally elected on November 25: Socialist Revolutionaries, 370; Bolsheviks, 175; Left Socialist Revolutionaries, 40; Cadets, 17; Mensheviks, 16; national groups, 86. The Constituent Assembly met in Petrograd on January 18, 1918, and, after holding one session, was dispersed by the Bolsheviks, who now had military power. Nevertheless, its makeup reveals the relative following of the various parties at that time.

One of the first measures of the new Bolshevik government was to fulfill the promise of peace. On March 3, 1918, it signed the Brest-Litovsk Treaty with Germany. The treaty's severe terms required the surrender by Russia of Poland, the Baltic provinces, Finland, the Ukraine, and parts of the Caucasus. The areas surrendered involved 62 million people and 1,250,000 million square miles of territory where, disastrously, three-fourths of Russia's iron and coal were produced. They also included half of its industrial plants and a third of its crop area. (see map of Russia in Revolution, 1917–1921, p. 579.)

In this manner Russia dropped out of World War I, and the new Bolshevik rulers proceeded to organize the Union of Soviet Socialist Republics.

V. GLOBAL PHASE OF THE WAR: AMERICAN INTERVENTION

When World War I began, President Wilson immediately called on his fellow citizens to be strictly neutral. This met with general approval, for the great majority of Americans wished to stay out of the war. And yet, by 1917, Wilson himself was leading the country into war. One reason for the shift from neutrality to intervention was the government's campaign for military preparedness culminating in the National Defense Act of June 3, 1916. The militaristic propaganda during the campaign helped to prepare the nation psychologically for intervention in the war. Another factor was the American armed intervention in Mexico (March 1916–February 1917) precipitated by Pancho Villa's raid on New Mexico. Nothing came of the intervention, but it provided the thrills of military action without much grief or sacrifice. Also favoring intervention were the American financiers and industrialists who had been supplying Britain and France with war materials on credit, and who would have been ruined if their customers were defeated. The drift to war was speeded up by Germany's unrestricted submarine warfare during which American lives and American ships were lost. Finally, the overthrow of the tsarist regime in March 1917 enabled the United States to join a league of democratic powers battling the autocracies of central Europe.

This combination of factors led President Wilson to declare war on Germany in April 1917. In his *Fourteen Points* he set forth specific and detailed war aims, including the end of secret diplomacy and the drafting of "open covenants of Peace," freedom of the seas, removal of barriers to international trade, reduction of armaments, impartial arbitration of all colonial claims on the principle that the interests of the colonial peoples must have equal weight with the claims of colonial powers, and the application of the principle of self-determination in dealing with the various subject minorities in central and eastern Europe.

VI. ALLIED VICTORY

How decisive was the American intervention is made clear in the statistics shown in Table 37.1 concerning the productivity of the belligerents. The intervention of the United States gave the Allies decisive superiority in manpower as well as in war supplies. In the month of March 1918, a to-

TABLE 37.1	Production of the Belligerent Powers (in millions of tons)*					
	August 1, 1914		September 15, 1914		1917	
	Allies	*Central Powers*	*Allies*	*Central Powers*	*Allies*	*Central Powers*
Pig Iron	22	22	16	25	50	15
Steel	19	21	16	25	58	16
Coal	394	331	346	355	851	340

* F. Sternberg, *Capitalism and Socialism on Trial* (Day, 1951), pp. 166–167.

tal of 84,889 American soldiers reached the western front, and in July the number rose to 306,350. Thus a fresh new army was made available to the Allied commanders each month. It is not surprising that during 1918 the Central Powers surrendered one by one.

The first to surrender were the Bulgarians, whose front crumbled when General Franchet d'Esperey, commander of the Allied forces in Saloniki, attacked in mid-September. On September 29, 1918, Bulgarian representatives signed an armistice, and on October 3 King Ferdinand abdicated in favor of his son Boris. Likewise in Turkey, British imperial forces were advancing victoriously in a two-pronged drive—one from Egypt up the Levant coast, and the other from the Persian Gulf up the Mesopotamian valley. At the same time an Allied force from Saloniki was marching on Constantinople. Staggered by these setbacks and isolated by Bulgaria's surrender, the Turks accepted an armistice on October 30, 1918.

Most desperate was the position of Austria-Hungary. The numerous minorities were organizing national assemblies and proclaiming their independence. Even German-Austrians and Hungarians, who hitherto had ruled the empire, now were talking in terms of independent states of their own. The ancient Hapsburg Empire finally reached its end on November 11, when Emperor Charles abdicated.

Meanwhile, the German position on the western front had steadily deteriorated. With American soldiers pouring in, Marshal Foch, the Allied commander-in-chief, was able to strike where and as he pleased. German casualties were outstripping replacements, and deserters were crowding into depots and railroad stations.

These setbacks, together with the news of their defecting allies, forced the Germans to begin armistice negotiations. A principal stumbling block was the kaiser's refusal to abdicate. The chancellor, Prince Max, forced the issue by announcing the abdication of the emperor November 9. Two days later the armistice was signed and fighting ceased on the western front.

Thus ended World War I—a war that lasted four years and three months, involved thirty sovereign states, overthrew four empires, gave birth to seven new nations, took approximately 8.5 million combatant and 10 million noncombatant lives, and cost $180.5 billion directly and $151.6 billion indirectly.

VII. PEACE SETTLEMENT

Separate peace treaties were signed with each of the Central Powers: the Versailles Treaty with Germany, June 28, 1919; the St. Germain Treaty with Austria, September 10, 1919; the Trianon Treaty with Hungary, March 22, 1919; the Neuilly Treaty with Bulgaria, November 27, 1919; and the Sèvres Treaty with Turkey, August 20, 1920. Three features of this overall peace settlement are significant for world history: the establishment of the League of Nations, the application of the principle of *self-determination* in Europe, and the failure to apply this principle outside of Europe.

The League of Nations was organized to attain two basic objectives. The most important was to preserve the peace. Its members were to give each other mutual protection against aggression, to submit disputes to arbitration or inquiry, and to abstain from war until three months after arbitration. The secondary purpose of the league was to concern itself with health, social, economic, and humanitarian problems of international scope. For this purpose there were established specialized league bodies such as the Health Organization, the Committee on Intellectual Cooperation, and the International Labor Organization, as well as numerous temporary advisory commissions. By and large, the league succeeded in its secondary functions. It proved invaluable in improving international labor conditions, promoting world health, combating the narcotic and slave traffics, and coping with economic crises. But we shall see that the league was not able to keep the peace, and since this was its chief aim, that failure spelled the end of the entire organization.

The post–World War I settlement was characterized also by the redrawing of European frontiers on the basis of the principle of self-determination. This, stated explicitly in the Fourteen Points, was officially implemented in the various peace treaties. The net result was a drastic revision of the map of Europe. Alsace-Lorraine was returned to France without question. Russia was deprived of most of its Baltic coastline by the establishment of the independent states of Finland, Latvia, Estonia, and Lithuania. An independent Poland was created, carved out of former Russian, German, and Hapsburg provinces; Czechoslovakia emerged from the former Hapsburg Empire. Yugoslavia also appeared, comprising prewar Serbia and Montenegro and various former Hapsburg territories inhabited by south Slavs. Rumania more than doubled in size as a result of its acquisitions from Austria-Hungary, Russia, and Bulgaria. Finally, from the remains of the old Hapsburg Empire, there emerged the two rump states of Austria and Hungary.

The principle of self-determination was not respected in every instance in drawing the new frontiers. Indeed, there were bitter protests concerning the sizable German minorities in Poland and Czechoslovakia; the Hungarian minorities in Yugoslavia, Rumania, and Czechoslovakia; and the Russian minorities in Poland, Czechoslovakia, and Rumania. The explanation for this friction is to be found partly in the fact that the numerous ethnic groups in central and eastern

Europe were so inextricably mixed that no frontiers could be drawn without creating considerable minorities on one side or the other. The inevitable minorities, however, were substantially increased because frontiers sometimes were drawn to satisfy strategic considerations as well as nationalist aspirations. This was why the Sudeten Germans were left in Czechoslovakia, why the Tyrol Germans were left in Italy, and why the union of Austria and Germany was specifically forbidden by the St. Germain Treaty even though it would have been in accord with popular will, at least in the immediate postwar years. Yet despite these deviations, the new frontiers were more in accord with nationalist aspirations than the old. And the number of minority peoples was much smaller after World War I than before. (See map of Europe After World War I, 1923, p. 583.)

Although the peacemakers generally applied self-determination in Europe, they definitely did not do so outside of Europe. This discrimination was clearly evident in Wilson's Fourteen Points, which specifically spelled out how the aspirations of the various European minorities were to be satisfied. By contrast, Point 5 declared that in the colonies "the interests of the populations concerned must have equal weight with the equitable claims of the government whose title is to be determined." The significant point here is the reference to the "interests" rather than to the "wishes" of the colonial peoples. Needless to say, it was the Europeans themselves who decided what these "interests" were, and the outcome was a modified form of imperial rule known as the mandate system.

Article 22 of the League Covenant referred to the inhabitants of the colonies taken from the Central Powers as "peoples not yet able to stand by themselves under the strenuous conditions of the modern world." The article accordingly provided that the "tutelage of such peoples should be entrusted to advanced nations who, by reason of their resources, their experience, or their geographical position, can best undertake this responsibility . . . and that this tutelage should be exercised by them as Mandatories on behalf of the League." It is significant that this provision for "tutelage" under "Mandatories" was not extended to the colonies of the victorious Allies, whose inhabitants in many

Europe After World War I, 1923

cases were at a similar level of development or lack of development.

The Mandatory Powers assumed specific obligations toward the inhabitants of the mandate territories. For fulfillment of these obligations they were accountable to the Permanent Mandates Commission and were required to report annually to the Council of the League of Nations. Though neither the commission nor the league itself had authority to force a recalcitrant Mandatory Power to fulfill its obligations, it is significant that European states for the first time accepted certain specified procedures. Although the *mandate* system represented a certain im-

provement over the traditional division of colonial booty by the victors in a war, nevertheless it is strongly reminiscent of the 1815 settlement because it ignored national aspirations. We shall see that the inhabitants of the Ottoman territories did not want mandate status and were violently opposed to France as Mandatory Power. Their wishes were directly flouted when Syria and Lebanon were allotted to France. It is not surprising, then, that just as the ignoring of nationalist wishes in 1815 led to a long series of revolutions in Europe during the nineteenth century, so this mandate system was to lead to uprisings in the colonial world during the postwar years.

VIII.   WORLD WAR I IN WORLD HISTORY

A glance at the globe before and after World War I reveals comparatively few changes. Europe's frontiers were different because of the disappearance of four empires, but as far as the world as a whole was concerned, European dominance appeared undiminished. Britain, France, and the other imperial powers still ruled as many overseas colonies as before 1914. Indeed, their possessions were even greater, for they now controlled territories in the Middle East that formerly had been under the sultan. Thus, Europe's global hegemony appeared to be more complete after World War I than before.

Beneath the surface, however, the situation was entirely different. In fact, the overriding significance of World War I from a global viewpoint is precisely that it began the undermining of Europe's supremacy—a process that was completed following World War II. The undermining was evident in at least three regards: the economic decline, the political crisis, and the weakening hold over the colonies.

Before 1914, Europe's economy was dependent to a considerable degree on massive overseas investments, yielding massive annual returns. During World War I, however, Britain lost a quarter of its foreign investments, France a third, and Germany lost all. The reverse of this trend may be seen in the new financial strength of the United States. In 1914 the United States owed about $4 billion to European investors, but by 1919 it had become a creditor nation to the tune of $3.7 billion; by 1930 this sum had risen to $8.8 billion. The same pattern is evident in industry, for many European industrial areas were devastated whereas American factories mushroomed spectacularly under the impetus of unlimited wartime demand. By 1929 the United States was responsible for no less than 42.2 percent of world industrial output, an amount greater than that of all the countries of Europe, including Russia. Thus, the economic relationships between Europe and the United States were reversed as a result of World War I. Europe no longer was the banker and the workshop of the world, as it had been during the nineteenth century. Leadership in both areas had crossed the Atlantic.

The war gutted Europe politically as well as economically. Prior to 1914 Europe had been the source of the basic political ideas and institutions of modern times. Their impact, as we have seen, had been felt in all corners of the globe. The holocaust of war, however, left Europeans demoralized and unbelieving. In all parts of the Continent the old order was being questioned and challenged. In a confidential memorandum of March 1919, the British premier, David Lloyd George, wrote, "There is a deep sense not only of discontent, but of anger and revolt, amongst the workmen against pre-war conditions. The whole existing order in its political, social and economic aspects is questioned by the masses of the people from one end of Europe to the other."[2]

In this revolutionary crisis, many Europeans looked for guidance to two non-Europeans, the American Wilson and the Russian Lenin. Wilson's Fourteen Points had stirred up a ferment of democratic hope and expectancy. When he stepped on the blood-soaked soil of Europe in December 1918, huge crowds greeted Wilson with delirious enthusiasm as "King of Humanity," "Savior," "Prince of Peace." They listened avidly to his plans for a future of peace and security.

At the same time another gospel of salvation was coming from the East. The millions of dead and wounded, the smoking ruins of cities and villages, made large masses receptive to the call for revolution and for a new social order. In imitation of the Bolshevik Revolution, soviets were set up in Berlin, Hamburg, and Budapest. Demonstrations were staged in the streets of London, Paris, and Rome. Wilson's confidant, Colonel House, wrote in his diary on March 22, 1919, "Rumblings of discontent every day. The people want peace. Bolshevism is gaining ground everywhere. Hungary has just succumbed. We are sitting upon an open powder magazine and some day a spark may ignite it."[3]

Finally, Europe's domination was undermined by World War I because of the repercussions in the overseas colonies. The spectacle of one bloc of European powers fighting another to the bitter end damaged the prestige of the white masters irreparably. No longer were they regarded as almost divinely ordained to rule over colored subjects. Equally disruptive was the participation in the war of millions of colonials as soldiers or as laborers. Indian divisions fought on the western front and in Mesopotamia; many Africans in French uniform fought in northern France; and large numbers of Chinese and Indochinese served in labor battalions behind the lines. Needless to say, the colonials who returned home after such experiences were not likely to be as obedient to European overlords as before.

Revolutionary ideas in the colonies were also spread by propaganda associated with the conduct of the war. It is true that Wilson's Fourteen Points had referred only to the "interest" rather than to the desires of the colonial peoples. But this was an overfine distinction in a time of war. The revolutionary phrase "self-determination of peoples" left its imprint on the colonial world as well as on Europe. Equally influential were the ideologies of socialism and communism. Before World War I, Asian intellectuals had been inspired by Western liberalism and nationalism. They had quoted Voltaire, Mazzini, and John Stuart Mill. But their sons now were likely to quote Marx, Lenin, or Harold Laski. Dr. Sun Yat-sen, on July 25, 1919, gave evidence of this shift when he declared, "If the people of China wish to be free . . . its only ally and brother in the struggle for national freedom are the Russian workers and peasants of the Red Army."[4]

All these repercussions of World War I on the colonial world inevitably had profound political consequences. One of the few who saw this clearly was the African-American leader W. E. B. Du Bois, who in 1918 wrote the following remarkable forecast of the world to come:

This war is an end and also a beginning. Never again will darker people of the world occupy just the place they had before. Out of this place will rise, soon or late, an independent China, a self-governing India, an Egypt with representative institutions, an Africa for the Africans, and not merely for business exploitation. Out of this war will rise, too, an American Negro with the right to vote and the right to work and the right to live without insult.[5]

SUGGESTED READINGS

The most recent of the numerous studies of the origins of World War I are G. F. Kennan, *The Fateful Alliance: France, Russia and the Coming of the First World War* (Pantheon, 1984); J. Joll, *The Origins of the First World War* (Longman, 1985); and G. Barraclough, *From Agadir to Armageddon: Anatomy of a Crisis* (Holmes and Meier, 1981), the latter stressing the domino effect of Agadir leading to Sarajevo and suggesting implications for the post–World War II cold war. For the broader significance of World War I, see H. Holborn, *The Political Collapse of Europe* (Knopf, 1951); and M. Ferro, *The Great War 1914–1918* (Routledge & Kegan Paul, 1973).

The most thorough study of the Russian Revolution is by E. H. Carr, *The Bolshevik Revolution, 1917–1923*, 3 vols. (Macmillan, 1953). See also the interpretation by H. Salisbury, *Black Night, White Snow: Russia's Revolutions 1905–1917* (Doubleday, 1978). Documentary materials are provided by J. Bunyan and H. H. Fisher, *The Bolshevik Revolution, 1917–1918* (Stanford University, 1934); and R. P. Browder and A. F. Kerensky, *The Russian Provisional Government, 1917*, 3 vols. (Stanford University, 1961). See also J. Bradley, *Allied Intervention in Russia 1917–1920* (Basic Books, 1968). The global impact of the Russian Revolution is analyzed by P. Dukes, *October and the World: Perspectives on the Russian Revolution* (St. Martin's Press, 1979).

For the Versailles settlement, see the definitive study by A. J. Mayer, *Politics and Diplomacy of Peacemaking: Containment and Counterrevolution at Versailles 1918–1919* (Knopf, 1967); the revealing analysis of the role of the United States by N. G. Levin, Jr., *Woodrow Wilson and World Politics: America's Response to War and Revolution* (Oxford University, 1968); and A. Walworth, *Wilson and His Peacemakers* (W. W. Norton, 1986).

38 Nationalist Uprisings in the Colonial World

Since the day of Japan's victory over Russia, the peoples of Asia have cherished the hope of shaking off the yoke of European oppression, a hope which has given rise to a series of independence movements—in Egypt, Persia, Turkey, Afghanistan, and finally in India. . . . If we want to regain our rights, we must resort to force.

World War I was followed by a wave of revolutions in the colonial territories. The roots of these revolutions go back to the pre–1914 years, but it was the war itself that provided the immediate stimulus. The final outcomes varied, with the Turks winning most of their objectives, whereas the Egyptians, Iraqis, Indians, and others won only modest constitutional concessions. These uprisings represent the prelude to the great upheavals that finally ended the European empires during the two decades following World War II.

I. TURKEY

The most spectacular and successful of all the post–World War I colonial revolts against European domination was that of the Turks. They had suffered disastrous defeat during the war and had then been compelled to accept humiliating armistice and peace terms. Yet they bounced back, defeating their enemies in armed conflict and winning a new treaty with more favorable terms. Thus, of all the Central Powers, only primitive and despised Turkey was capable of turning on the victorious Allies and forcing them to accept a revision of the peace settlement. To understand this extraordinary outcome it is necessary to review the tangled wartime diplomacy concerning the Ottoman empire. Britain was the prime mover behind most of the diplomacy involving the Middle East during the war years. It was responsible for three sets of often conflicting agreements—with its own allies, with Arab representatives, and with the Zionists.

The agreements among the Allies consisted of four secret treaties: the Constantinople Agreement of March–April 1915; the Treaty of London of April 26, 1915; the Sykes-Picot Agreement of April 26, 1916; and the Saint-Jean-de-Maurienne Treaty of April 1917. These treaties allotted to Russia Constantinople, the Straits, and a considerable portion of northeast Asia Minor; to Italy southwest Asia Minor; to Britain Mesopotamia and an enclave about Haifa and Acre; and to France the Syrian coast with the hinterland eastward to the Russian sphere. These secret treaties marked the death warrant of the Ottoman Empire, leaving to the Turks only 20,000 square miles in the northern

section of their homeland. More important, these secret treaties were in direct conflict with certain agreements that Britain was concluding at this time with Arab and Jewish representatives.

When Turkey joined the Central Powers in November 1914, the British negotiated a military alliance with the Arab leader Emir Hussein, Prince of Mecca. In return for an Arab revolt against the Turks, the British agreed to recognize the postwar independence of all Arab lands. This commitment conflicted with another that the British made to Lord Rothschild of the World Zionist Organization. Zionism was a nationalist movement that had developed among European Jews in the late nineteenth century as a reaction against mounting anti-Semitism. The World Zionist Organization, established in Basel in 1897, had repeatedly but vainly sought permission from the Ottoman government to establish a Jewish settlement in Palestine, the Jewish biblical homeland. With Turkey's involvement in World War I, Zionist leaders in England and the United States seized the opportunity to press for an Allied commitment to create a Jewish commonwealth in Pales-

A group of delegates at the Fifth Congress of the World Zionist Organization.

tine after the end of the Ottoman Empire. They succeeded when on November 2, 1917, Lord Balfour wrote to Lord Rothschild that the British Government favored the establishment in Palestine of a "national home for the Jewish people . . . it being clearly understood that nothing shall be done which may prejudice the civil and religious rights of existing non-Jewish communities in Palestine. . . ." It is evident that this Balfour Declaration conflicted with the commitment to Hussein, as well as with the secret treaties for the division of the Ottoman provinces among the Allies.

The final outcome was the Sèvres Treaty (August 10, 1920), by which France obtained Syria as a mandate, and Britain got Mesopotamia and Palestine, in additional to a protectorate over Egypt. The Dodecanese Islands were ceded to Italy, and Greece, thanks to the skillful diplomacy of its Premier Venizelos, obtained several Aegean islands, eastern Thrace, and the right to administer the Smyrna region for five years. After that its final disposition was to be determined by a plebiscite. Armenia and the Kingdom of Hejaz were recognized as independent. Finally, Soviet Russia, which was now in armed conflict with Allied interventionist forces and which had published and repudiated the secret treaties signed by the tsarist ministers, did not obtain Constantinople and the Straits. Instead, this strategic territory was left under Turkish sovereignty, though the Straits were to be demilitarized and placed under international control.

These provisions, so contrary to the promises made to the Arabs and to the professed Allied principle of self-determination, aroused a wave of armed resistance throughout the Middle East. A combination of factors enabled the Turks to scrap the Sèvres Treaty altogether, and the Arabs won piecemeal concessions after ten years of stubborn struggle.

A prime factor in the Turkish success was the personality of Mustafa Kemal, later known as Ataturk or Foremost Turk. He first won fame for his successful defense of the Dardanelles against the Allies. After the war he led the resistance against the Sèvres Treaty. He was willing to surrender the Arab provinces of the old empire, but he refused to accept the partition of Asia Minor and the loss of Constantinople and the Straits. In the elections of October 1919 Kemal's followers

Photo of Mustafa Kemal. taken at the window of his special train as he leaves Istanbul for Angora (present-day Ankara).

won a majority. When Parliament met in January 1920 it adopted a National Pact based on Kemal's program. In April 1920 Parliament dethroned the sultan, who was a virtual Allied prisoner in Constantinople, and established a republic headed by Kemal as president.

The young republic had to struggle against not only the sultan but also the victorious Allies. It succeeded against such odds because of Kemal's inspired leadership and because the Turkish people united behind him, especially after the landing of Greek troops at Smyrna in the spring of 1919. Kemal skillfully exploited differences among the Allies to conclude separate treaties with them, thereby isolating the Greeks in Smyrna. By September 1922 Kemal was riding triumphantly into Smyrna. Before him fled not only the Greek army but also Greek civilians who had lived in that coastal region since ancient times.

Kemal now was in a position to demand revisions of the Sèvres Treaty. After long negotiations the Lausanne Treaty was signed on July 24,

1923. This returned to Turkey eastern Thrace and some of the Aegean Islands. Also Turkey was to pay no reparations, and the capitulations were abolished in return for a promise of judicial reform. The Straits remained demilitarized and open to ships of all nations in time of peace or war if Turkey remained neutral. If Turkey was at war, enemy ships, but no neutrals, might be excluded. Finally, a separate agreement provided for the compulsory exchange of the Greek minority in Constantinople for the Turkish minority in western Thrace and Macedonia.

Having created a new Turkey, Kemal turned to the equally difficult task of creating new Turks. He ruthlessly swept away outdated institutions as reform followed reform in a great torrent. The capital was moved from vulnerable Constantinople to Ankara in the interior of Asia Minor. The caliphate was abolished; all religious orders and houses suppressed; a constitution adopted along with new civil, criminal, and commercial codes; and women given the right to vote and sit in the assembly. By the time of Kemal's death on November 10, 1938, the new Turkey was securely established.

II.   ARAB MIDDLE EAST

While the Turks were successfully scrapping the Sèvres Treaty, the Arabs were stubbornly resisting the Mandatory Powers to which they had been assigned. Contrary to the Hussein Agreement, Syria-Lebanon had been given as a mandate to France, Mesopotamia and Palestine had been made British mandates, and full British control had been established in Egypt. This high-handed parceling out of Arab lands was bound to lead to trouble because the war itself had stimulated tremendous national sentiment among the Arabs.

A common pattern developed in the postwar struggle for independence. First, an explosion of defiance and armed revolt occurred during the years immediately following the peace treaties. Then Britain and France gradually restored order and reasserted their authority. Finally, they granted varying degrees of autonomy, which did not entirely satisfy the nationalists but which did preserve an uneasy peace until World War II.

In Egypt, the mandatory relationship, strictly speaking, did not exist. But the situation was essentially similar because Britain at the beginning of the war had repudiated the nominal Ottoman suzerainty and had declared the country a British protectorate. Immediately, the nationalist Wafd party organized violent opposition. In 1922 Britain proclaimed Egypt "an independent sovereign state" but reserved for itself control of foreign affairs and of external security, as well as protection of minorities and of foreign interests. The nationalists rejected this fake independence and continued the struggle. They won repeated electoral victories and also conducted a terror campaign. Finally, in 1936 a compromise settlement was reached with the signing of a twenty-year alliance treaty. Britain understood to end its military occupation of the country and to arrange for Egypt's admission to the League of Nations. In return, Egypt agreed to stand by Britain in time of war, to accept the British garrison stationed for the defense of the Suez Canal, and also to continue the joint British-Egyptian administration of the Sudan. Nationalist leaders were far from satisfied with this settlement, but they accepted it as the best available under the circumstances.

Nationalist opposition in Iraq followed much the same course as in Egypt. A widespread armed revolt broke out in 1920. The British first restored order and then attempted to conciliate nationalist feeling by enthroning as king the third son of Hussein, Prince Faisal. The following year (1922), the British negotiated a treaty of alliance in which they retained such controls as they thought were needed to protect their interests. The nationalists remained dissatisfied and continued their agitation. Finally, an alliance treaty was concluded in 1930, by which Britain agreed to end the mandate and to support Iraq's application for admission to the League of Nations. In return, Iraq agreed that Britain should maintain three air bases in the country and also should have full use of railways, rivers, and ports in time of war. In 1932 Iraq became a member of the League of Nations, the first Arab country to gain that distinction. As in the case of Egypt, however, nationalist circles were still dissatisfied.

In Syria and Lebanon, the French were less flexible than the British and therefore less successful. Nationalist outbreaks occurred periodi-

ARAB OPPOSITION TO MANDATES

Virtually all Arabs opposed the Allied plan for replacing the Ottoman Empire with Western-controlled mandates. This was made clear by the following memorandum adopted on July 2, 1919, by the General Syrian Congress (Syria at that time included present-day Syria, Lebanon, Jordan, and Israel). The rejection of this memorandum embittered Arab nationalists and contributed to the turmoil that grips the Middle East to the present day.*

1. We ask absolutely complete political independence for Syria. . . .

2. We ask that the Government of this Syrian country should be a democratic civil constitutional Monarchy on broad decentralization principles, safeguarding the rights of minorities, and that the King be the Emir Feisal, who carried on a glorious struggle in the cause of our liberation and merited our full confidence and entire reliance.

3. Considering the fact that the Arabs inhabiting the Syrian area are not naturally less gifted than other more advanced races and that they are by no means less developed than the Bulgarians, Serbians, Greeks, and Roumanians at the beginning of their independence, we protest against Article 22 of the Covenant of the League of Nations, placing us among the nations in their middle stage of development which stand in need of a mandatory power.

4. In the event of the rejection by the Peace Conference of this just protest for certain considerations that we may not understand, we, relying on the declarations of President Wilson that his object in waging war was to put an end to the ambition of conquest and colonization, can only regard the mandate mentioned in the Covenant of the League of Nations as equivalent to the rendering of economical and technical assistance that does not prejudice our complete independence. And desiring that our country should not fall a prey to colonization and believing that the American Nation is farthest from any thought of colonization and has no political ambition in our country, we will seek the technical and economical assistance from the United States of America, provided that such assistance does not exceed 20 years.

5. In the event of America not finding herself in a position to accept our desire for assistance, we will seek this assistance from Great Britain, also provided that such assistance does not infringe the complete independence and unity of our country and that the duration of such assistance does not exceed that mentioned in the previous article.

6. We do not acknowledge any right claimed by the French Government in any part whatever of our Syrian country and refuse that she should assist us or have a hand in our country under any circumstances and in any place.

7. We oppose the pretensions of the Zionists to create a Jewish commonwealth in the southern part of Syria, known as Palestine, and oppose Zionist migration to any part of our country; for we do not acknowledge their title but consider them a grave peril to our people from the national, economical, and political points of view. Our Jewish compatriots shall enjoy our common rights and assume the common responsibilities.

* *Foreign Relations of the United States, Paris Peace Conference, 1919,* Vol. 12, pp. 780–781.

cally. The most serious was in 1925, when the French were forced to shell Damascus in order to retain control. Finally, in 1936 the French government negotiated treaties with Syria and Lebanon modeled after the Anglo-Iraqi treaty of 1930. Neither of these treaties, however, was ratified by the French Chamber of Deputies, so that the conflict remained unresolved when World War II began.

In Palestine the situation was unique because it quickly deteriorated into a bitter three-way struggle involving Britain, Arabs, and Jews. The Arabs maintained that the Balfour Declaration concerning a Jewish "national home" was in violation of prior commitments made to the Arabs. In 1921, Britain tried to appease the Arabs by setting apart the interior portion of the country as the independent state of Transjordan. This was exempt from all the clauses of the mandate concerning the establishment of a Jewish home. Furthermore, the British installed Faisal's elder brother, Abdullah, as ruler of Transjordan. This tactic was satisfactory as far as Transjordan itself was concerned. Abdullah always cooperated loyally with the British, particularly since the poverty

of his country made him dependent on subsidies from London. Probably the most effective military unit in the Arab world was Transjordan's Arab legion, supported by British funds and led by the British General John Glubb.

In Palestine proper, however, the triangle conflict became increasingly fierce as Jewish immigrants poured in and the apprehensive Arabs struck back against both the Jews and the British. Article 6 of the mandate required Britain to "facilitate" Jewish immigration and to "encourage close settlement by Jews on the land." But the same article also provided that "the rights and position of other sections of the population" were to be safeguarded. The British apparently felt at the time that the two orders were not necessarily contradictory. They expected that Jewish immigration would never reach such proportions as to threaten "the rights and positions" of the Arabs. They could not have foreseen the repercussions of Hitler's rise to power in 1933. Jewish immigration jumped from 9,553 in 1932 to 30,327 in 1933, 42,359 in 1934, and 61,854 in 1935. The total Jewish population in Palestine rose from 65,000 in 1919 to 450,000 in 1939.

Jewish colonists en route to a settlement in Palestine, 1920.

As long as the Jewish influx had been modest, the Arabs had not raised serious objections. In fact they had welcomed the Jews with their money and energy and skills. The Arabs themselves had benefited substantially from the success of the Jews in restoring exhausted land, founding industries, and checking diseases. But when the stream of immigration became a torrent, the Arabs reacted violently. They pointed out that there was no reason why they should lose their country because of western anti-Semitism. "Anti-Semitism is a deplorable Western disease. . . . We aren't anti-Semites; we are also Semites. Yet this Western problem is being smoothed over at our expense. Is that your idea of right?"[1]

Arab attacks against the Jews became increasingly frequent and serious. Highlights were the Wailing Wall disorders in 1929, the Arab "National Political Strike" in 1936, and the Arab Rebellion of 1938. The British response was to send Royal Commissions following the major outbreaks. By the time of World War II several commissions had investigated the situation and had vacillated in their recommendations as they sought to satisfy three distinct and conflicting interests—the Jewish Zionist aspirations, Arab nationalist demands, and British imperial interests. The White Paper of May 1939, for example, proposed that Palestine become an independent state in ten years and that definite limits be placed on Jewish immigration and land purchases. Both Arabs and Jews rejected the British proposals, and the Palestine controversy remained as far from settlement as ever when World War II began.

III. INDIA

At the turn of the century British rule in India seemed perfectly secure for the foreseeable future. In 1912, a great imperial durbar was held in Delhi to celebrate the coronation of King George V. Amid pageantry and splendor, King George received the homage of India's princes and potentates without a voice being raised in dissent. In 1914, India rallied solidly behind Britain at war. The princes contributed generous financial aid, and no fewer than 900,000 Indians served in the British army as combatants and another 300,000 as laborers.

Yet only three decades after World War I, British rule in India came to an end. One reason for this extraordinary outcome was the impact of the war itself—the influence of slogans about self-determination and the unsettling effect of overseas service on hundreds of thousands of soldiers who returned with new ideas and attitudes. Unrest was stimulated also by a series of disasters in the immediate postwar years. The failure of the monsoon in 1918 brought famine to many parts of India. The influenza epidemic of 1918–1919 killed no fewer than 13 million people! Another factor contributing to unrest was the repressive policy followed by Britain after the war, which ended with the infamous Amritsar Massacre of April 13, 1919. Seeking to impress the people with the strength of the government, General Dyer ordered his troops to fire without warning on a crowded political meeting of unarmed civilians. Nearly 400 were killed and 1,000 wounded. A wave of bitter protest swept India, and Gandhi denounced the government as "satanic."

Gandhi was by all odds the outstanding figure in this postwar anti-British movement. The Indian Congress, organized in 1885, did not seriously threaten the British before 1914 (see Chapter 32, Section V). It had remained essentially a middle-class movement with little support from village masses. Gandhi's great contribution was that he managed to break through to the villagers, establish rapport with them, and involve them in the struggle for independence. His message was simple and appealing. He pointed out that in 1914 the British were ruling 300 million Indians with a mere 4,000 administrators and 69,000 soldiers. This was possible only because all classes of the population were cooperating with the British in one way or another. If this cooperation were withdrawn, British rule inevitably would collapse. The task, then, was to educate and prepare the people for *satyagraha,* or nonviolent passive resistance. Gandhi also called on the people to practice *hartal,* or to boycott British goods. In place of imported machine-made goods, Gandhi preached the wearing of homespun cloth. This would undermine the economic basis of British rule and also revive village industries. He himself wore a loin cloth of homespun material and publicly worked at his spinning wheel. The combination of *satyagraha* and *hartal,* Gandhi

Gandhi and Nehru laughing and joking in Faizpur, India, 1937.

taught, would make possible the realization of *swaraj,* or home rule. Once India's villagers understood these teachings and acted on them, the days of British rule would be numbered.

In an effort to forestall the gathering storm, the London government introduced on December 23, 1919, the Montagu-Chelmsford reforms establishing an administrative system known as "dyarchy." This left important matters "reserved" for the governor and his executive council; the less important, such as sanitation, agriculture, medical relief, and education, were "transferred" to the Indian ministers. The theory was that more matters would be transferred from the "reserved" to the "transferred" list if this "dyarchy," or division of responsibilities, proved workable. The National Congress, led by Gandhi, rejected the British reform proposal. In September 1920, an all-out noncooperation campaign was launched. The response was impressive, but it gradually got out of hand. Gandhi insisted on strict nonviolence, yet strikes and riots broke out in many of the cities, and in the countryside the peasants rose up against the landlords and moneylenders. The shocked Gandhi promptly ordered suspension of the noncooperation campaign, but he was nevertheless arrested and sentenced to six years' imprisonment. He was released after two years because of his precarious health, but the nationalist campaign had largely petered out by then.

Another nationalist leader, Jawaharlal Nehru, was now coming to the fore alongside Gandhi. The son of a wealthy lawyer, Nehru had been educated at Harrow and Cambridge and had been admitted to the bar in 1912. On his return, he plunged into the nationalist struggle for freedom and became a follower and admirer of Gandhi. Nehru, however, was very different from his mystical and ascetic leader. He was a socialist and a firm believer in science and technology as the means for liberating humanity from its age-old misery and ignorance. Nehru nevertheless recognized Gandhi's extraordinary service in arousing India's peasantry. Even the National Congress, torn by personal rivalries and doctrinal disputes, was dependent on Gandhi. He returned to political life in December 1928 and persuaded Congress to accept a compromise resolution acceptable to both the radical and conservative elements. A few months later the British Labour party defeated the Conservatives and formed a new government. The outlook seemed promising, for the Labourites consistently had criticized the Conservatives for being so late in giving self-government to India. The promise, however, was not realized; the decade 1930–1939 was a disappointment.

One reason was the increasing dissension between warring Hindu and Moslem blocs. The All-India Moslem League was founded as early as 1919 but was of little significance until after

1935, when it came under the leadership of a Bombay lawyer, Mohammed Ali Jinnah. He offered to cooperate with the Congress on a coalition basis, but Congress would deal only with Moslems who joined the party as individuals. Jinnah retaliated by appealing to the Moslem masses with the cry "Islam is in danger." The response was enthusiastic, for many Indian Moslems felt they had more in common with the rest of the Moslem world than with their Hindu neighbors. Jinnah's electoral success made possible the future establishment of the independent Moslem Pakistan.

Finally, on August 2, 1935, the British Parliament passed the Government of India Act. It provided for new provincial arrangements that were implemented with the election of provincial legislatures in 1937. The Nationalists gained control in seven of the eleven provinces, and they promptly proceeded to liberate political prisoners, restore civil liberties, and prepare agrarian reform.

In 1939 all this abruptly ended when the viceroy proclaimed that India was a participant in the new world war. Since the Indians were in no way consulted, the Nationalist ministries in the seven provinces resigned. British governors then took over and governed by decree. Once again the Nationalists raised the cry for complete independence, and the Moslems under Jinnah demanded that the subcontinent be partitioned into two states, one Hindu, and the other, to be called Pakistan, Moslem.

IV.   CHINA

Although nominally independent, China experienced an anti-Western movement after World War I comparable to that in India. China entered the war in 1917 in hope of recovering Shantung province, which Japan had occupied in 1914. When the lost province was not restored by the peacemakers at Versailles, wild demonstrations broke out among the students and intellectuals in Peking. The protests soon spread to other cities, and the merchants joined by closing their shops. This developed into a boycott of Japanese goods attended by clashes with Japanese residents. The Western powers also were the targets

of this violent outburst because of their willingness to allow Japan to retain its booty on the mainland. Russia, by contrast, was regarded with sympathy and admiration because the Soviet government had renounced tsarist special privileges in China, as it also did at this time in Turkey and Persia.

These changes gave Dr. Sun Yat-sen the opportunity to make a fresh start with new policies and methods. After appealing in vain to the Western powers for aid against provincial warlords who were carrying on as independent potentates, he turned to the Soviet government. He got a positive response and so began in 1921 the Kuomintang-Communist Entente that lasted to 1927. Dr. Sun and the able Russian representative Mikhail Borodin together brought about three basic changes: They remodeled the Kuomintang party along Communist lines, organized an efficient modern army, and developed a more effective and appealing political ideology.

In the reorganization of the Kuomintang, Sun exercised control through a Central Executive Committee elected by a party Congress. For the first time the party was now able to function as a disciplined unit from headquarters to the smallest subdivision. At the same time a new army was being organized with the help of Russian arms and officers led by General Vasili Blücher. In May 1924, the Whampoa Military Academy was established in Canton to train officers. Officially, its director was Chiang Kai-shek, Sun's chief of staff, who had just returned from a period of study at the Red Army Academy in Moscow, but its real head was Blücher.

Sun Yat-sen died in 1925, at the very time when the instruments had been forged to fulfill his ambitions. Although he did not live to see the warlords humbled and the country united, he is today recognized, by both the mainland Communists and the Taiwan Nationalists, as one of the creators of modern China. With Dr. Sun's death, Chiang Kai-shek became the leading figure in the Kuomintang. In May 1926 he assumed command of the "Northern Expedition," a campaign to unify China by crushing the warlords in the north. The Kuomintang forces, preceded by propaganda corps that included Chinese Communists, swept everything before them, reaching the Yangtze by October. The capital was moved to Hankow, which was dominated by left-wing and Communist elements, the Chinese Communist party having been organized in 1921.

The military victories precipitated a split within the Kuomintang between the left wing in Hankow and the right wing under General Chiang. Chiang favored nationalism but not social revolution. He had become alarmed by the activities of the leftist propaganda corps that had been operating ahead of his divisions. Working among the peasantry and the city workers, these propagandists whipped up a revolutionary movement against the landed gentry, the urban bourgeoisie, and the Western business interests. Although Chiang had worked closely with his Russian advisers, he was definitely anti-Communist and determined to prevent the leftists from getting control of the Kuomintang.

The showdown between the incompatible forces of the right and left came when Nanking fell on March 24, 1927. As had happened in other cities, worker and student battalions were organized as the Kuomintang army approached. They

waged a general strike and were able to take over control of the city during the interval between the departure of the warlord forces and the arrival of Chiang. The latter was not at all happy to be greeted by a revolutionary committee. With the backing of conservative elements in the Kuomintang and of financial interests in Shanghai, Chiang now carried out a bloody purge of Communists and their leftist allies. Borodin returned to Russia, and Chiang reorganized the Kuomintang so that he was the undisputed head. In June 1928, his armies took Peking, destroying the power of the northern warlords and completing the official unification of the country. The capital of the new China was moved to Nanking.

During the following decade the country made appreciable progress under Chiang's guidance. Railway mileage almost doubled, and that of modern roads quadrupled. Internal tariff barriers were abolished in 1932, and a unified currency was created for the first time. Significant progress was also made in governmental procedures, public health, education, and industrial-

Under Chiang Kai-shek's reform of industry, steel rails help drive a steam train into northwest China for the first time in 1935.

Mao Tse-tung, leading figure of the Chinese Communists, speaking in Shensi Province, northwest China, 1937.

These weaknesses of the Kuomintang regime might have been gradually overcome if it had been given a long period of peace. But it did not have this opportunity because of two mortal enemies, the Communists at home and the Japanese abroad. The Chinese Communist party was organized in Shanghai in July 1921, and in the following years branches appeared in all parts of the country. Many students and intellectuals joined the ranks, attracted by the call for action and the assurances of a classless and equitable society for the future. As we have seen, the Communists first cooperated with Sun Yat-sen and then broke with Chiang Kai-shek in 1927. Most of the Communist leaders were killed off by Chiang, but a number managed to escape to the mountainous interior of south China. One of their leaders was Mao Tse-tung, who now worked out a new revolutionary strategy in defiance of the Communist International in Moscow. He rejected the traditional Marxist doctrine that only the urban proletariat could be depended on to carry through a revolution. From firsthand observation in the countryside he concluded that the poor peasants, who made up 70 percent of the population, were "the vanguard of the revolution. . . . Without the poor peasant there can be no revolution." This was pure heresy in Moscow, but Mao went his way, organizing the peasants and building up a separate army and government in the south.

ization. Equally striking were the government's successes in the diplomatic field. Control of the tariff was regained, some of the territories ceded to foreign nations were recovered, and many of the special privileges wrested by the Western powers were returned. By 1943 extraterritorial rights had been surrendered by all foreign nations.

But there were serious gaps in Chiang's reform program, and these ultimately proved fatal. Badly needed land reform was neglected because the Kuomintang party in the rural areas was dominated by landlords who opposed any change. And Chiang's authoritarian, one-party government prevented the growth of democracy, so that opposition groups could not assert themselves by constitutional means; revolution was the sole alternative. Finally, the Kuomintang failed to develop ideas that could attract the support of the people. Nationalist appeals had little attraction for land-hungry peasants and poverty-stricken city workers.

Chiang responded by launching five "bandit extermination campaigns," as they were called. The Communists managed to survive, thanks to the support of the peasants who were won over by the Communist policy of dividing large estates without compensation to the owners. The fifth campaign did succeed in dislodging the Communists, who were completely surrounded by the Kuomintang armies. Finally, 90,000 managed to break through, and, of those, less than 7,000 survived a 6,000-mile trek of incredible hardship. During this historic "Long March" of 368 days (October 16, 1934, to October 25, 1935) they fought an average of almost a skirmish a day with Kuomintang forces totaling more than 300,000. Finally, the Communist survivors reached the northwest provinces, where they dug in and established a base. Their land-reform policies again won peasant support, so that they were able to build up their strength to the point where they became serious rivals of the Kuomintang regime in Nanking.

While Chiang was involved in this domestic struggle with the Communists, he was being attacked from the outside by the Japanese. We shall see later (Chapter 42, Section I) that this aggression began with the occupation of Manchuria in 1931 and continued until, by the beginning of World War II, the Japanese were in control of the entire eastern seaboard. The combination of Communist subversion and Japanese aggression culminated in 1949 in Chiang's flight to Taiwan (Formosa), leaving Mao to rule the mainland from his new capital in Peking, or Beijing.

SUGGESTED READINGS

General surveys of the post–World War I colonial uprising are available in the relevant sections of H. Kohn, *The Age of Nationalism: The First Era of Global History* (Harper & Row, 1962); M. Edwardes, *Asia in the European Age, 1498–1955* (Thames & Hudson, 1961); and J. Romein, *The Asian Century* (George Allen & Unwin, 1962).

World War I diplomacy involving the Middle East is analyzed in M. Kent, ed., *The Great Powers and the End of the Ottoman Empire* (George Allen & Unwin, 1984). For Turkey's revival under Kemal, see S. R. Sonyel, *Turkish Diplomacy, 1918–1923: Mustafa Kemal and the Turkish National Movement* (Sage, 1975); and V. D. Volkhan and N. Itkowitz, *The Immortal Ataturk: A Psychobiography* (University of Chicago, 1984).

For the Arab nationalist awakening, see N. Safran, *Egypt in Search of Political Community* (Harvard University, 1961); Z. N. Zeine, *The Struggle for Arab Independence: Western Diplomacy and the Rise and Fall of Feisal's Kingdom in Syria* (Khayat, 1960); A. Hourani, *Arabic Thought in the Liberal Age 1798–1939* (Oxford University, 1962); and S. G. Haim, ed., *Arab Nationalism: An Anthology* (University of California, 1964).

On the outstanding figures in India, there are M. K. Gandhi, *An Autobiography: The Story of My Experiments with Truth* (Beacon Press, 1957); *All Men Are Brothers: Life and Thoughts of Mahatma Gandhi as Told in His Own Words* (UNESCO, 1958); E. Erikson, *Gandhi's Truth* (W. W. Norton, 1970); *Toward Freedom: The Autobiography of Jawaharlal Nehru* (Harper & Row, 1941); M. Brecher, *Nehru: A Political Biography* (Oxford University, 1959); and for the Moslem side, the biography *Jinnah* by H. Bolitho (J. Murray, 1954). An acute analysis of the British position is given by G. Wint, *The British in India,* 2nd ed. (Faber & Faber, 1955).

On the outstanding figures in China, there is H. Z. Schiffrin, *Sun Yat-Sen and the Origins of the 1911 Revolution* (University of California, 1969); E. Hahn, *Chiang Kai-shek: An Unauthorized Biography* (Doubleday, 1955); and M. Meisner, *Mao's China* (Free Press, 1977). The most useful works on the interwar period are by L. Bianco, *Origins of the Chinese Revolution 1915–1949* (Stanford University, 1971); H. R. Isaacs, *The Tragedy of the Chinese Revolution,* 2nd rev. ed. (Atheneum, 1968); and J. E. Sheridan, *China in Disintegration: The Republican Era in Chinese History, 1912–1949* (Free Press, 1975).

39 Revolution and Settlement in Europe to 1929

The failure to strangle Bolshevism at its birth and to bring Russia, then prostrate, by one means or another, into the general democratic system, lies heavy upon us today.

Winston Churchill
April 1, 1949

At the same time that the colonial world was in the throes of national revolution, Europe itself was seething with social revolution. All over the Continent the old order was being questioned, partly because of the trauma of the world war, and partly because of the impact of the Russian Revolution. Thus, European history during the decade to 1929 was largely a history of struggle between revolutionary and counterrevolutionary forces. In Russia, communism emerged triumphant after years of civil war and intervention. In central Europe the revolutionary forces were crushed and a variety of non-Communist regimes appeared, ranging from the liberal Weimar Republic in Germany to the rightist Horthy government in Hungary and to the fascist Mussolini state in Italy. Western Europe was spared such violent upheavals, but even here, the authority of traditional parliamentary institutions was being strained by economic difficulties, mass unemployment, and cabinet instability. By the late 1920s, some measure of order seemed to be returning to Europe. Prosperity was growing, unemployment was on the decline, and various international issues appeared to be resolved by the Dawes Plan, the Locarno Pacts, the Kellogg-Briand Pact, and the commitment of the Soviet Union to Five-Year Plans rather than to world revolution. Europe was returning to a normal state, or so it seemed, until the Great Depression precipitated the series of domestic and international crises that were to culminate in World War II.

I. COMMUNISM TRIUMPHS IN RUSSIA

By signing the harsh Brest-Litovsk Treaty on March 3, 1918 (see Chapter 37, Section IV), the Bolsheviks hoped that at last they would be able to turn from war to the more congenial task of building a new social order. Instead, they were destined to fight for three more years against counterrevolution and foreign intervention. The counterrevolution was in part the work of members of the propertied classes—army officers, government officials, landowners, and businessmen—who, for obvious reasons, wished to be rid of the Bolsheviks. Equally ardent in their counterrevolutionary activities, however, were the various elements of the non-Bolshevik Left. Of these the Socialist Revolutionaries were by far the most numerous. They agreed with the Bolsheviks on the need for social revolution, but they bitterly resented the fact that the Bolsheviks had monopolized the revolution when it finally came. They regarded the Bolshevik coup of November 7, 1917, as a gross betrayal, particularly because the Constituent Assembly elected on November 25, 1917, included only 175 Bolsheviks as opposed to 370 Socialist Revolutionaries and 159 other assorted representatives. Accordingly, the non-Bolshevik Left took the lead in organizing an underground opposition, while the elements of the right led armed forces in open revolt, beginning in the Cossack territories.

These anti-Bolshevik groups were encouraged and assisted by the Western powers, who were motivated by various considerations such as the strident Bolshevik campaign for world revolution. Both in Europe and in the colonial regions the Bolsheviks called on the "toiling masses" to "convert imperialist war into a class war." Many Western leaders naturally responded by seeking to crush these Marxist firebrands before they could ignite the smoldering tinder of revolution scattered throughout the world. Also, there was the problem of Allied war materials that had been accumulated in Russia in huge quantities—over 160,000 tons in Murmansk and 800,000 tons in Vladivostok. The Western powers were worried that the Bolsheviks, willingly or unwillingly, might allow these supplies to fall into German hands. And there were economic motives behind the Allied intervention: Bolshevik nationalization of foreign properties and refusal to pay foreign debts naturally alienated powerful vested interests, and these interests used their influence to help the forces of intervention and counterrevolution.

Under these circumstances several counterrevolutionary governments were set up all along the borders of Russia soon after the signing of the Brest-Litovsk Treaty—in the northern Archangel-Murmansk region, the Baltic provinces, the Ukraine, the Don territories, Transcaucasia, and Siberia. The Western powers provided these governments generously with funds and war materials, as well as with military advisers and small detachments of troops on certain fronts. At first the Bolsheviks suffered one reverse after another, simply because the old Russian army had disintegrated, and there was nothing else to take its place. The commissar for defense, Leon Trotsky, gradually built up a new Red Army, which numbered about 500,000 men by the end of 1918. At times this force had to fight on two dozen different fronts, as revolts broke out in all parts of the country and Allied forces landed in coastal areas. (See map of Russia in Revolution, 1917–1921, p. 579.)

The chief opponents of the Bolsheviks in 1919 were Admiral Kolchak in Siberia, General Denikin in the Crimea and the Ukraine, and General Yudenich in Estonia. A common pattern is evident in their campaigns. Beginning with sudden attacks from their bases, they gained easy initial victories; came within reach of full victory; then were stopped, gradually pushed back, and finally routed. In March 1919 Kolchak captured the city of Ufa to the west of the Urals; in August Denikin had advanced north to Kiev, and by October Yudenich had penetrated to the very suburbs of Petrograd. Lenin's regime now was limited to the Petrograd-Moscow regions, an area about equal to the fifteenth-century Muscovite principality. However, by the end of 1919 the tides had turned: Denikin had been driven back to the Crimea, Yudenich to the Baltic, and Kolchak not only was forced back over the Urals but also was captured and shot.

It appeared early in 1920 that the ordeal was finally over. But another full year of fighting lay ahead, owing to the appearance of the Poles and renewed large-scale intervention by the French. The Poles, determined to extend their frontiers as far eastward as possible, took advantage of the confusion and exhaustion to invade the Ukraine in April 1920. The pattern of the previous year's operations was now repeated. The Poles advanced rapidly and took Kiev on May 7, but five weeks later they were driven out of the city, and by mid-July were back in their own territory. The triumphant Bolsheviks pressed on, reaching the outskirts of Warsaw on August 14. But the Poles, strongly supported by the French, stopped the advancing Russians and managed to push them back. The campaign ended in mid-October, and on March 18, 1921, the Treaty of Riga defined the Polish-Russian frontier that prevailed until World War II.

Meanwhile, General Wrangel, who had replaced Denikin, had overrun much of southern Russia with the generous assistance of the French. But after the Bolsheviks were through with the Poles, they turned their forces against Wrangel, driving him south to the Crimea. This peninsula, once the playground of tsars and grand dukes, was now crowded with a motley host of refugees—high ecclesiastics, tsarist officials, aristocratic landowners, and the remnants of White

armies. As many as possible were evacuated in French warships and scattered in ports from Constantinople to Marseilles; the remainder were left to the mercy of the victorious Red Army.

The only foreign troops now left on Russian soil were the Japanese operating from Vladivostok. Originally there had been American and British as well as Japanese contingents in eastern Siberia, but the first two were withdrawn in 1920. The Japanese stayed on, hoping to keep control of these vast but sparsely populated regions through a puppet regime. The United States repeatedly brought diplomatic pressure on the Japanese to leave and finally persuaded them to do so at the Washington Naval Disarmament Conference in 1922.

With the departure of the Japanese, the tragic period of civil war and intervention mercifully came to a close. Lenin's Communist party was now in control of the entire country. One reason for this unexpected outcome was Allied disunity and vacillation. Aside from certain passionately dedicated anti-Bolsheviks who occupied subordinate posts, the Allied leaders regarded the intervention as little more than a sideshow, and they supported it fitfully with varied and conflicting motives. Another

Washington Naval Diarmament Conference, 1922—(left to right) L. Gonyo, Japanese Secretary of Foreign Affairs; S, Yada, Japanese Defense Consul; U.S. Secretary of State Hughes; General K. Tanaka; Vice-Admiral Kato; and assistant to Kato, E. R. Schipp.

reason for the triumph of the Bolsheviks was the disunity among the Whites, who were bitterly divided by conflicting ambitions of individual leaders and by the basic incompatibility of the leftist Socialist Revolutionaries and the assorted right-wing elements. The Communists, by contrast, enjoyed certain advantages that proved decisive in the end. Their monolithic party organization imposed a cohesion and discipline that was unmatched on the other side. The Communist party was effectively supported by an efficient secret-police organization, the Cheka, that ruthlessly ferreted out opposition groups. The commissar of war, Leon Trotsky, skillfully combined the enthusiasm of proletarian volunteers with the indispensable technical knowledge of former tsarist officers to forge a formidable new Red Army. Furthermore, this army enjoyed the substantial advantage of having internal lines of communication, in contrast to the tremendous distances separating the White forces from each other and from their sources of supplies in western Europe and the United States. Finally, the Bolsheviks were generally more successful in winning the support of the peasant masses. This does not mean that the Russian peasants were won over to Marxist ideology; indeed, most of them were fed up with both the Reds and the Whites and would rather have been left alone. But when forced to make a choice, they more frequently decided in favor of the Reds, who, they thought, would allow them to keep the plots they seized from the landlords.

In retrospect, the protracted civil war and intervention was a disaster for all parties concerned. It left the Russian countryside devastated from the Baltic to the Pacific and the Russian people decimated by casualties, starvation, and disease. Equally serious was the poisoning of relations between the new Soviet state and the Western world. The Soviet leaders were confirmed in their Marxist fears of "capitalist encirclement," and Western statesmen took all too seriously the futile manifestos of Communist International established in 1919. So deep and lasting was this mutual distrust that it poisoned international relations during the following decade and contributed significantly to the coming of World War II.

II. COMMUNISM FAILS IN CENTRAL EUROPE

Weimar Republic in Germany

While civil war was raging in Russia, the crucial question for Europe was whether communism would spread westward. Lenin and his fellow Bolsheviks assumed that if this did not occur, their cause would be doomed. In line with Marxist ideology, they could not conceive that their revolution might survive and take root in a single country, least of all in predominantly agrarian Russia. Accordingly, they followed closely and hopefully the course of events in central Europe—especially Germany, which was clearly the key country. If it went communist, the combination of German industrial strength and Russian natural resources would be unbeatable, and the future of the revolution would be assured.

At first it appeared that these Bolshevik hopes might be realized. The kaiser was forced to abdicate on November 9, 1918, following a mutiny in the navy and the spread of revolution from the Baltic ports into the interior (see Chapter 37, Section VI). Workers' and Soldiers' Councils, similar to the Russian soviets, appeared in all the major cities, including Berlin. So strong was the revolutionary movement that it seemed possible that communism would engulf the Continent, at least to the Rhine. The final outcome, however, was not a Soviet Germany but the bourgeois Weimar Republic.

Several factors that escaped attention at the time explain this fateful outcome. One was the prosperity of prewar Germany, which left the working class relatively contented and in no mood for revolution. It is true that the German Social Democratic party in 1914 was the strongest party in Europe, but it was conservative, committed to social reform rather than to revolution. Equally important was the prosperity of the German peasants, so that the Bolshevik slogan "Land to the Peasants," which had been so effective in Russia, made very little impact on Germany. Also, the war had already ended at the time of the German revolution, again in contrast to the situation in Russia. The demand for peace, which probably helped the Bolsheviks more than

PEASANTS AND BOLSHEVIKS

*C. R. Buxton, secretary to the British Labour party, visited Russia in June 1920. His report on the attitude of the Russian peasants explains why the Bolsheviks won, even though they were a small minority of the total population.**

My host's name was Alexander Petrovich Emilianov. He was of the "middle" type of peasant, which formed the great majority of the village. About one-fifth of its people were considered "poor" peasants. Of "rich" peasants there were only four or five, I was told. . . .

Before the Revolution my host had had eight acres—about the average holding in that region. He had now no less than eighty-five. This was the tremendous fact that I had turned over and over in my mind as we bumped along. Tremendous, surely; for my host's case was a type, not only of thousands, but of millions of others. . . .

"Look there," said Emilianov, pointing out from the edge of the village field over the limitless rolling steppe. "All that was the land of the landlords (barin)." . . .

"Who owned all this land?" I asked.

"All sorts of landlords. One was a Cossack. Two were Samara merchants. One was a German, Schmidt, who bought his from the Crown. Some was held by the Monks. One was an estate of Maria Feodorovna, the Tsaritsa."

"What has happened to them?"

"They are mostly gone," he replied in a matter-of-fact tone. "Some are in Samara. Most of them have left Russia, I suppose." . . .

"And what do the peasants think of it all now?" I asked Emilianov.

"It's a fine thing, the Revolution. Every one is in favour of it. They don't like the Communist Party, but they like the Revolution."

"Why don't they like the Communist Party?"

"Because they are always worrying us. They are people from the towns and don't understand the country. Commissars—powerful persons—are continually coming. We don't know what to do with them. New orders (prikazi) are always coming out. People are puzzled. As soon as you understand one of them, a different one comes along."

"What party do most people belong to here?"

"None at all. They are non-party (bezpartini)." . . .

The general attitude of the peasants, so far as I could judge, was that they owed much to the Soviet Government in the matter of the land; they approved of the "principle of everybody being equal"; they often talked of the "true" Communist as being an ideal sort of person. But they complained bitterly of the absence of necessities, of the compulsory contributions, and the worry of perpetual orders and appeals, often hard to understand. They considered that the Government was responsible for all these evils alike, and that the present was somehow in a position of inferiority to the townsman.

And yet, in spite of all these complaints, when the opportunity was offered them to choose between Kolchak on the one side and the Soviet Government on the other, the peasants do not seem to have had much hesitation. . . .

They were for the Revolution; and for the moment the Soviet power was the embodiment of the Revolution. They grumbled and cursed at it; but when the opportunity was offered to overthrow it, they said "No."

* C. R. Buxton, *In a Russian Village* (Labour Publishing Co., 1922), pp. 14–15, 19, 21, 26–27, 47–48.

anything else, was irrelevant in Germany. Furthermore, although the German army was defeated, it was far from being as demoralized and mutinous as the Russian army of 1917. The opponents of revolution in Germany were able to call on reliable military forces when the showdown came.

A final factor of major significance was the split in the ranks of the German socialists. This, of course, was not unique. All the European socialist parties had splintered to a greater or lesser extent in 1914 over the question of whether to support or oppose the war. In Germany, the Majority Social Democrats, led by Friedrich Ebert and Philipp Scheidemann, had supported the German war effort from the beginning. They were relatively conservative, and so they now strenuously opposed the revolutionary Workers' and Soldiers' Councils. "I hate the social revolution," Ebert declared candidly, "I hate it like sin." At the other end of the spectrum was the Spartacist League, the counterpart of Lenin's Bolsheviks, led by Karl Liebknecht, of a well-known German socialist family, and Rosa Luxemburg, of Polish-Jewish origin. The Spartacists, as might be expected, supported the Workers' and Soldiers' Councils and wished to establish a Soviet-type regime in Germany. Between the Majority Socialists and the Spartacists was the Independent Socialist party; it also favored a Soviet Germany but in addition wished to cooperate with the Majority Socialists.

When Prince Max announced the abdication of the kaiser, he himself resigned the chancellorship and handed the government over to Friedrich Ebert. The latter formed a cabinet, or council, of "Six Commissars," composed of three Majority Social Democrats and three Independent Socialists. The Spartacists chose to remain outside for the simple reason that they were interested only in forcing the revolution further to the left. Philipp Scheidemann had proclaimed the establishment of the German Republic from the balcony of the parliament building, but Liebknecht at the same time had proclaimed a Soviet Germany from the balcony of the Imperial Palace a mile away. The great question now was which side would win.

The situation was comparable to that in Russia when the Provisional Government was established in March 1917. Ebert was very much aware of the outcome in that country and had no desire to be another Kerensky. Accordingly, on November 10, the day after the kaiser's abdication, he formed a secret alliance with General Wilhelm Groener, chief of the General Staff, for the suppression of the Spartacists and the Workers' and Soldiers' Councils. Every night between 11:00 P.M. and 1:00 A.M., the two men talked on a special telephone linking the chancellory at Berlin and headquarters at Spa. With this powerful support, Ebert moved aggressively against the extreme left. The Independent Social Democrats refused to go along and resigned from the cabinet, but this made little difference. On December 30, the Spartacists renamed themselves the Communist Labor party of Germany and made plans for revolt, but before these were completed, Karl Liebknecht and Rosa Luxemburg were arrested and shot "while trying to escape." Over a thousand of their followers were killed during the ruthless street fighting that followed. By mid-January 1919, the danger from the left was over.

The critical turning point had been passed, and on January 19, 1919, elections were held throughout Germany for a National Assembly rather than for a Congress of Soviets. The delegates elected were overwhelmingly of the moderate left. The National Assembly met in Weimar, partly to escape the disorders of Berlin and partly to associate with the new Germany in world public opinion with peaceful cultural symbols such as Goethe and Schiller. Ebert was elected the first president of the Republic, and Scheidemann the first chancellor.

The constitution adopted in July 1919 was unimpeachably democratic. Its provisions included universal suffrage; proportional representation; a bill of rights; and separation of church, state, and school. But behind this new constitutional façade, much of the old Germany remained unchanged. The bureaucracy, the judiciary, and the police survived intact. In the universities, the most undemocratic and anti-Semitic faculties and fraternities continued untouched on the grounds of academic freedom. The new *Reichswehr* was the old imperial army in miniature. Except for the legal eight-hour day, virtually no social reforms were introduced. The industrial cartels and monopolies continued as before; the Junkers of East Prussia retained their landed estates, as did the kaiser and the various local rulers. In short, the German revolution had preserved more than it had changed. Power was left largely in the hands of the old ruling elements, which never accepted the new order. At first the Weimar Republic did succeed in stabilizing itself with foreign financial aid. But when the Great Depression undermined the foundations of the state, most of these unreconciled bureaucrats, army officers, and landed gentry turned on the Republic and helped in its destruction.

Revolution and Reaction in Central Europe

The suppression of the Spartacists and the establishment of the Weimar Republic ensured that the rest of central Europe would not go communist. Nevertheless, for a number of years this part of Europe seethed with unrest and revolt. The peasant masses between the Baltic and the Aegean were politically awake and active to an unprecedented degree. One reason for the unrest was that millions of peasant army recruits had widened their horizons immeasurably as a result of their war experiences. They had observed not only the differences between city and village life but also the differences in living standards and social institutions among various countries. The peasants were also profoundly affected by the overthrow of the Hapsburg, Hohenzollern, and Romanoff dynasties. In the light of centuries-old traditions, this was a shock that aroused nationalist aspirations and class consciousness. Finally, the unprecedented destruction and suffering that took place during the long years of war aggravated the revolutionary situation, especially in the countries that had suffered defeat.

The precise manifestation of this revolutionary ferment varied from country to country according to local circumstances. The Communist parties did not play an outstanding role except in the case of Hungary, where in March 1919 a Soviet republic was established under the leadership of Bela Kun. It lasted less than a year because of the hostility of the peasants and the invasion of the country by Rumanian troops. When the Rumanians departed in February 1920, a right-wing government headed by Admiral Mik-

lós Horthy was established with Allied support. Horthy remained in power for the whole interwar period, during which time Hungary was unique in central Europe for the almost complete absence of agrarian or other reforms.

In most of the other central European countries, agrarian or peasant parties were giving voice to popular discontent. The following peasant leaders assumed office in the postwar years: Aleksandr Stamboliski in Bulgaria in 1919, Stefan Radich in Yugoslavia in 1925, Wincenty Witos in Poland in 1926, and Iuliu Maniu in Rumania in 1928. Owing to their pacifism and distaste for violence, however, none of them was able to retain power for long. They were vulnerable to the entrenched military and bureaucratic elements that did not hesitate to seize power by force when their interests were threatened. Another reason for their failure was the increasing control that lawyers and urban intellectuals gained over the peasant parties. Under this leadership, the parties usually represented the interests of the wealthy peasants and had little contact with the great mass of poor peasants.

One after another the peasant leaders were ousted from office. Stamboliski was assassinated in 1923, and a dictatorship was established by King Boris. Radich was assassinated in 1928, and the following year King Alexander set up his dictatorship. In Poland, Witos lasted only a few days before he was removed by General Joseph Pilsudski, who dominated the country until his death in 1935. Maniu was eased out of office in 1930 by King Carol II, who made and unmade governments until forced to flee Rumania a decade later.

The same pattern prevailed in Austria and Greece where, for various reasons, agrarian parties never took hold. Yet Austria ended up with an authoritarian government under Chancellor Dollfuss in 1934, and Greece with an avowedly fascist regime under General Metaxas in 1936. Thus, by World War II, the whole of central Europe was under dictatorial rule, with one exception—Czechoslovakia. This country possessed certain advantages that explain its uniqueness: a high level of literacy, a trained bureaucracy inherited from the Hapsburgs, the capable leadership of Jan Masaryk and Eduard Benes, and a balanced economy that provided higher living standards and greater security than was possible in the predominantly agrarian countries to the east.

III.   ITALY GOES FASCIST

While bolshevism, agrarianism, and traditional parliamentarianism battled for primacy in eastern and central Europe, an entirely new "ism" was coming to the fore in Italy—fascism, the outstanding political innovation in Europe in the postwar years. Bolshevism had a history going back at least to the Communist Manifesto of 1848, and agrarianism was taking political form with the appearance of peasant parties at the turn of the century. Fascism, by contrast, appeared unexpectedly and dramatically with Mussolini's march on Rome in October 1922.

Postwar conditions in Italy provided fertile soil for a violent, melodramatic, and antiintellectual movement such as fascism. The Italy of 1919 had behind it only two generations of national independence and unity. Parliamentary government was, in practice, a morass of corruption in which party "bosses" manipulated short-lived coalition blocs. This unstable political structure was further weakened in the postwar years by serious economic dislocation. Many of the demobilized millions were unable to find jobs. Foreign trade and tourist traffic were declining in the aftermath of war. Emigration, which for decades had served as a safety valve and a source of overseas remittances, now petered out because of restrictive legislation in the United States and other countries. The popular unrest caused by this economic stress was aggravated by the slighting of Italian claims at the Paris peace conference. The resulting frustration and injured pride produced an inflammable situation.

Ready to exploit this situation was Benito Mussolini, the son of a Socialist blacksmith. He first attracted attention during the Tripolitan War of 1911 by his inflammatory speeches in which he referred to the Italian flag as "a rag fit only to be planted on a dung heap." The following year he became editor of the official Socialist paper, *Avanti!* When World War I began in August 1914, he was still a revolutionary and a pacifist, but the following month his great transformation took place, helped along by funds from the French government, which was anxious to secure Italy as an ally. Mussolini was able to start his own newspaper, *Il Popolo d'Italia,* in which he conducted a passionate interventionist campaign.

Premier Benito Mussolini of Italy, 1939.

Called to battle in September 1915, Mussolini fought in the trenches for a few weeks until he was wounded and invalided out of the army. He languished in obscurity until 1919, when he formed his first "combat troops," and organized the Fascist party. Unity and authority were his watchwords against the political anarchy and social strife of the period. At the outset he attracted the support of only a handful of frustrated students and demobilized soldiers. But in the early 1920s he forged rapidly ahead, partly because the passivity of the Socialists had created a vacuum that Mussolini promptly filled. Equally important was the substantial support that Mussolini was now receiving from industrialists, landowners, and other members of the propertied classes. Terrified by the widespread seizure of factories and estates, they now looked hopefully to the Fascist squadristi, or armed bands, as a bulwark against the dreaded social revolution. The government and the wealthy elements of society not only tolerated squadristi violence and terrorism but even secretly gave it their aid and support.

In the fall of 1922, Mussolini prepared for a coup by winning over both the monarchy and the Church with specific assurance that their interests would be respected. Since the regular army and the police already had shown their benevolent neutrality, Mussolini proceeded with assurance to mobilize his Blackshirts for a widely publicized march on Rome. Prime Minister Luigi Facta asked King Victor Emmanuel to proclaim martial law, but the king refused and instead called on Mussolini to form a government. Thus only a token march on Rome by the Blackshirts was necessary, and Mussolini arrived anticlimactically in Rome on October 27 in a sleeping-car.

Mussolini had become premier by technically constitutional methods, but it soon became apparent that he had no intention of respecting constitutional procedures. His party had won 35 seats in the 1921 elections, but these comprised only 6 percent of the total number. Parliament and the king gave Mussolini dictatorial powers until December 31, 1923, to restore order and introduce reforms. During this period he allowed a degree of liberty to the press, to the trade unions, and to the parliamentary parties. But at the same time he was gaining control of the state machinery by appointing prefects and judges of Fascist sympathies and organizing a voluntary Fascist militia.

The showdown came with the elections of April 6, 1924. Through liberal use of the squadristi, the Fascist party polled 65 percent of the votes and won 375 seats, compared to the 35 they had previously held. Two months later Mussolini faced a major crisis with the murder of a prominent Socialist deputy, Giacomo Matteoti. It was widely suspected, and later proven, that Matteoti had been killed on orders from Mussolini himself. Thanks to the indecisiveness of the opposition and the unwavering support of the king, Mussolini weathered the storm and, by the fall of 1926, felt strong enough to take the offensive. He disbanded the old political parties, tightened censorship of the press, and established an organization of secret police. Italy had become a one-party state, with the Chamber functioning as a rubber-stamp body for passing Fascist bills.

The new Fascist regime gradually evolved certain distinctive features. One was the corporative state in which deputies were elected as representatives not of geographical constituencies but rather of trades and professions. Theoretically it eliminated class conflict by bringing capital and labor together under the benevolent auspices of the state. Actually, only capital enjoyed true self-government, and labor was denied the right to strike or to select its own leaders. Neither the position of the workers nor that of the peasants was basically improved under the corporative state.

Another feature of Mussolini's Italy was the elaborate public works program designed to provide employment and to erect impressive structures for the glorification of fascism. Monuments of the past were restored, and many cities were adorned with large new buildings, workers' tenements, and stadiums. Certain marshlands were drained and made available for cultivation. Tourists were particularly impressed by the trains that "ran on time" and by the extensive new highways, or autostrade.

IV.   PROBLEMS OF DEMOCRACY IN WESTERN EUROPE

In western Europe there were no upheavals comparable to the civil war in Russia or to the bitter clash between right and left in central Europe. Democratic institutions had deeper roots in the West, and the prevailing social structures were healthier and enjoyed more popular support. In addition, the Western powers had been the victors rather than the losers in the war, a fact that further contributed to political and social stability. It does not follow, however, that western Europe had no difficulties in the postwar years. There were many problems. The most serious were economic in nature, though with far-reaching social and political repercussions. The experiences of the two leading Western countries, Great Britain and France, illustrate this point.

The chief problem in Britain was, by all odds, the severe and chronic unemployment. There was a short-lived boom immediately after the war when factories operated overtime to meet long-pent-up consumer demands. But the bust came in 1920, and by March 1921, over 2 million people were out of work. Unemployment persisted through the 1920s, and the situation grew worse in the 1930s. Thus the Depression actually began in Britain in 1920 rather than in 1929, and continued without interruption to World War II.

These economic difficulties stemmed in part from World War I which, by stimulating the industrialization of such countries as the United States, Japan, and the British dominions, reduced the overseas markets of British manufactures. The destruction of much of Britain's merchant marine also caused the invisible revenues to be reduced, as did the fact that Britain was no longer the world's financial center. The Bolshevik Revolution further hurt the British economy, wiping out an important market for manufactured goods as well as substantial investments. Finally, there was the failure of the British themselves to keep up with the rest of the world in industrial efficiency. Initially, they had led the world in the industrial revolution, but now they lagged behind in modernizing their equipment. Because they tended to keep machines until they were worn out rather than until they had become obsolete, productivity per man-hour lagged in comparison with other countries. For example, taking the year 1913 as 100, the output per man-shift in British mines rose by 1938 to a mere 113, compared to 164 in the German mines, and 201 in the Dutch.

This combination of circumstances was responsible for the almost unrelieved depression that gripped Britain during the interwar period. Millions of families subsisted on state relief, or the "dole" as it was popularly called. A whole generation grew up without an opportunity to work. Such a situation was as unhealthy psychologically as it was economically. Eventually the unemployed became demoralized, depending on the dole without hope for the future.

These conditions inevitably caused political repercussions. Most important was the decline of the Liberal party as the workers turned increasingly to the Labour party in the hope of finding relief. Thus the economic crisis tended to polarize British politics, with the propertied classes generally voting Conservative, the workers supporting Labour, and the middle class fluctuating between the two. Each party had its panacea for the country's ills: The Conservatives called for protection; the declining Liberals, for free trade; and Labour, for a capital levy and for the nationalization of heavy industry. The net result was a succession of alternating Conservative and Labour ministries under Stanley Baldwin and Ramsay MacDonald, respectively. None was able to improve significantly the national fortunes. In the May 1929 elections the Labourites won a plurality of the seats, and MacDonald formed his second government with the backing of the Liberals. He could not have known that within half a year the country would be hit by the Great Depression that was to cripple Britain's economy still more, ultimately sweeping away MacDonald's new administration.

France, too, was plagued by economic difficulties in the postwar years, although in certain respects it was better off than most of its neighbors. France had a well-balanced economy, so that it was not as vulnerable as the predominantly agrarian or industrial countries. The peace settlement strengthened its economy by adding the Saar Basin, with its coal mines, and the Alsace-Lorraine region, with its textile industry and rich potash and iron-ore deposits. Conversely, France had been weakened by the loss of 1.4 million men in the prime of life and by unprecedented destruction of property. The war on the western front had been waged mostly on French soil, causing $23 billion worth of damage to villages, towns, factories, mines, and railways. Also, France had financed the war by loans rather than taxes, which led to the depreciation of the franc after the war.

In contrast to Britain's two or three major parties, France had five or six, so that a government's life depended on its ability to organize a bloc of these parties to secure majority support. This explains the relatively rapid turnover of governments in France compared to that in Britain. The leading parties, from left to right, were the Communists and Socialists, who represented mostly urban and rural workers; the Radical Socialists, who were in the center and were supported by the lower-middle class; and various parties on the right, such as the Republican Democratic Union and the Democratic Alliance, which were usually strongly Catholic and represented big business and high finance.

For five years after the end of the war, France was ruled by National Bloc ministries based mostly on the parties of the right. The dominant personality during this period was Raymond Poincaré, who was determined to make the Germans pay the costs of reconstruction. His policy culminated in the French occupation of the Ruhr in 1923, an expensive operation that yielded little revenue. By early 1924 the franc had fallen from its prewar value of 19.3 cents to little more than 3 cents. The French public was alienated by this financial instability and by the Ruhr adventure, which aroused fears of renewed warfare. Accordingly, the May 1924 elections returned a majority for the Cartel des Gauches, or Left Bloc. Edouard Herriot, leader of the Radical Socialists, became premier with the support of the Socialists. In foreign affairs, he ended the Ruhr occupation, agreed to a settlement of the reparations issue, and recognized the Soviet Union. But the financial dilemma remained unsolved, and on this matter the laissez-faire Radicals and the quasi-Marxist Socialists were unable to reach agreement. The Socialists demanded a capital levy, Herriot was opposed, and his government fell in April 1925. The franc immediately decreased in value; by the following year it was worth only two cents—one-tenth of its prewar value.

France now turned once more to the right. In July 1926 Poincaré formed a National Union ministry of all parties except the Socialist and Communist. Poincaré adopted orthodox but stringent measures to reduce expenditures and increase revenues. By the end of 1926, the franc stood at four cents and was stabilized at that level. Since this was only one-fifth of its prewar value, the government had relieved itself of four-fifths of its debts, though this was achieved at the expense of French bondholders. The devaluation attracted many tourists, especially the Americans, and also facilitated the exportation of French goods. Poincaré's success enabled him to remain premier for three years, an interwar record. He retired in the summer of 1929, just in time to escape the economic cyclone that was to destroy the precarious stability he had achieved.

V. STABILIZATION AND SETTLEMENT IN EUROPE

The period from 1924 to 1929 was one of peace and settlement in Europe. The negotiation in 1924 of the Dawes Plan, an agreement concerning reparations payments, was the first phase of this process of stabilization. Germany had been required by the Versailles Treaty to accept responsibility for the war and to promise to make payments for the losses sustained. No agreement was reached at Versailles concerning the amount and the schedule of payments. The Reparations Commission, a body that had been appointed to work out the details, decided in 1920 that the payments from Germany should be divided as follows: 52 percent to France, 22 percent to Britain, 10 percent to Italy, 8 percent to Belgium, and the remaining 8 percent to the other Allied powers. The following year the commission set the total German indemnity at $32 billion, to be paid both in cash and in kind (coal, locomotives, textile machinery, and other products of German factories and mines).

Some payments were made in 1921 and 1922, but at the same time Germany was undergoing a disastrous inflation. The mark, worth twenty-five cents in 1914, had fallen to two cents by July 1922, and a year later it was worthless—two and one-half trillion to the dollar. The Germans requested a two-year moratorium on payments. The French, convinced that the Germans could pay if they wished to, occupied the Ruhr industrial region in January 1923. The Germans responded with a general strike, so that the French were forced to spend more on the occupation than they got out of it. With the German economy prostrate and the French stymied, the reparations issue was deadlocked.

A commission of economic experts, headed by an American banker, Charles Dawes, was called in. On September 1, 1924, the so-called Dawes Plan was approved by both sides and went into effect. The plan called for annual payments beginning at $238 million and reaching a maximum of $595 million. These amounts were adjustable depending on the index of prosperity for a given year. In return, Germany was to receive a foreign loan of $200 million, and France was required to evacuate the Ruhr. This arrangement, like so many others, was to be swept away with the onslaught of the Great Depression. Even during the four years that it operated, to September 1928, the Germans paid in cash and in kind only about half of what they borrowed from foreign markets, mostly American. Nevertheless, the Dawes Plan did ease tensions in Europe and prepare the way for the settlement of political issues.

European diplomacy in the years immediately following the war was dominated by France and its allies in central and eastern Europe. Owing to the disappearance of Austria-Hungary and the prostration of Germany and Russia, France was now the first power on the Continent. Because sooner or later both Germany and Russia would obviously seek to reassert themselves, the aim of French diplomacy was to organize some dependable and lasting basis for national security.

Theoretically, the League of Nations provided general security with Article 10 of the Covenant, which required member states "to respect and preserve against external aggression the territorial integrity and existing political independence of all members of the League." The difficulty was that the league lacked the power necessary to enforce this article. It possessed no weapons and no armed force. Having experienced two German invasions in fewer than fifty years, France refused to entrust its security to a league without authority. France turned to the smaller European states that shared its interest in supporting the peace settlement and opposing treaty revision. It negotiated a formal military alliance with Belgium in September 1920, with Poland in 1921, and with Czechoslovakia in 1924. Czechoslovakia had already organized the so-called "Little Entente" with Rumania and Yugoslavia in 1920–1921 for the purpose of providing mutual aid in case of either an attack by Hungary or the restoration of the Hapsburg dynasty. Poland was attached to the Little Entente in 1921 through an alliance with Rumania in which the two guaranteed reciprocal help in the event of attack by Russia. France's relationship with the Little Entente enabled it, then, to extend its own alliance system to include Rumania in 1926 and Yugoslavia in 1927.

This alliance system was basically anti-German, its primary purpose being to protect France and its allies by isolating Germany. About 1925, however, Franco-German relations improved, thanks to the temporarily successful operation of the Dawes Plan, and also to the foreign ministers of the two countries, Aristide Briand of France and Gustav Stresemann of Germany. The two foreign ministers decided that the security of their respective countries could be enhanced by direct negotiations and agreements. They were encouraged by British Foreign Minister Sir Austen Chamberlain, who also brought the Italians around to this view. The outcome was a series of agreements known as the Locarno Pacts, signed in October 1925.

These provided that Germany should enter the League of Nations and become a permanent Council member. In return, Germany agreed not to seek treaty revision by force and to settle peacefully every dispute with France, Belgium, Czechoslovakia, and Poland. Germany did reserve the right to seek modifications of its eastern frontiers by peaceful means, but it recognized the permanence of its western frontiers. Germany, France, and Belgium undertook to respect for all time their mutual borders, and Britain and Italy guaranteed observance of this provision.

The Locarno Pacts made a deep impression at the time. Chamberlain expressed the prevailing view when he declared that they marked "the real dividing line between the years of peace and the years of war." Likewise, Briand made eloquent speeches about "the Locarno spirit," which banned war and substituted "conciliation, arbitration, and peace." In the afterglow of this optimism, the American secretary of state, Frank Kellogg, acting on a suggestion of Briand, proposed that nations pledge themselves to renounce war as "an instrument of national policy." The proposal was implemented, and on August 27, 1928, the Kellogg-Briand Pact was signed. Since the pact only involved renunciation of war and made no provision for sanctions, it was quickly signed by over sixty countries. Although it depended exclusively on the moral pressure of world public opinion, the mere fact that so many countries signed contributed to a further lessening of international tension.

Equally promising were the improved relations with Germany. That country was admitted into the League of Nations in 1926 and was made a permanent member of the Council. Also, a further settlement was reached with Germany concerning the payment of reparations. The Dawes Plan had not stipulated the sum total of reparations that Germany should pay, so in 1929, a second commission of economic experts, under the chairmanship of another American financier, Owen Young, met in Paris and prepared a new payment schedule that was adopted early in 1930. The total amount to be paid by Germany was set at $8 billion, and the installment was to be extended over fifty-eight years. In return for Germany's acceptance of the Young Plan, France evacuated the Rhineland in 1930, four years earlier than was required by the Versailles Treaty.

There was a general feeling in the late 1920s that Europe had at last returned to normalcy: Germany and its former enemies appeared to be reconciled: French troops were out of the Rhineland, and the Germans were in the League of Nations; the problem of reparations appeared to be finally resolved; over sixty nations had renounced war "as an instrument of national policy"; prosperity was on the rise, and unemployment was correspondingly declining. Even the news from the Soviet Union was encouraging, for that country had launched in 1928 a novel and grandiose Five-Year Plan (see Chapter 40, Section I). Most authorities in the West regarded the plan as impractical and doomed to failure, but at least it diverted the Russians from international adventures to internal economic development. Thus the "Locarno spirit" appeared to have meaning and substance, and it was assumed that Europe now could settle back to enjoy decades of peace and prosperity as it had in the nineteenth century.

SUGGESTED READINGS

The standard accounts of the civil war and intervention in Russia are the three-volume work by E. H. Carr, *The Bolshevik Revolution, 1917–1923* (Macmillan, 1951–1953); J. Bradley, *Allied Inter-* *vention in Russia 1917–1920* (Basic Books, 1968); G. F. Kennan, *Russia and the West Under Lenin and Stalin* (Little, Brown, 1961); and D. Footman, *Civil War in Russia* (Praeger, 1962). The most recent and critical study of the Russian Revolution and of the subsequent Soviet regime is by R. Pipes, *Russia Under the Bolshevik Regime* (Knopf, 1993).

Several books deal with the critical developments in Germany in 1918 and after, including R. G. L. White, *Vanguard of Nazisms: The Free Corps Movement in Post War Germany, 1918–1923* (Harvard University, 1952); R. Coper, *Failure of a Revolution: Germany in 1918–1919* (Cambridge University, 1955); W. T. Angress, *Stillborn Revolution: The Communist Bid for Power in Germany, 1921–1923* (Princeton University, 1964); A. J. Ryder, *The German Revolution of 1918* (Cambridge University, 1967); and the collection of documents by C. B. Burdick and R. H. Lutz, eds., *The Political Institutions of the German Revolution 1918–19* (Praeger, 1966).

The best surveys of the forces molding central and eastern Europe in these years are by H. Seton-Watson, *Eastern Europe Between the Wars, 1918–1941* (Cambridge University, 1946); and F. L. Carsten, *Revolution in Central Europe 1918–1919* (University of California, 1972). See also L. S. Stavrianos, *The Balkans Since 1453* (Holt, Rinehart & Winston, 1959); and W. E. Moore, *Economic Demography of Eastern and Southern Europe* (League of Nations, 1945).

The standard works on Mussolini and fascism are by C. Seton-Watson, *Italy from Liberation to Fascism 1870–1925* (Methuen, 1967); I. Kirkpatrick, *Mussolini: A Study in Power* (Hawthorne, 1964); E. Wiskemann, *Fascism in Italy: Its Development and Influence* (Macmillan, 1969); M. Gallo, *Mussolini's Italy* (Macmillan, 1973); D. M. Smith, *Mussolini's Roman Empire* (Viking, 1976); and E. R. Tannenbaum, *The Fascist Experience: Italian Society and Culture, 1922–1945* (Basic Books, 1972).

Various aspects of Britain's development are analyzed in the general but meticulous survey by C. L. Mowat, *Britain Between the Wars, 1918–1940* (University of Chicago, 1955); and in the lively account by A. J. P. Taylor, *English History 1914–1945* (Oxford University, 1965). See also the excellent bibliographical guide by H. R. Winkler, *Great Britain in the Twentieth Century,* No. 28 (Service Center for Teachers of History, 1960). On France, see the detailed presentation by D. W. Brogan, *France Under the Republic, 1870–1939* (Harper & Row, 1940); the more lucid account by D. Thompson, *Democracy in France* (Oxford University, 1952); and the various works by the well-informed journalist. A. Werth, especially *France in Ferment* (Jarrolds, 1935).

Still useful for interwar diplomacy is the early study by E. H. Carr, *International Relations Between the Two World Wars* (Macmillan, 1947). More recent surveys are provided by F. P. Walters, *A History of the League of Nations,* 2 vols. (Oxford University, 1952); and S. Marks, *The Illusion of Peace: International Relations in Europe, 1918–1933* (St. Martin's Press, 1976).

The Five-Year Plans and the Great Depression

The year 1931 was distinguished from previous years in the "post-war" and in the "pre-war" age alike—by one outstanding feature. In 1931, men and women all over the world were seriously contemplating and frankly discussing the possibility that the Western system of Society might break down and cease to work.

Arnold J. Toynbee

As the 1920s drew to a close, Europe seemed to be settling down to an era of peace, security, and relative prosperity. This comfortable prospect was, however, destroyed completely by the onset of the Great Depression. The resulting economic dislocation and mass unemployment undermined the foundations of the settlement that had been reached in the preceding years. Everywhere governments rose and fell under the pressure of mounting distress and discontent. Such political instability affected directly—and disastrously—the international situation. Some governments resorted to foreign adventures as a means for diverting domestic tension, whereas others ignored the acts of aggres-

sion because of their own pressing problems at home. Thus the Depression represents the "Great Divide" of the interwar period. The years before 1929 were years of hope, as Europe gradually resolved the various issues created by World War I. By contrast, the years after 1929 were filled with anxiety and disillusionment, as crisis followed crisis, culminating finally in World War II.

The impact and significance of the Great Depression were heightened by Russia's Five-Year Plans. At the same time that the West's economy was a veritable shambles, the Soviet Union was proceeding with its unique experiment in economic development. Although they were accompanied by rigid repression and mass privation, the

Five-Year Plans did enable the Soviet Union to rise rapidly from a predominantly agrarian state to the second-greatest industrial power in the world. This unprecedented achievement had international repercussions, particularly because of the economic difficulties besetting the West at the time.

And so the Five-Year Plans and the Great Depression stand out in the interwar period, the one accentuating the other, and each having effects that are being felt to the present day.

I. FIVE-YEAR PLANS

War Communism

As soon as the Bolsheviks found themselves the masters of Russia, they faced the challenge of creating the new socialist society about which they had preached for so long. They soon discovered that it was a challenge they were unprepared to meet. There was no model in history to follow. Lenin himself admitted, "We knew when we took power into our hands, that there were no ready forms of concrete reorganization of the capitalist system into a socialist one. . . . I do not know of any socialist who has dealt with these problems. . . . We must go by experiments."[1]

At first there was little opportunity for experimenting because the struggle for survival took precedence over everything else. The so-called "War Communism" that prevailed between 1917 and 1921 evolved out of the desperate measures taken to supply the battlefront with needed materials and manpower. One feature of War Communism was the nationalization of land, banks, foreign trade, and heavy industry. Another was the forcible requisitioning of surplus agricultural produce needed to feed the soldiers and the city dwellers. The original plan was to compensate the peasants with manufactured goods, but this proved impossible because almost all factories were producing for the front.

The ending of the civil war meant that the stopgap system of War Communism was no longer needed, so it was promptly dropped. The peasants were up in arms against confiscation without compensation. At the same time, the economy of the country was paralyzed, owing largely to the uninterrupted fighting between 1914 and 1921. Industry had fallen to 10 percent of prewar levels, and the grain crop declined from 74 million tons in 1916 to 30 million tons in 1919. The crowning disaster was the widespread drought of 1920 and 1921, which contributed to the worst famine in Russia's history. Millions of people died of starvation, and millions more were kept alive only by the shipments of the American Relief Administration.

NEP

The practical-minded Lenin realized that concessions were unavoidable—hence the adoption in 1921 of *New Economic Policy*, or NEP, as it was commonly known, which allowed a partial restoration of capitalism. Peasants were permitted to sell their produce on the open market and private individuals were allowed to operate small stores and factories. Both the peasants and the new businesspeople could employ labor and retain what profits they made from their operations. Lenin, however, saw to it that the state kept control of title to the land and of what he termed "the commanding heights" (banking, foreign trade, heavy industry, and transportation). As far as Lenin was concerned, the NEP did not mean the end of socialism in Russia; rather, it was a temporary retreat, "one step backward in order to take two steps forward."

NEP did cope successfully with the immediate crisis left by the years of war. By 1926, industrial and agricultural production had reached pre-1914 levels. But the population had increased by 8 million since 1914, so the prewar per capita standards had not been reached. The Bolshevik leaders faced the basic problem of how to take the "two steps forward" that they had planned. Shortly before his death in 1925, Lenin appears to have decided that continuation of NEP offered the best road to socialism. Following Lenin's death, Nikolai Bukharin was the outstanding champion of the NEP. A warm and enthusiastic personality, with interests in sports, science, and the arts, as well as politics, Bukharin believed that NEP market relations could "grow into socialism." He favored such a course because it would require little coercion and would respect his favorite principle that "our economy exists for the consumer, not the consumer for the economy."[2]

Although Bukharin was Lenin's favorite and the most popular of the Bolshevik leaders, his views did not prevail. He was no match for Joseph Stalin, "the master builder of bureaucratic structures."[3] Stalin saw clearly that the Communist party was the only real power in the country, and he used his position as general secretary of the party to become the master of the party and of the country. After considerable wavering, Stalin decided to abandon the NEP in favor of a centralized economy in which both agriculture and industry would be managed and directed from Moscow. This meant not only continued government operation of factories, as had been the case under War Communism, but also government control of agriculture through collectivization of peasant plots. Stalin argued that collectivization was necessary for an economic reason (the small peasant plots were inefficient) and a political reason (the peasants, especially the wealthy kulaks, were hostile to the government and must be controlled).

These arguments have been generally accepted outside the Soviet Union as well as within. But recent research suggests that Stalin's Five-Year Plans by no means were necessary or desirable. The threat of the kulaks was exaggerated since they comprised in 1926–1927 only 3.1 percent of the total population, as against 67.5 percent for the middle-income peasants and 29.4 percent for the poor. The kulaks did market a disproportionately large percentage of farm produce, although that was still only 11.8 percent of the total. Likewise, the low productivity of peasant plots was due not so much to their small size as to the lack of simple necessities such as tools, seeds, and horses. Thus both the political and economic assumptions on which Stalin's Five-Year Plans were based appear to have been unjustified. Nevertheless, it was Stalin who was the party boss, and therefore it was he who set policy, and Bukharin was vilified and executed for "the most perfidious and monstrous crimes known to the history of mankind."[4]

SOVIET PLANNED ECONOMY

In 1928 Stalin launched the first of a series of Five-Year Plans, prepared by the *Gosplan* or State Planning Commission. The Gosplan members, appointed by the government, drafted each plan on the basis of general directives from Moscow and of statistical data received from all parts of the country. The first of these Five-Year Plans, though primitive when compared with the later computer-prepared ones, comprised a three-volume text of 1,600 pages.

In agriculture the Plans called for collectivization of the land. Many peasants, especially the kulaks, opposed the collective farms for they had to enter on the same terms as the poor peasants who brought little with them. In some cases, the kulaks burned the buildings of the collectives, poisoned the cattle, and spread rumors to frighten away other peasants. The Soviet government retaliated by uprooting hundreds of thousands of kulak families from their villages, putting them in prisons and in Siberian labor camps. Finally, the government had its way, though at a cost of many lives. By 1938 almost all peasant holdings had been amalgamated into 242,400 collective farms, or *kolkhozy*, and 4,000 state farms, or *sovkhozy*.

Although the Soviet government was successful in eliminating almost all private farms, the output of its collectivized agriculture proved very disappointing. With 50 percent more land being farmed, and with ten times more people working on it, the Soviet Union produced only three-fourths of the U.S. farm output. One reason for this difference was that the climate of the Soviet Union is much less favorable for agriculture than that of the United States. Another reason was that the Soviet government was more interested in developing industry and therefore starved agriculture. Soviet farmers used only half as much machinery and fertilizer per acre as did Americans. But the chief difficulty with Soviet agriculture was excessive control from Moscow. Soviet bureaucrats told the farmers what to plant, when to plant, when to cultivate, how much fertilizer to apply, and when to harvest. The farmers preferred to work hard on their own private plots, where they could farm as they thought best and then sell any produce on the open market for as high a price as they could get, rather than for a low, government-set price, as was the case with produce from the collective fields. Thus the private plots, which comprised only 3 to 5 percent of

Lenin's successor, Joseph Stalin.

the farmlands, yielded 25 to 30 percent of Soviet agricultural output.

Unlike the farms, most of the factories under Stalin's planned economy were not run as cooperatives, but were mostly owned and operated by the government. Besides providing industry with the necessary capital, the government also employed a combination of the "carrot" and the "stick" to stimulate maximum production. Both workers and managers were required to meet certain quotas on pain of fine or dismissal. On the other hand, if they surpassed their quotas, they were rewarded with bonuses. Trade unions were allowed and recognized but were denied the basic right to strike. Soviet industry grew rapidly because the government withdrew about one-third of the national income for reinvestment; in comparison, the United States withdrew about half that proportion. Furthermore, in a planned economy the government is able to allocate investment capital as it wishes. Thus about 70 percent of the total Soviet industrial output was made up of capital goods and 30 percent of consumer goods, whereas in the United States the ratio was roughly the reverse. By the end of the first Five-Year Plan, in 1932, the Soviet Union had risen in industrial output from fifth to second place in the world. This extraordinary spurt was due not only to the increase of productivity in the Soviet Union but also to the decline of productivity in the West that was brought about by the Depression. Nevertheless, Soviet *gross national product* (GNP), which included the lagging agricultural as well as the industrial output, increased three-and-a-half times during the quarter-century between 1928 and 1952—a rate of growth surpassing that of any other country during this period. From the viewpoint of world balance of power, which was Stalin's main concern, the Soviet share of total global industrial output rose from 1.5 percent in 1921 to 10 percent in 1939 to 20 percent in 1966.

We should emphasize that Soviet economic growth was achieved at the expense of the Soviet citizens, who were forced to work hard for the future and to endure privation in the present, regardless of their wishes. Consumer goods were scarce, expensive, and of poor quality. The GNP of the Soviet Union remained at 46 to 48 percent of the GNP of the United States. And in per capita terms, the Soviet GNP was only about two-fifths that of the United States, because the Soviet work force was about one-fourth larger than the American.

Significance for World History

For the Russian people the Five-Year Plans were a mixed blessing. On the positive side they made the country strong economically and militarily so that it was able to contribute substantially to the defeat of Hitler in World War II. The Five-Year Plans also transformed Russia from a primitive to a modern society. They increased literacy from 28.4 percent in 1897 to 56.6 percent in 1926, 87.4 percent in 1939, and 98.5 percent in 1959. In medical care, between 1913 and 1961, the number of physicians increased from 23,200 to 425,700; life expectancy rose from thirty-two to sixty-nine years; and infant mortality declined from 273 to 32 per thousand. Likewise in social services, the Five-Year Plans provided Soviet citizens with free medical care, old-age pensions, sickness and disability benefits, maternity leaves, paid vacations, and children's aid.

But the Russian people also endured negative experiences as a result of the Five-Year Plans. Most damaging was the ending of the alliance between the Bolsheviks and the peasants, which had made possible the 1917 revolution. The savage repression during the collectivization of the land was not soon forgotten. The peasants thereafter dragged their feet, regarding the kolkhozy as something alien that had been imposed on them—hence the contrast between their high productivity in their own small plots and their low productivity in the collective fields. The low productivity in agriculture in turn hurt the performance of Soviet industry. Since agriculture did not produce as much as was needed to finance the cost of industrialization, the factory workers also were squeezed to pay for the high cost of the successive Five-Year Plans. When the Soviet government withdrew one-third of the national income each year for reinvestment, it meant low wages and scarce consumer goods. The reaction of one Soviet worker was typical: "They pretend they are paying us, so we pretend we are working."

The Five-Year Plans had a mixed impact not only on the Soviet Union but also on the world. The impact was different on the Western world from what it was on the underdeveloped countries. Westerners at first were skeptical about Soviet plans for a new society, many assuming that they were bound to fail. As the successive Five-Year Plans unfolded, skepticism gave way to genuine interest. But those Westerners who were sufficiently interested to visit the Soviet Union were usually unimpressed, if not disillusioned. They were struck by the shabby clothing, the monotonous diet, the wretched housing, and the scarcity of consumer goods. They were also appalled by the lack of individual freedom as reflected in the one-party political structure, the hobbling of trade unions, the regimentation of education, and the rigid control of all communication media. Soviet society, despite the achievements of the Five-Year Plans, did not seem to most Westerners a socialist paradise worth copying. On the

other hand, most Westerners conceded that without the industrial growth under the Five-Year Plans, the Soviet Union would not have been able to contribute so much to Hitler's defeat in World War II.

Former colonial peoples in the underdeveloped world reacted differently. To them, the Soviet Union was the country that succeeded in transforming itself within a generation from a backward agrarian state into the second-greatest industrial and military power in the world. The institutions and the techniques that made this dramatic change possible were of vital concern to these peoples. Also noteworthy is the fact that the Soviet Union was a great Asian as well as European state. Its frontiers stretched from Korea, past Mongolia, Sinkiang, Afghanistan, and Iran, to Turkey. In almost all these regions, kindred people exist on both sides of the frontier, thus facilitating interaction and comparison of conditions. In most cases, the Soviet Union fared well by comparison, thanks to the revivifying effect of the Five-Year Plans on its eastern regions. The other side of the long frontier has had few counterparts to the substantial advances made in the Soviet central Asian republics, including irrigation works, textile mills, machinery plants, health services, and educational programs that raised literacy rates from about 2 percent in 1914 to 75 percent in 1940 to over 90 percent in 1960.

This mixed impact of the Soviet experiment changed after World War II to an almost totally negative impact. We shall see (Chapter 45, Section III) that in recent decades the Soviet planned economy fell steadily behind the Western market economy, while personal rights and freedoms remained conspicuous by their absence. Hence the disintegration and disappearance of the Soviet superpower, replaced in the 1990s by the Commonwealth of Independent States.

II. THE GREAT DEPRESSION

Origins of the Crash

In the beginning of 1929, the United States appeared to be flourishing. The index of industrial production in that country averaged only 67 in

1921 (1923–1925 = 100) but rose to 110 by July 1928 and to 126 by June 1929. Even more impressive was the performance of the American stock market. During the three summer months of 1929, Westinghouse stock rose from 151 to 286; General Electric, from 268 to 391; and U. S. Steel, from 165 to 258. Businesspeople, academic economists, and government leaders were all expressing confidence in the future. The secretary of the treasury, Andrew W. Mellon, assured the public in September 1929, "There is no cause for worry. The high tide of prosperity will continue."[5]

This confidence proved unjustified; in the fall of 1929, the bottom fell out of the stock market, and a worldwide depression, unprecedented in its intensity and longevity, followed. The serious international economic imbalance that developed when the United States became a creditor nation on a large scale (following World War I) seems to have been one reason for this unexpected denouement. Britain had been a creditor nation before the war, but it had used the proceeds from its overseas investments and loans to pay for its chronic excess of imports over exports. The United States, by contrast, normally had a favorable trade balance, accentuated by tariffs that were kept at high levels for reasons of domestic politics. In addition, money poured into the country in the 1920s in payment of war debts, and the American gold hoard rose between 1913 and 1924 from $1.924 to $4.499 billion, or half the world's total gold supply.

This imbalance was neutralized for several years by large-scale American loans and investments abroad: Between 1925 and 1928, the average annual total for American foreign investments amounted to $1.1 billion. In the long run, this, of course, intensified the imbalance and could not be continued indefinitely. As payments came due, debtor countries were forced to curtail imports from the United States, and certain branches of the American economy, especially agriculture, were hurt. In addition, some countries found it necessary to default on their debts, which shook certain financial firms in the United States.

As serious as the imbalance of the international economy was that of the American economy, the basic reason being that wages lagged behind the rising productivity. Between 1920 and 1929, hourly industrial wages rose only 2 percent, whereas the productivity of workers in factories jumped 55 percent. At the same time, the real income of the farmers was shrinking because agricultural prices were falling while taxes and living costs were rising. Whereas in 1910 the income per farm worker had been slightly less than 40 percent that of the nonfarm worker, by 1930, it was just under 30 percent. Such poverty in the countryside was a serious matter, because the rural population at the time was one-fifth of the total population.

The combination of stationary factory wages and falling farm income resulted in severe maldistribution of national income. In 1929, 5 percent of the American people received one-third of all personal incomes (compared to one-sixth by the end of World War II). This meant inadequate purchasing power for the masses, combined with a high level of capital investment by those who were receiving the high salaries and dividends. Production of capital goods during the 1920s rose at an average annual rate of 6.4 percent, compared to 2.8 percent for consumer goods. Eventually this led to the clogging of the economy; the low purchasing power was unable to support such a high rate of capital investment. As a result, the index of industrial production dropped from 126 to 117 between June and October 1929, creating a slump that contributed to the stock market crash that autumn.

The weakness of the American banking system was a final factor contributing to the crash of 1929. A great number of independent banking firms were operating, and some of these lacked sufficient resources to weather financial storms. When one closed its doors, panic spread, and depositors rushed to withdraw their savings from other banks, thus setting in motion a chain reaction that undermined the entire banking structure.

Worldwide Depression

The stock market crash in the United States began in September 1929. Within one month, stock values dropped 40 percent, and apart from a few brief recoveries, the decline continued for three years. During that period, U. S. Steel stock fell from 262 to 22; General Motors, from 73 to 8. Every branch of the national economy suffered correspondingly. During those three years, 5,000 banks closed their doors. General Motors had produced 5.5 million automobiles in 1929, but in 1931, they produced only 2.5 million. The steel industry in July 1932 was operating at 12 percent of capacity. By 1933, both general industrial production and national income had slumped by nearly one-half; wholesale prices, by almost one-third; and merchandise trade, by more than two-thirds.

The Great Depression was unique not only in its intensity but also in its worldwide impact. American financial houses were forced to call in their short-term loans abroad; naturally, there were repercussions. In May 1931, the Credit-Anstalt, the largest and most reputable bank in Vienna, declared itself insolvent, setting off a wave of panic throughout the continent. On July 13, the German Danatbank followed suit, and for the next two days all German banks were decreed on holiday; the Berlin Stock Exchange, the Börse, closed for two months. In September 1931, Britain went off the gold standard, to be followed two years later by the United States and nearly all the major countries.

The breakdown of the financial world had its counterpart in industry and commerce: The index of world industrial production, excluding the Soviet Union, fell from 100 in 1929 to 86.5 in 1930, 74.8 in 1931, and 63.8 in 1932, a drop of 36.2 percent. The maximum decline in previous crises had been 7 percent. Even more drastic was the shrinking of world international trade, from $68.6 billion in 1929 to $55.6 in 1930, $39.7 in 1931, $26.9 in 1932, and $24.2 in 1933. Again it might be noted that the maximum drop in international trade in the past had been 7 percent, during the 1907–1908 crisis.

Social and Political Repercussions

These economic catastrophes gave rise to social problems of corresponding magnitude. Most serious was the mass unemployment, which reached tragic proportions. In March 1933, the number of people out of work in the United States was estimated conservatively at over 14 million, or a fourth of the total labor force. In Britain, the jobless were numbered at nearly 3 million, representing about the same proportion of the workers as in the United States. Germany was the worst off, with more than two-fifths of trade-unionists unemployed and another fifth on part-time work.

Unemployment on this scale drastically lowered living standards in all countries. Even in the wealthy United States there was wholesale misery and privation, especially in the beginning, when relief was left to private and local agencies with inadequate funds. In England, where unemployment had been chronic through the 1920s, the situation now became even worse. A substantial proportion of a whole generation was growing up with little opportunity or prospect of finding employment. Some bitterly referred to their purposeless existence as a "living death." In Germany, with its higher percentage of jobless people, the frustrations and tensions were more acute. Eventually they made it possible for Hitler to triumph, for social dislocation on such a large scale inevitably had profound political repercussions.

Even in the United States, with its superior resources and its tradition of political stability, these were years of strange ideas and agitations. Various proposals were made for income redistribution, including the Townsend Plan for munificent old-age pensions and the Share-Our-Wealth movement of Senator Huey Long of Louisiana. Another manifestation of the political turbulence was Franklin Roosevelt's sweeping electoral victory in 1932. The New Deal that followed served as an escape valve for the political discontent and effectively neutralized the extremist movements.

Political developments in Britain and France during these years were generally the same as in the United States. Both countries were hit by political storms but managed to ride them out within the framework of their traditional institutions. The British Labour party, which had come into office in June 1929, was forced to give way in August 1931 to a new National government. This proved to be a mere façade for Tory rule, with the Conservatives making up the majority of the cab-

A breadline in Oklahoma.

inet. Three years later, the aging and ailing Mac-Donald resigned in favor of Stanley Baldwin, and so Britain passed under virtual Conservative rule, though the coalition still existed nominally.

In France, too, the left was forced out of office by the pressures of the Depression. It won the 1932 elections, and the Radical Edouard Herriot formed a government with Socialist support as had been done in 1924. The Radicals and the Socialists were hopelessly divided on the question of how to cope with the economic crisis. Herriot held office for only six months, and four other premiers followed in rapid succession. The showdown came in December 1933 with the Stavisky scandal involving a Russian-born promoter and a provincial pawnshop in a fraudulent bond issue. According to rumors, various important officials and politicians were implicated. Extreme rightist groups took advantage of the opportunity to stage street riots in an effort to overthrow the republic itself. Although they failed to do so, they did force the government to resign in February 1934. A number of conservative ministries fol-

lowed, none of which proved capable of coping with the country's basic ills.

Much more dramatic and fateful was the rise of Hitler to power in Germany. When the Depression hit that country, its government was a left-center coalition led by the Socialist chancellor Herman Müller, and the aging conservative war hero Paul von Hindenburg was functioning as president. Like Socialist ministries elsewhere, the Müller ministry in Germany was undermined by dissension over how to cope with unemployment and other problems created by the Depression. The ministry was forced to resign in March 1930, and from then on Germany was ruled by parties of the center and right.

At first a coalition government was organized by Heinrich Brüning, an intelligent and upright, though cold and rigid, centrist. Lacking a parliamentary majority, he fell back on Article 48 of the constitution, which empowered the president, in case of emergency, to issue decrees that would have the force of law unless specifically rejected by majority vote of the Reichstag. The

POVERTY AMID PLENTY IN THE UNITED STATES

The Great Depression was unprecedented in its intensity, scope, and longevity. Its effect on the United States is described in the following testimony before a congressional committee in February 1932.*

During the last three months I [Oscar Ameringer of Oklahoma City] have visited, as I have said, some 20 states of this wonderfully rich and beautiful country. Here are some of the things I heard and saw: In the State of Washington I was told that the forest fires raging in that region all summer and fall were caused by unemployed timber workers and bankrupt farmers in an endeavor to earn a few honest dollars as fire fighters. The last thing I saw on the night I left Seattle was numbers of women searching for scraps of food in the refuse piles of the principal market of that city. A number of Montana citizens told me of thousands of bushels of wheat left in the fields uncut on account of its low price that hardly paid for the harvesting. In Oregon I saw thousands of bushels of apples rotting in the orchards. Only absolutely flawless apples were still salable, at from 40 to 50 cents a box containing 200 apples. At the same time, there are millions of children who, on account of the poverty of their parents, will not eat one apple this winter.

While I was in Oregon the Portland *Oregonian* bemoaned the fact that thousands of ewes were killed by the sheep raisers because they did not bring enough in the market to pay the freight on them. And while Oregon sheep raisers fed mutton to the buzzards, I saw men picking for meat scraps in the garbage cans in the cities of New York and Chicago. I talked to one man in a restaurant in Chicago. He told me of his experience in raising sheep. He said that he had killed 3,000 sheep this fall and thrown them down the canyon, because it cost $1.10 to ship a sheep, and then he would get less than a dollar for it. He said he could not afford to feed the sheep, and he would not let them starve, so he just cut their throats and threw them down the canyon.

The roads of the West and Southwest teem with hungry hitchhikers. The camp fires of the homeless are seen along every railroad track. I saw men, women, and children walking over the hard roads. Most of them were tenant farmers who had lost their all in the late slump in wheat and cotton. Between Clarksville and Russellville, Ark., I picked up a family. The woman was hugging a dead chicken under a ragged coat. When I asked her where she had procured the fowl, first she told me she had found it dead in the road, and then added in grim humor, "They promised me a chicken in the pot, and now I got mine. . . ."

The farmers are being pauperized by the poverty of industrial populations and the industrial populations are being pauperized by the poverty of the farmers. Neither has the money to buy the product of the other; hence we have overproduction and underconsumption at the same time and in the same country.

---

* *Unemployment in the United States. . . . Hearings before a subcommittee of the Committee on Labor,* House of Representatives, 72nd Congress, 1st Session (Government Printing Office, 1932), pp. 98–99.

Reichstag did, in fact, vote against the first emergency decrees, but Brüning countered by persuading Hindenburg to dissolve the Reichstag and order new elections for September 1930. Thus Germany was ruled, well before the Hitler years, by legal but authoritarian presidential power. Brüning expected that a majority of the various center and right parties would be returned, enabling him to govern the country in regular parliamentary fashion. Instead, the elections marked the emergence of Hitler's National Socialist party as a national force.

The son of a minor Austrian customs official, Adolf Hitler went to Vienna early in life, aspiring to be a painter. According to his own account—which seems to be greatly exaggerated—he spent five miserable years working at the most menial jobs to keep body and soul together. From Vienna, Hitler drifted to Munich, where in 1914 he enlisted in a Bavarian regiment. At the end of the war, Hitler joined a struggling group called the National Socialist German Workers' party, of which he soon became the leader, or Führer. After making rabble-rousing speeches on nationalist and anti-Semitic themes, in 1923 he joined Field Marshal Ludendorff in an uprising in Munich. It was easily put down by the police, and Hitler was imprisoned for nine months. There, at the age of thirty-five, he wrote *Mein Kampf*—"My Battle"—a long and turgid autobiographical reflection into which he poured his hatred of democracy, Marxism, and Jews.

Upon release from prison, Hitler resumed his agitation but with disappointing results. In the December 1924 elections, his Nazi party won only fourteen seats and a mere 908,000 votes, and in May 1928 won even fewer—twelve seats and 810,000 votes, or 2.6 percent of the total number. The turning point came with the September 1930 elections, when the Nazis won 107 seats and 6,407,000 votes, or 18.3 percent of the total. This avalanche of ballots did not come from the workers. The Socialist and Communist parties between them gained thirteen more seats in 1930 than in 1928. Hitler was getting his newfound support from the middle-class elements that were looking desperately for safety in the fierce economic storm.

Recent studies of the German elections of the 1930s reveal that the wealthier the voters, the more likely they were to vote for Hitler. Such voters found comfort and hope in the Nazi platform, which promised economic relief without dismantling the existing social system. At the same time, all patriotic Germans were promised the smashing of the Versailles chains and the persecution of the Jews, who were branded as being both exploiting financiers and materialistic Communists. It should be emphasized that Hitler had been campaigning on this platform for years, with little response. It was the Depression that transformed him from a loud-mouthed fanatic to the beloved Führer who supplied scapegoats for misery and a program of action for individual and national fulfillment.

With the September 1930 elections, the Nazis increased their Reichstag representation from 12 to 107, thus becoming the second-largest party in the country. This unexpected outcome undermined parliamentary government in Germany because it denied a majority to both a center-right coalition desired by Brüning and a center-left coalition that had functioned under Müller. Consequently, Brüning had to rely for over two years on presidential decrees for all necessary legislation. The extent of his dependence on Hindenburg was demonstrated when he proposed legislation for the breakup of East Prussian estates; President Hindenburg, himself a Junker landowner, was strongly opposed, and he forced Brüning to resign in May 1932.

The new chancellor, Franz von Papen, headed a weak coalition government with negligible Reichstag support, so he held new elections in July 1932, in the hope of strengthening his position. Instead, the Nazis were the big winners: Their votes jumped to 13,799,000, or 37.4 percent of the total number, and their seats to 230. Hitler was now the head of the number-one party in the country, and since neither he nor the Communists would enter a coalition, no majority government support could be organized.

In November 1932, Papen held still another election in an attempt to break the deadlock. This time the Nazis lost 2 million votes and 34 seats in the Reichstag, reducing them to 196 deputies. They were still the strongest party in the country, but they could no longer pose as the irresistible wave of the future. Yet less than two months later, Hitler was the chancellor of Germany. One reason for this startling reversal was the large-scale financial support now given to the Nazi party by German business leaders, who were worried that millions of votes might shift to the left if the party disintegrated. The other reason was the morass of intrigues and cabals that passed for government in Berlin at the time. The aged Hindenburg was now senile and could function lucidly for only a few hours each day. Persuaded to get rid of Papen, he appointed in his place General Kurt Von Schleicher.

Schleicher cancelled the cuts in wages and relief that Papen had made, revived plans for partitioning East Prussian estates, and began an investigation of illegal profits made by landowners through government agrarian legislation. Both the landowners and businesspeople denounced him bitterly, and they won over Hindenburg. Schleicher was vulnerable for the same reason that Brüning and Papen had been: inability to organize a majority in the Reichstag. So on January 28, 1933, Schleicher was forced to resign, and, two days later, Hitler became chancellor with a coalition cabinet of Nationalists and Nazis.

Within six months Hitler had regimented Germany. A new Reichstag was elected on March 5 following a campaign of unprecedented propaganda and terrorism. The Nazis received 288 seats and 5.5 million votes, but they still made up only 44 percent of the total. When the representatives met, Hitler declared the Communist seats null and void and then made a deal with the Catholic center that gave him enough votes to pass the Enabling Act on March 23, 1933. This gave him authority to rule by decree for four years. But by the summer of 1933, he had eliminated or leashed virtually all independent elements in German life—trade unions, schools, churches, political parties, communications media, the judiciary, and the states of the federation.

Thus Hitler became master of Germany, and by technically legal methods, as he never ceased to boast. The Depression had made his triumph possible, though by no means inevitable. The possibility was translated into ac-

tuality by a combination of other factors, including Hitler's own talents, the support afforded by assorted vested interests, and the myopia of his opponents, who underestimated him and failed to unite in opposition. On August 2, 1934, Hindenburg conveniently died, enabling Hitler to combine the offices of president and chancellor in his own person. The following month the Nazi Party Congress assembled in Nuremberg, and Hitler proclaimed, "The German form of life is definitely determined for the next thousand years."

International Repercussions

The British foreign minister, Sir Austen Chamberlain, comparing the international situation in 1932 with that of the Lacarno era, observed,

I look at the world to-day and I contrast the conditions now with the conditions at that time, and I am forced to acknowledge that for some reason or other, owing to something upon which it is difficult to put one's finger, in these last two years the world is moving backward. Instead of approaching nearer to one another, instead of increasing the measure of goodwill, instead of progressing to a stable peace, it has fallen into an attitude of suspicion, of fear, of danger, which imperils the peace of the world.[6]

That "something" that Chamberlain could not identify was the Depression and its manifold repercussions, international as well as national. Various international agreements of the Locarno era became unworkable, particularly those concerning reparations and war debts. It soon became obvious that governments, pushed to the brink of bankruptcy by their slumping economies and mounting unemployment, would not be able to meet commitments undertaken a few years earlier. In July 1931, on the initiative of President Hoover, the powers agreed to a moratorium on all intergovernmental debts. The following summer, at the Lausanne Conference, the powers in fact, if not in theory, cancelled German reparations entirely. Simultaneously, the payment of war debts to the United States came to an end, though a few token payments were made in the following years. And so the sticky old issue of reparations and war debts was finally swept away by the economic storms let loose by the Depression.

Another effect of the storms was to accentuate the ever-present economic nationalism to the point where it disturbed international relations. Self-protective measures by individual nations took such forms as higher tariffs, more rigid import quotas, clearing agreements, currency-control regulations, and bilateral-trade pacts. These measures inevitably brought economic friction and political tensions among states. Various attempts were made to reverse the trend, but without success. The World Economic Conference that met in London in 1933 was a dismal fiasco. "Autarchy," or economic self-sufficiency, gradually became a commonly accepted national goal.

Closely related was the petering out of disarmament efforts, which gave way to massive rearmament programs. The Disarmament Conference that met intermittently for twenty months, beginning in February 1932, was as futile as the Economic Conference. As the 1930s progressed, countries devoted more and more of their energies to rearming. The trend was impossible to stop because armament manufacturing provided jobs as well as imagined security. Unemployment in the United States, for example, was not substantially reduced until the country began to rearm on the eve of World War II. Likewise, Hitler quickly disposed of the unprecedented unemployment he faced by launching a gigantic rearmament program.

The armaments now being accumulated were bound sooner or later to be used, and their use required some justification. The most obvious was that of *lebensraum,* or living space. This was the term coined by Hitler, but similar expressions and arguments were employed by Mussolini in Italy and by the military leaders in Japan. The unemployment and general misery, according to this doctrine, arose from the lack of lebenstraum. The few fortunate countries had seized all the colonies and underpopulated lands overseas, leaving the other nations without the natural resources needed to support their people. The obvious way out was to expand, by force if necessary, to remedy the injustices inflicted by the past. Such were the arguments used by the so-called "have-not" countries against the "haves."

The reasoning was obviously false in view of the fact that the Depression had devastated equally and impartially the United States, Canada, and Britain, along with Germany, Italy, and Japan. Nevertheless, the lebensraum ideology served to unite the people of the "have-not" countries in support of the expansionist policies of their respective governments. It also gave a superficial moral justification to aggression committed for the avowed purpose of providing food for the needy and work for the jobless. Indeed, certain elements even within the "have" countries accepted these rationalizations and defended the aggressions that followed.

Such, then, was the combination of forces behind the "suspicion," the "fear," and the "moving backward" that Chamberlain had observed in 1932. During the following years, these forces undermined completely the settlement that had been reached in the 1920s and precipitated one crisis after another, culminating finally in World War II.

SUGGESTED READINGS

A good brief summary of the Five-Year Plans from their beginning to their end is available in R. Munting, *The Economic Development of the USSR* (St. Martin's Press, 1982). Reappraising of the NEP and the plans is reflected in S. Cohen, *Rethinking the Soviet System* (Oxford University, 1985); M. Lewin, *The Making of the Soviet System* (Pantheon, 1985); C. Bettelheim, *Class Struggles in the USSR*, 2 vols. (Monthly Review Press, 1976, 1978); and S. Brucan, *The Post-Brezhnev Era: An Insider's View* (Praeger, 1983). The global impact of the plans is analyzed by E. H. Carr, *The Soviet Impact on the Western World* (Macmillan, 1954); by C. K. Wilber, *The Soviet Model and Underdeveloped Countries* (University of North Carolina, 1970); and more critically, by R. Pipes, *Communism: The Vanished Spectre* (Oxford University, 1994.

Analyses of the Depression are available in J. K. Galbraith, *The Great Crash, 1929* (Houghton Mifflin, 1955); G. Rees, *The Great Slump: Capitalism in Crisis* (Harper & Row, 1971); C. P. Kindleberger, *The World in Depression 1929–1939* (University of California, 1975); and J. A. Garrity, *The Great Depression* (Harcourt Bruce Jovanovich, 1986). On Hitler's rise to power there is the spirited account by W. L. Shirer, *The Rise and Fall of the Third Reich* (Simon & Schuster, 1960); and the competent biographies by A. Bullock, *Hitler: A Study in Tyranny* (Harper & Row, 1952; and J. Toland, *Adolf Hitler* (Doubleday, 1976). Conflict-ing views on the circumstances of Hitler's rise to power are presented by R. F. Hamilton, *Who Voted for Hitler?* (Princeton University, 1982); H. A. Turner, Jr., *German Big Business and the Rise of Hitler* (Oxford University, 1985); and D. Abraham, *The Collapse of the Weimar Republic: Political Economy and Crisis* (Princeton University, 1981).

41 Drift to War, 1929–1939

This is not Peace. It is an Armistice for twenty years.

Marshal Foch, 1919

The late 1920s were years of prosperity, stabilization, and settlement; the 1930s were years of depression, crises, and war. In Europe, the settlement of the 1920s was based on the French system of alliances, and in the Far East, on the Washington Conference agreements. The objective in each case was to preserve the status quo in the two regions. This objective was realized in the 1920s, but during the next decade everything was suddenly and decisively upset. New leaders appeared in Germany and Japan who were determined to revise the territorial settlement of World War I and who possessed the means and the will to do so. Their massive rearming programs and their breathtaking aggressions drastically altered the balance of power. No longer was the relatively weak Italy the only revisionist state attempting ineffectually to challenge the status quo. The Third Reich and Imperial Japan also gave strength to the revisionist drive, resulting in an entirely new balance of power.

A triangle situation developed, with Britain, France, and their Continental allies supporting the status quo; Germany, Italy, and Japan driving for revision; and the Soviet Union, strengthened by the Five-Year Plans, playing an increasingly important role. The interplay of these three forces explains the recurring crises of the 1930s and the final outbreak of World War II.

I.   JAPAN INVADES MANCHURIA

The first major act of aggression was made by Japan, in pursuit of long-cherished territorial ambitions on the mainland. The Japanese had entered World War I promptly in order to exploit what appeared to be a golden opportunity. They took over with little difficulty the German islands in the Pacific and the German holdings on the Shantung peninsula. The Japanese also had ambitions on the mainland, as evident in their

625

twenty-one demands on China (January 1915) and in their expeditionary force to Siberia, which remained there after the British and American troops left in 1920. These ambitions were, for the most part, unsatisfied. At the Paris Peace Conference, Japan did retain control of the former German islands, but as Class C mandates under League of Nations auspices rather than as outright possessions. President Wilson strenuously opposed Japanese claims to the Chinese Shantung peninsula. As a compromise, Japan was confirmed in "temporary" possession of the peninsula, but it conceded that it was its "policy" to restore the territory to China at an unspecified date, "retaining only the economic privileges [hitherto] granted to Germany."

At the Washington Naval Conference Japan formerly renounced any territorial ambitions it may still have cherished. The nine powers at the conference signed a Nine-Power Treaty (February 6, 1922) guaranteeing the territorial integrity of China and reiterating the principle of the Open Door. At the same conference the United States, Britain, France, and Japan signed the Four-Power Treaty (December 13, 1921), by which they agreed to respect one another's rights in "insular possessions" in the Pacific and to settle any future differences by consultation. In addition, Japan, after energetic American mediation, agreed to restore Shantung to China and to evacuate its troops from Siberia. Both commitments were fulfilled in 1922.

Having finished with foreign adventures, at least for the time being, Japan now turned to domestic economic problems. Japan, like the United States, had prospered greatly during World War I, supplying munitions and merchant shipping. Between 1914 and 1920, the value of foreign trade increased almost four times. The prosperity, however, was poorly distributed because of the unprecedented concentration of economic power in the so-called *Zaibatsu* (*zai* means, "wealth"; *batsu*, "clique"). This was the general name given to four giant family corporations (Mitsui, Mitsubishi, Sumitomo, and Yasuda) that by World War II controlled three-fourths of the combined capitalization of all Japanese firms. They held one-third of all deposits in Japan's private banks, three-fourths of all trust deposits, and one-fifth of all

life insurance policies. The peasants, comprising one-half the total population, were impoverished by high rents and heavy debts. Only 7 percent of these families owned five acres or more of land; the average holding was less than three acres. City workers suffered from high food prices, low wages, and lack of trade union freedom.

The depressed living standards of the workers and peasants meant a severely restricted domestic market. Consequently, Japanese industry was particularly dependent on foreign markets for the disposal of its products. This dependence spelled disaster with the coming of the Depression. Between 1929 and 1931, foreign trade decreased by almost 50 percent. The peasants, who had supplemented their meager incomes by silk cultivation, were badly hurt by the sharp slump in silk exports to Depression-ridden America. City workers suffered correspondingly from unemployment.

Army leaders and other champions of territorial aggrandizement argued persuasively that the source of Japan's trouble was its dependence on foreign markets. Japan should conquer an empire that would make it economically independent of the rest of the world. Military spokesmen had been preaching this doctrine for years, but the ravages of the Depression now provided them with a responsive audience, as had happened with Hitler in Germany. The Japanese expansionists were not only motivated by economic considerations. They were also concerned about the growing strength of the Soviet Union and the increasing success of Chiang Kai-shek in unifying China. In addition, they were fully aware of the unemployment situation and other problems that were then engrossing the attention of Western statesmen. These calculations figured in the Japanese decision to attack the Chinese province of Manchuria in 1931.

It was not accidental that Manchuria was the first objective of Japanese expansionism. This province in the northeast corner of China had the double advantage of being loosely connected with the central Nanking government and possessing abundant natural resources, including iron, coal, and extensive fertile plains. Furthermore, Japan had obtained through past treaty arrangements certain special privileges in Manchuria. These could be used to find pretexts for justifying aggressive measures.

On the evening of September 18, 1931, an explosion wrecked a small section of track on the Japanese-controlled South Manchuria railway to the north of Mukden. Baron Shidehara, who was foreign minister in 1931, testified before the International War Crimes Tribunal in June 1946 that the incident had been staged by army officers whom he had tried vainly to stop. His testimony is supported by the speed and precision with which the Japanese army swung immediately into action. Without declaring war, it captured Mukden and Changchun in the space of twenty-four hours and then fanned out in all directions. The taking of Harbin in late January 1932 signified the end of all organized resistance in Manchuria. In March 1932, the victors renamed their conquest Manchukuo, the "State of Manchu." They needed a puppet emperor, so they dragged out of retirement Henry P'u Yi, the surviving head of the old Manchu dynasty that had fallen in 1911, and solemnly installed him as regent.

Meanwhile, the Chinese government had appealed to the League of Nations under Article 11 and to the United States under the Paris Pact (Kellogg-Briand Pact). The result was much deliberation but no practical aid. On November 21, the Japanese delegation accepted the original Chinese proposal for an impartial commission of inquiry, but the members were not chosen until January 14, 1932, and they did not actually reach Mukden until April 21. By that time, Manchuria had become Manchukuo. The league commission, known as the Lytton Commission after its chair, Lord Lytton, submitted its report in October 1932. Carefully worded to avoid offending the Japanese, it denied that the Japanese aggression could be justified as a defensive measure and branded the new Manchukuo state a Japanese puppet regime. On the other hand, it refrained from ordering Japan to get out. Instead, the report proposed a settlement recognizing Japan's special interest in Manchuria and making that province an autonomous state under Chinese sovereignty but with the Japanese in control. On February 25, 1933, the league adopted the report, and the following month, Japan withdrew from that body.

In retrospect, the Manchurian affair stands out as the first serious blow leveled at the League of Nations and at the entire diplomatic structure designed to maintain the status quo—the Versailles settlement, the Washington Conference agreements, and the Paris Pact. The ease with which Japan had acquired its rich new possession was not lost on the revisionist leaders of Italy and Germany; Manchuria set off a chain reaction of aggressions that ultimately let to World War II. (See map of German, Italian, and Japanese Aggression, 1930–1939, p. 628).

II. DIPLOMATIC REACTIONS TO HITLER

The Japanese conquest of Manchuria was a rude challenge to the status quo in the Far East, but even more upsetting was Hitler's threat to the status quo in Europe. Hitherto the French system of alliances had dominated the Continent with little difficulty. Mussolini had tried to organize a counter bloc, but his agreements with third-rate revisionist states such as Austria, Hungary, Bulgaria, and Albania were of little value. Likewise, the Soviet Union was cut off by the "cordon sanitaire" and, in any case, was engrossed in "building socialism in one country." Only Germany was left, and under Stresemann, this country had made peace with its wartime enemies when it accepted the Locarno Pacts and entered the League of Nations.

This comfortable situation was drastically altered when Hitler became chancellor in 1933. The Nazi leader had for some time been demanding more lebensraum for the German people. It is scarcely surprising that there were immediate diplomatic repercussions when the champion of lebensraum became the master of Germany. The first move was the revitalization of the Little Entente, which had been dormant for several years. In February 1933, Czechoslovakia, Yugoslavia, and Rumania established a permanent council of their foreign ministers to facilitate the coordination and implementation of their diplomatic policies.

Even Mussolini, who later was to form the Rome-Berlin Axis with Hitler, at first reacted strongly against his fellow dictator. In view of the substantial German minority in the south Tyrol, Mussolini was apprehensive of an expansionist

Germany violated the Versailles Treaty, and Germany, Italy, and Japan defied the League of Nations by the following acts of aggression: Italy conquered (1) Ethiopia, 1935; and occupied (2) Albania, 1939. Germany seized (3) the Rhineland, 1936; (4) Austria, 1938; (5) the Sudetenland, 1938; (6) the rest of Czechoslovakia, 1939; (7) Memel and Danzig, 1939; and (8) Poland, 1939. Japan invaded (9) Manchukuo, 1931; (10) the Eastern Provinces, 1939; and (11) Hainan and Chinese Ports, 1939.

German, Italian, and Japanese Aggression, 1930–1939

628

HITLER, MUSSOLINI, AND LEBENSRAUM

Hitler and Mussolini both justified their conquests by claiming the need for lebensraum, or living space. They blamed their national problems on the lack of empires with resources and markets. This argument was made in the following statements by the two leaders.*

Hitler, 1930: If the German people does not solve the problem of its lack of space, and if it does not open up the domestic market for its industry, then 2,000 years have been in vain. Germany will then make its exit from the world stage and peoples with more vigor will come into our heritage. . . .

Space must be fought for and maintained. People who are lazy have no right to the soil. Soil is for him who tills it and protects it. If a people disclaims soil, it disclaims life. If a nation loses in the defense of its soil, then the individual loses. There is no higher justice that decrees that a people must starve. There is only power, which creates justice. . . .

Parliaments do not create all of the rights on this earth; force also creates rights. The question is whether we wish to live or die. We have more right to soil than all the other nations because we are so thickly populated. I am of the opinion that in this respect too the principle can be applied: God helps him who helps himself.

Mussolini, 1933: . . . Fascism, the more it considers and observes the future and the development of humanity quite apart from political considerations of the moment, believes neither in the possibility nor the utility of perpetual peace. It thus repudiates the doctrine of Pacifism—born of a renunciation of the struggle and an act of cowardice in the face of sacrifice. War alone brings up to its highest tension all human energy and puts the stamp of nobility upon the peoples who have the courage to meet it. . . .

For Fascism, the growth of empire, that is to say the expansion of the nation, is an essential manifestation of vitality, and its opposite a sign of decadence. Peoples which are rising, or rising again after a period of decadence, are always imperialist....

* *Voelkischer Beobachter*, May 7, 1930; and Benito Mussolini, "The Political and Social Doctrines of Fascism," *Political Quarterly* (July–September 1933), p. 356.

Nazi regime with its slogan of "Ein Volk, ein Reich, ein Führer." ("One People, One State, One Leader.") Accordingly, he took the initiative in concluding the Four-Power Pact on July 15, 1933, with Britain, France, and Germany. The agreement confirmed the adherence of the signatories to the League Covenant, the Locarno Treaties, and the Kellogg-Briand Pact, and also prohibited any change in the Versailles Treaty without the consent of all four powers. This was a futile exercise, for Hitler repeatedly violated these commitments—without even a reference to his fellow signatories. In October 1933, he announced Germany's withdrawal from the Disarmament Conference and from the League of Nations. Although he did not immediately reveal his rearmament program, its existence, if not its pace and magnitude, became generally known.

These developments stimulated the formation of another regional bloc made up of Turkey, Greece, Rumania, and Yugoslavia, the last two of which had considerable German minorities. On

Germany rearms in staggering numbers, as it renounces the Versailles Treaty
and gears up for war. SS troops at a Nazi Party rally in 1938.

February 9, 1934, the four countries signed the Balkan Pact, which provided for cooperation to preserve the status quo in southeastern Europe.

More significant than the formation of the Balkan Pact was the basic shift now occurring in Soviet foreign policy. Traditionally, the Soviet leaders regarded the League of Nations as an organization of imperialist powers. But with Hitler's rise to power, the apprehensive Russians began to view the League as a possible instrument for organizing collective resistance against anticipated Nazi aggression. This new attitude was encouraged by the French foreign minister, Louis Barthou. A conservative in domestic matters, Barthou's simple and consistent objective in foreign affairs was to build a coalition that would be strong enough to discourage Hitler from expansionist ventures. In addition to cementing the ties among France, the Little Entente, and Poland, Barthou now sought to add the Soviet Union to the status quo bloc. It was due largely to his efforts that the League of Nations invited the Soviet Union to join its ranks, and that the invitation was accepted on September 19, 1934.

The following month, in Marseilles, an assassin's bullets killed Barthou, along with King Alexander of Yugoslavia. It was a turning point in European diplomacy, for Barthou's successors followed a devious and ambivalent policy vis-à-vis Germany. This was particularly true of Pierre Laval, who concluded a pact with Mussolini on January 7, 1935, in which the two agreed to cooperate in case of action by Hitler. They also settled various differences concerning their African possessions. However, a verbal understanding regarding Ethiopia was to lead to much controversy: Mussolini claimed that he had been promised a completely free hand in that country, whereas Laval insisted that the understanding had been limited to economic matters.

Two months later, on March 16, 1935, Germany formally renounced the clauses of the Versailles Treaty concerning its disarmament, reintroduced conscription, and announced that its army would be increased to thirty-six divisions. Britain, France, and Italy responded on April 11 at the Stresa Conference where they agreed on common action against the German menace. The "Stresa front" proved as futile as the Four-Power Pact two years earlier. Each of the signatories promptly proceeded to go its own way: Italy busied itself preparing to invade Ethiopia; Britain made a separate naval agreement with Germany on June 18 permitting the latter to build up to 35 percent of British strength; France concluded on May 2 a five-year alliance with Russia, each promising to aid the other in case of unprovoked attack. On May 16, Czechoslovakia signed a similar pact with Russia, though Russian aid to Czechoslovakia depended on France also providing aid as required by the 1924 alliance.

In conclusion, Hitler's accession to power had stimulated within two years several new diplomatic groupings—the Balkan Pact, the revived Little Entente, the French-Russian alliance, and the Czech-Russian alliance—all designed to block any aggressive moves on the Führer's part. On the other hand, there were serious conflicts within this diplomatic lineup. The British-German Naval Pact was resented in Paris, the German-Polish Nonaggression Pact of January 1934 was not appreciated in Paris, and Laval basically distrusted his Soviet ally and preferred to make his own private deals on the side. With the outbreak of the Ethiopian crisis, these conflicts undermined the League of Nations and the entire postwar diplomatic structure.

III.   ITALY CONQUERS ETHIOPIA

On October 3, 1935, Mussolini's legions invaded the independent African kingdom of Ethiopia. Behind this naked aggression were several motivations: the Fascist yen for imperial glory, the hope that colonial expansion would relieve unemployment at home, and Mussolini's conviction that Laval had given him the green light and that opposition from other quarters would not be sufficient to stop him—an assumption that proved to be quite justified.

When the Italian army began its invasion of Ethiopia the council of the League of Nations declared Italy the aggressor, and the Assembly voted for economic sanctions. These sanctions,

which went into effect on November 18, 1935, included embargoes on arms, credits, and certain raw materials but did not include the key materials of oil, coal, iron, and steel. Despite such limitations, the sanctions did represent a significant beginning toward stopping the Italian advance. Also, world public opinion expressed itself overwhelmingly against Mussolini's aggression, and the Ethiopians resisted stoutly.

At this point, Laval squandered what chance there was of stopping the Italians. Early in December 1935 he persuaded the British Foreign Secretary Sir Samuel Hoare to accept a plan by which Italy would be given outright about half of Ethiopia and would control the remaining half of the country as a "zone of economic expansion and settlement." The two negotiators agreed to maintain secrecy until the plan had been submitted to the interested parties: Italy, Ethiopia, and the League. Laval, however, anticipated difficulties in Britain, so he leaked the plan to the French press. To his astonishment, the news of the deal aroused a storm of indignation in both London and Paris. Hoare was forced to resign and was succeeded by Anthony Eden. The following month, Laval also had to go, after a smashing defeat in the Chamber.

For a while it seemed like a clean sweep for the supporters of the League against aggression. But the basic issue still was whether the sanctions would be made effective by adding the key materials, particularly oil. Eden was in favor of doing so, but the new French foreign minister, Pierre Flandin, persisted in dragging his feet. Flandin's chief argument was that Mussolini would quit the League if oil sanctions were voted. He insisted that another attempt be made to reach a settlement. Since the British cabinet was not united behind Eden, Flandin had his way, and effective sanctions were never enforced. The significance of this decision is apparent in the following revelation by Hitler's interpreter, Dr. Paul Schmidt:

In 1938, on the eve of the Munich Conference, Mussolini admitted that the League of Nations had very nearly succeeded in countering aggression by means of collective security. "If the League of Nations had followed Eden's advice in the Abyssinian dispute," he said to Hitler, "and had extended economic sanctions to oil, I would have had to withdraw from Abyssinia within a week. That would have been an incalculable disaster for me."[1]

The death blow to any remaining hope of effective sanctions came with Hitler's occupation of the Rhineland on March 7, 1936. This was a fateful move with far-reaching repercussions (see Section IV). It made the British and French governments even more sensitive to the German threat and more determined to placate Mussolini to keep him on their side and within the League of Nations. Consequently, the Council voted on April 20, 1936, to continue the sanctions without oil, thus spelling the doom of the Ethiopian armies that in the meantime had been fighting the Italians.

The Ethiopian tribal leaders, in their suicidal pride and ignorance, scorned guerrilla warfare as unworthy and demeaning. Instead, attempting to wage a war of position, they were mercilessly bombarded, strafed, and even sprayed with mustard gas. After a campaign of seven months, the Italians triumphantly entered Addis Ababa on May 5, 1936. The same day, Mussolini proclaimed "a Roman peace, which is expressed in this simple, irrevocable, definite phrase— `Ethiopia is Italian.'" Four days later the "King of Italy" assumed the title of "Emperor of Ethiopia." And so, at a cost of 3,000 men and $1 billion, Mussolini had won an empire of 350,000 square miles, 10 million inhabitants, and rich natural resources.

As far as Europe and the rest of the world were concerned, the significance of the Ethiopian affair was that it undermined the League of Nations. Many small countries such as Greece, Rumania, and Yugoslavia had loyally supported the League during the crisis and enforced the sanctions against Italy. But their only rewards were heavy economic losses, and furthermore they were exposing themselves to the wrath of Mussolini, the triumphant Duce. The obvious moral was that, given the undependability of the leading Western powers, collective security was a delusion. Accordingly, the small countries henceforth looked only to their own interests and turned their backs on the League of Nations. Ironically, the sacrifice of the League did not keep Italy on the side of the Western powers against Germany, which had been the great objective of those who insisted on placating Mussolini. Instead, the appeasement had precisely the opposite effect. Both Mussolini and Hitler were im-

pressed by their striking victories in Ethiopia and the Rhineland, and they saw the vast possibilities of coordinated, aggressive activities. The final outcome was not the isolation of Nazi Germany but the formation of the Rome-Berlin Axis.

IV.   ROME-BERLIN AXIS

At the beginning of the Ethiopian crisis Hitler played a wait-and-see game. If Mussolini failed, a rival in central Europe would be eliminated; if he won, the collective security system would be undermined, and Hitler's lebensraum plans would be helped. On March 7, 1936, Hitler dramatically ended his passive policy by sending a force of 35,000 marching into the Rhineland. The Versailles Treaty had stipulated that Germany should have no fortifications or armed forces on the left bank of the Rhine nor in a zone of fifty kilometers from the right bank. Hitler's violation of this provision was a move of first-rate strategic significance. The French system of alliances was based on the accessibility of central Europe to the French army. With the reoccupation of the Rhineland and the building of the Siegfried Line fortifications, which was immediately started, the French no longer had this accessibility. France was cut off from its allies, whereas Germany's strength was immeasurably increased because its vitals were no longer left vulnerable by a demilitarized Rhineland. In short, Hitler's Rhineland coup represented a tremendous upset in Europe's military and diplomatic balance of power.

French Premier Sarraut and Foreign Minister Flandin wanted to stop Hitler by mobilizing the army and dispatching an ultimatum. This plan would have worked, for it is now known that the German armed forces were not yet ready to wage serious war. Hitler had ordered his divisions to retire without firing a shot if France mobilized and sent its army across the frontier. But France did not mobilize, because the British government now held back as much as the French government had done during the Ethiopian crisis. When Flandin consulted Prime Minister Baldwin, the latter replied, "You may be right, but if there is *even one chance in a hundred* that war would follow from your police operation, I have not the right to commit England. . . . England is not in a state to go to war."[2]

The French government, itself divided, was incapable of decisive action without Britain's support. Since this was not forthcoming, Hitler won a major victory with no opposition. One result of Hitler's triumph was the beginning of the end of the French system of alliances. At the same time that the construction of the Siegfried Line cut off France from central and eastern Europe, Germany conducted an economic offensive in southeastern Europe that made that region virtually an economic dependency. By 1936, Germany was taking 51 percent of Turkey's total exports, 48 percent of Bulgaria's, 36 percent of Greece's, 24 percent of Yugoslavia's, and 23 percent of Hungary's.

The Rhineland coup also served to bring together the hitherto antagonistic Führer and Duce. Mussolini deeply appreciated Hitler's role in distracting the attention of the League of Nations at a time when oil sanctions were still a possibility. Within a short time, the two dictators had formed a working partnership that quickly made a shambles of the existing diplomatic structure.

With the Austro-German accord of July 11, 1936, Hitler undertook to respect the integrity of Austria, thus removing the main source of discord between Rome and Berlin. A week later, civil war broke out in Spain, a tragic episode (see Section V) that was to drag on for three years. During that time Hitler and Mussolini worked together to overthrow the Spanish Republic. On October 24, 1936, the Rome-Berlin Axis was formally constituted. Italy and Germany agreed on general cooperation as well as on such specific issues as German recognition of Italian Ethiopia in return for economic concessions. The following month Japan associated itself with the Axis by concluding anti-Communist pacts with Germany and then with Italy.

And so by the end of 1936, the diplomatic balance was entirely different from what it had been when Hitler came into office. Italy and Germany now had a working partnership. France had lost its former hegemony and declined into relative isolation. Its old allies in central Europe were drifting away, and the new alliance with the Soviet Union remained largely a paper creation. The French governments distrusted the Soviet

regime to the point of refusing to conclude the military convention needed to make their alliance fully effective. Likewise, the relations of the French and the British were far from being close or trustful. The distrust within the status-quo bloc, together with the crippling of the League of Nations, enabled the Rome-Berlin Axis during the next three years to score triumph after triumph with virtually no opposition.

V.   SPANISH CIVIL WAR

The Spanish Civil War was of more than ordinary significance because it was essentially two wars in one—a deep-rooted social conflict generated by the decay and tensions of Spanish society, and a dress rehearsal for World War II arising from the clash of ideologies and of great power interests.

Spain in the twentieth century was very different from what it had been in the sixteenth, when that country was the most powerful and feared nation in Europe. Symbolic of the decline during the intervening centuries was the Spanish-American War of 1898. With humiliating ease, the United States stripped Spain of most of its remaining colonial possessions. The war exposed not only the military weakness of Spain but also the corruption and inefficiency of the entrenched oligarchy that ruled the country. Three principal elements made this oligarchy: the large landowners, the army, and the church.

The landowners, comprising about 35,000 families, possessed about 50 percent of the total arable land. They contributed nothing to the national economy, being absentee owners who squandered their incomes in Madrid or foreign capitals. The army was noteworthy for only two reasons: the extraordinarily large number of officers in proportion to the number of rank and file, and its constant intervention in the politics of the country. Finally, the Roman Catholic church in Spain was a wealthy and powerful institution. It controlled the educational system and exerted much influence through certain newspapers, labor groups, and various lay organizations. The Church's power engendered much anti-clericalism, and the attacks on priests, nuns, and Church property during the Civil War were by no means unique in Spanish history.

Such was the Spain that Alfonso XIII was called on to rule when he ascended the throne in 1902. His reign was marked by cabinet instability and numerous strikes, mutinies, and assassinations. Between 1923 and 1930 a surface calm was imposed by the dictatorship of General Primo de Rivera, who followed Mussolini's example in abolishing the constitution, censoring the press, and restricting the universities. After the dictator was gone, popular discontent turned against the king himself. The Depression made the situation still more unstable, until at last Alfonso decided to restore the constitution and to hold municipal elections in April 1931. The vote went heavily against the regime, the Republicans carrying forty-six of the fifty provincial capitals. The state of public opinion was evident, and Alfonso prudently left the country, as four of his predecessors had done since 1789.

A republic was proclaimed on April 14, 1931, and elections were held for a Constituent Assembly, or Cortes. When this body assembled in July, its members fell into three broad groupings: a conservative right, a republican center, and a left comprised of Socialists, Stalinist and Trotskyite Communists, and Anarcho-Syndicalists. The center and the left, which together constituted a large majority, combined to adopt a liberal constitution that provided universal suffrage for both sexes, complete religious freedom, the separation of church and state, secularized education, and nationalized church property.

The first prime minister under the new constitution, the Republican Manuel Azaña, who was supported also by the moderate Socialists, passed typical middle-of-the-road reforms. Government subsidies to the church were abolished, certain monastic orders were banned, the pay of farm laborers was raised above the usual twenty cents per day, a few large estates were divided among the peasants with partial compensation for the owners, hundreds of army officers were retired, and home rule was granted to the province of Catalonia. With the dissolution of the Constituent Assembly at the end of 1933, the first elections for a regular Cortes returned a conservative majority. The *bienio negro,* the "black two years" of clerical reaction, followed. Autonomy for Catalonia was revoked, and much of the legislation concerning the church

and land distribution was either repealed or not enforced.

In preparation for the elections of February 1936, the parties of the left and left-center now banded together to form a Popular Front similar to that which had just appeared in France. The coalition won a narrow victory and Azaña formed a new Republican cabinet, which the left parties supported but did not enter. Catalan autonomy was restored, and anticlerical measures along with mild social reform were resumed. In retrospect, the Republicans appear to have blundered in emphasizing anticlericalism rather than agrarian reform, which most Spaniards accepted. The anticlerical policy alienated the fervent Catholics and much of the middle class. At the same time, the Great Depression, with its widespread unemployment, strengthened the extremist and weakened the moderate parties. To hold the desperate workers, the Socialists had to move steadily to the extreme left. In reaction, much of the middle class allied itself with the extreme right—hence the mounting ideological passions and the polarization of political life to the point where parliamentary government became increasingly difficult.

At this juncture, the Spanish rightists, with the connivance of Germany and Italy, and under the leadership of General Francisco Franco, began a counterrevolution. On July 17, 1936, the army in Morocco revolted, and the next day a number of mainland generals took up arms. The rebels, or self-styled Nationalists, quickly overran the southern and the western regions, and these sections of the country remained their main bases throughout the long struggle. Franco had hoped that with the advantage of surprise, he would be able to capture the main cities and fortresses quickly and so gain control of the entire country. Instead, the struggle dragged on for almost three years with a savagery reminiscent of the sixteenth-century Wars of Religion.

The Loyalists lost about one-half the country in the first weeks of the revolt, but they then rallied and managed to retain control of Madrid in the center, the Basque provinces in the north, and the highly developed east coast with the large cities of Barcelona and Valencia. The Loyalists were now in a strong position. They had behind them the industrial centers, the most densely populated regions, and the capital, with its exceptionally large gold reserve. Despite these advantages, the Loyalists were eventually beaten, mainly because they were unable to obtain arms from abroad in quantities approaching those received by the Nationalists.

That such a turn of events should take place was paradoxical because the Loyalists had both the money to import arms and the right to do so under international law, since they constituted the legal government of the country. The British and French governments, however, refused to allow the sale of arms to the Republican regime. They were inhibited by the sharp division of public opinion in their respective countries concerning the Civil War, and they feared that an unrestricted flow of arms to the contending parties might escalate into a European war. Accordingly, Britain and France took the lead in sponsoring a nonintervention agreement, which was accepted by Germany, Italy, and the Soviet Union, as well as by several smaller countries.

The agreement provided that the signatories should refrain from shipping arms to Spain, but Germany and Italy violated their pledge from the beginning, and the Soviet Union soon was doing likewise. Italy sent not only arms but also regular army units, which rapidly increased in numbers as the war continued. Russia, like Germany, sent no ground troops but did provide war materials of all types in addition to technical advisers and pilots. The Loyalists were also aided by the International Brigades, which first went into action in November 1936 in the defense of Madrid. The brigades were made up of volunteers—mostly young idealists from Britain, France, and the United States—as well as antifascist émigrés from Italy and Germany. The majority were not Communists when they enlisted, but most of those few who survived did become members of that organization, partly because of their experiences and also because of indoctrination by their political commissars.

For two years there was a stalemate, with the Nationalists controlling the agrarian western and southern regions, and the Loyalists, the more developed northern and eastern sections together with the Madrid salient. But in mid-1938, the Soviet government decided to cut its losses and stop the aid to Spain because of the contin-

ued refusal of the Western democracies to end the nonintervention farce. The Soviet withdrawal enabled Franco's armies to break the stalemate. In late December 1938, the Nationalists began their great offensive against Catalonia. Within a month they had taken Barcelona. Madrid and Valencia were now helpless, but they held out for two more months. With their fall in late March, the Civil War ended.

For Spain, the long ordeal involved 750,000 casualties out of a population of 25 million, and one of every seven of the uninjured was left without shelter. For the Western powers, the Civil War represented another stunning defeat. As in the case of Ethiopia, they had again shown themselves to be weak and vacillating in the face of Axis aggression. The same pattern was to appear again during the German annexation of Austria and Czechoslovakia.

VI. END OF AUSTRIA AND CZECHOSLOVAKIA

Nineteen thirty-eight was the year of the great bloodless victories of the Axis powers. At the center of these fateful developments was Neville Chamberlain, who succeeded Stanley Baldwin as prime minister in May 1937. Little by little Chamberlain took over the direction of British foreign policy even though Anthony Eden was his foreign secretary. "The truth," wrote Eden, "was that some of my seniors in the Cabinet . . . could not believe that Mussolini and Hitler were as untrustworthy as I painted them. After all, had not Mussolini defeated the reds and made the trains in Italy run on time?"[3] Behind the fatuity implied by Eden, the conservatives in both Britain and France were motivated primarily by deep-seated distrust of Russia, and therefore by a determination to appease the dictators in order to gain time for rearmament. This conservative strategy explains in large measure the stunning Axis victories of these years. The Conservatives felt that they could do business with the dictators, and that this was preferable to "woolly" and "idealistic" projects based on the principle of collective security. Their counterparts in France likewise preferred to deal with Mussolini and Hitler rather than to turn to the Russians, with whom they were nominally

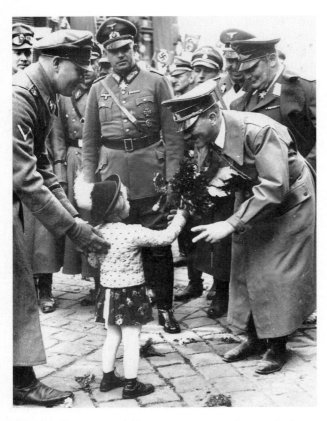

A smiling Adolf Hitler accepts a tribute from a little girl following his victory over and annexation of the Sudetenland. An approving General Hermann Göring, chief of the *Luftwaffe,* stands behind Hitler.

allied. The direct outcome of this way of thinking was the sacrifice of the independent states of Austria, Albania, and Czechoslovakia—a sacrifice that led, not to "peace in our time" as was fondly imagined, but to World War II.

On February 12, 1938, Hitler invited Austria's Chancellor Kurt von Schuschnigg to his Bavarian mountain retreat at Berchtesgaden. There the Führer demanded various concessions that would have seriously violated Austrian independence. Schuschnigg resisted by scheduling a plebiscite on March 13 on the following question: "Are you for a free and independent, German and Christian Austria?"

In the ensuing crisis, no great power went to the aid of Austria. France was caught between two ministries and had no government at all. Mussolini was resentful that he had not been

forewarned, but his hands were tied by the Rome-Berlin Axis. Chamberlain informed the House of Commons on February 22 that ". . . we must not try to delude small weak nations into thinking that they will be protected by the League against aggression and acting accordingly when we know that nothing of the kind can be expected."[4]

On March 11, Schuschnigg, in the face of two ultimatums, was compelled first to cancel the plebiscite and then to hand over the chancellorship to the Nazi minister of interior, Dr. Artur von Seyss-Inquart. The latter, who had been in continual telephone communication with Berlin, now issued a statement that had been dictated from Berlin and that requested the German government "to send in German troops as soon as possible . . . to restore peace and order . . . and to prevent bloodshed." On March 13, decrees from Berlin and Vienna declared Austria a part of Germany, and the next day Hitler made his triumphant entry into the land of his birth. Thus Austria was taken over by telephone. The event was not mentioned in the League of Nations.

With Austria safely annexed, Hitler turned against the neighboring state of Czechoslovakia, a larger and much stronger country with an efficient modern army and a considerable industrial establishment. But the presence of a German minority of 3 million in the Sudeten borderlands made Czechoslovakia vulnerable to Nazi propaganda and subversion.

With the disappearance of Austria, the Sudeten problem became a serious menace for Czechoslovakia. The country was now surrounded on three sides by the enlarged Reich. Even more serious were certain indications that the British and French governments were ready to abandon Czechoslovakia as they had Austria. This soon became apparent when Hitler precipitated the Czechoslovak crisis on September 12 with an inflammatory speech in which he violently attacked President Benes for his "persecution" of the Sudeten Germans and warned that "if these tortured creatures can find no rights and no help themselves, they will get both from us." The speech was followed by widespread rioting on the part of the Sudeten Germans. The Prague government proclaimed martial law, Nazi leaders fled to Germany, and Hitler concentrated troops along Czechoslovakia's frontier. Chamberlain feared that if Hitler actually invaded, a chain reaction might be unleashed that would embroil France and ultimately Britain. To avert this danger, Chamberlain and Daladier met with Hitler at Berchtesgaden on September 15.

Hitler baldly set forth his demand for annexation of the Sudeten areas on the basis of self-determination, and he indicated his readiness "to risk a world war" to attain his end. Chamberlain returned home and persuaded first his own cabinet, and then the French, to accept Hitler's terms. The two governments in turn urged acceptance on the Czechoslovak government. When the latter resisted, they brought every pressure to bear, including the threat of desertion. Prague finally capitulated on September 21, in return for an Anglo-French guarantee for the new frontier.

The next day Chamberlain flew to Godesberg in the belief that he only needed to work out with Hitler the technical details for the transfer of the territories. Instead, the Führer made new demands: immediate surrender of the predominantly German areas without waiting for plebiscites and without any removal or destruction of military or economic establishments. In addition, Hitler now supported territorial claims on Czechoslovakia made by Poland and Hungary. These new demands precipitated an acute international crisis. Czechoslovakia ordered full mobilization; France called up 600,000 reservists; and the Soviet foreign minister, Maxim Litvinov, declared on September 21 before the League of Nations Assembly, "We intend to fulfill our obligations under the Pact, and together with France to afford assistance to Czechoslovakia by the ways open to us."

"This public and unqualified declaration," as Churchill pointed out, was treated by the Western powers with "indifference—not to say disdain." Instead, they acted on Mussolini's suggestion for a four-power conference of Britain, France, Germany, and Italy. The meetings were held in Munich on September 29, and without either Czech or Soviet participation, it was decided that Hitler should be granted all his demands, the only modifications being the face-saving provisions that the Sudeten lands should be occupied in stages and that the final delimitation of the frontier should be determined by an international commission.

As Churchill pointed out in the House of Commons, "All that the Prime Minister has gained for Czechoslovakia has been that the German dictator, instead of snatching the victuals from the table, has been content to have them served to him course by course." Yet the Munich surrender was popular with the masses in both Britain and France. Chamberlain and Daladier were hailed as peacemakers by enthusiastic crowds. Loud cheers greeted Chamberlain when he declared, "I believe it is peace in our time." Hitler was gratefully believed when he avowed, "This is the last territorial claim I have to make in Europe." The events of the next year were to prove the worthlessness of such statements.

The first signs that further demands were in the offing was the gradual taking of substantial border regions of the Czechoslovak state. In accordance with the provisions reached at Munich, an international commission was appointed to determine the new frontiers. It soon became apparent that despite their commitments, Britain and France had no interest in the proceedings of the commission. Accordingly, no plebiscites were held, and the decisions were made by two German generals who were members of the commission. In the end, Germany acquired 10,000 square miles of Czechoslovak territory with a population of 3.5 million, of whom about one-fifth were Czechs. At the same time, Poland seized the Teschen area with its rich coal fields and Hungary occupied generous portions of Slovakia and Ruthenia. What remained of the Czechoslovak state now disintegrated into three fragments: an autonomous Slovakia, an autonomous Ruthenia, and the Czech provinces of Bohemia and Moravia.

The finale came in March 1939, when the puppet heads of the Czech and Slovak lands were summoned to Berlin to hear from Hitler the dissolution of their respective states. On March 15, German troops entered Prague. Bohemia and Moravia were declared a protectorate of the Reich, and Slovakia was also placed under German protection. Simultaneously, the Hungarians were allowed by Hitler to invade and annex Ruthenia in the east. So ended the state of Czechoslovakia, as well as the illusion that Hitler's objective was simply the redemption of German-populated lands. The partitioning of Czechoslovakia with its predominantly Slavic populations was a rude awakening for those who had taken the Führer at his word. Chamberlain was particularly shocked, for as an orthodox British businessman, he had assumed that Hitler would keep the pledge that he had no further territorial ambitions in Europe. The breaking of this promise forced Chamberlain, as well as Daladier, to reappraise painfully their policy and to take a firmer stand when Hitler now turned on Poland.

VII.   COMING OF WAR

With Austria and Czechoslovakia taken, and with Spain and Hungary in the Axis camp, it was becoming apparent that the Western powers and the Soviet Union needed to work together to stem further aggression. "The key to a Grand Alliance," wrote Churchill, "was an understanding with Russia." The Russian government, for its part, was more than ready for such an "understanding." On March 18, it informed Berlin that it refused to recognize the partitioning of Czechoslovakia. Three days later, the Soviet government proposed a six-power conference (Britain, France, Russia, Poland, Rumania, and Turkey) to consider measures against future aggression. London replied that the proposal was "premature," and so it was not pursued further. But in the same month, Hitler forced Lithuania to hand over the city of Memel, and he sent stiff demands to Warsaw concerning Danzig and the Polish Corridor. Faced by the prospect of limitless German expansion, Chamberlain, on March 31, pledged Anglo-French aid to the Poles in the case of "any action which clearly threatened Polish independence." A week later this commitment was expanded into a pact of mutual assistance. The next move of the Axis was Italy's invasion and conquest of Albania, which began on April 7. Again Britain and France countered by pledging on April 13 full support to Rumania and Greece in the event that their independence was clearly threatened. The following month, Anglo-Turkish and Franco-Turkish mutual assistance pacts were signed.

These commitments to various east European countries were worthless unless Britain acted in concert with the Soviet Union. As Churchill declared in the House of Commons on May 19, "Without an effective eastern front, there can be no satisfactory defence of our interests in the West, and without Russia there can be no effective eastern front."[5] Chamberlain finally opened negotiations with the Russians on April 15.

On the surface, both Russia and the Western powers favored the organization of a "Peace Front." However, given the current atmosphere, this was easier said than done. For example, on May 31, Vyacheslav Molotov, who had replaced Maxim Litvinov as Soviet foreign minister, declared that no Peace Front was possible unless Britain and France accepted the elementary principle of reciprocity and equal obligations. Specifically, he demanded that the border states of the Soviet Union—Finland and the three Baltic countries—must be given the same guarantees as had been extended to Poland, Greece, Rumania, and Turkey. But the Baltic states had concluded nonaggression pacts with Germany and refused any Soviet-Western guarantees. London took the position that this ended the possibility of guarantees, whereas the Russians interpreted it as legalistic quibbling and evading of the issue. Likewise, the Poles refused to agree to allow the Red Army to operate on Polish territory in case of war. Soviet aid, they insisted, should be limited to providing war materials. From the Polish viewpoint this view was understandable, but the Soviet Marshal Voroshilov retorted, "Just as the British and American troops in the past World War would have been unable to participate in military collaboration with the French armed forces if they had no possibility of operating in French territory, the Soviet armed forces could not participate in military collaboration with armed forces of France and Great Britain if they are not allowed access to Polish territory."[6]

Behind this sparring was the gnawing suspicion in London that the real objective of the Soviets was to obtain legal justification for marching into Poland and the Baltic states at their pleasure. The Russians, on their part, feared that if they agreed to go to war in the event of an attack on Poland and could not send their army into Polish territory to meet the advancing Germans, the latter would quickly overrun Poland and reach the Soviet frontier. Would Britain and France then wage serious war against Germany, or would they sit back and leave the Soviet Union to face the onslaught alone? Their apprehension was strengthened when, in July, two representatives of Chamberlain, acting on his instructions, broached to a German official in London the possibility of a British-German nonaggression pact that would enable Britain to rid itself of its commitments to Poland. Thus Chamberlain, who was not very happy about the guarantee to Poland, and was even less happy about the negotiations with the Soviet Union, was feeling out the Germans with a view to reviving his appeasement policy.

All of this was behind Stalin's fateful decision to turn to his hitherto mortal Axis enemies. On August 23 Russia and Germany signed a nonaggression pact and agreed to remain neutral if either were attacked by a third power. Significantly enough, the pact did not contain the so-called "escape clause," characteristic of Soviet nonaggression pacts with other countries, that would render the agreement inoperative if either party committed aggression against a third state. Perhaps this omission was related to a secret protocol in the pact stipulating that in the event of a "territorial or political rearrangement," Lithuania and western Poland were to come under the German sphere of influence, and the remainder of Poland, together with Finland, Estonia, Latvia, and Bessarabia, were to fall to the Russian sphere.

Now that he was protected on his eastern flank, Hitler felt free to strike. Early in the morning of September 1, 1939, without a declaration of war, German troops, tanks, and planes crossed Poland's frontier all along the line. On September 3, both Britain and France declared war on Germany. Mussolini, despite his oratory about the Axis "pact of steel," remained neutral. World War II had begun.

SUGGESTED READINGS

Conflicting interpretations of the diplomacy of the 1930s are presented by G. L. Weinberg, *Diplomatic Revolution in Europe 1933–1936*, and *The Foreign Policy of Hitler's Germany: Starting World War II, 1937–1939* (University of Chicago, 1970, 1980), who holds Hitler responsible for the war because of his demand for a free hand in central and eastern Europe; and A. J. P. Taylor, *The Origins of the Second World War* (Hamilton, 1961), who holds that war resulted primarily from Anglo-French blundering. A convenient brief survey of the steps to war is available in J. Remak, *The Origins of the Second World War* (Prentice Hall, 1975).

For the background to Japanese expansionism, see A. Iriye, *After Imperialism: The Search for a New Order in the Far East, 1921–1931* (Harvard University, 1965); D. M. Brown, *Nationalism in Japan* (University of California, 1955); Y. C. Maxon, *Control of Japanese Foreign Policy: A Study of Civil-Military Rivalry, 1930–1945* (University of California, 1957); and J. B. Crowley, *Japan's Quest for Autonomy* (Princeton University, 1966). Details concerning the actual expansion are available in D. Bergamini, *Japan's Imperial Conspiracy* (Morrow, 1971); J. M. Maki, *Conflict and Tension in the Far East: Key Documents, 1894–1960* (University of Washington, 1961); D. Borg, *The United States and the Far Eastern Crisis of 1933–38* (Harvard University, 1964); and F. C. Jones, *Japan's New Order in East Asia: Its Rise and Fall, 1937–1945* (Oxford University, 1954).

The Italian invasion of Ethiopia is considered in G. W. Baer, *The Coming of the Italo-Ethiopian War* (Harvard University, 1961); A. Mockler, *Haile Selassie's War: The Italo-Ethiopian Campaign* (Random House, 1985); G. W. Baer, *Test Case: Italy, Ethiopia and the League of Nations* (Hoover Institution, 1976); and A. Sbacchi, *Ethiopia Under Mussolini: Fascism and the Colonial Experience* (Zed Press, 1985).

For the background of the Spanish Civil War, see E. E. Malefakis, *Agrarian Reform and Peasant Revolution in Spain: Origins of the Civil War* (Yale University, 1970); and P. Preston, ed., *Revolution and War in Spain 1931–1939* (Methuen, 1985). The war itself is studied from various viewpoints in D. A. Puzzo, *Spain and the Great Powers, 1936–1941* (Columbia University, 1962); H. Thomas, *The Spanish Civil War* (Harper & Row, 1961); G. Jackson, *The Spanish Republic and the Civil War 1931–1939* (Princeton University, 1965); B. Bolloten, *The Grand Camouflage* (Hollis and Carter, 1961); and the two books by S. G. Payne, *Politics and the Military in Modern Spain* (Stanford University, 1967), and *The Spanish Revolution* (W. W. Norton, 1970).

The rapid drift to war after the Ethiopian invasion and the outbreak of the Spanish Civil War is described from various viewpoints by F. W. Deakin, *The Brutal Friendship: Mussolini, Hitler and the Fall of Italian Fascism* (Weidenfeld and Nicolson, 1962); G. F. Kennan, *Russia and the West* (Little, Brown, 1960); E. H. Carr, *German-Soviet Relations Between the Two World Wars* (Hopkins, 1951); M. George, *The Warped Vision: British Foreign Policy 1933–1939* (University of Pittsburgh, 1965); A. A. Offner, *American Appeasement: United States Foreign Policy and Germany 1933–1938* (Harvard University, 1969); and T. Taylor, *Munich: The Price of Peace* (Doubleday, 1979). The most recent study of the drift to World War II is D. C. Watt, *How War Came: The Immediate Origins of the Second World War, 1938–1939* (Pantheon, 1989), which uses effectively the captured archives of the German foreign ministry, and which includes revealing appraisals of the leading personalities on both sides.

42

World War II: Global Repercussions

The next World War will be fought with stones.

Albert Einstein

In signing the pact with Stalin, Hitler's aim was to secure Russia's neutrality while he disposed of Poland. Then he could, and did, marshal his armed forces against Britain and France. He declared privately at the time, "Let us think of the pact as securing our rear." As for Russia, that country also was on his list of future victims. "At present she is not dangerous," he stated. "We can oppose Russia only when we are free in the West. For the next year or two, the present situation will remain."[1] Thus, Hitler from the beginning had charted his schedule of conquest: first Poland, then the West, and finally Russia. He adhered to this schedule, and in doing so determined the course of World War II until Russia and the West became strong enough to seize the initiative.

World War II, like World War I, began as a European conflict precipitated by the issue of minorities in eastern Europe. During the first two years the campaigns were waged on European battlefields. Then Japan's attack on Pearl Harbor in 1941 transformed war into a global struggle, just as America's intervention in 1917 had transformed World War I. At this point, however, the similarity between the two wars ends. With Japan's lightning conquest of the entire East and Southeast Asia, World War II came to involve much more of the globe than did the preceding war. Moreover, the two wars differed fundamentally in the strategy and weapons employed. During the first war defense, based on trenches and machine-gun nests, proved superior to offense. During the second war offense, based on tanks and planes, proved stronger than defense. This explains the extraordinary fluidity of battle lines that characterized the later struggle. Whole countries, and even continents, changed hands back and forth in striking contrast to the bloody stalemate on the western front between 1914 and 1918.

I. EUROPEAN PHASE OF THE WAR

Partitioning of Poland

In Poland the Germans demonstrated for the first time the deadly effectiveness of their new type of *blitzkrieg,* or "lightning war." First came waves of dive bombers, or Stukas, blasting communication lines and spreading terror and confusion. Then followed the armored tank divisions, or Panzers, smashing holes in the enemy lines, penetrating deeply into the rear, destroying transportation and communication facilities, and cutting the opposing forces into ribbons. Finally, the lighter motorized divisions and the infantry moved in for the "mopping up" of the splintered and battered enemy forces, supported where necessary by air and artillery cover.

Unfortunate Poland, with its flat plains and obsolete army, was a "setup" for this type of warfare. Within ten days the campaign had been virtually decided. The German tank and plane teams raced through the Polish countryside against declining resistance. The speed of the German advance forced Stalin to move in order to take over the territories he had staked out in his pact with Hitler. On September 17, the Red Army crossed into eastern Poland, and two days later it established contact with the triumphant Germans. On September 27, Warsaw fell. The Polish government leaders fled to Rumania and thence to France. Their country was partitioned two days later. The Germans took 37,000 square miles with 22 million people, and the Russians took 77,000 square miles with a population of 13 million. Within less than a month, one of the largest countries of Europe had disappeared completely from the map. (See map of World War II: Axis Conquests, 1939–1943, p. 643.)

The Soviet government now took advantage of the secret protocol of the Moscow Pact to strengthen its strategic position in the Baltic area. In September and October 1939, it compelled Estonia, Latvia, and Lithuania to accept Russian military bases on their territories. Lithuania, by way of compensation, received the long-desired district and city of Vilna, hitherto a part of Poland. The Soviets next demanded from Finland certain

A motorized German cavalry sweeps into Poland in the early days of the German invasion.

World War II: Axis Conquests, 1939–1943

territories in the Karelian Isthmus and around Petsamo on the Arctic Ocean. The Finns refused, and on November 30 the Red Army attacked.

Finland appealed to the League of Nations, and that body expelled the Soviet Union from membership. The Finns resisted the Russian onslaught with unexpected success, repulsing repeated attacks on their Mannerheim Line. The Russians, who had grossly underestimated Finnish strength, brought up their regular forces with heavy artillery. By mid-March they cracked the Mannerheim Line and forced the Finns to sue for peace. The ensuing treaty gave the Russians somewhat more territory than they originally demanded, including the Petsamo region, the port of Viipuri, several islands in the Gulf of Finland, and a naval base at Hanko.

Perhaps the chief significance of these Russian moves against Finland and the other Baltic states was that they reflected the rivalry and distrust that existed behind the façade of Russo-German cooperation. This was demonstrated by Russia's insistence on the evacuation to Germany of the Baltic Germans who for centuries had dominated urban centers such as Memel and Riga.

Poland to France

Meanwhile, the western front had been disconcertingly quiet. The British and the French had stood helplessly by while Poland was being partitioned. They could not enter the Baltic Sea, which the Germans had sealed tight; their air forces were unable to operate across the breadth of the Reich; and their ground troops were confronted by the elaborate fortifications built by Hitler following his 1936 occupation of the Rhineland. Thus the French were forced to sit behind their Maginot Line, while the Germans made no move from behind their Siegfried Line or West Wall.

This surface calm proved deceptive. On April 9, 1940, the Wehrmacht suddenly erupted into action, sweeping through Denmark and making landings on the coast of Norway. The main objective was to gain control of the Norwegian fiords, which could provide invaluable bases for German submarines and also safeguard the shipment of Swedish iron ore down the coast to Germany. The Danes could offer no resistance, but the Norwegians, with British support, fought back stubbornly. But by early June France itself was in mortal peril, so the Allied expeditionary forces sailed away, accompanied by the Norwegian government, which took refuge in London. The Germans set up their own administration in Norway under the collaborationist *Quisling,* whose name became a synonym for a self-serving traitor.

The Allied setback in Norway was soon dwarfed by the stunning blitzkrieg that overran France and the Low Countries in seven weeks. On May 10 the Germans attacked Holland and Belgium, and two days later France. The Dutch defense collapsed in five days. The Belgians held out longer, but by May 28 King Leopold surrendered in person and the Belgian army capitulated. Meanwhile the Germans had skirted the northern end of the Maginot Line, which had never been extended to the sea, and drove through the Ardennes Forest, smashing a fifty-mile breach in the French lines at Sedan. The Panzer divisions now raced westward through Amiens to Abbéville on the English Channel, reaching it on May 21. The German breakthrough left the British, French, and Belgian forces in the north cut off from the main French armies. The Allied armies in Flanders, mostly British, retreated to Dunkirk, the only port still free of the enemy. The Royal Air Force covered the evacuation, and a flotilla of assorted boats ferried 366,000 soldiers back to Britain. Yet the British were forced to leave behind all their precious equipment, as well as 13,000 dead and 40,000 prisoners.

With the completion of the Dunkirk evacuation on June 4, the agony of France began. On the following day the German forces resumed their advance southward. By June 13 Paris was occupied, undefended and abandoned by the government. By this time the French premier, Paul Reynaud (who had succeeded Daladier in late March) was thoroughly demoralized and under the influence of appeasers within his cabinet. Originally he had planned to move his government to North Africa, but on June 16 he wearily resigned the premiership to Marshal Pétain. It was this "hero of Verdun" who, ironically, now sued for peace. On June 22, at Compiègne, the site of the signing of the 1918 German armistice, the French accepted the severe armistice terms, including release of all German prisoners of war; disbandment of French military forces; surrender of French warships; and occupation by Germany of slightly over half of France, including the principal industrial and food-producing areas and the entire French coastline to the Spanish border.

The staggering impact of the German blitzkrieg is reflected in the incredibly low casualty figures. During the entire campaign the French lost about 100,000 men, the other Allies 20,000, and the Germans 45,000. These losses were less than half those sustained in single offensives during World War I. The speedy collapse by what was considered to be the strongest Western power came as a most painful shock. Charges of treason and cowardice were leveled in explanation for the great disaster. Though these charges were not altogether unwarranted, other factors seem to have been more decisive. One was the effect of the Russo-German pact, which enabled Hitler to concentrate his forces on a single front. Perhaps most important was the German superiority in several fields, especially in the development of the new blitzkrieg technique.

Battle of Britain

After Dunkirk and the fall of France, Hitler assumed that Britain would see reason and would come to terms. But he failed to reckon with the British people and with Winston Churchill. A born fighter and maverick, Churchill had taken the lead in demanding a firm stand against Axis aggression during the years of appeasement under Chamberlain. This record made him the natural successor to Chamberlain when the latter was forced to resign on May 10, 1940, because of his failure to mobilize the country for a war of survival. Churchill formed an all-party cabinet, and he quickly proved himself an incomparable war leader. With characteristic resoluteness and audacity he told his people—and the world— "We shall fight on the beaches. We shall fight on the landing grounds. We shall fight on the fields and in the streets. We shall fight in the hills; we shall never surrender."

Meanwhile, Hitler was marking time, unsure what the next step should be. The unexpectedly rapid fall of France had caught him by surprise. First he tried to make a deal with the British, for whom he always had genuine respect. When his overtures were ignored, Reichsmarshal Hermann Göring unleashed his Luftwaffe, confident that it could subdue Britain by air attack alone, without resort to a hazardous sea crossing.

The ensuing air assault developed into the critical Battle of Britain, one of the major turning points of World War II. In this epic struggle in the skies, the Luftwaffe had the advantage of numbers—2,670 planes against the Royal Air Force's 1,475. But the RAF Spitfires and Hurricanes were more advanced, because Britain had gone into mass production of planes several years later than Germany. The British also had the use of radar, a new invention that enabled enemy aircraft to be "sighted" fifty to a hundred miles before reaching their targets. With these advantages, a few thousand British and dominion fighter pilots, with a scattering of Poles, Czechs, French, and Belgians, were able to repulse the Luftwaffe and thus end Hitler's chance for invading Britain.

Conquest of the Balkans

Because of his failure in the Battle for Britain, Hitler decided to invade Russia the following spring. Preparing for the projected invasion, in October 1940 Hitler sent troops into Rumania to ready the Rumanian army, which was to participate in the attack on the Soviet Union. At this point, when Hitler was occupying Rumania, Mussolini launched his blundering invasion of Greece. Il Duce, who for long had fancied himself the dean of the dictators, had become jealous of the spectacularly successful Führer. Although formally allied by the Axis Pact, Hitler had gone on from triumph to triumph without consulting or notifying his Italian partner. "Hitler always faces me with a fait accompli," complained Mussolini to his son-in-law and foreign minister, Count Ciano. "This time I am going to pay him back in his own coin. He will find out from the papers that I have occupied Greece."[2]

What Mussolini assumed would be an effortless occupation proved in fact to be a humiliating fiasco. On October 28, 1940, Italian troops crossed from Albania into Greece, expecting a triumphal procession to Athens. But after pushing some distance across the Greek-Albanian frontier, they suffered a decisive defeat at the battle of Metsovo on November 11. Taking advantage of the difficulties of the ponderous Italian armored divisions in the mountains of Epirus, the Greeks invariably made for the high ground and from there cut off and surrounded the enemy below. By mid-November they had driven the Italians back across the frontier into Albania. In the following weeks the Greeks captured the large Albanian towns of Koritsa, Argyrokastron, and Porto Edda. For a while it appeared that Mussolini might even have to endure a Dunkirk in the Adriatic.

At this point Mussolini was rescued from his mortifying predicament by the intervention of his Axis ally. Hitler could not sit back and watch the Italians flounder, particularly because the British were landing air units in Greece, which could prove troublesome once his invasion of Russia was under way. So on April 6 he launched his Operation Marita for the conquest of both Yugoslavia and Greece. As in Poland and France, the Panzer divisions and the Luftwaffe swept everything before them. The mountainous terrain of the Balkan peninsula did not prove an effective obstacle, as had been hoped, and the British ground and air units were too weak to halt the tide. By April 13, the Germans had entered Belgrade, and ten days later the British were evacuating their forces from southern Greece to Crete. The Germans then launched an airborne invasion of Crete, surprising the British who did not expect an air attack from the Greek mainland 180 miles to the north. Though they suffered heavy losses, the Germans finally gained complete control of the island by the beginning of June.

In addition to the triumph in the Balkans, Hitler's armies had won an equally impressive victory in North Africa under the able and energetic General Erwin Rommel. The British under General Wavell had gained the initial success in North Africa when, between December 1940 and February 1941, they had pushed the Italians back from the Egyptian frontier to Tripolitania. But immediately thereafter the British forces were weakened by the withdrawals for the Greek campaign. At the same time the Germans rushed reinforcements to North Africa to bolster their Italian allies. British intelligence underestimated the strength of these reinforcements, so that when Rommel attacked on March 31, 1941, he was able to sweep all before him. In less than a month he captured Benghazi, Bardia, and all of Cyrenaica. With the Balkans and North Africa under his control, Hitler ordered his Wehrmacht across the Soviet frontier on June 22, 1941. (See map of World War II: Axis Conquests, 1939–1943, p. 643.)

II.   GLOBAL PHASE OF THE WAR

Invasion of Russia

Stalin signed the August 1939 nonaggression pact with Hitler for a variety of reasons. He was deeply distrustful of the Western leaders and wanted to gain time to strengthen his military and industrial establishments. He also calculated that sooner or later Germany and the Western powers would clash in a war of attrition, whereas Russia, thanks to the pact, would be free to remain aloof until it was profitable to intervene. "If war begins," he told his comrades, "we cannot simply sit back. *We will have to get into the fighting, but we must be the last to join in.* And we shall join so as to cast the decisive weight onto the scales, the weight that will tip the balance."[3] This strategy was shrewd, yet it boomeranged and came very close to destroying the Soviet state. It was based on the assumption that the German and Western forces were evenly matched and would decimate each other, leaving the Red Army the dominant force on the Continent. Instead, the Wehrmacht crushed all opposition with incredible ease, leaving Germany the master of the Continent and the Soviet Union isolated and imperiled.

At first, it seemed that Russia would collapse as quickly as had Poland and France. The Panzer divisions, in their now familiar fashion, smashed through the frontier defenses and drove deeply into the rear, encircling entire Soviet armies and taking hundreds of thousands of prisoners. By the end of the year the Wehrmacht had penetrated 600 miles eastward, overrunning the most industrialized and populous regions of the Soviet Union.

One reason for the German triumph, apart from the important factor of surprise, was numerical preponderance at the outset. Hitler struck with an army of about 3 million as against approximately 2 million on the other side. The Russians, of course, had huge reserves to draw on, but the Luftwaffe's bombing made it difficult to utilize them promptly and efficiently. The German forces also had the telling advantage of battle experience under varied conditions in Poland, France, and the Balkans. In addition, Stalin had refused to take seriously many warnings of the imminent Nazi invasion, so a large part of his air force was destroyed on the ground the very first day. It should also be recalled that this was not a struggle between the Soviet Union and Germany but rather between the Soviet Union and the European continent. This meant that the Red Army had to cope with substantial Finnish, Rumanian, and Hungarian forces as well as German, and that Soviet armament plants were in competition with those of France and Czechoslovakia as well as Germany. Thus, whereas Soviet steel output in 1941 was almost equal to Germany's, it was considerably less than half that of Germany and the rest of the Continent. Finally, the invading German armies were assisted by very large numbers of Soviet citizens. Some of them were disaffected non-Russian minorities, and others were peasants who still resented Stalin's forced collectivization of their plots, and the ensuing mass deportations to Siberia. Consequently, many Soviet citizens collaborated with the Germans as the lesser of two evils.

Hitler's strategy was to advance all along the thousand-mile front from Finland to Rumania and to push eastward to a line running from Leningrad to Moscow to Kharkov to Rostov. The Red Army was to be encircled and destroyed to the west of this line, so that the Wehrmacht would not need to overextend its lines to the Urals and beyond. Thanks to the factors just indicated, the Germans attained almost all their territorial objectives. They captured both Kharkov and Rostov and almost completely encircled Moscow and Leningrad.

Despite these impressive gains, the 1941 German campaign failed in its basic strategic objectives. Neither Moscow nor Leningrad was taken, and the Red Army, though badly mauled, remained intact. In fact, it was able on December 10 to launch a counteroffensive that broke the German pincers around Moscow and Leningrad and also recaptured Rostov—the first city of any size that the Wehrmacht had taken and then been forced to surrender.

Hitler's failure, however, was more fundamental than the military inability to capture Moscow and Leningrad. After all, he was the master of all Europe and also of a large part of European Russia. In this vast area, far surpassing the domains of Charlemagne and Napoleon, Hitler introduced his "New Order." He promised Europeans a stern justice under which each nation would be assigned its fitting role. At first he won significant support, reflecting the degree of popular disillusionment with the interwar regimes. But like the Japanese plans for a "co-prosperity sphere" in east Asia, Hitler's New Order was very different in practice from the promised ideal. By 1942 the great majority of the populations of the occupied countries had turned against the New Order, and by the end of the war it was universally hated.

One reason for the shift in public opinion was that Hitler, like the Japanese, was forced by the demands of war to sacrifice his New Order priorities. The invasion of the Soviet Union absorbed all available German labor power, so the Nazis coerced millions of foreigners to work in German industry and agriculture. By the end of the war these workers had been degraded to the status of grossly exploited slave laborers. Many fled from the forced labor in the Reich and joined the resistance organizations that were springing up everywhere.

Even more antagonizing was Hitler's racial policy of classifying and treating eastern Europeans as inferior subhumans (*Untermenschen*) who were to be swept away and replaced by the superior Nordic Germans. His plans for a New Order in eastern Europe called for elimination of 30 million Slavs. Even worse was Hitler's decision for a "final solution" of the "Jewish problem" by the literal extermination of all Jews within his reach. Victory in Poland brought him between 2 million and 3 million Jews; victory in the West added a half-million more; and his invasion of Russia increased the figure by another 3 million. Special "action teams" (*Einsatzgruppen*) followed on the heels of the advancing German armies as extermination squads. Mobile gas vans began to be used in late 1941. They could not keep up with the growing number of victims, so five large extermination centers were constructed. Auschwitz achieved a grim record for efficiency in production-line murder—12,000 per day.

Thus perished an estimated 6 million Jews—three-fourths of Europe's Jews and two-fifths of the world's. But Jews were not the only victims. Five million Protestants and 3 million Catholics also disappeared in the extermination camps, along with half a million gypsies. This holocaust was so unique in the annals of world history that a new word was coined to define it. The word is *genocide*, from the Greek *genos* (race or nation) and the Latin *cide* (killing). Wholesale massacres of course are not peculiar to the twentieth century. Bloody religious wars have stained human history for many centuries, and Europe's overseas expansion was achieved at the expense of defenseless native peoples, some of whom completely disappeared from the face of the earth (Tasmania's aborigines and the Indians of the Caribbean).

Historian Arnold J. Toynbee has noted, however, that twentieth-century genocide is unique in "that it is committed in cold blood by the deliberate fiat of holders of despotic political power, and that the perpetrators of genocide employ all the resources of present-day technology and organization to make their planned massacres systematic and complete."[4]

The Nazis systematically used their prisoners as a source of labor while they were alive and as a source of "raw materials" after death. They ordered the ashes in the ovens carted off to be used as fertilizer, the hair from the corpses used for mattresses, the bones crushed for phosphates, the fat used to make soap, and the gold and silver fillings from teeth deposited in the vaults of the Reichsbank.

As far as the course of World War II was concerned, the unspeakable atrocities associated with genocide were as short-sighted as they were criminal. Millions who had been alienated in the interwar years by the excesses of Stalinism and of the assorted discredited regimes of the Continent would have supported the New Order had they not been even more cruelly oppressed by the German racists. The end result was that only a handful of compromised collaborators stood by the Nazis to the end. The great majority in the occupied lands supported in varying degrees the resistance forces and contributed significantly to Hitler's eventual defeat.

Japan Attacks Pearl Harbor

World War II was transformed from a European to a global conflict with the Japanese attack on Pearl Harbor on December 7, 1941. At the beginning of the war, almost all Americans were determined to remain neutral. But Hitler's unexpected victories, and particularly the fall of France, compelled American policy makers to question whether neutrality automatically afforded protection against involvement. If Hitler were to conquer England and then gain control of the Atlantic, might not the New World be next on the schedule of conquest?

These considerations led Washington to conclude that the best way to avoid involvement in the war was to give all aid short of war to those still fighting Germany. This explains the steady drift of the United States from neutrality to nonbelligerency with the Destroyers-Bases Agreement (September 2, 1940) and from nonbelligerence to undeclared war with the Lend-Lease Act (March 11, 1941), the signing of the Atlantic Charter (August 12, 1941), and the orders (August–September 1941) to provide naval escorts for all belligerent and neutral merchantmen between Newfoundland and Iceland and to shoot on sight any Axis warships in those waters.

While striving to limit Axis expansion in the West, President Roosevelt also attempted to restrain Japan from aggression in the Pacific. Successive Tokyo governments, however, became increasingly bellicose in response to what appeared to be golden opportunities provided by the course of events in Europe. Hitler's victories had left almost undefended the rich French, British, and Dutch possessions in east and Southeast

Pearl Harbor, Hawaii—
December 7, 1941.

Asia. Accordingly, on September 27, 1940, Japan signed the Tripartite Pact with Germany and Italy. This recognized the hegemony of Germany and Italy in Europe and of Japan in Asia and called for full mutual aid if any of the signatories were attacked by the United States.

The Japanese, however, had no direct interest in the war in Europe. In pursuit of their own advantage, they concluded a treaty with Russia on April 13, 1941, in which each power pledged neutrality should the other "become the object of hostilities on the part of one or several third powers." When Hitler invaded Russia in June 1941, he pressed Japan to join him and to attack from the east. The Japanese refused to oblige, distrusting German intentions in Asia. Furthermore, they perceived greener fields in Southeast Asia, which was seething with unrest and which offered obvious opportunity for them. By the summer of 1941 they had occupied bases in French Indochina, signed an alliance treaty with Thailand, and were demanding the oil and rubber output of the Dutch East Indies. The British were so hard-pressed in Europe that they had withdrawn from Shanghai and maintained only feeble forces in Hong Kong and Singapore. Thus the entire east and Southeast Asia appeared ripe for plucking if only the United States would not intervene.

Japan's leaders were divided on the question of relations with the United States. The army was ready to challenge Britain, France, and the United States directly, but the navy, the diplomats, and the industrialists mostly held back. The turning point came with the resignation in October 1941 of the premier, Prince Fumimaro Konoye, who favored a settlement with the United States. He was succeeded by General Hideki Tojo, at the head of a cabinet of army and navy officers. Tojo decided to settle accounts with the United States. Just as the Japanese forced the issue against the Russians in 1904 by attacking Port Arthur without a declaration of war, so now on December 7, 1941, they struck at Pearl Harbor. Within a few hours five of the eight battleships in Pearl Harbor had been destroyed, as well as three cruisers and three destroyers. At the same time another Japanese task force destroyed most of the U.S. army's planes in the Philippines. In conformity with the terms of the Tripartite Pact, Germany and Italy declared war on the United States. Thus America was fully involved in the war, both in Europe and in Asia.

1942: Year of Axis Triumphs

During the year 1942, Germany, Italy, and Japan were almost everywhere victorious. Great offensives overran large parts of Russia, North Africa, and the Pacific, like a huge three-taloned claw grasping the Eurasian hemisphere. At the same time, German submarines and surface craft were threatening Allied communication lines, their toll averaging about 400,000 tons a month in 1942.

The most spectacular triumphs were won by the Japanese, who quickly conquered a vast Pacific empire, stretching from the Aleutians to Australia and from Guam to India. The Japanese were successful for several reasons. One was right timing: They struck when France and Holland were occupied, when Britain was struggling to survive, and when the United States was only starting to convert from a peace to a war economy. The Japanese were successful also because during the years of fighting against Chinese guerrillas they had trained their men to infiltrate around enemy positions and to attack on the flanks and rear. These tactics worked well in the fighting against Western forces in the jungles of Southeast Asia. Finally, the Japanese benefited from the resentment of colonial peoples against their past exploitation by Western imperial powers. The Japanese invaders encouraged this sentiment with slogans such as "Asia for the Asians."

These factors explain the unbelievably swift Japanese advance from victory to victory—from Hong Kong to Guam to Singapore, and then around Southeast Asia to the Philippines, Malaya, Indonesia, and Burma, thus reaching the frontiers of India. In five months, at a cost of only 15,000 killed and wounded, the Japanese had won an empire that had a population of over 100 million and that supplied 95 percent of the world's raw rubber, 90 percent of the hemp, and two-thirds of the tin.

Meanwhile, on the Russian front, Hitler had launched another massive offensive in June 1942. Since Moscow and Leningrad had proven impregnable the previous year, he now directed his armies southward. His objective was to reach the Volga and the Caspian, thereby cutting the Soviet Union in two and depriving the Red Army of its oil supplies from the Caucasus. As in 1941, the Panzer divisions at first rolled swiftly across the flat steppe country. Then they crossed the Don River and fanned out southeast toward the Caucasus oil fields and northeast toward Stalingrad on the Volga. By August 22, Nazi tanks had taken the Maikop oil center, though they fell short of the major oil fields at Grozny. The main tank forces then drove through to the Volga slightly to the north of Stalingrad.

In North Africa also, 1942 was a year of victory for the Germans. Under the dashing General Rommel, the Afrika Korps in March 1941 had driven the British across Libya to the Egyptian border. In May 1942 Rommel resumed the attack, crossed into Egypt, and reached El Alamein, a scant fifty miles from Alexandria. So confident was Rommel of complete victory that he selected a white stallion for his triumphal entry into Cairo.

On every front the Axis powers were at the height of their fortunes. In North Africa Rommel was preparing to strike for Cairo, in Russia the Wehrmacht had reached the Volga, and in the Pacific the Japanese appeared to be ready to spring on Australia and India.

1943: The Turning Tide

During the first three years of the war the Axis powers had everything their own way. The turning point began at the end of 1942 with the Russian victory at Stalingrad, the British breakthrough in Egypt, and the Allied landings in French North Africa, and it continued in 1943 with the fall of Mussolini, the mounting aerial bombardment of Germany, and the defeat of Japanese fleets in the Pacific.

At Stalingrad the Russians had dug in with orders to defend the city to the last man. The battle for the city began on August 22. By mid-September the Germans had fought their way into the center, and there they bogged down. While the soldiers were fighting hand to hand in cellars, on rooftops, and in sewers, two Russian armies crossed the Volga from the east, one attacking to the north of Stalingrad and the other to the south.

With this gigantic pincers operation the besiegers became the besieged. The Germans on the banks of the Volga were hopelessly stranded. On February 3, 1943, the Russians accepted the surrender of 120,000 men, the frozen survivors of the original army of 334,000. Thereafter the Russians were on the offensive all along the front, forcing the Germans to fight defensive actions to prevent their retreat from becoming a rout. (See map of World War II: Axis Defeat, 1942–1945, p. 651.)

While the Germans were being forced out of Russia, they and their Italian allies were being driven out of North Africa. A new British commander, Sir Bernard Montgomery, attacked from Egypt and drove the Germans and Italians back along the coastal road, reaching Tripoli by January 1943. At the same time Anglo-American troops landed on the other end of North Africa, in Morocco and Algeria. They advanced eastward to Tunis and then invaded Sicily in July 1943. By the following month they were attacking across the Messina Straits to the Italian mainland.

Mussolini paid for these disasters with his office and eventually with his life. King Victor Emmanuel III was persuaded by monarchists and Fascist dissidents to dismiss and imprison Mussolini. A new government was formed, headed by Marshal Pietro Badoglio, the conqueror of Ethiopia. The latter concluded an armistice with the Allies on September 3, 1943. The Germans responded by seizing Rome and occupying the central and northern parts of the country. In a bold raid, Nazi parachutists rescued Mussolini from prison. The shopworn Duce established a "Fascist Republic" in northern Italy and proclaimed his intention of fighting to the bitter end. For the next year and a half Italy was to be a divided and war-wracked country—the Germans with their puppet Mussolini in the North, and the Allies with Badoglio's government in the south.

Meanwhile, the soil of the Third Reich itself was being subjected to steadily increasing aerial bombardment. By 1943, round-the-clock bombing became possible, the British raiding by night and the Americans by day. More explosives were now dropped on German cities in one hour than had been loosed during the entire Battle of Britain.

At the same time, the Japanese were suffering reverses comparable to those of their Axis partners in Europe. After their spectacular victo-

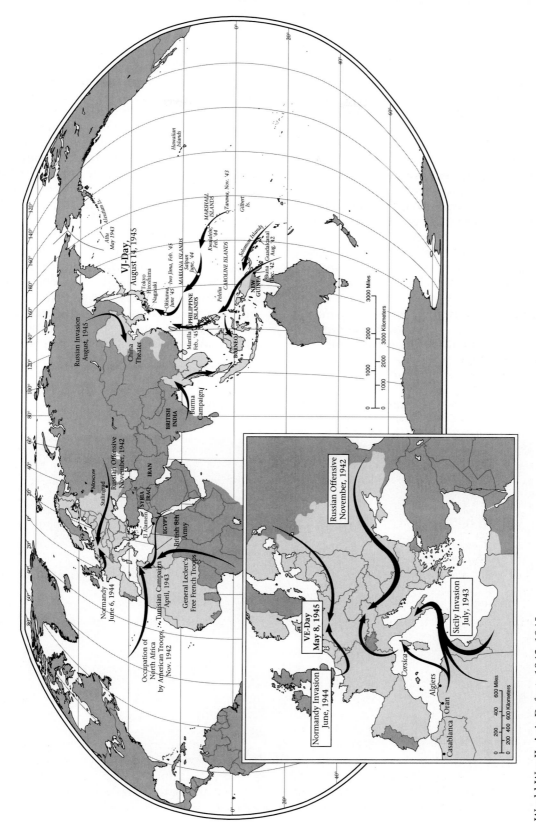

World War II: Axis Defeat, 1942–1945.

ries in the first six months, the Japanese finally were stopped and then pushed back at an accelerating pace. The basic reason for this shift in the course of the war was the overwhelming superiority of American resources and productivity. Once the American economy was converted to a war footing, it simply swamped the Japanese, despite their fanatic courage. For example, the disasters during the early part of the war left the United States with only three first-line aircraft carriers, but within two years of Pearl Harbor the number jumped to fifty. Likewise, the number of navy planes rose from 3,638 in 1941 to 30,070 in 1944; the construction of submarines increased from 11 in 1941 to 77 in 1944; and the production of landing craft, from 123 in 1941 to 54,206 in 1945.

The Japanese could not even begin to match this flood from American factories. The empire they had conquered had an abundant supply of raw materials, but they could not convert these into war goods. One reason was the decimation of their merchant marine by American planes and submarines. Equally serious was the weakness of Japanese heavy industry. Even if raw materials had been available in adequate quantities, Japan lacked the industrial resources to utilize them. If Japan could have had a decade or two of peace to exploit its newly won territories, it might have become a great world empire. But instead of peace, Japan was to suffer catastrophic defeat.

The first step on the long road to Tokyo was taken at Guadalcanal, where U.S. Marines landed on August 7, 1942. Slowly, and at heavy cost, American forces captured other enemy bases in the South Pacific. Very few Japanese were taken prisoners, for capture was considered a disgrace and was rarely accepted. Suicidal banzai charges by officers and soldiers refusing to surrender became

U.S. manufacture of warplanes increased by an astonishing number, as seen in this factory in Inglewood, California, 1942.

General Dwight D. Eisenhower gives the order of the day, "Full victory—nothing else," to paratroopers in England just before they board their airplanes to participate in the first assault in the invasion of the continent of Europe, June 6, 1944.

almost a routine climax to the taking of Japanese positions. In the face of such resistance, the American counteroffensive rolled on. By mid-1944 Saipan and Guam in the Marianas were taken, bringing the Japanese home islands within range of the new B-29 superfortresses. It was the beginning of the end of Japan's brief hour of glory.

Liberation of Europe

Europe was liberated in 1944–1945 primarily by the Red Army advancing from the east and by Anglo-American forces invading from the Normandy landing beaches in the west. Fighting also continued in Italy during this period, but it was peripheral compared to the campaigns in the north. Not until June 5 did the Fifth American Army of General Mark Clark enter Rome, where it was tempestuously welcomed by the inhabitants. Rome was the first of the Continental capitals to be freed from Nazi rule, but this triumph was overshadowed by the Allied landings in Normandy on the following day.

The invasion armada from England was made up of 4,000 merchant vessels and 700 warships. At 6:30 A.M. landings began, and by the end of the first day 326,000 men and 20,000 vehicles reached the shore. By D-Day plus five, the beachheads had been merged along a front of sixty miles. From the beginning, it should be noted, the Allied forces received invaluable aid from the French underground *maquis,* which wrecked bridges, cut communication lines, and derailed German troop trains.

By early August General George Patton was rushing headlong across northern France toward Paris. On August 15, a new American army under General Alexander M. Patch, with strong French reinforcements, landed on Riviera beaches and advanced rapidly up the Rhone valley. Meanwhile, central France was being liberated by the maquis, who descended from the hills and attacked enemy garrisons and communication lines. Belabored from all sides, the Germans now made a general withdrawal toward their own frontiers. On August 19, resistance forces began open insurrection in Paris, and six days later a French armored division and an American infantry division completed the liberation of the capital. General de Gaulle, now universally recognized as the leader of the French people, drove in triumph to Notre Dame.

While the Western powers were liberating France, the Red Army was advancing rapidly from the east. Having driven the Wehrmacht from the Crimea and the Ukraine by the spring of 1944, it then began a general offensive. In the north the Russians knocked Finland out of the war by September. In the center they crossed both the old and new frontiers of Poland and drove to the gates of Warsaw. In the south they reached the mouth of the Danube in the heart of Rumania. Young King Michael of Rumania seized the opportunity to pull his country out of the war in September, thus opening the Balkan peninsula to the Red Army. Bulgaria followed this example by suing for peace and reentering the war on the side of the Soviet Union. The German armies in the Balkans were now in danger of being trapped and began to pull out as fast as possible. As they did so, the Communist-led resistance forces in Yugoslavia and Greece descended from the mountains and took over control of their respective countries—a development that was to contribute to the forthcoming cold war between Russia and the Western powers. Aided by the local Communist-led guerrillas and by an exceptionally mild winter, the Red Army continued its westward drive to the frontiers of Austria and Germany. By April 1945 they had taken Vienna and were crossing the Oder, forty miles from Berlin. Meanwhile, American, British, and French armies were making corresponding progress on the western front. They were temporarily thrown off balance by a German offensive in December 1944 in the Ardennes in Belgium. After recovering from this setback, the Allies fought their way to the Rhine. There they discovered to their astonishment that the retreating Germans had neglected to blow up the Ludendorff railway bridge at Remagen, south of Bonn. The Allies swarmed over, and within a month they had conquered the Rhineland and taken a quarter-million prisoners. Seven allied armies raced through the collapsing Reich. They could have taken Berlin, since the Red Army still was on the Oder and since the Germans had concentrated their defenses against the Russians on the east, leaving the western approaches to their capital almost defenseless. General Eisenhower, the supreme Allied commander, decided against taking the prize for strategic and diplomatic reasons.

The Allied armies stood aside while Zhukov opened his final offensive against Berlin on April 16. Nine days later he had the capital surrounded. At the same time, on April 25, an American patrol linked up with the Soviet vanguard at the village of Torgau on the Elbe, cutting Germany in two. On the last day of April, Hitler and his companion, Eva Braun, committed suicide in a concrete bunker with shells thudding on all sides. On May 2, Berlin surrendered to the Russians. During the next week Nazi emissaries surrendered unconditionally to the Western powers at Rheims and to the Soviet Union in Berlin. At the same time German commanders in Italy signed terms of unconditional surrender. Mussolini tried to escape to Switzerland but was apprehended by guerrillas and summarily shot. His body and that of his mistress were hung up on display in Milan.

Surrender of Japan

The surrender of Germany and Italy made even bleaker the prospects for the Japanese in the Pacific. Already by mid-1944 their home islands were being bombarded by superfortresses based on Iwo Jima and Okinawa. Using these two islands as bases, American airmen subjected Japan's crowded cities to the same storm of explosives that had wracked Germany. The Japanese were even more vulnerable, for their flimsy wood and paper structures went up in flames like so much kindling. In the nine months from November 1944 to the surrender in September 1945, B-29 superfortresses made 32,000 sorties against Japan, or more than a hundred a day.

The militarists who had been responsible for Japan's intervention in the war were loath to acknowledge their error and to begin serious peace negotiations. While they were hesitating, a series of unprecedented cataclysms abruptly ended their indecision. On August 6, 1945, an American superfortress dropped an atomic bomb on Hiroshima, demolishing three-fifths of the city and killing 140,000 inhabitants. Two days later, Russia declared war on Japan, and the Red Army promptly drove across the frontier into Manchuria. The final blow was the dropping of a second atomic bomb on August 9 on the city of Nagasaki, resulting in 70,000 deaths. The extreme Japanese militarists still opposed a general surrender, and it

HIROSHIMA

*The dropping of an atomic bomb by the United States on Hiroshima on August 6, 1945, began a new era of military and human history. A study of the effect of the bomb was made by the U.S. Strategic Bombing Survey, and the following selection is taken from its report.**

The surprise, the collapse of many buildings, and the conflagration contributed to an unprecedented casualty rate. Seventy to eighty thousand people were killed, or missing and presumed dead, and an equal number were injured. The magnitude of casualties is set in relief by a comparison with the Tokyo fire raid of 9–10 March, 1945, in which, though nearly 16 square miles were destroyed, the number killed was no larger, and fewer people were injured. . . .

When the atomic bomb exploded, an intense flash was observed first, as though a large amount of magnesium had been ignited, and the scene grew hazy with white smoke. At the same time at the center of the explosion, and a short while later in other areas, a tremendous roaring sound was heard and a crushing blast wave and intense heat were felt. The people, even those who lived on the outer edge of the blast, all felt as though they had sustained a direct hit, and the whole city suffered damage such as would have resulted from direct hits everywhere by ordinary bombs. . . .

Such a shattering event could not fail to have its impact on people's way of thinking. . . .

Typical comments of survivors were:

"If the enemy has this type of bomb, everyone is going to die, and we wish the war would hurry and finish."

"I did not expect that it was that powerful. I thought we have no defense against such a bomb."

"One of my children was killed by it, and I didn't care what happened after that."

Other reactions were found. In view of their experiences, it is not remarkable that some of the survivors (nearly one-fifth) hated the Americans for using the bomb or expressed their anger in such terms as "cruel," "inhuman," and "barbarous."

". . . they really despise the Americans for it, the people all say that if there are such things as ghosts, why don't they haunt the Americans?" . . . .

The reaction of hate and anger is not surprising, and it is likely that in fact it was a more extensive sentiment than the figures indicate, since unquestionably many respondents, out of fear or politeness, did not reveal their sentiments with complete candor. . . .

* U.S. Strategic Bombing Survey, *The Effects of the Atomic Bombs on Hiroshima and Nagasaki* (Government Printing Office, 1946), pp. 3–5, 8–9.

The formal Japanese surrender being signed aboard the USS *Missouri,* as General MacArthur looks on.

seemed at one point that the war would deteriorate into a struggle of individual guerrilla groups led by diehard officers. But the emperor, on the advice of the cabinet and the elder statesmen, decided to capitulate, and on August 14 the Allied ultimatum was accepted. The formal ceremony of surrender took place on board the USS *Missouri* in Tokyo Bay on September 2 in the presence of General MacArthur, Admiral Nimitz, and ranking Allied officers.

Thus ended World War II—a war even more destructive and savage than the first. In contrast to the 28.4 million casualties in World War I, the cost now was 50 million, including 20 million Russians, 15 million Chinese, 5 million Germans, 2.5 million Japanese, 1 million British and French, and 300,000 Americans. Most appalling was that of the 50 million deaths, no less than one-fifth repre-

sented cold-blooded murder. Those 10 million victims had been "exterminated" as "undesirables" for racial, religious, political, or other reasons.

III.   WORLD WAR II IN WORLD HISTORY

World War II completed the undermining of Europe's global hegemony that had been started by World War I. Thus, the two wars had a similar significance for world history. There were significant differences, however, that are of prime importance for the contemporary scene. The Nazis and the Japanese militarists were infinitely more destructive of the old orders in Europe and Asia than the Hohenzollerns and the Hapsburgs had ever been. The Germans had overrun the entire continent of Europe; and the Japanese, the whole of east and Southeast Asia. But these vast empires were short-lived. They disappeared in 1945, leaving behind two great power vacuums embracing territories of great economic and strategic significance. It was the existence of these vacuums, as much as any ideological considerations, that was responsible for the outbreak of the cold war and the inability to conclude a general peace settlement immediately after 1945.

Another difference between the two postwar periods was the successful upsurge of colonial subjects after 1945, in contrast to the enforcement of imperial authority after 1918. Within a period of two decades the farflung European empires had all but disappeared. Thus the two outstanding global developments in the immediate postwar years were the worldwide colonial revolutions and the cold war. These are the topics of the following two chapters.

SUGGESTED READINGS

The most fascinating and revealing introduction to the second world war is by S. Terkel, *"The Good War": An Oral History of World War II* (Pantheon, 1984). A useful bibliographical guide is provided by L. Morton, *Writings on World War II* (Service Center for Teachers of History, 1967). The best general histories are by B. H. Liddell Hart, *History of the Second World War* (Putnam's, 1970); G. Wright, *The Ordeal of Total War 1939–1945* (Harper & Row, 1969); M. B. Hoyle, *A World in Flames: A History of World War II* (Atheneum, 1970); and R. A. Divine, *Causes and Consequences of World War II* (Quadrangle Books, 1969).

A fascinating account of the fall of France is provided by W. L. Shirer, *The Collapse of the Third Republic* (Simon & Schuster, 1969). The German-Russian war in its various phases is treated by B. Whaley, *Codeword Barbarossa* (MIT, 1973); G. I. Zhukov, *Marshal Zhukov's Greatest Battles* (Harper

& Row, 1969); A. Werth, *Russia at War, 1941–1945* (E. P. Dutton, 1964); W. Craig, *Enemy at the Gates: The Battle for Stalingrad* (E. P. Dutton, 1973); and H. E. Salisbury, *The 900 Days: The Siege of Leningrad* (Harper & Row, 1969). Hitler's extermination policies and actions in eastern Europe are set forth in M. Gilbert, *The Holocaust* (Holt, Rinehart and Winston, 1985); G. Fleming, *Hitler and the Final Solution* (University of California, 1984); and the revealing documentary collection by A. Eisenberg, *Witness to the Holocaust* (Pilgrim Press, 1981).

The diplomacy leading to Japan's intervention is analyzed by H. Feis, *The Road to Pearl Harbor* (Princeton University, 1950); and J. M. Meskill, *Hitler and Japan: The Hollow Alliance* (Atherton, 1966). The circumstances of the attack are authoritatively analyzed by R. Wohlsetter, *Pearl Harbor: Warning and Decision* (Stanford University, 1964). An excellent anthology of the Pacific War, edited by D. Congdon and published as a Dell paperback, is *Combat: The Pacific Theater: World War II* (1959). The war from the Japanese viewpoint is described by J. Toland, *The Rising Sun: The Decline and Fall of the Japanese Empire* (Bantam Books, 1970). American use of the A-bomb is defended by H. Feis, *The Atomic Bomb and the End of World War II* (Princeton University, 1970), and attacked as an anti-Soviet move by G. Alperowitz, *Atomic Diplomacy: Hiroshima and Potsdam* (Random House, 1965). For the human implications of the A-bomb, see R. J. Lifton, *Death in Life: Survivors of Hiroshima* (Random House, 1968). An important contribution is by J. Dower, *War without Mercy* (Pantheon, 1986), which reveals the prevalence of racism in both the American and Japanese camps during the Pacific war.

Finally, the entire August 1985 issue of the *Bulletin of the Atomic Scientists* is worth reading for the collection of important articles interpreting the nature and consequences of World War II and the current prospects for the human race.

43 End of Empires

Hereafter, perhaps, the natives of those [overseas] countries may grow stronger, or those of Europe may grow weaker, and the inhabitants of all the different quarters of the world may arrive at that equality of courage and force which, by inspiring mutual fear, can alone overawe the injustice of independent nations into some sort of respect for the rights of one another. But nothing seems more likely to establish this equality of force than that mutual communication of knowledge and of all sorts of improvements which an extensive commerce from all countries to all countries naturally, or rather necessarily, carries along with it.

Adam Smith

A major difference between the first and second world wars lay in their colonial aftermaths. Europe's hold over the colonial empires was weakened but not broken by World War I; indeed, the colonial holdings were expanded by the acquisition of Arab lands as mandates. After World War II, by contrast, an irrepressible revolutionary wave swept the colonial empires and ended European domination with dramatic speed. Just as most of Europe's colonies had been swiftly acquired in the last two decades of the nineteenth century, so most of them now were lost in an equally short period following World War II. Between 1944 and 1985, a total of ninety-six countries had won their independence. These included about a third of the world's total population (see T.43.1). After so many epoch-making triumphs and achievements overseas, the Europeans appeared in the mid-twentieth century to be retreating back to the small Eurasian peninsula whence they had set forth half a millennium earlier (see map of World of New Global Relationships, 1985, p. 659). Table 43.1 also reveals that the breakaway of overseas Afro-Asian colonies was followed by the breakup of multiethnic European states into several ethnic succession states. The table shows that in 1991 and 1992, the USSR was replaced by thirteen succession states, Yugoslavia by three, and Czechoslovakia by two.

I. ROOTS OF COLONIAL REVOLUTION

During the course of World War II, the leaders of the imperial nations made it clear that they were determined to hold on to their colonies. Yet de-

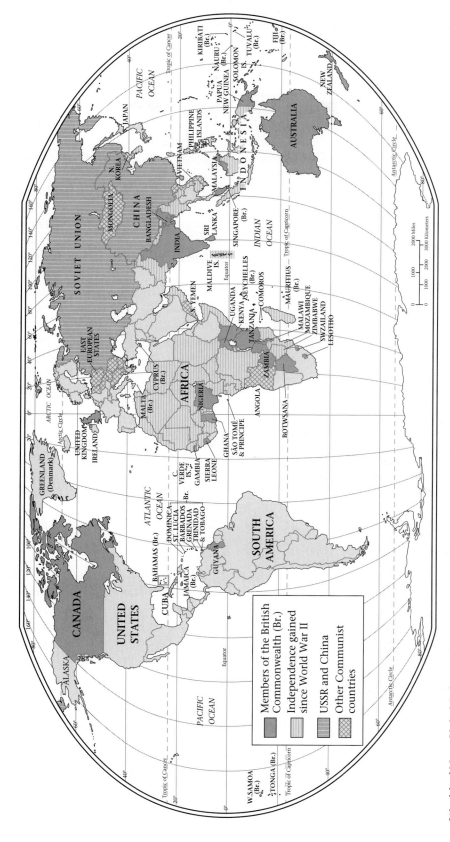

World of New Global Relationships, 1985

Members of the British
Commonwealth (Br.)

Independence gained
since World War II

USSR and China

Other Communist
countries

TABLE 43.1   March to Independence

Country	Became Independent of	Year	Country	Became Independent of	Year
Syria	France	1944	Jamaica	Britain	1962
Lebanon	France	1944	Rwanda	Belgium	1962
Jordan	Britain	1946	Trinidad and Tobago	Britain	1962
Philippines	United States	1946	Uganda	Britain	1962
India	Britain	1947	Western Samoa	New Zealand	1962
Pakistan	Britain	1947	Kenya	Britain	1963
Burma	Britain	1948	Zanzibar[b]	Britain	1963
North Korea	Japan	1948	Malta	Britain	1964
South Korea	Japan	1948	Malawi	Britain	1964
Israel	Britain	1948	Zambia	Britain	1964
Sri Lanka (Ceylon)	Britain	1948	Gambia	Britain	1965
Indonesia	Netherlands	1949	Maldive Islands	Britain	1965
Libya	Italy	1952	Singapore	Britain	1965
Cambodia	France	1954	Guyana	Britain	1966
Laos	France	1954	Botswana	Britain	1966
North Vietnam	France	1954	Lesotho	Britain	1966
South Vietnam	France	1954	Barbados	Britain	1966
Sudan	Britain-Egypt	1956	South Yemen	Britain	1967
Morocco	France	1956	Mauritius	Britain	1968
Tunisia	France	1956	Swaziland	Britain	1968
Ghana	Britain	1957	Equatorial Guinea	Spain	1968
Malaya[a]	Britain	1957	Nauru	Australia	1968
Guinea	France	1958	Fiji	Britain	1970
Republic of the Congo	Belgium	1960	Tonga	Britain	1970
Somalia	Italy	1960	Bangladesh	Pakistan	1971
Nigeria	Britain	1960	Bahrain	Britain	1971
Cameroon	France	1960	Bhutan	Britain	1971
Mali	France	1960	Oman	Britain	1971
Senegal	France	1960	Qatar	Britain	1971
Malagasy	France	1960	United Arab Emirates	Britain	1971
Togo	France	1960	Bahamas	Britain	1973
Cyprus	Britain	1960	Grenada	Britain	1974
Ivory Coast	France	1960	Guinea-Bissau	Portugal	1974
Upper Volta	France	1960	São Tomé and Principe	Portugal	1975
Niger	France	1960	Mozambique	Portugal	1975
Dahomey	France	1960	Cape Verde Islands	Portugal	1975
Congo Republic	France	1960	Comoro Islands	France	1975
Central African Republic	France	1960	Seychelles	Britain	1976
Chad	France	1960	Djibouti	France	1977
Gabon	France	1960	Solomon Islands	Britain	1978
Mauritania	France	1960	Tuvalu	Britain	1978

TABLE 43.1   March to Independence *(continued)*

Country	Became Independent of	Year	Country	Became Independent of	Year
Sierra Leone	Britain	1961	Saint Lucia	Britain	1979
Tanganyika[b]	Britain	1961	Kiribati	Britain	1979
Algeria	France	1962	Zimbabwe (Rhodesia)	Britain	1980
Burundi	Belgium	1962	St. Vincent and Grenadines	Britain	1980
Antigua and Barbudo	Britain	1981	Uzbekistan	USSR	1992
Belize	Britain	1981	Armenia	USSR	1992
Vanuatu	Anglo-French condominium	1981	Tajikistan	USSR	1992
St. Christopher and Nevis	Britain	1983	Turkmenistan	USSR	1992
Brunei	Britain	1984	Azerbaijan	USSR	1992
Namibia	South Africa	1990	Georgia	USSR	1992
Marshall Islands	U.S. Trust Territory	1991	Slovenia	Yugoslavia	1992
Russian Federation	USSR	1991	Bosnia and Herzegovina	Yugoslavia	1992
Estonia	USSR	1991	Croatia	Yugoslavia	1992
Latvia	USSR	1991	Czech Republic	Czechoslovakia (Dissolved on Dec. 31, 1992)	
Lithuania	USSR	1991	Slovak Republic	Czechoslovakia (Dissolved on Dec. 31, 1992)	
Moldova	USSR	1992			
Kazakhstan	USSR	1992			
Kyrgyzstan	USSR	1992			

[a] *Combined in 1963 with Singapore, Sarawak, and Sabah (British North Borneo) to form the state of Malaysia with a population of 10 million.*
[b] *Tanganyika and Zanzibar combined in 1964 to form the United Republic of Tanganyika and Zanzibar, or Tanzania.*

spite their statements, virtually all the Asian colonies were free within a decade after the war, and virtually all the African colonies, within two decades after the war. One reason for this unexpected outcome was the unprecedented weakening of the foremost colonial powers during World War II. France and Holland were overrun and occupied, and Britain was debilitated economically and militarily. Equally important was the growth of democratic, anti-imperialistic sentiment within the imperial countries themselves. Gone were the days when whites in the colonies confidently asserted, "We are here because we are superior." Now their presence was questioned, not only by their subjects but also by their own

fellow Europeans. Mussolini's attack on Ethiopia in 1935 was widely regarded in western Europe as a deplorable throwback, and the Anglo-French assault on the Suez in 1956 aroused much popular opposition in both Britain and France. The end of the Western empires was due as much to the lack of will to rule as it was to the lack of strength.

The short-lived Japanese Empire in Asia also contributed substantially to the colonial revolution. Western military prestige was shattered by the ease with which the Japanese drove the British out of Malaya and Burma, the French out of Indochina, the Dutch out of Indonesia, and the Americans out of the Philippines. The political foundations of Western imperialism were undermined by Japanese propaganda based on the slogan "Asia for the Asians." When the Japanese were at last forced to surrender their conquests, they deliberately made the restoration of Western rule as difficult as possible by leaving arms with local nationalist organizations and by recognizing these organizations as independent governments—as in the case of Ho Chi Minh's Viet Minh in Indochina and Sukarno's Putera in Indonesia.

We should note, however, that the Africans who escaped Japanese invasion also won freedom along with the Asians, thus pointing up the fact that important as the Japanese impact was, it merely strengthened the great unrest and awakening that had been gathering momentum since the beginning of the century. The series of colonial uprisings following World War I reflected this growing movement (see Chapter 38). In the intervening years it had gained strength and purpose with the growth of a Western-educated native intelligentsia. It was not accidental that the successful nationalist leaders were people who had studied in Western universities and observed Western institutions in operation—for instance, Gandhi, Nehru, Sukarno, Nkrumah, Azikwe, and Bourguiba.

The worldwide colonial awakening was further stimulated during World War II with the service of millions of colonials in both Allied and Japanese armies and labor battalions. Many Africans fought under the British, French, and Italian flags. Over 2 million Indians volunteered for the British forces, and an additional 40,000 Indian prisoners captured in Hong Kong, Singapore, and Burma signed up for the Japanese-sponsored Indian National Army. When all these men returned to their homes, they inevitably regarded in a new light the local colonial officials and native leaders. Finally, the civilian populations were affected at this time, as during World War I, by the Allied propaganda regarding freedom and self-determination.

II.   INDIA AND PAKISTAN

By far the most important single event in the colonial revolution was the winning of independence by India and Pakistan. When Britain declared war on Germany on September 3, 1939,

the viceroy, the Marquis of Linlithgow, on the same day proclaimed India also to be at war. Leaders of Congress protested bitterly that they were not consulted on this momentous decision. London curtly rejected their protests until Japan's precipitous conquest of Southeast Asia in early 1942 fundamentally changed the Indian situation. With Japanese armies poised on Bengal's borders, Churchill responded by sending to India on March 22 cabinet member Sir Stafford Cripps, bearing a momentous message: Major change was excluded for the duration of the war, but as soon as it was over, India could become fully autonomous, with the right to secede from the Commonwealth. Congress, however, turned down Cripps's offer and on August 7, 1942, passed a "Quit India Resolution" demanding immediate freedom, "both for the sake of India and for the success of the cause of the UN." Congress further threatened, if its demand was not met, to wage "a mass struggle on nonviolent lines." Britain replied with wholesale repression. Over 60,000 people were arrested—including all the Congress leaders—14,000 were detained without trial, 940 were killed, and 1,630 were injured in clashes with the police and military.

It was a most critical moment for the Allies as well as for India. The Germans had by then reached the Volga and were only thirty miles from Alexandria, and the Japanese had overrun Burma. The gigantic German and Japanese pincers were separated only by India, which was seething with disaffection, and by the Arab countries, which sided more with the Axis than with the Allies. Britain's position in the subcontinent would have been precarious, if not impossible, had Congress made any preparations for armed revolt. Instead, under Gandhi's influence, only nonviolent resistance was offered. Despite this lack of militant leadership, the arrest of the Congress leaders precipitated strikes and riots in the cities and the countryside. But the resistance was unplanned and uncoordinated, so the British were able to crush the centers of violence one after another.

During the remaining years of the war, the British stood firm in refusing to release the Congress leaders unless they modified their "Quit India" demand. The leaders, in turn, refused to do so, and they stayed locked up for the duration.

The last British troops leave India.

Meanwhile, Mohammed Jinnah, head of the Moslem League, took advantage of the hobbling of Congress to win India's Moslems to his organization and thus prepare the ground for an independent postwar Moslem state.

A new and decisive turn in Indian affairs was taken with the Labour party victory in the British elections of July 1945. Labour traditionally had championed Indian freedom, and now Prime Minister Attlee acted swiftly to carry out his party's promises. Actually apart from his party's commitments and sympathies, the fact is that Attlee had little choice but to accept independence. Indian nationalism, inflamed by the wartime experiences, no longer could be repressed by sheer physical force. This became apparent at the end of 1945, when the government brought to trial some officers of the Japanese-sponsored Indian National Army. These men immediately became national heroes, not because they had cooperated with the Japanese, but because their aim had been to oust the hated British. So strong was the feeling throughout the country that the trial had to be dropped. The truth was that Britain could no longer rule the country against the wishes of its people. Nor was there much desire any longer to try to do so. The Indian Civil Service had become even more Indianized during the war, and British investments in India had shrunk drastically. Also the British

public had become weary of the never-ending Indian problem. Thus Attlee was now able to sever ties with the former "jewel of the empire" with relatively little opposition at home.

In March 1946 a three-man cabinet mission went to India to make arrangements for self-government. Two months later a plan was made public, but it failed to reconcile the demands of the feuding Congress party and Moslem League. The Labour government then sent out Admiral Lord Louis Mountbatten as the new viceroy. After hurried conferences, he concluded that no plan for preserving Indian political unity was feasible and recommended partition, with the two governments each to have dominion status. By this time the Congress leaders had realized that partition was inevitable, so they accepted the plan. In July 1947, the British Parliament passed the Indian Independence Act, and on August 15, both Pakistan and the Union of India became free nations in the British Commonwealth.

III. SOUTHEAST ASIA

Southeast Asia, in contrast to India, was occupied by the Japanese during the war. A common pattern is discernible throughout the area during this brief occupation period between 1942 and 1945. In almost every country, widespread disaf-

fection against Western rule had contributed substantially to the swift conquests of the Japanese (see Chapter 42, Section II). The latter then proclaimed, like the Germans, that their conquests inaugurated the beginning of a "New Order." The watchwords of this New Order were "Asia for the Asians," "Greater East Asia Co-Prosperity Sphere," and "no conquests, no oppression and no exploitation."

If these principles had been applied, the Japanese could have mobilized solid popular support in most of Southeast Asia. The Japanese military, however, had other plans, so that the principles remained propagandist slogans that soon sounded hollow and unconvincing. These military leaders viewed Greater East Asia not as a "Co-Prosperity Sphere" but as a region consisting of satellite states under varying degrees of control. The Japanese armed forces everywhere lived off the land as much as possible, frequently creating severe local shortages of food and supplies. Also, they ruthlessly expropriated whatever foodstuffs and industrial raw materials were needed for the home islands. In return, the Japanese were able to offer little, since their economy was not strong enough to produce war materials and consumer goods.

After the initial honeymoon period, relations between the Japanese and the local nationalists rapidly deteriorated. If the occupation had been prolonged, the Japanese undoubtedly would have been faced with serious uprisings. Fortunately for them, they were forced to pull out during 1945. In doing so, they did everything possible to create obstacles in the way of a restoration of Western rule. In Indochina they overthrew the Vichy regime and recognized Ho Chi Minh's provisional government; in Indonesia they handed over the administration to the nationalist leader Sukarno; and in many regions they distributed arms to local revolutionary groups.

It is not surprising that within ten years of the Japanese withdrawal, all Southeast Asia was independent. The manner in which the various countries won their freedom varied, depending on the imperial rulers involved. The British, having been forced to face facts in India, were the most realistic in coping with Southeast Asian nationalism. In January 1948 they recognized Burma as an independent republic outside the Commonwealth, and in the next month they granted Ceylon (now Sri Lanka) full dominion status within the Commonwealth. Malayan independence, however, was delayed until February 1957. One reason for the delay was the country's mosaiclike ethnic composition. It included Malayans and Chinese—each a little over 40 percent of the total population—as well as Indians, Pakistanis, and a few Europeans. The Chinese were the prime movers behind a Communist uprising that began in 1948. The ensuing jungle

A veiled woman votes in an Indian village.

warfare was very costly and dragged on until 1955. In 1963, Malaya combined with Singapore, Sarawak, and Sabah (British North Borneo) to constitute the new state of Malaysia. Tension between Malaya and the predominantly Chinese Singapore led in 1965 to the secession of Singapore, which became an independent state in the Commonwealth.

The French and the Dutch, whose subjects also demanded independence, were less adjustable and fared much worse. The Dutch were willing to grant Sukarno's nationalists some measure of self-government but not enough to satisfy their demand. The negotiations broke down, and the Dutch resorted to armed force to reassert their authority. The war dragged on until 1947, when the Dutch finally recognized the independent United States of Indonesia. This legacy of armed conflict embittered the future relations between the two countries. Although a Dutch-Indonesian Union with a common crown existed for a few years, it ended when Sukarno withdrew in 1954. Relations became more strained in the following years because the Dutch refused to yield Netherlands New Guinea to the new republic. In 1957, in retaliation, Indonesia seized more than $1 billion worth of Dutch assets, and, in 1960, it severed diplomatic relations with The Hague. Three years later Sukarno gained control over West Irian, thus liquidating the last remnant of an empire older than most of the British Empire.

The French in Indochina fought longer to retain their colony, but in the end they, too, were forced out. Indochina consisted of three nations: Vietnam, Laos, and Cambodia. Resistance against the restoration of French rule was led by the Viet Minh, or League for the Independence of Vietnam. Though comprising many elements, the Viet Minh was led by a Communist, Ho Chi Minh, who had lived in Paris, Moscow, and China. In 1945, after war's end, Ho Chi Minh proclaimed the provisional Republic of Vietnam. The French refused to recognize the new regime, and war ensued. Laos and Cambodia were easily reoccupied by the French, but an exhausting struggle dragged on in Vietnam.

With the advent of the cold war, the United States backed up the French financially as a part of the policy of "containment." By 1954, most of northern Vietnam was in the hands of the Viet Minh, and in the same year, the French suffered a major defeat at Dien Bien Phu. The ensuing Geneva settlement recognized the independence of all Vietnam, divided the country temporarily at the seventeenth parallel, and called for supervised elections to be held in 1956 to reunify the country. This settlement in effect gave Ho Chi Minh half the country and the expectation of the other half within two years, since his resistance record had made him a national hero.

To avert this outcome the United States supported in the south the anti-Communist Catholic leader Ngo Dinh Diem. His policies aroused such fierce opposition among the peasants and the powerful Buddhist monks that in 1963 his regime was overthrown and a succession of coups followed until the rise to power, with Washington's support, of Nguyen Cao Ky and then of Nguyen Van Thieu. They were able to hold out in Saigon only because of accelerating American intervention, beginning with money and arms and progressing to "advisers," combat troops, and after the Tonkin Bay incident (August 1964), the bombing of North Vietnam. The bombing was designed to coerce Hanoi, which had been sending troops southward, to disengage and to recognize South Vietnam as a separate state. Although the bombing far surpassed World War II levels, and although over a half-million American troops were committed, victory remained elusive. The enemy's January 1968 Tet offensive strengthened the growing antiwar movement in the United States—hence President Johnson's decision to end the bombing of North Vietnam and to begin peace talks in Paris.

His successor, President Nixon, had been elected on a promise of a plan to end the war. This plan involved withdrawal of American troops, a move that in any case had become unavoidable because of the growing disaffection of the troops and of the home population. But the Nixon plan also involved continued support to President Thieu, whose regime was thought to be essential for American interests. Accordingly it was buttressed with U.S. funds, arms, noncombative military personnel, and supportive bombing on a scale surpassing that of the Johnson administration. Despite the magnitude of the American assistance, the position of the Thieu government remained so precarious that Nixon felt it necessary to launch incursions, supported by American troops and airpower, into Cambodia (April–June 1970) and Laos (February–March 1971).

These moves provoked intense dissension and mass demonstrations in the United States. But at the same time Nixon was conducting secret diplomacy with China and the Soviet Union, culminating in his well-publicized visits to Peking (February 1972) and to Moscow (May 1972). In October 1972, on the eve of the presidential election, Nixon announced an American–North Vietnamese agreement for a cease-fire. But the announcement proved premature, as Nixon ordered the heaviest bombing of the entire war directed against North Vietnam's industrial heartland on December 18–30, 1972. Finally, a ceasefire was signed in Paris on January 27, 1973, with terms essentially similar to those of the 1954 Geneva accords. Both agreements called for a temporary partition of Vietnam into a Communist North and a non-Communist South, for the determination of the future of South Vietnam by an election, for the neutralization of Laos and Cambodia, for the withdrawal from all Indochina of all foreign troops—French in 1954, American in 1973—and for the supervision of both settlements by a small and largely powerless international committee.

The cost of obtaining in 1973 what the United States had opposed in 1954 was the longest war in American history, 46,000 American deaths, 600,000 civilian and military deaths in South Vietnam, and an estimated 900,000 deaths in North Vietnam. Also, there was incalculable damage to the American social fabric, including G.I. drug addiction, bitter domestic discord, and festering national problems neglected with the financial drain of war expenditures totaling $146 billion. Nor did the 1973 Paris agreement finally end the fighting. The war dragged on until April 1975, when the demoralized Thieu regime collapsed like a house of cards before a North Vietnamese offensive.

IV.   TROPICAL AFRICA

In Africa the colonial revolution was even more dramatic than it was in Asia. The triumph of nationalism in the latter area was not altogether unexpected, given ancient cultures and local political organizations that had been agitating for some decades. In Africa, by contrast, the nationalist movements were much younger and weaker. Also the continent had not been jarred and aroused by Japanese occupation. And yet, just as the first postwar decade witnessed the liberation of Asia, so the second witnessed the liberation of Africa. During that decade, no fewer than thirty-one African countries won their independence. The few remaining colonies in turn got rid of foreign rule during the following years. The course of this nationalist awakening differed fundamentally from region to region because of the varying historical backgrounds. Accordingly, the colonial revolution will be considered not on a continent-wide basis but individually in tropical Africa, in South Africa, and in North Africa.

Nationalist movements, at least of the Western variety, did not appear in tropical Africa until after World War II. Before that time, only a few Western-educated leaders were awake and active. The mass of the people were politically uninvolved. The few nationalist organizations were more like debating societies than political parties, and they devoted more energy to sniping at the European administrators than to communicating with their own peoples. World War II drastically altered this traditional African pattern. In the first place, a tremendous economic expansion occurred during the war years because of the pressing demand for African raw materials and foodstuffs. Between 1939 and 1953, the value of exports from the Congo increased fourteen times, and from Northern Rhodesia they multiplied ninefold. This economic upsurge led to a boom in the building of schools; the construction of roads; and the improvement of housing, sanitation, and medical services. At the same time, the Africans saw the Asian peoples gaining their independence and naturally asked why they, too, should not be rid of the bonds of colonialism. The question became acute with the return of the war veterans, large numbers of whom had served for the French in Europe and for the

Accra, Ghana, with corrugated iron
shanties. These are quite a contrast to the
city's modern buildings.

British in Burma and the Middle East. All these
factors combined to shake up and awaken tropical Africa.

The first outburst occurred on the Gold
Coast in 1948. The small farmers now had more
income than ever before, but consumer goods
were in short supply and very expensive. They
suspected the European traders of profiteering
and organized a widespread boycott of their busi-
nesses. This was followed by rioting in the towns
and general ferment in the countryside. A new
leader appeared who exploited this disaffection
with startling success. Kwame Nkrumah had
studied in American and English universities,
where he had become converted to the Marxist
socialism current among colonial students and
had met other African leaders, such as Jomo
Kenyatta from Kenya. Nkrumah quickly overshadowed the older West African nationalists by
demanding immediate independence. In 1949 he
organized the Convention People's party on a
genuine mass basis.

In a general election held in 1951 under a
new constitution, that party won an overwhelming majority. Nkrumah was in prison on election
day, charged with sedition, but the British governor, sensing the trend of events, released
Nkrumah and gave him and his colleagues leading posts in the administration. In the next few
years the cabinet became all-African and was entrusted with full authority except for defense and
foreign affairs. With this apprenticeship in self-
government, it was possible to make the transition to full independence without violence or
dislocation. By 1957, thanks to the initiative of
Nkrumah and the statesmanship of the British,
the Gold Coast became the independent Commonwealth country of Ghana.

Once the colonial dam had been broken in
Ghana, it was impossible to keep it from breaking
elsewhere. Most decisive was the course of events
in Nigeria, with its 68 million people the most
populous country in Africa. The three regions of
the country—the north, west, and south—differed basically from each other in ethnic composition, cultural traditions, and economic development. This diversity led to serious interregional
conflicts that delayed the winning of independence to 1960. The other British West African
colonies, Sierra Leone and Gambia, followed in
1961 and 1963, respectively. Their delay was due
primarily to poverty and small size.

The British did not foresee how quickly
their new colonial policy would affect the rest of
tropical Africa. Repercussions were felt first in the
surrounding French holdings. In 1956 the Paris
government issued a "framework law" that
granted representative institutions to their
twelve West African territories and to the island
of Madagascar. Two years later the new de Gaulle
regime, brought into power by the crisis in Algeria (see Section VI, this chapter) decided to avoid
a similar ordeal in tropical Africa. The sub-Saharan colonies were given the option of voting either for full independence or for autonomy as
separate republics in the French "Community"

that was to replace the Empire. In the ensuing referendum, all the territories except Guinea, which was under the influence of the trade union leader Sékou Touré, voted for autonomy. The arrangement, however, was transitory. In 1959, Senegal and the French Sudan asked for full independence within the Community as the Federation of Mali. When this was granted, four other territories—the Ivory Coast, Niger, Dahomey, and Upper Volta—went a step further and secured independence outside the Community. By the end of 1960, all the former colonies of both French West Africa and French Equatorial Africa had won their independence, and all but one had become members of the United Nations.

In contrast to the smooth transition to independence in French and British West Africa, the Belgian Congo endured a bitter and costly struggle involving the great powers as well as Belgium and assorted Congolese factions. One source of this trouble was the rigid paternalistic character of Belgian rule. Though they were often enlightened in their measures for economic advance and technical training, Belgian officials allowed no opportunity for political training to the Africans, or for that matter, to the resident Belgians. The educated native elite were few in number and inexperienced. Tribal alliances and rival-

ries were prominent. Such was the situation when the French colonies across the Congo were given self-rule. This stimulated latent hostility to Belgian rule and brought to the fore Patrice Lumumba, the only Congolese leader with more than a regional following. His radical and nationwide approach to the problem of Congo independence won him a substantial following within his country as well as among pan-Africanists everywhere.

Early in 1959, after the Congo capital had been shaken by nationalist riots, the Belgians hastily decided that they could best protect their vast economic interests by allowing free elections and immediate independence. The predictable outcome was conflict and chaos. Lumumba became the first premier, but he found he could govern only with the help of Belgian army officers and civil-service officials. Some of the soldiers mutinied against the remaining officers, and attacks on whites occurred in various parts of the country. At the same time, fighting broke out between tribes taking advantage of the opportunity to repay old scores. Most serious was the virtual secession of the rich mining province of Katanga, owing to an unholy alliance of local African politicians and Belgian mining interests. The spreading anarchy caused the Belgian gov-

An overview of a copper mining town in Southern Rhodesia, now Zimbabwe.

ernment to reconsider and to return its troops to key points and airfields.

The cold war now intruded. The Soviet Union threatened unilateral intervention under the guise of supporting the Congolese against a restoration of imperialist rule. The United Nations responded by assuming the responsibility of policing the Congo with an international force made up largely of Africans. After months of confused violence some semblance of order was restored, though not without the sacrifice of Lumumba, who was murdered by Katanga secessionists, and of the UN Secretary-General Dag Hammarskjold, who died in an airplane crash during a mediatory mission in the Congo. Finally, the former Belgian Congo ended up as the Republic of Zaire, ruled as a one-party dictatorship headed by General Mobutu.

Meanwhile, across the continent in East Africa, the nationalist cause was encountering much stiffer resistance because of the presence of white settlers. In Kenya, the conflict between Africans and settlers was particularly acute since the settlers had appropriated much of the best farming land. This contributed to the uprising of the *Mau Mau*, a secret terrorist society made up of members of the Kikuyu tribe. Before the fighting was over, nearly 7,000 Mau Mau had been killed, over 83,000 were in prison, and many more were held in temporary detention camps. The uprising, though it led to sickening excesses on both sides, did force the British to recognize the futility of attempting to follow a conciliatory policy in West Africa and a rigid one in the East. Accordingly, they released from prison the outstanding Kikuyu leader Jomo Kenyatta. Educated in London and author of an anthropological study of his people, Kenyatta had been imprisoned for suspected sympathies with the Mau Mau, though actual collaboration was never proven. Now he was released, and, like Nkrumah, he won a majority vote in an election and was allowed in 1963 to become premier. In the same year, Kenya became an independent state amid wild rejoicing in Nairobi for the cherished uruhu, or freedom.

In neighboring Uganda, where the whites had not been allowed to take land, the issues were simpler, and independence had been granted peaceably in 1962. Tanganyika, a Ger-

man possession before World War I, had become a British mandate in 1922, with two segments, Rwanda and Burundi, becoming Belgian mandates. All three territories were granted independence in 1962, with Julius K. Nyerere of Tanganyika playing a key role in the transition. Under his leadership, Tanganyika and Zanzibar combined in 1964 to form the republic of Tanzania.

The Central African Federation, made up of Southern Rhodesia, Northern Rhodesia, and Nyasaland, was organized to the south of Tanganyika in 1953. Though it was created with the declared objective of "racial partnership," the federation was beset by crises and violence. The root cause was the political and economic domination of more than 9 million Africans by 300,000 Europeans, most of whom lived in Southern Rhodesia. The nationalist movement made strong gains in Northern Rhodesia and Nyasaland, and in 1962 both were given self-rule under African prime ministers. Since Southern Rhodesia refused to follow suit and to give Africans the vote, the federation became impossible and was dissolved on January 1, 1964. Later in the year, Northern Rhodesia became fully independent as Zambia, and Nyasaland as Malawi.

The center of strife then shifted to Southern Rhodesia, now known as Rhodesia, where the black majority demanded the vote. The London government sought a compromise settlement looking toward gradual enfranchisement of the Africans. The white minority was adamantly opposed. Under the leadership of Prime Minister Ian Smith it rejected British rule in 1965 and became officially independent in 1970. The constitution of the new state of Rhodesia gave fifty seats in Parliament to the 230,000 whites, as against sixteen seats to the 4.5 million Africans. In explanation of this discrepancy, Smith claimed that the Africans sixty years earlier had been "savages walking around in skins" and that although they had made some progress, they still "have a long way to go."[1] By 1973, however, these "savages" were organizing increasingly successful guerrilla attacks from Zambia. A major setback for the Smith regime was the 1975 collapse of Portuguese rule in Mozambique, which then became another base for guerrilla attacks. The guerrillas continued their armed struggle until

December 1979, when they agreed to a cease-fire and to new elections monitored by a Commonwealth contingent. The ensuing election (February 1980) gave an overwhelming majority to the Marxist leader Robert Mugabe, whose guerrilla forces had been the most active. In April 1980, after seven years of armed resistance, the independent African state of Zimbabwe was born.

Meanwhile, African nationalism had triumphed in the Portuguese colonies of Mozambique, Angola, and Guinea-Bissau. South Africa strongly supported Portuguese rule as a barrier against spreading African nationalism. Nevertheless, insurrections broke out in all the colonies, and, as the colonial wars dragged on, the financial burden was too much for poverty-stricken Portugal. Forty percent of the Portuguese budget was being spent on the military, and army recruits were deserting and fleeing abroad like their American counterparts during the Vietnam War. Finally, on April 12, 1974, Portugal's dictatorship was overthrown in a military coup. By the following year all three colonies were internationally recognized as independent states.

V.   SOUTH AFRICA

The basic difference between tropical Africa on the one hand and North Africa and South Africa on the other is the relative absence of European settlers in the former region and their presence in large numbers in the latter two. This difference explains the brutal armed struggle that ravaged Algeria between 1954 and 1962, as well as the undercover conflict that wracked South Africa until apartheid's end in 1994. The colony of South Africa, as noted earlier, was established by the Dutch but came under British rule in 1814. The Dutch farmers, or *Boers*, rejected British rule and trekked northward, where they established the independent republics of the Transvaal and the Orange Free State. With the discovery in these republics of diamonds in 1871 and gold in 1886, the British made moves to annex them. The resulting Boer War (1899–1902) ended with the Boers accepting British sovereignty, but in return they were promised self-rule. This promise was fulfilled in 1909, when South Africa became a self-governing dominion in the British Commonwealth.

A little more than half a century later, in May 1961, South Africa left the Commonwealth to become an independent republic. The main reason for the separation was the clash between South Africa and new African and Asian Commonwealth members, such as Nigeria and India, over the issue of *apartheid*. Apartheid involved two basic policies: the exclusion of all nonwhites from any share in political life; and the confinement of the Africans to separate areas known as Bantustans, or preserves for the "Bantu," as the Africans have been known. These Bantustans comprised only 14 percent of South Africa's land, whereas the Africans made up 73.8 percent of South Africa's total population of 31.7 million (in 1984). The whites, by contrast, made up only 14.8 percent, and the Afrikaners comprised three-fifths of the white minority. The other ethnic elements are the Coloreds, or mixed race (9.3 percent), and the Asians (2.9 percent).

The Afrikaner minority controlled South Africa partly because parliamentary representation was weighted in favor of the predominantly Afrikaner rural areas, and also because many English-speaking whites supported apartheid for economic reasons. This was especially true of white labor, which feared competition in employment from nonwhites if the latter were given equal opportunities. In fact, the first Afrikaner (Nationalist) government was able to take office in 1924 because of support from the South African Labour party.

It is generally agreed that apartheid was not a viable program, either economically or politically. If the Africans were in fact segregated on the proposed Bantustans, the entire economy of South Africa would collapse. Their labor, as well as that of the Coloreds and the Indians, has been essential for agriculture and commerce as well as mining and other industries. In addition, Bantustans had not been able to support the African population, and the government was unwilling to spend the large sums needed to increase their absorptive capacity. Most important of all, the great majority of Africans had no desire to be isolated as separate "tribal" entities. Instead, they demanded a fair share in the united South Africa of which they were an integral part. In this demand they were backed by the growing power of African nationalism in the rest of the continent.

Apartheid was long preserved in South Africa primarily because the government possessed by far the most powerful military forces on the continent of Africa and did not hesitate to use them, as demonstrated in the mass killing of black demonstrators in Sharpeville (1960) and Soweto (1976). This strategy proved workable until the 1980s. Then it was hit by a veritable tidal wave of opposition, external as well as internal, which for the first time threatened the future of apartheid. The opposition consisted of several elements. Most important was the "angry generation"—young Africans who were completely alienated, and who were determined to destroy apartheid whatever the cost. Another important opposition element was the black trade unions, which were given the right to bargain with their employers but which used their organizational strength in the political struggle against apartheid. The resulting turmoil prompted leading businesspeople in South Africa to call publicly for the abolition of apartheid and even to meet with leaders of the banned African National Congress. Likewise, leading South African clergy, such as Nobel Laureate Archbishop Desmond Tutu, rejected apartheid and criticized the government's use of "law and order" and the specter of communism to justify its campaign to crush black political aspirations.

Finally, the Pretoria government for the first time encountered powerful opposition in foreign countries, especially in church, student, and trade union circles. This movement was strong enough to persuade the American government in

Long lines of people queue outside the polling station in the black township of Soweto in the Southwest suburbs of Johannesburg on April 27, 1994. The majority of South Africa's 22 million voters were voting in the country's first all-race elections.

A South African policeman dances with a black woman during President-elect Nelson Mandela's speech at City Hall after taking the oath of Parliament on May 9.

September 1985 to adopt certain economic sanctions against South Africa, including a ban on loans, on the sale of computers, and on the importation of the Krugerrand gold coin. These pressures proved too much for President Pieter W. Botha, who resigned in 1989.

Whereas Botha's strategy had been to rely on the government's overwhelming military power to impose "grand" apartheid by force on the disfranchised African majority, Botha's successor, Frederick W. de Klerk, stated by contrast that some way must be found to reconcile the African demand for "one person, one vote" with the Afrikaner response of "never." De Klerk began his search dramatically in February 1990 by legalizing the African National Congress and by releasing its leader, Nelson Mandela, from prison where he had been incarcerated for twenty-eight years. De Klerk went further by stating publicly that in the South Africa of the future, all adults must have the vote, though he added that this enfranchisement must be balanced by "checks and balances" to protect minorities, including the hitherto dominant whites.

Despite the powerful ideological and economic forces buttressing apartheid society, it proved possible to achieve a peaceful transition to a new nonracial, democratic South Africa through four-day free elections based on universal suffrage. Held in late April 1994, these elections gave Mandela's African National Congress 62.7 percent of the votes (252 seats in the new parliament); de Klerk's National party received 30.4 percent of the votes (82 seats); Mangosuthu Buthelezi's Zulu-based Inkatha Freedom party got 5.8 percent of the votes; and the Freedom Front led by former army chief Constand Viljoen, which favors a white homeland, received 2.8 percent of the votes. As leader of the largest party, Mandela became the president of South Africa in place of de Klerk, who, as leader of the second-ranking party, became deputy president.

The contrast between the new South African state and its apartheid predecessor is evident in its constitution, which states forthrightly, "there is a need to create a new order in which all South Africans will be entitled to a common South African citizenship in a sovereign and democratic constitutional state in which there is equality between men and women and people of all races so that all citizens shall be able to enjoy and exercise their fundamental rights and freedoms."

The significance of this statement is apparent if it is recalled that the apartheid system was constructed by Afrikaners using as their model the Jim Crow segregation laws of the American

South. South Africa's citizens transcended this heritage of segregation-apartheid, and they did so at the time when in the United States Rodney King, following his beating and the ensuing rioting and looting in Los Angeles, asked his agonized question, "Can we all get along?"

South Africans cannot claim to have answered that question at this writing, but thanks to inspired leadership from both sides, they have taken a first step toward an answer.

VI.   NORTH AFRICA

In North Africa, as in Indochina, the French fought long and stubbornly to retain their possessions. A principal reason was the substantial number of French settlers (colons) in this region—250,000 in Tunisia, 400,000 in Morocco, and 1 million in Algeria. These colons, in league with powerful French economic interests in North Africa, bitterly opposed all proposals for self-rule and sabotaged a number of provisional moves in this direction made by certain Paris cabinets.

Tunisia and Morocco had the legal status of protectorates, which France claimed to administer in behalf of their traditional rulers. Both territories were governed autocratically—not even the resident Europeans were allowed political rights. This foreign domination stimulated movements for national liberation: in Tunisia, the Neo-Destour party, established in 1934 and led by Habib Bourguiba; and in Morocco, the Istiqlal party, founded in 1944 and given some support by Sultan Mohamed Ben Youssef.

Tunisia and Morocco won their freedom relatively easily following World War II. The French were determined to hang on to Algeria and were willing to accept losses elsewhere in order to concentrate on this prime objective. Accordingly, when armed resistance began in Tunisia in 1952, the French, after two years of guerrilla warfare, agreed to grant it autonomous status, and having made this concession in Tunisia, they were ready to do likewise in Morocco. Sultan Mohamed, who had been exiled for his pro-Istiqlal sympathies, was allowed to return to his throne. He then demanded complete independence, which the French conceded on March 2, 1956. In the same month, Tunisia also became fully independent, with Bourguiba as president of the new republic.

The French now were able to deal with the crucial Algerian problem without distractions. Legally, Algeria was not a colony but an integral part of France, with representatives in the National Assembly in Paris. In practice, a double standard of citizenship prevailed in Algeria, so that the country was dominated economically and politically by the Europeans, who comprised only one-tenth of the total population of 10 million. On the other hand, the colons, like the Afrikaners at the other tip of the continent, did not regard themselves as mere colonists. Algeria was their homeland as much as that of the native Algerians. Their fathers and grandfathers had worked and died there, and they were resolved to defend their patrimony. This meant unalterable opposition to any concessions to the Algerian nationalists.

Armed revolt against French rule began in the fall of 1954. The French had been ousted from Indochina only four months earlier and were in no mood for compromise. With the enthusiastic approval of the colons and of the army officers, who were still smarting from the Indochina humiliation, the Paris government resolved to crush the uprising. The result was an exhausting, brutalizing struggle that dragged on until 1962. At its height, the French were forced to send a half-million men into Algeria and to spend nearly $1 billion annually. The Algerians paid much more heavily in human terms, including 1 million dead, or one-ninth of their total numbers.

In May 1958, a North African "Committee of Public Safety" seized power in Algeria in order to replace the republic with an authoritarian regime that presumably would be more successful in holding the empire together. The demoralized National Assembly bowed to this show of force, especially since most of the armed forces were in Algeria. In June 1958, the National Assembly voted full power to de Gaulle to rule France in whatever manner he wished for six months and to prepare a new constitution for the country. Before the end of the year, the Fourth Republic had given way to the Fifth, and political power had been shifted decisively from the legislative to the executive branch—specifically to the president.

Veiled Moslem women cast ballots in the referendum of July 1, 1962, in which Algerians voted for independence.

President de Gaulle now used his unprecedented popularity to end the Algerian bloodshed, despite the opposition of the colons and the military, who had made possible his rise to power. In March 1962, after a referendum in France had approved such a move, de Gaulle agreed to a cease-fire and to a plebiscite to determine Algeria's future. On July 3, 1962, he proclaimed the independence of Algeria after its people had voted overwhelmingly in favor of it. All of North Africa was now free for the first time since French soldiers had landed in Algeria in 1830. The granting of independence to Algeria marked the virtual end of a French African empire that once covered nearly 4 million square miles and contained more than 41 million people.

VII.   MIDDLE EAST

Meanwhile, Arab nationalism had been as militant in the Middle East as it had been in North Africa. During the interwar years the British had given up their hold on Egypt and Iraq, and both countries had entered the League of Nations. Arab nationalists, however, were far from appeased, since the British still exercised controlling authority over these countries. They had reserved various privileges, including the right to maintain a garrison along the Suez Canal, to maintain three air bases in Iraq, and to administer the Sudan together with Egypt. More galling had been the stiff-necked attitude of the French, who continued to hold Syria and Lebanon as mandates. Above all, Arab nationalism had been aroused by large-scale Jewish immigration into the British-held Palestine mandate during the 1930s.

Because of these unhappy experiences during the interwar years, most politically conscious Arabs during World War II were either neutral or openly hostile to the Western powers—hence the pro-Axis uprising in Iraq in May 1941 and the extremely reluctant assistance that King Farouk I of Egypt gave to the British despite his treaty obligations.

Although the Arab nationalists had been unable to satisfy their aspirations during World War II, the new postwar balance of power offered them a unique opportunity, which they promptly exploited. Britain and France, who had dominated the Middle East before the war, now emerged drastically weakened. A power vacuum was created, which the United States and the Soviet Union attempted to fill. The Arabs skillfully took advantage of the Anglo-French weakness and the American-Russian rivalry to play off one side against the other, thus enabling them to win

NASSER NATIONALIZES THE SUEZ CANAL

*On July 26, 1956, Egyptian Premier Nasser nationalized the Suez Canal. The following passages from his speech proclaiming the nationalization reflect Egyptian bitterness toward the Suez Canal Company of Paris and toward imperialism in general.**

Is history to repeat itself again with treachery and deceit? Will economic independence . . . or economic domination and control be the cause of the destruction of our political independence and freedom?

Brothers, it is impossible that history should repeat itself.

Today, we do not repeat what happened in the past. We are eradicating the traces of the past. We are building our country on strong and sound bases.

Whenever we turn backwards, we aim at the eradication of the past evils which brought about our domination, and the vestiges of the past which took place despite ourselves and which were caused by imperialism through treachery and deceit.

Today, the Suez Canal where 120,000 of our sons lost their lives in digging it by corvee, and for the foundation of which we paid 8 million pounds, has become a state within the state. It has humiliated ministers and cabinets. . . .

Britain has forcibly grabbed our rights, our 44 percent of its shares. Britain still collects the profits of these shares from the time of its inauguration until now. All countries and shareholders get their profits. A state within the state; an Egyptian Joint Stock Company.

The income of the Suez Canal Company in 1955 reached 35 million pounds, or 100 million dollars. Of this sum, we, who have lost 120,000 persons, who have died in digging the Canal, take only 1 million pounds or 3 million dollars! This is the Suez Canal Company, which was dug for the sake of Egypt and its benefit!

Do you know how much assistance America and Britain were going to offer us over five years? 70 million dollars. Do you know who takes the 100 million dollars, the Company's income, every year? They take it of course. . . .

We shall not repeat the past. We shall eradicate it by restoring our rights in the Suez Canal. This money is ours. This Canal is the property of Egypt because it is an Egyptian Joint Stock Company.

The Canal was dug by Egypt's sons and 120,000 of them died while working. The Suez Canal Company in Paris is an impostor company. It usurped our concessions. . . .

Therefore, I have signed today the following law which has been approved by the Cabinet: [Article 1 of the decree read, "The Universal Company of the Suez Maritime Canal (Egyptian Joint-Stock Company) is hereby nationalized. All its assets, rights and obligations are hereby transferred to the Nation . . . "].

* Mimeographed copy of speech from Egyptian Embassy, Washington, D.C.

concessions that would have seemed preposterous only a few years earlier. The Arabs were further aided by their control over vast Middle East oil reserves, which appeared particularly indispensable to the fuel-hungry West during the postwar years.

In October 1944, the Arabs organized a league of Arab states to coordinate their policies and maximize their effectiveness. The Arab League won its first success against the French in Syria and Lebanon. In May 1945, a French expeditionary force landed in Beirut and proceeded to bombard Damascus in an attempt to cow the local nationalists. Such tactics had prevailed in the 1920s, but they did not work now. The Arab League Council promptly met and passed a resolution demanding the evacuation of all French forces. Churchill supported the Arabs, especially since the war was not yet over, and he had no desire to cope with an aroused Arab nationalism in the Middle East. Under British pressure the French withdrew their troops, and in July 1945 they accepted the end of their rule in the Middle East. As a result of the French withdrawal, the Arab states of Lebanon and Syria won their independence.

In Egypt, the aim of the nationalist leaders after the war was to end or modify the 1936 treaty, which was the legal basis for Britain's control of the Canal Zone and of the Sudan. The Egyptians tried various measures, including direct negotiations, appeals to the UN Security Council, and desultory guerrilla activity. All proved futile, and the resulting frustration, together with the general resentment against the disastrous failure in the Palestine War, culminated in an army revolt in July 1952. General Muhammad Naguib assumed power and forced King Farouk to abdicate.

Naguib removed one of the sources of friction between Egypt and Britain when he concluded an agreement with Britain on February 12, 1953, by which the Sudanese were to be given a choice of independence, union with Egypt, or some other course. The decision was for independence, and in 1956 the Sudan joined the ranks of free nations. The remaining Egyptian grievance—the British presence at the Suez—was ended by Gamal Abdel Nasser, who displaced Naguib as head of the new Egyptian regime. After prolonged negotiations, Nasser signed an agreement with Britain on October 19, 1954, by which under certain stipulated conditions, the British garrison was to be removed and the British installations transferred to Egypt.

Arab nationalism was successful in Syria and Lebanon, and in Egypt and the Sudan, but it failed disastrously in Palestine. The mass extermination of Jews in Hitler-controlled Europe created strong pressures for opening up Palestine to the desperate survivors. In August 1945, President Truman proposed that 100,000 Jews be allowed to enter the mandate. In April 1946, an Anglo-American investigating committee reported in favor of the president's proposal. The Arab League responded by warning that it was unalterably opposed to such an influx, and that it was prepared to use force to stop it. The United Nations then sent a fact-finding commission to Palestine, and the General Assembly, after receiving the commission's report, voted on November 29, 1947, in favor of partitioning the mandate. On May 14 of the following year, the Jews invoked the partition resolution and proclaimed the establishment of a Jewish state to be called Israel. On the same day, President Truman extended recognition to the new state. The following day, the Arabs carried out their long-standing threat and sent their armies across the Israeli border.

The course of the war went contrary to expectations. The Arab armies lacked discipline, unity, and effective leadership. The Israelis, fighting literally with their backs to the sea, possessed all three qualities to a high degree. They not only repulsed the Arab attacks from all sides but also advanced and occupied more territory than had been awarded to them by the UN Assembly's resolution. After two abortive truces, the Israelis finally signed armistice agreements with the various Arab states between February and July 1949.

A peaceful settlement did not follow the cessation of fighting. The main reason was that the armistice agreements left Israel with more territory than had been allotted by the United Nations. The Arabs demanded that this extra territory be surrendered. Israel maintained that it was won in a war that the Arabs themselves started and that the extra land was needed for the Jewish immigrants pouring in from all parts of the world.

This issue resulted in renewed warfare in 1956, 1967, and 1973. Israel attacked Egypt in 1956 to stop repeated border raids, and Britain and France joined in the attack because Nasser had nationalized the Suez Canal. Both the United States and the Soviet Union strongly opposed the invasion and forced the three aggressors to withdraw. Quite different was the outcome of the six-day Israeli blitz of June 5–10, 1967. Claiming that the surrounding Arab states were planning invasion, the Israeli forces quickly advanced to the Suez Canal and the Jordan River and also occupied Jerusalem, the Gaza Strip, and Sharm el-Sheikh on the Tiran Strait. The UN Security Council on November 22, 1967, passed a resolution requiring both withdrawal of the Israeli armed forces from the overrun territories and Arab acknowledgment of the independence and integrity of Israel. The resolution remained inoperative because Israel demanded direct peace negotiations with the Arab states, whereas the latter demanded Israeli withdrawal before negotiations.

The deadlock persisted for six years, marked by an unending succession of attacks and counterattacks. On October 6, 1973, the fourth round in the Arab-Israeli struggle exploded with the Egyptians attacking across the Suez Canal and the Syrians into the Golan Heights. In successfully crossing the Suez Canal and occupying a wide strip in the Sinai along the northern half of the canal, the Egyptians destroyed the myth of Israeli invincibility, even though the Israelis counterattacked and occupied an equally wide strip of Egyptian territory along the southern half of the canal. On January 17, 1974, Egypt and Israel agreed that Israeli forces should withdraw to a north-south line roughly twenty miles east of the canal and that a UN buffer force should be installed between the two armies. On May 31, a similar agreement was signed by Israel and Syria concerning the Golan Heights.

It was hoped that these agreements would clear the way for a lasting peace, but this did not happen. The main reason was that the Palestinians demanded an independent state on the West Bank, whereas an increasing number of Israelis referred to the West Bank by the old biblical name of Judea and Samaria and viewed it as an integral part of the land of Israel ceded to the Jews in the Bible. Egypt's President Anwar Sadat tried to break this stalemate with his famous peace trip to Jerusalem in November 1977. The outcome was the Camp David accord, or Egyptian-Israeli Peace Treaty of March 26, 1979, which provided that the two countries would establish full diplomatic relations; Israel would evacuate the Sinai within two years; Egypt would end its economic embargo of Israel and allow Israel shipping through the Suez Canal; and the two countries would negotiate on the future of Palestine, with the aim of holding elections for local representative councils within one year.

The treaty lessened the danger of a Mideast war because the Arab states lost their most powerful member. On the other hand, the basic problem of Palestine remained unresolved. Rather than reaching some settlement, the Israelis and the Palestinians drifted further apart.

On the one hand the Israelis were embittered that their cession of the large Sinai territory did not lead to rapprochement with the Arab world. Instead, Sadat incurred the enmity of Islamic fundamentalists because of his accord with Israel, and in 1981 he was assassinated. His successor, Hosni Mubarak, tried to walk the same tightrope but faced much opposition. The extent of Israeli disillusionment and frustration was reflected in the growing popular support for Rabbi Meir Kahane, who was elected to the Israeli Parliament in 1984 on a program calling for the forcible expulsion of all Arabs from Israel (where they comprise a 14 percent minority) and from the West Bank territories (where they comprise a 94 percent majority).

On the other hand the Palestinians were equally disillusioned and frustrated by the course of events, so militant elements gained ground among them also. The principal Palestinian grievance was the continued planting of Israeli settlements in the West Bank. The number of settlers rose from 3,200 in 1977 to 17,400 in 1980, to 51,600 in January 1985, to 70,000 in 1989 (as against 800,000 native Palestinians). When Gorbachev allowed Jews to emigrate freely from the Soviet Union, many chose Israel as their destination. Consequently, the number of Jewish settlers in the West Bank and the Gaza Strip rose to 130,000 by December 1993. Those Israelis who had favored the expulsion of Palestinians saw the Soviet influx as a welcome means for transforming the West Bank from a predominantly Palestinian land to a predominantly Jewish land.

Faced with this bleak prospect, Palestinian resistance now assumed a third new form. The first, until 1948, depended on the outside Arab states to repulse the Israelis. The second phase depended on the Palestine Liberation Organization (PLO), whose forces also were outside Israel. With the failure of both the Arab states and the PLO, younger Palestinians decided that delivery would come not from the outside but only from direct action by themselves. This direct action took two forms. One is the *intifada*, or uprising of stone-throwing youth who have lost their fear of Israeli soldiers and are making life miserable for them by constant pinprick harassing. The other resistance action is by assorted fundamentalist Islamic organizations such as the Islamic Resistance Movement or Hamas, the Islamic Holy War, and the Party of God. These organizations are more militant than the PLO because they reject on religious grounds the PLO's willingness to recognize and accept the existence of the state of Israel. Hamas states in its charter: "The soil of all Palestine is a *wakf* (Muslim property) that belongs to the Muslims forever."[13]

On the other side, Israeli's Prime Minister Yitzhak Shamir gave similar religious reasons to support his stand that Israel never will give up one square inch of the West Bank lands. "We will not withdraw from these territories which we believe belong to us. We believe that all this country that is called Palestine—or in the Bible is called the Land of Israel—this country belongs to us, the Jewish people."[14] With the fundamentalists becoming stronger in the Moslem camp, and the fundamentalists becoming stronger in Israel, the spiral of violence and counterviolence continued in the Middle East.

The downward spiral was checked, at least for the time being, on September 13, 1993, by the signing of an agreement by Prime Minister Yitzhak Rabin of Israel and Yasir Arafat, chairman of the PLO. The agreement calls for the establishment of an elected interim Palestinian council representing Gaza and the West Bank "for a transitional period not exceeding five years, leading to a permanent settlement." In the interim, the PLO will have authority over the Gaza Strip and

the West Bank town of Jericho regarding education and culture, health, social welfare, direct taxation, and tourism. This agreement was possible because more basic and controversial issues, such as the status of Jerusalem, Israeli settlements, borders, and relations and cooperation with neighboring states, were all left for negotiation and settlement during the "transitional period." The Palestinians will be free during that interim to organize a "strong police force" to maintain order and security, while Israel will remain responsible for defense against external threats.

This agreement is only a first step toward a stable Middle East peace. Many obstacles still block such a peace, including the bitter opposition of the fundamentalists on both sides. In the Israeli camp they still yearn for a "greater Israel," and they still fear Arafat and the PLO as terrorists, with whom no peace can be expected. Likewise, the Palestinian fundamentalists distrust Israel as a powerful expansionist state—an intolerable thorn in the flesh of Islam—hence the recurring clashes between Israeli settlers in the West Bank and the surrounding Palestinian villagers. The common strategy of these antagonists is to unravel the Rabin-Arafat agreement by forcing postponement of any settlement of the remaining unresolved issues.

In addition to the fundamentalist obstacle, the Rabin-Arafat agreement faces political rivalries that have made it a political football in both camps. Some Palestinians reject Arafat's leadership, charging that he is corrupt and high-handed, making decisions and deals without proper consultation. Likewise in Israel, Rabin is being challenged by the opposition Likud Party headed by Benjamin Netanyahu, who states that he feels no obligation to respect the Rabin-Arafat accord. He argues that Arafat already has violated the agreement by failing to stop anti-Israeli attacks. Rabin also faces opposition from Israeli religious leaders such as the former Chief Rabbi Shlomo Goren, who has called on Israeli soldiers to disobey if ordered to evacuate the settlements.

These are serious impediments blocking a stable settlement, yet the accord is by no means stillborn. Two important factors are keeping it alive, one military and the other economic. The military factor emerged from the Gulf War, which demonstrated the decisive superiority of American arms (which Israel uses) over arms (on which the Arabs largely depended). So conclusive was the superiority that an Israeli military expert declared, "It is no longer possible for the Arabs to push Israel into the sea."[15] So Rabin decided that the West Bank no longer was so essential for Israel's security, and that therefore he could safely negotiate a deal with Arafat.

The economic factor is that over the years the Palestinians and the Israelis have developed mutually profitable economic ties, so that now they need each other. This became clear when a wave of lethal attacks led the Israeli government to stop the daily influx of over 100,000 Palestinian workers. This seriously harmed the West Bank Palestinians, who derived about one-third of their total income from jobs in Israel. It was worse in the Gaza Strip, where half the income came from such jobs. But Israel also suffered, having become dependent on cheap Palestinian labor in agriculture and construction, and also on an export trade to the territories, estimated at $1 billion a year. Thus an Israeli economist has concluded that the model of economic relations between Israel and Palestine should be "the Free Trade agreement that exists between Mexico and the U.S."[16] If that is so, then the Rabin-Arafat accord may be as necessary for both sides as the Nafta accord was in North America, and may attract as widespread support for that reason.

In fact, support has been forthcoming. The interim Rabin-Arafat agreement was implemented on May 4, 1994, by an accord formally beginning Israel's withdrawal from Gaza and Jericho, and granting Palestinians a measure of self-government. Simultaneously, the World Bank announced a three-year, $1.2-billion program to provide an economic foundation for Palestinian self-rule. The program includes construction of housing, roads, health centers, waste disposal facilities, and telecommunications. The objective of the program is to improve rapidly the currently abysmal living conditions of the Palestinians in order to win their support for the peace process.

SUGGESTED READINGS

The post–World War II colonial revolutions are analyzed from various viewpoints by R. Emerson, *From Empire to Nation: The Rise to Self Assertion of Asian and African Peoples* (Harvard University, 1960); D. Horowitz, *Imperialism and Revolution* (Penguin, 1969); L. Kaplan, ed., *Revolutions: A Comparative Study* (Vintage, 1973); and R. J. Barnet, *Intervention and Revolution* (World, 1968).

For the winning of independence by India, see M. J. Akbar, *Nehru: The Making of India* (Viking, 1989); and V. P. Menon, *The Transfer of Power in India* (Princeton University, 1957). The long Vietnam struggle has stimulated many studies, of which the following are the most recent and noteworthy: General B. Palmer, Jr., *The 25-Year War: America's Role in Vietnam* (Simon & Schuster, 1985); G. M. Kahin, *Intervention: How America Became Involved in Vietnam* (Knopf, 1986); and G. Kolko, *Anatomy of a War: Vietnam, the United States and the Modern Historical Experience* (Pantheon, 1986).

For general surveys of Africa's awakening, see I. Wallerstein, *Africa: The Politics of Independence* (Random House, 1963); P. Gifford and W. R. Louis, eds., *The Transfer of Power in Africa: Decolonization, 1940–1960* (Yale University, 1982); R. Emerson and M. Kilson, eds., *The Political Awakening of Africa* (Prentice Hall, 1965); and R. I. Rotberg and A. A. Mazrui, *Protest and Power in Black Africa* (Oxford University, 1972).

For the rise of nationalism in the Middle East, see G. Lenczowski, ed., *The Political Awakening in the Middle East* (Prentice Hall, 1970); A. Home, *A Savage War of Peace: Algeria 1954–1962* (Viking, 1977); P. J. Vatikiotis, *Nasser and His Generation* (St. Martin's Press, 1978); and A. Hourani, *A History of the Arab Peoples* (Harvard University, 1991). Differing interpretations of the Arab-Israeli conflict are given in T. Draper, *Israel and World Politics* (Viking, 1967); *The Israeli-Arab Reader* (Bantam Books, 1969); E. W. Said, *The Question of Palestine* (Times Books, 1980); M. Benvenisti, *Conflicts and Contradictions* (Villard, 1986); D. K. Shipler, *Arab and Jew: Wounded Spirits in a Promised Land* (Times Books, 1986); Y. Harkabi, *Israel's Fateful Hour* (Harper & Row, 1988); and T. L. Friedman, *From Beirut to Jerusalem* (Farrar, Straus and Giroux, 1989).

44 Grand Alliance, Cold War, and Aftermath

It is not so difficult to keep unity in time of war since there is a joint aim to defeat the common enemy, which is clear to everyone. The difficult task will come after the war when the diverse interests tend to divide the Allies.

Stalin, at Yalta

World War I was followed by revolution in central and eastern Europe and by the threat of revolution in western Europe. World War II stimulated no comparable disturbances. Revolutions did not convulse the Continent, despite the fact that the second war inflicted greater material damage and political dislocation than the first. One reason was the sheer fatigue of the civilian populations. For six years they had been subjected to constant bombardment from the air; to wide-ranging ground operations; and to mass uprooting through flight, forced labor, or imprisonment. More than 15 million soldiers were killed, as well as 10 million civilians, including 6 million Jews. This was approximately twice the casualties and thirteen times the material damage of World War I.

Those who survived had experienced unprecedented privation and dislocation. In the first three-and-a-half years of the war alone, 30 million Europeans had fled or were driven from their original homes. At the end of the hostilities, Allied armies and international relief agencies returned more than 12 million "displaced persons" to their homes, yet there still remained a hard core of more than a million—mostly anti-Communists from eastern Europe—who refused to go home. The wholesale reshuffling of peoples, together with cold, hunger, and disease, left most Europeans too exhausted and dispirited to think of revolution.

Equally decisive was the occupation of all Europe by the forces of the victorious Allies. The Red Army, no less than the British and the American, stamped out opposition and disorder. A revolution in the social structure did occur in eastern Europe, but it was an imposed revolution directed from Moscow. The Communist parties throughout Europe were obedient instruments of

Soviet foreign policy rather than fomenters of indigenous revolutions. Thus, the Soviet Union, Britain, and the United States effectively controlled developments in Europe after the downfall of Hitler. It was these powers that were responsible for the policies and events that gradually disrupted the wartime Grand Alliance and brought on the cold war.

I. WARTIME UNITY

During the war years, the Western powers and the Soviet Union were forced to present a common front against the menace of a mortal enemy. On the very day of Hitler's invasion of Russia, Churchill proclaimed, "The Russian danger is . . . our danger, and the danger of the United States, just as the cause of any Russian fighting for his hearth and home is the cause of free men and free peoples in every quarter of the globe."[1]

Two months later, on August 14, 1941, Churchill and Roosevelt issued their Atlantic Charter, in which they set forth in idealistic terms their common aims and principles. More specific expressions of Allied cooperation were the twenty-year mutual-aid pact signed by Great Britain and the Soviet Union in May 1942 and the American-Russian Lend-Lease Agreement of the following month. Another manifestation of cooperation was the decision of the Soviets in May 1943 to abolish the Communist International, which they had established in 1919 to overthrow world capitalism. In view of their friendly relations with the Western powers, the Soviets now decided that the Comintern had outlived its usefulness. However, this decision meant little in practice because the top Comintern officials had been transferred to the Party Secretariat, where they continued to function. Still another result of Allied wartime cooperation was the establishment in November 1943 of the UN Relief and Rehabilitation Administration (*UNRRA*). UNRRA followed in the wake of the armed forces and provided relief of all kinds to the liberated countries until the new national administrations could assume responsibility. It began work in the spring of 1944, and, by the time of its dissolution in September 1948, it had distributed 22 million tons of supplies including food, clothing, and medicines, mostly of American origin. Its main operations were in Greece, Yugoslavia, Poland, Czechoslovakia, Austria, and Italy. Without its contributions the deprivation and distress in postwar Europe would have been substantially worse than it was.

As the war neared its end, the cooperation forced by mutual danger began to falter. The partners were more and more inclined to sacrifice unity for what they considered to be their postwar national interests. Thus with peace, the Grand Alliance was rent by discord and, within two or three years, was replaced by a cold war that constantly threatened to become hot.

The breakup of the Grand Alliance was hastened by the failure of the Allied leaders during the war years to make serious plans for the postwar settlement. The Atlantic Charter provided for a postwar world based on self-determination in form of government, equal economic opportunity for all nations, and disarming of aggressive powers. Unfortunately, little effort was made to apply these idealistic principles specifically and realistically to the many issues that awaited the conclusion of peace. The conferences held in 1943 in Casablanca, Quebec, and Teheran were all devoted primarily to military strategy. Postwar matters were referred to only incidentally and in general terms.

By the fall of 1944, political issues no longer could be evaded. The advance of the Red Army up the Danube valley was forcing the Germans to evacuate the Balkan peninsula, and the Communist-led resistance fighters were filling in the vacuum. The prospect of a Communist-dominated Balkans caused Churchill, in October 1944, to meet with Stalin in Moscow. These two leaders quickly agreed on spheres of influence in the disputed peninsula. Bulgaria and Rumania were to be in the Soviet sphere, Greece in the British, and Yugoslavia a buffer zone under joint British-Soviet influence. Thus Churchill was forced, by the unfavorable strategic situation, to accept Soviet predominance in the northern Balkans in order to preserve Britain's traditional primacy in Greece.

At the same time that Churchill was bargaining with Stalin in Moscow, British troops were beginning to land in Greece. They advanced northward on the heels of the retreating Germans but

CHURCHILL AND STALIN DIVIDE THE BALKANS

Prime Minister Winston Churchill and Communist Party Secretary Joseph Stalin met in Moscow the evening of October 9, 1944. Churchill has left the following colorful account of how the two men divided the Balkan peninsula between them into British and Russian spheres of influence.*

The moment was apt for business, so I said, "Let us settle about our affairs in the Balkans. Your armies are in Rumania and Bulgaria. We have interests, missions and agents there. Don't let us get at cross-purposes in small ways. So far as Britain and Russia are concerned, how would it do for you to have ninety per cent predominance in Rumania, for us to have ninety per cent of the say in Greece, and go fifty-fifty about Yugoslavia?" While this was being translated I wrote out on a half-sheet of paper:

Rumania	
Russia	90%
The others	10%
Greece	
Great Britain	90%
(in accord with U.S.A.)	
Russia	10%
Yugoslavia	50–50%
Hungary	50–50%
Bulgaria	
Russia	75%
The others	25%

I pushed this across to Stalin who had by then heard the translation. There was a slight pause. Then he took his blue pencil and made a large tick upon it, and passed it back to us. It was all settled in no more time than it takes to set it down. . . .

After this there was a long silence. The pencilled paper lay in the centre of the table. At length I said, "Might it not be thought rather cynical if it seemed we had disposed of these issues, so fateful to millions of people, in such an off-hand manner? Let us burn the paper." "No, you keep it," said Stalin.

* W. S. Churchill, *The Second World War: Triumph and Tragedy* (Houghton Mifflin, 1953), pp. 227–228.

found the Greek resistance forces preceding them in all the towns and cities. No opposition was offered by these forces, led by disciplined Communists who obediently followed the current Kremlin line. They welcomed the small British units, although, had they wished, they could have easily barred them at that time just as the nationalist-minded Tito was doing in Yugoslavia.

Despite the compliance of the Greek resistance forces, the fact remained that they were the preponderant military power in the country as the Germans withdrew. This was an intolerable situation for Churchill. To ensure the British dominance in Greece that he and Stalin had agreed on in Moscow, it was essential to disarm the resistance forces and transfer state power to the royal Greek government-in-exile that he favored. Various disarmament formulas were proposed, but none satisfied both sides. This dispute precipitated an armed clash that developed into the bitter and bloody Battle of Athens. British and Indian troops were rushed in from Italy, and after a month of fighting the resistance forces withdrew from the Athens area.

On February 12, a peace agreement (the Varkiza Pact) was signed by which the resistance troops surrendered their arms in return for a promise of elections and a plebiscite on the question of the return of the king. Thus Churchill secured the sphere allotted to him in Moscow: Greece was to be on the side of the West during the postwar years. Equally significant was Stalin's eloquent silence while Churchill was dispersing the leftist resistance fighters. The British-Soviet deal on the Balkans was in operation and was working.

The fighting in Athens had barely ceased when, in February 1945, Roosevelt, Churchill, and Stalin met at Yalta for the last of their wartime conferences. With the Allied armies converging on Germany from all sides, the problems of a postwar settlement now had to be considered specifically and realistically. Little difficulty was encountered in reaching an agreement on the Far East. Stalin agreed to declare war against Japan within sixty days after the end of hostilities in Europe. In return, the USSR was to regain the Kuril Islands and also the concessions and territories lost to Japan in 1905, including the southern part of Sakhalin Island, the lease of the Port Arthur naval base, and joint Russo-Chinese operation of the Chinese Eastern and South Manchuria railroads. On Germany, the conference postponed decisions about most issues, including reparations and frontiers. It was agreed, however, that the country should be divided into four occupation zones (including one for France) under an Allied Control Council. Berlin, located within the Soviet zone, was to be occupied and administered jointly.

Most of the negotiating at Yalta had to do with the newly liberated countries in eastern Europe. Stalin was in a strong position in this area, for his armies had done the liberating and were in actual occupation. Given this context, the agreements that were made on eastern Europe

"The Big Three"—Stalin, Roosevelt, and Churchill—meet for the last time at Yalta, 1945.

were, *on paper*, satisfactory from the Western viewpoint. The USSR was to receive the Polish territory east of a modified Curzon Line, which had been drawn after World War I but subsequently ignored. Poland was to be compensated with territory in east Germany. Concerning the Polish and Yugoslav governments, Stalin agreed that the Communist regimes already established under Soviet auspices should be broadened by the admission of representatives from the West-oriented governments-in-exile. The latter were understandably apprehensive about this arrangement, which left the Red Army and the Communist governments in physical and legal control. Their doubts were met, in theory, by a broad statement of policy known as the Yalta Declaration on Liberated Europe. This committed the three powers to assist the liberated peoples of Europe "to form interim governmental authorities broadly representative of all democratic elements in the population and pledged to the earliest possible establishment through free elections of governments responsive to the will of the people. . . ."

Taken at face value, this declaration represented a substantial concession on the part of Stalin. Despite his domination of eastern Europe, he had consented to free elections that might well bring anti-Soviet governments to office. The substance of this concession, however, was negligible. The declaration turned out to be meaningless and was a constant source of friction, because it was interpreted very differently by the various signatories. The United States interpreted it literally—that is, free elections and no spheres of influence in eastern Europe. The United States was free to take this position because it was not bound by the agreement reached by Churchill and Stalin in Moscow the previous October.

Stalin, by contrast, clung to the Moscow agreement and regarded the declaration as mere window dressing. He had scrupulously kept quiet while the British crushed the Greek resistance forces. In return, Stalin expected the Western powers to respect his primacy in the northern Balkans. He was surprised and outraged when the British gradually joined the Americans in demanding strict enforcement of the declaration. Stalin refused to budge on this point, regarding "friendly" governments in eastern Europe as pre-

requisite for Soviet security. He made this clear at the next three-power conference at Potsdam (July–August 1945), where the American secretary of state, James Byrnes, demanded freely elected governments in eastern Europe. "A freely elected government in any of these countries," responded Stalin, "would be anti-Soviet and that we cannot allow."[2] The contradiction between "friendly" and "freely elected" governments was one of the main causes for the disruption of the Grand Alliance in the months to come.

II.   PEACE TREATIES

Despite the seeds of discord at Yalta, the conference was generally welcomed and interpreted as the climax of the wartime cooperation of the allies. Cooperation was shown again with the organization of the *United Nations* (*UN*). The final charter was signed by the representatives of fifty nations at the conclusion of a conference held in San Francisco from April to June 1945. By 1990 UN membership had more than tripled. Some of the newcomers were wartime enemies or neutrals, but the majority were newly independent states in Asia and Africa. The UN, like its predecessor, the League of Nations, was set up to accomplish two basic tasks: to preserve peace and security and to cope with international economic, social, and cultural problems. Also like the league, the UN was established as an association of sovereign states. The charter specified that the organization might not "intervene in matters which are essentially within the domestic jurisdiction of any state."

The task of maintaining peace was entrusted primarily to a *Security Council* made up of five permanent members—the United States, the Soviet Union, Britain, France, and China—and six other members elected for two-year terms by the General Assembly on the recommendation of the council. In all substantive matters the unanimous vote of the permanent members was required (together with the vote of two of the nonpermanent members), for it was recognized that peace could be maintained only if the great powers were in agreement.

The second task of the UN—the fight against hunger and disease and ignorance—was en-

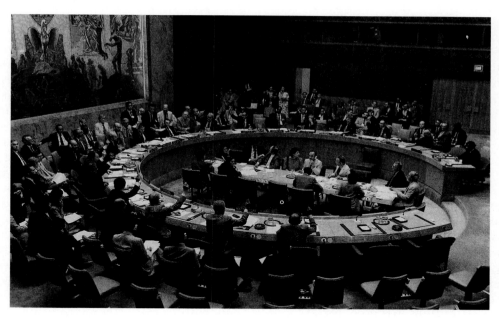

The United Nations Security Council in session.

trusted to the *Economic and Social Council*. It established programs designed to provide more food for the half of the world's people who were hungry, cure the one-eighth of the world's population that had malaria, save the 40 percent of the children who died before the end of their first year, and teach the 50 percent of the world's adults who were illiterate to read and write.

Like the League of Nations, the UN has been quite successful in these various nonpolitical activities. But again like the League, the UN has had a spotty record in its main job of keeping the peace. It has helped to prevent all-out war between the great powers by providing a medium for maintaining rapport. It has stopped fighting in areas such as Indonesia and Kashmir, where vital interests of the major powers were not involved. But it was not able to forestall a series of local, or "brush-fire," wars in Korea, Algeria, the Middle East, and Vietnam. Nor was there any consultation of the UN during the highly dangerous Cuban crisis of 1962 or the prolonged Vietnam agony. The basic difficulty of the UN, as of the League, was that in a world of sovereign states it could provide machinery for settling disputes but could not compel use of that machinery.

Two months after the establishment of the UN, Japan surrendered and the war in the Far East was over. The victorious Allies could now devote full attention to the making of peace. Their foreign ministers on February 10, 1947, signed peace treaties with Italy, Rumania, Hungary, Bulgaria, and Finland. All the treaties imposed reparations on the defeated countries, limited their armed forces, and redrew their frontiers. Italy lost the Dodecanese Islands to Greece; Saseno Island to Albania, small enclaves to France; Venezia Giulia to Yugoslavia; and the Trieste region, which was set up as a Free Territory. When the last-named arrangement had proved unworkable by 1954, Italy annexed the city itself with its predominantly Italian population, and Yugoslavia took the surrounding rural part of the Free Territory. Italy's African colonies were placed under the temporary trusteeship of Great Britain, their ultimate status to be determined later.

In the Balkans, Bulgaria restored the Greek and Yugoslav territories that it had occupied, but it acquired southern Dobruja, which it had lost to Rumania in 1919. Rumania lost Bessarabia (which had been Russian from 1812 to 1918) and the northern Bucovina (inhabited largely by Ukrainians) to the Soviet Union, but it regained northern Transylvania, which Hungary had seized during the war. Other territorial changes in eastern Europe not covered by the satellite treaties included the acquisition by the USSR of the predominantly Ukrainian Carpathian—Ruthenia from Czechoslovakia—and of the three Baltic states—Latvia, Lithuania, and Estonia. Though the USSR claimed the Baltic states on the ground that they had been a part of the tsarist empire, the Western powers withheld official recognition of their annexation.

III.   COLD WAR IN EUROPE

The satellite treaties were not followed by corresponding pacts with the other enemy countries. The breakdown in peacemaking reflected the growing dissension between East and West. This, in turn, may be explained to a large degree by the immense power vacuums in Europe and Asia following the collapse of the German and Japanese empires. These vacuums required some fundamental readjustments of power relationships. Under the best of circumstances such readjustments are difficult to arrange, as evidenced by the crises following the Napoleonic Wars and World War I. Now, after World War II, the process of readjustment was made even more complicated and perilous by the addition of ideological issues to the traditional power struggle.

In the Far East, the situation was simplified by the fact that the United States had the leading role in the war against Japan and did not hesitate to assume a leadership role also in the peace settlement and in postwar affairs. In Europe, the issues were considerably more complicated because the Soviet Union was entrenching itself within its east European preserve. Its objectives were territorial expansion toward the pre–World War I tsarist frontiers, large-scale reparations to help pay for the crushing war devastation, and "friendly" governments in eastern Europe that would prevent more invasions from the West. In striving for these objectives the Soviet Union came into direct and progressively sharper conflict with the Western powers. The latter opposed strenuously the so-called "Peoples' Democracies" as being representative more of the Soviet proconsuls than of the peoples concerned. In reply, the Soviets repeatedly drew attention to the rightist terrorism in Greece, where the governments ever since the Battle of Athens were supported by Britain.

More serious was the East-West clash in Germany, where the stakes were higher. The end of the war had left Germany with no central government. Only local officials were left, and in the East even these were lacking as they fled before the advancing Red Army. For purposes of occupation the Allies divided Germany into four zones—the Soviets in the east, the British in the northwest, the Americans in the south, and the French in a smaller southwest zone bordering their own country. A similar four-way division of Berlin was arranged, with an Allied Control Council located in the city to ensure uniformity of policy.

When the occupying powers faced the concrete problems of administering Germany, they discovered basic differences in aims and policies. The differences came to a head over reparations. It had been agreed at the Potsdam Conference in July 1945 that the USSR was to receive $10 billion indemnity from Germany, to be collected from German foreign assets and through the removal of industrial equipment—from the Soviet zone and from the Western zones insofar as the equipment was not needed by the local economies. The Soviets promptly proceeded to dismantle and ship East German factories to their own country, and also to tap current German factory output. The latter practice was a violation of the Potsdam agreement, as was also the refusal by the Soviets to allow any inspection of the East German economy. In retaliation, the Americans and the British stopped the delivery of reparations from their zones in May 1946 and repeatedly raised the permitted level of German industry. The next step occurred in December 1946, when the British and the Americans combined their zones into an economic "Bizonia."

By early 1947 the four-power administration of Germany had broken up. In an effort to resolve the conflict, a Big Four conference was held in Moscow in March 1947. The Americans and the British insisted on the economic unification of Germany; the French and the Russians were opposed. After six weeks of futile wrangling, the conference adjourned. Its failure, together with the proclamation of the Truman Doctrine at the same time, are considered to mark the beginning of the cold war.

The most dramatic manifestation of the oncoming cold war was President Truman's intervention in the Greek Civil War in March 1947. Communist-led guerrillas had appeared the preceding fall in the mountains of northern Greece. One reason for the renewed civil strife was the wretched economic condition that drove many impoverished peasants to the rebel ranks. Another was the deteriorating international situation, which led the Soviet bloc to incite and aid the guerrillas against the British-supported Athens government. Finally, there was the rightist persecution of political opponents despite the provision for amnesty and normal political procedures in the Varkiza Pact terminating the Battle of Athens.

These circumstances engendered considerable popular support for the insurrection, which spread from the northern mountains to the Peloponnesus and the larger islands. The likelihood for suppressing the revolt appeared bleak, so that Greece faced the prospect of prolonged civil war with the possibility of an eventual Communist victory. The possibility became a probability when on February 24, 1947, the British government announced that it could not afford the large-scale aid necessary to ensure victory over the rebel bands. President Truman met the emergency by proclaiming the doctrine named after him. Stating that "the very existence of the Greek state is today threatened," he requested Congress to appropriate $400 million for aid to Greece and Turkey. Thus Britain surrendered its century-old primacy in Greece. The United States assumed the responsibility for preventing the extension of Communist influence in the eastern Mediterranean.

The task proved more expensive than anticipated. The United States between March 1947 and June 1949 spent approximately $400 million for military purposes and $300 million for economic aid. Even with this lavish support, both the 1947 and 1948 campaigns were inconclusive. In 1949 the balance shifted decisively in favor of the Athens government. The Tito-Stalin split led Marshal Tito to close the Yugoslav border and stop all aid to the guerrillas who had sided with Stalin. At the same time the Athens armies were being retrained by American officers to fight a mobile offensive war instead of garrisoning key towns and communication routes. Thus, in the fall of 1949 the national armies were able to drive

the guerrillas from their mountain strongholds and to reach and seal the northern frontiers.

The counterpart to the Truman Doctrine in the economic sphere was the European Recovery Program, commonly known as the Marshall Plan. By the time of its termination on December 31, 1951, a total of $12.5 billion was spent in support of Marshall Plan operations. This extraordinary investment, together with the human and material resources of Europe, brought about a rapid recovery that raised production and living standards to above prewar levels. But from the viewpoint of East-West relations, the Marshall Plan marked the final step toward the *cold war*. In January 1949, Moscow established the Council for Mutual Economic Assistance (Molotov Plan) as the Eastern counterpart to the Marshall Plan.

Thus the line was drawn between the Communist and Western worlds. The cold war now was in full sway, and for the next half-decade one crisis followed closely on another. The moves and countermoves culminated in the establishment of the two confrontational military alliances: the *North Atlantic Treaty Organization*, or *NATO* (April 4, 1949), which included the United States, Canada, and western European states, and the *Warsaw Pact* (May 1955), comprising the Soviet Union and its eastern European allies. Thus Europe, as well as Germany, was cut in two by the cold war. (See map of World of New Global Relationships, 1985, p. 659.)

IV.   COLD WAR IN THE FAR EAST

In 1950, the focus of the cold war shifted from Europe to the Far East. By this time a balance had been reached in Europe between East and West. But in the Far East the balance was upset by the triumph of the Communists in China. Just as the Bolshevik Revolution was the outstanding byproduct of World War I, so the Chinese Communist Revolution was the outstanding byproduct of World War II.

Chiang Kai-shek had become the head of the Chinese government in 1928, but from the outset his Kuomintang regime was threatened by two mortal enemies, the Communists within and the Japanese without. During World War II his position became particularly difficult. The country was divided into three sections: the east, controlled by the Japanese and administered through a puppet government at Nanking; the northwest, controlled by the Communists operating from their capital at Yenan; and the west and southwest, ruled by Chiang's Nationalist government from its capital in Chungking.

It was during the war years that Chiang's regime was fatally undermined. Chiang traditionally had depended on the support of the conservative landlord class and of the relatively enlightened big businesspeople. The latter were largely eliminated when the Japanese overran the east coast, and Chiang was left with the self-centered and short-sighted landlords of the interior. His government became increasingly corrupt and unresponsive to the needs of the peasants suffering from years of war and exploitation. In contrast to the decaying Kuomintang, the Communists carried out land reforms in their territories, thereby winning the support of the peasant masses. They also had a disciplined and efficient organization that brought order out of political and economic chaos in the areas under their control. Also their leadership in the anti-Japanese struggle won them popular support as patriots fighting to rid the country of foreign invaders and to restore China's unity and pride.

Such was the situation when Japan's surrender in August 1945 set off a wild scramble by the Nationalists and Communists to take over the Japanese-occupied parts of China. The Communists issued orders to their troops to take over the areas held by the Japanese. Chiang Kai-shek promptly canceled these orders and insisted that the Communists make no move without instructions from him. He was ignored, and clashes occurred between Communist and Kuomintang forces. With civil war imminent, the United States sent a mission under General George Marshall to attempt to negotiate a settlement. But neither side could overcome its fear and suspicion of the other, and Marshall's mediation failed. By 1947 the final showdown was at hand.

The Communists occupied the countryside around the major cities. They were helped by the Russians, who turned over to them the arms the Japanese had surrendered in Manchuria. The Nationalists, aided by the transportation services of the U.S. Navy and Air Force, won all the main

cities, including Nanking, and also rushed troops north to Manchuria. The latter move was a strategic blunder. The Kuomintang forces found themselves in indefensible positions. In the fall of 1948 they were forced to surrender to the Chinese Red Army. A chain of comparable military disasters followed in quick succession. The Communist armies swept down from Manchuria through the major cities of North China. By April 1949 they were crossing the Yangtze and fanning out over south China. The Communist steamroller advanced even more rapidly in the south than in the north. By the end of 1949 it had overrun all of mainland China. Chiang fled to the island of Taiwan (Formosa), and on October 1, 1949, in Peking, the Communist leader, Mao Tsetung, proclaimed the People's Republic of China.

In the years after 1949 the Communists transformed China at an unprecedented rate. In place of the flabby and decentralized political state of the past, they imposed a monolithic structure, extending into every city, every village, and every household. The Communists at the head of this structure were able to reach down to individual citizens, moving them to new occupations and forcing them to live and think in new ways. They uprooted the traditional Confucian culture by changing the old family relationships; raising the inferior position of women; and ignoring the old classics in favor of a new literature, art, and educational system. The Communists indeed left their mark on China, but at a price. At the outset they enjoyed wide support because of their leadership in resisting the Japanese invaders and in tackling the many problems China faced at the end of the war. But the longer they remained in power, the more opposition they aroused, as shown when students erected their Statue of Liberty in Tiananmen Square in the summer of 1989. The aging Communist leaders ordered their army to crush the students, and then hunted them down throughout China as "counterrevolutionaries" and "ruffians."

The victory of communism in China was a serious setback for the United States, although it dominated the postwar occupation in Japan. Japan, in contrast to Germany, was governed by a single Supreme Command of the Allied powers, which included Allied representatives. The Supreme Commander General Douglas

MacArthur and the bulk of the occupation forces were American.

MacArthur's instructions were to disarm and demilitarize the country, develop democratic institutions, and create a viable economy. Accordingly, he disbanded the imperial army and navy, banned patriotic organizations, stripped Emperor Hirohito of his divine rights, and purged education of its militaristic elements. In 1947 he proclaimed a democratic constitution that transferred sovereignty from the emperor to the people, guaranteed individual rights, and granted women equal status with men. In the economic field the most important measure was wholesale redistribution of land. By 1952, 90 percent of the arable acreage was owned by former tenants. Less successful was the attempt to break up the large family corporations, or zaibatsu, that had dominated the prewar industry, finance, and foreign trade. The initial measures against the zaibatsu were dropped because it was felt that they hampered economic recovery.

By 1951, when the occupation had accomplished most of its aims, a peace treaty was concluded and signed by the United States and most of the Allies. The exceptions were China and the Soviet Union, who considered the terms too generous. The treaty restored Japanese sovereignty, but only over the four main islands. There were no military or economic restrictions, except that the United States was permitted to maintain military bases in Japan. The United States also gained trusteeship over the Ryuku and Bonin islands and over Japan's former Pacific mandates. Japan relinquished the Kuril Islands and southern Sakhalin (which had been allotted to the USSR) as well as Formosa, but the future disposition of these islands was left open. In effect, this treaty made Japan the main bastion of the American position in the Far East. In support of this bastion the United States spent about $2 billion in the first six years after the war. With the demand for a wide variety of goods during the Korean and Vietnam wars, Japan made such remarkable economic progress that by 1985 it had become the second greatest industrial power in the world, surpassed only by the United States.

In the Far East, as in Europe, World War II was followed by the cold war. Russia backed Mao Tse-tung, although belatedly, whereas the United States vainly attempted to maintain Chiang Kai-shek as master of China. Conversely, in Japan the United States dominated the occupation and utilized it to further its interests, while

Tanks roll through the streets of Beijing.

the Soviet representatives impotently protested. Once the outcome had apparently been settled in both countries, there was hope, as expressed by Secretary of State Dean Acheson, for "the dust to settle" and for a balance to be reached, as in Europe. The hope was shattered when in 1950 fighting broke out in Korea, and the cold war heated up.

Since 1895—and formally since 1910—Korea had passed under Japanese rule. During World War II, at the 1943 Cairo Conference, the United States, Britain, and China declared that "in due course" Korea should once more be free and independent. But a generation of Japanese rule had left Korea without the necessary experience for self-government. The victorious Allies decided, therefore, that for a period of not more than five years Korea, though independent, should be under the trusteeship of the United States, the USSR, Britain, and China.

With the surrender of Japan, American and Soviet troops poured into Korea. For purposes of military convenience the thirty-eighth parallel was set as the dividing line in their operations. The coming of the cold war froze this temporary division in Korea as it did in Germany. The Soviets set up in their zone a regime dominated by the Communist New People's party. In the south, the Americans depended on English-speaking Koreans, who usually were members of the conservative upper class. In August 1948, a Republic of Korea was proclaimed in the south, with Dr. Syngman Rhee as president. A month later the North Koreans formed their People's Democratic Republic under Kim Il-sung. A UN commission attempted without success to mediate between the regimes headed by these two men. So strong were the feelings that the commission warned in September 1949 of the danger of civil war.

On June 24, 1950, civil war did begin when North Korean troops suddenly crossed the thirty-eighth parallel. On June 27 the Security Council asked UN members to "furnish such assistance to the Republic of Korea as may be necessary to repel the armed attack and to restore international peace and security in the area." Forty UN member states responded to the Security Council's appeal and provided supplies, transport, hospital units, and, in some cases, combat forces. But the main contribution, aside from that of South Ko-

rea, came from the United States, and General MacArthur served as commander-in-chief.

The course of the Korean War fell into two phases—the first before, and the second after, the Chinese intervention. The first phase began with the headlong rush of the North Korean forces down the length of the peninsula to within fifty miles of the port of Pusan at the southern tip. Then on September 14, 1950, an American army landed at Inchon, far up the coast near the thirty-eighth parallel, and in twelve days retook the South Korean capital, Seoul. The North Koreans, their communications severed, fell back as precipitously as they had advanced. By the end of September the UN forces had reached the thirty-eighth parallel.

The question now was whether to cross or not to cross. The issue was transferred to the General Assembly, because the Soviet Union, with its veto power, had returned to the Security Council. On October 7, 1950, the assembly resolved that "all constituent acts be taken . . . for the establishment of a unified, independent, and democratic government in the sovereign state of Korea." The next day American forces crossed the thirty-eighth parallel and quickly occupied Pyongyang, the North Korean capital. By November 22 they reached the Yalu River, the boundary line between Korea and the Chinese province of Manchuria.

At this point the second phase of the Korean War began with a massive attack by Chinese "volunteers" supported by Soviet-made jets. The Chinese drove southward rapidly in what looked like a repetition of the first phase of the war. Early in January 1951 they retook Seoul, but the UN forces now recovered and held their ground. In March, Seoul once more changed hands, and by June the battle line ran roughly along the thirty-eighth parallel.

By mid-1951 it was apparent that a stalemate prevailed at the front. After two years of stormy and often-interrupted negotiations, an armistice agreement was concluded on July 27, 1953. The terms reflected the military stalemate. The line of partition between North and South Korea remained roughly where it had been before the war. The Western powers had successfully contained communism in Korea and had vindicated the authority of the United Nations. The

Chinese had secured North Korea as a Communist buffer state between Manchuria and Western influences. And meanwhile, most of the Korean countryside had been laid waste and about 10 percent of the Korean people had been killed.

V. RELAXATION OF THE COLD WAR

At the end of World War II, both western and eastern Europe were forced to turn for support to the two new superpowers, the United States and the Soviet Union. In military affairs western Europe depended on the American-organized NATO, and eastern Europe depended on the Soviet-organized Warsaw Pact. In economic matters western Europe relied on the Marshall Plan financed by the United States, and eastern Europe depended on the Council for Mutual Economic Assistance, which theoretically funneled in Soviet aid, though in practice it did the opposite.

The primacy of Washington and Moscow was accepted because their support was needed in the face of the pressures produced by the cold war. But after building up for several years, the cold war began to subside in 1953. One reason was the death in April 1953 of Joseph Stalin, who had become increasingly paranoid and inflexible in his later years. The younger men who succeeded him were ready for a relaxation of both the cold war abroad and the dictatorship at home. At the same time, the new Eisenhower administration was replacing that of Truman in the United States. This also contributed to the international "thaw," for Eisenhower was able to make a compromise peace in Korea, whereas domestic political considerations would have made this extremely difficult for Truman. Thus the Korean War was ended in July 1953, eliminating the most serious single source of international tension.

The following month the Soviet government announced that it also possessed the secret of the hydrogen bomb. Paradoxically, this strengthened the movement for a settlement. It was known that the hydrogen bomb exploded by the United States at Bikini was 750 times more powerful than the Hiroshima atomic bomb, which had killed 78,000 people. All but the most fanatic cold warriors sensed that war was no longer a feasible instrument of national policy.

The deterring effect of the H-bomb was manifested during the 1962 Cuban crisis, precipitated when American air reconnaissance revealed that Soviet missile bases were under construction in Cuba and that a large part of the United States soon would be within range. In a dramatic broadcast on October 22, 1962, President Kennedy proclaimed a "quarantine" to halt ships carrying offensive weapons to Cuba and demanded the removal of the Soviet strategic missiles. But he did not demand the removal of the Castro regime or even of the Cuban defense missiles. It was clear that neither country wanted war when Soviet vessels bound for Cuba altered course and the United States permitted a Soviet tanker to proceed when satisfied that it carried no offensive weapons. Finally, on October 28, Khrushchev announced that he had ordered Soviet missiles withdrawn and all Soviet bases in Cuba dismantled under UN inspection. In return, the United States ended its blockade and pledged not to invade Cuba.

Although the Cuban crisis ended peaceably, it was a very near thing—so near that it stimulated several agreements for the limitation of nuclear weapons: controls on tests of nuclear weapons (1963), prohibition of nuclear weapons in space (1967), a nonnuclear zone in Latin America (1967), nonproliferation of nuclear weapons beyond the nations already possessing them (1968), prohibition of nuclear weapons on the seabed (1971), prohibition of the use of biological weapons (1971), and the first Western-Soviet Strategic Arms Limitation Treaty (1972). These agreements together helped to lessen substantially the international tensions of the cold war.

The Cuban missile crisis was a narrow squeak, narrower than a scared world realized at the time. This became clear to American and Soviet officials who met in Moscow a quarter-century later, in January 1989, to review and reflect on what had happened. Robert S. McNamara, Secretary of Defense at the time of the crisis, reached this conclusion from the Moscow discussions:

The missile crisis is replete with examples of misinformation, misjudgment, miscalculation. . . . This must lead to the conclusion that, insofar as it is achievable, we must seek to return to a nonnuclear world.[3]

VI.   END OF THE COLD WAR

During the 1960s and 1970s the cold war slowly and painfully thawed. During the 1980s, the cold war suddenly and unexpectedly ended. The reason was simple and dramatic. It takes two to wage a cold war, and the two after the second world war were the American and Soviet superpowers. But in the 1980s the Soviet superpower weakened rapidly to the point of actual disintegration. An astonished world witnessed the disappearance of the USSR from our world map, replaced by the Commonwealth of Independent States (CIS). How and why the Soviet Union gave way to the Commonwealth will be analyzed in the following chapter.

As startling as the breakup of the Soviet Union was the breakup of the Soviet-Chinese alliance. When the victorious Chinese Communists established the People's Republic in 1949, they were promptly recognized by the Soviet Union. A score of other countries, including Britain and India, did likewise. The United States, however, continued to treat Chiang Kai-shek's exiled regime in Taiwan as the legal government of China. Peking therefore turned to Moscow and, in 1950, signed a thirty-year treaty of "friendship, alliance, and mutual assistance." Under the terms of the treaty, the Soviet Union helped China to build a large modern army and to begin an ambitious program of industrialization.

The Soviet-Chinese alliance began to show signs of disruption in the late 1950s. The roots of this dramatic and fateful rift in the Communist world appear to be partly a conflict of national interests and partly a conflict of ideologies. The national issues arose from traditional material considerations such as frontier demarcation. The 2,000-mile frontier separating the two countries has been drawn in precise detail in Soviet maps. On Chinese maps certain sections have been depicted as "undemarcated," including the eastern margins of the Pamir highlands, some islands at the confluence of the Amur and Ussuri rivers, and almost the entire frontier with Mongolia. These territories, formerly a part of the Chinese Empire, were annexed by tsarist Russia during the nineteenth century and now are claimed by Communist China. Many armed clashes have occurred along these disputed frontiers.

At the outset of the Soviet-Chinese dispute it appeared that ideological issues were more important than frontier lines. Years of revolutionary struggle in China had stimulated a new vision of human and social relations—a vision of an egalitarian Communist order in which the individual is motivated by the desire for social service rather than personal gain. Thus, although the Soviet-type Five-Year Plans were successful in furthering industrialization and raising productivity, Mao was unwilling to accept the increasing income differentiation and bureaucratic elitism on which these plans were based. This explains the Great Leap Forward of 1958 and the Cultural Revolution of 1966, with their slogans such as "organization without bureaucracy" and "serve the people." The Soviets regarded this as utopian romanticism doomed to failure, which was one reason why they stopped their aid to Mao.

Since Mao's death in 1976 the ideological differences between China and the Soviet Union (now the CIS) have become blurred. Mao's successors launched a "modernization" drive, which not only included measures hitherto denounced as "revisionist" but also went much further down the revisionist path toward "market socialism." These measures included restoring family farms in place of communes; substituting individual managers for revolutionary committees in factories; rewarding good workers and penalizing poor ones; and moving away from industrial self-reliance and toward mass importation of factories and technologies.

This post-Mao program has changed fundamentally the cold war world. No longer are the Russian and Chinese Communist giants close allies in a global feud with the capitalist West. Rather, they are competing with each other in a search for practical economic strategies to satisfy the rising consumer expectations of their respective peoples. In this way the cold war world is giving way to a very different world that will take shape gradually in the 1990s and in the twenty-first century.

SUGGESTED READINGS

World War II diplomacy and the ensuing cold war have been the subject of vigorous debate by historians. The traditional view, holding the Soviet Union primarily responsible for the cold war, is set forth by H. Thomas, *Armed Truce: The Beginnings of the Cold War 1945–6* (Atheneum, 1987); R. J. Maddox, *The New Left and the Origins of the Cold War* (Princeton University, 1973); and J. L. Gaddis, *The United States and the Origins of the Cold War, 1941–1947* (Columbia University, 1973). The revisionist interpretation that holds the West responsible, or more so, than the Soviet Union, was first propounded in detail by D. F. Fleming, *The Cold War and Its Origins, 1917–1960*, 2 vols. (George Allen & Unwin, 1961). This thesis has been elaborated by other writers such as G. Kolko, *The Politics of War: The World and U.S. Foreign Policy 1943–1945* (Random House, 1969); W. La Feber, *America, Russia and the Cold War* (John Wiley, 1968); T. G. Paterson, ed., *Cold War Critics: Alternatives to American Policy in the Truman Years* (Quadrangle Books, 1972); N. D. Houghton, ed., *Struggle against History: U.S. Foreign Policy in an Age of Revolution* (Simon & Schuster, 1972); and B. A. Weisberger, *Cold War, Cold Peace: The United States and Russia since 1945* (Houghton Mifflin, 1984). For the Truman Doctrine and the Near East, see B. Kuniholm, *The Origins of the Cold War in the Near East* (Princeton University, 1980);

and L. S. Wittner, *American Intervention in Greece* (Columbia University, 1982). Finally, American-Soviet relations since 1966 are examined by R. L. Garthoff, *Detente and Confrontation: American Soviet Relations from Nixon to Reagan* (Brookings, 1985).

Varying interpretations are available also concerning Far Eastern diplomacy in works such as Y. Nagai and A. Iriye, *The Origins of the Cold War in Asia* (Columbia University, 1977); Tang Tsou, *America's Failure in China 1941–50* (University of Chicago, 1964); W. I. Cohen, *America's Response to China* (John Wiley, 1971); B. Cumings, *The Origins of the Korean War* (Princeton University, 1984); and J. Halliday and B. Cumings, *Korea: The Unknown War* (Pantheon, 1988).

On the ending of global bipolarism, see W. S. Vucinich, ed., *At the Brink of War and Peace: The Tito-Stalin Split in a Historic Perspective* (Columbia University, 1982); W. G. Rosenberg and M. B. Young, *Transforming Russia and China: Revolutionary Struggle in the Twentieth Century* (Oxford University, 1982); and R. J. Barnet, *The Alliance: America, Europe and Japan* (Simon & Schuster, 1983).

45

Second Industrial Revolution: Global Repercussions

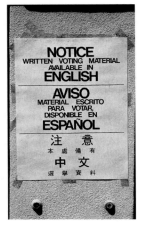

Ours is a time of problems, of gigantic problems. Everything is being transformed under the magic influence of science and technology. And everyday, if we want to live with open eyes, we have a problem to study, to resolve.

Pope Pius VI, May 18, 1969

We are amidst the biggest technological revolution men have known, far more intimate in the tone of our daily lives, and of course far quicker, either than the agricultural transformation in Neolithic times, or the early industrial revolution . . .

C. P. Snow, 1966

The major problems of our day confront all human beings in all societies. In 1985, about $1 trillion was invested in armaments in a desperate search for security. Yet the more money spent, the greater the insecurity. By far the largest hoards of arms were accumulated by the two superpowers of the time, yet Americans and Soviets were no more secure than the peoples of tiny Switzerland or Sri Lanka. Likewise, unemployment and poverty are scourges usually associated with underdeveloped Third World coun-

tries, but today they are afflicting millions in western Europe and North America as well as in Asia, Africa, and Latin America. Ecological deterioration is normally attributed to shortsighted policies of Third World countries that allow their tropical forests to be denuded and their deserts to advance into arable lands. Yet the topsoils of the American Midwest continue to erode as in dust-bowl days; parts of California's fertile Central Valley are becoming salt deserts; and in the northeastern United States, eastern Canada, and northern Europe, acid rain is turning forests brown and lakes a lifeless blue, not to mention the corrosion of famous monuments in London, Paris, and Cologne.

What is responsible for these afflictions ravaging all societies in all parts of the globe? Many forces are at work, but probably most basic is the second industrial revolution that began during World War II. We noted in Chapter 28 how decisive was the impact of the first industrial revolution on both European and non-European lands. Much deeper, swifter, and all-pervasive is the impact of today's second industrial revolution. In this concluding chapter we shall examine the origin and nature of the new industrial revolution and then analyze its impact on various regions of the world, and on various aspects of our lives.

I. SECOND INDUSTRIAL REVOLUTION: ORIGINS AND NATURE

World War II stimulated several technical breakthroughs of such magnitude and significance that they warrant classification as the second industrial revolution.

Example: Nuclear Energy. The first industrial revolution created new energy sources such as steam power, electricity, and the gasoline engine. During World War II an explosion on the desert floor of New Mexico marked the harnessing of the power of the atom. This power was used first for military purposes with the dropping of atom bombs on Hiroshima and Nagasaki. Today it is used for numerous other purposes, such as nuclear powered ships, biomedical research, medical diagnosis and therapy, and nuclear power plants.

Example: Labor-Replacing Machines. Whereas the first industrial revolution created labor-*saving* machines, the second is creating labor-*replacing* machines. The roots of these new machines go back to Britain's World War II antiaircraft batteries, which were filled with computers—a combination of electric memory and programs that told the machine how to process the stored data. Thanks to microconductors, or silicon chips, computers now are much smaller and faster.

They have become the backbone of modern economies, being used in power stations, business offices, supermarket checkout stands, textile mills, telephone switching systems, and factory production lines. They are the "brains" in robots, which are used today for welding and painting and moving materials and which will be used tomorrow for chores in homes.

Example: Space Science. When the Germans bombarded London with their V-2 rockets, they were using arms that led to the space age a few years later. On October 4, 1957, the Soviet shot Sputnik I into orbit around the earth. For the first time human beings had burst the bonds of gravity and were free to explore outer space. No one can foresee precisely what the repercussions will be. Outer space offers many advantages for manufacturers because of the absence of gravity and the limitless supply of vacuum and of super-high and super-low temperatures. Hence projects are now under way for automated pharmaceutical space factories producing vaccines and pure tissue cultures for enzymes, automated space factories creating near perfect crystals for use in electronic circuits, and giant solar collectors bearing energy from the sun to earth stations via microwave. More futuristic are the speculations of scientists such as American physicist Gerald K. O'Neill and Soviet astrophysicist Iosif S. Shklovsky, who foresee the construction in outer space of huge platforms or islands where eventually more humans might live than on earth.

Example: Genetic Engineering. Scientists discovered in 1953 the structure of DNA (deoxyribonucleic acid), the chemical that carries the genetic code of all living things. Since learning how to read the messages of genes through DNA, scientists have also learned how to write their own genetic messages by cutting apart and splicing the genes, by making animal and human genes grow in bacteria, and even by manufacturing totally new and artificial genes in the test tube. Thus scientists now can read genetic codes, modify them, and create new ones. Humans have been tampering with genes since they began domesticating plants and animals about ten thousand years ago. But now the tampering is direct and instantaneous. Instead of choosing among plants and animals through many generations, scientists now choose among individual genes and manipulate them. Such genetic engineering opens up possibilities for a new agricultural revolution. In the field of medicine, genetic engineering already has created insulin and growth hormone as well as several new vaccines, including one against the highly infectious hoof-and-mouth disease of cattle.

Example: Information Revolution. This is a revolution of two parts—accumulating information and distributing information. The rate at which knowledge is being accumulated today is unprecedented and explosive. The amount of scientific information alone that is being published around the world every twenty-four hours would fill seven complete twenty-four-volume sets of the *Encyclopaedia Britannica.* Equally unprecedented and explosive is the rate at which information can be stored and retrieved by computers, and also distributed throughout the world at the speed of light, especially via satellites. Any person, in any country, can receive this information through a newspaper, magazine, radio, television set, or computer.

Example: New Agricultural Revolution. The first industrial revolution was accompanied by an agricultural revolution (Chapter 29, Section IV) characterized by enclosures, improved seeds, scientific stock breeding, and new agricultural machinery. The second industrial revolution also has been accompanied by an agricultural revolution ("Green Revolution") stimulated by the steep rise in the demand and prices for farm products during World War II. New hybrid varieties of major cereals greatly increased crop yields when used in conjunction with irrigation, fertilizers, and pesticides. Because of genetic engineering the first "green revolution" is being followed in the 1990s by a second, in which scientists are mixing and matching genetic materials from different organisms. Just as this technique has yielded useful substances such as human insulin and interferon, so it is being applied to agriculture to produce plants that can grow in salty or dry soils; that will make their own nitrogen fertilizers; that are less susceptible to diseases caused by viruses, bacteria, fungi, and worms; and that will yield larger and more nutritious crops. This is

one reason why food output in the Third World since World War II has increased more than has the population growth.

The first industrial revolution had a profound impact on the European continent, where it originated, and also on the rest of the globe. So it is now with the second industrial revolution. But since this revolution is infinitely more powerful and dynamic, its impact everywhere is correspondingly more disruptive and encompassing.

II.   IMPACT ON THE DEVELOPED FIRST WORLD

Postwar Prosperity and Recession

The quarter-century after World War II was the golden age of capitalism. World industry during those years grew at the unprecedented annual rate of 5.6 percent, and world trade at 7.3 percent. The prolonged boom was caused by several factors, including the need to make up for wartime damage, the enormous pent-up demand for goods and services neglected during the war, civilian spinoffs from military technology in fields such as electronics and jet transport, and the large military purchases during the Korean and Vietnam wars and throughout the cold war years.

Multinational corporations spearheaded the global economic expansion during this boom. They now had available for the first time the technology necessary for global operations because of certain innovations of the second industrial revolution, including containerized shipping, satellite communications, and computerized cash management systems. Such facilities have made it possible for the median multinational corporation of this period to produce twenty-two products in eleven different countries. Corporations now can export not only their manufactured goods but also their plants to Third World countries, where daily wages often are no more, and sometimes less, than hourly wages at home. Thus the multinationals during the quarter-century boom grew at an average rate of 10 percent a year, as opposed to 4 percent for noninternational corporations.

The global prosperity filtered down to the working classes, at least in the industrialized countries. Real wages rose substantially, providing enough money for weekend outings; annual vacation trips; and the purchasing on credit of private homes, cars, and other durable goods. Many economists were persuaded that their monetary and fiscal policies created the necessary purchasing power to avoid the boom-slump business cycles of the past. Their optimism proved as unfounded as that of earlier economists on the eve of the 1929 crash.

In the mid-1970s the boom gave way to "stagflation"—a disconcerting combination of stagnation in the economy and inflation in prices. The wartime damages had been repaired, the consumer needs deferred during the war had been satisfied, and expanding industrial capacity had ended up by creating overcapacity. The overcapacity resulted in surpluses because the majority of the human race living in the Third World had not been included in the global boom, at least not as consumers. The low wages paid in overseas plants put a cap on local purchasing power. World Bank statistics show that in 1950, per capita income in the industrialized countries was ten times that of the underdeveloped countries. By 1965 the ratio was fifteen to one, and by the end of the century the World Bank predicts it will be thirty to one.

A basic structural weakness of the post–World War II boom was that it rested on integrated global production but it lacked global consumption. The imbalance was worsened by the disproportionate drop in prices of raw materials exported by Third World countries and by their heavy external debts. By 1986 the debts neared $1 trillion, and interest payments for the debts absorbed between one-quarter and one-half of the export earnings of the Third World countries. To meet the interest payments, Third World governments reduced their social expenditures and their imports. But one-third of all industrial countries' exports have gone to the Third World, so reduction of Third World imports promptly increased First World unemployment. Among fifteen members of the Organization for Economic Cooperation and Development, unemployment averaged 3.4 percent in 1973, 5 percent in 1979, and 8.3 percent in 1983. Unemployment in turn triggered demands for protective tariffs, which revived memories of the 1920s protectionism that contributed to the onset of the Great Depression.

These economic attacks dispelled post–World War II confidence and euphoria. Economists who believed that at last they had exorcised the boom and bust cycle now expressed bewilderment and apprehension. Scholars from fifteen countries agreed during a meeting of the International Federation of Institutes for Advanced Study (June 1983) that neither capitalist nor socialist economies were functioning satisfactorily. "We are living in a disjointed planet which is based on economic concepts which have nothing to do with present-day reality. . . . We want to question the basic tenets to see if they can be modified or adjusted."[1] In line with this thinking, the federation embarked on a project entitled "Adapting Economic Thinking to Changing Global Conditions."

Social Repercussions

The economic setbacks after the mid-1970s were intellectually unsettling for economists, but they were much more disruptive for the many who had become accustomed to relative affluence. American farmers had been encouraged by the federal government during the 1970s to increase their output for overseas markets to counterbalance growing trade deficits. The farmers responded enthusiastically, so that agricultural exports jumped from $8 billion in 1971 to $43.8 billion in 1981. Then the foreign market suddenly shrank because of Washington's embargo on exports to the Soviet Union after its invasion of Afghanistan; the overvalued dollar, which in effect imposed in 1984 a 32 percent surcharge on all American exports; and the cutback on all imports by financially strapped Third World governments. American agricultural exports between 1981 and 1983 dropped 21 percent in price level and 20 percent in volume.

American farmers found themselves caught in a squeeze, especially because many had borrowed heavily at high interest rates to buy more land and equipment to meet the government appeal for more output. Bankrupt farmers were dispossessed, and the number of family farms dropped from a peak of 6.8 million in the mid-

1930s to 2.8 million in 1980 to 1.9 million in 1994. The U.S. Census Bureau found that farm family incomes in 1985 were only three-fourths that of nonfarm families, and that the poverty rate among those living on farms was 24 percent, compared with 15 percent for nonfarm residents. The resulting emotional and social disruption was reflected in suicide rates, which in 1984 were twice as high in rural Iowa counties as the national average. Iowa State University extension service booklets traditionally had dealt with subjects such as insect infestations and soil erosion. Now they deal also with "soul erosion," as indicated by booklets on crisis management and advice to wives on signs of impending suicide in their husbands. Furthermore, the economic and social malaise is not confined to the Midwest; its sorry symptoms are being reported also from rural areas in eastern and western states.[2]

Disruption has been evident in urban communities as well as rural because of high unemployment. Although the unemployment rate in the 1980s and 1990s has been far below that of the Great Depression, many urban workers consider themselves to be worse off now. During the 1930s the unemployment was assumed to be typically cyclical, and therefore bound to end with the transition from bust to boom. Today it is realized that this assumption cannot be made, for several reasons. First, with factories being transplanted from expensive-labor to cheap-labor countries, Western workers no longer can demand and receive the high wages to which they have become accustomed. Second, the spread of automation and robots is displacing white-collar workers in offices along with blue-collar workers in factories. The number of unemployed in the entire Western world rose from 10 million in January 1970 to 31 million in January 1983. It is true that although factory jobs are decreasing, service jobs (for instance, bank tellers, fast-food workers, hotel clerks, recreation and health attendants) are increasing rapidly. But wages in the service sector are substantially lower than in manufacturing.

All this adds up to social disruption as severe for urban workers as for rural. For the latter, disruption means loss of farms and of traditional ways of life. For urban workers, disruption means loss of jobs and income shrinkage, forcing them out of middle-class status. In the 1950s and 1960s, workers could expect to earn one-third more than their fathers. In the 1970s and 1980s, workers could expect to earn 15 percent less than their fathers, a situation that jeopardized such prized attainments as home ownership and college education for children (see T.45.1).

The human implications of these statistics have been spelled out in the 1985 report of the twenty-two-member Physician Task Force on Hunger in America, headed by J. Larry Brown, chair of the Harvard School of Public Health. The task force interviewed governors, teachers, ministers, and social workers, as well as the hungry people themselves, in the search for "the human face of hunger." The investigators concluded that about 20 million American citizens were suffering from hunger, meaning specifically that they were unable to purchase an adequate diet and periodically ran out of food altogether. "Hunger in America," stated the physicians, "is a national health epidemic. It is our judgment that the problem of hunger in the United States is more widespread and serious than at any time in the last ten to fifteen years. . . . We believe that today hunger and malnutrition are serious problems in every region of the nation. We have, in fact, returned from no city and no state where we did not find extensive hunger."[3]

As revealing as this report on hunger in the United States was an October 1993 report from Fordham University, where social scientists issue an annual "Index of Social Health." This monitors the well-being of American society by examining reports from the Census Bureau on sixteen major social problems, including unemployment, teenage suicide, high school dropout rates,

TABLE 45.1	Class Distribution in the United States	
	1979	1983
Upper Class (over $41,000)	15%	18%
Middle Class ($17,000 to $41,000)	54%	43%
Lower Class (under $17,000)	31%	39%

Source: CBS Evening News, September 10, 1984; *New York Times*, February 7, 1986.

and supply of affordable housing. The first report of the scientists measured social health for the year 1970, which they indexed at 75. But in 1991, the most recent year for which complete data were available, the index was down to 36, which the director of the study described as "awful." "These results," he added, "reveal as much about what is happening to us as the economic indicators that we watch closely every day."[4]

III. IMPACT ON THE SOCIALIST WORLD

The second industrial revolution has had a profound impact on the socialist world as well as the capitalist, so much so that the socialist world disintegrated. We noted (Chapter 41, Section I) that Stalin's Five-Year Plans had accelerated the economic development of the Soviet Union, making that country the second-greatest industrial power by 1932. Then the Soviet economy suffered a grievous setback with the staggering human and material losses sustained during World War II. But recovery was swift, with sharp gains achieved during the 1950s and 1960s. This success encouraged Khrushchev to boast in 1961 that Soviet industrial output would surpass that of the United States by 1980. In fact, the opposite happened. The Soviet rate of growth slowed during the 1970s, so that the Soviet economy fell further behind the American economy, rather than catching up to it and surpassing it.

One reason for the Soviet slowdown was a shrinking supply of labor and natural resources, in contrast to the Stalin period, when both were plentiful. Another reason was the growing size and complexity of the economy, which made it increasingly difficult and inefficient to direct everything from the center. Perhaps the chief reason for the Soviet economic slowdown was political—the unwillingness of Soviet workers, technicians, and scientists merely to carry out orders from above with no role in decision making. Such a one-sided arrangement was feasible during the early years, when Stalin was dealing mostly with illiterate *muzhiks* fresh from the villages. But today the Soviet labor force includes many highly educated engineers, managers, and professionals, whose creative energies need to be

tapped if the former Soviet Union is to participate actively in the ongoing second industrial revolution. This has not been done, and the consequences have been disastrous, as noted most perceptively by the famous Soviet physicist and dissenter Andrei Sakharov. In March 1970 Sakharov, along with a fellow physicist and historian, addressed an *Appeal of Soviet Scientists to the Party-Government Leaders of the U.S.S.R.* Its penetrating analysis of Soviet ailments merits quotation:

Why have we not only failed to become the pioneers of the second industrial revolution but, as it transpires, are we even incapable of keeping abreast of the developed capitalist countries in this revolution? Can it be that the socialist system does not present the same opportunities as the capitalist system for the development of productive forces and that in the economic competition between capitalism and socialism, capitalism will emerge victorious?

Of course not. The source of our difficulties does not lie in the socialist system at all, but, on the contrary, in those features and circumstances in our life which run counter to socialism and are alien to it. This source lies in the anti-democratic tradition and norms of public conduct which were laid down during the Stalinist period and which have not been eradicated even to this day. . . .

The obstacles blocking the development of our economy lie in the sociopolitical sphere, and all measures which fail to remove these obstacles are doomed to inefficacy. . . .

From our friends abroad we sometimes hear the U.S.S.R. compared to a huge truck, whose driver presses one foot hard down on the accelerator and the other on the brake. The time has come to make more intelligent use of the brake! . . .

What has our country to expect if a course leading towards democratization is not taken? It can expect to lag behind the capitalist countries in the second industrial revolution and to gradually revert to the status of a second-rate provincial power.[5]

During Leonid Brezhnev's long stewardship from 1964 to 1982, Sakharov's plea for "more intelligent use of the brake" was ignored. Instead, the brake continued to be pressed down hard. The Soviet bureaucracy squelched periodic pro-

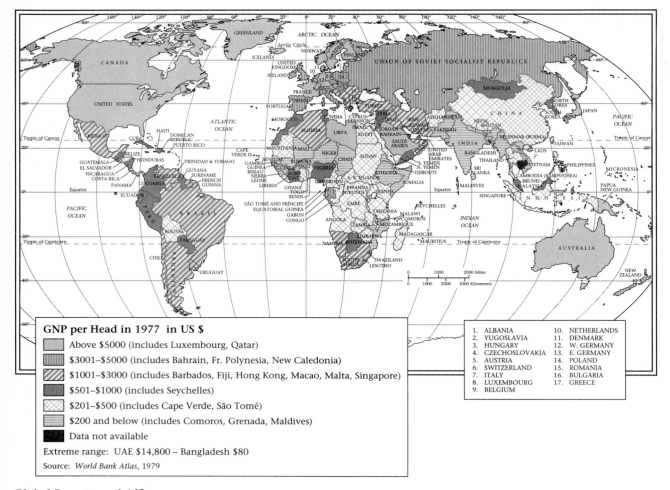

GNP per Head in 1977 in US $

Above $5000 (includes Luxembourg, Qatar)

$3001–$5000 (includes Bahrain, Fr. Polynesia, New Caledonia)

$1001–$3000 (includes Barbados, Fiji, Hong Kong, Macao, Malta, Singapore)

$501–$1000 (includes Seychelles)

$201–$500 (includes Cape Verde, São Tomé)

$200 and below (includes Comoros, Grenada, Maldives)

Data not available

Extreme range: UAE $14,800 – Bangladesh $80

Source: *World Bank Atlas*, 1979

1.	ALBANIA	10.	NETHERLANDS
2.	YUGOSLAVIA	11.	DENMARK
3.	HUNGARY	12.	W. GERMANY
4.	CZECHOSLOVAKIA	13.	E. GERMANY
5.	AUSTRIA	14.	POLAND
6.	SWITZERLAND	15.	ROMANIA
7.	ITALY	16.	BULGARIA
8.	LUXEMBOURG	17.	GREECE
9.	BELGIUM		

Global Poverty and Affluence

posals to decentralize the Soviet economy and allow some initiative to local factories and administrative bodies. Even copiers were viewed as potential instruments of subversion and were kept under lock and key, with access to them strictly regulated and recorded.

The repercussions of brake-slamming have been precisely what Sakharov foretold. Regimentation and ossification have proven incompatible with participation in the second industrial revolution. Today's global economy is characterized by a fast tempo of technological innovation, constantly changing consumer tastes, and keen competition in an integrated world market. All this demands flexibility, efficiency, and adaptability—qualities notably lacking in the multilayered party and state bureaucracies of the former Soviet Union. Hence the average annual growth of the Soviet GNP declined from 5 to 6 percent between 1950 and 1970, 3.7 percent between 1971 and 1975, and 2.7 percent between 1976 and 1980. Instead of the USSR surpassing America, as Khrushchev expected, Japan now has surpassed the former Soviet Union and has become the world's second-greatest industrial power.

With the death of Brezhnev and of his short-lived successors (Yuri Andropov and Konstantin Chernenko), the founding generation of Soviet leaders departed from the historical stage. Mikhail Gorbachev assumed power in 1985 as the first of a younger generation, which realizes that in this age of the second industrial revolution, the Soviet "truck" will be left behind as long as one foot presses on the brake and the other on the accelerator. At the Twenty-seventh Congress of the Communist Party, which opened on February 25, 1986, Gorbachev criticized the failings of the Brezhnev years in terms that recalled and validated Sakharov's warning in 1970:

The inertness and stillness of our administration, the decline of dynamism in our work and an escalation of bureaucracy—all this has done no small damage. . . . Difficulties began to build up in the economy in the 1970s, with the rates of economic growth declining visibly. . . . A lag ensued in the material base of science and education, health protection, culture and everyday services. . . . Unfortunately, there was a widespread view that any change in the economic mechanism should be regarded as being practically a retreat from the principles of socialism. . . . The situation called for a change, but a peculiar psychology— How to improve things without changing anything?—took the upper hand.[6]

Once in power, Gorbachev proceeded to reverse the policies of his predecessors with a gusto reminiscent of Tsar Peter the Great. In June 1987, he spoke frankly to the Communist Party Central Committee about his determination to make a clean break with the past: "Ours is a rapidly changing society. . . . We are in for new problems, considerable complexities. We are not insured against mistakes. . . . Yet I am confident that the greatest mistake is fearing to err."[7]

Gorbachev's phrase, "fearing to err," is strikingly similar to President Roosevelt's phrase, "nothing to fear but fear itself." In fact, a parallel may be drawn between Roosevelt's New Deal in the 1930s and Gorbachev's *perestroika*, or restructuring, in the 1980s. Both programs were designed in response to traumatic crises—Hoover's Great Depression in the United States and Brezhnev's great stagnation in the Soviet Union. Both programs were headed by leaders who came not from below but from above— from the national elites. Both Roosevelt and Gorbachev were interested not in a revolution that would overthrow their social systems, but in reform substantial enough to rejuvenate and preserve those systems. Despite the conservative objective of their reform programs, both leaders were strenuously opposed by conservatives who

feared an uncertain future, and by radicals who demanded societal surgery rather than first aid. Thus, FDR was excoriated from the right as a traitor to his class, and from the left by radicals such as Louisiana's Huey Long, with his "Share-Our-Wealth" program.

In the end, FDR and his New Deal were rescued by World War II, which opened factories, created jobs, and thus ended the nightmare of the Great Depression. Fortunately for the world but perhaps unfortunately for Gorbachev, no World War III occurred to rescue him from his predicament. So he had no alternative but to struggle directly with a host of problems even more formidable than those that confronted FDR. These problems included the restive minorities living in the sixteen republics that comprised the Union of Soviet Socialist Republics (USSR). Their hostility increased because of an economic crisis at least as severe as the American Great Depression of the 1930s. Gorbachev's perestroika program for economic restructuring raised expectations for improved economic conditions. Instead, there was economic deterioration. Because inefficient enterprises were forced to trim payrolls or even to close down, unemployment increased sharply. The resulting social distress heightened ethnic unrest and conflicts, as it has in the United States and western Europe, where minority immigrants have been blamed for lost jobs and low wages.

These mounting problems proved too much for Gorbachev. By 1991 he had been replaced as leader by Boris N. Yeltsin, and the USSR itself had disintegrated, being replaced by a looser political structure known as the Commonwealth of Independent States. Another sign of the popular dissatisfaction with the old Communist order was the decision of the citizens of Leningrad to restore the old tsarist name of their city, St. Petersburg.

Yeltsin tried to give the Commonwealth a fresh start by making changes that dismantled the old Communist system much more than Gorbachev had been willing to do. In agriculture, he abolished the state-owned and collective farms. In industry, he turned over by 1993 one-third of formerly state-owned enterprises to private ownership. Another change that was unplanned and unwelcome was the mass emigration of highly trained scientists who had been left unemployed and unpaid during the economic crisis in their country. With the lifting of restrictions on emigration, 39,000 citizens left in 1987; 600,000 in 1991; and 1 million in 1992. In the past, most emigrants had been disaffected minorities such as Jews, Volga Germans, and Armenians. Now, so many of the top scientists are leaving that it is feared that not enough will remain to train the next generation of scientists.

Just as alarming for many Russians is the ideological vacuum they are now facing. In the past, the official Stalinist ideology had answers for all their questions. True socialism, they were taught from childhood, required government ownership of the means of production and a central planning board to prepare plans for the economy and to supervise its functioning. At first, this strategy seemed to work satisfactorily.

But by the 1990s the Russians had to face up to the fact that their country, as Sakharov had warned back in 1970, seemed to be sinking down to "the status of a second-rate provincial power." So despite their past bragging about "surpassing" the United States, Russia's leaders began looking abroad for advice and for models, especially after the advent of Gorbachev. They did not find abroad guidelines they were looking for. Instead, they found confusion and uncertainty in former socialist countries that had abandoned their planned economies for the Western market

mechanism. Poland was a leader in this trend, so that its economy by 1993 was the fastest growing in Europe. A new class of affluent Poles was enjoying the many luxuries now appearing in stores. But at the same time, a new class was appearing that lacked not only luxuries but also necessities. The gap between the two classes widened as Polish unemployment rose by August 1993 to 15.2 percent of the work force. Poland's President Lech Walesa, who had led the successful struggle against the previous Communist regime, declared in February 1992 before the Council of Europe: "Our own people are not getting the feeling that they are better off. The fruits of victory have turned sour. Democracy is losing its supporters."*

At a time when the second industrial revolution is unfolding at breakneck speed, millions throughout the world must cope with the task of devising social systems suitable for this age of high technology. It is a difficult and uncomfortable task requiring careful sorting out of the good from the bad in the numerous contending social systems. This brings us back to a key problem that has plagued humans from their beginnings (as noted in Chapter 1, Section I)—the problem of the chronic time lag between technological and social change. We defined that problem as one of balancing our expanding knowledge with wisdom in how we use that knowledge.

*The New York Times, February 6, 1992.

Many women put a career in the outside work force on hold to stay home and raise children.

With luck, this task can be fulfilled, in which case the twentieth century, which has witnessed so much barbarism, may yet close in a blaze of creative innovation. On the other hand, if the twentieth century closes with ill luck rather than good, then the end result of the second industrial revolution might well prove grim, as indicated by the savagery now rampant from Northern Ireland to Rwanda to Bosnia to the Commonwealth emerging from the wreckage of the former Soviet Union.

IV. IMPACT ON THE UNDERDEVELOPED THIRD WORLD

Third World history since World War II has been made up of a combination of political triumphs and economic disasters. The political triumphs culminated in the dismantling of colonial empires and the creation of new independent states on the imperial ruins (see Chapter 44). But the accompanying economic disasters culminated in a decline of living standards in Third World countries. One important cause for economic deterioration has been the impact of the second industrial revolution on the daily lives of Third World peoples.

In agriculture, the new seeds and new techniques of the Green Revolution resulted in greater productivity. But this did not benefit most of the peasants, who lacked the capital required for the hybrid seeds, fertilizers, and irrigation equipment. Only medium- and large-scale farmers were able to participate in the Green Revolution, and they tended to shift from domestic staple food crops to the more profitable export crops. Also, they were likely to introduce labor-saving machines, which forced the already underemployed peasants to flee to city slums, where they usually found themselves as superfluous as they had been in the countryside. This pattern is clear in Mexico, where the most efficient farms are now producing winter fruits and vegetables for the American market while corn and bean staples are imported from the United States, and where millions of uprooted peasants are crossing the frontier in search of work. Meanwhile, the capital, Mexico City, grew by 1980 to an almost unmanageable population of 14 million, with an

increase of another 14 million expected in the next two decades.

Runaway urbanization is under way on all continents, so that by the year 2000 there will be an estimated forty metropolitan areas in the Third World with populations of 5 million or more, but only twelve of that size in the First World. In 1900 the largest metropolitan areas in descending order were London, New York, Paris, Berlin, Chicago, Vienna, Tokyo, St. Petersburg, Philadelphia, and Manchester. In 2000 they are expected to be Mexico City, São Paulo, Tokyo, New York, Shanghai, Beijing, Rio de Janeiro, Bombay, Calcutta, and Jakarta. The important point about this global urbanization is that there is no accompanying industrialization. Therefore the newcomers to the cities are forced into the kind of marginal employment that saves them from outright starvation but that contributes little to the national economies. They spend their lives in such work as street vending, shining shoes, running errands, and pushing a cart or pedaling a rickshaw.

The second industrial revolution has distorted the industry as well as the agriculture of underdeveloped countries. In the immediate post–World War II period, the newly independent countries tried to overcome their underdevelopment by import-substitution industrialization—that is, by helping local industries to manufacture the products formerly imported from abroad. This was done with such measures as protective tariffs, cheap credit for local firms, and government help in building infrastructure facilities and providing cheap energy and labor. The import-substitution strategy was successful during the global boom of the 1950s and 1960s, but as the boom shrank, so did the local industries. However, they suffered even more from domestic conditions than from global ones. The chief reason for the failure of import-substitution industrialization was that the poverty-stricken peasants lacked purchasing power and therefore could not buy the products of local industries, whereas the wealthy who did have money preferred to spend it for fancier goods made abroad.

This failed economic strategy was replaced by export-directed industrialization, in which the Third World countries turned away from the stunted domestic markets and looked instead to the larger world market. The calculation was that Third World industries would be able to compete successfully against foreign competitors because of the low production costs at home. Multinational corporations took the lead in export-directed industrialization because the technology of the second industrial revolution enabled them to manufacture simultaneously many products in many countries. Third World industrial output increased, as had the agricultural, so the new economic strategy aroused hopes that it would end, at last, Third World underdevelopment. But the hopes for Third World industry proved as short-lived as they had for agriculture.

World markets were found to be more limited than had appeared at first. They shrank with the end of the global boom, especially when the unemployed in the developed countries demanded protective tariffs to regain their lost jobs. Also, the factories established in Third World countries did not generate the expected benefits, partly because of the low wages and partly because the unskilled jobs did not provide the technical training needed for local development. Consequently, in the Third World as a whole, one-third to one-half of the total labor force remains chronically unemployed.

Between 1950 and 1976, Third World economies grew at an impressive 5 percent annual rate. Between 1981 and 1984, the rate shrank to 1.1 percent, which if population growth is taken into account, represents an actual decrease in per capita income during that period.[8] (See map of Global Poverty and Affluence, p. 700.) In 1981 the richest fifth of the world's population received 71 percent of the world's product, whereas the poorest fifth received 2 percent. The end result of these statistics is that an estimated 15 million to 20 million people die each year in the Third World from starvation or malnutrition-related diseases. This is the equivalent of a Hiroshima every two days.

These statistics are being questioned and revised because estimates of national incomes vary greatly depending on whether they are

Global Illiteracy

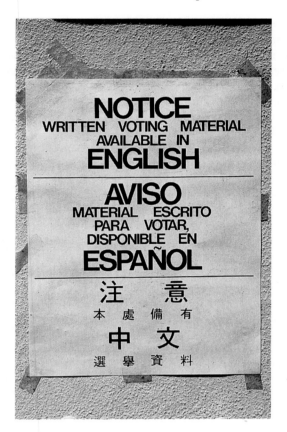

The ethnic mix of America is seen in this sign at a voting site.

based on the purchasing power of the different currencies, or on their exchange value. When the yardstick is the exchange value, then if a country's exchange drops 10 percent, that country's economy automatically is considered to be smaller by the same degree. A more realistic system is to calculate what goods and services a country's currency will buy compared with the purchasing power of other countries' currencies. More specifically, the International Monetary Fund (IMF) now looks at the price of a set bundle of goods and services, including food, clothing, housing, and transportation, and uses that yardstick to compare the total value of output in different countries. On the basis of that measure, the IMF calculated China's per capita income to have been about $1,600 in 1992, compared with $370 using the old system based on exchange rates. So China's economy now is seen as the third largest in the world, surpassed only

by the economies of the United States and Japan, and growing faster than all others. An American journalist, after five years' residence in China, reported the paradox of a "Beijing government that fights leprosy as aggressively as it attacks dissent. It inoculates infants with the same fervor with which it arrests its critics. Partly as a result, a baby born in Shanghai has a longer life expectancy than a baby born in New York City." However, the same American journalist noted the comments about this paradox made by a Chinese dissident living in California: "When Hitler held power, the German economy enjoyed a boom. And Japan grew very quickly during the militarist years before World War II. So we shouldn't regard economic development as our sole objective."[9]

V   IMPACT ON THE GLOBE

The second industrial revolution is having not only a specific impact on the societies of the first, second, and third worlds but also a profound general impact on all peoples of all societies. We have seen that throughout human history, technological change has deeply affected daily life. The shift from hunting-gathering to agriculture necessitated a shift from nomadic band life to sedentary village life. Equally far-reaching was the effect on human existence of the first industrial revolution. More pervasive and disruptive is the impact of the ongoing second industrial revolution, corresponding to the unprecedented power of its new technology. We shall analyze four of the most important aspects of this global impact: on ecology, on race relations, on gender relations, and on war.

A.   Impact on Ecology

So powerful is the second industrial revolution that it is leaving its imprint on planet Earth as well as on its inhabitants. This is an ecological impact, since the planet is the *oikos,* or home of the human species. All peoples in all ages have affected their environment, simply by virtue of being human with human needs and with human technology, even if it consisted only of stone tools and fire. But today their impact is infinitely greater because of their combined technological

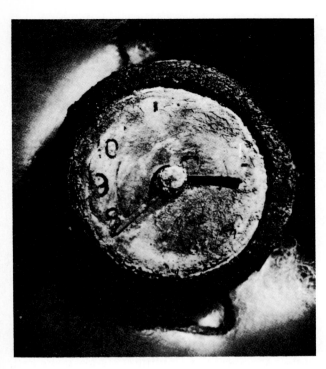

A clock is melted and frozen at 8:15 on August 6, 1945 at Hiroshima.

and population explosions.

The contrast between past and present ecology is illustrated clearly in the livelihood of the Semang, a group of 2,000 to 3,000 nomadic forest foragers in Malaysia. They appear to be ecologically irresponsible in their everyday life, using their river as a bath, laundry, toilet, fishing ground, and source of drinking water. Likewise, they freely set fire to the surrounding forest in the course of their slash-and-burn cultivation. They plant seeds in the fire-cleared ground, then resume their nomadic foraging, returning only to collect whatever the animals have left in the unprotected plots.

With this mode of life, the average per capita daily consumption of energy by the Semangs is under 5,000 kilocalories (40 percent from human labor and 60 percent from burning firewood) in contrast to the 250,000 kilocalories used by the typical U.S. citizen. So the Semang, living on such a modest scale, have no appreciable impact on their river and on the surrounding forest, despite activities that would be catastrophic in our world with its proliferating ma-

chines and its billions of inhabitants rather than a few thousand.[10]

Since both machines and inhabitants are increasing at an accelerating pace, the ecological situation may well deteriorate. World population has been growing rapidly because it could be supported by increasingly productive agriculture and industry, and because advances in medical science and in public health measures reduced death rates. So whereas the human race required millions of years to reach its first billion in 1830, it needed only one century to reach its second billion, only thirty years to reach its third billion, a mere fifteen its fourth billion, and eleven years its fifth.

These new billions of human beings crowding the planet were provided with numerous new machines produced during the first and second industrial revolutions. The inevitable result has been infinitely greater stress on our oikos than that exerted by our ancestors. Even in the United States, which is relatively underpopulated and richly endowed, evidence of the stress can be seen everywhere—in the depletion of the great Ogallala Aquifer, which supplies irrigation water to the Great Plains from Nebraska to the Texas Panhandle; in the conversion of California's orchards and Long Island's potato fields into housing developments; in the clear-cutting of remnant primeval forests in the northwest; and in the 99 percent of known toxic dumps that have not been cleaned up and that are contaminating water supplies throughout the country.

The most dramatic report on this ecological dilemma came on April 9, 1983, from Paul J. Weitz, commander of the first flight of the space shuttle *Challenger*. Returning to his home base on planet Earth, he was struck as he neared his destination by the deterioration of what originally had been a beautiful blue planet. "It was appalling to me to see how dirty our atmosphere is getting. Unfortunately, this world is rapidly becoming a gray planet. Our environment apparently is flat going downhill. . . . What's the message? We are fouling our nest."[11]

Cleaning up our fouled global "nest" is not an easy task in the age of the second industrial revolution. This is evident in California, the original "golden state" which became the state of

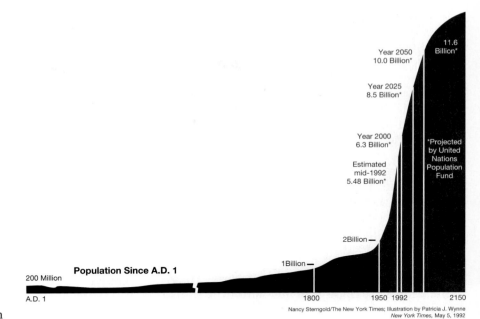

Year 2050
10.0 Billion*

11.6
Billion*

Year 2025
8.5 Billion*

Year 2000
6.3 Billion*

*Projected
by United
Nations
Population
Fund

Estimated
mid-1992
5.48 Billion*

2Billion —

1Billion —

Population Since A.D. 1

200 Million

A.D. 1

1800

1950 1992

2150

World Population Growth

Nancy Sterngold/The New York Times; Illustration by Patricia J. Wynne
New York Times, May 5, 1992

smog with the influx of military and space industries, and millions of newcomers attracted by plentiful, high-paying jobs. The sequel to crowded cities and freeways was increasingly frequent "smog alerts," during which people were advised to stay indoors. An aroused citizenry generated state legislation mandating car pooling and regulating pollution from lawn mowers, motor vehicles, and factories and power plants. By the 1990s air quality had improved dramatically, and the California legislation became the model for other states, which experienced similar relief from air pollution. Paradoxically, this success has provoked a backlash from private corporations and local governments, which fear that restrictive regulations will frighten away business—an urgent fear in southern California, where the end of the cold war has undercut military industries and aggravated unemployment. Enforcement of air-quality legislation is slackening, so that an official of the Environmental Protection Agency in Washington has observed: "California has been on the leading edge of air quality. Now it is leading the backlash."[12]

The ecological impasse is not confined to California or to the United States. It has become a worldwide problem with the spread of the sec-

ond industrial revolution. China offers a good example, as it is now the second-largest industrial power and is growing the fastest. Its headlong industrialization is powered mostly by the country's huge reserves of coal. But coal is the dirtiest of fuels in carbon emissions, so that China now ranks second in such emissions, and may well be the first by 2025. Chinese consumers (of which there are over 1 billion) doubtless will behave like consumers everywhere in striving for an ever-higher living standard with more cars, more refrigerators, more home heating, and more consumer goods, all requiring more energy to produce and to operate. When Mao began his rule in China in 1949, the popular clamor was for the "big four" (bicycle, sewing machine, radio, and watch). Since then, consumer expectations have escalated to the "big six" (color TV, washing machine, radio-cassette player, refrigerator, electric fan, and motorcycle) and most recently to the "eight big things" comprising the "big six" plus modern furniture and a camera.

Such is the consumerism generated by the second industrial revolution, and such is the resulting ecological impasse.

B.   Impact on Race Relations

All through history, technology has affected race relations profoundly by determining population growth and population movements. For example, when our earliest ancestors in Africa's savannas developed their technology to the point where they could make fire, fashion clothes, and build shelters, they were able to expand from their African base and strike out across Europe and Asia, ultimately reaching the Americas and Australia. Likewise, the first industrial revolution, with its advances in agriculture and industry, triggered a jump in Europe's population from 100 million in 1650 to 463 million in 1914. This made possible during the eighteenth and nineteenth centuries a great emigration of Europeans to the underpopulated lands of Siberia and the Americas. Today, with the second industrial revolution, a similar emigration flood is occurring, though in reverse— from underdeveloped to developed lands. Increased food production and improved health technology (mass immunization, DDT, and oral rehydration therapy) have reduced sharply the death rates in underdeveloped countries, while birthrates have remained high. Consequently, between 1950 and 1970, annual population growth rates in developed and underdeveloped countries were 1.1 percent and 2.2 percent, respectively. Third World population growth now is twice that of the developed world, and this new pattern will be hard to change because Third World populations are predominantly young. What this means for the future is evident in T.45.2, which shows total world population is increasing at a constantly accelerating pace, and how most of the population growth is in underdeveloped countries.

The rapidly growing populations in the Third World are finding it hard to support themselves because most Third World economies have bogged down, as noted above. Therefore, these hard-pressed people have migrated, whenever possible, from their poverty-stricken countries and taken any jobs available in the developed lands. During the post–World War II boom years, many jobs were open, so approximately 15 million to 20 million workers flocked to northwestern Europe— to Germany, Britain, France, and the Scandinavian states. Many of the immigrants came from southern European countries: Spain, Portugal, Italy, Greece, Yugoslavia, and Turkey. The remainder came from overseas countries, chiefly from North Africa, Pakistan, India, and the West Indies.

The Europeans at first welcomed the immigrants as "guest workers," assuming that after a few years they would return to their homelands with their savings. But the newcomers did not act as expected. As the years passed, they sank roots in their adopted countries and naturally were unwilling to relocate again. Their children, born in the new countries, regarded themselves as Germans or French or Swedes rather than as Turks or Pakistanis or West Indians. Nevertheless, when the postwar economic boom ended, unemployment became a serious problem for Europeans, and former "guest workers" found themselves no longer welcomed as "guests." Instead, they were now resented, and sometimes even attacked, by the unemployed. In May 1993, five Turkish nationals were killed in an arson attack in their family home in the western German city of Solingen. By that date, 6 million foreigners were living in Germany, of which 1.7 million were Turks. Some governments tried to resolve the dilemma by of-

TABLE 45.2	Population Projections: 1950–2100 (population in millions)					
	1950[a]	1980[a]	2000[b]	2025[b]	2050[b]	2100[b]
Underdeveloped countries	1,670	3,284	4,922	7,061	8,548	9,741
Developed countries	834	1,140	1,284	1,393	1,425	1,454
Total world	2,504	4,424	6,206	8,454	9,973	11,195

[a]Estimated.
[b]Projected.
Source: UN and World Bank estimates and projections.

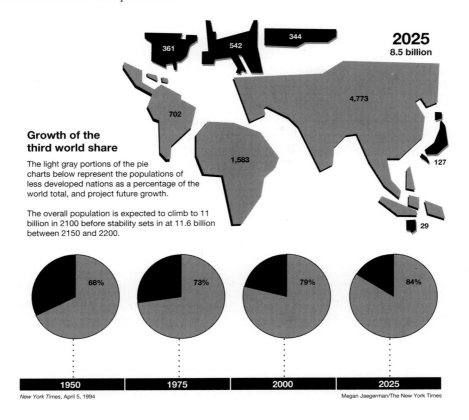

2025
8.5 billion

Growth of the third world share

The light gray portions of the pie charts below represent the populations of less developed nations as a percentage of the world total, and project future growth.

The overall population is expected to climb to 11 billion in 2100 before stability sets in at 11.6 billion between 2150 and 2200.

68% | 73% | 79% | 84%

1950 | 1975 | 2000 | 2025

New York Times, April 5, 1994   Megan Jaegerman/The New York Times

fering to pay the fares for immigrants willing to go back home, but few accepted the offer.

Gradually and reluctantly, Europeans are being forced to recognize that they face not a temporary problem of foreign minorities, but the permanent fact of a new multiethnic, multicultural, and multireligious continent. It is a jarring experience for hitherto insulated Europeans to see the minarets of new mosques rising amidst their cities, to hear calls to prayer issuing loudly from those mosques several times each day, to have television and radio stations broadcasting full-time in foreign languages, and to receive protests when Moslem children are taught in state schools to sing "Onward Christian Soldiers." These are especially difficult dilemmas for countries lacking the "melting pot" tradition of the United States. In Britain, for example, there is no agreement as to whether an individual can be both a Briton and a black, whereas in the United States, African Americans are taken for granted, as is also their right to decide for themselves whether they should be addressed as blacks or as African-Americans.

It should not be assumed, however, that the United States always has been a melting pot accessible to all newcomers. Until recently, non-Europeans (except for Africans who arrived early in chains) were excluded or strictly limited by legal quotas that were avowedly designed to preserve the existing ethnic composition of American society. This explains why only 6 percent of all migrants to the United States between 1820 and 1979 came from Asia. The quota system was repealed in 1965, so that by 1983, half of all immigrants were from Asia, and most of the remainder from Latin America. Consequently, European immigrants, who traditionally have comprised the great majority, now are a small minority. In 1983, the country that sent the largest number of emigrants to the United States was Mexico, with 59,298. Next were China, Hong Kong, and Taiwan, which together sent 48,668. The next-largest sources were the Philippines (41,725), Vietnam (39,821), Korea (33,453), India (25,535), and Laos (23,917).

So large and so different is today's new wave of immigrants that some observers believe the United States is moving from being a "melting pot" of Europeans to a "world nation" with links to virtually every inhabited part of the globe.[13] If such a transformation actually occurs, then the United States will become the first "world nation" in history, just as earlier it pioneered as the first European melting pot in history. The change will be so far-reaching that some foresee a change in the complexion of Americans. "We are probably going to have a browning of America over time," declares an expert on the subject. "It will take six or seven generations, but ultimately, I believe a majority of the population will be nonwhite. That is likely to occur because of immigration and increasing rates of intermarriage between darker-skinned peoples and whites."[14]

Demographic changes of such magnitude do not arouse the outcry in the United States that they might in European countries. On the other hand, some Americans do question the desirability of large-scale influx of such different peoples. A 1986 poll in southern California found 55 percent agreement with the statement "immigration is a change for the worse," and a 1989 poll in the same region found 47 percent of the residents agreed that there are "too many" immigrants here.[15]

Looking back on the flow of migrations through history, basic technological change has triggered correspondingly basic demographic change. The agricultural revolution enabled farming people such as the Bantu to push aside the food-gathering Bushman and Pygmy. (See map of Global Race Distribution, p. 18.) Likewise, the first industrial revolution enabled Europeans to expand from their small continent into Siberia and the Americas. (See map of Racial Distribution in the World, p. 414.) Today, the second industrial revolution is responsible for the migrations of millions of people, though this time the result is not the displacement of entire ethnic blocs, but rather the intermingling of peoples from all quarters of the globe.

It is tantalizing to speculate what the demographic repercussions might be if our current high technology continues to develop at its present accelerating tempo and if, as some scientists expect, huge platforms or islands are constructed in outer space, and are inhabited by as many human beings as live now on planet Earth. Inter-

planetary migrations would be a fitting sequel to the interregional and intercontinental migrations of past millennia.

C.   Impact on Gender Relations

Gender relations, as well as race relations, have been affected deeply throughout history by technological developments. During the food-gathering millennia, women enjoyed equal status because as food gatherers they contributed at least as much to their families' food supplies as did their husbands. With the advent of the agricultural revolution, women gave up nomadic band life for village life; they spent most of their time at home raising children and doing housework, and no longer were they able to contribute equally to family food needs. The first industrial revolution opened new horizons for women, as factories and wage-paying jobs offered an alternative to child rearing housework (Chapter 28, Section VI).

Somewhat later, women benefited from the establishment of public schools, where they were able to get an education alongside male students. By the beginning of the twentieth century, women were winning the right to vote. By 1900 they had won the *franchise* in national elections in only one country; by 1950 they could vote in sixty-nine countries; by 1975, in 129. Today, women have the vote virtually everywhere except for a few Arab countries (Oman, Qatar, Saudi Arabia, and the United Arab Emirates). During the first half of the twentieth century, however, women did not benefit much from their access to voting booths. Women's rights appear to have been overshadowed by more immediate and traumatic concerns such as the Great Depression and World War II.

The second industrial revolution has affected women as deeply as did the first. Contraceptives made available by medical technology have given women control over their own reproductive function. No longer are they bound by traditional assumptions about what "nature intended" concerning the social roles of males and females. Motherhood can be assumed or refused. Family planning enables women to raise their children, and then renew old careers or even begin new ones. However, only about 50 percent of the world's women have access to contraceptives. And some of that 50 percent cannot make effective use of the devices for various reasons, including opposition by governments or churches or husbands who want to prove their virility or to have sons to carry on the family name or to inherit the family lands.

A second important change in the status of women today is the opening of doors to education. Global illiteracy is decreasing rapidly among women as well as men. In the developed countries, there are about equal numbers of males and females in school at all levels. In Third World schools, males still outnumber females, but the gap is narrowing. In 1960 only 59 percent of the world's women were literate, but in 1985 this number had increased to 68 percent. However, women also face the problem of differences in content as well as quality of education. From the earliest years in school, girls in all countries tend to be directed toward subjects that are of more use in the kitchen and living room than in the outside world. They are encouraged to study art, literature, domestic science, and dressmaking, whereas boys are studying engineering, mathematics, physics, and mechanics. (See map of Global Illiteracy, p. 704.)

The contrast in the content of education is an important factor in the corresponding contrast in the content of paychecks. One of the most dramatic changes in the role of women in recent years has been their influx into the global labor force. In the United States only 18.9 percent of adult women worked outside the home in 1890. By 1940 the percentage had increased to 25.8 percent, and by the end of World War II (1945) it had risen to 35 percent. Furthermore, a survey in that year disclosed that 80 percent of the female employees wanted to keep their jobs rather than return to their homes at the end of the war. Consequently, by 1984, 54 percent of adult American women were in the labor force, comprising 44 percent of all workers.

The flow of women out of the home and into the workplace has been even more marked in the former Soviet Union because of the tremendous labor demands of the Five-Year Plans. The percentage of women in the Soviet work force rose from 24 percent in 1928 to 35.4 percent in 1937 to 50 percent in 1984. In Third

World countries, women substantial portion of t dition to their house they have been more the men usually have h the countryside to the cities, le with an extra workload as well as sponsibility of managing family concern cisely what this means is evident in the following report from the Kenya countryside:

One-third of all rural households are headed by women, largely because men have migrated to the cities and towns in the hope of finding salaried work. Their wives continue to work the family plots of land and are always busy with some scheme to earn a bit of cash. Everywhere one sees women walking to market with basketloads of vegetables on their heads, infants strapped to their backs, and older children following behind. Even while they walk to market, these women are often weaving baskets or fashioning other handiwork that they hope to exchange for cash needed for the family's support or the children's education.[16]

Participation in the economy outside the household has been a mixed blessing for women. It has made them less dependent and has opened up new horizons and new opportunities for realizing their potential. The increased involvement of women in national economies also has correspondingly increased national productivity and wealth. In the United States, for example, two paychecks have enabled many families to enjoy larger homes, more luxurious automobiles, regular vacations, and more education for the children.

On the other hand, the new status of women has brought grievances along with the benefits. One is that having taken on outside work, women find themselves overloaded with both inside and outside work. In addition to the hours they spend on their jobs, American women work an average of 24.2 hours per week on household chores, compared to 12.6 hours by their husbands. In the former Soviet Union the disparity is greater: 25 to 28 hours per week by women, compared to 4 to 6 hours by the men.

In recent years gender inequality in workloads has been decreasing in the United States,

has been increasing in the former Soviet
and eastern Europe. "Men on all economic
," states American psychologist Joyce Broth-
"are worrying about the family and putting it
d children's welfare front and center in their
ives. For 80 percent of men, family and children
were the most important things in life, beyond
even work, career and leisure time."[17] This tendency was reinforced by a message to families issued on November 17, 1993, by the U.S. Roman
Catholic bishops. The bishops urged men to view
"their traditional role as provider for a family in
more than an economic sense. Physical care of
children, discipline, training in religious values
and practices, helping with school work and
other activities, all these and more can be provided by fathers as well as mothers."[18]

This message may have had some influence,
judging from what is happening in "home economics" courses in schools across the country. For
decades these courses have been regarded as
"girls' classes" for female teenagers preparing to
be good wives. Now, however, "home ec" courses
have a new focus, and in some cases, a new name:
"life-management education." These courses are
changing also in enrollment as well as in name.
Of the estimated 5.3 million U.S. students enrolled in these classes in 1993 in grades 7 through
12, 41.5 percent were boys, compared with 4.2
percent (of 2.2 million students) in 1968.[19]

Impressive as these statistics are, it must be
noted that long-standing habits and inequities
do not disappear overnight. A study by the Har-
vard-based Project on Human Sexual Development, which surveyed 1,400 Cleveland parents
with children aged 3 to 11, discovered that 90
percent of the wives and 85 percent of the husbands believe that women do all or most household chores.[20]

Meanwhile, the trend in eastern Europe has
been the reverse of that in the United States. The
old Communist regimes are being replaced by
new market economies, in which all enterprises
must pay their way or be shut down. This has
meant heavy unemployment and reduction of
public services in health, education, child care,
and so forth. The general retrenchment has been
especially hard on women, who usually are the
first to be sent home and to be pressured to remain in the kitchen and nursery. In Poland, 80
percent of the unemployed are women, day care
is no longer subsidized, and job protection during parental leave has been eliminated. Yugoslav
sociologist Sonja Licht refers caustically to the
new regimes emerging in eastern Europe as "male
democracies."[21]

Another grievance of female workers
throughout the world is wage discrimination. We
read in the Bible that the Lord said to Moses:
"Your valuation of a male . . . shall be 50 shekels
of silver . . . if the person is a female, your valuation shall be 30 shekels" (Leviticus 17:1–4). In the
2,000 years since this biblical injunction, the relative working value of the two sexes has remained unchanged. In the United States the *median* income of full-time women workers in 1983
was 63.6 percent of male median income. In the
former Soviet Union the disparity is similar, ranging from 60 to 70 percent.

One reason for the wage differential is that
women enter the work force later in life and with
less training. Also, some forgo overtime work and
promotions that might interfere with domestic
obligations. But perhaps the main reason for the
wage gap is that men and women do not perform
the same jobs. Women are in the "pink-collar
ghetto," working in service industries and helping professions that traditionally pay less than
male-dominated jobs. Despite the gains of recent
decades in the United States, 99 percent of all sec-
retaries are still women, as are 95 percent of registered nurses, 87 percent of restaurant workers,
and 83 percent of elementary school teachers.
Even where men and women work side by side in
the same occupations, men usually fill the higher
positions and women the lower. In American
universities in 1983, women comprised only 10
percent of full professors as compared to 21 percent of associate professors, 36 percent of assistant professors, and 52 percent of instructors.
Outright discrimination also is a factor in this inequity. Women are given different titles for the
same work that men do, and then are paid less.
Furthermore, salaries are lowered in professions
after they become largely female, as in the case of
teachers and bank tellers.

Wage inequity between the sexes has not
been affected significantly by the second indus-

trial revolution. Contrary to common assumption, high technology accentuates gender inequality in the workplace, reinforcing the segregation of women in low-skilled, low-paid clerical and service jobs. Computers, automated data processors, and computer-aided design systems are eliminating such stereotypically female jobs as stenographer, bank teller, keypunch operator, bookkeeper, and librarian. The jobs opening up in the new technologies are as sex-segregated as those that already exist. In 1980, men held 88 percent of managerial and professional high technology jobs, whereas women comprised 75 percent of the operative and clerical work force.

In recent decades, the income gap between the sexes has widened because of the rising rate of divorce. In 1970, 70 percent of all households in the United States were composed of married couples. By 1985, the percentage had dropped to 57.5. Because male incomes are about a third greater than female, the effect of divorce is to further depress the disposable income available to women who no longer share in the higher income of their spouses, and to further increase the disposable income of men following divorce. This income disparity becomes greater if children are involved because women commonly assume financial responsibility for the children with minimal child support. Thus in 1985, the average divorced woman's income in the United States was only $8,249, compared to a divorced man's income of $16,467.

In addition to this economic subordination, women all over the world face, in varying degrees, the constant threat of violence. In almost all cultures, violence against wives and against women in general has such deep historic roots that it is condoned as the acceptable norm. If a person is killed because of his or her politics, the act is commonly denounced as a violation of human rights. But if a person is beaten or killed because she is a female, the case commonly is dismissed as "cultural tradition." Nor is this a shortcoming only of aberrant or less-developed cultures. In the United States, a woman is beaten every fifteen seconds, and one is raped every five minutes.

In many cultures, the violence against females begins even before birth. Strong social pressure to bear sons is causing women in India and China to use amniocentesis—a genetic test designed to screen for birth defects—to determine the sex of their fetus. When the test reveals a girl, the fetus is usually aborted. Of 8,000 abortions performed at a clinic in Bombay, for example, 7,999 were female. The motivation behind this thriving business is reflected in sex-detection clinic advertisements, which proclaim that it is better to spend $38 on terminating a girl than to spend $3,800 later on her dowry. Likewise, China's single child per family policy triggered so much female infanticide that in 1982 in a village in Hupei province, the male-female ratio of one-year-olds was 503 to 100 (the norm being 106 to 100).

The end result of this female infanticide is that an estimated 100 million females are missing around the world.[22] They are missing because they were aborted or killed at birth, or died because they were given less food than males, or because family members view a daughter with diarrhea as a nuisance, but a son with diarrhea as a medical crisis requiring a doctor. "If a boy gets sick," acknowledges an official in China's State Family Planning Commission, "the parents send him to the hospital at once. But if a girl gets sick, the parents may say to themselves, `Well, we'll see how she is tomorrow.' "[23]

In parts of Africa and the Middle East, young girls endure another form of violence known as female circumcision. The operation removes all or part of the external genitalia, a form of mutilation that deprives the victims of all sexual feeling as well as endangering their lives during the operation and later during childbirth. The rationale of this custom is to dampen the sexual desire of young females and thus to ensure their virginity until marriage. Efforts to eradicate female circumcision are opposed on the ground that foreign organizations and ideologies are jeopardizing "an important African tradition." The Kenyan women's magazine *VIA* responds that "There is nothing `African' about injustice or violence, whether it takes the form of mistreated wives, mothers, or slums, or circumcision. Often the very men who . . . excuse injustice to women with the phrase, `it is African,' are wearing three-piece pinstriped suits and shiny shoes."[24]

D.   Impact on War

The impact of the second industrial revolution has been most clearly evident in the field of war, and naturally so because the technology of the second industrial revolution stems directly from World War II military inventions. These wartime breakthroughs were radar (British), the nuclear bomb (American), the ballistic missile (German), and the electronic computer (American).

As important as these technological advances was the integration of the activities of military men, of scientists, and of industrialists. This proved to be a highly efficient combination, leading to what has been termed "invention on demand." Experience in battle stimulated demand for improvement of existing weapons or development of new ones, such as (during World War I) tanks, poison gas, and submarines. The demand was referred to the new scientist-military-industrialist trio, which usually responded so efficiently that military technology made unprecedented advances during the two world wars.

This arrangement was institutionalized after World War II, to the point that President Eisenhower was moved to warn of the dangers of a "military-industrial complex." The scope of the complex was demonstrated when the Strategic Defense Initiative (SDI, or "Star Wars") was adopted, and Congress began authorizing appropriations in 1983. By 1987, contracts had been signed with eighty universities (led by MIT, with $350 million) and with 460 corporations (led by Lockheed, with $1 billion).

Under these circumstances, the torrent of "demand" inventions continued unabated during the cold war years that followed World War II. Even though Einstein had warned, when the first nuclear bombs were detonated, that "we drift to unparalleled catastrophe," nevertheless an arms race proliferated, with each new invention triggering counter-inventions. The 1945 American A-bomb was followed by a Soviet one in 1949; the 1952 American H-bomb by a Soviet one in 1953; and the 1968 Soviet antiballistic missile by an American one in 1972. The end result of this arms race was the accumulation of a global arsenal of 50,000 nuclear weapons.

The implication of this stalemate was made clear by a consortium of scientists from several countries, who warned in November 1983 that if only a small fraction of existing weapons were detonated, a "nuclear winter" would ensue. Firestorms and massive amounts of smoke, oily soot, and dust would blot out the sun and plunge the earth into a freezing darkness for three months to a year or more. "Global environmental changes sufficient to cause the extinction of a major fraction of the plant and animal species on the earth are likely. In that event, the possibility of the extinction of Homo sapiens cannot be excluded."[25]

This shocking statement prompted scientists in several countries to conduct follow-up studies. Some questioned whether the global chilling would be severe enough to be described as "winter," and proposed in its place the term "nuclear fall." On the other hand, they also agreed that nuclear war would deplete the ozone layer, which protects humans from solar ultraviolet radiation. They warned also that direct blast and radiation effects of nuclear war might cost several hundred million lives, but that an additional 1 billion to 4 billion of the world's 5 billion people could die of famine following worldwide crop failures. Thus a country such as India, with its huge population dependent on food imports, could suffer the heaviest loss of life, even though not a single bomb fell on its territory. Such was the dismal prospect confronting humanity at a time (1982) when $650 billion was being spent annually on arms, or $1 million each minute. Thus astronomical expenditure had brought not the desperately desired security, but the bleak alternative of nuclear fall at best, or nuclear winter at worst.

The much-discussed possibility of human self-destruction is particularly ironic, coming as it does at a time when everything imaginable by the human mind seems to be attainable by human technology. Yet this paradox fits in with our survey of human evolution, indicating that it was precisely past advances in technology that made possible the escalation of human violence from personal vendettas to full-scale warfare. (See "The Nature of Human Nature" in *The World to 1500*, Chapter 2.) So long as humans were food gatherers, they had neither the incentive nor the means for large-scale fighting. They did not acquire either means or incentive until their technology improved to the point where they had accumulated possessions worth fighting over. This oc-

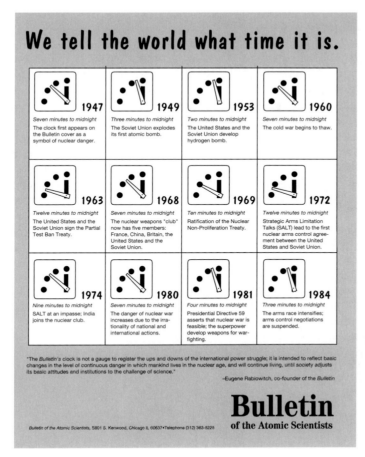

We tell the world what time it is.

1947 Seven minutes to midnight
The clock first appears on the Bulletin cover as a symbol of nuclear danger.

1949 Three minutes to midnight
The Soviet Union explodes its first atomic bomb.

1953 Two minutes to midnight
The United States and the Soviet Union develop hydrogen bomb.

1960 Seven minutes to midnight
The cold war begins to thaw.

1963 Twelve minutes to midnight
The United States and the Soviet Union sign the Partial Test Ban Treaty.

1968 Seven minutes to midnight
The nuclear weapons "club" now has five members: France, China, Britain, the United States and the Soviet Union.

1969 Ten minutes to midnight
Ratification of the Nuclear Non-Proliferation Treaty.

1972 Twelve minutes to midnight
Strategic Arms Limitation Talks (SALT) lead to the first nuclear arms control agreement between the United States and Soviet Union.

1974 Nine minutes to midnight
SALT at an impasse; India joins the nuclear club.

1980 Seven minutes to midnight
The danger of nuclear war increases due to the irrationality of national and international actions.

1981 Four minutes to midnight
Presidential Directive 59 asserts that nuclear war is feasible; the superpower develop weapons for war-fighting.

1984 Three minutes to midnight
The arms race intensifies; arms control negotiations are suspended.

"The *Bulletin's* clock is not a gauge to register the ups and downs of the international power struggle; it is intended to reflect basic changes in the level of continuous danger in which mankind lives in the nuclear age, and will continue living, until society adjusts its basic attitudes and institutions to the challenge of science."

–Eugene Rabinowitch, co-founder of the *Bulletin*

Bulletin
of the Atomic Scientists

Bulletin of the Atomic Scientists, 5801 S. Kenwood, Chicago IL 60637•Telephone (312) 363-5225

1994

curred with the agricultural and industrial revolutions, which increased productivity dramatically and created affluent civilizations fundamentally different from all the preceding subsistence societies. Their cultivated fields, overflowing granaries, and urban centers filled with treasures were all valuable prizes for predators. Thus war became profitable and endemic, waged by nomads erupting out of their deserts and steppes, by Roman senators seeking new provinces to loot, by conquistadors overrunning whole continents with their muskets and crosses, and by their successors who won worldwide empires with their gunboats and machine guns, and most recently with their helicopters and computers.

The great paradox of our age is that as the agricultural and industrial revolutions made war profitable and rational, so our second industrial revolution has made war unprofitable and suici-

dal. This is why Einstein warned us that we now face the choice of new "ways of thinking" or "unparalleled catastrophe." Our species is not unique in facing such a challenge. Innumerable other species have been confronted with similar threats, and usually they have failed and disappeared because their genetic mode of adaptation was too slow for sudden environmental change such as the onset of the Ice Age. We humans are fundamentally different because we have been able thus far to use our brains to create our own environments (by technologies such as the use of fire, the making of clothes, and the building of shelters) to suit our own needs. But now the second industrial revolution, with a powerful and dynamic technology, is creating and altering environments at an accelerating pace that requires quick and unceasing adaptation. So the supreme question now is whether we can once more use our brains adequately, this time to adapt to a new world of our own creation. In coping with this challenge, the primary advantage we enjoy over all other species that have perished in the past is that we are not buffeted by something mysterious and unknowable, such as the Ice Age. Our problem is not one of adapting to an environment beyond our control and ken, as has been the case with past species, but rather one of adapting our own human-made environment to our own human needs.

The recent adjustment of the minute hand of the "doomsday clock" of the *Bulletin of the Atomic Scientists* from three minutes to seventeen minutes before midnight offers some hope that Bertrand Russell may have been overly pessimistic in stating that "Man will sooner die than think." But any historian, reviewing the millions of needless human deaths during the last hundred years alone, would be rash to reject out of hand the validity of Russell's commentary. We cannot foresee in what direction the minute hand will move during the twenty-first century; or whether the clock still will be ticking; or whether it will be silent like the one unearthed at Hiroshima with the hand, melted and frozen, at 8:15.

SUGGESTED READINGS

Like all ages of transition this one also has stimulated many works on human prospects. Most recent and most thought-provoking is the interdisciplinary analysis by biologist M. E. Clark, *Adriadne's Thread: The Search for New Modes of Thinking* (St. Martin's Press, 1989). This study is especially useful in providing explanations and guidelines because the author conscientiously and ably pursues the search indicated in her subtitle. Also noteworthy are the following publications presenting various interpretations of current human prospects: A. Toffler, *Previews and Premises* (South End Press, 1984); L. S. Stavrianos, *Lifelines from Our Past* (M. E. Sharpe, 1992); M. G. Raskin, *The Common Good: Its Politics, Policies and Philosophy* (Routledge and Kegan Paul, 1986); F. M. Lappé, *Rediscovering America's Values* (Ballantine Books, 1989); and R. N. Bellah et al., *Habits of the Heart: Individualism and Commitment in American Life* (Harper & Row, 1986). Especially useful and revealing is the UN survey, *Human Development Report 1993* (Oxford University, 1993).

What It Means For Us Today

HUMAN PROSPECTS

We have reached the end of this study of our human past. In the course of the study we have paused for stock-taking at the end of each major period. We have asked ourselves, "What does it mean for us today?" We have asked this question several times—at the end of each of the eight parts into which this text is divided. The answer for this final part is more difficult than for the preceding ones, simply because more history is crowding now into each year than in past decades or centuries.

In the preceding chapter we ended our survey of global history with the question of whether the "doomsday clock" will continue ticking in the twenty-first century, or whether it will be melted and frozen like the one at Hiroshima. The immediate impulse is to answer negatively, living as we do at a time when the Tutsi and Hutu are butchering each other in Rwanda; and when Serbs, Croats, and Moslems are doing likewise in Bosnia. Indeed, it has become almost fashionable to forecast Armageddon for our species. But if we review the actual record, as set forth in this text, it may be argued that we are on the way up, not down.

For starters, thanks to our technology we are producing enough today so that we can begin treating each other as fellow humans rather than as competitors in a dog-eat-dog relationship. Those of us who live in affluent societies tend to minimize the significance of this attainment, but we should remind ourselves that in the past we human beings lived in a world of scarcity. All past historic civilizations have been what economists call *zero-sum civilizations*. They had available only finite pies of natural wealth which were claimed and fought over by many contenders, both within nations (class wars) and between nations (state wars). The Roman Empire was typical in that it required 80 percent of its population to work the land in order to feed the whole. Roman cities seem to have always been about three weeks from starvation. This was a zero-sum situation in that one claimant could get more only by others' getting less.

Today the situation is precisely the opposite, because the main source of wealth is not natural resources but scientific knowledge and technological knowhow. Therefore, the available pie is potentially no longer trapped in a zero-sum contest in which one's gain must be another's loss. No longer are we forced to pursue a policy of "me first and devil take the hindmost." Such a policy may have been profitable in the past, as demonstrated by the fortunes garnered by Alexander the Great in the ancient Near East; by the Spanish conquistadors in the New World; by British nabobs in India; and by Americans when they defeated Mexico (1846–1848) and annexed Texas, New Mexico, and California.

Today, however, war and conquest are hardly the road to riches, as the Germans and the Japanese discovered during and after World War II. The problem we face now is not one of a finite pie necessitating a struggle for the largest slice. Thanks to the first industrial revolution, with its labor-*saving* technology, and the second industrial revolution, with its labor-*replacing* technology, the problem we face now is one of a large and growing pie resulting in a global glut. The reality of the glut is reflected in the chronic overproduction, the chronic unused capacity, and the multitude of overt and covert trade restrictions designed to keep out the flood of foreign goods seeking markets. Although the Germans and the Japanese were defeated in World War II, they emerged the economic victors after the war because of their technological comeback. After this experience, it is unlikely that future German or Japanese leaders will use the *lebensraum* (living space) argument for war, as Hitler and Tojo did in the 1930s.

Skeptics will reply that our new plenty does not necessarily mean better human relationships, as demonstrated recently in Bosnia and Rwanda. Of course, we have all heard about the atrocities perpetuated at those two localities, but before going overboard we should ask how many have heard of Niota, which may well prove more significant in the long run than either Bosnia or Rwanda. Niota is a small Illinois town on the Mississippi, where an overlooked event occurred during the 1992 Midwest floods.

A team of convicted black and Hispanic drug dealers stationed in a nearby boot camp were sent to Niota to sandbag the levee threatened by rising waters. As they approached the town, one of the inmates remarked apprehensively, "Watch this—how long before someone calls us nigger?" Months later, reflecting on his experience, the inmate observed, "We was wait-

ing, but it never happened." Not only did it not happen, but the opposite did happen. After working nine days from dawn to dark, the inmates won the respect and gratitude of the townspeople. "They brought us Pepsi," reminisced one of the inmates. "They let us sit down in the shade and drink from their water hose. They were just nice people. . . . They gave us roast beef and chicken dinners. Meat loaf, apple pie, as much as you wanted. And they thanked us every night." The significance of this experience was not lost on the participants, though the media did ignore it amidst the hourly reports on water levels. One of the songs that they sang while hurling sandbags was written by an inmate:

They say Niota
The eatin's mighty fine.
They feed me twice a day
and now they're friends of mine.
Oh, Lord, we won't let you flood
'cause there is lots of love.
They say in Niota
the people's mighty fine.
Our skin's a different color
they don't pay it mind.[1]

Minds were changed on both sides, as demonstrated when it came to clean-up time. The townspeople were offered a choice of more inmates or a group of student volunteers. The unanimous decision was for the inmates. So within a short period a diverse group of Midwesterners was able to replace old fears and prejudices with mutual discovery and mutual respect.

Skeptics again will argue that this conversion was possible because the entire group was forced by the rising waters to work together, and in doing so was able to transcend old fears and prejudices. The same thing happened during the cold war, when Americans and their allies banded together in face of the threat from the "Evil Empire." But now that the threat is removed, former allies are bickering over trade terms, and even within the United States there is so much strife and hostility that prison construction has become the growth industry.

The obvious rejoinder is that plenty of substitutes for the old "Evil Empire" are available, if we must have a sword of Damocles dangling over our heads to prod us into turning mutual differences and suspicions into mutual discovery and respect. For example, more threatening than rising river levels is the growing danger from worldwide degradation of oceans, earth, and air. Also, social degradation is as threatening as the ecological variety. We have plenty to worry about when in Japan, *karoshi,* or death from overwork, becomes the second leading cause of death after cancer,[2] and when in the United States, Fordham University's annual report, *The Index of Social Health,* registers a drop in the index from 75 in 1970 to 36 in 1991. This index decline has been verified by a three-year study of young American children issued by the Carnegie Corporation of New York in 1994.[3]

The fact is that all humans today are subject to pressures as severe, if not as visible, as those endured by the beleaguered group at Niota. Evidence is to be found in the results of an international team that studied 39,000 randomly chosen men and women in the United States, Canada, Italy, Germany, France, Taiwan, Lebanon, and New Zealand. The team found that these people now are experiencing major psychological depressions three times more frequently than did their grandparents. Likewise, a study in the United States disclosed that only 1 percent of Americans born before 1905 have suffered a depression by age 75, as against 6 percent of those born since 1955.[4]

Is this black mood justified? Must we assume, as many do, that we are irretrievably trapped on a downhill toboggan? Not everybody thinks so. Much high-level thinking is going on to find a way out of our predicament. Pope John Paul II has called on both capitalist and socialist leaders to reappraise their dogmas and practices.[5] Mikhail Gorbachev did likewise with his *glasnost* and *perestroika* projects. The Chinese since Mao have been groping for a "Communism with a Chinese face." The Parliament of the World's Religions, which met in Chicago from August 28 to September 5, 1993, called for "a just social and economic order, in which everyone has an equal chance to reach full potential as a human being."

Such creative thinking is not limited to a few at the top. Mass activization is evident all over the globe. Villagers in the Himalayan foothills are organizing to reforest barren slopes;

rubber tappers in the Amazon basin also are organizing grass-roots resistance against ecological ravages; and in blighted Brazilian urban neighborhoods (*favelas*), young doctors work with teams of local women to teach preventive health care.

This movement is surging also in the United States in the form of self-help or mutual-aid groups, of which there were some 500,000 in 1980, with an estimated membership of 12 million to 15 million. These are people facing a common concern or condition, and banding voluntarily for emotional support and practical assistance. Inspired partly by Alcoholics Anonymous, formed in the 1930s by two alcoholics, the movement now includes Parents Anonymous, Emphysema Anonymous, Overeaters Anonymous, Pill Addicts Anonymous, Gamblers Anonymous, Kleptomaniacs Anonymous, Molesters Anonymous, Cocaine Anonymous, and WWL2M (Women Who Love Too Much), after the bestseller of that title.

Such worldwide awakening calls not for melancholia but for anticipation. It suggests that Niota may be a preview of things to come, with global pressures sublimating the fears and tensions expressed in the statistics about worldwide depression. Responsible historians, lacking crystal balls, cannot forecast one outcome or another. But neither can they dismiss the real possibility of the twenty-first century being not a dreary era of melancholia, but rather a vibrant era of creative innovation.

This conclusion will seem over-sanguine to many, but their reaction may reflect not so much present-day realities as a common underestimation of our proud heritage as a species. It is a heritage that we have surveyed in this text, and that comprises a succession of remarkable achievements through the ages. Best known are those in technology, beginning with the earliest tool making and mastery of fire, and continuing through the agricultural revolution, to the first and second industrial revolutions, to our present-day explosive high technology era. But at least as significant, though less conspicuous, have been our achievements in ways of thinking. Here we have been able to shed blinders and to attain new insights that are particularly relevant for us on the threshold of the twenty-first century.

Before Copernicus, we thought we were the center of the universe, and that all the heavenly bodies revolved around the earth, but the great astronomer corrected that conceit, teaching us that our planet is one of many circling the sun. Before Charles Darwin, we believed our species was separate and apart from the animal kingdom, but the great biologist proposed that Homo sapiens is the product of a vast evolutionary process whose laws are no different for us than for any other form of animal life. Before Sigmund Freud, we assumed that what we said and did were the results of our conscious will alone, but the great psychologist uncovered the existence of another part of our mind that functions in darkest secrecy and can even rule our lives.

Given this matchless record of our species, it is reasonable to expect that we will cope successfully with current challenges less strenuous than those overcome by our ancestors. On the other hand, innumerable species have disappeared in the past simply because they proved incapable of adapting to their changing environments. And today our environment is changing at a dizzying and ever-accelerating pace. But we have a fundamental advantage that no other species ever enjoyed. Our environment is our own human-made creation, so it is easier for us to adapt it to our human needs than it was for those countless other species to adapt to environments beyond their comprehension and control.

It does not follow that we will use wisely the opportunities we have in our grasp. The historical record shows that despite our past achievements, we rarely have refrained from any folly of which we were capable. Nevertheless, thanks to our genes and our technology, we are free today to be the creators of our destiny rather than its victims, as some would have it.

The choice is ours. It remains open. Bosnia need not be the symbol of the twenty-first century. It can be Niota in our own heartland.

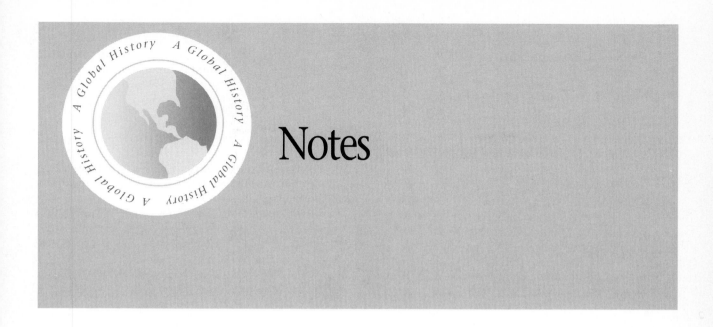

Notes

CHAPTER 18

1. F. Boas, "Racial Purity," Asia, XL (May 1940), p. 231.

CHAPTER 19

1. Mehmed Pasha, *Ottoman Statecraft: The Book of Counsel for Vezirs and Governors,* W. L. Wright, ed. and trans. (Princeton University, 1935), p. 21.
2. C.T. Foster and F.H.B. Daniell, eds., *The Life and Letters of Ogier Ghiselin de Busbecq* (London, 1881), pp. 221, 222.
3. *Ibid.*, pp. 154, 155.
4. Cited by W. Eton, *A Survey of the Turkish Empire* (London, 1808), p. 10.

CHAPTER 21

1. Cited by K.O. Dike, *Trade and Politics in the Niger Delta,* 1830-1885 (Oxford University, 1956), p. 7.
2. Cited by A.G. Price, *White Settlers and Native Peoples,* (Melbourne University, 1949), p. 121.

CHAPTER 22

1. Cited in manuscript by L.V. Thomas, "Ottoman Awareness of Europe, 1650-1800."

2. Cited by S.M. Wyntjes, "Women in the Reformation Era," in R. Bridenthal and C. Koonz, eds., *Becoming Visible: Women in European History* (Houghton Mifflin, 1977), p. 174.
3. Cited by C. Hill, The World Turned Upside Down (Viking, 1972), p. 257.

CHAPTER 23

1. A.G. Keller, "A Byzantine Admirer of 'Western' Progress: Cardinal Bessarion," *Cambridge Historical Journal,* XI (1955), pp. 343-348.
2. S.B. Clough and C.W. Cole, *Economic History of Europe* (D.C. Heath, 1952), p. 66.
3. T.K. Rabb, "The Expansion of Europe and the Spirit of Capitalism," *Historical Journal,* XVII (1974), 676.
4. Cited by J. Needham, *Science and Civilization in China: IV, Civil Engineering and Nautics* (Cambridge University, 1971), p. 533.
5. *Ibid.*, p. 534.
6. R.H. Tawney, *Religion and the Growth of Capitalism* (Murray, 1925), p. 68.

WHAT IT MEANS FOR US TODAY

1. C.L. Riley et al., *Man Across the Sea: Problems in Pre-Columbian Contacts* (University of Texas, 1975), pp. 448, 452-53.

2. *Los Angeles Times,* September 14, 1975.
3. *Ibid.,* April 21, 1985.

CHAPTER 24

1. Cited by K.M. Panikkar, *Asia and Western Dominance* (Day, 1953), p. 42.
2. Cited by *The New Cambridge Economic History*, I (Cambridge University, 1957), p. 454.

CHAPTER 25

1. Cited by L. Huberman, *Man's Worldly Goods* (Harper & Row, 1936), p. 103.

CHAPTER 26

1. R.J. Kerner, *The Urge to the Sea* (University of California, 1942), p. 86.
2. Cited by G.V. Lantzeff, *Siberia in the Seventeenth Century* (University of California, 1940), p. 105.

CHAPTER 27

1. Cited by F. Whyte, *China and Foreign Powers* (Oxford University, 1927), p. 38.
2. Cited by A.C. Wood, *A History of the Levant Company* (Oxford Unviersity, 1935), p. 230.
3. Cited by L.S.S. O'Malley, ed., *Modern India and the West* (Oxford University, 1941), p. 51.
4. H. Blount, "A Voyage into the Levant," in J. Pinkerton, ed., *A General Collection of the Best and Most Interesting Voyages...X* (London, 1808-1814), p.222.
5. Cited by D. Lach, "Leibniz and China," *Journal of the History of Ideas*, VI (October 1945), 440.
6. Cited by A. Reichwein, *China and Europe: Intellectual and Artistic Contacts in the Eighteenth Century* (Knopf, 1925), p. 152.
7. Cited by O'Malley, *op. cit.*, p. 546.
8. Cited by Reichwein, *op. cit.*, p. 151.

WHAT IT MEANS FOR US TODAY

1. *New York Times,* November 30, 1979. (c) 1979 by The New York Times Company. Reprinted by permission.

2. V.R. Mehta, *Beyond Marxism: Towards an Alternative Perspective* (New Delhi: Manohar, 1978), p. 92.
3. *New York Times*, February 4, 1980.

PART VII

1. E.J. Hamilton, "American Treasure and the Rise of Capitalism (1500-1700)," *Economica* (November, 1929), 356.
2. Cited by C.E. Robinson, "The English Philosophies and the French Revolution," *History Today*, VI (February , 1956), 121.

CHAPTER 28

1. T. Sprat, *The History of the Royal Society of London, for the Improving of General Knowledge* (London, 1734), p. 72.
2. *Siderius nuncius*, trans. E.S. Carolos (1880). Cited by M. Nicolson, Science and Imagination (Cornell University, 1956), p. 15.
3. Charles Darwin, *Origins of Species,* Vol. I (New York, 1872) p. 3.
4. H. Butterfield, *The Origins of Modern Science, 1300-1800* (Bell, 1957), p. 179.
5. Cited by L. Huberman, *We, the People,* rev. ed.(Harper & Row, 1947), p. 218.
6. Cited by N. McKendrick, *The Birth of a Consumer Society* (Indiana University, 1982), p. 98.
7. Cited by Huberman, *op. cit.*, p. 263.
8. Definition from W.L. Langer, *Diplomacy of Imperialism 1890-1902,* 2nd ed. (Knopf, 1935), p. 67.
9. P. Deane, *Colonial Social Accounting* (Cambridge University, 1953), p. 37.

CHAPTER 29

1. Cited by G. Wint, *The British in Asia* (Institute of Pacific Relations, 1954), p. 18.
2. Sir Edwin Sandys, in a speech in Parliament. Cited by J.L. Laski, *The Rise of Liberalism* (Harper & Row, 1936), p. 117.
3. P. Zagorin, "The English Revolution, 1640-1660," *Journal of World History*, II (1955), p. 903.
4. A.S.P. Woodhouse, *Puritanism and Liberty* (Dent, 1938), p. 55.
5. T. Kolokotrones and E.M. Edmonds, *Kolokotrones, Klepht and Warrior* (London, 1892), pp. 127-28.

6. B.C. Shafer, *Nationalism: Myth and Reality* (Harcourt Brace Jovanovich, 1955), p. 105.
7. Cited by D.W. Morris, *The Christian Origins of Social Revolt* (George Allen & Unwin, 1949), p. 34.

CHAPTER 30

1. Cited by B. Pares, *A History of Russia* (Knopf, 1953), p. 117.
2. Cited by F. Nowak, *Medieval Slavdom and the Rise of Russia* (Holt, Rinehart and Winston, 1930), p. 91.

CHAPTER 31

1. Ch. Photios, *Apomnemoneumata peri tes Hellenikes Epanastaseos* [Memoirs on the Greek Revolution], Vol. 1 (Athens, 1899), p. 1.

CHAPTER 32

1. Cited by K. Goshal, *The People of India* (Sheridan, 1944), p. 129.
2. Cited by A.B. Keith, ed., *Speeches & Documents on Indian Policy 1750-1921,* I (Oxford University, 1922), p. 209.
3. Cited by E. Stokes, "The First Century of British Colonial Rule in India: Social Revolution or Social Stagnation," *Past & Present* (February 1973), p. 153.
4. Cited by W.T. de Bary et al., *Sources of Indian Tradition* (Columbia University, 1958), p. 601.
5. D. Naoroji, *Speeches and Writings* (Madras: Natesan, N.D.), p. 2.

CHAPTER 33

1. S. Teng and J.K. Fairbank, *China's Response to the West: A Documentary Survey, 1839-1923* (Harvard University, 1954), p. 28. Reprinted by permission of the publishers. Copyright 1954 by the President and Fellows of Harvard College.
2. Cited by E. Swisher, "Chinese Intellectuals and the Western Impact, 1838-1900," Comparative Studies in Science and History, I (October 1958), p. 35.
3. Cited by J.R. Levenson, *Confucian China and Its Modern Fate* (University of California, 1958), p. 105.
4. Cited by J.K. Fairbank, "China's Response to the West: Problems and Suggestions," *Journal of World History,* III (1956), p. 403.

5. Cited by J.K. Fairbank, *The United States and China* (Harvard University, 1958), p. 150.

CHAPTER 34

1. E. Reynolds, *Stand the Storm: A History of the Atlantic Slave Trade* (Schocken, 1985), p. 13.
2. Cited by H. Russell, *Human Cargoes* (Longman, 1948), p. 36.
3. Cited by T. Hodgkin, *Nationalism in Colonial Africa* (New York University, 1957), p. 98.

CHAPTER 35

1. *The Education of Henry Adams: An Autobiography* (Constable, 1919), pp. 319-20.
2. H.C. Lodge, *Studies of History* (Boston, 1884), p. 352.

CHAPTER 36

1. S. Banerjea, cited in L.S.S. O'Malley, *Modern India and the West* (Oxford University, 1941), p. 766.
2. From "The White Man's Burden," in *Rudyard Kipling's Verse: Definitive Edition* (Doubleday).
3. Cited by R. Emerson, *From Empire to Nation* (Harvard University, 1960), p. 403.
4. Cited by J. Israel, " 'For God, for China and for Yale' —The Open Door in Action," *American Historical Review* (February 1970), p. 801.
5. W.T. Stead, *The Last Will and Testament of Cecil Joyn Rhodes* (London, 1902), p. 190.
6. E.G. Browne, *The Persian Revolution of 1905-1909* (Cambridge University, 1910), pp. 120-23.

CHAPTER 37

1. Cited by J.C. Adams, *Flight in Winter* (Princeton University, 1942), p. 29.
2. Cited by R.S. Baker, *Woodrow Wilson and World Settlement,* Vol. 3 (Doubleday, 1922), p. 451.
3. C. Seymour, ed., *The Intimate Papers of Colonel House,* Vol. 4 (Houghton Mifflin, 1928), p. 389.
4. Cited by K.M. Panikkar, *Asia and Western Dominance* (Day, 1953), p. 364.
5. Cited by R. Emerson and M. Kilson, "The American Dilemma in a Changing World: The Rise of Africa and Negro America," *Daedalus,* Vol. 94 (Fall 1965), 1,057.

CHAPTER 38

1. Cited by W.R. Polk, "What the Arabs Think," *Headline Series,* No. 96, p. 38.

CHAPTER 40

1. Cited by S. and B. Webb, *Soviet Communism: A New Civilization,* Vol. 2 (Gollanez, 1937), p. 605.
2. Cited by S.F. Cohen, *Rethinking the Soviet Experience* (Oxford University, 1985), p. 77.
3. M. Lewin, *Russian Peasants and Soviet Power* (W.W. Norton, 1968), p. 517.
4. Cited by Cohen, *op. cit.,* p. 78.
5. H.E. Salisbury, *New York Times,* September 29, 1953.
6. Cited by J.K. Galbraith, *The Great Crash, 1929* (Houghton Mifflin, 1955), pp. 20, 75.
7. *London Times,* February 4, 1932.

CHAPTER 41

1. P. Schmidt, *Hitler's Interpreter* (Heinemann, 1951), p. 60.
2. W.S. Churchill, *The Second World War: The Gathering Storm* (Houghton Mifflin, 1948), p. 197.
3. A. Eden, *Facing the Dictators* (Houghton Mifflin, 1962), p. 636.
4. *Bulletin of International News,* XV (March 5, 1938), 9.
5. Churchill, *op. cit.,* p. 376.
6. *New York Times,* August 27. 1939.

CHAPTER 42

1. Cited by A. Dallin, "The Fateful Pact: Prelude to World War II," *New York Times Magazine* (August 21, 1948), p. 40.
2. *Ciano's Diary 1939-1943,* Malcolm Muggeridge, ed. (Heinemann, 1947), p. 297.
3. Cited by Dallin, *op. cit.,* p. 163.
4. A.J. Toynbee, *Experiences* (Oxford University, 1969), p. 241.

CHAPTER 43

1. *New York Times School,* March 27, 1990.
2. *New York Times,* August 5, 1985; *Middle East Report,* November-December, 1988, p. 22.

3. *Ibid.,* May 16, 1990.
4. *Ibid.,* September 18, 1988.
5. *Los Angeles Times,* April 23, 1989.

CHAPTER 44

1. W.S. Churchill, *The Second World War: The Grand Alliance* (Houghton Mifflin, 1950), p. 373.
2. P.E. Mosely, "Face to Face with Russia," *Headline Series,* No. 70 (July-August 1948), p. 23.
3. Cited by M. Kaldor, *The Disintegrating West* (Allen Lane, 1978), p. 151.
4. *New York Times,* October 26, 1989.

CHAPTER 45

1. *New York Times,* February 20, 1985.
2. *Ibid.,* June 21, 1983.
3. *Ibid.,* November 20 and December 11, 1984; March 3. 1986; *Los Angeles Times,* January 10, 1986.
4. *Hunger in America: The Growing Epidemic* (Harvard University School of Public Health, 1985), pp. XIII, XIV.
5. *New York Times,* April 3, 1970.
6. *New York Times,* February 26, 1986.
7. *Los Angeles Times,* June 27, 1987.
8. *New York Times,* November 1, 1989.
9 A. Aganbegyan, "New Directions in Soviet Economics," *New Left Review,* No. 169 (May-June 1988), p. 95.
10. *UN World Economic Survey 1985,* p. 31, Table 3/2.
11. *The State of the World's Women, 1985,* UN Decade for Women (Nairobi, Kenya, 1985), pp. 4-5.
12. P. Huston, *Third World Women Speak Out* (Praeger, 1979), p. 8.
13. Cited by L. Heise, "Crimes of Gender," *WorldWatch,* March-April 1989, p. 19.
14. *State of the World's Women, op. cit.,* pp. 3, 17.
15. J. Kotkin, "America's Capacity for Renewal," *New Perspectives Quarterly,* Summer 1988, p. 5.
16. Professor Lawrence Fuchs of Brandeis University, quoted in *New York Times,* October 2, 1984.
17. J. Kotkin, "Fear and Reality in the Los Angeles Melting Pot," *Los Angeles Times Magazine,* November 5, 1989, p. 6.
18. *New York Times,* March 6, 1986.
19. *Ibid.,* April 23, 1985.
20. P.R. Ehrlich et al., "The Long-Terms Biological Consequences of Nuclear War," *Science,* 222, (1983), 1,299.

21. *New York Times*, January 23, 1990.

WHAT IT MEANS FOR US TODAY

1. H. Jennings, *Pandaemonium 1660-1886. The Coming of the Machine as Seen by Contemporary Observers* (Free Press, 1985), p. 8.
2. *Los Angeles Times,* January 15, 1989; January 29, 1989.
3. *World-Watch,*-October 1989, pp. 9-10.
4. *Los Angeles Times,* November 5, 1989.
5. *New York Times,* October 1, 1987.
6. *New York Times,* November 11, 1948.
7. Cited by H.S. Commager, "The Revolution as a World Idea," *Saturday Review,* December 13, 1975, p. 13.
8. J.K. Nyerere, *Man and Development* (Oxford University Press, 1974), pp. 166-67.
9. *Nation*, July 8-15, 1978.
10. *Los Angeles Times,* November 26, 1989.

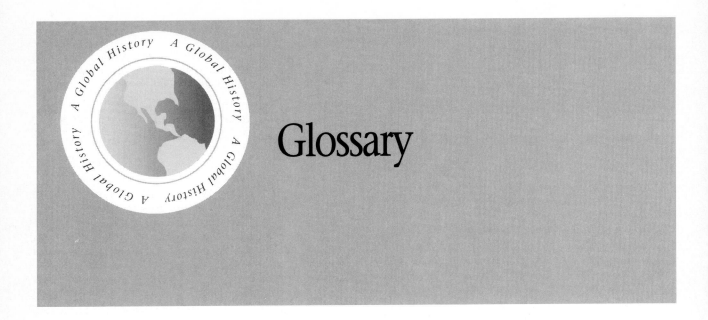

Glossary

agriculture cultivating the soil, producing crops, and sometimes raising livestock

Ainus Caucasoid people who originally inhabited the Japanese islands

Anabaptists members of a radical Protestant sect that arose in Zurich in 1524; it required adult as opposed to infant baptism, as well as nonresistance, mutual help, and separation of church and state

apartheid South African policy that excludes all non-whites from any share in political life and confines Africans to separate areas known as Bantustands (preserves for the "Bantu" Africans)

arts: liberal vs. servile in the Middle Ages, liberal arts were done with the mind; servile arts involved a change in matter; e.g., a physician didn't change matter so his work was considered liberal, whereas a surgeon changed matter so his work was servile

audiencas courts into which the huge vice-royalties of New Spain were divided

Bantu Negroid linguistic group originating in the Cameroon Highlands and later infiltrating into the Congo Basin at the expense of the Bushmen and Pygmies; predominant ethnic group when the Europeans arrived in sub-Sahara Africa

benevolent despots rulers such as Frederick the Great of Prussia (1740-1781), Catherine the Great of Russia (1762-1796), and Joseph II of the Hapsburg Empire (1765-1790) who used their governmental authority for the benefit of the people

Bhopal city in India where a chemical accident in a Union Carbide Corporation pesticide plant in December 1984 resulted in over 2,000 deaths

blitzkrieg new type of "lightning war" used by the Germans in World War II; first came dive bombers, then armored tank divisions called Panzers, and finally the lighter motorized divisions and infantry

Boers inhabitants of South Africa of Dutch descent

Bolsheviks literally "majority" in Russian; Lenin's followers

bourgeoisie the middle class, e.g., merchants, industrialists, professionals, etc.

boyars large landowners in tsarist Russia

Brahmins one of the highest Hindu castes; theoretically their occupation was that of priest or teacher; see *caste*

Buddhism a movement that was begun by Guatama Buddha in India in the fifth century B.C.; became full-fledged religion throughout Asia

bureaucracy a body of nonelected workers in any unit of government; first appeared in China

burghers middle-class townspeople

capitalism a system in which the desire for profits is the driving motive and capital is accumulated and used to make profits in a variety of ways

caste one of many hereditary groups in India that were originally based on color and occupation; there are four broad divisions with thousands of subdivisions; still in existence in rural India despite efforts to abolish them

Chernobyl town in the Soviet Union where a damaged nuclear reactor resulted, in April 1986, in radiation contamination of air, soil, water, and food supplies in the Soviet Union and in surrounding countries

civilization a stage of development in which people have achieved all or most of the following: writing, arts and sciences, cities, formal political organization, social classes, taxation

classical liberalism program by which the growing middle class proposed to get the benefits and control in government that it wanted; see also *democratic liberalism*

class struggle Marx's proposition that it is through conflict between opposing interests of classes that humankind has passed from one type of social organization to another

cold war name given to the series of crises after World War II that resulted from bad relations between the Communist and Western worlds

Common Market an economic association with six original members: Italy, West Germany, Belgium, Netherlands, Luxembourg, and France; then in 1973 Britain, Ireland, and Denmark joined

Confucianism name given to the teachings of Confucius and his followers; mainly a practical moral system concerned with problems of everyday life and emphasizing conformity, propriety, and social responsibility

conquistadors New World solders of fortune from Spain; Cortes, conqueror of the Aztec Empire, is one of the best known

Cossacks Russian frontiersmen, mostly former serfs, who fled to the wild steppe country and became hunters, fishermen, and pastoralists

Crusaders people from Christian Europe who went on expeditions during the eleventh, twelfth, and thirteenth centuries seeking to capture the Holy Land from the Moslems

daimyo local lords in sixteenth-century Japan who fought each other to extend their domains

democratic centralism principle adopted by Lenin for the operation of the Social Democratic party; major issues were discussed freely, and decision reached by democratic vote; once a vote was taken every party member had to support the "party line" or be expelled

democratic liberalism doctrine that holds that the state is responsible for all its citizens; reforms of democratic liberalism were the prelude to the welfare state; see also *classical liberalism*

diffusionists people who believe that human civilization developed by diffusion fro the Middle East to northwest Europe, north Africa, south Asia, and east Asia

Duma Russian elective national assembly created after the Russian Revolution of 1905 and swept away by the Bolshevik Revolution of 1917

dynasty a succession of rulers of the same family

ecological pertaining to ecology, the science dealing with the relations between organisms and their natural environment

ecosystem the complex of human community and natural environment, forming a functional whole

Economic and Social Council UN Council whose task was fighting hunger and disease; set up such agencies as the ILO; Food and Agriculture Organization; UN Educational, Scientific and Cultural Organization; World Health Organization; and International Monetary Fund

enclosures land closed off in England in the fifteenth to nineteenth centuries; left yeomen without grazing land or land for wood cutting; between 1714 and 1820 over six million acres were enclosed

enlightened despots see *Enlightenment* and *benevolent despots*

Enlightenment movement dating from the century prior to the French Revolution of 1789; leaders believed they lived in an enlightened age of reason and progress in contrast to the previous times of superstition and ignorance

Europeanization term used to include political domination and cultural penetration by Europe as well as actual biological replacement of one people by another, as in the relatively empty territories of the Western Hemisphere and South Pacific that were inundated by European emigrants

evolution theory that all animals and plants have their origins in preexisting types and differences gradually evolved because of modifications in successive generations

extraterritoriality right of foreigners to be exempt from the laws of a nation in which they are living; e.g., most ambassadors and diplomats are not subject to the laws of the nation in which they live but only to the laws of their own country

feudalism political system that flourished in Europe from about the ninth to fifteenth centuries; a lord gave land to vassals, who in return, gave the lord military service

fluyt flyboat; a large, cheap Dutch merchant ship that was unarmed and had great capacity for carrying goods

food-gathering culture culture in which people collect food as distinct from cultures in which people grow their food

Fourteen Points Wilson's specific, detailed aims including open diplomacy, freedom of the seas, removal of international trade barriers, armament reduction, and application of the principle of self-determination to subject minorities in central and eastern Europe

franchise right to vote

giaours nonbelievers; derogatory term used by the Moslems to refer to their Christian subjects

Gosplan Soviet State Planning Commission, which prepared plans on the basis of general directions from the government and statistical data received from all parts of the country

gross national product (GNP) total output of goods and services of a country

hidalgos Spanish aristocrats who had most of the territorial wealth, were exempt from taxes, and looked down on people engaged in commerce and industry

Hinduism major religion of India

hominids humanlike ancestors of modern human beings who had a smaller brain that was less developed than that of humans

Homo sapiens "thinking" humans; includes all members of the human race

hybrid vigor the superior qualities produced by interbreeding

ideographic writing writing in which symbols represent ideas or objects; used in early China, Mesopotamia, and Egypt

imperialism the rule or control, political or economic, direct or indirect, of one state, nation, or people over similar groups; see also *new imperialism*

independent inventionists people who believe that civilizations developed independently in the various regions of the globe

injunction an order prohibiting a specified act

Islam the religion of the Moslems, based on the monotheistic teachings of the prophet Mohammed and spread by the Arabs; not only a religion but also a political system and social code

janissaries Ottoman infantrymen

joint-stock companies stock or shares sold to investors who risked only the amount invested in the shares regardless of what losses a company might have—a characteristic that encouraged investors to risk their money, and thus mobilized the large sums necessary for European economic expansion overseas

Koran bible of the Islamic faith; provided guidance for all phases of life: manners, hygiene, marriage, divorce, commerce and politics, crime and punishment, peace and war

kulaks well-to-do Russian peasants who were hostile to the Soviet regime; finally eliminated when agriculture was collectivized

Kuomintang Chinese National People's party founded by Sun Yat-sen

League of Nations created by the Versailles Treaty; its two basic objectives were (1) to preserve the peace and (2) to concern itself with health, social, economic, and humanitarian problems of international scope; failed in its first objective but succeeded in its second

Levellers group drawn mainly from the English lower-middle class agricultural tenants who favored a democratic government and social reform

literocracy hierarchy of learned people such as that which ruled China before the intrusion of the West

mandates people of the colonies taken from the Central Powers after World War I were regarded as unable to stand on their own feet; their tutelage was entrusted to "advanced nations" who were to exercise their tutelage on behalf of the League of Nations; this tutelage was not extended to the colonies of the victorious allies

materialist interpretation of history Marx's theory that in every historical epoch the mode of economic production and exchange gives rise to a particular social organization and is the basic foundation for the political and intellectual history of that epoch

Mau Mau secret East African terrorist organization made up of members of the Kikuyu tribe

median situated at the midpoint between the two extremes, so that when nine incomes are arranged in order, the median income is the fifth from the top and from the bottom, whereas the average income is the sum of the nine incomes divided by nine

Mensheviks literally "minority" in Russian; Lenin's opponents within the Russian Social Democratic party

mercantilism early modern rigid regulation of economic life in contrast to no regulation or "laissez faire" policy

Mesoamerica central and south Mexico, Guatemala, and Honduras

mestizo person in Spanish America of mixed European and Indian origin

millennium one-thousand-year period

modernization economists define modernization as the process by which humans have gained control over their physical environment by increasing output; sociologists and anthropologists term such features as the awakening and activation of the masses; more interest in the present and future than in the past; belief that human affairs are understandable rather than the result of supernatural manipulation; and until recently, faith in the beneficence of science and technology

monoculture cultivation of a single crop

multinational corporations business corporations that conduct commercial, industrial, or banking activities in many countries, and which are today's counterpart of the earlier *joint-stock companies*

muzhik a Russian peasant

nationalism allegiance to the cause of the nation rather than to the church and region as before the nineteenth century

natural selection an important part of the process of evolution; in the struggle for existence, the organisms whose genes are best adapted to the environment are selected and will survive and reproduce; the less well adapted will die out

New Economic Policy (NEP) plan adopted by the Soviet government in 1921 that made some concessions; e.g., peasants were allowed to sell their produce on the open market, private individuals could operate small stores and factories and keep the profits

new imperialism the great European expansion of the late nineteenth century; differed from the old imperialist control of a state over another because it did not simply demand tribute but completely transformed the conquered countries

North Atlantic Treaty Organization (NATO) a mutual defense organization consisting of the United States, Canada, and several western European countries who agreed that "an attack on one or more of the signers is an attack upon all"

Orthodox Christians Greek Christians who rejected the leadership of the pope and instead were under the patriarch of Constantinople

ostracism a form of punishment involving isolation or exclusion from a social group

ostrogs fortified posts or blockhouses built by the Cossacks as they advanced eastward

Palestine Liberation Organization (PLO) an organization consisting of several Palestinian nationalist groups; all are opposed to Israel but disagree about how an independent Palestinian state should be created

Panchayat elected council of five or more, usually caste leaders and village elders, who governed the traditional Indian village

paradox something absurd, false, and self-contradicting

philosophes a group who believed in the existence of natural laws that regulated the universe and human society

photosynthesis the process by which green plants utilize the energy of sunlight to manufacture carbohydrates from carbon dioxide and water—a process on which all plant and animal life on this planet depends

proletariat the working class in industrial societies, e.g., workers in factories, mines, the docks, etc.

Quisling a Norwegian who collaborated with Hitler and whose name became a synonym for the self-serving traitor

Reformation basic upheaval that shattered the unity of Western Christendom; Martin Luther triggered the Protestant Reformation when he reacted against abuses in the Roman church

Renaissance literally "new birth" or "revival"; an intellectual and cultural awakening that took place in Europe during the fifteenth to seventeenth centuries

revisionism a movement among twentieth-century socialists to adopt a "revised" strategy that depends on gradual reform instead of revolution to bring about a socialist society

sans culottes literally "those who lacked the knee breeches of genteel society"; French revolutionaries who wanted a more egalitarian state with equitable division of land; government regulation of prices and wages, and a social security system

savannas tropical or subtropical grasslands; treeless plains

Security Council UN Council made up of five permanent members, the United States, USSR, Britain, France, and China, and six two-year members elected by the General Assembly whose task is to maintain peace

self-determination the principle that all peoples should have the right to self-rule

Shiite sect a Moslem sect that repudiated the first three successors of Mohammed; Persians (Iranians) identified with this sect

shogun generalissimo; a general who commanded military forces for the Japanese emperor

socialism ideology calling for social and economic change and political reform; the government owns and operates the means of production and the main parts of the economy, e.g., banks, mines, factories, railroads, foreign trade, etc.; emphasizes community and collective welfare rather than the individual

soviets workers' elected councils that originated in the Russian Revolution of 1905 and reappeared in the 1917 revolution; soviets supplied the government with close rapport with the masses

steppe open, treeless plains with fertile black earth

suffragist one who favors extending suffrage, or the right to vote, to women

Sunnite sect a Moslem sect to which Turks and other surrounding peoples belonged and which set them apart from the Persian Shiites

surplus value Marxist theory that workers who provided the labor receive substantially less in wages than the price charged the consumer; hence the workers cannot buy what they produce; this leads to overproduction, unemployment, and finally, depression

taiga forest belt or zone

Taoism Chinese doctrine that stressed the importance of living naturally, conforming to nature's pattern; ambition was abandoned and honors and responsibilities rejected in favor of a meditative return to nature

technology the body of knowledge and skills evolved by human beings to produce goods and services

tundra barren, frozen land along the Arctic coast

United Nations (UN) organization of nations set up in 1945 to carry out two basic tasks: (1) preserve peace and security and (2) set up international economic, social, and cultural programs; originally fifty charter members, with membership doubling by 1980

UNRRA UN organization set up to provide relief of all kinds to liberated countries; originated in the spring of 1944 and was to continue until the new national administrations could assume responsibility

Utopian Socialists school of social reformers who produced blueprints for the operation of their projected model communities but did not indicate how these principles could be put into practice in the larger society

Versailles Treaty treaty with Germany, signed on June 28, 1919, which ended World War I; this treaty, together with separate treaties with the other Central Powers, are significant for world history because they applied the principle of self-determination to Europe but failed to apply it in overseas colonies

Warsaw Pact formal military alliance concluded in May 1955 between Russia and the east European countries

white man's burden theory that Europeans were a superior race who had the duty to direct the labor and guide the development of inferior races; allowed Europeans to cloak their imperialism with a mantle of idealistic devotion to duty

World Zionist Organization nationalist Jewish movement established in Basle in 1897; wanted a Jewish commonwealth in Palestine after the end of the Ottoman Empire

Young Turks pioneer group of Turkish nationalist who wanted a new modern government in place of the Ottoman Sultanate

Zaibatsu literally "wealth-clique"; general name given to four giant family corporations that by World War II controlled three-fourths of the combined capital of all Japanese firms, three-fourths of all trust deposits, and one-fifth of all life insurance policies

Photo Credits

Chapter 18: Page 291, The Granger Collection; **p. 292**, Reuters/Bettmann.

Chapter 19: Page 298, United Nations; **p. 299**, United Nations; **p. 303**, The Granger Collection; **p. 305**, Trevor Wood/Tony Stone Images.

Chapter 20: Page 314, Bettmann; **p. 316**, Bettmann.

Chapter 21: Page 320, American Museum of Natural History; **p. 324**, Eugene Gordon; **p. 325**, American Museum of Natural History; **p. 328**, Stuart Rome, Albuquerque Museum/Belize Department of Archaeology, Belmopan.

Chapter 22: Page 334, Accademia Campo Della Carita', Venezia; **p. 336**, Accademia Campo Della Carita', Venezia; **p. 337**, Alinari/Art Resource.

Chapter 23: Page 347, Courtesy of New York Public Library; **Page 348**, Giraudon/Art Resource; **p. 350**, New York Public Library; **p. 357**, New York Public Library.

Chapter 24: Page 365, The Granger Collection; **p. 369**, Gramstorff Bros., Inc.; **p. 370**, The Granger Collection; **p. 371**, The Granger Collection; **p. 372**, Culver Pictures, Inc.; **p. 373**, The Granger Collection; **p. 376**, The Granger Collection; **p. 378**, The Granger Collection.

Chapter 25: Page 382, Astor, Lenox and Tilden Foundations/Rare Book Division, The New York Public Library; **p. 384**, New York Public Library; **p. 385**, Courtesy of Stavrianos; **p. 386 (bottom)**, National Maritime Museum; **p. 389**, Astor, Lenox and Tilden Foundations/Rare Book Division, The New York Public Library; **p. 393**, Library of Congress.

Chapter 26: Page 396, National Museum, Copenhagen; **p. 401**, National Museum, Copenhagen; **p. 402**, The Granger Collection; **p. 405**, Astor, Lenox and Tilden Foundations/Rare Book Division, The New York Public Library.

Chapter 27: Page 412, New York Public Library; **p. 414 (top)**, Culver Pictures, Inc.; **p. 414 (bottom)**, Peabody Museum, Harvard University; **p. 415**, The Granger Collection; **p.**

417, New York Public Library; **p. 418**, Bettmann; **p. 419**, The Granger Collection; **p. 423**, Courtesy of Stavrianos; **p. 426**, The Granger Collection; **p. 428**, Culver Pictures, Inc.

Chapter 28: Page 437, International Museum of Photography at George Eastman House; **p. 443**, Ford Motor Company; **p. 446,** The Granger Collection; **p. 447,** Culver Pictures, Inc.; **p. 454**, The Granger Collection; **p. 455,** International Museum of Photography at George Eastman House.

Chapter 29: Page 461, Hulton Deutsch Collection Limited; **p. 462**, Library of Congress; **p. 468**, Library of Congress; **p. 475**, Hulton Deutsch Collection Limited; **p. 479**, V. Mastjukov Sovfoto/Eastfoto.

Chapter 30: Page 484, PH Archives; **p. 485**, PH Archives; **p. 486**, The Granger Collection; **p. 491**, McCutcheon/Pro Pix from Monkmeyer Press.

Chapter 31: Page 497, Bettmann; **p. 498**, Bettmann; **p. 500**, The Granger Collection; **p. 502**, Hulton Deutsch Collection Limited.

Chapter 32: Page 508, John Isaac/United Nations; **p. 509**, John Isaac/United Nations; **p. 511**, New York Public Library Picture Collection; **p. 513**, Bettmann; **p. 516**, Bettmann.

Chapter 33: Page 520, Library of Congress; **p. 526**, Library of Congress.

Chapter 34: Page 533, The Granger Collection; **p. 535**, Library of Congress; **p. 536**, Library of Congress; **p. 538**, The Granger Collection.

Chapter 35: Page 546, United Pacific Railroad; **p. 549**, Public Archives of Canada. From a watercolor by James Duncan; **p. 550**, United Pacific Railroad; **p. 553**, Library of Congress; **p. 556**, Copyright Rodman Wanamaker, 1912/American Museum of Natural History.

Chapter 36: Page 558, Bettmann; **p. 559**, The British Museum, London; **p. 560**, Library of Congress; **p. 561**, Bettmann.

Chapter 37: Page 569, Library of Congress; **p. 570**, Na-

Index

HIKING THE WASATCH

HIKING THE WASATCH

**A Hiking and Natural History Guide
to the Central Wasatch**

Second Edition

BY JOHN VERANTH

PHOTO CREDITS

FRONT COVER/   Albion Basin, Trudy Healy
                Columbine, Trudy Healy

BACK COVER/   Aspen in Willow Fork, Charles Ranney
                Lake Mary, Ruth Frear
                Lone Peak Summit Ridge, Rich Gregersen
                Red Pine Lake, Ruth Frear

INSIDE PHOTOS/ John Veranth
MAPS/   Dan Welton
COVER DESIGN/   Easton Design Group
TYPESETTING/   Design Type Service

Published by The Wasatch Mountain Club, Inc.
c/o Wasatch Publishers,
        4460 Ashford Drive
        Salt Lake City, Utah 84124

Library of Congress Catalog Number: 88-050444
ISBN Number: 0-915272-32-6

PREFACE

The Wasatch Mountains, east of Salt Lake City, are a mountain treasureland with three Wilderness Areas and miles of trails. These mountains are within an hour's drive of nearly a million people, but the steep, rugged terrain can seem intimidating to new hikers and many parts of the Wasatch are relatively unknown and are seldom visited

This book began as an updating of the original "Wasatch Trails," published by the Wasatch Mountain Club in 1973. The project expanded into a totally new guidebook covering hikes, off-trail routes, and alpine scrambles in Salt Lake County and in the the Lone Peak Wilderness. Included are lists of hikes according to the best season, the time required, the objective, and the desired level of difficulty. The descriptions range from nearly level walks, requiring less than an hour, to ascents that challenge experienced mountaineers.

Understanding the mountain environment enhances hiking enjoyment. The geology, the flora and fauna, and the human history are discussed for the curious amateur. Getting people onto the trails where they can listen to the birds, smell the flowers, and marvel at the forces which carved the land, is a key step in building support for preservation of the Wasatch and other precious natural areas. This book is a plea for citizen involvement in the protection and wise management of the mountains, deserts, and rivers of Utah.

My thanks go to the countless hiking leaders who introduced me to various trails over the years, and to all the companions who have walked with me. Special thanks are given to the Governing Board of the Wasatch Mountain Club for supporting this project, to Dale Green for serving as an invaluable reference on trails and place names, and to Mel Davis and Alexis Kelner for their advice regarding the mechanics of publishing a book. Individuals who reviewed the manuscript for accuracy include; Charles Keller, Trudy Healy, Mike Treshow, Dave Wallace, Chris Biltoft, Mary Fleming, Oscar Robinson, Earl Cook, John Kennington, Gail Cordy and Karin Caldwell. Additional comments were received from George Nickas of Utah Wilderness Association, Mark Wilson of Solitude, Rick May of Snowbird, and from the Salt Lake City Water Department. The cooperation of the Forest Service staff including Richard Klein, Salt Lake District Ranger, Ollie Jones, Al Soucie, Kevin Plettenberg, Jeff Larson, John Hougland, Neil Hunsacker, Frank Grover and Dale Gerry is also appreciated. The maps were drawn by Dan Welton, book design was by Julie Easton, and copy editing was performed by Dan Felsen and by Martha Veranth. My wife, Martha, deserves very special thanks for tolerating the endless hours this project consumed.

The extensive revision and updating found in this second edition were made possible through the efforts of Dale Green who has meticulously mapped the Wasatch trails and by Alison Hottes who did much of the editorial work.

CONTENTS

LIST OF MAPS

	Scale	Page

SUMMIT PANORAMA SKETCHES

	Page

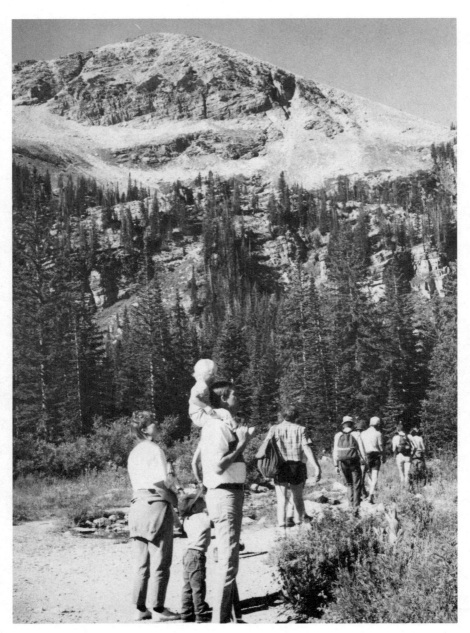

Hiking is healthful recreation for anyone; young or old. Head up a canyon and discover the trails of every description that lie beyond the roads.

1

INTRODUCTION TO HIKING IN THE WASATCH

The Wasatch is a hiker's paradise only a few minutes' drive from the cities of the Wasatch Front. This guidebook covers all the trails and major off-trail routes in the central portion of the Wasatch Range from the south end of Davis County through Salt Lake County to American Fork Canyon in Utah County; a 15- by 30-mile area. The hike descriptions include 323 miles of hikes that span the full range from excellent trails to scrambles defined only by terrain features.

Some hikes follow ski area service roads or old mining, logging, and dam access roads. Due to watershed impacts, motor vehicles are restricted on most of these primitive roads which make well-graded, easy-to-follow walking paths. Other hikes are along official Forest Service trails that are well-constructed and maintained, creating a distinct foot path for easy walking. Some well-used and popular trails are not part of the official Forest Service "system." Travel on these secondary trails is not difficult, but you have to contend with climbing over occasional logs and with picking your way through brush, across mud, and over rocks.

Extending beyond the official trails are numerous routes along foot tracks or game trails which often disappear, especially in grassy areas, requiring detours and searching for the route. Finally, all trails end, and you reach the brush thickets, rock ridges and snowfields where the only choice is cross-country travel, picking your way from landmark to landmark and looking for the *least difficult* line.

USING THIS GUIDEBOOK

Some hikes in this book are suitable for families with small children, while others are a challenge for experienced mountaineers. This section explains the route descriptions so a hiker can understand the length and difficulty involved in reaching a particular destination.

The amount of detail in the descriptions varies with the type of trail and the difficulty. On a maintained trail, little description is needed to follow the obvious path. Descriptions of maintained trails emphasize locating the trailhead and pointing out the highlights that add interest to the hike. Since vandalism of trail signs is a problem, descriptions of maintained trails also include hiking times, distances, and physical landmarks. To preserve the challenge and adventure, less detail is provided on the harder routes which are traveled only by experienced hikers. On unmaintained routes, the entire description comes from landmarks and compass bearings.

The chapters are arranged by the starting location (foothills, Millcreek Canyon, etc.) and the individual hikes are in a west-to-east or north-to-south order. The Hike Number (M-01, WF-7, etc.) matches the descriptions to the maps used in this book. The index is arranged alphabetically by hike name, with cross reference to hike number and page number.

Route Difficulty

Difficulty depends on distance, elevation change, trail condition, and required routefinding. Adjectives used to describe trail difficulty are defined as follows:

BEGINNER — A well-maintained trail with a good walking surface and no unsafe terrain. The route is well defined and has adequate signs.

EASY — Hikes with less than 4 miles round trip and with less than 2000 feet elevation gain. Round trip hiking time is 45 minutes to 3 hours but inexperienced hikers may take longer.

INTERMEDIATE — Longer hikes with more elevation gain that may involve sections where the trail is in poor condition. Round trip hiking time is typically 3 to 7 hours.

ADVANCED — Long routes requiring 5 to 10 hours round trip, and routes with difficult terrain involving extensive route finding.

EXPOSURE — Routes where there is little danger of falling — but if you fall, there is risk of serious injury. Crossing ledges or ridge crests with a precipitous drop below causes a feeling of being exposed to danger.

SCRAMBLING

Routes that are intermediate between steep hiking and technical mountaineering. Scrambling involves using your hands for balance when moving across rock but does not include using your arm strength to pull yourself up, except possibly for single short climbing moves. Scrambles also include routes on hard spring snow where an ice axe is required. Reasonably athletic persons can handle the scrambling on the hiking routes in this book if they are accompanied by someone experienced enough to coach them through the hard spots.

MOUNTAINEERING

Any route involving dangerous terrain where technical skill and experience are required. The routes described as mountaineering scrambles should be attempted only by persons who have had some previous training such as a basic mountaineering or rock climbing course.

The photographs illustrate the contrast between an easy walk up a graded road in White Pine Canyon and an exposed scramble on the summit ridge of Devils Castle.

Trail Condition

Throughout the descriptions, certain words were used to describe the type and condition of the walking surface. "Roads" are paved or graded surfaces maintained for vehicles and include roads open to the public and limited access roads blocked by gates. "Jeep roads" or "4WD roads" are unmaintained routes used by off-road vehicles. Wheel tracks are usually evident and limited construction may have been done to create the route.

"Trails" are maintained or constructed footpaths. For a path to be called a trail, at least the brush has been cleared in recent years. "Tracks" and "game trails" are footpaths where the soil and the vegetation show evidence of repeated travel. "Routes" describe a general direction of cross-country travel with no defined footpath. A "bushwhack" is a route where hikers must force their way through sections of brush. Short pants are not recommended for bushwhacks. "Improvised bridges" are logs thrown across a stream. Routes that cross major streams on improvised bridges may be dangerous or impassable during the peak of the spring runoff.

Accuracy

Trail locations, distances, and elevation changes were determined from a combination of field checking with sketch pad, compass, and altimeter and the most recent USGS maps. All trails in this book have been hiked by the author, and most descriptions were personally field checked during 1986 and 1987. Dale Green walked and mapped the major trails in 1992 and 1993. The manuscript was also reviewed by knowledgeable hikers, but conditions change rapidly — avalanches and rockfall can obliterate a trail that was in excellent condition a

"Easy-Beginner" and "Advanced-Scrambling" Hikes. Left — White Pine Canyon (Trail L-05), a wide well-graded dam access road leading to overlook. right — Devils Castle (Trail L-13.3), a ridge crest route to a summit.

year ago. Brush is periodically cleared, and sections of trails are occasionally relocated. Where trails cross private property, a housing development may appear where hikers have walked for years.

Neither the text nor the sketch maps attempt to accurately describe every bend in the trail. Use the information with a degree of skepticism and common sense.

Maps and Names

The maps published in this book were compiled from field notes and from the United States Geological Survey (USGS) topographic maps. The trail locations are shown as accurately as possible given the limits of scale.

Hikers will find that additional maps are useful supplements to this book. Serious hikers will eventually accumulate a set of the 7-1/2 minute series USGS topographic maps. Drawn at 1:24,000 scale (approximately 2-1/2 inches per mile), these are the most accurate maps available for topographic features but the trail information is badly out of date. The USGS maps covering this area were originally issued between 1948 and 1963 and have received only minor revisions, based on aerial photographs, since then. Hike descriptions in this book point out the map errors when they are significant, but don't be surprised if the USGS map shows a trail on the wrong side of a stream. Comments regarding errors on the USGS maps refer to the most recent edition as of 1986.

"Hiking the Wasatch—The Official Wasatch Mountain Club Trail Map For the Tri-Canyon Area—Mill Creek, Big Cottonwood, and Little Cottonwood," published by the Wasatch Mountain Club and the University of Utah Press, covers most of the popular hikes and has been updated by Wasatch Mountain Club member Dale Green on the same scale as the USGS 7-1/2 minute series maps. It accurately shows trail locations and is cross referenced to this book. The new 1:50,000 scale (approximately 1-1/4 inches per mile, 20 millimeters per kilometer) metric dimensioned USGS topographic map series is an ideal scale for hiking use.

Lack of official names for many geographic features is a problem. Unnamed peaks can often be identified by the summit elevations found on topographic maps. Many names used in the route descriptions are unofficial names used by local hikers for peaks and drainages. The geologic maps and the 1903 USGS "Cottonwood Map" were additional sources of names. Other names were derived from a related feature (e.g., Reynolds Peak is the summit, Peak 9422, at the head of Reynolds Gulch).

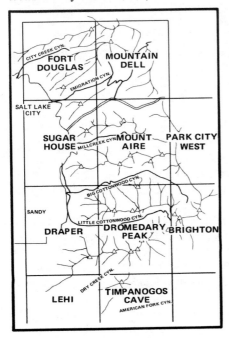

USGS Topographic Maps. Ten maps at 1:24,000 scale cover the area discussed in this book. Other useful maps are the 1:50,000 scale "Brighton" map and the 1:100,000 scale "Salt Lake City" map.

Distances and Directions

Short distances along trails are generally stated in yards if estimated by hiking time or scaled from a map. Longer distances are rounded off to the nearest quarter mile unless measured. Highway mileages given in decimal fractions were determined from odometer readings.

The best method to judge distances in a trail description is to convert the distance into hiking time. A quick mental conversion is that 1/4 mile requires six minutes on level trail and up to 14 minutes on a very steep trail. In the descriptions, "immediately" means very short distances, typically within sight, or less than one minute's walk.

The words "right" and "left" are for travel in the direction of the route description. Most descriptions are written for travel in the uphill direction, so referring to the "left side of the stream" is the reverse of the usual geographic convention.

Hiking Times

Hiking times are based on a typical pace for experienced hikers who are in good physical condition. The durations are walking time only and do not include long rest breaks or sightseeing. A strong hiker can easily beat these times, while a family with children will take much longer. These times are consistent; if you require 3 hours to do a hike that has a book time of 2 hours, you will require 6 hours to do a hike with a 4 hour book time. Once you have done a few hikes you will learn how to adjust these times for your own pace.

The basic formula is: 2 miles per hour on normal trail, plus 1/2 hour for every 1000 feet of ascent. Adjustments were made for trail condition, intermediate summits, and high altitude. The route descriptions list a one-way time to the destination. For most trails, the return will require about 3/4 of the time required for the uphill portion, but very flat and very steep trails with rough terrain require about equal time in either direction.

Hiking Pace

The proper pace, not extraordinary strength, is the key to hiking without becoming over tired. On longer hikes, take a slower pace or stop and rest often, and you will be more likely to reach your objective. Avoid becoming out of breath or developing a racing heart beat.

The "rest step" is a proven method to conserve your leg strength by allowing a short period where the muscles are relaxed on each step. The idea is to take a step uphill, setting your foot down but not putting any weight on it while simultaneously locking the knee of your back leg. With practice, this can be accomplished while maintaining a steady pace. Take small steps on steep uphill sections. An upward movement of 4 to 7 inches per step puts much less strain on your thighs than do 10 or 12 inch steps.

Data Tables

The data tables included with major hikes show the distance, elevation gain, highest elevation and hiking time to one or more destinations. Usually, the destinations will be a series along a trail starting with a short hike and continuing farther and higher. At other times, the destinations will be alternative branches that fork from a single trailhead. This will be evident from the text description or the map. If the measurements are from a point other than the trailhead, this is noted at the bottom of the table.

If the hike is described as a one-way route, the table reflects the more common direction of travel. If the route crosses significant intermediate summits, an additional line gives the total ascent, rather than the difference from the trailhead to the destination.

HIKER RESPONSIBILITY

The freedom of traveling in a natural environment requires judgment and responsibility from each hiker. Each hiker is personally responsible for being physically fit for the intended trip; for having proper equipment, clothing, water, and food; for evaluating the route conditions and weather; and for protecting the environment and the rights of others.

Private Property

Many trails, especially along the Wasatch Front, cross private land. This complex issue is discussed in Chapter 3. Where no official right-of-way exists, access is by the permission of the owner and may be revoked at any time.

Respect all private property and avoid behavior which would cause owners to object to hikers crossing their land. Park where you will not cause congestion on adjacent streets, stay on the trail until you are on Forest Service land, and don't litter or cause excessive noise. Observe any signs or fences which would indicate a change in the owner's policy to hikers.

If challenged on the trail and told that you are trespassing, act respectfully and leave. The Wasatch Mountain Club has a strong interest in trail access. If you are told that hikers are not welcome on a trail, the club would like to hear about the problem. Call or write to the club's Hiking Director or the author.

The trails included in this book are routes which have been used by the public for many years with few landowner conflicts; however, occasional trail closures are likely as the foothills and canyons become more developed.

Protection of traditional access routes to the mountains requires the cooperation of landowners, public agencies, and citizen groups. Elected officials are becoming more involved in trail access and planning departments are considering trail access when approving new subdivisions.

Watershed Protection

The national forests were created for watershed protection, and water quality remains an issue today. Watershed concerns necessitate restricting traffic in City Creek Canyon and prohibiting swimming in the lakes. Dogs and horses are forbidden on the watershed including City Creek, Big Cottonwood, and Little Cottonwood Canyons. Animals have been allowed in Millcreek Canyon since the water is used for irrigation, but restrictions have been proposed.

Hikers and wilderness lovers must learn to enjoy an area without damaging it. Toilet facilities have been placed at popular trailheads — **use them**. With a little planning, you can reduce the need to "go behind a bush" especially on short day hikes, but if nature calls be sure you go away from the trail and at least 200 feet from streams. When defecating, dig a hole six inches deep in organic soil and cover it thoroughly when done. Lightly compact the soil and cover the excavation with loose twigs and rocks to reduce both the erosion potential and the visual impact.

Litter is both a health problem and an aesthetic issue. Do your part and carry out what you carry in on your hike. Better still, carry out some of the garbage left by less considerate hikers.

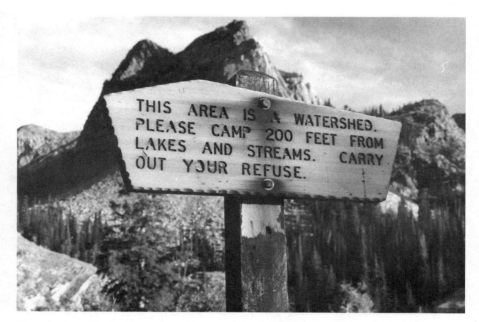

Many popular hiking destinations are at lakes and reservoirs. Avoid leaving anything in the water that you would not want to drink.

Camping on the Watershed

For many years, prohibition of camping on the watershed severely limited the opportunity to spend more than a few hours in some of the more remote parts of the Wasatch. Except for the City Creek and Red Butte drainages, camping is now allowed, and the opportunity should not be abused.

Obviously, this means staying the required distance (200 feet) from lakes and streams; not fouling the water with human waste, soap suds, or food scraps; and packing out all garbage. Locate your camp to minimize visual impact by getting off the trail and utilizing natural topographic and vegetative screening. Don't chop down trees or build new fire rings for a massive bonfire. Use of a camping stove is highly recommended. Also, the Wasatch has a high forest fire risk. For resource protection, camp fires are now prohibited in most of the popular lake basins. The Wasatch is not particularly suitable for camping; backpackers should consider alternative destinations.

Trail Etiquette

The Wasatch is a heavily used and fragile area. Hikers must strive to minimize their impact.

Shortcutting switchbacks on the trails damages vegetation and causes serious erosion. Much trail maintenance labor goes into restoring areas damaged by shortcutting. Hikers who prefer steeper trails can avoid the switchbacks by choosing an alternative trail or a totally off-trail route.

Large groups can be very intrusive and affect the experience of other hikers. This is especially true when a huge group shows up at an already popular destination in a fragile area. Camping has an official limit of 10 to a group. Although there are no limits for day use, leaders are encouraged to limit group size in the designated Wilderness Areas. The Forest Service manages the upper canyons for "developed recreation," and these areas are more appropriate for large hiking groups.

Being Prepared

Each hiker must take responsibility for being physically prepared and adequately equipped for the intended trip. Good physical condition is not a prerequisite for hiking, and regular hiking is an enjoyable way to exercise; however, hikers must select routes that match their health and strength.

Equipment

Hiking does not require a large investment in equipment, but for a safe trip there are a few essentials, including:
- Good comfortable boots with adequate tread.
- Extra clothing appropriate to the season.
- FULL water bottle.

- Sun glasses and sunscreen.
- A small pack to carry everything.

As hikes become longer and more serious you will also need:

- A map or trail guide.
- Food including some extra for emergencies.
- Raingear or other clothing for a change in the weather.
- A small first aid kit.
- Insect repellent in July and August.
- A flashlight if there is any chance of a twilight return.

Wasatch Weather

Normal atmospheric conditions result in a decrease in temperature with altitude, and mountains generate their own weather. Air passing over a mountain range is forced upward and cools as it rises and expands. Colder air holds less water vapor, so moisture condenses, forming clouds, rain, and snow. The ridges and canyons also redirect the surface winds and affect the local climate.

The climatic difference between the valley at 4300 feet and the Brighton parking lot at 8700 feet is roughly comparable to the change experienced when going north from Salt Lake City to central Canada or parts of Alaska. In mid-June when the city is hot and dry, Alta and Brighton are still buried in snow.

At high elevation, the mid-day sun is intense. The air directly above a mountain becomes warmer than the surrounding air at the same altitude and begins to rise. This rising air forms the towering cumulus clouds which are often seen above the Wasatch on an otherwise clear summer afternoon. They can produce anything from an overcast to an incredibly violent thunderstorm mixed with hail. Lightning is a special danger to hikers on summits and ridges.

The physics are simple, but the magnitude of the effects resulting from the great vertical relief must be experienced first-hand before it is fully appreciated. I have started hiking on a bright, hot summer afternoon and returned home drenched with rain, only to discover that not a drop fell in the valley. I have sat on top of Mount Olympus feeling chilled while wearing a pile jacket and mountain parka, yet knowing there was shirtsleeve weather down in the city. Taking proper clothing along is important at any time of year.

Drinking Water

You are unlikely to find drinking water on foothill hikes or on trails that follow ridges or minor drainages. Small streams, such as the one on the Mount Olympus Trail, usually dry up by mid-summer, and only major drainages and lakes are reliable water sources. Water quality at higher elevations in the Wasatch is generally good, but treating lake and stream water is always recommended and prudent.

There are diverse opinions about which treatment method is best. Personally, I have used Halazone tablets, iodine tablets, iodine crystals, a dropper bottle of chlorine bleach, a high-efficiency filter, and boiling. Filtering and boiling are the most certain but are too much hassle for a day hike. All chemical treatments require 15 to 20 minutes, are less efficient in cold water, and leave a residual taste. For occasional day hikes, the iodine treatment tablets are economical and convenient, have a good shelf life, and are readily available in outdoor stores.

For short day hikes, carrying enough water for the full trip is easiest. A quart bottle and maybe a canned beverage to enjoy with lunch are enough in cool weather. For a long hike such as Twin Peaks or Olympus in July and August, carry two or even three quarts plus treatment chemicals.

Judgment

Reaching the objective is glorious, but knowing when to turn around is prudent. Gauge your progress and allow yourself enough time and energy to return to the trailhead safely. Many avoidable accidents have occurred when an exhausted hiker was hurrying down a trail in twilight. When traveling beyond the maintained trails, be sure you are capable of handling the terrain. This is especially true with any route described as exposed scrambling or mountaineering.

Other Ways Of Enjoying the Wasatch Trails

Mountain running is a demanding sport which combines alpine hiking with distance running. The distances and terrain that runners cover seem truly astounding to hikers. Runners travel very light compared to hikers, and depend on strength, speed, and knowledge of the route to avoid bad weather and to get themselves to a road or aid location. Meeting a runner wearing shorts and running shoes and carrying only a water bottle is a humbling experience when you are panting uphill with a full pack. Many of the longer trails and ridge routes, especially the rolling terrain north of Parleys and along the Wasatch Crest, are popular with runners. The Wasatch Mountains are the site of races which are attracting runners nationwide.

Mountain bicycles are a controversial innovation on the trails. Conflicts between ascending hikers and descending bicycles on a narrow trail and erosion damage caused by the continuous wheel track are major concerns. Bicycles are vehicles and are officially prohibited in Wilderness Areas even though they are muscle-powered.

Routes suitable for bicycles include the Big Water Trail, the Millcreek to Brighton ridge route, the ski area roads, and the old mining roads. Bicyclists should keep to established routes and avoid fragile meadows and alpine areas. They should also evaluate trail conditions and avoid riding steep hiking trails, especially when trails are wet and are easily eroded.

Organizations and Instruction

The best way to learn about the mountains and routes and about wilderness ethics is to hike with knowledgeable companions. The Wasatch Mountain

Club has introduced thousands of people to the local mountains since it was founded in the 1920's. There are currently over 1100 members ranging in age from teenagers to octogenarians. The outing schedule includes four to seven hikes per weekend during the April through September season. Most hikes are open to non-members and are an excellent way to meet people and see the mountains. The Salt Lake and Ogden chapters of the Sierra Club also schedule hikes which are open to non-members.

The University of Utah outdoor recreation program conducts a number of courses ranging from hiking to technical climbing. The schedule and fees are listed in the catalog published by the Division of Continuing Education.

The Wasatch has many seldom visited places which can be reached by unmaintained trails or by moderate off-trail hiking. This area is a short way from the Mill B North Fork Trail.

2

NATURAL HISTORY OF THE WASATCH

This chapter addresses some of the frequently asked questions about the rocks, trees, and wildflowers. Understanding the natural environment is fun, and hiking allows plenty of time for observing and learning. The Wasatch is a marvelous outdoor classroom—the complex geology and the numerous life zones provide unusual diversity in a small area. An extensive bibliography is included since there is insufficient space to provide all the geological and biological detail that can be found in more technical works.

THE LAND

The Wasatch Mountains form part of the Middle Rocky Mountain geographic province, an area characterized by recent uplift, complex folding of the rock strata, and rapid erosion into peaks and valleys. The Wasatch Range extends about 160 miles, from near the Idaho border south to Mount Nebo, where the Rocky Mountain Province, the Colorado Plateau Province, and the Basin and Range Province meet. The Provo and Weber River valleys separate the Wasatch from the Uinta Mountains, which continue the Rocky Mountain Province eastward into Wyoming and Colorado.

The Rocky Mountain Province ends abruptly at the Wasatch Fault. The Salt Lake Valley and all the land west to the Sierra Nevada Mountains are in the Basin and Range Province. This province results from widespread uplifting and stretching of a thin area of the earth's crust and is characterized by isolated mountain ranges about 20 miles apart, separated by flat, sediment-filled valleys.

The Wasatch Mountains were carved from an uplifted block which has been incised into peaks and canyons. The result is a spectacular west face with high summits overlooking the valley. Wasatch Front hikes, such as Lone Peak or Mount Olympus, are long and steep. Hikers soon notice that the rugged alpine ridges and summits around Little Cottonwood Canyon change to rolling, moderate-elevation terrain north of Parleys Canyon. This is a result of an overall folding of the rock layers which form the uplifted block.

The rocks in the south part of Salt Lake County are folded upward in an arch, and the Traverse Mountains south of Draper and the Alpine Ridge are actually an extension of the broad uplift which forms the crest of the Uintas. This upward folding has been magnified by the injection of molten rock from below which pushed up the older layers. This molten rock solidified deep below the surface and formed the granite found between the mouth of Little Cottonwood Canyon and Lone Peak. In the northern part of Salt Lake County, the layers are folded downward, with the low point of the fold following Emigration Canyon. The downward folding slowed the erosion, and the surface here is formed by relatively soft, younger sedimentary rocks which were completely removed from the highlands to the south.

Noted geologist Max Crittenden wrote: "The wealth and variety of geological features to be found in Salt Lake County are, for an area of its size, probably unexcelled anywhere in the world." How did all this form? What forces produced the bewildering array of steep cliffs, rounded ridges, tilted layers, igneous rocks and loose gravel that we hike over? How did the rich mineral deposits and alpine basins form?

A Billion Years On Mount Olympus

Let us imagine the summit of Mount Olympus, appropriately named for the home of the gods, as a stationary vantage point where we can sit and observe a billion-year drama. The modern geographical names and directions will serve as our landmarks as the continents drift, twist, sink, rise, and are eroded away again.

Our mountain spirit awakens on a vantage point high above a barren and lifeless land near the edge of a shallow sea containing algae and tiny soft-bodied creatures. The earth is already old, and the violent convulsions which formed the oldest rocks in the area are lost in the dimness of time. To the north, near Farmington Canyon, and south, near Deaf Smith-Little Willow Canyon, are rocks already a half-billion years old. These ancient sediments have already been injected with igneous intrusions, buried, heated, recrystallized, folded and exposed again.

For millions of years we watch sand and clay wash into shallow bays beneath us. The seabed gradually sinks until 16,000 feet of material has accumulated. This will become the rusty quartzites and red, greenish, and purple shales of the massive Big Cottonwood Formation, which lies between Tolcat Canyon and the crest of the Cottonwood Ridge. The process is interrupted by an extensive ice age, which carves smooth-bottomed basins deep into the Big

The Geology of Mount Superior Viewed From the Peruvian Gulch Trail.

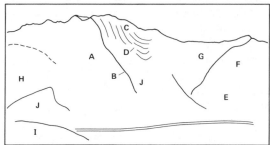

Key to Photo Above

A. *Big Cottonwood Formation — Precambrian Age.*
B. *Unconformal Contact — A period of erosion occurred between deposition of the two formations.*
C. *Mineral Fork Tillite — Precambrian Age.*
D. *Folding and tilting of originally horizontal sediments.*
E. *Ophir Shale and Maxfield Limestone — Cambrian Age.*
F. *Fitchville Formation, Gardison and Deseret Limestone — Mississippian Age.*
G. *At least five major faults are in this small area.*
H. *Quartz monzonite, commonly called granite. Molten rock was forced below the older formations during the Tertiary Period.*
I. *Geologically recent glacial deposits.*
J. *Talus deposits which are still accumulating.*

Cottonwood series of sediments and deposits moraines of boulders, cobbles, pebbles, sand and silt which will become the rusty-weathering Mineral Fork Tillite found between Snowbird and Hidden Falls.

The Cambrian Period begins with an explosion of marine life. Within a few million years, creatures with hard body parts appear and the seas teem with trilobites. The land continues to subside as sand and limey muds are deposited in shallow water and become the Tintic Quartzite, Ophir Shale and Maxfield Limestone which form the north flanks of Mount Olympus and the walls of Mill B North below Mount Raymond. At times the coastline is in Nevada, and at other times, the sea covers all of Utah. Most of the deposition is taking place in western Utah while the area to the east is part of a large, relatively stable continent. The equator extends northward through our skewed vantage point. The warm climate, the low-lying land, and the shallow seas are a preview of Florida and the Bahamas.

This pattern continues as vascular plants invade the land and as Cephalopods (ancestors of snails and squids) reach a peak and then are replaced by fish as the dominant large marine animals. The deposition continues to the west and north, but only occasional outcrops record this period in the central Wasatch.

Our overlook is now above shallow seas which flood the edge of the single world continent of Pangaea. Winged insects and small reptiles appear on land as limestone, occasionally mixed with sand, is being deposited in these shallow seas. These Carboniferous Age and Permian Age limestone layers will form colorful cliffs around Alta and much of Mount Raymond, Gobblers Knob, and lower Mill D Fork.

The Triassic Period begins with reptiles dominating the land while early mammals appear. Pangaea begins to separate, and an arc of islands rises to the west, separating the sea between the Wasatch and central Nevada from the open ocean. Periods of continental and marine deposition continue below us. These deposits will become the shales and limestones found between Millcreek and Parleys Canyons.

For 400 million years, a continent to the east has been eroding and depositing sand and mud into a shallow sea to the west. Now this pattern ends as the earth hinges along the approximate location of the Wasatch. New highlands rise to the west, forming a 3000-mile long mountain chain extending from southern Nevada to Alaska. The Wasatch is near the coast as the sea floods into eastern Utah and the massive sandstones of the redrock country begin to accumulate.

Great dinosaurs and early birds inhabit the coastal sand dunes and swamps during Utah's Jurassic period. The dunes which will form the Navajo sandstone cliffs of Capitol Reef, Zion National Park and the Escalante drainage in southern Utah are contemporaneous with the Nugget Sandstone found in the Wasatch around Parleys Canyon and Red Butte Canyon.

Flowering plants appear as the last dinosaurs vanish from the coastal plain below us. Conifers are abundant and deciduous trees such as maple and cottonwood are now present. High land resulting from a mountain building period (the Sevier Orogeny) lies west of the Wasatch, while in Summit County,

16

alluvial fans of sand and gravel are washing eastward into a shallow sea. This sea spreads across the flooded continental shelf and reaches all the way to Texas. Organic debris, the precursor of Utah's Cretaceous coal seams, is accumulating in coastal swamps from Coalville in Summit County south to the Kaiparowits Plateau.

The land to the west is slowly moving eastward in a series of great thrusts which will eventually narrow Utah by 40 miles. Around Mount Timpanogos, this leaves older (Carboniferous Age) rocks from the Oquirrhs on top of younger (Jurassic) rocks. These uplifted areas erode rapidly and, in Salt Lake County, the overthrust material is washed into the eastern sea.

The Tertiary Period opens with mammals taking over the land and a new series of tectonic forces shaping the continent. The Rocky Mountains begin to rise to the east, ending marine deposition in Utah. A north-to-south compression grips Utah; the Emigration Canyon area folds downward and the area to the south rises in a series of folds that extend east along the Uinta Mountains.

This period of violent movement causes igneous activity throughout the area. A series of hot spots form under Clayton Peak, under the Alta/Brighton area, under lower Little Cottonwood Canyon, and across the valley at Bingham Canyon. Molten magma is forced below the ancient rocks, pushing them upward. The silica-rich magma cools far below the surface forming the light-colored, large-crystalled rock commonly called granite. Geologists will call it quartz monzonite to distinguish it from other varieties of granite, based on grain size and composition. Volcanos in Wyoming fill the valleys of Summit County with ash and surround the Uintas with a broad piedmont. We are overlooking a spectacular place much like Yellowstone, the Hawaiian volcanos, and Mount St. Helens on a statewide scale.

The intense heating and the effects of hot pressurized water result in local concentrations of various minerals. Where the molten rock directly contacts limestone, carbon dioxide is released and minerals such as iron and copper sulfides are deposited. Different rates of crystallization result in concentration of certain minerals near the apex of the underground chamber. Hot water migrates through recently solidified rock, dissolving and redepositing quartz, forming veins of large crystals. At times, this hot water passes through areas of partially concentrated minerals and becomes mineralized. Then this solution follows fissures into the Maxfield Limestone and the Ophir Shale formation where the alkaline lime neutralizes the water, precipitating lead, zinc, copper, and silver. The result is a scattering of rich ore bodies ranging from narrow veins to massive deposits.

During all this time our vantage has been far above the low ridges, coastal swamps and shallow seas. Only 25 million years before our story ends, the Wasatch begins to rise. The whole of western North America is uplifted nearly a mile, and the Great Basin and Rocky Mountain provinces begin to take shape. In the Great Basin, the mountains rise, while the stretching causes the intervening blocks to drop. The Salt Lake Valley and other newly-formed valleys fill with thousands of feet of sediment washing from the rising mountains.

The vertical movement on the Wasatch Fault averages only six one-thousandths of an inch per year, but a 10,000- to 15,000-foot movement accumulates before humans arrive. Meanwhile, the Great Basin is stretching by 1/4 inch per year, eventually adding 30 to 60 miles to the distance between the Wasatch and California.

At the beginning of the Quaternary Period, *Homo habilis* is already walking upright and using tools in Africa, but the familiar peaks, ridges and canyons of the Wasatch are still in their infancy. As the climate turns colder and wetter, glaciers begin to scour the land shaping the cirques and canyons. For 700,000 years, glaciers advance and retreat as continental ice ages pass. In the final 90,000 years the fourth major ice age sculpts the Wasatch into recognizable form.

At the peak of this ice age, 33 glaciers are found in Salt Lake County, ranging from the short glaciers in Deaf Smith and Ferguson Canyons to the icefield which connects the Brighton and Albion Basin cirques across Catherine Pass. A 14-mile-long glacier winds down Little Cottonwood Canyon with six tributary glaciers joining from the south. Lower Little Cottonwood Canyon is carved into a characteristic "U"-shaped glacial valley with steep-walled cirques, steep sidewalls, and a fairly wide low-angled floor. Moraines are being deposited along the sides and ends of glaciers. As reinvigorated glaciers override older moraines, at least seven minor periods of advance and retreat leave evidence during this last ice age alone. At the mouth of Little Cottonwood Canyon, a huge tongue of ice reaches out from between the granite walls and crosses the gravel beach to end on the shore of Lake Bonneville. Silty-grey water pours from streams under the glacier and washes into the lake, giving it a distinct green tint.

Glaciers occupy the heads of all the north-facing side canyons of Big Cottonwood. Five major tributary glaciers from Brighton to Days Fork feed into the main valley glacier, which ends just below Cardiff Fork. A multi-branched glacier is scouring out the Lake Blanche basin and descends Mill B Fork but does not continue down the main canyon. Since glaciers do not reach the canyon mouth, lower Big Cottonwood Canyon retains a narrow stream-cut "V"-shape.

Short glaciers on the north flanks of Lone Peak, in Bells Canyon, and in Neffs Canyon are visible from the lake shore. From Mount Olympus, we cannot see the far shores of Lake Bonneville, which reaches from Idaho on the north, to Nevada on the west, and south nearly to Cedar City.

Volcanic activity in Idaho diverts the Bear River from the Snake River drainage into the Bonneville Basin, causing the lake level to rise. As the lake tops Red Rock Pass in southern Idaho, it carves an outlet to the Pacific, causing one of the greatest floods in the earth's history. The torrent pouring from Lake Bonneville cuts a gorge 300 feet deep and fills the Snake River Canyon at Twin Falls to overflowing. This is the lake's climax. The lake drops from the 5135-foot Bonneville level to the 4800-foot Provo level in only a few years, just as the climate changes and a warmer and drier period begins. The lake rises and falls several more times, but never again reaches its past glory.

Now, a new creature appears on the lake shore: a hunter and gatherer seeking the herds of mammoth, musk ox, deer and mountain sheep. These great herbivores will disappear from the mountains, unable to withstand the climatic change combined with hunting pressure from this new predator. In a geological instant this creature will fill the earth, altering the landscape with its works and interrupting processes which have been going on for billions of years. Yet, this new species brings a unique and precious trait, for it has the curiosity to inquire, the language to record, and the wisdom to preserve.

The Legacy Today

Geological history did not end with our arrival. The forces and processes continue—at times mocking our folly when we ignore the geological evidence. The climate continues to fluctuate. The glaciers are temporarily gone from the area, but elsewhere the process of advance and retreat continues. On nearby Mount Timpanogos, small moraines record the most recent minor advance which began 800 years ago and ended about 1850. The Great Salt Lake will continue to grow into an inland sea and shrink into a sun-baked mudflat as it has 85 times during the Quaternary Period.

The Wasatch continues to rise, and the Great Basin continues to stretch. Fault scarps are clearly visible in the gravel moraines between Little Cottonwood and Bells Canyons recording an earthquake scarcely more than a century old. Avalanches, landslides, and rockfall onto trails and highways all serve to remind us that the canyons are still cutting into the uplifted block. Likewise, the unstable nature of the unconsolidated foothill soils makes some areas permanently unsuited for development. In August of 1945, a cloudburst caused a major landslide in Perrys Hollow which washed debris across 11th Avenue and on into the cemetery. Subdivisions climb farther up the foothills than they did 40 years ago, increasing the risk of major damage.

The Wasatch geology presents us with hazards but also provides unparalleled opportunities. The scenic beauty of the Wasatch is unsurpassed for a location adjacent to a major city. The abrupt, mile-high uplift is an efficient water collector for the thirsty city. The foothills provide a bountiful supply of sand, gravel, lime, and quarried stone for constructing a technological civilization. In the last century the mountains yielded fortunes in silver and base metals. Today, recreation and the tourist industry are not only major employers, but are also a significant factor in the quality of life available to persons living in Utah.

Geologic Period Or Epoch	Million Years Before Present	Wasatch Geological Features	Local Conditions Events	Evolutionary, Global and Regional Events
Early Precambrian	?? to 1400	Farmington Canyon Complex	Mutiple episodes of igneous activity and mountain building.	
Late Precambrian	1100 to 700	Big Cottonwood Formation, Mutual Formation, and Mineral Fork Tillite. Covers most of area between north face of Mt Olympus & the Twin Peaks – Mt Superior ridge.	Continent to the southeast. Deposition of shallow water marine and glacial sediments which were later meta-morphosed and folded.	Barren land. Bacteria & algae in the seas.
Cambrian	600 to 500	Tintic Quartzite, Maxfield Limestone, and Ophir Formation. Found in narrow strip between Neffs Canyon & Cardiff Fork.	Beginning of long period of shallow water marine deposi-tion in a slowly sinking basin to the west.	Explosion of marine life. Sponges, jellyfish and trilobites dominate.
Ordovician Silurian Devonian	500 to 360	Deposits from this period are well represented near Logan and in West Desert but are largely removed from the Wasatch.	Salt Lake Area is a peninsula of uplifted land with sea to north and south.	Cephalopods. First vascular land plants. Fish dominate sea. Early amphibians and giant ferns on land.
Carboniferous Mississippian Pennsylvanian	360 to 280	Colorful limestone outcrops near Cardiff Fork, Alta & in American Fork Canyon. Includes the black & white cliff north of Snowbird. Weber Quartzite; covers much of south side of Millcreek, Mt. Raymond & Gobblers Knob.	Shallow seas cover all of Utah.	Warm climate, lush forests which later form coal in Eastern states. Winged insects and first reptiles appear. Uplift begins in Colorado and spreads into eastern Utah.
Permian	280 to 240	Park City Formation found low in Millcreek Cyn from Rattle-snake Gulch to Big Water Gulch. Also in Butler Fork and Mill A.	Earth hinges along the Wa-satch line. Continent to east sinks and land rises in west.	Conifers spread, trilobites disappear. All land joined in continent of Pangaea.
Triassic	240 to 200	Woodside, Thayne, and Ankareh Formations. Shales & limestones found along the north side of Millcreek.	Marine deposition ends in Wasatch.	Reptiles dominate land. First mammals appear. Pangaea splits.
Jurassic	190 to 140	Nugget Sandstone, Twin Creek Limestone – Continental de-posits found between Millcreek and Emigration Canyons.	Dune fields on a coastal plain with sea to north.	Great dinosaurs & early birds. Widening of Atlantic Ocean. Massive sandstones being deposited in shallow seas in southeastern Utah.

Geological Period Or Epoch	Million Years Before Present	Wasatch Geological Features	Local Conditions Events	Evolutionary, Global and Regional Events
Cretaceous	136 to 66	Older rocks (Oquirrh Formation) above younger strata on Mt. Timpanogos. Overthrust material eroded from Salt Lake County area.	East-West compression thrusting rocks from the west on top of the Wasatch.	Dinosaurs vanish. Birds spread. Flowering plants appear. Formation of a mountainous highland to the west and shallow sea to the east. Sevier Orogeny
		Conglomerate sediments found in Summit County.	Coastal plain at foot of the Sevier Mountains.	
Tertiary	65 to 1.8			Rocky Mountains begin to form. Mammals spread. North America and Europe separate.
Paleocene	65 to 58	Eastward trending folds lowering Emigration and Parleys area and raising land to the south near Little Cottonwood.	Compression in North-South direction. Uplift of Uinta Mountains.	
Eocene	58 to 37			
Oligocene	37 to 24	Clayton Peak, Alta, Little Cottonwood & Bingham stocks.	Intrusion of molten rock which cooled beneath the surface, forming granite.	Similar intrusions forming LaSal, Henry and Abajo Mountains.
Miocene	24 to 5	Wasatch Mountains Basin & Range terrain to the west.	Uplift begins along Wasatch Fault.	Great Basin begins to stretch resulting in block faulting. Basin and range pattern forms. Valleys fill with sediments.
Pliocene	5 to 1.8			
Quaternary	1.6 to Present			Climatic change brings ice ages.
Pleistocene	1.6 to 0.01	The familiar canyons, cirques and foothill benches form.	Glaciers in upper canyons. Lake Bonneville fills the valley.	Humans migrate from Central Africa and reach Europe and Asia.
Holocene	Last 10000 years.	Forests reclaim the cirques, scoured canyons, and glacial moraines. Earthquakes slice through recent deposits.	Humans arrive in the Wasatch.	
	Last 100 years.	Roads, mines, ski lifts and deforestation.	Civilization arrives.	

Note: This chart is highly simplified and utility for an amateur was favored over technical accuracy. Readers wishing a more complete presentation are encouraged to consult the references found in the bibliography.

TREES AND WILDFLOWERS

Adapted from the forthcoming *Wildflowers of the Wasatch* by Mike Treshow

Hikers travel through an environment shaped by the terrain and the vegetative cover. Geologic history has created the terrain. Contemporary patterns of sun, rain, wind, and soil along with human activities such as logging, ski area development, and fire suppression determine the vegetation found along the trails. Learning about the trees and other plants adds to hiking enjoyment and helps in understanding the complex ecological relationships which exist in natural places. Wildflowers play vital ecological roles and are a delight for hikers. A casual glance at a summer hillside reveals a carpet of color, but the beauty is even greater when you see and recognize the individual flowers.

Plant Associations

The concept of "plant associations" or "plant communities" is very useful in understanding what you see along a trail. Each type of plant needs specific conditions of temperature, moisture, soil, and exposure to the sun for best growth. Because these conditions vary with elevation, the plant life at any given elevation will be much the same from one site to another. The resulting plant communities are named for the most prominent plants in any given area.

The dominant plants form the habitat for the other plants, as well as for birds, mammals, and insects. The plant associations also determine the "feel" of a trail. Walking an open, sun-baked ridge with only a few mountain mahogany trees is totally different from hiking a stream-bottom willow thicket with birch and cottonwood overhead.

Starting in the lower foothills at 5000 to 6000 feet the "grasslands" association is most prominent. This is also known as the plains or prairie zone. This zone is dominated by various grasses with some sage and other species present. In April and May, numerous wildflowers bloom here, including our State flower, the mariposa or sego lily. But these areas soon dry out, and by the end of June they have turned brown and the plants now wait for the next winter's moisture to resume their growth.

The "mountain brush" or chapparal association, dominated by Gambel oak, appears at about 5500 feet and extends 1000 to 2000 feet higher. We also find a few other woody shrubs or trees including mountain mahogany, with its grey bark and small, dark green leaves, and junipers. Big tooth maple appears in shady or moist sites, mostly along streams. The draws and ravines found here lend to varied habitats that support a rich diversity of wildflowers.

Passing through the mountain brush community, more and more fir trees and aspen begin to appear, first in ravines and on north-facing slopes, and finally providing a full cover of trees at 6500 to 7000 feet. The conifers and aspen can occur as much as 1500 to 2000 feet lower in elevation on moist north-facing slopes than on more arid south-facing slopes. This "needle-leaf" community, characterizing the montane zone, is typically represented by Douglas fir, white fir, and blue spruce. Areas of deciduous forest, dominated by the aspen association, occupy the moister sites. Beneath the shaded canopy, we find several other woody plants such as the low growing mountain lover, currants, elderberry, and mountain ash. Mountain lilac, characterized by thick evergreen leaves, grows in more open areas while along streams we find big tooth maple, river birch, alder, and dogwood with its distinctive red bark.

The species of fir and spruce change at roughly 8000 feet but the forest looks much the same. Now we have Engelmann spruce and subalpine fir, which form the principal components of the subalpine zone. Aspen may continue to appear near the streams, which are often bordered by flowering meadows. By the time we reach 9000 to 9500 feet, again depending largely on the exposure, the trees become less frequent, the forest opens up, and we begin to leave the subalpine community. Here we find shrubby species and an occasional subalpine fir, with limber pine on the harshest sites of rocky outcrops.

We must get above 10,000 feet before all the trees have disappeared and we have entered the distinct Wasatch alpine zone or community. Here we find mostly short grasslands and rock fields, intermixed with patches of sedge in the marshy spots, and gardens of wildflowers on the drier sites. The flowers are often short-stemmed and form a cushion or carpet. At the very highest elevations in the Wasatch, near the summits of such peaks as the Twins or Lone Peak, we find mostly the rich flora of lichens covering the otherwise bare rock, and an occasional sprig of grass and small perennial plants between the rocks.

Plant Identification

The local flora is easy and fun to recognize. With only a little background, you will be able to identify most of the trees and many of the wildflowers along the Wasatch trails.

Space does not permit providing adequate information for identifying individual species. Excellent regional field guides ranging from colorful picture books to scholarly tomes are listed in the bibliography. The minimum essential book for serious plant identification is Anderson and Holmgren, *Mountain Plants of the Northeast Wasatch,* which is inexpensive and easy to follow, and uses well-written text and line drawings to describe all the common plants in the area.

A few hints will help you get started in plant identification. Learning the common trees is the best way to get started. This will enable you to recognize the major plant associations on sight and will also help you understand the effects of slope direction, angle, soil conditions, and other factors on the distribution of species. Also, learning the trees is relatively easy, since there are few species within the limited geographical area of the Wasatch. For example, only one pine, one oak and two maples are common in the Wasatch. Since the number of species is so limited, trees can be identified by any of several characteristics such as the leaf, the bark texture or the overall shape.

The small herbaceous plants can occasionally be identified by secondary characteristics, but the best approach is to identify them by the flowering parts. These parts change more slowly than characteristics such as leaf shape, color, and size which can vary widely even within a species. The flower is the key to recognizing the deeper evolutionary relationships of the plant families. Learning to recognize the major wildflower families rather than memorizing individual species organizes your growing knowledge, makes using the technical books much easier, and enables you to make a partial identification with difficult specimens. Identify only a few (four to six) species on a single hike, then review them by looking for additional specimens along the trail.

Wildflowers can be studied throughout the hiking season. Plants found at lower elevations early in the spring often make a later appearance higher up. Once you become familiar with a plant, say in the grasslands zone, you will recognize it a month or two later as it comes into bloom along a trail in the fir forest.

Wildflowers can be enjoyed throughout the hiking season.

Vegetation Zones of Wasatch Trails

The predominant zones and the best season for wildflowers for some of the more popular trails can be categorized as follows:

Trails mostly in the grassland and mountain brush zones. Best wildflower season: April or May.

Mount Olympus to Stream	Little Mountain
Ensign Peak	Big Beacon
Little Black Mountain	Grandeur from West

Trails mostly in the mountain brush and conifer or montane zone. Best wildflower season: June.

Grandeur from Church Fork	Mule Hollow
Thayne Canyon	Ferguson Canyon
Terraces to Elbow Fork	Lone Peak from Corner Canyon
Mount Olympus	Bowman Fork

Trails beginning in the montane zone and climbing into the subalpine zone. Best wildflower season: June and July.

Mill B North Fork	Butler Fork
Mineral Fork	Cardiff Fork
Mill D North Fork	Box Elder Peak
Lake Blanche	Broads Fork

Trails predominantly subalpine and leading to the alpine zone. Best wildflower season: July and August.

Brighton –Twin Lakes	Lake Catherine
White Pine	Red Pine
Peruvian Gulch	Collins Gulch
Secret Lake (Albion Basin)	Lone Peak Cirque

Wildlife in the Wasatch

The land and the ecological relationships in the area have been drastically altered by human activity — often in ways not noticeable to the casual forest visitor. Loss of winter range to foothills urbanization limits the population of deer. The elk heard is also sensitive to human disturbance, both on their winter range and in their spring calving areas. Large carnivores such as bear, lynx, bobcat, and cougar are rare due to disturbance and predator control efforts. Highways impair migration routes, destroy and alter streams, and result in road kills.

LEGEND

Glacial drift of
later epoch

Former névé fields

Glacial drift of
earlier epoch

Glacial striae

Morainic ridges

Note:
Catchment basins 1 to 63
inclusive are referred to by
number in the text.

PORTION OF SALT LAKE QUADRANGLE, UTAH
Showing distribution of glacial formations

Scale 1:250000

Triangulation and topography
by the King and Power surveys

Rollin D Salisbury, Geologist in charge
Glacial geology by Wallace W. Atwood

Map from Wallace W. Atwood, Glaciation of the Uinta and Wasatch Mountains, 1909. Showing both the extent
of Pleistocene glaciation and the extent of human settlement at the beginning of the century.

HISTORY AND ENVIRONMENTAL PROTECTION

When the pioneers arrived in Utah, the canyons offered a wealth of water, minerals, timber, wildlife, grazing and open space. Since then, our technology has stripped the canyons of old-growth timber, depleted the mineral deposits, and built dams, roads, cabins, condominiums and ski lifts. The Wasatch, like all natural places, is finite and fragile, yet the demands of the adjacent urban area are enormous and growing. The opposing forces of development and conservation have shaped the Wasatch for 140 years. The foresight of early conservationists created the forest preserves which evolved into the National Forests and Wilderness Areas of today. For persons who know and love the Wasatch, the challenge of the next century will be to manage this unique resource wisely by setting priorities and resolving use conflicts.

HUMAN HISTORY AND THE RESULTS

Only wildlife witnessed the highest level of Lake Bonneville lapping the flanks of the mountains while glaciers pushed from the canyons onto the beaches. The earliest evidence of humans in northern Utah is the 11,000-year-old debris in Danger Cave near Wendover. Only a few local sites survive from the Fremont culture which flourished in Utah from 400 A.D. to about 1300. From

1300 until the arrival of the mountain men and government explorers in the early 1800's, the Wasatch was a sparsely populated area between the Shoshone, Ute, and Goshute lands.

The Mormon pioneers arrived in July, 1847, and immediately began using the water and timber to build Zion. They also introduced a conservation ethic and publicly controlled water, timber, and grazing ground for the good of the community. Communal ownership was followed by *privatization* and increased exploitation. The main influences on the mountains during the 1800's were grazing, hunting, lumber cutting, mining, and development of transportation routes.

Grazing had an amplified effect on the mountains since Utah has a very limited supply of upland summer range compared to the greater supply of winter range in the desert. Wildlife was overexploited for meat and fur and to reduce depredation of livestock and crops. The numbers of large mammals were substantially reduced, and some species such as Rocky Mountain bighorn sheep, elk, and grizzly bear ceased to inhabit the area.

Lumbering, which began at the mouth of City Creek, had reached all the way to Tanners Flat in Little Cottonwood Canyon by 1851. About 50 sawmills operated in the canyons adjacent to Salt Lake City at various times leaving behind names such as Alexander Basin and Mill A Gulch. Mining brought increased demand for large timbers, and the Alta and Brighton areas were denuded. By 1900 the timber near the Wasatch Front had run out and lumber began to arrive by railroad.

Mining in Utah began in Bingham Canyon in September, 1863, and the Wasatch Mining District was organized the next year. The greatest production occurred between 1870 and 1880, followed by a second maximum between 1901 and 1910. Mining claims quickly covered the mineralized parts of the Wasatch, resulting in today's land ownership pattern in the canyons. The overlapping claim locations were defined by trees and piles of rock, and today many of the boundaries between private and Forest Service lands are still not surveyed.

Many trails began as wagon roads that were carved up the side canyons to reach mine sites. Some logging roads were also constructed, but most trees were horse-skidded to the mills in winter. A narrow-gauge railroad, with snow-sheds across avalanche paths, reached Alta in the early 1870's. Horses pulled the empty ore cars up the tracks, and descent was by gravity with a brakeman attempting to control the cars. About 1915, passengers were transported up the canyon in a GMC truck mounted on railroad car wheels, a precursor of today's transit proposals. The decline of mining made the railroad obsolete, and the tracks were removed from Little Cottonwood in 1935.

Beginnings of Preservation

Throughout the west, the mountains were unable to withstand the grazing, logging and mining. Concern about hillside erosion and decreasing water quality led to public concern, restrictions on grazing of watersheds, and the beginning of protection for public lands.

As Chief Grazing Officer in the Department of Interior, Albert F. Potter visited the Wasatch during the summer of 1902 while conducting a personal survey of the condition of forest lands. His diary records the deforestation around Brighton: "It would be difficult to find a seedling big enough to make a club to kill a snake." Regarding grazing, he wrote, "The transient herd cutting feed and mountain cover to ribbons as it rushed the season to beat some other tramp to a bit of grass was a common phenomenon."

The contrasting conservation attitudes which we see today between the urbanized Wasatch Front and the sparsely populated counties were already evident. Cache Valley welcomed Potter's survey and requested that a forest preserve be quickly established. Meanwhile, Beaver County, which had experienced neither a timber shortage nor watershed damage, was opposed to the entire concept of conservation. At the April, 1902 General Conference, the Mormon Church voted to support federal withdrawal of public lands for watershed protection.

In 1891 Congress provided for forest reserves, and in 1897 a presidential order designated part of the Uinta Mountains as Utah's first reserve. By the end of 1902, 4 million acres of additional forest reserves, including much of the Wasatch, had been established in Utah. In 1905, the forests were transferred from the Interior Department to the new Forest Service within the Agriculture Department.

Bringing herd sizes in line with the summer range capacity was the Forest Service's initial priority. The 1930's brought new programs including the Soil Conservation Service and the Civilian Conservation Corps. The terraces constructed on local peaks to stabilize and revegetate overgrazed slopes and the realigned automobile roads up the canyons are a result of these programs. The Forest Service eventually became aware of the recreational potential of the mountains, and by 1935 the agency was promoting ski development at Brighton.

Conservation efforts were changing ownership of the Wasatch Mountains. Salt Lake City purchased much private land, including numerous sections of railroad land, for watershed protection. In 1937, George Watson sold 80 mining claims to the Forest Service for $1 to help create the Alta ski area. In the early 1970's the Forest Service acquired surface rights to 2500 acres of patented mining claims that covered most of the Brighton basin using $2 million from the Land and Water Conservation Fund. After the mid-1970's, the acquisition of critical lands slowed drastically due to political shifts in Washington which dried up funding.

CONTEMPORARY ISSUES

The legacy of these conservation efforts is a mountain resource which provides high-quality water, hiking, mountaineering, world-class skiing, and three superb Wilderness Areas overlooking an urban area. Now, nearly a million people live within 20 miles of the mountain area covered by this book. The exploding population requires more water, housing, transportation, and recreation. Watershed protection, control of canyon development, preservation of access to public lands, and wilderness protection are a few of the issues facing the Wasatch.

Water and Recreation Development

Since pioneer times watershed protection has been emphasized, and Salt Lake now has excellent drinking water. The economic benefits of a nearby watershed far outweigh timber, grazing, minerals, or even skiing. The stream quality ranges from pristine in Red Butte Canyon, to acceptable in Big and Little Cottonwood Canyons, to irrigation quality in Millcreek, to heavily polluted in Emigration Canyon.

Increased human activity on a watershed often results in lower quality water. Coliform bacteria count is a measure of direct fouling with human waste. The runoff from roads and parking areas contains salt and oil products. Soil erosion resulting from construction, devegetation, or even from trail erosion causes both silt and bacterial contamination of the streams. Pets and domestic animals add to the burden.

Fortunately human impacts can be mitigated. Healthy ecosystems produce high quality runoff as natural processes decompose wastes and riparian zones act as filters for silt and other pollutants. Proper sanitation practices by backcountry users and appropriate technology in developed areas can decrease the contamination resulting from a given level of use.

Today, sewage disposal in Emigration Canyon is based on holding vaults, but spills occur when tanks are pumped out and leaks contaminate the streams. The new Big Cottonwood sewer will improve water quality but will also open the door to increased development and more traffic.

Early water developments diverted streams after they left the mountains, but dams to capture the runoff and conduits to convey water to the city were soon built farther up the canyons. Today, in-stream flow is a major issue. The lower sections of Big Cottonwood and Little Cottonwood creeks are often dry in late summer because all the water disappears into pipelines. Proposals are still on the drawing board for diverting water from Lambs Canyon and upper Millcreek into the new Little Dell Reservoir. The energy crunch of a few years back brought a renewed interest in hydropower, and serious proposals were made for dams in sensitive locations such as City Creek Canyon and at Tanners Flat in Little Cottonwood.

Protecting the riparian habitat in the local canyons while providing water to the city requires balancing objectives. Well-placed small dams reduce the peak runoff and extend it into the summer. Also, depending on local water resources is less costly and damaging than importing water from the Uintas.

Access To Public Lands

Large areas, in both the foothills and in the upper canyons, have historically been reached by routes that cross a strip of private land between the public road and the public land. Generally landowners have not objected to persons crossing their land, so there has been little concern about whether these commonly used routes had a legally recorded right-of-way. However, sale of land to a developer or to an owner who wants privacy can result in challenges to the historical use of a route.

The years between the first and second editions of this guidebook brought repeated challenges to trail access along the foothills, but they also brought the first signs of real progress. Landowners have put up fences and posted signs on traditional access routes to Mount Olympus, Hounds Tooth, Deaf Smith Canyon, and Bells Canyon. The Corner Canyon road was closed at the Draper end and washed out at the Alpine end. New foothill developments have been proposed continuing the irreversible loss of open space, recreational opportunities, and winter wildlife habitat.

On a positive note, the first section of the Bonneville Shoreline Trail is now in place and the University of Utah's master plan includes this recreational corridor. The Bonneville Shoreline Trail provides access to four foothill trails listed in this book and extension of the trail to the north and south will ensure access to many more. The long-simmering debate over the Mount Olympus trail right-of-way appears to be resolved. Public agencies such as the Forest Service, Salt Lake City, Salt Lake County, and Sandy City all recognize foothill access as a planning issue. Agencies are including designated trail right-of-ways as part of new subdivision approvals. There is a vision of a county-wide network of urban trails and bike paths linking the Jordan River with the mountains.

The most effective way to protect historic access routes is for trail users to work through the planning and zoning process. In principle, asking a developer to grant an easement for a trailhead is no different than requiring that the subdivision leave room for a future street (a fairly routine requirement). The local planning departments support protecting access.

Trailhead protection requires strong public support. Hikers must express this support to elected and administrative officials at both the Federal (congressional delegation and Forest Service) and local levels (Salt Lake and Utah Counties, Salt Lake City, Sandy City, Draper, and Alpine) levels.

Good previous relations between recreational users and adjacent landowners will be an advantage when negotiating trailheads. Parking congestion, noise, litter, and travel off of the designated trail are typical conflicts which we should all strive to prevent.

Wilderness Protection

Wilderness represents many things: scenic natural vistas, intact ecosystems with abundant wildlife, pure water, and unconfined recreational opportunities; or, locked-up resources, a threat to one's livelihood, and a restriction against taking a motorcycle up every hill it can climb. To some, wilderness means any undeveloped land, and to others it means only the most isolated and remote places on earth. With a capital "W" it usually refers to a designated Wilderness Area with protection guaranteed by an act of Congress. The Wilderness Act of 1964 created the Federal Wilderness Preservation System and serves as the basis for the subsequent laws which designate specific areas.

Wilderness Areas were defined as " . . . an area where the earth and its community of life are untrammeled by man, where man himself is a visitor who does not remain." The Wilderness Act further defined wilderness as an area at least 5000 acres in size which has outstanding opportunities for solitude or for primitive and unconfined recreation. The act directed that these areas are to be managed for "the public purposes of recreational, scenic, scientific, educational, conservation, and historical use."

Wilderness areas are protected by prohibiting roads and structures, and by restricting motorized transportation within the area to emergencies and similar essential uses. Contrary to popular misconceptions, grazing and hunting are identified as allowable uses of Wilderness. Exceptions also exist for water projects, mining claims, oil leases, and private inholdings which predate the wilderness designation.

Wilderness is not an exclusive playground for elite backpackers. Much Wilderness is readily accessible to anyone willing to walk. This book includes many hikes into Wilderness Areas which require less than two hours round-trip.

Wilderness is used by and is valuable to everyone — including persons who never enter a Wilderness. First, there is the emotional and intellectual satisfaction of knowing that wild places exist and are preserved for future generations. Wilderness Areas are ecological reservoirs where species that are intolerant of human disturbance can thrive. Wilderness users include anyone who looks up from the road and watches a soaring eagle or sees mountain goats perched on a cliff. Actually, everyone along the Wasatch Front who looks up at Lone Peak,

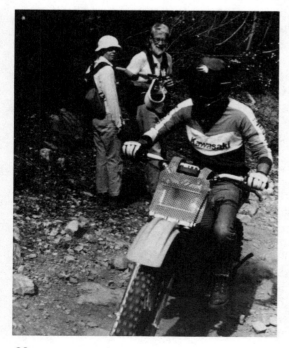

Conflict between different groups of recreational users is one of the major issues in the Wasatch.

Twin Peaks, or Mount Olympus and enjoys the view of unscarred land is a Wilderness user.

There is also the global perspective. The health of our planet depends on natural systems, especially the tropical rain forests, for genetic diversity, winter habitat for migratory species, and climate regulation. How can we justly encourage poor, overpopulated nations to preserve their rain forests if we, a rich nation, do not set an example by preserving our own wild places? Wilderness designation is a way of saying that we value preserving the earth more than we value a few more barrels of oil or truckloads of lumber.

Utah's Wilderness Areas — Now and Tomorrow

After a long battle by local conservationists, the 30,000-acre Lone Peak Wilderness was included in the Endangered American Wilderness Act of 1977 and became Utah's first Wilderness. An extensive public relations campaign was required to educate the public and local officials about the concept of wilderness and its compatibility with other land uses such as watershed.

Wilderness preservation is a slow process. The Wilderness Act of 1964 required an inventory of all roadless areas on National Forest Lands and a report to the President on their suitability for designation as Wilderness. The inventory process in Utah began in 1971 and climaxed with the Utah Wilderness Act of 1984 which designated 12 Forest Service Wilderness Areas statewide. The Alexander Basin controversy illustrates how complex wilderness issues can become due to differing priorities and objectives.

Protection for Alexander Basin, on the magnificent north side of Gobblers Knob, was a high priority throughout the inventory and review process. But this area is also coveted by helicopter skiers. To obtain the wilderness designation, many groups and individuals were willing to accept a special clause which would have allowed continued helicopter skiing "subject to Forest Service regulation," believing that any protection was better than none and that the helicopter issue could be resolved later through regulation. Others, concerned about national priorities, feared that this non-conforming use would set a bad precedent for future wilderness legislation. The issue split the local environmental groups when a united effort was needed. The last days of the legislative process were hectic and the final bill was a compromise which resulted in the peculiar shape of the Mount Olympus Wilderness boundary. The north-facing bowls were excluded and a few more acres around Dog Lake were added in exchange. Which is more important — protection or precedent?

Wilderness battles are not over. There are still roadless forest areas which do not have the protection they deserve. Locally, these include White Pine Canyon, Alexander Basin and the area east toward Desolation Lake, and the area around Mount Aire. Many more such areas exist statewide.

Planning and Development

The Forest Service responds to numerous influences including political decisions in Washington, executive actions, technical input from professional staffers, and comments from local agencies and forest users. Citizen input is vital throughout this process.

These influences become codified in laws, in Forest Service regulations, and in management plans. The Forest Plans allocate lands for various uses (developed recreation, timber harvest, primitive areas, etc.) and set specific management objectives for a 10- to 15-year period. The plan for the Salt Lake Ranger District was issued in 1979, and the plan for the entire Wasatch-Cache National Forest was issued in 1984. Generally, both plans were sensitive to environmental protection issues and tried to balance the competing interests of various users. Continued citizen monitoring and input are needed since the plan only sets goals, and many specific actions, such as the location of an access road or the extent of trail reconstruction, need to be worked out year by year.

The primary responsibility over private lands in the canyon is with the county commission acting through the planning and zoning function. When the county commission candidates were asked, at a 1986 pre-election meeting, what their vision was for the canyons in twenty years, each answered with the idea that they wanted to see the canyons remain as they are. Achieving this vision will be difficult due to legal, environmental, economic, and social issues. Private land-owners will want to sell and develop their lands and ski resorts want to expand. Many valid mining claims remain, including several within the Wilderness Areas. Current "assessment work" has limited impact on the environment but increasing metal prices may someday make full-scale mining operations feasible.

There are also conflicts between various recreational users. Each expansion request by a ski area raises the question of how to allocate land between developed and dispersed recreation. Since nearly all of the *gentle* terrain in the canyons is already developed, the issue is more than one of relative acreage. Ski development also affects hikers, since ski roads, ski lifts and ski run clearing drastically alter the character of an area in summer.

Land exchanges between public and private owners and between the Forest Service and Salt Lake City will alter the management of the canyons. The Forest Service and Salt Lake City are making a change to eliminate the "checkerboard" pattern north of Parleys Canyon. The land exchange which resulted in the Forest Service acquiring the south side of lower Little Cottonwood Canyon is a model for future conflict resolution. Cooperation between the Whitmore estate, which had owned the land for many years; the Trust for Public Land, a private conservation organization skilled in negotiating land transfers; Salt Lake City, which provided temporary financing; and the Forest Service, which sold several other parcels to pay for the land, finally preserved these pinnacles and but-tresses.

Wild and Natural Places Tomorrow

Can wilderness coexist with urban areas? Trampling of vegetation is caus-ing severe erosion on popular trails and at heavily used developed forest sites. Many do not yet understand the devastation caused by mountain bikes and

ATVs climbing hills and consider limiting travel to designated routes to be an infringement on their freedom. A new appreciation and ecological conscious- ness must be developed. Our local challenge of preserving our mountains is truly an experiment in low-impact living on Earth which will have to be repeated elsewhere many times if future generations are to appreciate healthy ecosys- tems and the freedom of natural places.

Public education and involvement are essential if natural areas are to be preserved. If people know the area only from a distance and do not understand it at close range, the protection effort will have no support. Getting people walking the Wasatch trails is one step in building a constituency for preserva- tion. Protection of the mountains requires letters to agencies and to elected officials to reinforce the commitment to preservation. Sensitive ecosystems cannot be saved solely through political action. Much more remains to be done. Concerned individuals can become involved in many ways ranging from volun- teer work on trail clearing projects to active membership in several local conservation and environmental organizations.

36

4

TRAILS AND TRAILHEADS

When I visit an unfamiliar mountain range, I buy the maps and guidebooks and start thumbing through descriptions of challenging trails and interesting destinations. But choosing is difficult. There are many routes and so little time. Worse, the descriptions are confusing to someone who is unfamiliar with the area and who must sift through the entire book looking for routes appropriate for the time available and desired level of difficulty. When I listen to hikers talking to a ranger at a visitor center, the second question always seems to be, "What do *you* recommend?"

This chapter sorts through the descriptions and recommends hikes by length, level of difficulty, and the best season. For beginning hikers and for newcomers to the area, there are trails for the first few hikes. For those who are busy, there are many worthwhile hikes that require 3 hours or less round-trip from the car. Experienced hikers will find new areas to explore, including rarely visited summits and interesting bushwhacks.

SHORT HIKES AND EASY HIKES

Beginner Hikes

All of these hikes are relatively short and ascend gradually on a maintained trail. The trails are well marked and easy to follow. In addition, the hikes marked "Family" have plenty of interesting features along the way, have no cliffs or dangerous stream crossings, and are recommended for families hiking with small children. Of course, any adults who are hiking with children should be sufficiently experienced to recognize hazards and to evaluate trail and weather conditions.

BEGINNER HIKES		Trail
Desolation Trail to the Salt Lake Overlook		M-04
Big Water Trail to Mill D Pass & Dog Lake		M-16
Elbow Fork to Terrace Picnic Area		M-11
Elbow Fork to Lambs Canyon	(Family)	M-10
Lake Mary or Dog Lake from Brighton	(Family)	B-24
Twin Lakes from Brighton	(Family)	B-22
White Pine Trail to the canyon overlook	(Family)	L-05
Secret Lake from Albion Basin	(Family)	L-13

No Routefinding Problems

Trail maintenance has improved in recent years, but some Wasatch trails are still full of false branches and overgrown sections where the trail nearly disappears. These trails are intimidating until you develop your routefinding skill. If you want a longer hike than the beginner trails but prefer trails that are easy to follow, try these roads. Vehicles are restricted so walking is pleasant.

HIKE	Trail
Lower City Creek (Road along stream)	CC-2
Mineral Fork (Abandoned mining road)	B-06
White Pine Trail to lake (Dam access road)	L-05
Collins Gulch to Germania Pass (Ski area road)	L-11

Short Hikes — Requiring Less Than Three Hours.

One of the greatest benefits of living in Salt Lake is the wealth of accessible short hikes. You can go hiking after work on summer afternoons, or you can go hiking on a Saturday morning and be home before lunch. All the routes listed here are short enough that an average hiker can do the round trip in one to three hours. Many of these short hikes follow a longer trail only as far as a meadow, an overlook, or other feature that makes a logical destination. There are enough suggestions for one hike per week from May through September.

SHORT HIKES	Miles Round Trip	Feet Elev. Gain	Standard Time Round Trip	Trail
FOOTHILLS				
City Creek North Rim	2	500	1h 25m	CC-1
Mount Van Cott	2	1148	1h 50m	F-04
Avenues Twin Peaks	1 to 2	1100	1h 55m	F-01
Olympus to Tolcat stream crossing	3	1100	2h 20m	WF-2

SHORT HIKES	Miles Round Trip	Feet Elev. Gain	Standard Time Round Trip	Trail
MILLCREEK				
Elbow Fork to Terrace (one-way)	1-3/4	-430	1h	M-11
Pipeline Trail (one-way)	2	630	1h 20m	M-07
Church Fork to start of switchbacks	2	880	1h 40m	M-01
Elbow Fork to Mt. Aire Pass	2	1170	1h 50m	M-09
Bowman Trail to White Fir Pass	3	1240	2h 30m	M-06
Elbow Fork to Lambs Pass	3	1490	2h 40m	M-10
Alexander Basin	3	1640	2h 50m	M-12
Desolation to Salt Lake Overlook	4	1300	2h 50m	M-04
BIG COTTONWOOD				
Storm Mountain — Stairs Gulch	1/2	300	30m	B-01
Mineral Fork to canyon overlook	1-1/2	450	1h 5m	B-06
Brighton Lake Mary	2	760	1h 35m	B-24
Lake Solitude from Brighton	3	300	1h 45m	B-21
Mill B North to overlook	2-1/4	840	1h 45	B-05
Twin Lakes Dam	2-1/2	710	1h 50m	B-22
Mill D Dog Lake	3	1010	2h 20m	B-09
Broads Fork to bridge	1-1/4	1300	2h 20m	B-03
Greens Basin	3-1/4	1050	2h 30m	B-14
Mule Hollow to mine	2-3/4	1400	2h 30m	B-02
Lake Blanche Trail to meadow	3	1600	2h 45	B-04
Lake Catherine	4	1200	2h 55m	B-24
Circle-All Peak	3-1/2	1587	3h	B-08
LITTLE COTTONWOOD				
Secret Lake from Albion	1-1/2	420	1h 5m	L-13
White Pine to Overlook	2-1/2	500	1h 40m	L-05
Red Pine to Overlook	3	500	1h 55m	L-01
Cardiff Pass	2	1360	2h 5m	L-08

Accessible Summits

Reaching a summit is always a satisfying accomplishment and the panorama makes the effort worthwhile. The most accessible summits in the Wasatch are:

SUMMIT	TRAIL	
Circle-All Peak	B-08.1	Just off the Butler Fork Trail
Mt Aire	M-09	Trail all the way
Grandeur Peak	M-01	Trail all the way
Clayton Peak	B-25	Trail all the way
Reynolds Peak	B-09.1	Short bushwhack up from Dog Lake
Sunset Peak	L-14.1	Easy from Catherine Pass
Mt Olympus	WF-2	Last 600 feet steep but well marked. Some use of hands
Hidden Peak		Snowbird Tram

Accessible Without A Car

If you do not have a car, there are a few hikes that can be reasonably reached from the Utah Transit Authority bus routes. The UTA schedule can be obtained by calling 287-4636 (BUS-INFO).

The Neffs Canyon Trail and all of the foothill hikes are located within a mile or less of a bus route. The lower City Creek Canyon area is within walking or running distance of downtown. The "Union" bus route passes near the mouth of Big Cottonwood Canyon, and drivers in the canyon are usually willing to pick up hitchhikers.

A HIKE FOR EVERY SEASON

The hiking season follows the retreating snow line up the mountain. The low, sunny foothills are snow-free as early as March, while the ski season is still at its peak. By May, the lower portions of the south-facing canyon trails are often wet and still have occasional patches of snow, but they are generally passable. June opens up many more trails and is also the best month for alpine hiking on consolidated summer snow. Nearly all trails are snow-free by July, but snow lasts all summer in sheltered areas above about 10,500 feet. The high trails remain usable until the first heavy snowfall, which ushers in another ski season.

The limits of the receding snow pack vary with elevation and with the direction that the slope faces. The maps give a general idea of the snow conditions during the spring and early summer.

Early Summer Hikes

These trails are generally snow-free by late May or early June, but you may encounter small patches of snow, especially in shady locations at higher elevations.

Grandeur Peak	Elbow Fork
Ridge between Emigration and Parleys	Mill B North Fork
Mount Olympus	Lone Peak to the Cirque
Ferguson Canyon	Mule Hollow

Early Summer Snow Hikes

In June, the higher basins develop consolidated summer snow as the daily freeze and thaw cycle causes the snow to settle and recrystallize. In the morning you have firm, almost icy snow, allowing a steady ascent, and by afternoon the snow has softened, allowing rapid descent by plunge stepping or by glissading. Many areas are most easily visited at this time of year since the snow covers the loose rock and boulders which make summer travel exhausting.

Summer snow is not for the inexperienced. Anyone venturing onto the

SNOW COVER BY MONTH

JULY 1

JUNE 1

MAY 1

SNOW PATCHES IN SHELTERED AREAS —

CONTINUOUS SNOW COVER ——

41

snow-covered cirque headwalls and ridges should be carrying an ice axe and *should know how to use it.* Also, some of the steeper areas are susceptible to afternoon avalanches. A basic mountaineering course is the best way to learn how to deal with these conditions.

The summer snow routes in the Wasatch are first-class alpine adventures and the conditions are as exciting and as beautiful as climbs in the Tetons, in the Wind River Range, or in the Pacific Northwest. The finest snow routes are:

The Pfeifferhorn	The Beatout Hike (Red Pine to Bells)
Tanners Gulch-Triple Traverse	Hogum Cirque
Mt Superior from Lake Blanche	Broads Fork Twin Peaks

Fall and Early Winter Hikes

Fall hiking offers the widest opportunities of the year, since all trails and routes are snow-free and the cooler weather makes long, strenuous hikes more pleasant than in mid-summer. The changing leaves make September and early October an especially nice time to be in the mountains. The best hiking area to see the fall foliage is along the Desolation Trail east of Gobblers Knob. By November or December, hiking is again limited to the foothill and low south-facing trails.

SUGGESTIONS FOR EXPERIENCED HIKERS

An unavoidable impact of a guidebook is increased use of the areas described. To help mitigate this impact, a number of less- known and less-used routes are identified. Start doing a little exploring once you have gained some experience in the Wasatch.

Little-used Trails That Deserve More Attention

Although the Wasatch is adjacent to a major metropolitan area, there are many trails that are under-utilized. Some constructed trails have one hiking group on a summer weekend, and unofficial trails are disappearing into the undergrowth due to lack of foot traffic. These trails are identified to encourage hikers to visit some new areas.

Thayne Canyon	Neffs Canyon
Ferguson Canyon	Alexander Basin to Bowman Fork
Mule Hollow	Upper Silver Fork West Branch
Beartrap Fork	Maybird Lakes
American Fork Silver Lake	Alpine Dry Creek

Highest Summits In Salt Lake County

"Peak baggers" are hikers and climbers who set a goal of climbing most or all of some defined group of summits, be it all the peaks over 4000 feet in New Hampshire or the highest summits on the seven continents. Peak-bagging gives an incentive to visit places that you might never otherwise consider.

Thirty-two summits in Salt Lake County are over 10,000 feet high. For this list, a point is considered a distinct summit if it is at least 200 feet above the saddle connecting it to the next peak on a ridge. Neither Sundial nor Flagstaff is included since they are connected by continuous ridges to higher summits.

HIGHEST POINTS IN SALT LAKE COUNTY	Elevation
1. American Fork Twins (West Summit)	11,489
2. Broads Fork Twins (East Summit)	11,330
3. Pfeifferhorn	11,326
4. White Baldy (between White Pine and Red Pine)	11,321
5. Sunrise (1/4 mile west of Dromedary)	11,275
6. Lone Peak	11,253
7. Red Baldy (1 mile southwest of Am. Fork Twins)	11,171
8. South Thunder Mountain	11,154
9. North Thunder Mountain	11,150
10. Monte Cristo	11,132
11. Dromedary	11,107
12. Mount Baldy	11,068
13. Sugarloaf	11,051
14. Unnamed (1/2 mile east of Dromedary)	10,910
15. Upper Bells Peak (1/2 mile east of Lone Peak)	10,877
16. Mount Wolverine	10,795
17. Clayton Peak	10,721
18. Sunset Peak	10,678
19. Unnamed (Reed and Benson Ridge north of Flagstaff)	10,561
20. Hogum Divide (1/4 mile west of Maybird Lakes)	10,516
21. Bells Cleaver (northeast of Upper Bells Reservoir)	10,488
22. Honeycomb Cliffs	10,479
23. Pioneer Peak	10,440
24. Unnamed (between Clayton Peak and Guardsman Pass)	10,420
25. Kessler Peak	10,403
26. Unnamed (Between Pioneer Peak and Snake Creek Pass)	10,316
27. Rocky Mouth Canyon Peak	10,292
28. Gobblers Knob	10,246
29. Mount Raymond	10,241
30. Scott Hill	10,116
31. Guardsman Peak (1/4 mile north of Guardsman Pass)	10,026
32. Silver Peak (Wasatch Crest above Beartrap Fork)	10,006

Challenges For The Expert

These routes involve off-trail travel, route finding, and considerable elevation change. The reward is some of the most spectacular and remote areas of the Wasatch and the satisfaction of traveling an extraordinary route.

Mount Olympus from the north
Mule Hollow to Neffs Canyon
Dromedary Peak
Alta to White Pine Canyon
Pfeifferhorn from Dry Creek

Wildcat Ridge
Upper Mill B North Fork Canyon
Twin Peak from Ferguson Canyon
Red Pine to Bells Canyon
Box Elder Traverse

Author's Favorites

Finally, to answer the question, "What do *you* recommend?" I will admit to having a few favorites. I try to hike these trails at least once each year and I always enjoy doing them again. At the risk of overcrowding a few trails, the favorites are:

Mount Olympus
Broads Fork
Red Pine

Grandeur Peak
Mount Aire
Pfeifferhorn

TRAILHEADS

The following road logs will help you locate trailheads and landmarks as you drive the local canyons. Trailheads are crowded on popular summer weekends and parking is limited. Whenever possible, meet your friends in town or at the canyon mouth and carpool into the canyons.

Millcreek Canyon Trailheads (Fee Area)

The road into Millcreek Canyon starts at 3800 South on Wasatch Boulevard. This is a block north of the Olympus Hills Shopping Center, which is a good carpool meeting point. All mileages to Millcreek trailheads are measured from the stop light on Wasatch Boulevard. The road is narrow, especially the upper portion beyond Elbow Fork. During the winter, the Millcreek road is plowed only as far as the Terrace Picnic Area.

Miles	Elev.	
0.0	4960	Wasatch Blvd. and 3800 South.
0.3		Parkview Drive, Access to Neffs trailhead.
0.7		Entrance Fee Station
1.4		Wasatch National Forest boundary.
3.2	5680	Church Fork trailhead (Grandeur Peak).
3.4	5720	Desolation trailhead (Desolation & Thayne).

Miles	Elev.	
4.1		Log Haven Inn.
4.4	5956	Porter Fork.
4.5	6020	Lower end of Burch Hollow Trail (Pipeline Trail).
4.7	6200	Terrace Picnic Area (Bowman Fork & Terrace to Elbow Fork).
4.9		Gate, road is closed above here until mid-June.
6.4	6547	Elbow Fork (Mt. Aire, Lambs Canyon pass, Pipeline Trail).
7.8	7080	Alexander Basin trailhead.
9.2	7500	Wilson Fork.
9.5	7600	Big Water Trail (lower trailhead) and Soldier Fork.
9.6	7640	End of Millcreek road, large parking lot. Access to Big Water Direct Trail, Little Water, and Upper Millcreek.

Big Cottonwood Canyon Trailheads

The road into Big Cottonwood Canyon starts on Wasatch Boulevard at 7200 South (Fort Union Blvd.). The large parking lot on the northeast corner is a popular meeting point. Big Cottonwood mileages are measured from the stop light at the intersection.

Miles	Elev.	
0.0	4960	Intersection stoplight.
2.9	5800	Storm Mountain picnic area (Stairs Gulch).
3.2	5800	Mule Hollow Trail.
4.5	6200	S-Turn (Mill B North Fork, Lake Blanche, and Broads Fork).
6.1	6709	Mineral Fork.
7.1	6960	Mill A Gulch (no cleared trail).
8.5	7080	Butler Fork.
9.3	7268	Cardiff Fork Road Turnoff. New Mill D North trailhead.
9.9	7320	Mill D North Fork old trailhead
10.1	7360	Spruces campground & Days Fork Trail.
11.3	7560	Beartrap Fork Trail.
12.2	7850	Willow Creek.
12.7	8120	Solitude lower lot (Silver Fork & Honeycomb Fork Trails).
13.1	8200	Solitude Ski Area upper lot.
13.4	8300	Redman campground.
14.3	8600	Guardsman Pass Road turnoff.
14.7	8730	Start of Brighton one-way loop.
14.8	8730	Silver Lake trailhead.
15.1	8760	Brighton Ski Area parking lot.

Little Cottonwood Canyon Trailheads

The road into Little Cottonwood Canyon is reached either by driving south on Wasatch Blvd. or by driving east on 9400 South. These two roads meet at a sharp Y-junction at the mouth of the canyon. All mileages to Little Cottonwood trailheads are measured from the electric road condition sign at the Y-junction.

Miles	Elev.	
0.0	5400	Start, electric road sign.
0.2		Forest Service boundary sign.
1.3		Gate Buttress rock climbing area.
1.9	6040	Hydro power station (Coalpit Gulch area).
2.9	6400	Lisa Falls.
4.4	7200	Tanners Gulch, Tanners Flat campground.
5.5	7700	White Pine Trailhead (Also access to Red Pine, Maybird Gulch, Hogum Fork and beyond.)
6.2	7850	Snowbird lower parking lot.
6.6	8040	Snowbird Tram turnoff.
7.1	8300	Bypass road lower turn-off.
7.7		Town of Alta boundary.
7.9	8460	By-pass road upper end.
8.1	8560	Alta Ski Area main parking lot.
8.3	8650	Forest Service garage (Cardiff Pass, Mt. Superior, Grizzly Gulch road.)
8.7	8800	End of paved road, upper Albion parking lot.
9.2	8920	Gate on right to ski area service road. (Walking route to Albion Basin).
11.2	9400	Side road on left — Start of Catherine Pass Trail.
11.3	9400	Albion Basin campground (Catherine Pass, Secret Lake, Devils Castle, Sugarloaf).

American Fork Canyon Trailheads

American Fork Canyon, in Utah County, is reached by State Highway 92. Coming from the Salt Lake Valley, take Interstate 15 south across the Traverse Mountains and take the first exit in Utah County, which is marked with signs for Alpine and Timpanogos Cave. Turn east and follow Utah 92 for 7 miles directly to the mouth of the canyon. Highway 146 from Pleasant Grove approaches American Fork Canyon from the south.

Miles	Elev.	
0.0	5044	Mouth of Canyon, junction of Utah 146 and Utah 92.
0.1		Uinta National Forest boundary sign.
2.7	5600	Timpanogos Cave visitor center. End of plowed road.
5.2	6073	North Fork Road (Utah 144) branches left.

Log continues up north fork.

7.4	6360	Tibble Reservoir.
7.8		Dirt road to Pittsburg Lake branches right.

Log continues up paved road.

Miles	Elev.	
8.6	6720	Granite Flat campground. Silver Lake Flat road branches right.
8.7	6760	Deer Creek trailhead in campground.
8.8	6760	Box Elder trailhead behind Group Site "C."

Log of Silver Lake Flat Road

Miles	Elev.	
8.6	6720	Begin dirt road to Silver Lake Flat.
9.3	7000	Upper access to Deer Creek Trail.
10.8	7440	Summer home area.
11.2	7520	Silver Lake Flat Reservoir.
11.8	7550	Silver Lake trailhead and upper parking area.
		Jeep road fords stream and continues northeast.

Dry Creek–Alpine Trailhead

Approaching from Interstate 15, take Utah 92 east 5 miles, then turn north on Utah 74, which goes directly to the town of Alpine. Continue to 2nd North in Alpine, then turn right, go to 2nd East, and turn north onto Grove Drive, which curves northeast. Follow the paved street until it makes a sharp right turn and becomes a gravel road.

This area is undergoing rapid urbanization, so the description is likely to change. Follow the main road past an area on the right enclosed by chain link fence and across a bridge. The road ends in a large turnout and parking area on private land just short of the Forest Service boundary. The road continues as a track up a short hill, where you reach a Forest Service trailhead sign.

Miles	Elev.	
0.0	4957	Intersection of Utah 74 and 2nd North in Alpine.
1.8	5200	End of pavement (1987).
1.9	5240	Turn left for Schoolhouse Springs trailhead.
2.7	5600	Schoolhouse Springs.

Continuing East on Main Road

Miles	Elev.	
2.2	5340	Road crosses stream, turn left for Dry Creek.
3.0	5420	Dry Creek trailhead.

5

FOOTHILLS AND WASATCH FRONT

The distinction between foothill hikes and Wasatch Front hikes is arbitrary and reflects seasonal preferences. The foothills are popular in spring and fall since they are snow-free and relatively dry when the canyon trails are accessible only to skiers. The Wasatch Front hikes are longer and go higher than the foothill hikes and are generally considered summer hikes.

The foothill hikes are appropriately in the "foothill" or "transition" ecological zone. The dominant vegetation communities on the exposed slopes are open grasslands, Gambel oak, and mountain brush. Sheltered areas have stands of maple and aspen and the drainage bottoms contain cottonwoods and willows. The foothills are vital winter habitat for deer. The Wasatch Front hikes start in the foothills and lead through successive ecological zones, finally climbing above treeline.

The experience of hiking from the suburbs to a wilderness summit is a unique and precious part of living in Salt Lake County but this opportunity is threatened as subdivisions push closer to the mountains. Only a few of these routes currently have a public right-of-way which will protect future access.

The foothills have few hiking trails, but this does not severely limit opportunities for walking since there are numerous jeep roads, random vehicle tracks, deer trails, and footpaths created by repeated travel. The destinations or major landmarks are clearly visible and the routes follow terrain features such as ridges or gullies while avoiding areas of brush.

The high peaks of the Wasatch Front, Grandeur, Mount Olympus, Twin Peaks, and Lone Peak, are well known even by non-hikers. The huge vertical relief and the west-facing aspect make the hikes steep, sunny, and dry. Spectacu-

North and East Area

lar canyons incise the face of the Wasatch uplift. Neffs Canyon, Ferguson Canyon, Deaf Smith-Little Willow Canyon, and Bells Canyon all have trails climbing between steep walls through meadows and on to the passes and summits above. Heughs Canyon, Rocky Mouth Canyon, and Lone Peak Little Willow Canyon are largely unvisited and unknown to even experienced hikers due to the rugged terrain.

NORTH RIM OF CITY CREEK CANYON
(No. CC-1)

Destination:	Ensign Peak	Antennas Loop	Ridge Exploration
One-Way Miles:	1/2	6-1/2	1 to 10
Elevation Gain:	600	1300	500 to 2000
Highest Point:	5414	6150	Varies
Hiking Time One Way:	40m	3h 50m	1h to 6h

The low ridge above the state capitol northeast of Salt Lake City stays snow-free for much of the winter and can be hiked very early in the spring. The area is open grass-covered hills and many variations are possible, ranging from a short stroll to an all day hike on the jeep road which follows the ridge. Most of City Creek Canyon is owned by Salt Lake City, and all of the canyon is municipal watershed. Dogs and camping are strictly prohibited, and hikers should be careful to protect water quality.

Ensign Peak, the hill with a prominent stone monument, has a long history as a site for commemorative events and casual hikes. These south and west facing slopes are dry and snow free from very early in the spring to late in the fall. A short hike offers outstanding views of the Salt Lake Valley and of the lake. Once on the ridge, you can hike for miles along the north side of City Creek Canyon. After years of meetings and public hearings, the final plan for the Ensign Downs subdivision included a land transfer that created a city-owned nature park to connect the streets with the hills above. Hiking opportunities at the upper end of East Capitol Blvd. were permanently lost, but a recreational right-of-way into Antennas Road was preserved. The process, though often emotional, was always conducted with mutual respect and the result demonstrates what can be accomplished when citizen groups, the municipal planning department and developers seek a mutually beneficial project design.

Ensign Peak (No. CC-1.1)

To hike directly up Ensign Peak (Elev. 5414), start from the city-owned land along Greenstroke Drive northwest of the LDS Chapel. To get there take East Capitol Blvd. to North Sandrun Drive (940 N) and turn right at the chapel. The trailhead is currently undeveloped, but designated parking and other improvements are planned. Ensign Peak towers above the subdivision and the route up the open, grassy slope is obvious.

The Antennas Hike — Ensign Peak to City Creek (No. CC-1.2)

To reach the service road which climbs to the communication antennas, follow Edgecombe Drive (800 N) to Dorchester Drive and continue to the end. A sign indicates the end of the public street and states that the road beyond is closed to vehicles. Hikers and mountain bikes are allowed to continue up the road through the subdivision to reach the city-owned land beyond. The road traverses north to a junction where the left branch continues toward Bountiful and the right branch climbs to the antennas.

After the third major antenna station, the road levels off then drops a short way to a saddle. Beyond the saddle a set of vehicle tracks drops down to the City Creek road. A small square microwave reflector a short way below the ridge marks the correct turn. The mouth of the canyon is a 20-minute walk from the large satellite dish visible near the road. Including a walk back to Dorchester Drive, this loop requires about four hours.

North Ridge to Rudys Flat (No. CC-1.3)

The jeep road continues east along the ridge and becomes faint in spots. The maintained motorcycle trails coming up from North Canyon and Mueller Park in Bountiful meet the ridge at Rudys Flat, 3-1/2 miles beyond the antennas.

LOWER CITY CREEK (No. CC-2)

This beautiful nature preserve is only a few minutes' walk from downtown. Take Canyon Road (120 E. North Temple) to Memory Grove, walk up through the park, and continue across Bonneville Blvd. into the canyon. Cars can take Bonneville Blvd., a one-way road starting at 11th Avenue and B Street, to the mouth of City Creek. Turn right into the canyon where the road crosses the stream and park just before the traffic control gate.

City Creek Road: Traffic is restricted on the City Creek road making the lower canyon a popular area for hiking and jogging. The narrow paved road follows the stream for 3.6 miles to the water treatment plant and continues for another 2 miles to end at Rotary Park. The stream and heavy forest along the canyon bottom are a pleasant contrast to the open hills above.

City Creek Ski Trail: A ski touring trail follows the power lines on the north side of the road from the gatehouse to the treatment plant. In summer, this makes a nice walking path. Signs mark points where the ski trail joins the road.

North Ridge from City Creek: Walk up the road about 1-1/4 miles. A large blue pipeline valve station near the road and a large satellite dish hidden in a gully mark where a vehicle track heads up to the ridge. Follow the road past a "Danger Road Damaged No Vehicles Allowed" sign. The ridge crest jeep road is just beyond the microwave reflector which you can see high on the ridge.

AVENUES TWIN PEAKS (No. F-01)

Distance: 1 to 2 miles to peak depending on starting point
Elevation Gain: 1100 feet
Highest Point: 6291 feet
Hiking Time One Way: 45 minutes to 1-1/4 hours

A pair of small peaks on the ridge above the Avenues provide an outstanding view of the city and of City Creek Canyon. The hillsides are a good place for spring wildflowers. All routes cross Salt Lake City and private lands. The watershed damage and erosion have resulted in closing the area to off-road vehicles.

A jeep road follows the ridge above City Creek and numerous tracks once connected this high road with the road shown on the topographic map at about 5200 feet. Subdivisions block historic routes but the Salt Lake City Planning Commission is trying to preserve access. The routes that are likely to survive are from Morris Reservoir, Limekiln Gulch, and Dry Creek.

Morris Reservoir is reached from 18th Avenue at 650 East. A track heads north past the reservoir and leads to a City Creek Canyon overlook 1/2 mile ahead. The best route to the ridge is the first distinct set of tracks heading east after you cross under the powerline. From here, the route to Twin Peaks is about 2 miles across intermediate hills. An alternative start is from the end of Terrace Hills Drive near 900 East and 1000 North where a gate blocks an eroded road which leads up to the ridge.

Perrys Hollow can be reached from Perry Hollow Drive at 1250 East and 640 North or from North Bonneville Drive at 1055 East and 775 North. A city owned trail right-of-way is planned as this area is developed. The jeep roads and tracks leading northeast from the hollow all converge on the ridge crest road west of Twin Peaks.

The summits are just south of the ridge crest and are obvious from any direction. The jeep road just north of Twin Peaks continues east past the head of Dry Creek toward Little Black Mountain.

BONNEVILLE SHORELINE TRAIL
(No. F-07)

An urban trail for walkers, runners, and bicycles follows the hillside from the University Medical Center to Pioneer Trails State Park. The trail is wide and nearly level as it follows the pipeline above Research Park, and the view of the city is spectacular. This two mile section is the first part of a long-range vision to create a trail from Davis County to Utah County following on or near the bench formed by ancient Lake Bonneville's highest level. (Due to urban development in the foothills, most of the trail will actually be above the bench.)

The Bonneville Shoreline Trail provides access to several foothill hikes including Dry Creek, Mount Van Cott, and Big Beacon. Current access points are near the University Medical Center, the entrance road to Red Butte Gardens, and the Emigration Canyon road east of Pioneer Trails State Park.

There is a trailhead access point on Sunnyside Drive at 2700 East. A gap in the fence allows hikers and mountain bikes through and there is a trail sign just beyond. This trail climbs up the pipeline where you can continue north toward the university. It is also the best place to start the hike up the south side of Big Beacon.

Mount Van Cott, just east of the University, is an easy foothill hike with excellent views.

DRY CREEK (No. F-02)

Distance: 1 to 3 miles one way
Elevation Gain: 1000 to 1500 feet
Hiking Time One Way: 30 minutes to 2 hours

Dry Creek, directly northeast of the University Medical Center, offers nice canyon bottom hiking and leads to the ridges above City Creek and Red Butte Canyons. Most of the land is owned by the University.

The route starts at the northeast corner of the University Medical Center parking lot. On weekends there is generally no parking problem but observe posted regulations. Follow the dirt road leading north for about 1/4 mile then turn east into Dry Creek, which is the first drainage you cross. Official trails are planned to connect Dry Creek with the city-owned land near Avenues Twin Peaks.

The beginning of the canyon is unsightly but it soon turns into a beautiful natural area. A foot trail continues up the drainage for about 1/2 mile before reaching a fork.

The north fork trail continues along the bottom. Where the trail fades out, you can climb up onto the left hill and continue through aspen and several clearings to reach the ridge just east of the Twin Peaks. This hike involves about 1000 feet of elevation gain in 1-1/2 miles and is one approach to Little Black Mountain. Another faint trail follows the south fork of Dry Creek for about 2 miles to the head of the canyon.

LITTLE BLACK MOUNTAIN (No. F-03)

Distance: 4 1/4 miles one-way
Elevation Gain: 3100 feet
Highest Point: 8040 feet
Hiking Time One Way: 3 hr 40 min

Little Black Mountain is a high point on the ridge forming the south side of City Creek Canyon, and its forested slopes are a prominent feature as you approach Salt Lake City from the west. Little Black Mountain was my first hike with the Wasatch Mountain Club and has always been one of my spring hiking favorites.

There are two commonly used starting points for Little Black Mountain: Dry Creek from the University Medical Center and the upper Avenues to Twin Peaks. Both routes converge on the ridge crest jeep road just east of Twin Peaks. Follow the jeep trail for another two miles to the summit of Little Black Mountain. There is one steep section where the erosion damage caused by ORV use is evident, and the last half mile is a narrow limestone ridge with a little scrambling.

Veeroceras X1

A Cephalopod, This ancestor of snails and squids is a common fossil in the Thayne Formation. The small gulch (Hike F-04) is a collecting area used by geology students. From Sharp, "Guide Fossils For The Layman" in Geology of Salt Lake County p53.

Most hikers stop at the the first rock outcrop just before the ridge drops about 200 feet to a saddle. A trail once descended from this saddle into the second minor drainage above Rotary Park. Advanced hikers can continue east from Little Black Mountain and make a 15-mile off-trail hike above Red Butte Canyon, eventually reaching Big Beacon.

Dry Creek Ridge Variation: At the first fork in Dry Creek a faint track makes a series of tiny switchbacks up onto the dividing ridge. This ridge merges with the main ridge 1/4 mile west of the summit of Black Mountain. The best route is generally on the south slope near the ridge crest. Descending this ridge one October we watched a bald eagle soaring above Dry Creek; a reminder of the ecological richness in the foothills.

CEPHALOPOD GULCH
And Mount Van Cott (No. F-04)

Destination:	Head of Gulch	Mount Van Cott	Head of Dry Creek
One-Way Miles:	1/2	1	3
Elevation Gain:	700	1148	1800
Highest Point:	5900	6348	7000
Hiking Time One Way:	40m	1h 5m	2h 20m

An eroded vehicle track on the ridge directly north of the upper University Medical Center parking lot is the start of a jeep road which follows the ridge crest to Mount Van Cott. The destination is an overlook 200 feet south from where the jeep road levels off. The jeep trail becomes fainter but continues northeast along the ridge. This is open grassland and many longer hikes are possible, including continuing to the head of Dry Creek and returning along the drainage.

Cephalopod Gulch is the drainage immediately to the northeast of the parking lot. A jeep trail contours the hillside above the parking lot and leads to the gulch, where a foot track leads up the dry streambed. The gulch soon closes in, and brush fills the bottom. Here, most hikers work their way up onto the more open side hills and climb to the jeep road above.

Red Butte Canyon

Red Butte Canyon is managed as a Research Natural Area and access is restricted. This area was once part of Fort Douglas and serves as an ecological baseline since it was never heavily grazed or developed. The Forest Service has experimented with an open weekend when hikers could visit the canyon. This policy should be encouraged.

BIG BEACON

Approach Route:	From Georges Hollow	From Pioneer Park
One-Way Miles:	2	1-1/2
Elevation Gain:	2140	2140
Highest Point:	7143	7143
Hiking Time One Way:	2h 5m	1h 50m

The two large microwave reflectors, which bounce telephone signals from downtown to Park City, make this summit between Red Butte Canyon and Emigration Canyon easy to identify from anywhere in the valley. The other structure on the summit is an abandoned aircraft beacon which was paired with "Little Beacon" on the hill directly south. The summit is called "Mount Wire" on the USGS maps, but the name is rarely used.

From Pioneer Monument Park (No. F-06)

Start from the Bonneville Shoreline Trail access point on Sunnyside Drive east of the Pioneer Trails State Park exit gate. Hike up to the pipeline road which follows the foothills from the University to Emigration Canyon.

Follow the pipeline road east over a couple of ridges until you are on the top of a ridge directly north of the condominiums on Donner Way. Here, a foot track branches left up the hill. This junction is on the last ridge before the powerline crosses the pipeline. The distinct foot track follows the ridge crest to the summit. This is a pretty ridge with limestone outcrops, mountain mahogany, and an occasional cactus.

A service road which offers changing views down into Red Butte Canyon follows the ridge crest northeast from the summit. A jeep track descends into Emigration Canyon after about 1-1/2 miles along the ridge.

From Georges Hollow (No. F-05)

The other route starts in Research Park from the Bonneville Shoreline Trail and goes up Georges Hollow. This route is slightly longer, but it has the same elevation gain and is more scenic. From Sunnyside Avenue, turn north at the Research Park Post Office and take Chipeta Way, the first street on the right. As you pass the Fort Douglas Cemetery you will see two drainages immediately to the east. Georges Hollow is the left drainage with the small red rock outcrop on the north, but the trail actually starts in the right drainage.

The Bonneville Shoreline Trail follows the pipeline right-of-way above Research Park. Currently hikers are parking on Colorow Drive behind the Fort Douglas Cemetery and following informal paths up to the pipeline. Eventually signs will mark the designated access points.

From the Bonneville Shoreline Trail, take the footpath into the drainage to the right of Georges Hollow. Eventually the trail turns north and continues to climb along the side of Georges Hollow. Route finding is necessary as there are a number of dead-end footpaths in the area and the trails shown on the USGS map bear no relation to reality.

The trail follows the bottom of the south drainage for 1/2 mile then crosses the ridge to the north and follows the Georges Hollow drainage. Part way up, a route branches back to the west and traverses to the top of the Red Butte, while the main trail continues east to the minor pass overlooking Red Butte Canyon. Here, the trail makes a sharp right turn toward the summit of Big Beacon, 1/2 mile due south. The slopes are open and the indistinct trail passes to the west of the minor summits.

Descending, remember that the trail turns down at the third saddle. If you turn down the wrong drainage, you will encounter dense oak brush.

EMIGRATION CANYON TO PARLEYS
Foothill Hikes

The foothills between Emigration Canyon and Parleys Canyon contain several historic hiking routes which are now almost inaccessible due to housing developments. The Salt Lake City planners are trying to establish permanent trailheads in this area. There is now a city-owned right-of-way starting near the "H" rock south of Carrigan Canyon. Take 21st South east from Wasatch Blvd. which becomes Hyland Hill Road. Turn left onto Lakeline Drive and park near the end. The route follows the ridge between Carrigan Canyon and spring Canyon over several minor summits. A narrow ridge connects the last minor summit with the main ridge beyond. This is the best current access to Perkins Peak from the west. There are currently no maintained trails in the area but there are plenty of opportunities for foothill exploration.

Perkins Peak (elev. 7520) is the high point on the ridge east of Hogle Zoo. The direct route up the spectacular west ridge is now blocked by development. Poor access is still possible by fighting through the brush from the mouth of Emigration Canyon. Perkins Peak is also reached by traversing the ridge from Little Mountain Summit (See No. E-01).

Pencil Point (elev. 6130) is a sharp outcrop on the ridge between Carrigan Canyon and Parleys Canyon directly above the Regency Theater parking lot. Both the Pencil Point ridge and the ridge to the south have footpaths.

GRANDEUR FROM THE WEST (No. F-09)

Distance: 1 3/4 miles one way to summit
Elevation Gain: 3100 feet
Highest Point: Summit - 8299 feet
Hiking Time One Way: 2 hr 25 min

The streets below Grandeur are reached from Wasatch Blvd. at 33rd South. The Forest Service land starts well above the houses and both routes cross private land. A proposed development here mobilized neighborhood activists and forced the county commission to become more active in foothill issues.

The north approach is reached from about 2900 South on Cascade Way which is the frontage road above the freeway. At the end of the street, there is a "Limited Access" sign, and beyond are power poles and a right-of-way belonging to Utah Power and Light. Climb east a short way, then turn right on a road which contours south above the houses. The trail starts in a gully where the road

Foothill Hiking. Ferguson Canyon (Hike WF-4) in the center of the picture leads to Storm Mountain on the left skyline. The Hounds Tooth (Hike F-10) is the flat-topped outcrop above Ferguson Canyon and is reached by hiking the slope to the right.

crosses the drainage between the first and second ridges south from Parleys Canyon. The footpath rapidly climbs to the south side of the first ridge and continues all the way to the summit. This is the most distinct trail of the two, but it fades out rapidly when you get higher up. Some skill is needed to follow the game trails through the oak brush high on the ridge.

The south access is from the service road which starts at 3401 Crestwood Drive and leads to the water tanks. In 1990, there was a "Foot Travel Only" sign posted. The road gives access to the ridge which is distinguished by the prominent "S" shaped rock outcrop. The trails, which are deer tracks, start steeply on the second ridge south of Parleys Canyon. There are no hiking difficulties if you stay to the south of the outcrop, and a foot track exists all to way to the ridge crest.

HOUNDS TOOTH (No. F-10)

Distance: 1-1/4 miles one way to outcrop
Elevation Gain: 2600 feet
Highest Point: 7800 feet at base of outcrop
Hiking Time One Way: 1 hr 55 min

Hounds Tooth, the farthest south of the popular foothill hikes, is the prominent granite outcrop high on the ridge above Golden Hills and immediately south of Ferguson Canyon. The Forest Service land is about 1/4 mile up the hill, and the first part of the trail crosses private land. Recent changes in ownership have blocked the direct access from the Top of the World Drive. The area can now be reached by traversing south from the Ferguson Canyon Access.

Hike up the ridge east of the LDS chapel. The brush is less thick on the south side of the ridge, and game trails are plentiful. The open hillside makes distances deceptive, and the hike is longer than it looks. This is winter range for deer, so be on the lookout, especially in areas with cover.

The hike stops at the base of the cliffs that looked so small from the valley. This outcrop has several technical rock routes and the north side drops steeply into Ferguson Canyon. To climb higher on the ridge, pass south of the Hounds Tooth.

UPPER CITY CREEK (No. CC-3)

Destination:	Lower Meadow	Grandview via Cottonwood	Hardscrabble Canyon Pass	Lookout Peak via Ridge
One-Way Miles:	3	3-1/2	4-3/4	6-1/4
Elevation Change:	1436	3366	2176	2910
Highest Point:	7480	9410	8220	8954
Hiking Time One Way:	2h 15m	4h 30m	3h 30m	4h 50m
Special Difficulties:		Bushwhack		

All measurements are from Rotary Park.

Upper City Creek Canyon offers spectacular limestone fins, the massive landslide on Grandview Peak, meadows, and abundant wildlife. The seldom-visited ridges above City Creek are a delight for the long-distance hiker and mountain runner. City Creek was the first watershed utilized by the pioneers and remains an important source of culinary water today. Watershed protection is the main management objective; recreation is definitely secondary.

Vehicles are restricted in City Creek. Advance reservations are required to drive up the canyon. Currently, automobiles are allowed on even numbered days, and odd days are for bicycles. Reservations may be made by phoning the Department of Public Utilities at 483-6757. The current regulations overlooked hikers, and the required procedure is to request and pay a small fee for a picnic site to get a car permit. Persons showing up at the gate without reservations can get a permit only if space is available in the canyon.

The gatehouse is just off Bonneville Blvd., and a paved road continues for 5-3/4 miles to a large turnaround at Rotary Park. A steep unofficial trail connects Rotary Park to Rudys Flat on the north ridge. The main City Creek Canyon trail begins beyond the turnaround. A jeep road continues east and fords the stream three times before becoming a distinct foot trail on the north side of the stream. The route is through heavy brush in a narrow gorge, but the canyon opens up higher up. A mile from the start, the trail crosses a narrow eroded gully, and the trail into Cottonwood Gulch immediately branches left.

Three miles beyond Rotary Park the trail crosses a small moraine and comes to a large meadow pocketed with small lakes in the landslide debris that came off the huge white scar on Grandview Peak. Here the trail degenerates to a track along the south side of the meadow, then continues up the drainage. At the head of City Creek is a pass overlooking Hardscrabble Creek, which drains north into Morgan County. Grandview is to the northwest and Swallow Rocks and Big Mountain are southeast. The Great Western Trail follows this ridge.

The surrounding ridges are open, rolling, grassy terrain offering opportunities for cross country exploration to those with energy and the ability to use a topographic map. The area is a mix of Forest Service, Salt Lake City Corporation, and private lands. A recent land exchange allowed Salt Lake City and the Forest Service to block up their lands for more efficient management.

Grandview Peak (No. CC-3.1)

Grandview, the highest peak in the north area, has panoramic views but no easy trails. Some bushwhacking is required by every route. Turn north into Cottonwood Gulch and follow the trail a short way to the Treasure Box Mine. Beyond here, careful routefinding and use of game trails are necessary to avoid thick oak brush. The Riley Ridge route is the grassy ridge in the center of the left fork of Cottonwood Gulch. This fairly open ridge will take you to the main City Creek Ridge directly above the Burro Mine, shown on the USGS map. Remnants of an abandoned trail along the ridge are then followed east for over a mile to Grandview.

A longer but easier route up Grandview is to continue up the main canyon to the area marked "City Creek Meadows" on the USGS map, then ascend the grassy ridges northwest to Grandview. Also, the main fork of Cottonwood Gulch can be descended by carefully following faint game trails and occasionally following the streambed.

Lookout Peak (No. CC -3.2)

From Hardscrabble Pass, a trail follows the ridge toward Lookout Peak, the distinct summit to the southwest. The trail traverses below Lookout on the east side so in about 1/2 mile you will have to climb up on faint game trails to reach the summit ridge. Lookout Peak can also be reached by bushwhacking up the drainage leading to the pass 1/2 mile north of the peak. Trail No. E-02 leads south from Lookout Peak to Affleck Park and to Killyon Canyon.

NEFFS CANYON (No. WF-1)

Destination:	Meadow	Thayne Canyon Pass	Mill B Pass
One-Way Miles:	2-3/4	3-1/2	3-1/4
Elevation Change:	2450	3190	3650
Highest Point:	8000	8740	9200
Hiking Time One Way:	2h 40m	3h 20m	3h 30m
Special Difficulties:			No Trail

Neffs Canyon is the west-facing bowl directly above Olympus Cove. This canyon is never crowded even though it is within walking distance of homes. The lower canyon is heavily forested, and the upper canyon has jagged limestone cliffs and views of the city. The trail starts at the water tanks in White Park. From Wasatch Blvd., drive east on 3800 South and turn right on Parkview Drive (3700 East) at the stop sign. Follow this street around a left and then a right bend heading generally southeast until it meets Parkview Terrace (4175 East 4245 South). Turn left on Parkview Terrace; the second street on the right leads to White Park. The road ends at the Forest Service trailhead.

The trail starts to the south of the fence enclosing the water tanks and follows the jeep road heading southeast into Neffs Canyon. After 1/2 mile there is an open area of unusually tall Gambel oak and a side stream coming from Norths Fork.

The Neffs Trail follows the old road for 1-1/4 miles, crossing the stream twice on improvised bridges, before becoming a foot trail south of the stream. The route climbs up the side of a small ridge then drops back to a stream crossing. The trail becomes faint as it crosses a broad meadow 2-3/4 miles from the trailhead. When the grass is high, the trail can be found again by heading directly east across the meadow. Next, the trail climbs an aspen-covered hill and crosses an upper meadow with evidence of frequent avalanches. The trail now makes a long switchback, first heading south, then turning back north as it climbs the headwall of Neffs Canyon. The trail passes through a series of cliffs, then reaches a notch in the ridge where it joins the Thayne Canyon Trail.

Neffs Trail to Mill B Pass

Neffs Canyon provides access to Wildcat Ridge between Mount Olympus and Mount Raymond. At the extreme south end of the long switchback, leave the trail and continue southeast, climbing 450 vertical feet through wide-spaced trees to an open saddle at the head of Mill B Gulch. An old watering trough is part way up the hill. This saddle marks the end of the difficult scrambling along Wildcat Ridge. From here, an unmaintained trail heads east along the south side of the ridge to the junction with the Desolation Trail at the head of Porter Fork.

MOUNT OLYMPUS (No. WF-2)

Destination:	Tolcat Canyon Stream	South Summit
One-Way Miles:	1-1/2	3
Elevation Gain:	1290	4050
Highest Point:	6240	9026
Hiking Time One Way:	1h 20m	3h 35m
Special Difficulties:		Scrambling (Easy)

The distinctive shape of Mount Olympus dominates the view from much of the valley's east side, and the summit is a popular objective. The trail has switchbacks up open foothills, a climb through dense forest, an easy rock scramble at the top, and spectacular views all along the way. This well-maintained trail is sunny and is a good choice for spring and fall.

The new trailhead is at about 5700 South on Wasatch Boulevard, 1.7 miles south of the 45th South overpass and 2.6 miles north of the Big Cottonwood intersection. The trail starts at the Forest Service sign just south of the prominent rock outcrop known at Petes Rock. A lot of work by the Forest Service went into securing a trail easement at this location and in constructing the new trail. This was one of the big successes of recent years.

The trail climbs steeply up switchbacks to the bench where it levels off then continues up the hill where it turns north along the alignment of the old trail that started from Tolcat Canyon.

The trail now ascends in a series of switchbacks passing through areas of Gambel oak, juniper, and mountain mahogany. It eventually enters Tolcat Canyon where there is a seasonal stream. Formerly the trail continued directly up the steep slabs known as Blister Hill, but new switchbacks to the left make the next section much easier. The trail continues east through the trees with the prominent west ridge of Mount Olympus on the left and a smaller rock rib on the right. Eventually the trail reaches a saddle with a fine stand of Douglas fir and signs of picnic and camping use. On the way back down, be sure to watch for the top of the switchbacks.

From the saddle to the summit is 600 vertical feet in 1/4 mile of easy scrambling requiring occasional use of the hands. The trail turns north and heads for a couloir in the rock face directly ahead. Foot traffic has made a distinct track up the couloir. There is no exposure and the major danger is that a careless hiker might kick rocks loose. If you find yourself overlooking a cliff or facing an unscalable wall, look around and you will see the correct route a few feet away. About 2/3 of the way up, the couloir runs into an abrupt wall where the route jogs east for about 150 feet to a notch behind a pinnacle, then turns left and continues directly up. At the top, turn right and boulder-hop along the ridge for about 200 feet to the summit. All routes from the summit other than the ascent route involve expert hiking and elementary rock climbing skills.

Dry Hollow (No. WF-3)

An historic route starts from the water tank on the southeast side of the Canyon Cove subdivision and follows vehicle tracks up the ridge between Heughs Canyon and Dry Hollow. A trail traverses into the Dry Hollow drainage, then ascends the open slopes on the north side of Dry Hollow to reach a pass overlooking Mule Hollow.

FERGUSON CANYON (No. WF-4)

Destination:	Ridge Overlook	Upper Meadow	Storm Mountain Summit
One-Way Miles:	1-1/2	2-3/4	3-1/2
Elevation Change:	1600	3200	4324
Highest Point:	7000	8400	9524
Hiking Time One Way:	1h 35m	2h 55m	3h 50m
Special Difficulties:			Scrambling

Ferguson Canyon is the short, steep canyon located immediately south of the mouth of Big Cottonwood Canyon and east of the Prospector Hill subdivision. The lower canyon is enclosed by granite walls popular with rock climbers, while the upper canyon contains open meadows. The current, unofficial access is from the water tanks south of the canyon. The Forest Service is working to provide a legally guaranteed and well-designed access.

The water tanks are reached by turning left at the stoplight at 7800 South and Wasatch Blvd. Follow Honeywood Cove Drive to Top-of-the World Drive, turn left, and then turn right on Timberline Drive (7780 South). To avoid homeowner conflicts with excess numbers of cars parked on the street, hikers are strongly encouraged to park at the Park and Ride lot on Wasatch Blvd. and walk up through the subdivision to the water tanks. This adds a little bit to the hike, but for anyone with enough energy to go up Ferguson Canyon it is a small hardship and helps maintain goodwill with the homeowners.

Trails that begin directly in urban neighborhoods create unique problems. Homeowner concern over late night parties held in the canyon caused the Forest Service to institute a closure between 10 PM and 6 AM and a ban on fires and camping for the lower 2 miles of Ferguson Canyon.

Descend from the water tanks and follow the trail that soon crosses the Twin Peaks Wilderness boundary. The trail stays in the canyon bottom and crosses the stream twice on logs and once on boulders as it climbs steadily. After about 1-1/4 hours you will reach the bottom of the switchbacks which climb up the north side of the canyon.

In a sandy area near the top of the ridge, the trail to Storm Mountain makes a sharp switchback to the east, and a well defined track branches left and heads west to a spectacular overlook on the crest of the narrow ridge above Big

Cottonwood Canyon. A track continues down the crest of this ridge, but it is a very steep route on rock and gravel.

After the overlook junction, the trail continues east, traversing through brush high on the canyon side until it again approaches the now-dry stream bed. There is a trail from here all the way to the upper meadow. If you lose the trail (or are searching for it on descent), look for it 15 yards from the south wall of the obvious narrows at about 7800 feet. Above the narrows the trail climbs on the south side of the drainage until it reaches an open boulderfield where it jogs to the north, then begins a very steep climb up an open slope. The easiest route here is along the stream; fragments of the old trail are seen nearby. The trail disappears soon after reaching the upper meadow so locate landmarks for the return. Storm Mountain is visible 1/4 mile ahead. To the right are a higher summit on the ridge leading around Stairs Gulch toward Twin Peaks, and farther right, a saddle overlooking Deaf Smith Canyon.

The best route to Storm Mountain is to go up the center of the bowl, aiming for the saddle south of the peak. An alternative is to ascend the north ridge and follow the crest, crossing one minor peak on the way. Both routes are enjoyable.

Anything beyond Storm Mountain is a mountaineering scramble. The east face of Storm Mountain is a technical rock climb and the north ridge is either a very difficult scramble or a technical climb depending on the route. The traverse from Storm Mountain to Twin Peaks is long and involves routefinding along an exposed ridge.

DEAF SMITH CANYON (No. WF-5)
Also Called Little Willow Canyon

This is a very steep, narrow canyon leading from the Golden Hills subdivision to the summit of Twin Peaks.

There have recently been "No Trespassing" signs and fences in the area around the mouth of this canyon. Various agencies are attempting to secure a proper public access, but the current situation is very uncertain. The only access to this canyon that does not require scrambling is to follow the private road from Golden Oaks Drive up past homes and into the canyon. Alternatively, an experienced hiker can enter the canyon by traversing over from the area near Hounds Tooth or by scrambling cross-country from the south. This is a magnificent canyon with a long record of use by the public.

A reasonably-defined trail follows the stream up the north side of the north fork then crosses to the south side before fading out 2 miles from the mouth at about 8800 feet. Above here the terrain is open and you can continue up the scree slopes following either branch of the drainage to the summit of Twin Peaks.

BELLS CANYON (No. WF-6)

Destination:	Meadow	Upper Bells Reservoir	Thunder Mountain Pass
One-Way Miles:	2-3/4	3-3/4	4-3/4
Elevation Change:	2600	4100	5420
Highest Point:	7900	9400	10,720
Hiking Time One Way:	2h 40m	3h 50m	5h 10m

This is a long canyon that rises from the sage-covered foothills, past a popular rock climbing area, to an alpine cirque with Lone Peak and Thunder Mountain towering above. From high in Bells Canyon, the huge north face of Lone Peak dominates the view. The lower portion is on private land, and suburban development is rapidly blocking traditional routes.

Currently there is no official trailhead although hikers are able to get into Bells Canyon from the end of a new subdivision street near 10000 South. The Wasatch National Forest Management Plan recognizes the access problem and the Forest Service and Sandy City are currently trying to secure a right-of-way and construct trails at the mouth of Bells Canyon. Hikers, especially those who live in Sandy City, are urged to contact their public officials and express support for a Bells Canyon Trailhead.

The historic trail begins as a road past the now-drained Bells Reservoir. The trail ascends on the north side of the stream then crosses to the south at about 6100 feet. The steep trail continues up past the spectacular Bell Towers, then recrosses to the north side at about 7400 feet. The USGS map shows portions of this trail on the wrong side of the stream. The stream crossings are on improvised bridges. Soon after the second crossing, the trail reaches a swampy meadow. The north branch of the canyon leads to Thunder Bowl, the prominent cirque below Thunder Mountain ridge. The trail to the upper reservoir can be found on the spur ridge separating the branches and continues up the south branch of the canyon.

The trail ends at the upper reservoir. The pass on the ridge between Thunder Mountain and Upper Bells Peak is reached by continuing up past the reservoir. All routes out of Bells are difficult off-trail hiking with some scrambling.

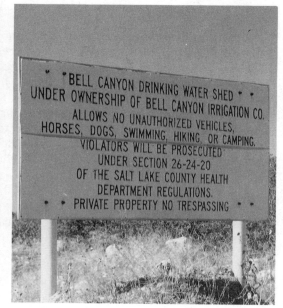

BELL CANYON DRINKING WATER SHED
UNDER OWNERSHIP OF BELL CANYON IRRIGATION CO.
ALLOWS NO UNAUTHORIZED VEHICLES,
HORSES, DOGS, SWIMMING, HIKING, OR CAMPING.
VIOLATORS WILL BE PROSECUTED
UNDER SECTION 26-24-20
OF THE SALT LAKE COUNTY HEALTH
DEPARTMENT REGULATIONS.
PRIVATE PROPERTY NO TRESPASSING

Mouth of Bells Canyon 1993 — Urban development, historic land uses, and the public demand for recreation clash here. Public agencies are trying to resolve the trail access problems at Bells Canyon and at other locations along the Wasatch Front. With strong public support open-space corridors can be preserved for wildlife and for recreation.

Descending Bells Canyon on consolidated snow in June. The granite ridge ahead separates Bells Canyon from Little Cottonwood and is a popular rock climbing area.

Dimple Dell Regional Park

This creek bottom area was designated by the County Commission as a nature park after a long battle between preservationists and golf course promoters. The trails in this 3 mile long park are for walking, running, bicycling, and horse riding.

Urban trails can provide high quality muscle-powered outdoor recreation and need to be a major part of recreation planning. Overuse of primitive backcountry and Wilderness areas can be reduced by providing more opportunities in areas that can be hardened and managed for high use. If you want solitude visit the Wilderness but if you want fresh air and exercise consider Dimple Dell Park.

LONE PEAK

This rugged summit, visible from North Salt Lake to Provo, was the centerpiece of Utah's first congressionally designated Wilderness. The trail is steep, hot, and dry, but the experience of standing in an alpine cirque only a few miles from the city is unique. The cirque is ringed with near-vertical granite walls and angular summits; the view from the lower end of the cirque is one of the most photogenic in Utah.

This is a huge massif and there are several major routes. The most popular route is Jacobs Ladder (Movie Road) from Corner Canyon. The Draper Ridge route is a variation that starts lower on the Corner Canyon road, then follows the skyline ridge to join the Jacobs Ladder route high on the mountain. A route starting from Dry Creek leads to the south (lower) summit. Mountaineers can approach Lone Peak from Bells Canyon.

Note: Corner Canyon Road was closed at the time of the revision. The Corner Canyon road crosses sections of forest Service land and Draper City has stated that they are committed to maintaining access. To reach Corner Canyon, drive to Draper Corners (700 E and 12300 South), go one block south, head east, cross the railroad tracks, and continue 1.1 miles from the tracks to the end of the pavement. Take a sharp right turn onto a dirt road that heads south and gradually up onto the foothills. The road is rough and washed out but is passable with most passenger cars if the driver is careful. The Draper Ridge trailhead is 3.0 miles from Draper. The Movie Road Trail starts across from the large turnout 4 miles from Draper. The south end of the Corner Canyon road is reached by taking a left turn at the four-way stop in Alpine. Go straight until the road starts winding through some subdivisions. A dirt road branches off one of the loops and heads up towards Corner Canyon. In 1993 this road was washed out about two miles before Jacobs Ladder. Due to rapid development in both Draper and Alpine, road status and landmarks are likely to change.

The routes up Lone Peak from the south are described in chapter ten.

Jacobs Ladder Route (No. WF-8)

Destination:	Lone Rock Jeep Road	Draper Ridge Trail	Lone Peak Cirque	Lone Peak Summit
One-Way Miles:	1-1/2	2-3/4	3-3/4	5
Elevation Change:	1340	3600	4000	5643
Highest Point:	6940	9200	9600	11243
Hiking Time One Way:	1h 20m	3h 10m	3h 50m	5h 45m
Special Difficulties:				Scrambling Exposure

Start hiking up the deeply rutted 4WD road (now closed) across from the turnout. Almost immediately, you climb a ridge where the road branches. The easier route turns right and follows a jeep trail and foot path up the crest of the

68

Lone Peak Cirque — *a rugged alpine Wilderness. The true summit is the on the left side of the picture.*

ridge. This route connects with a road coming in from the south that is frequently used by motorbikes. After about a mile, you reach an abrupt dropoff overlooking Utah County where there is a wilderness boundary sign. Here, a cleared trail heads northeast directly up the spur ridge called "Jacobs Ladder." Climb for two hours to the junction with the Draper Ridge route.

The alternative route at the first junction is to continue straight ahead, down into a gully, and up a very steep road on the other side. This is the "Movie Road" which climbs to an outcrop used for filming a commando movie some years ago. The road ends at the outcrop, and a cross-country route heads up and northeast into the brush, crossing several open slabs as it follows minor ridges to meet the maintained trail up Jacobs Ladder.

The hardest part ends where the Jacobs Ladder Ridge meets the main Draper Ridge. The trail now heads east through a large meadow and crosses a small stream which is a reliable source of water as late as July. The unwary occasionally follow this stream by mistake, but the route continues east across a ridge and into the cirque. The trail gets faint as it crosses the granite ridge, but there are cairns all the way. The elevation gain is only 250 feet from the junction with the Draper Ridge route to the cirque.

The trail ends soon after entering the cirque, and in early summer the route beyond here will be on snow. The prominent rock outcrop on the end of the ridge above marks where the trail enters the cirque, and will be a landmark for the return. The true summit is the triangular point farthest left along the top of the sheer wall. The ridge on the right leads to a series of minor summits.

The normal route stays on the left of the stream (reliable most years) draining the cirque, and heads north to the obvious saddle. The most energy-efficient route is to ascend the grassy slope to the granite dome on the far left side of the cirque staying about 200 feet from the cliffs. Next, traverse a boulder-filled cove, and cross another area of exposed rock before reaching the short scramble to the saddle. From the boulder-strewn saddle, the route follows the ridge east toward the summit. The last few hundred feet involve scrambling with extreme exposure. Know your abilities and be very cautious if the rock is wet. The summit is a small flat-topped rock.

Draper Ridge Route (No. WF-7)

Destination:	Movie Road Trail Junction	Lone Peak Cirque	Lone Peak Summit
One-Way Miles:	3-1/4	4-1/2	5-1/2
Elevation Change:	3900	4300	5943
Hiking Time One Way:	3h 35m	4h 25m	6h 5m

The start of the Draper Ridge route is marked by incredibly steep jeep tracks carved into the hillside. There is a parking turnout across the road. A jeep road with switchbacks leads to some private land high on the ridge, but 4WD adventurers have clawed their way directly up. Follow the jeep road up about eight switchbacks to a point where the road approaches the drainage to the south. Here, a cairn marks the trail, which drops slightly into the gully before beginning the steady climb up through oak and mountain mahogany. It ascends the south side of the minor ridge between the Movie Outcrop and Cherry Canyon. The trail is deeply eroded in spots, and there are a few forks which soon rejoin. A climb of 1800 feet leads to an open grassy ridge which is followed to the junction with the Jacobs Ladder route.

An alternative is to continue past the previously mentioned trail and follow the jeep road northeast to its end on the skyline ridge above Cherry Canyon. A cross-country hike from the end of the jeep road passes on the south of a rock outcrop and joins the other route at about 7800 feet.

6

MILLCREEK CANYON

Millcreek has a good system of maintained trails leading up from the narrow stream-cut gorge. The area was not heavily glaciated and much of the area is covered by soft sedimentary rock, resulting in rounded summits and rolling ridges. Millcreek was logged in pioneer times but the north-facing slopes are still heavily forested.

The Millcreek Ridge, on the north between Parleys Canyon and Millcreek Canyon, offers short hikes to Mount Aire and Grandeur Peak. The vegetative cover is mixed grass, mountain brush, and stands of aspen, with limited forest in sheltered areas. There are a few small cliffs but no serious obstacles to off-trail hiking. A herd of elk inhabits the area around Lambs Canyon, and they are frequently seen farther west.

The ridge on the south, between Millcreek Canyon and Big Cottonwood Canyon, is higher and has two topographically distinct portions. The western section from Mount Olympus to Neffs Canyon is called Wildcat Ridge. Narrow rock spurs separate nearly impassable couloirs and gulches. This rugged cockscomb formed by tilted layers of the Big Cottonwood and Mutual formations is a place for mountain goats, alpinists, and adventurous hikers. Farther east, from Mount Raymond to the head of Millcreek, the Raymond Ridge is wider and much gentler. Here, the complex geology consists of layers which have been folded and shoved horizontally by the Raymond thrust fault. Trails lead up the main drainages and connect into a network of constructed trails, which run the full length of this ridge, from Neffs Canyon to Park City and Brighton.

Millcreek is undergoing rapid change. The new vehicle access fee, $2 per car (bicycles free), has provided funds for road, picnic area, and general maintenance of the canyon. Plans to use Millcreek for municipal water will result in more restrictive watershed management probably including a ban on dogs and horses.

GRANDEUR PEAK (No. M-01)

Destination:	Bottom of Switchbacks	Grandeur Peak
One-Way Miles:	1	2-3/4
Highest Point:	6600	8299
Elevation Change:	880	2619
Hiking Time One Way:	55m	2h 40m

Grandeur Peak forms the west end of Millcreek Ridge and is prominent on the Wasatch skyline. It is the most accessible and the easiest of the major peaks overlooking the Salt Lake Valley. The trail starts from the Church Fork picnic area, on the north side of the road, 3.2 miles from Wasatch Blvd.

Hike or drive the paved road north through the picnic area to a gate where the trail begins. A footpath continues along the west side of the stream for 1/2 mile to a small clearing where the trail leaves the stream and turns sharply west. Well constructed switchbacks lead up to a saddle on the Millcreek ridge crest where you get an outstanding view of Salt Lake Valley. The trail from the saddle follows the ridge west to Grandeur summit 1/2 mile away and 680 feet higher.

Several trails branch from the trail to Grandeur. An unmaintained route follows Millcreek Ridge east toward Church Fork Peak and Mount Aire (See Trail R-1). An alternative descent is the west side of Grandeur Peak (Trail F-09). The Lower Pipeline Trail (Trail M-02) starts from the dirt road just past the gate and continues along the 6200 foot contour.

Church Fork Peak Trail (No. M-01.1)

The Church Fork Peak Trail is an old route that follows a distinct constructed bench across the hillside. It branches from the Grandeur Peak Trail after the seventh switchback where there is a long curve to the west. The Church Fork Peak Trail leads in a straight line east to a meadow at the head of the Church Fork drainage. From the meadow the route goes north through the trees and ascends the ridge to Church Fork Peak (elev. 8316).

THAYNE CANYON (No. M-03)

Destination:	Desolation Trail	Neffs Canyon	Thayne Peak
One-Way Miles:	1-1/2	2-1/4	2-3/4
Highest Point:	7950	8760	8676
Elevation Change:	2150	2960	2876
Hiking Time One Way:	1h 50m	2h 40m	2h 55m

The trail follows the Thayne Canyon drainage and offers a steep but easy climb to the upper portion of the Desolation Trail and a direct route to the pass at the head of Neffs Canyon.

The trail starts at the Desolation trailhead on the south side of the road, 3.4

LEGEND

———————— MAIN ROAD

– – – – – TRAIL

- - - - - - - ROUTE (UNMAINTAINED)

←———→ DIRECTION OF CROSS-
COUNTRY TRAVEL

WILDERNESS AREA

NOTE:

ROUTES STARTING WITH "MS" ARE
MOUNTAINEERING SCRAMBLES.

N

0   1   2   3
MILES

miles up Millcreek Canyon from Wasatch Blvd. The trailhead is at the lower end of the picnic area just east of the Millcreek Inn. Head south past the outhouse and look for the Desolation Trail sign. After about 100 yards the trails separate as the Desolation Trail makes a switchback to the right onto the hillside.

The Thayne Trail continues as a cleared path along the bottom of the drainage, and it eventually makes a short, sharp switchback to the left, immediately below a reliable spring and an old watering trough. A short distance above, the trail meets the Desolation Trail which has been making endless switchbacks. The two trails combine for one long switchback, then separate. The separation, marked by a cairn, is at the edge of a small ravine where the Desolation Trail turns back east.

The Thayne Trail continues up along the east side of the ravine until the drainage opens into a bowl. Here the trail becomes less distinct. One route heads generally up and west, directly toward the pass to Neffs Canyon, which is just to the left of a prominent rock outcrop. The more popular route goes higher and to the east but eventually curves to reach the pass.

Marine fossils are abundant in the limestone near the pass. The peak to the south (elev. 9776) is a triple divide between the Millcreek, Big Cottonwood, and Neffs Canyons. This peak is most easily reached from the Big Cottonwood side. Thayne Peak (elev. 8656) is visible on the divide between Thayne Canyon and Porter Fork. The Neffs Canyon Trail continues from the pass to Olympus Cove.

DESOLATION TRAIL
— Millcreek Portion (No. M-04)

Destination:	Salt Lake Overlook	Thayne Trail Junction	Thayne Peak Junction	Porter Fork
One-Way Miles:	1-3/4	3	4-1/2	6-3/4
Elevation Change:	1250	2150	2906	3570
Highest Point:	7000	7900	8656	9320
Hiking Time One Way:	1h 30m	2h 35m	3h 40m	5h 10m

This well maintained trail climbs by gentle switchbacks to a viewpoint overlooking the city. It is also the beginning of the Desolation Trail, which continues for 17 miles along the Raymond Ridge to Desolation Lake.

The Desolation trailhead is just east of the Millcreek Inn, on the south side, 3.4 miles up Millcreek Canyon. Head south past the outhouse and look for the Desolation Trail sign. The Desolation Trail soon makes a switchback to the right and up out of the stream bed.

Desolation Trail to Salt Lake Overlook

This trail is an obvious constructed path and the Hiking the Wasatch Map accurately shows the series of easy switchbacks. The hillside is steep and susceptible to erosion, so avoid the temptation to shortcut the switchbacks. A minor trail branches to the west and heads down into the Boy Scout camp. There are excellent views both up and down the canyon from the Salt Lake overlook on the crest of a rocky ridge. To the north, just off the trail, there are a few sheltered resting spots. If you are using a topographic map, the overlook is on the end of the sharp ridge (elev. 7000 feet) above Greens Canyon.

Salt Lake Overlook to Porter Fork

Beyond the overlook, the trail re-crosses the ridge and begins a long winding ascent of upper Thayne Canyon. It crosses the main stream drainage and meets the Thayne Canyon Trail after one hour of hiking. A spring and an old watering trough are located on the Thayne Trail a hundred yards below the junction.

From the junction, the Thayne and Desolation Trails combine for one long switchback. They then separate and the Desolation Trail continues east to reach the small saddle just south of Thayne Peak (elev. 8656). Beyond the saddle there are endless switchbacks as the trail continues across Porter Fork, finally reaching the Porter Fork Trail a few switchbacks below the pass into Big Cottonwood. The remainder of the Desolation Trail is covered as Trail No. B-11.

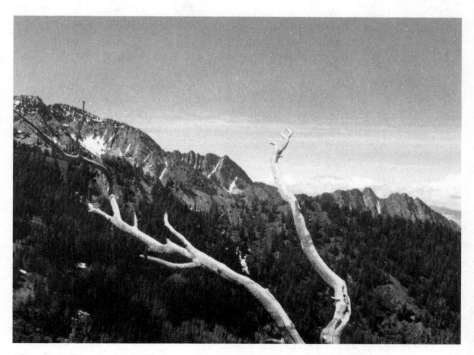

View from Thayne Peak. This summit is a few minutes' climb from the Desolation trail and offers excellent views in every direction. Mount Olympus is on the right skyline.

Thayne Peak is a short scramble up deer trails from the pass. The summit has a panoramic view and is a popular destination.

The Desolation trail was originally constructed as a motorcycle trail but it is now in the Mount Olympus Wilderness. Prior to Wilderness designation, the irresponsible behavior of a few motorcycle riders who could not resist the challenge of climbing the nearest hill led to trail closures to prevent serious watershed damage. Hikers are generally responsible users of trails, but everyone must practice walking softly in the wilderness.

Forest Service trail standards specify an unrealistic grade which makes sense for wheeled vehicles but results in a trail of limited use to hikers. It simply takes too long to get anywhere-hence, the continued popularity of the more direct Thayne Canyon Trail and the appearance of switchbacks with a more realistic grade on the Forest Service trail from repeated cross-country travel. Also, constructing trails at these gentle grades consumes the limited budget which could be used to maintain existing trails.

Porter Fork and Mount Raymond viewed from Burch Hollow. The Bowman Trail (Hike M–06) climbs to Baker Pass on the left of Mount Raymond and the Desolation Trail crosses the pass on the right of the peak, then continues west across Porter Fork towards Thayne Canyon.

PORTER FORK (No. M-05)

Destination:	End of Road	Porter Fork Pass
One-Way Miles:	1-1/2	3-1/4
Highest Point:	6800	9320
Elevation Change:	1140	3660
Hiking Time One Way:	1h 20m	3h 25m

The route begins as a road through a summer cabin area on Forest Service leased land and continues into the Mount Olympus Wilderness to a junction with the Desolation Trail and to the Porter Fork West Pass.

Mount Raymond Area.

The Porter Fork road starts 4.4 miles up Millcreek Canyon. A small sign identifies Porter Fork, and there is a gate just after the bridge at the start of the side road. The road is a public right-of-way for foot traffic, but respect the cabin owners' privacy as you hike through the summer home area.

After 1-1/2 miles the road is blocked by the gate marking the Wilderness boundary. A jeep trail continues up to a mine site which pre-dates the Wilderness designation. A mile beyond the Wilderness boundary, the road turns west and the foot trail branches left. The junction with the Desolation Trail is about 400 vertical feet below the Porter Fork West Pass. A series of switchbacks takes you up the steep headwall to the pass on the Raymond Ridge, where you can continue east on the Desolation Trail or can turn west on an unmaintained trail which follows the Big Cottonwood side of the ridge to Neffs Canyon.

Porter Fork can be used in combination with the Bowman Fork Trail, Desolation Trail, or Mill B North Fork Trail to create a one-way outing.

BOWMAN TRAIL (No. M-06)

Destination:	White Fir Pass	Baker Spring	Baker Pass
One-Way Miles:	1-1/2	3	3-3/4
Highest Point:	7520	8880	9320
Elevation Change:	1260	2660	3080
Hiking Time One Way:	1h 20m	2h 50m	3h 20m

The first part of the Bowman Trail up to White Fir Pass is an easy hike through dense forest. An intermediate hike takes you past Baker Spring, across open slopes, and on to the pass overlooking Big Cottonwood. Ambitious hikers can climb either Mount Raymond or Gobblers Knob.

The trail starts near the Terraces picnic area which is on the south, 4.7 miles up Millcreek Canyon. Drive across the bridge, take the right branch at the top of the hill, and park near the end of the road. A signboard marks the trailhead which is the start of both the Bowman Trail and the trail to Elbow Fork. The Bowman Trail is the one to the right. The trail becomes a distinct constructed tread as it traverses a hillside and heads into the Bowman Fork drainage. This trail is shown on the USGS map, but the route location is inaccurate in several places.

A spur trail at the first stream crossing leads to the Porter Fork cabin area. After a mile, the trail leaves the stream and climbs to White Fir Pass, a nice overlook with a good view of most of Porter Fork. A good place for lunch is just a few feet north along the ridge.

About 1-1/2 miles beyond White Fir Pass, there is a junction with the connecting trail from Alexander Basin. The Bowman Trail continues up a lush gully to Baker Spring (a reliable water source), then begins a long ascending traverse of the avalanche-swept slopes below Gobblers Knob to reach the saddle between Mount Raymond and Gobblers Knob.

There is a four-way junction at Baker Pass. Unmaintained trails lead to the summits in either direction (see B-08.2 and B-08.3). A short spur trail descends the Big Cottonwood side of the pass to the Desolation Trail immediately below. For a longer return to Millcreek, you can follow the Desolation Trail west around Mount Raymond and descend by the Porter Fork Trail, making a 10-mile loop.

Baker Spring is an historical site where several mine workings were located. The miner's cabin burned down in the early 1980's. A stock watering trough was constructed here to service sheep grazing which continued in Porter Fork until 1973.

BURCH HOLLOW TRAIL
And Pipeline Trail

Destination:	Lookout Rock	To Elbow Fork	From Elbow Fork	Millcreek Ridge
One-Way Miles:	3/4	2	2	2
Elevation Change:	56	640	-640	2080
Highest Point:	6480	6640	6640	8120
Hiking Time One Way:	40m	1h 20m	1h 10m	2h 10m

Mount Raymond viewed from the Bowman Trail just beyond Baker Spring.

Pipeline Trail (No. M-07)
Burch Hollow to Elbow Fork

This bike trail offers a short climb of about 600 feet, followed by a level walk through the woods for a mile parallel to the Millcreek Road. The Burch Hollow Trail branches from the Pipeline Trail and climbs to the ridge crest.

The trailhead is on the north side of the Millcreek Road and about 250 feet west of the service road to the Forest Service Millcreek Guard Station. The trail heads northeast and crosses the end of the service road, then continues up the Burch Hollow drainage. After 1/4 mile, the trail makes a sharp switchback to the right, climbs south out of Burch Hollow, crosses the ridge separating Burch Hollow from Millcreek, and turns east. From here to Elbow Fork, the trail follows the level grade cut for the pipeline supplying a long gone hydroelectric plant. It is free of brush and is easy walking. Remains of pipeline can be seen where side drainages cross the route. Mountain bike riders have provided much of the volunteer work to reconstruct this trail.

The Elbow Fork end of the trail can be found by leaving the road at the black rock outcrop that is 200 feet west of the Mount Aire trailhead.

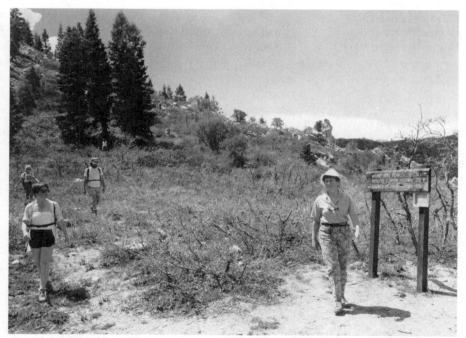

Mount Aire Pass. The ridge between Millcreek Canyon and Parleys Canyon is rounded and at relatively low elevation. Trails lead to summits and an unmaintained hiking route follows the ridge crest for its entire length.

Lookout Rock

Where the trail climbs out of Burch Hollow and turns east, a path through the woods following the old pipeline route can be seen heading southwest and slightly downhill to Lookout Rock. This outcrop, on the end of the ridge separating Burch Hollow from Millcreek, offers an outstanding view of Porter Fork. Although the road is clearly visible directly below, the best choice is to return the way you came as the slopes below are steep and easily eroded.

BURCH HOLLOW TO THE RIDGE(No. M-08)

The trail to the ridge branches from the Pipeline Trail 900 feet east of the point where the trail levels off. The trail starts as a wide swath cut through the brush, but it takes a very sharp turn back to the northwest and is easy to miss. Look carefully for the trail starting up the hill. The trail ascends the east side of the Burch Hollow drainage with occasional switchbacks. A few spots have washed out and some areas are slightly overgrown, but the track is distinct all the way. The route passes beneath spectacular outcrops of Thayne Formation limestone and heads for the obvious saddle on the ridge. The saddle overlooks Mount Aire Canyon, a Y-shaped area of private land with roads and summer homes.

If you are hiking the ridge and want to descend Burch Hollow, the trail starts at the low point west of the prominent pinnacle on the crest and heads southeast, passing below the first cliff.

ELBOW FORK TRAILHEAD

Four trails start from this trailhead, located at the sharp right-angle bend 6.4 miles up the Millcreek Canyon road. Elbow Fork is the side-canyon directly north of the bend, and the trails to Mount Aire and the Lambs Canyon Pass share a common route for the first 1/4 mile up this drainage. An old pipeline grade leads along the north side of the road back to the Millcreek road at Burch Hollow. On the south, a bridge across the stream is the beginning of the trail that winds up onto a spur ridge, then descends to the Terraces picnic area. The Pipeline and Terraces trails make good one-way hikes, or the two can be combined as a loop. Parking space along the road is limited so park carefully to leave room for others and get completely off the road to avoid creating a traffic hazard.

MOUNT AIRE (No. M-09)

Destination:	Mt. Aire Pass	Mt. Aire Summit
One-Way Miles:	1	1-3/4
Elevation Change:	1170	1991
Highest Point:	7800	8621
Hiking Time One Way:	1h 10m	1h 50m

When I want an outstanding view without too much hiking time or effort, I often choose the panorama from the summit of Mount Aire. The trail follows a pleasant south-facing slope and is especially good in the spring and fall, but it has enough shade to be a good summer trail as well.

The trail starts up the east side of the drainage from the Elbow Fork trailhead. After about 1/4 mile, the Lambs Canyon Trail branches east and the Mount Aire Trail crosses the stream on a sturdy bridge. The trail becomes steeper, but you soon reach the saddle at the head of Mount Aire Canyon. The trail turns east and follows a series of well-defined switchbacks through the Gambel oak to reach the summit.

LAMBS CANYON FROM ELBOW FORK
(No. M-10)

Distance: 1-1/2 miles one-way
Elevation Gain: 1490 feet
Highest Point: Lambs Canyon pass — 8120 feet
Hiking Time One Way: 1h 30m

Start at the Elbow Fork trailhead and turn right just before the bridge where the Lambs Canyon Trail and the Mount Aire Trail separate. A sign marks the junction.

The trail follows the stream into a gully which is filled with moss and fallen logs and is reminiscent of the forests found in wetter areas. Near the head of the gully, the trail bends right and traverses to an excellent Millcreek overlook on the top of a minor ridge. Across the ridge, the terrain becomes more open and you walk through a grove of small aspen before climbing a short hill to the pass.

At the pass is the junction with the Great Western Trail coming up from Lambs Canyon, a major side-canyon of Parleys Canyon. The ridge trail (R-1) is the faint track heading east along the ridge crest toward Murdock Peak.

ELBOW FORK
To Terraces Trailhead (No. M-11)

Destination:	Terrace Picnic Area	Return From Terrace
One-Way Miles:	1-3/4	1-3/4
Elevation Change:	-430	430
Total Ascent:	690	1120
Hiking Time One Way:	1h 25m	1h 35m

This nice short hike has good views down Millcreek Canyon and up into Porter Fork and involves little elevation gain. The trail is on a north-facing slope

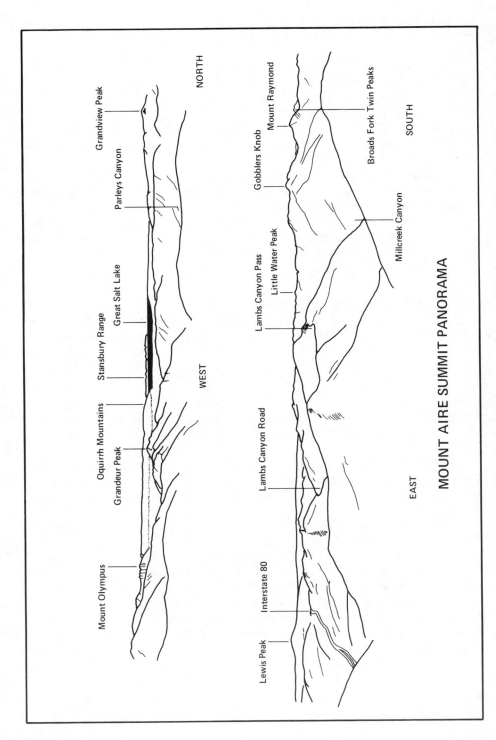

MOUNT AIRE SUMMIT PANORAMA

85

and is shaded, so it makes a good summer hike even though it is at a relatively low elevation. You can start at either the Elbow Fork trailhead, 6.4 miles up Millcreek Canyon, or at the Terraces trailhead, 4.7 miles up the canyon.

The Elbow Fork end of the trail begins at the footbridge on the south side 200 feet beyond the sharp turn in the road. The trail climbs a series of steep switchbacks and reaches an excellent viewpoint after only 10 minutes of walking. From here, the trail continues generally south as it gradually ascends to the crest of the ridge above Bowman Fork. The trail follows this mountain mahogany covered ridge for 3/4 mile before descending a series of switchbacks to the Terraces trailhead.

It is an excellent trail for observing the effect of the direction of the slope on the microclimate and on the vegetation as you walk through dense stands of tall fir and more open areas of aspen and Gambel oak.

To get the Terraces end of the trail, drive across the bridge leading to the picnic area at the top of the hill, take the right fork and park at the end of the road. A signboard marks the beginning of both the trail to Elbow Fork and the Bowman Trail.

ALEXANDER BASIN TRAIL (No. M-12)

Destination:	Alexander Basin	Gobblers Knob	Start of Trail to Bowman	Bowman Trail Junction
One-Way Miles:	1-1/2	2-1/4	1	2-1/2
Elevation Change:	1640	3086	1040	1440
Total Ascent:	1640	3086	1040	1740
Hiking Time One Way:	1h 35m	2h 40m	1h	2h 5m

Alexander Basin was the center of intense controversy during the final stages of the Utah National Forest Wilderness Bill in 1984. Hike up to this beautiful glacial cirque and discover why local conservationists fought so hard to protect the area.

The new Alexander Basin trailhead is on the south side of Millcreek Canyon, 7.8 miles up from Wasatch Blvd.

A trail mileage sign and a wilderness boundary sign are located where the trail turns and climbs directly up the hill. The next section is one of the steepest trails in the Wasatch. Soon, two well-graded switchbacks wind through stands of fir on the steep slope. After climbing 600 feet, the slope becomes more gradual and the trail straightens out and heads southwest. To reach the Alexander Basin viewpoint, continue south up an aspen-covered hill, climbing another 600 feet in the next 1/2 mile.

Alexander Basin to Gobblers Knob (No. M-12.1)

The trail ends at the edge of the Alexander Basin cirque, but a definite track continues. This route climbs 1000 feet up steep and loose slopes to the east ridge of Gobblers Knob. Carefully pick your way and make switchbacks where necessary to avoid erosion. In June much of the route will be snow-covered and the ridge-top cornice will still be present. At the saddle, turn west and follow the ridge crest for 1/4 mile to the summit.

Alexander Basin to Bowman Fork (No. M 13)

Most hikers have not discovered the pleasant walking and spectacular views of Alexander Basin, Porter Fork, Mount Raymond and the Salt Lake Valley that this under-utilized trail offers. A maintained trail traverses across the ridge and connects with the Bowman Trail about 1-1/2 mile beyond White Fir Pass. The junction with the connecting trail to Bowman Fork is located in a small clearing, a mile from the trailhead, at about the 8200-foot elevation.

From the junction, the trail to Bowman Fork heads west and drops a short way before beginning to climb across the first ridge. The trail rises and falls as it crosses a series of ridges and gullies but stays between 8200 and 8600 feet. The route alternates between open brush, wide-spaced aspen, and dense stands of fir. Soon, the huge Porter Fork Basin comes into view, and you can see the Bowman Trail below. You can make a loop by descending the Bowman Trail to Terraces, then taking the trail to Elbow Fork, followed by walking a mile up the road from Elbow Fork to the start.

SOLDIER FORK AND WILSON FORK

Destination:	Soldier Fork Pass	Wilson Fork Pass
One-Way Miles:	1-1/2	1-1/4
Elevation Gain:	1380	1622
Highest Point:	8880	9122
Hiking Time One Way:	1h 40m	1h 40m

These are both short, north-facing drainages which provide an alternative access to Raymond Ridge and the Desolation Trail. Soldier Fork has an abandoned trail, while Wilson Fork is off-trail hiking through open forest and meadows. This is a delightful area to explore, and the two routes can be combined into a loop.

Wilson Fork (No. M-14)

The Wilson Fork trailhead is 9.2 miles up the canyon. A closed jeep road starts up this drainage but ends in 1/4 mile. From here, find your own route, staying on game trails on the left side or near the center of the drainage. The area is open forest with little brush. Use the surrounding ridges as landmarks and aim for the low point on the main ridge to the southwest. From the saddle, the head of Soldier can be reached by traversing the minor summit to the east. Also, the ridge going west is a nice route to Gobblers Knob.

Soldier Fork (No. M-15)

The Soldier Fork Trail starts at the east end of the lower Big Water parking area, 9.5 miles up Millcreek Canyon. The well-graded Big Water Trail heads west from here and makes a wide loop before recrossing the Soldier Fork Trail higher up. The unmaintained Soldier Fork Trail goes directly up the drainage. Occasional fallen trees block the foot track. As you approach the head of the drainage, the slope becomes steeper and the game trails become as prominent as the human trail. The route makes several switchbacks just below the pass. If you lose the trail, work your way up through open forest. A trail continues from the pass to the Desolation Trail, about 200 yards downhill.

BIG WATER FORK
And Little Water Fork

To Dog Lake Junction via:	Big Water Official Trail	Big Water Direct Trail	Little Water Trail
One-Way Miles:	2-1/2	1-1/4	1-1/2
Elevation Change:	1200	1200	1200
Hiking Time One Way:	1h 50m	1h 15m	1h 20m

Note: All measurements are from the parking area to the junction at 8780 feet.

The upper trailhead at the end of the road, 9.6 miles up Millcreek Canyon, offers the shortest access to the Desolation Trail, Dog Lake, and Reynolds Peak. Mountain bikes are allowed except for even-numbered weekend days.

Three routes lead from here to the Dog Lake/Desolation Trail junction. The well-constructed Big Water Trail is the official Forest Service trail. The Little Water Trail, shown on the USGS map, is an old jeep road and is reached from the new Forest Service trail that leads from the Big Water Trail to the Great Western Trail. Another unofficial route is the foot track which runs directly up Big Water Gulch.

Big Water–Official Trail (No. M-16)

The Big Water Trail starts at the southwest corner of the upper parking area. It heads west and climbs gradually to join a side trail comeing from the lower parking area. The trail is a wide, obvious constructed path with frequent switchbacks and there is no difficulty staying on the route. The trail turns back to the east and crosses the stream. Here the unofficial direct route can be seen going more steeply up the drainage. Near the top of a minor ridge there is the junction with the newly-constucted section of the Great Western Trail which traverses east. The Great Western Trail soon crosses the Little Water Trail then continues east to join the Upper Millcreek Road. The Big Water Trail heads generally south in a series of switchbacks until it reaches the four-way junction where it crosses the Little Water Trail. Five more minutes up either branch will take you to the junction with the Desolation Trail near Dog Lake.

To reduce the conflict between hikers and mountain bikes, the Forest Service has instituted even/odd day restrictions on the weekends. Mountain bikes are allowed on odd weekend days (Saturdays and Sundays) only; the even days are reserved for hikers. These restrictions also apply to the Little Water Trail and the part of Great Western Trail in Millcreek Canyon.

Big Water–Direct Route (No. M-16.1)

This alternative route follows a reasonable grade, has signs of water bar construction, and provides a faster way to the Desolation Trail while avoiding the bicycles.

This is the foot track on the east side of the stream coming from Big Water Gulch. Avoid the meadow restoration just beyond the parking area. The trail follows the stream to the point where the official trail crosses the stream. The direct route continues up the drainage and rejoins the official trail one switchback below the four-way junction.

Little Water Trail (No. M-17)

The historic access to this trail was to go about 1/4 mile east from the upper Big Water parking area then turn south and follow the stream coming from Little Water Gulch. The official access, which bypasses the private land, branches from the Big Water Trail, described above. The Little Water Trail ascends through an open area, crosses the stream, and continues through forest and occasional small meadows until it reaches the four-way junction. Most of the way there is an obvious track and evidence of a road bench in the hillside.

Dog Lake Junction

All these routes converge at the Dog Lake junction on the Desolation Trail. From the junction you can descend to Dog Lake or climb Little Water Peak or Reynolds Peak. The Desolation Trail (Trail B-11) provides a connection to all the major trails from both Big Cottonwood and Millcreek, so many loops and extended hikes are possible in this area.

Upper Millcreek, Dog Lake and Reynolds Peak Area.

UPPER MILLCREEK CANYON (No. M-18)

Destination:	Meadow	Wasatch Crest Ridge (South)	Park West Pass	Murdock Peak
One-Way Miles:	2	3	2-3/4	3-1/4
Elevation Change:	1200	1900	1420	2002
Highest Point:	8800	9500	9020	9602
Hiking Time One Way:	1h 35m	2h 25m	2h 5m	2h 40m

The Great Western Trail follows the paved Millcreek Canyon road from Elbow Fork to the Upper Big Water trailhead. Here the Great Western Trail (No. R-2) continues up Millcreek Canyon to the Wasatch Crest Ridge that overlooks the Wolf Mountain Ski Area. (When was the last wolf in Utah?)

From the Upper Big Water parking area follow the Big Water Trail, described above, to the junction with the new trail which continues east. This trail traverses along the south side of the canyon and crosses the Little Water Trail. It stays nearly level until it meets the Upper Millcreek road in the canyon bottom.

The road enters a meadow where the trail forks. The north branch is the main road and leads to the pass just southeast of Murdock Peak. A ski lift is 1/4 mile east at the same elevation. The Murdock Peak area is easy cross-country hiking. Immediately before the pass, the road turns sharply south and follows the Wasatch Crest Ridge staying on the Millcreek side. A road runs east and descends into Summit County, and the ridge road, part of the Great Western Trail, continues as a trial (No. R-2) around the head of Millcreek and on toward Brighton. Most of the land on the Park City side are privately owned, as is Murdock Peak.

The south branch leads into the wide upper bowl where the road fades out just below the ridge, 300 vertical feet above. The trail goes back to the west, climbs up on the ridge, and then swings back to join the ridge crest trail. The ridge directly south of the bowl is the divide to the Mill D North Fork of Big Cottonwood Canyon. Desolation Lake is just over this ridge. A nice loop can be made by following the Raymond Ridge west over Little Water Peak and then descending to the parking area by the Big Water Trail.

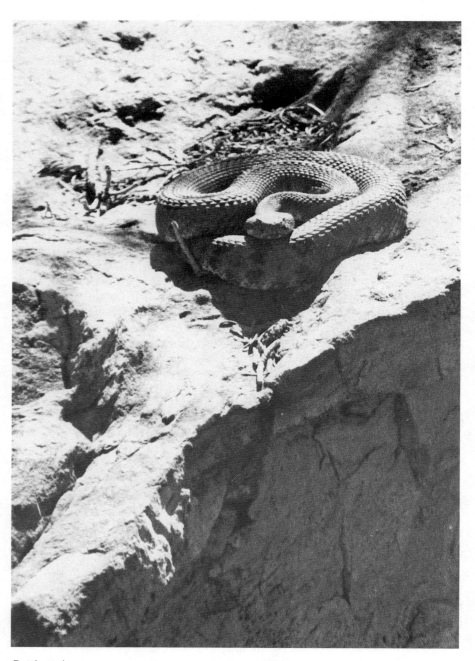

Rattlesnake—The author met this canyon resident while solo hiking off-trail in Big Cottonwood. Watch where you walk especially when crossing boulder fields.

7

BIG COTTONWOOD CANYON

This long canyon cuts east between Mount Olympus and Twin Peaks, then turns south as it approaches Brighton. The lower canyon is a narrow, stream-cut gorge with wild, steep walls that limit hiking. The upper canyon is a wide, glacier carved valley with numerous side drainages leading to lakes and alpine cirques. The mouth of the canyon is flanked by hard, Precambrian metamorphic rocks forming spectacular red and pink cliffs and buttresses. The upper canyon is a geologist's nightmare of hard and soft, young and old rock which has been thrust, folded, and intruded into endless scenic variety. The canyon offers the full range of ecological transitions from foothill brush to alpine tundra, and from swampy streambeds to forest zones to dry grasslands.

The trails near the canyon mouth lead into the Wilderness Areas on either side. The canyon has had a long mining history and many of the trails, especially from Mineral Fork to Brighton, are actually on old road grades. The best easy hiking is in the Brighton area, where the glacier-scoured bowls have resulted in delightful lakes a short walk from the highway.

Raymond Ridge to the north is crossed by several trails, and the area is mostly gentle to moderate terrain. Cottonwood Ridge to the south is asymmetrical. The north side offers a long gradual ascent, but the south side drops sharply into Little Cottonwood Canyon and, west of Cardiff Pass, there are no hiking routes across this ridge.

Big Cottonwood is in a cultural transition. It is far less developed then Little Cottonwood, and most of the resorts, restaurants, and residences are remnants of a more low-key era. Cabins and folksy stores and cafes contrast with the concrete high-rise condominiums and private clubs of Little Cottonwood, but Big Cottonwood has much potentially developable private land. A sewer has been constructed recently, and both the Brighton and Solitude ski areas have proposed new projects.

STAIRS GULCH (No. B-01)
Storm Mountain Trail

Distance: 1/2 mile one way to end of trail.
Elevation Gain: 300 feet.
Highest Point: Water Intake — 6100 feet.
Hiking Time One Way: 20 min

This short trail takes you into the lower portion of Stairs Gulch, an avalanche-swept couloir with the east face of Storm Mountain towering above. The cliffs, towers and pinnacles combine with summer snowfields to provide an easily accessible glimpse of the conditions experienced by climbers on the upper portions of major peaks.

The trail starts on the south side of the road directly across from the Storm Mountain picnic area, 2.9 miles up Big Cottonwood Canyon. Park 100 yards up the road near the geology sign. The trail follows the ramp up to the west and then turns directly south into Stairs Gulch. It follows the east side of the gulch along a water pipeline, and the constructed trail ends at the intake. The terrain beyond is suitable only for climbers or very experienced hikers and is described in the Mountaineering Scrambles chapter.

The snowfields in Stairs Gulch are frequently used by mountaineering classes for ice axe training, and the cliffs have several intermediate to difficult rock climbing routes. Rockfall from the frost-fractured quartzite walls accumulates to form the boulder-covered floor of the gulch. Stairs Gulch was a major obstacle to travel up the canyon before the modern graded road was constructed across the stair-like waterfall where the gulch meets Big Cottonwood Creek.

MULE HOLLOW (No. B-02)

Distance: 1-1/2 miles one way to the mine
Elevation Gain: 1400 feet
Highest Point: Mine at 7200 feet
Hiking Time One Way: 1 hr 30 min to mine

Mule Hollow is a nice hike to an abandoned mine in a seldom visited side canyon. The trail is south-facing and relatively low, so it is passable when other routes are snow-covered. There are spectacular cliffs on both sides of this steep-walled canyon, and Stairs Gulch and Storm Mountain are visible from the mine.

The trail starts on the north side of the road, 3.2 miles up Big Cottonwood Canyon, just above the Storm Mountain picnic area. A fence intended to keep vehicles out of the reservoir area is installed along the road at the end of Mule

Hollow. The best parking is at the geology sign on the south side of the road across from the picnic area and about 100 yards before the trailhead.

The well-defined trail starts on the right side of the stream coming from Mule Hollow and climbs steadily up the drainage. The canyon is narrow, and the trail makes frequent stream crossings. The trail never gets far from the stream, and in several places the water overflows onto the trail during high runoff periods. The trail ends at the mine dump where there are a collapsed tunnel, the ruins of a cabin, and a few pieces of equipment. A short way farther up there is another tunnel on the west side of the stream that has a large flow of water coming out; numerous cascades can be heard inside. Another mine dump is a few hundred feet farther up.

Beyond the mines, the hollow is filled with dense brush and loose rock, but deer trails and natural clearings can be used by adventurous hikers wishing to bushwhack higher. The west wall of the hollow can be climbed from the mine to a pass at the head of Dry Hollow overlooking the Salt Lake Valley. An experienced hiker can scramble up the head of the drainage and reach Wildcat Ridge. Mule Hollow Wall, a rock climbing area with many challenging routes, is on the west side of the hollow about 1/2 mile from the road.

S-TURN TRAILHEADS

The S-turn, 4.5 miles up Big Cottonwood Canyon, is the location of a very short walk to a waterfall and of three major trailheads. A spur road branches from the lower turn and follows along the stream for 1/4 mile to the Lake Blanche trailhead. The Broads Fork Trail starts from the spur road just after it crosses the bridge. The Mill B North Trail and the short walk to Hidden Falls start from the upper turn.

Parking is provided at a small area between the loops and on the spur road that follows the stream. Space is very limited and the trails are popular so park carefully.

BROADS FORK (No. B-03)

Destination:	Stream Crossing	Meadow (Trail End)
One-Way Miles:	1-1/4	2
Elevation Gain:	1300	2200
Highest Point:	7500	8400
Hiking Time One Way:	1h 15m	2h 5m

This trail starts on heavily timbered slopes, follows a stream through open stands of aspen, and reaches an alpine meadow with fine views of Dromedary Peak (elev. 11,107) and Sunrise Peak (elev. 11,275). The trail starts from the lower loop of the S-turn. Immediately after the spur road crosses the bridge, the Broads Fork Trail begins by heading west up the hill.

The trail climbs around the end of the ridge into the Broads Fork drainage, making one switchback along the way. After a mile through fir and spruce forest, the trail crosses the stream on a sturdy bridge. Several small, shady clearings and the natural cooling of the stream make the bridge a nice destination on hot summer days. After crossing to the west side of the stream, the trail passes through open brush and stands of aspen. A couple of small ridges give the feeling of "we're there," followed by disappointment when the crest is reached and more trail comes into view. Finally, the trail curves around the left side of a small knob, and the meadow opens up beyond.

The maintained trail ends at the bottom of the meadow, but a footpath continues left across the stream and up the east side of the bowl toward Twin Peaks. Another faint footpath leads up the right side of the meadow, passing above the swampy and brushy area and continuing up the open west side slopes. Both of these routes converge farther up. The upper part of Broads Fork is exposed to severe avalanches coming off the steep, smooth slopes of Twin Peaks to the west. Massive ridges of avalanche debris remain through June.

If you enjoy routefinding and scrambling, you can cross the ridge to the east and descend to the Lake Blanche Trail. The notch north of the end of the Broads Fork Trail is probably the best, but all ridge crossings involve steep slopes of loose rock and gravel.

Broads Fork Basin. The maintained trail ends at this viewpoint with Sunrise Peak ahead. The routes to Dromedary Peak and to Twin Peaks continue up the left side of the drainage.

BROADS FORK TWIN PEAKS

Distance: 4-1/2 miles one way from trailhead
Elevation Gain: 5130 feet
Highest Point: East summit at 11,330 feet
Hiking Time One Way: 4 hr 45 min to 5 hr 30 min depending on route conditions.
Special Difficulties: Scrambling, snowfields, boulder-hopping.

The beautifully matched summits of Twin Peaks form the west end of the rugged ridge separating Big Cottonwood and Little Cottonwood canyons. Panoramic views, the magnificent alpine setting, the enormous vertical relief, and the prominent position on the Salt Lake skyline make this peak a popular objective for intermediate and advanced hikers. From the end of the Broads Fork Trail there are several routes up Twin Peaks and all require some scrambling.

Standard Route (No. B-03.1)

The standard route continues from the meadow up the main drainage to a notch on the Cottonwood Ridge, then follows the ridge west to the summit. Upper Broads Fork is a boulderfield with much loose gravel and some brush. In May or June much of the route will be on snow making travel easier but an ice axe is advisable for climbing the steep headwall.

An unmaintained footpath continues east from the trail-end knoll, crosses the stream, and climbs up the east side of Broads Fork. After climbing about 1000 feet, there is another, less distinct basin, with Sunrise Peak directly ahead and the spectacular north face of Dromedary Peak to the left. Head toward the saddle to the right of Sunrise Peak. From this saddle you can see most of the remaining route to the summit, 1/4 mile to the northeast and 550 feet higher. There are two variations — the choice depends on the snow conditions and preferences for couloir *versus* ridge scrambling. Both routes have moderate exposure.

The high route follows the crest of the ridge until you come to an abrupt 20-foot cliff. This cliff is bypassed by traversing a series of ledges on the south side of the ridge for about 100 feet until you reach the crack which can be ascended back to the ridge crest. This traverse involves difficult scrambling. Use caution! Continue along the ridge then climb the switchbacks worn into the gravel of the summit cone.

The low route drops from the saddle and follows the slope on the Little Cottonwood side for about 200 yards to a couloir next to the cliffs that form the south ridge of the summit. Ascend this couloir, which may be snow-filled early in the season, to the ridge crest and continue up the summit cone.

Deaf Smith Canyon (Trail WF-4) is an alternative descent from Twin Peaks. The best way to avoid the cliffs north of Twin Peaks is to descend southwest from the west peak into a rounded gully with steep rock ridges on both sides. Follow this drainage until it curves back north into the main canyon.

Robinson Variation (No. B-03.2)

An exciting variation of the Broads Fork approach is to ascend the wide, steep gully southwest of the end of the knoll at the end of the trail. The route looks forbidding, but with some routefinding a way can be found through the slabs to the ridge above. The right side of the gully leads to a saddle overlooking Stairs Gulch and the left saddle overlooks Deaf Smith Canyon. There is considerable scrambling and exposure along the jagged north ridge to Twin Peaks but no technical climbing.

DROMEDARY PEAK
From Broads Fork

Distance: 3-3/4 miles one way from Broads Fork trailhead.
Elevation Gain: 4907 feet.
Highest Point: 11,107 feet.
Hiking Time One Way: 4h 30m to 5h depending on conditions.
Special Difficulties: Scrambling, snowfields, boulder-hopping.

The route to Dromedary from Broads Fork is the shortest and easiest approach. Both this route and the route from Lake Blanche converge on the upper mountain. Starting from the end of the Broads Fork trail, continue up the east side of the drainage as described for Twin Peaks. At about 9800 feet the Twin Peaks route turns southwest toward the notch and the route to Dromedary turns east. Aim for the shoulder of the mountain, about 200 feet above and south of the saddle on the ridge between Broads Fork and Lake Blanche Fork. At the shoulder, you are a few feet above the "sloping boulderfield" traverse described in the route from Lake Blanche. Traverse south on the Lake Blanche side, passing below the summit slopes, to the couloir leading up to the Cottonwood Ridge then continue scrambling the east ridge to the summit.

LAKE BLANCHE TRAIL (No. B-04)
Mill B South Fork

Destination:	Lower Clearing	Lake Blanche	Lake Lillian
One-Way Miles:	1-1/2	2-3/4	3-1/4
Elevation Gain:	1600	2720	2720
Extra Up & Down:			120
Highest Point:	7800	8920	8920
Hiking Time One Way:	1h 30m	2h 45m	3h

A well-maintained trail climbs past smooth rock slabs crowned with sawtooth spires to a photogenic basin containing Lake Blanche, Lake Florence,

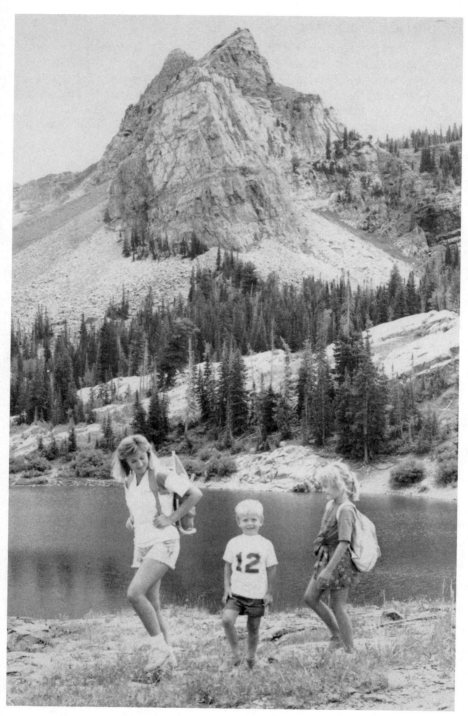

Lake Blanche and Sundial Peak. This trail is fairly long but these hikers managed the climb.

and Lake Lillian. The view of Sundial Peak above Lake Blanche is the emblem of the Wasatch Mountain Club, and the Salt Lake Valley is visible from the glacier-scoured rocks which ring the lakes. The USGS Map calls this drainage "Mill B South Fork" but the name "Lake Blanche Fork" is commonly used.

The trailhead is on the spur road that follows the stream for 1/4 mile from the lower bend of the S-turn to a picnic area with limited parking. The trail starts a few yards before the end of the road on the right (west) of the side stream coming from Lake Blanche. About 1/4 mile beyond the trailhead, the route crosses to the east side of the drainage on a fine bridge. For the next mile, the trail stays close to the stream and climbs steadily. Halfway to the lake, there is a clearing with fine views of the surrounding ridges and of Sundial Peak rising above the rounded red cliffs which rim the lakes.

The trail avoids the cliffs by leaving the stream and climbing the side slopes to the east. The Forest Service has done extensive trail work constructing switchbacks to bypass the erosion-prone steeper sections. Just before the lake the trail crosses a short area of bare rock where the track disappears, but just keep heading in the same general direction. It helps to pick out a few landmarks here to help find the start of the trail on the return. The trail ends at Lake Blanche, which is the highest of the three lakes in the basin.

Footpaths head in various directions. Using these paths, you can follow the north side of Lake Blanche to reach Lake Florence and Lake Lillian or you can make a circuit of the three lakes. Separate descriptions are provided for ascending each of the three peaks and for crossing the passes into Broads Fork and Mineral Fork.

ADVANCED HIKES
From Lake Blanche

Destination:	Sundial Peak	Dromedary Peak	Mount Superior
One-Way Miles:	3-3/4	4-3/4	4-3/4
Elevation Gain:	4120	4907	4932
Extra Up & Down:			120
Highest Point:	10,320	11,107	11,132
Hiking Time One Way:	3h 55m	4h 55m	5h15m
Special Difficulties:	Scrambling Exposure	Scrambling	Scrambling Exposure

Note: All distances and elevations are from the road.

West Branch – Dromedary and Broads Fork
(No. B-04.1)

Dromedary is a rugged and seldom-visited summit overlooking the major drainages on the far side of Little Cottonwood from White Pine to Hogum.

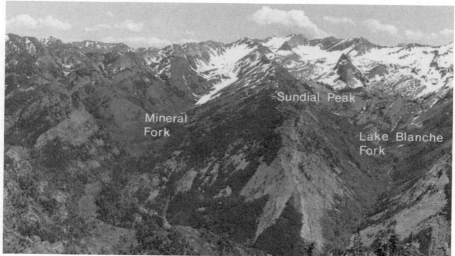

The south side of Big Cottonwood Canyon viewed from Wildcat Ridge in mid-June.
Excellent trails lead up Mineral Fork, Lake Blanche Fork, and Broads Fork. The trail in Stairs Gulch ends in
1/4 mile; above is mountaineering terrain.

Top Photo — Lake Blanche to Stairs Gulch. The skyline summits, from the left, are Dromedary, Sunrise,
and Twin Peaks.

Lower Photo — Mineral Fork and Lake Blanche Fork. Mount Superior and Monte Cristo are on the skyline
and part of Kessler Peak is visible on the far left.

The most direct route from Lake Blanche is to climb up the grassy gully which is south southwest (200 degrees) from the Lake Blanche Dam. The gully headwall is an upward "V" of cliffs. On the left side, near the point of the "V," there is a crack which requires about 20 feet of easy rock scrambling with no exposure. After reaching the grassy slopes above, note landmarks so you can find the crack on your return. Continue directly up the slopes toward the couloir southeast of Dromedary and ascend to the Cottonwood Ridge. The summit is 300 vertical feet of moderate ridge crest scrambling to the northeast.

The longer route up Dromedary is to ascend the wide scree-filled gully which is southwest (220 degrees) from Lake Blanche. Turn left just below the headwall into the steep couloir that takes you up 200 vertical feet through the cliff bands and onto the upper slope of Dromedary. An indistinct pass can be seen about 300 feet above the top of the couloir. This pass is the junction with the route to Dromedary from Broads Fork. From the top of the couloir, the route traverses for 1/2 mile south across a sloping boulderfield. Traversing low is easier, while the high traverse from the pass is shorter. The traverse ends at the couloir leading to the Cottonwood Ridge, which was described above.

Sundial Peak (No. B-04.2)

The towering north face of Sundial is a difficult route for technical rock climbers, but hikers can scramble up the back side. Most hikers start by going around Lake Blanche on the north, crossing at the dam, and heading south up the rounded rock ribs ahead. When you are level with the talus slope at the base of Sundial, turn left and scramble up through the cliff band into the hanging canyon which is immediately on the west side of Sundial. Follow the side of Sundial southeast for 3/4 mile climbing 600 feet to a saddle on the Sundial ridge. From this saddle, scramble along the knife-edged ridge for 300 yards heading back northwest to the summit. There are a few tricky spots with dangerous slabs below so pick your route carefully and turn back if you question your ability.

An alternative to the hanging canyon is to continue up the rock ribs until the drainage curves to the southeast and you can turn back toward Sundial. This is a longer route, but the area is well worth exploring for its own sake.

East Branch–Regulator Johnson Pass
Cardiac Pass, and Mount Superior (No. B-04.3)

The east fork of the Lake Blanche drainage is a pair of glaciated canyons with sheer cliffs overlooking a spring-fed lake, meadows, moraines, and boulderfields. An unmaintained trail continues from the east end of Lake Blanche, traverses high on the wall of the east branch of the drainage, and leads to old mine workings just below the pass leading into Mineral Fork. This trail, which can easily be seen from the lake, avoids the cliff bands which make hiking the east branch a routefinding challenge. The start of the trail is lost among the tracks around the lake, so look for the distinct track leading east up between the first pair of rock ribs beyond the lake. After climbing 600 feet, the trail turns southeast and traverses through the dark cliffs and continues into the upper hanging canyon.

The trail ends above the ruins of a mine and near a small pond. The pass to the Regulator Johnson Mine in Mineral Fork is a 200 foot scramble directly up the slope from the trail end. The canyon beyond the pond is an open boulderfield heaped into a series of moraines. The easiest way to continue up the east branch of Lake Blanche Fork is to drop down to the mine workings then follow the drainage.

A steep, glacier-carved headwall rings the end of this drainage. The prominent notch on the left (east) is Cardiac Pass, which leads into Cardiff Fork. Mount Superior (elev. 11,050) is the indistinct high point to the south, while Monte Cristo (elev. 11,132) is the dark mass on the right. Superior can be reached by climbing to Cardiac Pass then scrambling along the narrow ridge, or by ascending the headwall directly below the summit. Monte Cristo is reached by continuing along the ridge from Superior. These summits offer a view of Snowbird's developments as well as a panorama of Big and Little Cottonwood canyons.

The Twin Peaks Wilderness boundary follows the jagged ridge between Mineral Fork and Lake Blanche Fork to the summit of Mount Superior. The original conservationist proposal was to use the old mine road in Mineral Fork as the boundary, but this was opposed by helicopter skiing interests.

MILL B NORTH FORK (No. B-05)
Hidden Falls Trail

Destination:	Overlook Trail	Desolation Pass	Porter Fork Pass	Baker
One-Way Miles:	1	3-1/4	3-3/4	4-3/4
Elevation Gain:	840	2960	2960	3120
Highest Point:	7040	9160	9160	9320
Hiking Time One Way:	55m	3h 5m	3h15m	3h 50m

Spectacular views of the Wilderness to the south highlight this well-maintained trail as it winds upward through cliffs and across streams. Mount Raymond, Porter Fork, and Mill A Basin are reached from this trail, and it is often used as a descent from hikes starting at Butler Fork. The trail is named after the stream at the start, but it actually crosses both branches of the next drainage east before reaching the Desolation Trail.

Two trails start on the north side of the road on the upper loop of the S-turn, 4.5 miles up Big Cottonwood Canyon. A very short trail leads along the stream to Hidden Falls. The main trail heads diagonally up the slope to the right, makes a series of switchbacks, and rejoins the stream above Hidden Falls. A half mile from the start, the trail passes the Wilderness boundary sign. A few yards beyond, the trail makes a sharp 180-degree turn, leaves the stream, and heads south through open forest. Two more switchbacks bring you to the overlook.

The viewpoint is on the rock outcrop, 20 feet south of the trail, just as the trail begins to turn back to the north. Cliffs drop 600 feet from the overlook to the road.

The trail now heads north along the crest of a ridge for another 1/2 mile to another overlook and a cliff band. Next it crosses into the Elbow Fork drainage, a remarkable area of riparian vegetation, follows the drainage a short way, then begins a last series of switchbacks up the ridge to the east. The Desolation Trail junction is not correctly shown on the USGS map due to trail relocation. The Desolation Trail makes a loop around Mount Raymond, staying between 9200 and 9400 feet, and the junction is now about 200 yards farther east.

Connections along the Desolation Trail From Mill B

The Desolation Trail can be followed west about 1/4 mile to reach Porter Fork West Pass. From here, the Porter Fork Trail descends to the Millcreek road. The Desolation Trail crosses the ridge and traverses high across the Porter Fork drainage toward Thaynes Canyon. Immediately before the pass are the steep, open southwest slopes of Mount Raymond. Experienced hikers can ascend these slopes by staying well to the left, thereby avoiding the cliffs below the Mount Raymond summit. The easier route up Mount Raymond is to follow the Desolation Trail east one mile to Baker Pass then climb the east ridge.

MINERAL FORK (No. B-06)

Destination:	Overlook	Wasatch Mine	Regulator Johnson
One-Way Miles:	3/4	3	4-1/2
Elevation Gain:	450	1940	3510
Highest Point:	7160	8650	10,220
Hiking Time One Way:	35m	2h 30m	4h

Mineral Fork has no routefinding problems and is well suited to large groups. A well-graded mining road, currently closed to vehicles, leads to a spectacular overlook then continues past the Wasatch Mine. This mine is at the transition between forest and open alpine terrain. Above are the switchbacks across talus slopes to the Regulator Johnson Mine.

The Mineral Fork trailhead is on the south side of the road, 6.1 miles up Big Cottonwood Canyon. Look for a heavy gate which blocks the Mineral Fork road where it joins the highway. The dirt road crosses the stream, then heads west into the canyon. Both the USGS map and the Hiking the Wasatch Map accurately show the road with all its switchbacks.

The road makes four switchbacks and then arrives at an overlook that provides a fine view down and across Big Cottonwood Canyon. The road eventually arrives at the Wasatch Mine where a stream of rusty water discharges from the portal. From here you have a view back toward Kessler Peak and ahead toward the upper bowl of Mineral Fork. To reach the Regulator Johnson Mine, continue up the 24 switchbacks until you reach the scattered artifacts which mark the site. The upper portion of the fork is loose scree and is swept by winter avalanches, so there is little vegetation except low, well-rooted or fast-growing species.

The pass 200 feet above the Regulator Johnson Mine is reached by scrambling up the boulders on the right of the mine. The route described for the east branch of Lake Blanche Fork is directly below the pass on the other side.

Mineral Fork is unusual in that the upper cirque is not on the main ridge line. The triple divide of Cardiff Fork, Mineral Fork, and Lake Blanche Fork is separated from the main canyon divide by a short, jagged ridge. This peak at the head of Mineral Fork can be reached by scrambling the ridge from the Regulator Johnson pass. The area is broken by cliffs, narrow ridges, and rock pinnacles, so careful routefinding is needed.

Mineral Fork and Cardiff Fork. This rugged area is viewed from near Carbonate Pass (Hike B-12.4) The old road climbing to the Regulator Johnson Mine is visible on the right in Mineral Fork (Hike B-06). The Mount Superior area on the skyline is usually approached from the Alta side (Hike L-08.1).

106

BUTLER FORK TRAILHEAD

The Butler Fork Trail provides the best access to a large area on the north side of Big Cottonwood Canyon between Dog Lake and Mount Raymond. The east-branch trail climbs below the south slopes of Gobblers Knob to reach Dog Lake and Reynolds Peak. The west-branch trail climbs past a viewpoint on the ridge between Butler Fork and Mill A Gulch, then continues north. The Desolation Trail crosses high in the Butler Fork drainage, connects the east and west branch trails, and continues west below Mount Raymond.

The Butler Fork trail starts on the north side of the road, 8.5 miles up Big Cottonwood Canyon. A large parking area is on the south side of the road 100 yards up the canyon from the trailhead. The trail starts on the west side of the stream, then crosses on a bridge and climbs quickly up the steep-sided gulch. After 1/2 mile, the drainage widens and forks. A sign marks the junction where a maintained trail to Dog Lake turns east along the stream and the main trail continues left (west) toward the saddle above Mill A Basin.

East Branch of Butler Fork (No. B-07)

Destination:	Dog Lake	Loop Via Desolation Trail
One-Way Miles:	2-1/4	6-1/2
Elevation Gain:	1640	1640
Highest Point:	8760	8760
Hiking Time One Way:	1h 50m	4h 10m

This route to Dog Lake passes through an incredible range of plant communities in a short distance. The mixture of sagebrush, stream-side willow, Gambel oak, aspen, and spruce-fir communities is an excellent example of the effects of microclimate and soil conditions.

From the trail junction 1/2 mile up Butler Fork, the trail to Dog Lake crosses a bridge and heads east along the stream. The side canyon between Gobblers Knob and Reynolds Peak is narrow, and the trail crosses the stream five times before the stream disappears in a meadow. The trail climbs to a saddle where it joins the Desolation Trail. The combined trail continues nearly level for 1/4 mile along the head of Big Water Gulch, a side canyon of Millcreek, before crossing another saddle into the Mill D drainage just above Dog Lake.

The two branches of Butler Fork and the Desolation Trail can be combined into an excellent loop, or you can return to the Big Cottonwood road by the Mill D Trail from Dog Lake. Another option is to climb Reynolds Peak from Dog Lake and hike west along the ridge then drop back to the Butler Fork Trail.

West Branch of Butler Fork (No. B-08)
Circle-All Peak, Mill A Basin and Mount Raymond

Destination:	Circle All Peak	Desolation Trail	Baker Pass
One-Way Miles:	1-3/4	2	3-1/2
Elevation Gain:	1587	1520	2050
Highest Point:	8707	8640	9200
Hiking Time One Way:	1h 40m	1h 45m	2h 45m

At the trail junction 1/2 mile from the Butler Fork trailhead, a well-maintained trail continues left and follows a small stream coming from the west branch for a short way. The USGS map shows the old route, now overgrown, continuing up the stream bed, but the trail turns right and ascends switchbacks which were constructed to avoid trail erosion. The trail then crosses back to the

Raymond Ridge viewed from Kessler Peak summit. The Desolation Trail (B-11) provides a high connection from Dog Lake, across Butler Fork, around Mount Raymond, and into Porter Fork. The routes up Mount Raymond and Gobblers Knob follow the ridge crest. Circle-All Peak is an easy hike with excellent views.

left side of the drainage and makes another series of switchbacks up the steep, aspen-covered slope leading to the ridge crest.

Circle-All Peak (elev. 8707) is a hundred yards south from where the trail reaches the ridge. A foot track leads to this popular viewpoint. To the south, Kessler Peak dominates the foreground, with Cottonwood Ridge in the background. Mount Raymond and Gobblers Knob complete the panorama. This peak is named after the avalanche slide area below but the origin of the slide area name is obscure.

The trail continues north along the ridge above Mill A Basin for 1/4 mile to the Desolation Trail. Several other tracks can be seen, including the now abandoned trail that drops down into Mill A Basin and follows a moraine back up to Baker Pass. To reach the Mount Raymond area and Baker Pass, turn left on the Desolation Trail and follow an ascending traverse, gaining 450 feet in the next mile. The trails in this area have recently been relocated. Just below the saddle, the Desolation Trail continues east and a short branch trail leads to Baker Pass and the Bowman Trail junction. The Desolation Trail may be followed on a nearly level grade for a mile southwest around the Mill A Basin to the Mill B North Fork Trail.

SUMMITS FROM BAKER PASS

Destination:	Mount Raymond		Gobblers Knob	
Approach Route:	From Butler Fork	From Bowman Fork	From Butler Fork	From Bowman Fork
One-Way Miles:	4-1/4	4-1/2	4	4-1/4
Elevation Change:	3161	4041	3166	4046
Highest Point:	10,241	10,241	10,246	10,246
Hiking Time One Way:	3h 40m	4h 15m	3h 35m	4h 10m

Note: Both summits are reached from Baker Pass, where the Bowman Fork and Butler Fork trails join. Measurements are from the road.

Mount Raymond (No. B-08.2)

Mount Raymond overlooks nearly all of Big Cottonwood and Millcreek canyons and is one most popular peaks in the Wasatch. Three well-defined ridges join at the angular summit, and cliffs drop to Porter Fork and Mill A Basin. The standard route heads up from Baker Pass and follows occasional switchbacks, keeping near the crest of the east ridge of Mount Raymond. Near the top, the ridge narrows to a knife-edge and there is some scrambling, but the route is suitable for most hikers. An alternative route is the steep slope on the west side of the mountain, which leads from the Desolation Trail near Porter Fork West Pass to the summit.

Gobblers Knob (No. B-08.3)

This massive mountain is the highest point on the ridge between Millcreek and Big Cottonwood. From Baker Pass, a faint track heads northeast up the ridge toward Gobblers Knob. There is no scrambling and little brush along the ridge. The true summit is the second high point on this route. The ridge continues east and is described as Hike M-12.1, the route up Gobblers Knob from Alexander Basin. The upper portion of Gobblers Knob is largely treeless creating excellent views and off-trail routes for hikers who like exploring.

MILL D NORTH FORK TRAILHEAD
Dog Lake and Desolation Lake

The Mill D North Fork is one of the most popular canyons for easy hikes in summer and for ski tours in winter. These trails are also extremely popular with mountain bikes. The drainage is "Y" shaped, with maintained trails leading to both Dog Lake in the west branch and Desolation Lake in the east. Hiking in this valley gives an intimate, enclosed feeling. Connecting trails and routes continue beyond the lakes in all directions, and the easy peaks around the perimeter of the basin can be reached by short off-trail hikes. The Mill D Trail can be combined with the Butler Fork Trail to create a loop hike which requires only a short return walk along the road.

The trail starts from the Mill D trailhead parking area, at the bottom of Reynolds Gulch and just across the highway from the road into Cardiff Fork, 9.6 miles up Big Cottonwood. The trail begins in the clearing east of the Reynolds Gulch stream and makes a gradual ascending traverse across the south-facing slope between Reynolds Gulch and the Mill D drainage. It then turns north and continues almost level for 1/2 mile until it reaches the stream in Mill D Fork. The trail continues up the west side of the drainage for another 3/4 mile to the trail junction.

This trailhead was relocated by the Forest Service. The historic trailhead on is on the north side of the road 9.9 miles up the canyon. The old route curves northwest into the drainage then follows the west side of the stream across from the summer homes. This route crosses the stream twice before joining with the new trail.

DOG LAKE (No. B-09)

Destination:	Y Junction	Dog Lake	Big Water Junction
One-Way Miles:	1-1/2	2	2-1/4
Elevation Gain:	1010	1520	1560
Highest Point:	8250	8760	8800
Hiking Time One Way:	1h 15m	1h 45m	1h 50m

Most Wasatch lakes are in alpine cirques, but Dog Lake is set in a forested area with rolling hills and grassy meadows. Nearby, there is a major trail junction with connecting routes in every direction.

From the trail junction where Mill D North Fork branches, turn left and follow the wide trail along the bottom of the gully for 1/2 mile to the lake. This section is steep for a beginner hike, but the trail is excellent and the steep section is short. There is a foot track all around the lake. If you want a little privacy, the meadow just south of the lake is off the main trails and drains into a gully which offers an interesting alternative return to the main Mill D Trail.

The trail continues along the north shore of the lake and climbs 50 feet to the junction on a small saddle. The Big Water Trail and Little Water Trail coming from Millcreek Canyon and the Desolation Trail converge here. The Butler Fork East Branch Trail separates from the Desolation Trail 1/4 mile west of this saddle.

DESOLATION LAKE (No. B-10)

Destination:	Desolation Lake	Beartrap Fork Pass
One-Way Miles:	3-1/2	4
Elevation Change:	1890	2450
Highest Point:	9240	9800
Hiking Time One Way:	2h 40m	3h 15m

Desolation Lake is a large mountain lake with no surface outlet—the water drains through the loose glacial deposits which formed the lake cirque. This was the last grazing allotment in the Tri-Canyon Area. Grazing was suspended in 1993.

Starting at the Mill D trailhead, hike 1-1/2 miles to the junction where the canyon branches and take the right (east) branch to Desolation Lake. The trail makes a switchback at the start, then joins the east drainage near an overlook. There are excellent views of the Mount Superior and Cardiac Pass area on the far side of Big Cottonwood Canyon. The route follows the drainage through a meadow, up a short hill, then past a small pond. From the pond the trail goes northeast through the woods, then climbs over the final moraine to reach the lake in an open cirque.

The trail continues past the north side of the lake and ascends 300 feet to the Wasatch Crest Ridge overlooking Summit County where it joins Trail No. R-2 from Millcreek to Scotts Hill. The trail to the ridge has switchbacks and is part of the Great Western Trail. Mountain bicycle use has carved an eroded track up the slopes on the south side of the lake.

A good loop hike is to climb to the ridge and cross into Beartrap Fork, which is immediately south of Desolation Lake. Beartrap Fork can be followed back to the Big Cottonwood road, where you will be only 1 mile from the old Mill D trailhead.

REYNOLDS PEAK (No. B-09.1)

Approach Route:	Mill D Trail	Big Water Trail	Butler Trail
One-Way Miles:	2-1/4	2	2-3/4
Elevation Gain:	2182	1822	2302
Starting Elev:	7240	7600	7120
Hiking Time One Way:	2h 15m	1h 55m	2h 30m

Note: All measurements are from the trailhead to the summit (elev. 9422).

Reynolds Peak, an easy summit for hikers, is reached by a short off-trail ascent from Dog Lake. The line drawing identifies some of the features which can be seen from here.

The route to the summit starts on the low ridge southwest of Dog Lake and follows the north ridge of Reynolds Peak. A foot track goes from the south side of Dog Lake, passes the route to Reynolds, and eventually connects with the maintained trail a few hundred feet west of the main Dog Lake trail junction. If you don't find the start, just head south keeping near the crest of the ridge. From the saddle to the summit is 1/2 mile and 650 vertical feet. The climb is through open aspen with some brush.

The southeast ridge of Reynolds Peak can be descended back to the start of the Mill D Trail. There is quite a bit of brush but no other difficulties. Another alternative is to hike along the west ridge for a way, then drop down to the Butler Fork Trail and return to the road at the Butler Fork trailhead. If you follow this ridge too far west, you get into an area with a lot of fallen trees, brush and cliffs, so drop off the ridge while you can still see open areas among the fir trees below.

LITTLE WATER PEAK (No. B-09.2)

Approach Route:	Mill D Trail	Big Water Trail
One-Way Miles:	3	2-1/4
Elevation Gain:	2365	2005
Starting Elevation:	7240	7600
Hiking Time One Way:	2h 40m	2h 5m

Note: All measurements are from the trailhead to the Little Water Peak summit (elev. 9605 feet).

This is another relatively easy summit for hikers. The route up Little Water Peak from Dog Lake starts as a track up the hillside on the north side of the lake, then turns right and follows the ridge northeast to the summit. There are several alternative tracks up the brushy hillside at the start. Once on the ridge, the terrain is open with grass and widely spaced aspen. Hiking is possible just about anywhere, but the game trails near the crest are the best route.

A good off-trail hike is to continue east from the summit to the Wasatch

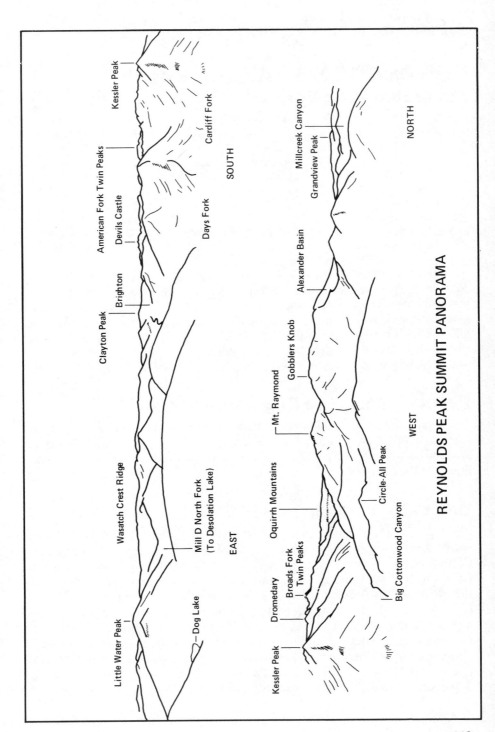

REYNOLDS PEAK SUMMIT PANORAMA

Kessler Peak
American Fork Twin Peaks
Devils Castle
Cardiff Fork
Days Fork
Brighton
Clayton Peak
Millcreek Canyon
Grandview Peak
Alexander Basin
Gobblers Knob
Mt. Raymond
Little Water Peak
Wasatch Crest Ridge
Mill D North Fork
(To Desolation Lake)
Dog Lake
Oquirrh Mountains
Broads Fork
Twin Peaks
Dromedary
Kessler Peak
Circle-All Peak
Big Cottonwood Canyon

EAST
SOUTH
WEST
NORTH

113

Crest at the head of Millcreek. If you get tired following the ridge, you can easily drop down to the Desolation Lake Trail.

DESOLATION TRAIL (No. B-11)
Big Cottonwood Portion

Trail Segment:	Desolation Lake to Dog Lake Junction	Dog Lake Junction to Butler Fork West Trail	Butler Fork to Baker Pass	Baker Pass to Porter Fork
One-Way Miles:	2-1/2	3	2	2
Elevation Change:	-400	-200	600	100
Highest Point:	9200	8800	9200	9400
Hiking Time One Way:	1h 20m	1h 30m	50m	1h 10m

The Desolation Trail was constructed by the Forest Service as a well-graded route from Thaynes Canyon on the Millcreek road to Desolation Lake. This long trail provides a nearly level connection among the numerous routes coming up from Millcreek and from Big Cottonwood, creating possibilities for extended hikes. The best hike in the Wasatch for seeing fall foliage is to ascend Big Water Gulch, then follow the Big Cottonwood portion of Desolation Trail west and return to Millcreek by either the Bowman Trail or the Porter Fork Trail.

Desolation Lake to Dog Lake Junction

The Desolation Trail follows the drainage from Desolation Lake down to the junction in Mill D North Fork, then back up the drainage to Dog Lake. The route is described as part of the Mill D North Trail, since that is how nearly everyone thinks of the route.

Dog Lake Junction to Butler Fork

This section is wide, level, and in good condition. The trail provides a constantly changing view of Butler Fork and of the peaks on both sides of Big Cottonwood Canyon. From the junction with the Big Water Trail west of Dog Lake, this trail winds around the south side of Gobblers Knob, staying between the 8600 and 8800 foot contours. Five minutes after leaving the Dog Lake junction, the trail forks. The left trail leads down the east branch of Butler Fork, and the right trail is the Desolation Trail. The area west of this junction is in the Mount Olympus Wilderness. The slopes above are brushy, but a foot track leads to the head of Soldier Fork, and bushwhacking to the ridge above Wilson Fork is also possible. The trail descends 200 feet to a pleasant meadow, then climbs past a series of small cliffs to the junction with the Butler Fork west-branch trail.

114

Butler Fork to Porter Fork

From the junction with the Butler Fork Trail, the route continues west. It ascends 450 feet in one mile then passes about 200 vertical feet below Baker Pass, the saddle between Mount Raymond and Gobblers Knob. A switchback leads up to Baker Pass and the Bowman Fork Trail junction. The Desolation Trail continues along a contour around the head of the Mill A Basin and hooks around the end of the sharp southeast ridge of Mount Raymond. After a mile the Desolation Trail reaches the small saddle above Maxfield Basin, where it joins the Mill B North Fork Trail. The nearly level trail continues another 1/2 mile to the pass west of Mount Raymond leading down into Porter Fork. The continuation of the Desolation Trail on the Millcreek side is described as Trail No. M-04.

Porter Fork West Pass to Neffs Canyon (No. B-11.1)

There is a little-known route along the Big Cottonwood side of the ridge which leads to the pass between the head of Mill B Fork and Neffs Canyon. This is apparently an abandoned trail since some sections were obviously constructed while other sections are no more than game trails. Follow the ridge west from the Porter Fork pass. The route traverses below some of the minor peaks rather than following the crest. Stay high and watch for the track and an occasional cairn.

Descending Kessler Peak by the north route (Hike B-12.3). Mill A Gulch and Mount Raymond are visible across the canyon.

CARDIFF FORK (No. B-12)
Mill D South Fork

Destination:	Donut Falls	Cardiff Mine	Cardiff Pass
One-Way Miles:	3/4	2-1/2	3-1/4
Elevation Gain:	280	1660	2720
Highest Point:	7200	9140	10,200
Hiking Time One Way:	30m	2h 5m	3h

Cardiff Fork is a long, straight canyon with steep cliffs on both sides. Upper Cardiff Fork is quite nice and contains many relics of the mining era. The road over Cardiff Pass was a major route connecting Alta with the extensive mines in Cardiff Fork. The rich history resulted in a patchwork of Forest Service and private land. The main road leading up Cardiff Fork to the mine currently receives heavy use from pickup trucks, motorcycles, and ATVs, but the steep side roads and trails are pleasant hiking.

The road into Cardiff Fork turns south from the Big Cottonwood road, 9.3 miles up the canyon. The road is paved to the Jordan Pines group picnic area, then becomes a gravel road that continues south through a summer home area. There is a trailhead for Donut Falls and Cardiff Fork 3/4 miles from the Big Cottonwood Road just before the stream crossing. At this point, a gate closes the road to all vehicles except mountain bikes.

Donut Falls (No. B-12.1)

This is one of the easier hikes in the Wasatch. Park in the developed trailhead just before the stream crossing and follow the trail that starts on the east side of the creek. After walking 1/2 mile, you will come to a major fork in the road. The left fork leads to the falls, and the right fork continues up to the mine. Continue along the road to the falls.

Cardiff Fork Road To Mine and Pass (No. B12.2)

The Cardiff Fork road stays on the west side of the canyon as it follows the stream. There are several points where the road forks and rejoins, and there are branch roads which go to mines high on the canyon wall. The main road passes several mine dumps on the way to Cardiff Mine, where rusting machinery and buildings in various stages of collapse mark the site. Beyond the mine, the road soon degenerates into a trail which continues over Cardiff Pass at the head of the canyon and descends to Alta. Just below the mine, there is a major branch road which works its way up the west side of the canyon and passes through a meadow before it fades out near Montreal Hill on the west ridge.

KESSLER PEAK

Destination:	North Route to Summit	Carbonate Pass Route to Summit	Montreal Hill Route to Summit
One-Way Miles:	2-1/4	3	4
Elevation Change:	2953	2953	2953
Hiking Time One Way:	2h 40m	3h	3h 30m
Special Difficulties:	Steep	Scrambling	Long

Note: All measurements are from the stream crossing to the summit. (elev. 10,403).

Kessler Peak, the high point on the north end of the ridge separating Cardiff Fork and Mineral Fork, is a challenging hike that offers a spectacular view of Flagstaff, Mount Superior, Dromedary, Twin Peaks, Mount Raymond, Gobblers Knob, and the entire upper end of Big Cottonwood Canyon.

There are at least two well-defined trails up Kessler Peak from the Cardiff Fork road and several bushwhacking variations. Use a topographic map to supplement these descriptions.

North Route (No. B-12.3)

This route is the shortest and the easiest to follow. It climbs very steeply but involves no scrambling. The trail starts from the main Cardiff Fork road less than 1/4 mile beyond the road to Donut Falls. An excellent landmark is a large, lone fir tree on the left, about 100 feet beyond where the north route trail starts by heading up the slope on the right. The USGS map shows the start of this trail. The trail passes through a meadow, then continues climbing. About 9200 feet, watch carefully for a distinct junction where the trail begins a traverse across an avalanche gully to connect with another trail on the far ridge. After crossing the gully, the trail crosses to the west side of the ridge and begins a very steep climb up a path which connected two mine workings. This brings you to the ruins of a cabin on the saddle between the north and main summits. From here, follow the west side of the ridge to the main summit.

Carbonate Pass Route (No. B-12.4)

If you find this trail, which is an old mining wagon road, the route is quite easy. If you miss the trail, you are in for brush and steep scrambling on loose rock.

To locate the start of this trail, watch for the first mine dump on the right-hand side of the road. Contour around the mine dump and you will see a trail starting up to the south which eventually curves back north and climbs to Carbonate Pass. As you walk up the road, note the prominent yellow spur ridge near the top of Kessler Peak. The trail goes on the south side of this ridge.

The trail ascends through the aspen and soon leads to a steep, grassy meadow. If you lose the trail, search for this meadow. The trail goes up the left side of the meadow and at the top it traverses to the north. From here on, the route is a distinct track that follows switchbacks as it ascends past the huge mine dump to the south of the yellow spur ridge just before reaching the saddle between Cardiff and Mineral Fork. Several ruins of mine buildings are on the saddle.

From the saddle, a track heads north along the Mineral Fork side of the ridge, dropping about 100 feet before reaching the steep couloir leading to the summit. There is considerable scrambling and routefinding, but there are no difficulties that would stop an experienced hiker.

Montreal Hill Route (No. B-12.5)

A long route to Kessler Peak is to hike up the mine roads above the Cardiff mine and gain the ridge near Montreal Hill. This ridge can be followed back to the north, with occasional scrambling through small cliff bands, to Carbonate Pass.

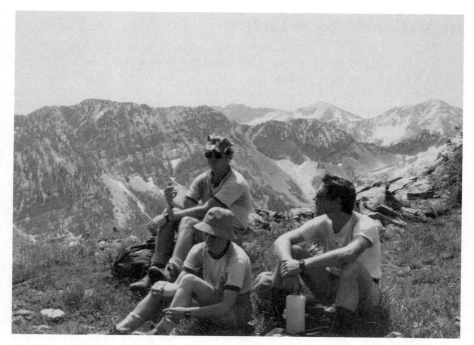

Rest stop at Carbonate Pass. The view is looking across Cardiff Fork with the high peaks of the Alta area visible across the ridge.

DAYS FORK (No. B-13)

Destination:	Lower Meadow	Eclipse Mine	Silver Fork Pass	Flagstaff Peak
One-Way Miles:	1-1/2	2-3/4	3	3-3/4
Elevation Gain:	850	2250	2570	3180
Highest Point:	8200	9600	9920	10,530
Hiking Time One Way:	1h 10m	2h 30m	2h 45m	3h 35m
Special Difficulties:				Scrambling

Days Fork is a long side canyon leading south from the Spruces campground. The upper basin features a well-preserved boiler and steam engine and several old mine workings in a beautiful alpine cirque with a steep headwall. Mount Superior, Silver Fork, Twin Lakes Pass, and the Alta parking lot are all within a mile of the upper end of Days Fork.

The trail starts at the Spruces campground on the south side of the road 10.1 miles up Big Cottonwood Canyon. Turn right on the side road to cross the bridge. At the concession booth, ask for directions to the hiker parking area. From the gate at the southwest corner of the hiker parking area, walk past the cinder block toilet building and continue straight south toward the group picnic area. The Days Fork Trail starts as a jeep road beyond the locked gate ahead.

Days Fork to the Mine

The road makes a curve to the east side of the drainage where it enters a steep chute that is a nightmare for ski tours in the winter. After a climb of 300 feet, the trail levels off and climbs gradually for the next mile to the lower basin. The Greens Basin Trail branches left soon after the top of the steep portion. Ahead, the hiking trail goes left around a large wet area then quickly rejoins the road.

The lower basin at 8200 feet is a nice meadow with wooded cliffs on both sides. Here, the road loops to the right side of the drainage as the slope gets steeper. Looking back to the north, you can see much of the Mill D North Fork drainage and Reynolds Peak. After passing the remains of an old mine cabin, the trail continues on a long ascent along the west side of the stream. The road finally rejoins the stream after climbing about 1000 feet from the meadow to the Days Fork Mine. The trail crosses the stream, then ascends a steep hill. Above, the slope levels off, and the trees give way to an open bowl surrounded by steep, loose rocks mixed with smooth slabs. The road continues intermittently to the Eclipse Mine.

Days Fork to Silver Fork (No. B-13.2)

This trail follows an old mining road that leads to the crest of Cottonwood Ridge. The trail is easy to follow if you start at the right place which is about the

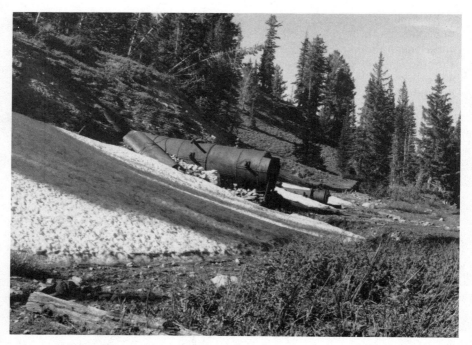

Upper Days Fork (Hike B-13). *The abandoned boiler at the site of the Eclipse Mine is a reminder of the era when the canyons were filled with mining camps.*

9400 foot elevation and just a few minutes below Eclipse Mine. After making a long swing to the west, the Days Fork Trail crosses to the east side of the stream and then climbs a steep hill. Part way up the hill, the trail to Silver Fork branches left and heads back to the northeast.

The trail curves east, then south, as it makes an ascending traverse to the edge of a steep gully that drains into Days Fork. The route then runs parallel to this gully until it reaches a relatively wide and level pass in the ridge above Silver Fork. The route continues as a distinct track on the Silver Fork side, makes a traverse below an unnamed peak, and soon reaches Cottonwood Ridge. This destination overlooks Alta and Snowbird, and is less difficult than the climb up Flagstaff. To continue along the ridge, see Trail No. R-4.

Flagstaff Peak from Days Fork (No. B-13.1)

Experienced hikers can reach Flagstaff Peak by ascending the steep head-wall of Days Fork, but the easiest route up Flagstaff is Trail No. L-09 from the Alta side.

From the Eclipse Mine, one route continues along the drainage to the low point on the ridge east of Flagstaff. A faint foot track marks the best route. The steep, smooth rock slabs hold snow well into July, so careful routefinding and confidence in scrambling are needed.

The alternative route from Days Fork is up the slopes to the west of the mine. Remnants of a mining road head west toward the high point on the Reed and Benson Ridge. This route leads to the summit north of Flagstaff, which is slightly higher but does not have as good a view of Alta. To reach Flagstaff, you will need to scramble the difficult ridge connecting the peaks.

GREENS BASIN (No. B-14)

Distance: 1-3/4 miles one way
Elevation Gain: 1050 feet
Highest Point: Basin at 8300 feet
Hiking Time One Way: 1 hr 25 min

Greens Basin is a meadow hidden part way up the south side of Big Cottonwood Canyon on the ridge separating Days Fork from Silver Fork. A good trail through forest leads to this secluded spot.

Start from the Days Fork trailhead described previously. Follow the Days Fork Trail up the steep chute. About 100 yards after the slope eases, watch carefully for a cleared, constructed trail heading back to the northeast. The trail makes two switchbacks as it climbs through the aspen on the east side of Days Fork; then it crosses a minor ridge and makes an ascending traverse along the south side of Big Cottonwood Canyon. A half-mile after the second switchback, you arrive at the flat meadow. It is about 100 yards across and is walled in by the steep slope on one side and by a low ridge on the other. The trail ends in the meadow, but a faint track continues from the far side of the meadow and climbs up onto the ridge above Silver Fork.

Just before reaching the basin, there is a junction with a steep trail that comes up from a cabin area on private land down along the highway.

BEARTRAP FORK (No. B-15)

Destination:	Upper Bowl	Desolation Lake Overlook
One-Way Miles:	1-3/4	2
Elevation Change:	1940	2240
Highest Point:	9500	9800
Hiking Time One Way:	1h 50m	2h 10m
Special Difficulties:		No Trail

Beartrap Fork is a short side canyon with an under-utilized trail along the streambed. The ridge trail, (No. R-2), from Millcreek Canyon to Guardsman Pass, crosses high in Beartrap Fork and is part of the Great Western Trail. The trail begins on private land, and cabin development can change future access. Currently several jeep roads wind around the mouth of Beartrap Fork and converge at the stream about 1/4 mile from the Big Cottonwood highway where a foot trail continues up the drainage.

The most direct start is an unmarked dirt road on the north, 11.0 miles up Big Cottonwood and about 150 yards beyond the "Pine Tree Village" cabin area on the opposite side of the road. Another start is 0.2 mile farther up the canyon, where the Forest Service has placed a sign for Beartrap Fork. Follow either road uphill, working toward the center of the drainage to find the hiking trail continuing up the east side of the stream.

The trail is in good condition and is easy to follow. Not all of the stream crossings have bridges, but except during peak runoff, none is a problem. The trail fades out in the grassy upper bowl, but just continue on up. The pass to Desolation Lake is not the low spot on the ridge to the northwest. The correct pass is due north from where the trail fades out. The Great Western Trail from Millcreek to Scotts Hill crosses high in the bowl, and the track is obvious once you climb up to it.

If you are descending into Beartrap Fork or down the bowl, pick up the trail along the west side of the eroded gully. The trail eventually crosses to the east side of the drainage where the canyon bottom first narrows down and enters the trees.

Desolation Lake. The view from Beartrap Pass near the junction of hikes B-10, B-15, and R-2. Mount Raymond and Gobblers Knob are in the background.

WILLOW HEIGHTS (No. B-16)

Destination:	Willow Lake	Great Western Trail
One-Way Miles:	3/4	2
Elevation Change:	640	1960
Highest Point:	8480	9800
Hiking Time One Way:	40m	1h 55m

This drainage is across the road from Silver Fork and is a delightful place for hiking through open aspen forest to a lake and several meadows. The area below the lake is private land. Gradual terrain leads to the ridges above. Preserving access to Forest Service lands, such as the area above Willow Lake, when the bottoms of side canyons are subdivided and developed is a challenge for the next decade.

A distinct hiking trail starts from the road, 12.1 miles up Big Cottonwood Canyon and follows the east side of the drainage to Willow Lake. The jeep road shown on the USGS maps starts in the cabin area and stays on the west side of the stream until just below the lake. The terrain above the lake is open, rolling ridges, and foot tracks and game trails lead up toward the Great Western Trail.

SILVER FORK (No. B-17)

Destination:	Lower Mine	Upper Bowl	Grizzly Gulch	Days Fork
One-Way Miles:	2-1/4	3	3-3/4	4
Elevation Change:	420	1500	1940	1740
Highest Point:	8520	9600	10040	9840
Hiking Time One Way:	1h 20m	2h 15m	2h 50m	2h 55m

The hike up the Silver Fork road to the mine is easy but not exceptional. In contrast, the upper portion of Silver Fork is a spectacular bowl with dramatic geology, abandoned mines, and access routes to Days Fork and Little Cottonwood. Silver Fork is another patchwork of Forest Service and private land. Current access is from the Lower Solitude parking area 12.7 miles up the canyon. Park along the highway and don't block the gate, which is used by cabin owners. Walk to the west end of the lot, pass behind the Inspiration Lift station, and continue on the road straight ahead. The Forest Service is planning a new trailhead and parking area for Silver Fork.

Silver Fork Mine

This is an easy, almost level walk along the road which starts at Solitude and passes along the upper edge of the summer home area in the mouth of the canyon. About 1/4 mile of this road crosses private land, so stay on the road and respect the cabin owners' wishes. Follow the paved road until you pass a large building which was formerly a church lodge and which is now called "Silver Hill." Here, the pavement stops and a dirt road, which is closed to unauthorized vehicles, continues up the canyon. About 1/2 mile beyond the pavement, a jeep road branches left into Honeycomb Fork. The road to upper Silver Fork branches right less than 1/4 mile after the Honeycomb Fork road. The main road stays low, crosses the stream, and climbs to the top of the large flat area formed by the mine dump. Most of the stream flow comes out from the mine portal.

Upper Silver Fork Basin

The road to upper Silver Fork is an obvious bench cut in the hillside which starts from the open area below the mine. Follow this road along the west side of the canyon until it crosses the stream in an area of white rock outcrops a short way above the mine. From here, the route follows a mining road that occasionally degenerates to a footpath as it climbs steeply along the east side of the stream past numerous small waterfalls. The canyon narrows to a V-shaped gorge, then opens up into two magnificent bowls. The road leads to mine workings in the east bowl below the steep headwall which separates Silver Fork from Grizzly Gulch.

The Prince of Wales Mine, with its abandoned steam engine, and the wagon road leading to Grizzly Gulch are high on the east side of the bowl. The wagon road is reached by scrambling up the spur ridge which lies just north of the end of the lower road, then following the ridge a short way southeast.

Upper Silver Fork—West Bowl (No. B-17.1)

The west bowl of Silver Fork is much larger than the east bowl and contains a small marshy lake. To reach the west bowl, watch for a foot track branching left from the road and crossing the stream about 200 vertical feet below the east bowl. A good landmark is the white-black-white striped cliff on the east side of the canyon. The foot track makes a single switchback, then climbs into the west bowl.

To continue into Days Fork, look for the road bench crossing the ridge on the west side of the bowl. The easiest route is to go slightly right (north) and make an ascending traverse of the open alpine slopes.

Big Cottonwood Canyon, south side from Cardiff Fork to Brighton.

HONEYCOMB FORK (No. B-18)

Destination:	Lower Honeycomb Junction	Upper Pass (Summit Lift)
One-Way Miles:	1-1/4	2-1/2
Elevation Change:	380	1840
Highest Point:	8500	9960
Hiking Time One Way:	50m	2h 10m

Honeycomb Fork was an area of intense mining activity and the canyon is nearly all private land. Most is now managed as part of the Solitude ski area. The best access is to start from the lower Solitude parking area (see description for Silver Fork) and hike the "Honeycomb Return Trail" ski run from the Inspiration Lift. The correct route is the dirt road that turns west about 100 feet above the lift and begins a gradual ascending traverse around the end of the ridge. The other (higher) road from the start of the Inspiration Lift climbs up to the top of the lift in a series of switchbacks.

The bulldozer cut for the Honeycomb Return ski run ends in a meadow in lower Honeycomb Fork across the stream from the badly eroded jeep road coming up from Silver Fork. The jeep road climbs up to the Woodlawn Mine and a trail eventually reaches the summit ski lift at the head of Honeycomb Fork.

SOLITUDE AREA ROAD (No. B-19)
Mill F South Fork

Destination:	Lake Solitude	Mount Evergreen Pass
One-Way Miles:	1-3/4	2-1/2
Elevation Change:	900	1440
Highest Point:	9020	9600
Hiking Time One Way:	1h	1h 40m

This trail leads from the upper Solitude parking lot to Lake Solitude, then continues on to the top of the Summit Lift. It is longer than the approach from Brighton, but it makes a nice alternative descent.

The service road starts west of the upper Solitude parking lot behind the Main Street Grill and climbs along "Sesame Street" ski run, first west, then turning back under the Moonbeam Lift into the Mill F drainage. The road forks and the right branch leads up to the Inspiration Lift, while the left branch crosses under the Powderhorn Lift and continues to Lake Solitude. The road passes the west side of Lake Solitude, then makes a series of switchbacks up the headwall to a junction immediately south of the pass near Mount Evergreen. The hike from Brighton to Twin Lakes Pass joins the service road for a few hundred feet.

Then, the route to Twin Lakes Pass recrosses the ridge and the service road begins a final series of switchbacks to the Summit Lift which overlooks the top of Honeycomb Fork.

BRIGHTON AREA

Brighton is a former mining town and present-day ski area at the head of Big Cottonwood Canyon. Brighton is named after William Stewart Brighton who, with his wife Catherine, built a hotel near Silver Lake in 1874. Much of the private land in the area dates from Brighton's original 80 acre homestead and his later mining claims.

The area has relatively easy terrain with good trails leading to lakes and overlooks. The natural beauty and the short distances combine to make Brighton a popular beginner hiking area; however, the parking lot at Brighton, at 8700 feet, is nearly as high as the summit of Mount Olympus on the Wasatch Front. The weather is much colder than in the valley, and snow lasts well into June, so the hiking season here is only from July through mid-September.

Persons who are not well acclimatized will feel the effect of high altitude when hiking at Brighton. I first hiked at Brighton on a summer vacation in 1972. I had been living at sea level and my hiking had been in the Appalachians, where summits are lower than the Salt Lake Valley. We hiked only as far as the Lake Mary Dam and I was totally exhausted and out of breath. Take it easy and rest often when you start hiking at high elevations.

Unfortunately, the Brighton trails are often confusing. The area is mixed with service roads, winter ski runs, and private in-holdings. Construction activities and lack of summer trail maintenance have resulted in a multitude of false trails. The Forest Service attempts to keep the trails marked, but sign vandalism is a problem. The USGS map of the area is badly out of date, but the Hiking the Wasatch Map will help you find the correct trail.

It is easy to lose your sense of direction when hiking around Brighton. You drive east up the canyon and expect the direction at the end of the road to be east. Actually, the road turns at the Guardsman Pass junction, and you are driving south as you arrive at the start of the loop road. Once you start thinking of the Brighton Store as being to the north, everything falls into place.

SILVER LAKE AND LAKE SOLITUDE
From Brighton Store

Destination:	Silver Lake	Lake Solitude
One-Way Miles:	300 yards to 1/2 mile	1-1/2
Elevation Gain:	Level	300
Highest Point:	8730	9020
Hiking Time One Way:	15 minutes to 1h	55m

The Silver Lake and Lake Solitude hikes both start on the right (west) side of the road, across from the Brighton Store. Drive 14.7 miles up Big Cottonwood Canyon to the beginning of the one-way loop road and park in the area on the left or along the road on the right.

Silver Lake (No. B-20)

Silver Lake is the easiest hike in this book. Signs, wide paths, and a new boardwalk provide easy access to the lake. This area has been extensively reconstructed and rehabilitated by the Forest Service and provides a high quality recreational opportunity for those who do not want to go far from their cars. A new trail continues all the way around Silver Lake, and there is now a bridge that gets you across the inlet stream and avoids the private land further south. Try to walk softly and use existing routes.

As you cross the meadow from the parking toward the lake, the trail to the right crosses a narrow bridge at the outlet of the lake and continues along the north shore. On the north side of the lake, there is trail junction where the routes to Twin Lakes and to Lake Solitude turn right and the lake shore trail turns south.

Lake Solitude (No. B-21)

Tiny Lake Solitude is set in a steep-walled bowl at the head of Mill F South Fork. Start by hiking around the north side of Silver Lake to the trail junction at the northwest side of the lake one quarter mile from the start. The trail turns right and heads north for about 200 yards and then forks again. The trail straight ahead continues in a generally northwest direction and gradually climbs toward Lake Solitude. The trail to the top of the Evergreen Lift and to the Twin Lakes Dam switches back to the south.

Continue the gradual climb north through an open, park-like forest of fir and aspen and cross the ski trail leading from Brighton to Solitude. The hiking route continues in the same direction, crosses under Solitude's Sunrise Lift, and then turns south into the Mill F drainage. Two more downhill ski runs cross the route before the last short hill to the lake.

On the west side of the lake is the road from Solitude to the Summit Lift (see Trail B-19). Some rare flowering plants grow around the lake, and hikers should stay on existing routes to avoid trampling vegetation unnecessarily.

The Solitude Tunnel, just above the lake, was the lowest entrance into the Michigan Utah group of mines. Most of the development and ore production from this group was conducted on the Alta side of the divide from the head of Grizzly Gulch. Work in these mines ceased in 1928, and in the 1970's the surface rights were acquired by the predecessor of Solitude.

Brighton Area 1:24,000

TWIN LAKES AND TWIN LAKES PASS
(No. B-22)

Destination:	Twin Lakes Dam	Twin Lake Pass
One-Way Miles:	1-1/4	2-1/2
Elevation Gain:	710	1260
Highest Point:	9440	9993
Hiking Time One Way:	50m	1h 50m

The two original lakes are now merged behind a concrete arch dam, forming a large lake in a spectacular setting. The lake is set in a bowl with rocky slopes and bare summits above. The area can be reached by either of two easy trails: the ski area maintenance road or the hiking trail from Silver Lake.

Looking across Silver Lake, you can see a trail heading left and upward on the hillside toward Twin Lakes. Start by walking around the north side of the lake as described for Lake Solitude. From the northwest side, continue along the trail toward Lake Solitude for 150 yards, then take the sharp switchback. The trail to Lake Solitude continues north and the route to Twin Lakes turns south and climbs steadily. After Silver Lake comes into view, you will pass a wide but overgrown cut in the hillside heading back north. This is another downhill ski trail to Solitude. As the hiking trail enters the trees again, it turns right and begins to climb more steeply. This next section is wet early in the summer. A spur trail on the left will take you 100 feet to a level area that is a nice overlook and resting spot. Continue up the trail until the Evergreen Lift comes into view. The Twin Lakes Dam is 500 feet west of the ski lift. If you return this way, the top of the trail is indistinct, but you can easily pick up the trail about 50 feet left (north) of the top lift tower.

An unmaintained trail leads along the north side of the lake, generally staying close to the shore. This trail leads to the far end of the lake directly below Twin Lakes Pass.

The alternative route to Twin Lakes Dam starts next to the Millicent ticket booth in the Brighton Ski Resort parking lot and follows the maintenance road up a series of switchbacks through the downhill ski runs. This route is sunny and open and is a better early summer route than the trail from Silver Lake. Take the right fork just after the start, then follow the wide road directly to the top of the Evergreen Lift. This road and the trail from Silver Lake can be combined to make a nice short loop. Distances and times for either route are about the same.

Twin Lakes Pass (No. B-21.1)

The best route from the lake to Twin Lakes Pass begins up the service road (part of the Solitude-to-Brighton ski connection) which climbs the hill to the north of the Twin Lakes Dam. Just past a retaining wall of railroad ties, the road crosses through a notch into Mill F Fork (See Trail B-19). Lake Solitude is about

500 feet lower along the road. Continue horizontally on the Mill F side for about 1000 feet, passing under a series of ridge top pinnacles, then climb the steep slope to your left to reach another notch in the ridge. After crossing the notch, look for the good foot track leading directly to Twin Lakes Pass which is 1/2 mile away but only 200 feet higher. Twin Lakes Pass is at the head of Grizzly Gulch (Trail No. L-10) and has an outstanding view looking west down Little Cottonwood Canyon.

Granite Lakes Trail To Lake Mary (No. B-23)

This trail starts from the south end of the Twin Lakes Dam and climbs a small rise. Immediately ahead, the trail passes directly left of the base of a 15-foot-high cliff, then becomes a distinct trail as it begins to descend and cross under the Millicent Lift. The USGS topographic map shows this trail incorrectly; it starts higher and goes directly to Lake Mary.

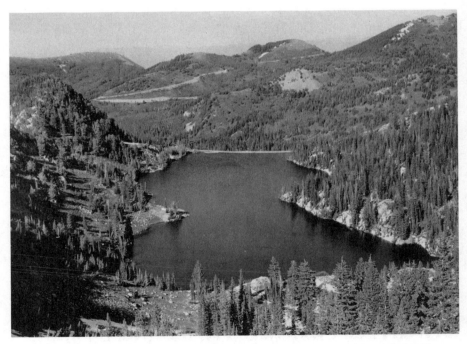

Twin Lakes from Twin Lakes Pass (Hike B-22). Mount Evergreen overlooks the lake on the left. The recently (1986) controversial powerline is in the foreground.

TWIN LAKES AREA SUMMITS

Destination:	Mount Evergreen	Mount Millicent	Mount Wolverine	Honeycomb Cliffs
One-Way Miles:	1-3/4	2	2-1/2	2-1/2
Elevation Change:	1110	1722	2065	1749
Highest Point:	9840	10,452	10,795	10,479
Hiking Time One Way:	1h 30m	2h	2h 30m	2h 15m

These summits can all be reached by moderate off-trail hiking starting from the Twin Lakes Dam, and they are worthwhile objectives for intermediate hikers.

Mount Evergreen is the forested ridge directly north of Twin Lakes. Follow the route described for Twin Lakes Pass and turn northeast at the saddle where the ski area road crosses into Mill F Fork. Scale the very steep slope ahead and continue along the ridge to the summit.

The top of Honeycomb Cliffs can be reached by hiking to Twin Lakes Pass, then scrambling north along the ridge. The hike can continue above Honeycomb Cliffs to Silver Fork.

Mount Millicent is reached from the ski area service road that climbs from the Twin Lakes Dam to the top of the Millicent Lift in a series of switchbacks. Climb south along the rocky ridge from the Millicent Lift to the summit. There is some boulder-hopping on this ridge.

Wolverine is the highest peak in the area and overlooks both Big Cottonwood and Little Cottonwood canyons. The route to the summit of Wolverine continues southwest along the ridge from Millicent. Alternatively, Wolverine can be reached by hiking south from Twin Lakes Pass, following the crest of the curving ridge. This is a longer route, but it offers a spectacular view of Wolverine Cirque.

GREAT WESTERN TRAIL

The Great Western Trail descends from the Wasatch Crest Ridge into Big cottonwood Canyon along the Guardsman Pass road. It follows the paved road to Brighton then ascends the Brighton Lakes Trail to Catherine Pass.

BRIGHTON LAKES TRAIL—(No. B-24)

This trail winds past four lakes and then climbs to the pass into Little Cottonwood. It is a popular area for easy hikes and is one of the nicest areas in the Wasatch for all levels of hiking. The trail up to Catherine Pass is part of the Great Western Trail.

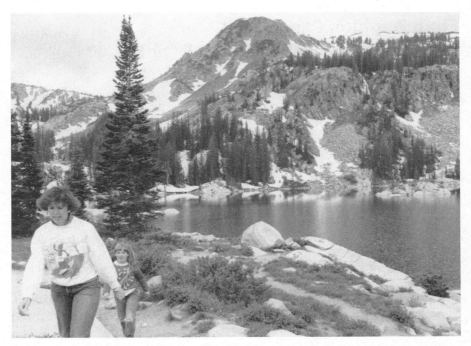

Lake Mary an easy hike from Brighton. The trail continues along the lake shore past Lake Martha and on to Lake Catherine.

Easy Hikes on the Brighton Lakes Trail

Destination:	Dog Lake	Lake Mary
One-Way Miles:	3/4	1
Elevation Gain:	600	760
Highest Point:	9360	9520
Hiking Time One Way: (Leisurely Pace)	40m	55m

The trail starts from the signboard at the north end of the Brighton Ski resort lot and climbs north. The trail crosses the road which gives access to the Wasatch Mountain Club Lodge and the LDS camp, but there is no public parking on this road. It then curves west towards the ski runs and then crosses and continues along the creek.

As you start up the trail, you will pass a large log structure on the far side of the stream. This is the Wasatch Mountain Club Lodge built in 1930 and now on the National Register of Historic Places.

From Brighton Parking Lot
to Dog Lake Junction and Lake Mary

Yes, there are two "Dog Lakes" in Big Cottonwood Canyon: this one near Brighton and the other in Mill D North Fork. The routes to Dog Lake, Clayton Peak, Lake Mary, and Catherine Pass share a common trail for the first 1/2 mile.

The main hiking trail is fairly straight and wide and heads south, staying in the trees between the stream and the Mary Lift. Fifteen minutes up the main trail you will cross a tiny side stream just before the top of the Mary Lift comes into view.

Just below the ski lift, the hiking trail joins the maintenance road which provides an alternative route from the parking lot. To hike the maintenance road, start from the southeast corner of the parking lot near the Alpine Rose. This road also services several cabins to the east, so take the right-hand forks at the junctions. The road crosses under the Majestic Lift and arrives at the top of the Mary Lift.

From the Mary Lift, continue up for about 200 yard to a large rock outcrop, where the ski run makes a sharp turn left. The hiking trail turns right, heads west up the hill, and reaches the stream and the Dog Lake junction in 200 yards. The left branch leads to Dog Lake and Clayton Peak, and the trail straight ahead continues to Lake Mary and Catherine Pass.

South of Dog Lake there is an abandoned road making a loop to some mining claims. The cut in the hillside is very evident once the snow melts off.

Lake Mary

From the junction at Dog Lake, cross the stream and continue west along a narrow gully for 1/4 mile to Lake Mary. The connecting trail to Twin Lakes Dam branches right a short way below the Lake Mary Dam. The Lake Mary Trail crosses the stream just below the dam, then climbs to the lake.

Lake Mary is in a glacial basin which was dammed in 1916 to create a water supply reservoir. Lake Martha is a much smaller lake in the same basin as Lake Mary. Lake Phoebe was merged with Lake Mary by the dam, but it reappears in the fall when the water is low. This group of lakes is called "Granite Lakes" on old maps.

LAKE CATHERINE (No. B-24.3)
Intermediate Hikes on Brighton Lakes Trail

Destination:	Lake Catherine	Catherine Pass	Sunset Peak
One-Way Miles:	2	2-1/4	2-1/2
Elevation Gain:	1200	1450	1950
Highest Point:	9950	10,220	10,648
Hiking Time One Way:	1h 35m	1h 50m	2h 15m

There are two trails to Lake Catherine: the official trail which goes past Lake Mary, and an alternative trail directly from Dog Lake following the winter ski tour route. Both trails converge above Lake Martha.

The direct trail starts on the west side of Dog Lake as a foot track which ascends the ridge to the southwest. Two switchbacks and an ascending traverse bring you to the top of the ridge where you join the official trail.

The official trail continues from the left (southeast) side of Lake Mary to Lake Martha. Above Lake Martha, the trail makes a switchback to the left and ascends the ridge separating Lake Mary from Dog Lake. From the ridge crest, the trail contours through stands of fir and passes along the top of the cliffs above Lake Martha. Soon the cliffs coming off Pioneer Peak come into view on your left as you approach the cirque containing Lake Catherine. A spur trail to the left leads to Lake Catherine, and the trail to the pass goes to the right of a small ridge dividing the cirque.

When hiking back to Brighton, remember that the trail traverses high after leaving the lake. A false trail leads into the steep cliffs above Lake Martha. The stream draining Lake Catherine disappears into a sinkhole located near the junction of the Lake Catherine spur trail with the trail continuing to the pass.

Catherine Pass

This pass is the obvious low spot on the ridge above the lake. Follow the trail to the right of the small ridge and make one long switchback as you ascend the headwall of the cirque. The other side of the pass is densely forested, but a short walk up either ridge provides excellent views of Albion Basin and Little Cottonwood Canyon.

The trail on the Alta side leads down to Albion Basin, and the Brighton Ridge Run crosses the hiking trail here on the way from Sunset Peak to Mount Tuscarora. Sunset Peak (elev. 10,648) is reached by the excellent foot track described in the Little Cottonwood chapter.

Brighton Lakes viewed from Sunset Peak. Lake Catherine is directly below. Beyond are tiny Lake Martha and the irregularly shaped reservoir formed from the formerly separate Lake Phoebe and Lake Mary.

GRANITE LAKES TRAIL (No. B-23)
From Lake Mary to Twin Lakes

Distance: 1 mile from Lake Mary to Twin Lakes.
Elevation Gain: No net change but 300 feet of down and up.
Hiking Time One Way: 40m between the lakes.

This constructed trail provides the opportunity to make a loop hike and offers good views of Brighton as it passes through both forested and open areas. The actual trail is higher than the route shown on the USGS map.

This trail branches right from the Lake Mary Trail a short way below the dam and makes a switchback up a rock slope, then passes a cabin before reaching the north end of the Lake Mary Dam. The trail descends gradually as it continues north through stands of fir, then makes a pair of sharp switchbacks down to the base of a cliff band. A trail branches downhill from the low point and follows a stream for 1/4 mile to the road near the Wasatch Mountain Club Lodge. The main trail crosses the boulderfield, ascends the open slopes under the Millicent Lift, and crosses a small ridge just before the Twin Lakes Dam.

MAJESTIC TRAIL (No. B-25)
Snake Creek Pass and Clayton Peak

Destination:	Snake Creek Pass	Clayton Peak
One-Way Miles:	2	2-1/2
Elevation Gain:	1310	1960
Highest Point:	10,040	10,721
Hiking Time One Way:	1h 40m	2h 15m

This area is undergoing rapid change due to the expansion of Brighton Ski Resort. Construction of the access road to the Snake Creek Pass and construction of the Great Western Lift devastated a section of the hiking trail. Fine stands of forest that were enjoyed by hikers and challenging to cross-country skiers were cut down to create new ski runs. Still, the area has some of the finest views for the hiking effort. The hillside scars will heal, and wildflowers will grow in the new clearings.

Snake Creek Pass

There are two routes from the Brighton parking lot to the pass. The scenic route follows hiking trails through the woods beside the ski runs. A shorter, direct route is to walk the service roads from the Brighton parking lot.

For the scenic route, follow the Lake Mary Trail to the junction near Dog Lake. Take the Dog Lake fork (left), and in another 200 feet turn left again. The trail now heads east and climbs gradually. Above the Majestic Lift, the trail crosses a jeep road and continues into a stand of fir, then passes under the new Snake Creek Lift. The split rock just ahead is a memorable landmark. The trail crosses a second ski run swath cut through the trees. At this point, the service road is clearly visible about 50 feet down from the trail. A short section of trail remains before the route disappears onto the service road. On the return, you can find the start of the trail just below the closely spaced pair of curves on the road. From here, the route follows the road up two more switchbacks to the pass. Plans have been made to sign the trail to Snake Creek Pass.

From the pass, Mt. Timpanogos is visible to the south, and the Heber Valley and the Uintas lie to the east. The service road turns west and follows the ridge over one minor summit to the ski lift.

Clayton Peak (Mount Majestic)

The peak is called by both names. The 1903 Cottonwood Map shows a "Majestic Trail" leading to "Clayton Peak". The trail to Clayton Peak continues northeast along the ridge from Snake Creek Pass.

The route follows the service road for 1/4 mile before making a steep ascent to the summit. There is occasional boulder-hopping along the way, but no real

Snake Creek Pass with Mount Timpanogos in the distance. This pass is reached by a moderate hike and offers the best views of the Heber Valley and the area to the south and east.

difficulties. The summit offers a bird's-eye view of the area above Park City as well as a panoramic view of Big Cottonwood and the area to the south.

No trails lead from here to the north or east, but there is opportunity for off-trail exploration. The land between here and Guardsman Pass is private. To the east there is a mix of private and Wasatch Mountain State Park lands.

8

LITTLE COTTONWOOD CANYON

Here is a canyon of superlatives and contrasts. It has the steepest walls, the most heavily glaciated topography, the highest trailhead, and the highest peaks in the area. The mouth is flanked by granite cliffs which challenge the best technical rock climbers, but the upper canyon has the best meadows for easy walking and for finding wildflowers. The lower canyon is bounded by two Wilderness Areas while the upper canyon is the home of two world-class ski resorts.

The canyon has been subjected to development pressure ever since pioneer days, and the conflicts continue. Granite for the Salt Lake Temple was quarried at the mouth of the canyon, and the Wasatch Resort today marks the site of an early work camp. Railroads and tramways served the rich silver mines of Alta. The forests were stripped as sawmills supplied lumber for the mines. An early hydroelectric plant was built in the canyon to provide power for production of oxygen. Lakes were dammed to form reservoirs. Now, tramways carry skiers, and pipelines for natural gas and sanitary sewer have been constructed to heat and drain the luxury condominiums. The upper canyon was an active mining district from the 1860's until 1967, when the last activity ceased at the Wasatch Drain Tunnel near Snowbird. Many mining claims are still active and much of the land around Alta is still owned by mining companies.

Through all this the canyon has survived. It is still a wild and natural place with recreational opportunities for everyone from mountaineers to families with children.

The topography controls and limits hiking opportunities. The north side is a steep wall of buttresses and couloirs, without a route or pass suitable for hikers down-canyon from Cardiff Pass. The side canyons on the south between White Pine and the mouth are hanging valleys perched high on the wall, with cliffs and waterfalls separating the side drainages from Little Cottonwood Creek. Hikers enter the lower side canyons by starting at the White Pine trailhead and traveling west across the dividing ridges above the cliffs. Maintained trails lead as far as Red Pine Lakes and Maybird Lakes.

The south side of Little Cottonwood above the White Pine trailhead is dominated by the Snowbird and Alta ski resorts. The service roads provide easy walking and the combination of mining-era logging, frequent avalanches, and contemporary ski run construction has resulted in open, grassy slopes with excellent vistas.

Alta was the mining center, and roads lead from the town to Cardiff Fork, Silver Fork, and the Twin Lakes Pass area. Alta is at 8600 feet, so the approaches from Alta to the Mount Superior and Flagstaff Peak areas are much shorter (but steeper) than the routes from Big Cottonwood.

WHITE PINE TRAILHEAD
(Lone Peak Wilderness)

This excellent trailhead is the main access for the south side of Little Cottonwood Canyon and the northeast portion of the Lone Peak Wilderness. Two easy hikes, suitable for beginners, follow good trails from this trailhead to overlooks. Intermediate hikes continue up the trails to the lakes in White Pine Canyon, Red Pine Canyon, and in Maybird Gulch. Travel beyond the lakes requires off-trail hiking and some scrambling. All these hikes share a common route for the first mile.

The White Pine trailhead is on the south side of the road, 5.5 miles up Little Cottonwood Canyon and 0.7 mile below Snowbird. The turnoff for the parking area is just after a turn and is easy to miss. Start slowing down just after the "White Pine Slide Area" sign. An asphalt path leads from the parking area to a footbridge across the stream.

The trail continues on the other side of the stream as a wide jeep road and soon turns west as it climbs the hill. This road is closed to motor vehicles except for permitted uses such as maintaining the dam in White Pine Canyon. The road ascends in a generally southwest direction then turns south as it curves into White Pine Canyon. A mile from the parking lot, the road meets the stream coming down White Pine Canyon. Here, the road up White Pine turns east and makes a switchback up the hill, and the trail to Red Pine and Maybird crosses the stream.

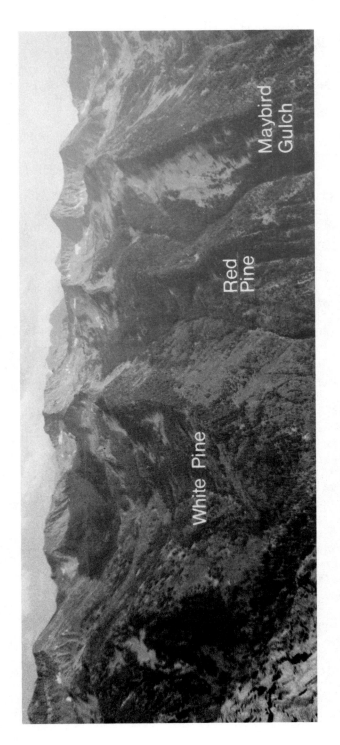

The south side of Little Cottonwood viewed from Dromedary Peak. *From the left, the skyline peaks are: American Fork Twin Peaks, Red Baldy, White Baldy, Mount Timpanogos in the distance, and the Pfeifferhorn on the ridge between Maybird Gulch and Hogum Fork.*

White Pine

Red Pine

Maybird Gulch

RED PINE CANYON (No. L-01)

Destination:	Canyon Overlook	Mine & Maybird Trail	Lower Red Pine Lake	Upper Red Pine Lake
One-Way Miles:	1-1/2	2-1/2	3	3-1/2
Elevation Gain:	500	1400	1940	2300
Highest Point:	8200	9100	9640	10,000
Hiking Time One Way:	1h	1h 55m	2h 30m	2h 50m

Red Pine Canyon is the most accessible canyon in the Lone Peak Wilderness and is the start for many longer trips to remote canyons and summits. A well-maintained trail leads up this narrow canyon, and spectacular rock formations crown the ridges. Lower Red Pine Lake is a very popular mountain lake, set in forest just below tree line. Upper Red Pine Lake is set in alpine boulderfields with the jagged cirque headwall above. Snow here lasts into July.

The trail starts from the White Pine trailhead and follows the previously described road to the junction at the stream, 1 mile from the start. The Red Pine Trail crosses the stream on a footbridge which is about 50 yards upstream from the switchback in the White Pine road. The area immediately beyond the stream is wet, and logs have been laid to reduce trail erosion. The trail heads back downstream, turns west, and begins a fairly level traverse around the end of the ridge. As the trail enters the Red Pine Canyon drainage it begins to climb again. A half-mile after the stream crossing there is a spectacular view down the U-shaped, glacier-carved canyon toward the farmland and suburbs of the valley.

Red Pine Creek is far below the overlook, but the trail and stream converge as you climb through aspen. Ahead you will see an excellent landmark: a rock buttress on the east wall of the canyon. An old mine dump and the bridge across Red Pine Creek leading to Maybird Gulch are directly below this ridge, which is reached 2-1/2 miles from the start of the trail.

Beyond the mine dump, the trail continues up through the trees on the east side of the canyon and is separated from the stream by a minor ridge. An alternative route, when the canyon is still snow-covered in early summer, is to go up the open slopes a few hundred feet farther east. About 45 minutes past the mine dump, you arrive at the top of a small rise overlooking the lake. There is a track all the way around the lake.

Upper Red Pine Lake, set in a small depression about 400 feet higher in the canyon, is reached by walking around the east side of the lower lake, then following the foot track up through the trees from its southeast corner. This means losing altitude, but it is easy walking. A high traverse across the slope from the trail directly to the upper lake is an alternative route in early season.

The entire upper end of Red Pine Canyon is worth exploring. If you are good at routefinding and scrambling, look for the notch which provides a moderately difficult access to White Pine Canyon. You can also bushwhack down the west side of the canyon and meet the main trail at the mine dump. Climbing up to the

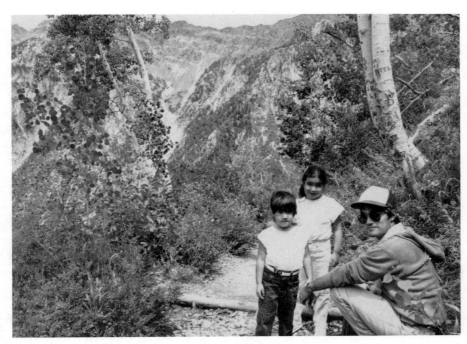

Red Pine Lake Trail Overlook. These hikers made it past the canyon viewpoint about an hour up the trail. The Cottonwood Ridge is in the background.

ridge provides outstanding views of Timpanogos and Utah County and is the start of the Pfeifferhorn route.

MAYBIRD LAKES (No. L-02)

Destination:	Maybird Lake	Hogum Fork Pass
One-Way Miles:	3-3/4	4-1/2
Elevation Change:	1946	2536
Highest Point:	9650	10,240
Hiking Time One Way:	2h 50m	4h 5m

Maybird Gulch is less crowded than nearby Red Pine, and the rock formations are more dramatic. Maybird Gulch has a chain of small lakes and a majestic view of the Pfeifferhorn towering above.

The trail into Maybird Gulch branches from the Red Pine Trail at the bridge at the landmark buttress. After crossing the stream, the Maybird Trail makes a switchback up the hill and heads generally west as it crosses over the ridge. After crossing into Maybird, the trail climbs steadily to the lake, passes below

Lower Red Pine Lake. The trail is visible on the far side of the lake and Red Baldy Peak, which overlooks White Pine Canyon, is in the background across the ridge.

spectacular pinnacles which crown the ridge and ends at the upper lake. The trail was recently cleared and relocated, and the USGS map does not show the current route.

A challenging descent from Maybird Lakes is to follow the stream down past the waterfall and then search for the overgrown wagon road that connected Maybird to the Red Pine Trail just above the canyon overlook. Hint: On the way up look carefully for the road scar on the hillside across from the Red Pine Trail.

ADVANCED HIKES
From Red Pine Canyon

Southwest of Maybird Gulch lies the most isolated part of the Wasatch. There are no easy routes. Sheer cliffs wall the canyons, and all approaches involve long distances and thousands of vertical feet of climbing. This section lists only the most popular of the many routes which are accessible to strong hikers.

PFEIFFERHORN VIA RED PINE (No. L-03)

Distance: 4 1/2 miles one way from trailhead to summit
Elevation Gain: 3700 feet
Highest Point: Summit at 11,326 feet
Hiking Time One Way: 4 hr 20 min
Special Difficulties: Scrambling on ridge, snow in early season

The Pfeifferhorn is the perfectly-shaped triangular peak on the divide between Maybird Gulch, Hogum Fork, and Dry Creek. The summit views, the alpine terrain, and the exposed scrambling on a knife-edged ridge make this an excellent route for strong hikers who want a taste of mountaineering. In June the summit pyramid is still snow-covered, and this is a very popular spring snow climb.

Take the trail to Red Pine Lake and continue to the upper lake. Look for the minor ridge heading southwest from the upper lake to Alpine Ridge above. This minor ridge barely shows on the topographic maps but is obvious on the ground. The headwall is steep, and there may be a snow cornice at the top. From the Alpine Ridge head west, traversing on the south side of the minor summit between Red Pine and Maybird. Then, cross the knife-edged ridge, picking your

The Pfeifferhorn. *The hiker is on the standard route from Red Pine which crosses the foreground ridge and then ascends the summit snowfield staying just left of the rock ridge crest directly ahead.*

way through and over the massive boulders. The final section up the summit pyramid stays slightly to the left of the rock crest of the east ridge.

The summit is surrounded by scrambling and mountaineering routes. The steep granite headwall of Hogum Cirque to the west contains many difficult technical climbing routes and a few difficult scrambling routes. The north ridge of the Pfeifferhorn is a technical rock climb, but the west ridge is moderate hiking and is the continuation of the Beatout Hike to Bells Canyon.

Maybird Lakes with Broads Fork Twin Peaks visible on the far side of Little Cottonwood Canyon. This viewpoint is a short off-trail hike beyond the lakes.

UPPER MAYBIRD GULCH
And Hogum Cirque (No. L-04)

Exploring Maybird Gulch above the lakes involves either spring snow hiking or boulder-hopping after the snow retreats, but the scenery makes it worthwhile. The Maybird headwall is a steep scrambling route leading directly to the Alpine Ridge and the Pfeifferhorn. The wide notch in the ridge immediately north of the Pfeifferhorn leads to Hogum Fork.

Hogum Fork is a wild and magnificent drainage that ends with a steep drop into Little Cottonwood Canyon. At the head, two huge cirques are ringed by vertically-jointed granite pillars, and popular technical rock climbing routes ascend from Hogum to the ridge. The summits and smooth flanks of Thunder Mountain dominate the view west.

The normal route into Hogum Cirque is from Maybird Lakes, crossing at the notch in the ridge between the Pfeifferhorn and Peak 10,516 at the 10,240 foot elevation. Climb through the notch and descend 200 feet into the east branch of Hogum. The west branch is 3/4 mile away around the end of the ridge. This is an easy traverse if there is still snow.

WHITE PINE CANYON (L-05)

Destination:	Overlook	Meadow	Lake
One-Way Miles:	1-1/4	2	4-1/2
Elevation Gain:	500	800	2460
Highest Point:	8200	8500	10,000
Hiking Time One Way:	1h	1h 25m	3h 30m

White Pine Canyon has been a focus of controversy between advocates of ski development and of wilderness. Hike up this magnificent side canyon and discover why everyone wants it. The wide, U-shaped valley, with angular ridges above, combines with the well-graded road to provide excellent terrain for hikers, ski-tourers — and for downhill skiers. The dam access road leads past a canyon overlook, through a meadow, across the barren rock fields of the upper cirque, and ends at White Pine Lake. This road is closed to vehicles and makes an excellent, easy-to-follow trail. The hikes to the overlook and to the meadow are both excellent beginner hikes.

Start at the White Pine trailhead and follow the main service road all the way to the lake. After one mile, the Red Pine Trail turns right and crosses the stream, while the road to White Pine makes a switchback east. At the top of the next sharp switchback there is a nice overlook with views of the Cottonwood Ridge summits to the north and of the Salt Lake Valley to the west. Continue up two more switchbacks to the meadow, another good destination for a short hike.

Above the meadow, the road makes a series of short switchbacks along the east side of the drainage. The road eventually climbs over a small ridge, then descends 200 feet to the south end of the lake. An alternative hike is the old trail, shown on the USGS map, which branches west well below the dam and climbs as a footpath along the stream.

White Pine is full of opportunities for off-trail hiking. From the west side of the dam you can follow the 10,000-foot contour to a notch leading into Red Pine Canyon. Walking around the lake is difficult unless you stay quite high due to the cliffs which drop to the high water line. The Bullion Divide ridge from Alta to White Pine can be reached at several points by moderate hiking up the headwall. The upper canyon is loose scree and boulderfields, so expect slow off-trail travel after the spring snow is gone.

The original boundary proposal for the Lone Peak Wilderness followed the road up White Pine Canyon. At the time, Snowbird's representatives supported the general concept of wilderness designation and even supported expanding the wilderness area on the American Fork Canyon side, but they requested that White Pine be excluded. The wilderness bill moved the boundary to the crest of the ridge above Red Pine. For now, the area is managed primarily as culinary watershed.

The "white pine" for which the canyon was named are actually Engelmann spruce, a major source of lumber. A mature Engelmann spruce averages 110 feet high and 24 inches in diameter.

White Pine Lake from the highest point on trail L-05. The background skyline is the difficult mountaineering scramble across Dromedary, Sunrise, and Twin Peaks (Route MS-5).

SNOWBIRD AREA

Snowbird Village is an anomaly in the Wasatch. Excellent restaurants, fancy lodging, and high-tech are thrust between two Wilderness Areas and are next to old, familiar Alta. But Snowbird brings to the mountains summer visitors who might otherwise never venture up the canyon, and the tram allows multitudes to sample the alpine environment that hikers and climbers find so precious.

Snowbird has been controversial ever since it was first proposed, but the worst construction-era scars have healed, the grass and wildflowers are reclaiming the slopes, and there is no reason for hikers to ignore the delights which still can be found here. Snowbird welcomes hikers, publishes a trail map, and keeps the hiking routes well marked, especially the descent from the tram. Ski run signs provide additional landmarks.

GAD VALLEY (No. L-06)

Destination:	Hidden Peak Via Gad Valley Road	White Pine Overlook Above Gad II Lift	American Fork Twin Peaks via White Pine Ridge
One-Way Miles:	4	3	4
Total Ascent:	2890	2100	3549
Highest Point:	10,990	10,200	11,489
Hiking Time One Way:	3h 45m	2h 40m	4h 20m
Special Difficulties:		Bushwhack	No trail on ridge.

Most of Gad Valley is Forest Service land within the Snowbird permit area, and the valley is in a more natural state than Peruvian Gulch. Dense forest, streams, and small ponds are mixed with the Mid-Gad Restaurant (closed in summer) and the swaths cut for ski runs. The White Pine overlook and the ridge leading to Twin Peaks from the west are reached from the service road leading to the Gad II Lift. The other service road leads through the scree-filled bowl below Twin Peaks to Hidden Peak.

The service road into Gad Valley starts from the lower Snowbird parking area. This road can also be reached from Snowbird Center by following the foot trail up the "Dick Bass Highway" ski run. The road to the Gad II Lift branches right at 9100 feet, descends slightly to cross the stream, then resumes climbing to the west. As you approach the top of the lift, a distinct saddle is visible on the ridge to the west, about 400 feet higher. This saddle, overlooking White Pine Canyon, is a steep bushwhack from the road up your choice of either grassy slopes or forested boulders.

To continue from the White Pine overlook to American Fork Twin Peaks, climb south along the ridge between Gad Valley and White Pine Canyon to the minor summit 1/4 mile west of Twin Peaks, descend to the saddle, then climb the ridge to the higher twin. This route is easier than the knife-edge traverse from Hidden Peak.

PERUVIAN GULCH (No. L-07)

Destination:	Hidden Peak From Snowbird via Peruvian Gulch	Snowbird From Hidden Peak via Peruvian Gulch
One-Way Miles:	3-1/2	3-1/2
Elevation Change:	2880	-2880
Highest Point:	10,980	10,980
Hiking Time One Way:	3h 25m	2h 35m

Peruvian Gulch was the site of much activity during the mining era and is largely private land, now managed as part of Snowbird. Another legacy of the mining era is that this area, like Alta and Brighton, was largely deforested. This hike is along service roads and is a popular descent from the tram. Fascinating geology is displayed on the towering south face of Mount Superior, across Little Cottonwood Canyon.

Starting from Snowbird, there are two routes into Peruvian Gulch. The west approach is reached by taking the foot trail which follows the "Dick Bass Highway" ski run up and west onto the Wilber Ridge, then by following the marked trail (road) back east into Peruvian Gulch at 8800 feet. The east route joins this road near the top of the Peruvian Lift. A single service road continues from here on a steady grade as it winds its way up to the top of Hidden Peak.

The east route is reached by hiking up the bypass road past the Cliff Lodge until you come to a foot trail, marked by a sign, which follows a restored jeep road directly up the hill. Above is a service road which starts farther east along the bypass road and goes below the condominiums on the ridge. This service road is blocked by a gate just past the top of the restored jeep road. Beyond the gate, the road climbs the east side of the Peruvian Gulch, staying near the cliffs, to the junction with the west route.

CARDIFF PASS FROM ALTA (No. L-08)

Distance: 1 mile one way
Elevation Gain: 1360 feet
Highest Point: Pass at 10,000 feet
Hiking Time One Way: 1 hr 10 min

The old mining road leading north from Alta to Cardiff Pass provides access to Flagstaff Peak, Mount Superior, and Cardiff Fork. The best hiking is in morning or in cool weather since the route is south-facing and has few trees. On the way up, you have a changing perspective of the Alta and Snowbird ski areas and of Albion Basin. From the pass, you can see the knife-edged ridges and magnificent summits of the Mount Superior area. Much of the Cottonwood Ridge above Alta is a maze of private lands resulting from mining claims.

The road to Cardiff Pass starts at the Forest Service garage, a low, stone-

Little Cottonwood Trails 1:50,000

151

faced building across the highway from the Alta Lodge, 8.3 miles up Little Cottonwood Canyon. There is ample parking along the road in Alta.

Start on the right (east) of the garage and follow the road up behind the modern wood buildings and around two switchbacks. The first two roads branching left dead-end at cabins, and the third road branching left is the route to Cardiff Pass. It ascends in a series of switchbacks and generally follows the power line to the pass.

About halfway up, the road forks and the more distinct road turns right to the Flagstaff Mine, while the Cardiff Pass road continues northwest. This fork is immediately after two closely spaced switchbacks and before the road crosses under the power line. Higher up, the Cardiff Pass road becomes a foot track through open meadows, but the pass and power line provide clear landmarks.

Mount Superior and Monte Cristo (No. L-08.1)

Destination:	Mount Superior	Monte Cristo
One-Way Miles:	2-1/4	2-1/2
Elevation Gain:	2400	2492
Extra Ascents:	320	400
Highest Point:	11,040	11,132
Hiking Time One Way:	2h 45m	3h

These summits on the Cottonwood Ridge southwest of Cardiff Pass overlook much of the Twin Peaks Wilderness. All around are jagged knife-edged ridges and steep headwalls. To the south you can see the full vertical scale of Snowbird, and the Salt Lake Valley is visible in the distance. There is a perennial debate about which peak is named "Superior," but most hikers do both summits anyway. Local usage, and the 1903 Cottonwood Map, identify the east summit overlooking Alta as Mount Superior. The west peak is higher and provides the best views of the Lake Blanche area.

The route continues west from Cardiff Pass following the ridge crest across several minor summits. It involves exposed scrambling but is suitable for experienced hikers. The first major summit is Mount Superior. The scrambling continues along the very exposed ridge to Monte Cristo. The ridge continuing west beyond these summits is mountaineering terrain.

Flagstaff Peak from Alta (No. L-09)

Distance: 1-1/4 miles one way
Elevation Change: 1890 feet
Highest Point: Summit, 10,530 feet
Hiking Time One Way: 1 hr 40 min

The climb from Alta to Flagstaff Peak is a shorter and easier approach than the route from Days Fork. The hike starts up the road from Alta to Cardiff Pass,

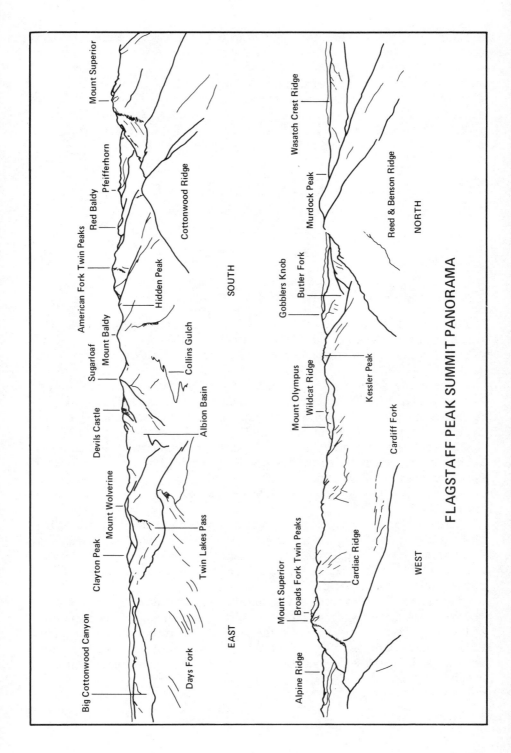

FLAGSTAFF PEAK SUMMIT PANORAMA

153

described previously. Take the right branch of the Cardiff Pass road and continue to the large mine dump where the road ends. A wide, grass-covered slope continues up to a clearly visible pass 400 feet higher. From this pass, turn right and follow the rounded ridge crest to the Flagstaff summit.

From Flagstaff, hikers can continue east along the Cottonwood Ridge toward Grizzly Gulch on an intermittent unmaintained trail. The route along the ridge between Flagstaff and Cardiff Pass involves serious scrambling. The route along the Cottonwood Ridge is described in Chapter 11.

GRIZZLY GULCH (No. L-10)

Destination:	Twin Lakes Pass	Prince of Wales Mine
One-Way Miles:	1-3/4	2-1/4
Elevation Gain:	1353	1460
Highest Point:	9993	10,100
Hiking Time One Way:	1h 30m	1h 50m

This hike follows a road up a narrow gulch rich in mining history. Most of this area is private land, and the Forest Service shows the route as "road on lands of uncertain status." This drainage is the site of one of the proposed interconnect ski lifts.

The Grizzly Gulch Road and the Cardiff Pass hike both start from the Forest Service garage, 8.3 miles up Little Cottonwood Canyon. Start on the right (east) of the garage and follow the road up behind the modern wood buildings. After the second switchback, the main road to Grizzly Gulch continues east. For the first 3/4 mile the road gradually ascends parallel to the highway. It then turns northeast into Grizzly Gulch and stays on the left side of the drainage. Grizzly Gulch crosses the main Little Cottonwood Canyon road near the end of the pavement. Many hikers park there and bushwhack directly to the Grizzly Gulch road.

The road forks about 1/2 mile up Grizzly Gulch. Twin Lakes Pass is visible straight ahead up the drainage. The left branch goes generally north and ascends the side of the gulch to reach a saddle between Honeycomb Cliffs and Davenport Hill. From here, the road continues along a contour into Silver Fork, ending at the Prince of Wales Mine.

Operations at the Prince of Wales mine ceased in the 1880's. Today, the shaft opening and the rusting steam-powered hoisting equipment provide a glimpse of the past. The gratings covering the shafts are a recent attempt at mine restoration. They protect skiers from falling into a snow-covered shaft, yet the grating can be removed if favorable prices ever make reopening the mines a feasible venture.

Boiler and hoisting equipment at the Prince of Wales Shaft between Silver Fork and Grizzly Gulch. The gratings are a recent addition and are intended to prevent skiers from falling into the 900-foot-deep shaft.

Geologic plan of Alta tunnel workings, with projection parallel to Prince of Wales fissure.

The mountains between Cardiff Fork and Alta are full of mine workings as this illustration from a geology report shows. Drawing from James, 1979.

COLLINS GULCH TO GERMANIA PASS
(No. L-11)

Distance: 2 1/2 miles one way
Elevation Gain: 2000 feet
Highest Point: Pass at 10,600 feet
Hiking Time One Way: 2 hr 20 min

Collins Gulch is a good hiking area with sub-alpine meadows, similar to Albion Basin. Alta ski service roads ascend the gulch, and the open ski runs provide long-distance views. The road leads to Germania Pass, which can also be reached by a shorter route from Albion Basin. This area is seldom crowded during the summer, and it provides a good place to contemplate the impact of ski development on other recreational use.

The service road up Collins Gulch starts at the east end of the main Alta parking lot near the Collins and Wildcat ski lifts. Walk uphill between the lifts and follow the obvious road that soon turns left and begins the first of many switchbacks.

The road forks near the base of the Germania Lift. The right branch goes to the top of Wildcat Lift on the ridge to the west and gives a view of Snowbird and Peruvian Gulch. The left branch continues to the top of Germania Lift, then crosses the spur ridge to the east. Across the minor pass, it connects with the Sugarloaf road then climbs the last 200 feet to the ridge.

ALBION BASIN AREA

The highest trailhead in the area is in Albion Basin, a beautiful cirque 800 feet above the town of Alta. A variety of sub-alpine and alpine environments near the road make this a popular area for finding wildflowers during July and August. The basin is an excellent walking area for beginners, while providing the shortest access to the spectacular summits which ring the head of Little Cottonwood Canyon. Secret Lake, Catherine Pass, and Sunset Peak can be reached by good trails. Mount Wolverine, Devils Castle, Sugarloaf, and Mount Baldy all involve routefinding along the ridges. Most of the basin is Forest Service land, with several in-holdings of private land with summer homes. High on the ridges are additional areas of private land resulting from mining claims.

Albion Basin is at the end of the road, 11.3 miles from the mouth of Little Cottonwood Canyon. The last 2-1/2 miles beyond Alta are unpaved but are suitable for passenger cars. There are two hiker parking areas in Albion Basin. One is for the Catherine Pass Trail and the other is just outside the Albion Basin campground.

If you decide to walk up to Albion Basin, the ski area road is a shorter and nicer hike than walking up the automobile road. Start up the Albion Basin road and turn right at the gate which is 1/2 mile beyond the end of the pavement at the upper parking lot and just before the first left turn in the automobile road. The service road leads up the drainage and past the Sugarloaf road, and ends at Albion Basin a few yards from the hiker parking area.

Collins Gulch. The road climbs from Alta to Germania Pass near Sugarloaf Peak. In late summer this gulch becomes a delightful area for finding wildflowers.

SECRET LAKE (No. L-13)

Distance: 3/4 miles one way
Elevation Gain: 420 feet
Highest Point: Lake at 9220 feet
Hiking Time One Way: 35 min

Secret Lake is an excellent beginner hike to a sparkling lake set below the dark cliff face of Devils Castle. This hike is at a high altitude, so adjust your hiking pace.

The Secret Lake Trail has been rerouted to start below the campground

Albion Basin Area

about 1/2 mile away from its original starting point. Follow the trail around the right-hand side of the campground and turn west towards Secret Lake.

The foot trail heads west, crossing a small stream. Locate the small cliff and mine dump to your left. Secret Lake is above these landmarks and in the general direction of the Sugarloaf summit. There are several alternative routes to the lake, which is only 200 yards away. As you approach the cliff the main trail heads right, then makes a switchback to the left above the mine. A few yards of steep trail cross over the rock and the lake comes into view. An alternative route continues west at the switchback and follows an old road around the end of the ridge before reaching the lake.

SUGARLOAF ROAD
To Germania Pass (No. L-12)

Route to Germania Pass:	Along Sugarloaf Road	Direct From Secret Lake
One-Way Miles:	2-1/2	1-3/4
Elevation Gain:	1300	1100
Highest Point:	10,500	10,500
Hiking Time One Way:	1h 45m	1h 30m

The hike from Albion Basin to the Sugarloaf road is the easiest route to Sugarloaf Peak and to the Bullion Divide, Mount Baldy and Hidden Peak (Snowbird tram). The road is a pleasant walk through high meadows and past abandoned mines.

The actual service road starts at the base of Sugarloaf Lift, about 1/2 mile west and 160 feet below the the Albion Basin trailhead. This area is reached from the ski area road which runs parallel to the Albion Basin auto road. Alternatively, start from the Albion Basin trailhead and continue northwest past Secret Lake for 1/4 mile, ascending about 100 feet to connect with the Sugarloaf road.

The road climbs in a series of switchbacks to the top of Sugarloaf Lift. Near the top, the road forks and the right branch crosses the spur ridge to the Collins Gulch road. The Sugarloaf road leads past Germania Pass, a saddle on Bullion Divide overlooking American Fork Canyon, and ends at the top of the ski lift. Either Sugarloaf Peak to the east or Mount Baldy to the west can be reached by off-trail hiking along the ridge.

MOUNT BALDY (No. L-12.1)

Distance: 2-1/4 miles from Albion Basin to Summit via Germania Pass
Elevation Gain: 1668 feet
Highest Point: Summit at 11,068 feet
Hiking Time One Way: 2 hr
Special Difficulties: Unmaintained trail on summit ridge

Mount Baldy is on the ridge separating the Alta and Snowbird ski areas and is only a short ridge hike from Hidden Peak, the destination of the Snowbird Tram. The shortest hiking route up Baldy is to take the service road from Albion Basin to the top of Sugarloaf Lift and then follow the ridge west up the short but very steep slope, making small detours around rock outcrops and brush. There is no exposure, and there is a distinct foot track. From Baldy toward Hidden Peak, the ridge is fairly narrow, but a footpath follows along the crest.

DEVILS CASTLE AND SUGARLOAF
From Albion Basin Trailhead

Destination:	Devils Castle	Sugarloaf Peak
One-Way Miles:	1-1/2	1-1/2
Elevation Change:	1520	1651
Highest Point:	10,920	11,051
Hiking Time One Way:	2h	1h 50m
Special Difficulties:	Exposure Scrambling	

Devils Castle (No. L-13.3)

Devils Castle is the dark, rugged peak whose spires tower above Secret Lake. It is a challenging objective for self-confident hikers who do not mind exposed scrambling on blocks and ledges. The ridge route from the saddle to the summit is an incredible emotional experience and gives hikers a sense of the satisfaction that rock climbers seek.

If you have not done much rock scrambling, climb this peak with someone more experienced. It is a great place to learn about scrambling, and anyone in good condition can follow the route with some coaching. The individual moves are easy, but the consequences of a fall would be serious.

Hike the trail to Secret Lake and continue around the east side of the lake. A foot track with switchbacks climbs 800 vertical feet up the loose scree to the saddle between Devils Castle and Sugarloaf. Turn left at the saddle and follow the ridge which soon becomes a knife-edge. The scrambling route is generally on the right (American Fork Canyon) side of the crest. Routefinding is required

— if the moves seem too difficult, back up and look around. Hands and arms should be used only for balance. One short climb up an inside corner on the left side brings you to the first summit of Devils Castle, where most hikers stop.

The crossing to the next two summits along the ridge crest is still scrambling but is more difficult and time-consuming than the approach to the first summit. From the third summit, the fastest descent is to continue east to the next saddle where you can descend to Albion Basin.

Secret Lake and Sugarloaf Peak. This is a spectacular lake and the trail is short and easy.

Sugarloaf Peak (No. L-13.2)

Sugarloaf is the rounded, scree-covered peak between Devils Castle and the top of the Sugarloaf Lift. It can be approached from either direction by following the ridge crest on moderate off-trail terrain. In contrast to Devils Castle, there is no exposure.

The direct route from Secret Lake continues up the scree slope to the pass as described for Devils Castle but turns right (west) at the pass. The summit is a short walk up the east ridge of Sugarloaf. The other route is from the Sugarloaf road, described previously, and ascends the west ridge across loose rock with some brush.

CATHERINE PASS
And Sunset Peak (No. L-14)
From Albion Basin

Destination:	Catherine Pass	Sunset Peak
One-Way Miles:	1	1-1/2
Elevation Change:	800	1248
Highest Point:	10,200	10,648
Hiking Time One Way:	1h	1h 25m

Catherine Pass

The short but steep trail to Catherine Pass leads through a variety of sub-alpine environments to a fine view of the Brighton area and upper Little Cotton-wood Canyon. Intermediate hikes continue along the ridges in both directions.

The trail starts from the hiker parking area on the spur road 0.1 mile before the Albion Basin campground. The spur road continues to some cabins. The trail begins by making switchbacks up the steep hill. At the top of this hill, the slope levels off, and a short hanging valley leads directly to Catherine Pass.

The trail turns right and levels off after you pass beneath a prominent rock outcrop near the top of the hill. Follow the obvious tracks which lead to an alpine meadow in the hanging valley. Alternatively, the road to the cabins continues to the stream where it makes a switchback and then rejoins the direct trail to the top of the hill. Next, the combined trail crosses the meadow, then becomes steeper as it enters a stand of fir and ascends the last 150 vertical feet to the pass. Across the pass, a trail descends past Lake Catherine and Dog Lake to Brighton.

Sunset Peak From Albion (No. L-14.1)

Sunset Peak is the second summit to the southeast of Catherine Pass and is reached by an informal trail which is in very good condition. This is one of the most accessible summits in the Wasatch and I have seen many children reach the top.

From Catherine Pass a trail heads south, starting on the right side of the ridge crest. The first peak to the south of the pass is a triple divide between Big Cottonwood, Little Cottonwood, and American Fork canyons. The main trail passes to the right of this summit, then turns east, crosses the ridge crest for a short way, and crosses back. One last short switchback brings you to the summit of Sunset Peak.

The good trail ends at Sunset Peak, and the Brighton Ridge Run continues toward Snake Creek Pass. From the saddle near the triple divide, a trail descends into upper American Fork Canyon. Also, the ridge leading south toward the Point Supreme Lift is open meadow and is easy off-trail hiking. There

SUNSET PEAK SUMMIT PANORAMA

163

are several tracks leading from the ridge down toward Lake Catherine, but since this steep slope has high erosion potential, please don't use them for a descent.

Upper Maybird Lake from the end of the maintained trail with the Pfeifferhorn on the skyline.

9

NORTH AND EAST AREAS

The north and east areas of Salt Lake County are not as spectacular as the tri-canyon area, and few hikers venture here — partly because few hikers know the area. The rolling, open terrain is excellent for long-distance travel. Mountain runners frequent these routes, and the "Wasatch Steeple Chase" and "Wasatch Front 100 Mile Endurance Run" are annual events. The relatively low elevation makes this area good for early and late season hikes when the higher ridges are snow-covered.

This is a huge place for wandering. The area covered by this chapter is nearly equal to the acreage covered by the rest of the book. Beyond the jeep roads and constructed trails are miles of footpaths, sheepherder trails, and open, grass-covered slopes and ridges. Only a few of the major routes are included in this chapter.

Historically, grazing and watershed (a strange combination) were the major uses of this area. In recent years, there has been increased interest in managing this area for recreation as well. Land exchanges allowed Salt Lake City and the Forest Service to block up their holdings. The Great Western Trail project has created an officially designated hiking route through the area and has linked many of the previous trails and cross-country routes. Some of these trails are shown on the map in the foothills chapter.

This area does not yet have the level of recreational trails that it deserves. Landowner negotiations to secure access and volunteer construction efforts are continuing.

The Great Western Trail

The Great Western Trail is a national recreation trail extending from Yellowstone to the Grand Canyon. The section through Utah generally follows the crest of the Wasatch Range. The portion described in this guidebook is from Interstate 84 in Ogden to American Fork Canyon.

The current northern access is at the Forest Service Fernwood Picnic Area in Layton. The picnic area is reached by taking US 89 to a point 0.6 miles south of the junction with Utah 193 to Hill Air Force Base. Turn east onto Valley Drive and continue for 0.7 mile then turn east onto Fernwood Road. Follow Fernwood Road as it winds up through the new subdivisions and eventually goes straight into the Forest Service picnic area.

In about the middle of the picnic area, a service road, blocked by a gate, heads steeply up the hill toward a water collection site. A few hundred feet up this road, another road branches north and contours for 1/4 mile above the houses then begins following the Middle Fork of Kays Creek. After climbing 800 feet the trail crosses to the north side of the creek then climbs onto the spur ridge between Kays Creek and Hobbs Canyon and continues east up to the main ridge. Work is currently underway on the section, so access points and routing are subject to change. The trail turns south and follows the rugged ridge crest toward the air traffic control antennas on Francis Peak.

At Francis Peak the Great Western Trail meets a gravel road which heads south into the head of Farmington Canyon where there is a junction with the Forest Service road that loops from Farmington to Bountiful. The next section of the Great Western Trail follows the gravel road from Francis Peak, down past Farmington Lakes, and back up around Bountiful Peak, eventually reaching the trailhead near the head of Centerville Canyon. There are plans for a trail to be constructed from Farmington Flats up to Bountiful Peak but for now the choices are cross-country hiking along the ridge or following the road.

To drive up from Farmington, take exit 325 from Interstate 15 and go to 600 North 100 East in Farmington. A gravel road, marked with a Forest Service sign, heads up the canyon. It is rough, very steep, and winding but passenger cars can make it all the way. It is 8 miles from the end of the pavement to the Farmington Flats junction and 13 miles from the pavement to the north end of the of the spur road at Francis Peak.

The next vehicle access point is at the head of Centerville Canyon which is reached on the road that comes up from Bountiful. To get to this access point, take 400 North to 1300 East in Bountiful. Turn north at 1300 East and follow the main street up two switchbacks through the homes until you are below the prominent letter B on the hillside. Here the gravel road starts and turns up into the canyon and passes a Forest Service sign after 11/2 miles. It is 9 miles from the start of the gravel road to the parking area high on the ridge.

At the head of Centerville Canyon the Great Western Trail leaves the road and continues along the ridge separating Davis and Morgan counties. The next 5 miles to the Sessions Mountains are a mix of old four-wheel drive roads and

Great Western Trail North of Parleys Canyon

new constructed trail. The Kenney Creek Trail which starts at Mueller Park climbs to join the Great Western Trail high in the Sessions Mountains. From the Sessions Mountains the Great Western Trail continues in a generally southeast direction along the ridge above City Creek and passes east of Grandview Peak. As this trail gets more use, it will become the most popular but longest access to Grandview Peak.

From the head of City Creek Canyon, the trail heads east towards Swallow Rocks and then continues on to Big Mountain where a series of switchbacks drops down to Big Mountain Pass on the paved road between Mountain Dell and East Canyon. On the south side of the road, a dirt track heads up the hill, continues past a gate and quickly becomes a foot trail that follows the ridge crest, mostly on Salt Lake City land, over Bald Mountain then descends towards Parleys Summit. New Great Western Trail signs have been put up along this section of ridge.

The Great Western Trail then goes back west 2 1/2 miles from Parleys Summit to the Lambs Canyon Road. There is currently no constructed trail along I-80, so some ingenuity is needed to follow the incomplete frontage roads along Interstate 80 to get between Parleys Summit and Lambs Canyon.

Beyond Lambs Canyon the Great Western Trail generally follows existing roads and routes that are described elsewhere in this book. From the mouth of Lambs Canyon, it follows the Lambs Canyon road to the Lambs Canyon trailhead, follows the Lambs Canyon Trail (No. E-04) to the ridge where it joins the trail going down to Elbow Fork (No. M-10) in Millcreek. From the Elbow Fork trailhead in Millcreek, it goes up the Millcreek road to the Upper Millcreek Trail (No. M-18) which is followed to the Millcreek Ridge (No. R-2). From there the trail follows the ridge between Salt Lake and Summit Counties south towards Scotts Hill. At Scotts Hill, the Great Western Trail currently goes down the Guardsman Pass road to Brighton although it is also possible to continue crosscountry along the ridge crest above Brighton. At Brighton the Great Western Trail takes the Brighton Lakes Trail (No. B-24) up past Lake Mary to Catherine Pass and from Catherine Pass goes up to the triple divide between Big Cottonwood and American Fork Canyon where it leaves the Wasatch National Forest and drops down into American Fork Canyon.

BOUNTIFUL AREA

There are two major Forest Service trailheads southeast of Bountiful. A graded motorcycle trail, which is also excellent for human-powered bicycles, makes a loop from the North Canyon trailhead up to Rudys Flat on the City Creek ridge and back down to the trailhead at Mueller Park. This low-elevation area is well suited to spring and fall hiking. It is heavily forested due to the increased local precipitation resulting from the lake effect.

MUELLER PARK TO RIDGE (No. N-01)

Destination:	Rudys Flat via Bike Trail	Rudys Flat via Stream
One-Way Miles:	4-1/2	2-1/2
Elevation Change:	1870	1870
Highest Point:	7120	7120
Hiking Time One Way:	3h 10m	2h 15m
Special Difficulties:		Bushwhack

To reach Mueller Park from Salt Lake, take I-15 to Exit 318 (Utah 93) and head east. The main road curves north and becomes Orchard Drive. Follow this road to 1800 South, which leads east directly into the mouth of the canyon. The road ends in a large park and picnic area.

The official trail starts about 50 feet before the Forest Service sign at the entrance to Mueller Park. A bridge crosses the stream, and the first of an endless series of switchbacks begins to wind up the hillside. This is a wide, well-constructed trail that climbs slowly as it traverses above the picnic area, crosses the right-hand fork of the drainage, meanders over to Big Rock, and then winds back into the right fork for the final switchbacks to the ridge at Rudys Flat. The trail is open to motor vehicles less than 40 inches wide, *i.e.,* ATVs and motorcycles.

Mueller Park Direct Route

A more direct foot trail formerly followed the drainage from Mueller Park to the ridge, but it was partially washed out several years ago and is now a bushwhack. The remnants of the old trail are reached by walking up the road beyond the park until the canyon branches, then continuing up the right hand fork directly to the ridge. Those wishing a more direct route to the ridge should be prepared for routefinding and bushwhacking through streamside brush on steep hillsides.

NORTH CANYON
To Rudys Flat (No. N-02)

Destination:	Rudys Flat	Loop Hike to Mueller Park
One-Way Miles:	2-1/2	7
Elevation Change:	1120	-750
Total Ascent:		1120
Highest Point:	7120	7120
Hiking Time One Way:	1h 50m	4h 15m

The North Canyon trailhead can be reached by following the route to Mueller Park as far as the intersection of 1800 South and Bountiful Blvd. Follow Bountiful Blvd. back south to about 3400 South, where you turn east on a street which follows the north side of the drainage. Park at the end of the pavement.

From the end of the pavement in North Canyon, continue up the dirt road which eventually becomes a series of switchbacks that climb to the ridge. At Rudys Flat, on the ridge, this trail meets the trail coming from Mueller Park. This is a shorter route to the ridge and is part of the motorcycle trail loop.

View from Emigration Ridge near Dale Peak (Hike E-01). The peak overlooking the city is Big Beacon. Hike WF-6 follows the ridge forming the left skyline of Big Beacon. The oil and natural gas pipeline route is visible snaking across the hillside.

Connecting Trails from Rudys Flat

An unmaintained trail with evidence of vehicle use leads along the ridge above City Creek from the antennas above Ensign Peak, past Rudys Flat, and on towards Grandview Peak. A trail from Rudys Flat down into City Creek was recleared in 1989.

SESSIONS MOUNTAINS (No. N-03)

The Sessions Mountains are a spur ridge extending west from the divide between Davis and Morgan Counties. The Kenny Creek Trail starts in Mueller Park on the west side of the stream and across the road from the lowest parking lot. The trail climbs north and generally follows the route shown on the USGS map. This trail connects with the Great Western Trail.

The Great Western Trail north of Parleys Canyon offers long-distance hiking along open ridges with great views.

EMIGRATION CANYON RIDGE (No. E-01)

Destination:	Dale Peak	Perkins Peak
One-Way Miles:	2-1/2	4-1/4
Elevation Change:	1146	1261
Highest Point:	7376	7491
Hiking Time One Way:	1h 50m	3h
Special Difficulties:		No Trail

The best access to the ridge between Emigration and Parleys canyons is from Little Mountain Summit, the pass at the head of Emigration Canyon just after the hairpin turns. Park in the turnout at the pass. A jeep road, which is blocked by a gate, branches to the south and makes a switchback to turn west. After 1/4 mile, there is a second gate where the road becomes a set of distinct wheel tracks continuing along the ridge crest. After about two miles, the wheel tracks start up a steep hillside and disappear. Beyond, a game trail near the crest provides the best route through the brush. The first major high point (marked Dale on the USGS map) has an excellent panorama of the Salt Lake Valley, Big Beacon, Millcreek Ridge, and of Emigration, Mountain Dell, Parleys and Mount Aire canyons.

The next major high point is Perkins Peak, two miles farther along the ridge. The route is off-trail hiking over minor summits, utilizing game trails to avoid the worst brush. At Perkins Peak the ridge splits; branches lead to the mouth of Emigration Canyon and to the Pencil Point Ridge.

LOOKOUT PEAK
From Affleck Park (No. E-02)

Destination:	Birch Springs Pass	Lookout Peak Summit	Killyon Trailhead
One-Way Miles:	1	3-1/2	2-1/2
Elevation Change:	520	2754	-160
Total Ascent:			520
Highest Point:	6720	8954	6720
Hiking Time One Way:	45m	3h 10m	1h 35m

Note: All measurements are from Affleck Park.

Lookout Peak is on the ridge between City Creek Canyon, Emigration Canyon, and Mountain Dell Canyon. This route starts from Affleck Park, a picnic area in Mountain Dell Canyon 2.2 miles from the junction of Utah Highway 65 with the Emigration Canyon road and 5.1 miles north of the East Canyon exit from Interstate 80. The entrance is marked by a small sign on the west side of the road. A gravel road descends into the park.

From the parking area at the bottom of the hill, walk across the bridge, then take the road to the north. Follow this road for 1100 feet until just past Site #6, then look for a trail which turns sharply back southwest and starts up the hill. This is the jeep road shown on the USGS map. The "road" is a well-defined trail which heads west through oak brush to a pass on an open ridge crest where there is a four-way junction.

Lookout Peak is clearly visible from here. The trail turns north and follows the ridge to the summit. The trail straight ahead drops into Killyon Canyon, and the trail to the south goes to the Emigration Canyon road.

From the four-way junction the trail is distinct up to the point where it leaves the ridge and traverses to City Creek and Hardscrabble Pass. From this point, the faint trail follows the ridge crest over minor peaks to the Lookout Peak summit. Nice views exist all of the way. Areas of oak in this region were recently burned, but they are recovering rapidly as roots send up new shoots.

Killyon Canyon

Killyon Canyon is an alternative approach to the Birch Springs Pass. Take the Emigration Canyon road and turn north on the branch leading to Pinecrest. In 0.3 mile, turn right onto the road into Killyon Canyon and continue for another 0.5 mile. Where the road makes a sharp switchback, there is a small turnout. The Killyon Trail goes straight ahead past the corral and follows the drainage. The trail starts on Forest Service land but there have been conflicts with cabin owners along the road so park carefully and respect their privacy. This route to Birch Springs Pass is somewhat longer than from Affleck Park, but it is a nice, low-elevation canyon for hiking.

MOUNTAIN DELL CANYON (No. E-03)

As you walk up the road described for the hike to Birch Springs and Lookout Peak you are following the stream draining upper Mountain Dell Canyon. There is a washout just beyond the end of the picnic area road but an unmaintained trail continues up the drainage past spectacular rock formations.

EMIGRATION CANYON – LITTLE MOUNTAIN (No. E-04)

This trail starts north of the road at the pass between Emigration Canyon and Mountain Dell Canyon. This distinct trail traverses on the west of the ridge crest over several minor spur ridges, passes under power lines, and ends at a four-way junction where it joins the trails coming from Killyon Canyon and Affleck Park. Because this trail has little elevation change, it gets extensive mountain bike use.

To reach the summit of Little Mountain, go cross country across the open slopes on the south side of the ridge.

Mormon Pioneer Trail (No. E-05)

The Mormon Pioneer Trail is a national historic trail that goes from Navoo, Illinois to Pioneer Trails State Park in Salt Lake City. The trail eventually connects with the Pony Express National Historic Trail and the California National Historic Trail.

Pioneer Trails State Park maintains a 4.2 miles section of this footpath which starts at Big Mountain Pass and descends into Summit County. One trailhead is located at Big Mountain Pass on the divide between Mountain Dell Canyon and East Canyon. Take Utah Highway 65 from the Mountain Dell exit on I-80 to reach the pass. The trail descends through aspen forest along Little Emigration Canyon to the lower trailhead at Mormon Flats in the East Canyon drainage. To get to the Mormon Flats trailhead, go up Interstate 80 to the Jeremy Ranch turnoff. Go past the clubhouse and follow the Summit County gravel road. The trail is 5.1 miles past the clubhouse. A monument marks both trailheads.

LAMBS CANYON (No. E-06)

Distance: 1-3/4 miles one way
Elevation Gain: 1540 feet
Highest Point: 8140 feet at pass
Hiking Time One Way: 1 hr 40 min

The trail from Lambs Canyon, which climbs through fir and aspen forest to the Millcreek Ridge, is the only Forest Service hiking trail on the Parleys Canyon side of the ridge. The trailhead is reached by taking the Lambs Canyon exit from I-80 and continuing south on a narrow paved road for 1.6 miles from the off-ramp to a parking area on the left. The trail starts across the road from the parking area and immediately descends to the bridge across the stream. The trailhead has recently been relocated from the location shown on the USGS map, and there has been recent trail construction, but a few areas are overgrown with grass.

The trail makes a couple of switchbacks, then joins a small spring-fed stream. The trail continues southwest and crosses the stream four times before the flow disappears. Here, the trail turns slightly right and soon becomes steeper as it continues up the drainage. A series of short switchbacks completes the climb to the pass where the Lambs Canyon Trail joins with the trail from Elbow Fork and with the Millcreek ridge route. Both the Lambs Canyon Trail and the trail from down to Elbow Fork are part of the Great Western Trail.

10

DRY CREEK AND AMERICAN FORK CANYON
(Utah County)

The south part of the Lone Peak Wilderness contains dense forests, three sparkling lakes, and spectacular summits. The complex geology has produced steep cliffs which are part of the beauty of this area, but which also channel hiking into a limited number of routes and drainages. Access is from the Dry Creek trailhead northeast of the town of Alpine, from the north fork of the American Fork Canyon road, or by scrambling across the ridge from Little Cottonwood Canyon.

Box Elder Peak, the major peak between Lone Peak and Timpanogos, is one of my favorite routes in Utah County. The summit provides a different perspective of Lone Peak and the Pfeifferhorn, and of the towns to the southwest. There are two routes up Box Elder, but both require off-trail hiking to reach the summit. The north route from Deer Creek is longer but less difficult, and the summit is visible most of the way. The south route leads to a steep and spectacular drainage, which presents moderately difficult scrambling on loose rock since the old trail has been obliterated by rockslides.

The terrain south of Box Elder has no maintained trails and the area is broken by steep cliff bands and narrow drainages which plunge toward American Fork Canyon. This book ends at the roads along the south edge of the Lone Peak Wilderness. The Utah County public lands are administered by the Pleasant Grove Ranger District, Uinta National Forest.

DRY CREEK TRAIL (No. DC-1)

Destination:	Pipeline Intake	Dry Creek Divide
One-Way Miles:	1-3/4	4-1/4
Elevation Change:	1900	3950
Highest Point:	7600	9650
Hiking Time One Way:	1h 50m	4h 10m

This wide horse trail climbs to a grassy pass where it meets the trail coming up Deer Creek from the Granite Flat trailhead. The name is misleading; the southwest-facing canyon has a flowing stream and dense forest. The upper drainages of Dry Creek lead to the south side of Alpine Ridge overlooking Little Cottonwood Canyon. This area is full of old roads and trails which are now little used and overgrown but are still passable by those who like to explore.

From the end of Utah Highway 79 at 2nd North and Alpine go to 2nd East and turn north onto Grove Drive. Continue northeast along the main paved road and go past a chain link fence with large white boulders along the side of the road. The road makes a turn to the right and then goes back to the left and ends at a turnaround 2.6 miles from the end of the State Highway.

The main Dry Creek Trail follows an old pipeline road northeast up a short hill, past a Forest Service wilderness boundary sign, and on up the drainage,

This meadow is the junction of the Dry Creek Trail (DC-1) and the Deer Creek Trail (AF-1). From here, the Silver Fork Overlook Trail leads north and the route to Box Elder leads south.

Lone Peak Wilderness to American Fork Canyon 1:100,000

climbing steadily and staying south of the stream. This trail continues northeast to reach the grassy pass where it joins the trail coming up from Deer Creek.

Another trail also leaves from the parking area. The Phelps Canyon Trail (No. DC-4) heads southeast into the smaller drainage immediately south and climbs to join the Box Elder Canyon Trail.

NORTH MOUNTAIN TRAIL
Dry Creek to Lake Hardy Trail (No. DC-3)

A trail branches right from the Dry Creek Trail, about 1 1/2 miles from the start, and heads to an abandoned intake structure at the stream. Across the stream there is a meadow where you can find the end of a trail which heads west for a mile to connect with the trail from Schoolhouse Springs to Lake Hardy. Look for cairns in the meadow and for a distinct track on the west side of the clearing. The trail is overgrown in spots but is not difficult to find. It winds over ridges and around gullies, staying near the 7800 foot contour.

SCHOOLHOUSE SPRINGS TRAILHEAD
(No. DC-2)

Northwest of the Dry Creek trailhead, a jeep road can be seen climbing the hillside in a series of switchbacks. This is the hiking route to the First Hammongog (a meadow), to Lone Peak, and to Lake Hardy. A connecting trail traverses between the Lake Hardy Trail and the trail up Dry Creek.

Follow the directions for the Dry Creek Trailhead, but watch for a street marked Alpine Cove Drive, which is just before a chain link fence and a series of large white rocks alongside of Grove Drive. Follow Alpine Cove Drive to Aspen Drive, 0.3 miles. Aspen Drive is 13560 N. 4300 W on the Alpine Street Grid. A road heads up from the end of Aspen Drive. A short way beyond the end of the pavement, the road passes through a fence and becomes steeper and rougher. Park in a clearing alongside the road. As you hike up, the main road is generally the branch to the right; there are a couple of false branches to the left. This road crosses private land as it climbs up to the Wilderness Area boundary about 1500 hundred vertical feet above. Currently the road is badly eroded, but four-wheel drive vehicles do make it up to the point where the road is closed at the Wilderness boundary. If you head north and find an intimidating gate with an imposing house just beyond, you are one road too far east. This area is being developed, so the directions are subject to change.

Lake Hardy is at the end of the Schoolhouse Springs Trail (DC-2). Off-trail routes climb above the lake to the ridges above Hogum Cirque and Bells Canyon. The Beatout Hike (R-6) passes high above Lake Hardy.

LAKE HARDY (No. DC-2.1)

Destination:	First Hammongog	Dry Creek Trail	Lake Hardy
One-Way Miles:	2-1/4	3	5
Elevation Change:	1800	2300	4700
Highest Point:	7100	7600	10,000
Hiking Time One Way:	2h	2h 40m	4h 50m

This beautiful lake is perched in a small bowl high on the ridge. The hike starts in foothill brush, climbs through mid-elevation forest and grassland, then passes below sheer cliffs before entering a narrow, glacier-carved valley with the lake at the head.

Follow the main jeep road up the switchbacks avoiding the minor roads which branch off to the left and dead-end. Immediately before the First Hamongog is the Wilderness boundary where a dirt ridge blocks the road. This charming meadow has a fine view of Lone Peak and is a worthwhile objective. Halfway across the meadow the trail forks. The trail to the left leads to the Second Hamongog and Lone Peak. The foot trail to Lake Hardy makes a sharp right turn and heads uphill into the trees.

The Lake Hardy Trail climbs across a minor ridge before reaching the reliable creek draining the lake. The trail then continues east a short way, turns north, and follows a small dry drainage which parallels the stream. About 250 yards beyond the stream crossing is the junction with the crossover trail leading to Dry Creek. The trail to the lake continues up the dry drainage for 1000 vertical feet. Where it reaches the cliffs the faint trail, marked by cairns, jogs slightly west and continues ascending. A cluster of dead snags and a huge limber pine mark where the trail leaves the base of the cliffs and climbs across the open slabs to meet the stream, 500 feet higher. The walls of a canyon now close in and suddenly you are in a forest of old-growth sub-alpine fir. Follow the east side of the stream up to a large meadow at 9500 feet. Climb the last steep section to the lake by starting up the west side of the drainage, crossing back east where the slope eases, then continuing up the rounded granite ridge.

The area around the lake is very fragile, due to the altitude and the thin soil, and shows severe impact from camping. Those staying overnight should consider camping in the meadow below rather than at the lake.

Two moderate angle slopes, separated by a cliff, lead up from the lake. The east slope leads to the saddle near Chipman Peak and the ridge overlooking Hogum Cirque. The west route leads to a pass into Bells Canyon. The divide ridge above these slopes is described as part of the Beatout Hike (See Route No. R-6).

Lone Peak by Hamongog Trail (No. DC-2.2)

The road up from School House Springs ends at a large flat meadow known as the First Hamongog. In the middle of the meadow there is a T-junction in the trail. The trail to the right is the route to Lake Hardy and the trail to the left goes up to the Second Hamongog. This is a well defined trail through the oak brush that climbs up to a second beautiful meadow known as the Second Hamongog.

Here there is another trail junction. The Hamongog Trail continues west and traverses across the heads of several drainages and eventually ends at a trailhead on the road in Hog Hollow. The trail to Lone Peak continues north. From the Second Hamongog you can see the entire route to Lone Peak Summit. Looking up, you will see a long steep cliff wall on the right. This is the edge of Upper Bells Peak. In the center of the drainage you will see a prominent outcrop which divides the drainage, and to the left you will see the jagged ridge which forms the eastern edge of Lone Peak Cirque. The route goes up the east side of the drainage along a poorly defined but visible trail and ends at the base of a cliff. Here the more distinct trail goes east, and the route to Lone Peak goes west across the open slabs eventually crossing the ridge that divides the middle of the drainage and climbs to a point overlooking Bells Canyon. From here you follow the obvious slope to the south summit of Lone Peak.

To reach the west end of the trail that goes from the First Hamongog to Hog Hollow, turn left from the Fort Canyon Road. Park before the gate and walk up the road to the trail.

GRANITE FLAT TRAILHEAD

To reach the Granite Flat area, drive east on Utah 80 to the junction 2.5 miles past the Timpanogos Cave Visitor Center. Continue 2.4 miles up the north fork to Tibble Fork Reservoir. At the upper end of the reservoir, a paved road turns left, passes a horse unloading station, and continues into the campground. The south route to Box Elder Canyon and the Deer Creek Trail leave from here. Immediately before the campground gate, a dirt road branches right. This road leads to the upper Deer Creek trailhead (limited parking) and on to Silver Lake Flat.

DEER CREEK TRAIL (No. AF-1)

Destination:	Dry Creek Divide	Box Elder Summit	Silver Lake Overlook
One-Way Miles:	2 3/4	4 1/2	3 1/2
Elevation Change:	2700	4341	3240
Highest Point:	9640	11,010	10,200
Hiking Time One Way:	2h 45m	4h 25m	3h 25m
Special Difficulties:		No Trail	

A Lone Peak Wilderness trailhead sign is on the right, just inside the campground. This lower trailhead leads to the upper Deer Creek trailhead

Box Elder Peak. Straight ahead is the north route (Hike AF-1.2) which follows the ridge crest to the summit.

which is about 1/4 mile north along the gravel road. From the campground, follow the maintained trail north until it meets the road. Walk five minutes up the road then turn west on the Deer Creek Trail, a wide swath with motorcycle barriers across it. (Trail construction may soon eliminate the walk along the road.) About 15 minutes from the road, the trail crosses a creek, then makes a sharp right turn to the north at a four-way junction. The other two branches eventually fade out.

Next, a series of switchbacks crosses an open south-facing slope. There are sections of aspen and Gambel oak but much of this slope is covered with sage and mountain mahogany. The summit of Box Elder is visible above the far side of the Deer Creek drainage. Follow the trail to the grassy saddle, where the Dry Creek Trail continues west toward Alpine.

Silver Lake Overlook and Beyond (No. AF-1.1)

From the Deer Creek divide, an eroded horse track leads north along the ridge, then crosses a grassy bowl. Suddenly you are at the top of a limestone cliff overlooking Silver Lake, 1000 feet below.

The unmaintained trail ends at the overlook, but either the overlook ridge or the easier ridge to the west can be followed higher. The knob where these ridges converge has excellent views of Dry Creek, the Pfeifferhorn, and the Silver Lake Basin. Beyond this knob, the granite ridge has been carved to a knife-edge, and serious scrambling is required to continue north to the headwall of Red Pine Canyon.

North Route to Box Elder (No. AF-1.2)

From the Dry Creek saddle, follow the ridge crest for 1-1/2 miles over two minor summits to reach Box Elder Peak. There is a track through the brush, and there are no major difficulties. The last part near the summit involves boulder-hopping and some easy scrambling.

BOX ELDER CANYON TRAIL (No. AF-2)
South Route to Box Elder Peak

Destination:	Cabin and Wide Hollow Overlook	Box Elder Summit	Phelps Canyon Trailhead
One-Way Miles:	2	3-1/2	7
Elevation Change:	1960	4301	-1050
Total Ascent:	1960	4301	3120
Highest Point:	8760	11,101	9920
Hiking Time One Way:	1h 50m	4h 15m	5h 40m
Special Difficulties:		Scrambling	Faint Trail

182

Lone Peak, the Alpine Ridge, and Dry Creek viewed from Box Elder Peak. The Dry Creek Trail *(DC-1) and the Schoolhouse Springs Trail (DC-2) provide access into this area. The ridges are rugged off-trail hiking.*

The trail starts behind the cinder block outhouse in the "C" group campground and turns sharply right (northwest), following the stream for a short way before turning west and beginning a series of switchbacks. The trail climbs steadily through forest, passes an unusual dirt headwall, and climbs to the spur ridge, where you overlook Wide Hollow. There are some false trails here. The route to Box Elder goes right and passes a cabin ruin immediately after the overlook. The trail enters a meadow, then goes around to the south of a minor peak (elev. 10,138). Ahead is the steep-sided upper portion of Wide Hollow, where the trail forks.

Box Elder Summit from the South (No. AF-2.1)

Ten years ago, the right branch of the trail (shown on the USGS map) continued high along the north side of the drainage to reach the pass. Rockslides have wiped out several sections, but a strong hiker can still follow this route. The easier route is to take the left branch to the stream, then follow the drainage up to the saddle. This route requires considerable scrambling, and there are a few difficulties with loose rock, which average hikers can handle. At the saddle, turn north and follow the scree-covered ridge to the summit.

West to Phelps Canyon (No. AF-2.2)

The left branch crosses the drainage and climbs southwest to a pass where it crosses into Box Elder Canyon. The trail then heads back north into Phelps Canyon and descends to the Dry Creek trailhead near Alpine. The trail is faint in spots, but it is the best access to the huge area between Box Elder Peak and the American Fork Canyon road.

The hillsides in this area were terraced in the 1930's to counteract the effects of overgrazing. The soil stabilization work left a number of overgrown trails, which can be followed if you explore for them.

American Fork Silver Lake An excellent trail leads to this lake which is ringed by cliffs. Silver Glance Lake is reached by off-trail hiking up the slope to the right.

AMERICAN FORK SILVER LAKE TRAIL
(No. AF-3)

Destination:	Silver Lake	Silver Glance Lake	White Pine West Pass
One-Way Miles:	1-3/4	2-3/4	3-1/4
Elevation Change:	1440	2320	3080
Highest Point:	9000	9880	10,640
Hiking Time One Way:	1h 35m	2h 30m	3h 20m
Special Difficulties:		No Trail	Scrambling

This "other" Silver Lake is a secluded place just over the ridge from White Pine. The lake is ringed by cliffs, and the setting is similar to Secret Lake but is more spectacular. The maintained trail ends at Silver Lake, but hikers can continue up to Silver Glance Lake and beyond to a pass in the ridge leading to Little Cottonwood Canyon.

The trailhead is at the north end of the Silver Lake Flat Reservoir, 11.8 miles from the mouth of American Fork Canyon. Follow the paved road past Tibble Reservoir to the campground entrance. Immediately before the Granite Flat Campground gate, turn right on a gravel road and continue for another 3.2 miles to a large parking area, where the road fords the creek.

From the parking area, the trail heads north through aspen and follows the west side of the creek. Soon, a spur ridge with several mine dumps separates the trail from the main drainage, and a cliff begins to wall in the trail on the west side. The trail continues up a single major switchback through a steep section and leads to the dam at Silver Lake. Towering above is a black and white limestone layer cake (Donut Formation), and to the south is a magnificent view of Mount Timpanogos. The top of the cliffs on the west can be reached from the Deer Creek Trail.

Silver Glance Lake (No. AF-3.1)

Silver Glance Lake is reached by continuing up the minor ridge northeast from the dam. There is no trail but the hiking is through widely-spaced trees with little brush. Red Baldy looms ahead as you approach the divide to Little Cottonwood Canyon. From Silver Glance Lake to White Pine Lake is less than a mile, but the ridge crossing is steep and requires some routefinding.

11

RIDGE HIKES AND MOUNTAINEERING SCRAMBLES

The ridge hikes are most often done as part of a loop connecting two trails. They provide access to remote summits and hanging canyons, and they let an experienced hiker spend a full day traveling over peaks and crossing above drainages while enjoying an alpine environment, ever changing scenery, and solitude. These routes are seldom traveled, so be capable of handling changes in the weather, accidents, or emergencies. Good physical condition is essential for routes involving multiple ascents and descents.

Except for the hike from Millcreek to Brighton, these ridge hikes are *routes*, not *trails*. At most, you will find a track indicating where others have walked. Ridges are frequently interrupted by rock pinnacles and outcrops that require detours or scrambling. The second part of this chapter describes mountaineering scrambles that require excellent physical condition and previous training in mountaineering techniques. Mountaineering scrambles are not for casual hikers.

Routefinding is part of off-trail hiking. The descriptions for these routes are directed toward trip planning, identifying connecting trails, and negotiating tricky sections. Where the route follows an obvious ridge, you are on your own. Carry a topographic map if you are not familiar with the major drainages and landmarks.

MILLCREEK RIDGE (No. R-1)
Grandeur to Murdock Peak

Trail Section:	Grandeur Peak to Burch Hollow	Burch Mt. Hollow to Mt. Aire Pass	Mt. Aire Pass to Lambs Pass	Lambs Pass to Murdock Peak
One-Way Miles:	2-3/4	1-1/2	2-1/2	4-1/4
Elevation Change:	-179	-320	320	1482
Total Ascent:	1327	374	1801	2402
Highest Point:	8306	8194	8621	9602
Hiking Time One Way:	3h	1h 20m	3h5m	4h 15m
Special Difficulties:	No Trail	No Trail Scrambling	No Trail Brush	No Trail

Note: Measurements are for ridge segments only, and do not include the hike from the road to the ridge.

The peaks and ridges of the divide separating Millcreek from Parleys Canyon are rounded, with only a few rock outcrops. The ridge is long but not difficult. Although maps show a trail, the route is a faint unmaintained track

The ridge from Millcreek to Brighton (Hike R-2) *is a fairly level long-distance hike following jeep roads and horse trails. Mountain bikes are popular but controversial.*

which is occasionally lost in the brush. An elk herd is frequently seen from this ridge.

Starting from the trail at the saddle 1/2 mile east of Grandeur Peak, the route to Mount Aire follows near the ridge crest with occasional detours around rock outcrops, and after a mile it reaches the trail to Church Fork Peak. A short section of the ridge crest near Church Fork Peak is private land and the Mount Aire Canyon summer home area is climbing toward the ridge. Today this section of ridge offers solitude; someday, you may encounter roads. In another mile, the Burch Hollow Trail joins the ridge near a series of massive rock outcrops. A faint track continues from here to the maintained trail at Mount Aire Pass.

Beyond the summit of Mount Aire, the ridge is narrow and rocky, and easy scrambling is required to reach Lambs Canyon Pass. Continuing east, the ridge becomes more wooded, with alternating brush and fir-aspen forest. There is a track along the ridge, but you have to search. Try to stay near the ridge crest; it is easy to get off onto a side ridge and be forced to double back. The ridge route crosses the section of private land in upper Millcreek, then continues toward Murdock Peak. Beyond Murdock Peak are the jeep road along the Wasatch Crest Ridge and the Park West Ski Resort.

GREAT WESTERN TRAIL (No. R-2)
Millcreek to Brighton

Trail Section:	Park West Saddle to Desolation Lake Pass	Desolation Lake Pass to Scotts Pass
One-Way Miles:	2-1/2	4
Elevation Change:	840	-360
Total Ascent:	1280	596
Highest Point:	9800	10,116
Hiking Time One Way:	2h	2h 35m

Note: Measurements are for ridge segments only, and do not include the hike from the road to the ridge.

The ridge separating Salt Lake Country from Summit County overlooks the Park West Ski Resort and Park City. A jeep road follows this ridge around upper Millcreek Canyon, then a trail continues along the ridge past Desolation Lake and Beartrap Fork to Scotts Hill where another jeep road appears. Gates restrict motorized vehicles, so the roads are pleasant for walking and are popular with mountain bicycles. The Great Western Trail follows this ridge from the head of Millcreek Canyon to Scotts Hill, then drops down to Brighton along the Guardsman Pass road.

The upper Millcreek road (Trail No. M-18) leads directly to the ridge crest road at Park West Pass. The jeep road, which is used by a sheepherder, generally stays on the west of the ridge crest, following contours around the minor summits. The road turns east and descends into Summit County, and a trail continues along the ridge. The ridge can also be reached by bushwhacking up from the south road in Millcreek.

Beyond Millcreek Canyon, the trail continues to the Desolation Lake junction, where a trail descends to the lake 350 feet below. The loop from upper Millcreek to Desolation Lake, returning by the Mill D and Big Water Trails, is a good 9-mile hike. Just beyond Desolation Lake, the trail crosses a ridge and traverses high in Beartrap Fork. The top of the Beartrap Fork Trail can be found on the east of the stream, where the canyon first narrows.

Farther along the ridge the trail becomes wider, and near Scotts Hill it becomes a road again. From Scotts Pass, a service road, described in the Thayne Canyon section of Raye Ringholtz's *Park City Trails,* descends through the ski area to the golf course. The road to the south descends through the summer cabin area in Mill F Fork which is private land. The Guardsman Pass road, which is open to automobiles during summer months, is another 3/4 mile southeast along the ridge.

BRIGHTON RIDGE RUN (No. R-3)

Trail Section:	Snake Creek Pass to Catherine Pass	Catherine Pass to Twin Lakes Via Twin Lakes Pass	Catherine Pass to Twin Lakes Via Millicent
One-Way Miles:	2-1/2	2-1/2	1-3/4
Elevation Change:	160	-760	-760
Total Ascent:	1328	635	835
Highest Point:	10,648	10,795	10,795
Hiking Time One Way:	2h 30m	2h 20m	2h 5m

Note: Measurements are for ridge segments only, and do not include the hike from the road to the ridge.

This peak-bagger's delight crosses six summits above 10,000 feet, as the route follows the ridge crest forming the perimeter of the Brighton bowl. It involves off-trail hiking but no serious rock scrambling or exposure. Many hikers double back and also include Clayton Peak as a seventh summit.

From Snake Creek Pass, the route follows the road south past the ski lift and then continues as a faint foot track on the ridge. Go directly over the first unnamed summit (elev. 10,315), then continue past the second summit (elev. 10,321). The track occasionally disappears in the brush along this section. Just before Pioneer Peak there is a mine working that still shows the vivid colors that guided the early prospectors. The ridge becomes narrow and rocky over Pioneer Peak and Sunset Peak. From Sunset Peak to Catherine Pass there is a trail.

From Catherine Pass, the route climbs the steep ridge leading to the summit of Mount Tuscarora, with Mount Wolverine, the high point of the ridge, just beyond. There is a little brush here and some tricky boulder-hopping, but no real difficulty if you search for the easiest route. Beyond Wolverine, you have a choice. The curving ridge toward Twin Lakes Pass is longer but avoids most of the loose rock and offers great views of Wolverine Cirque. The alternative is to go northeast over Mount Millicent, then boulder-hop down to the top of the ski lift, where you meet the service road.

An alternative hike, sometimes called the Alta Ridge Run, ascends from Albion Basin to Point Supreme and continues to Catherine Pass, then follows the Brighton Ridge route to Twin Lakes Pass and descends Grizzly Gulch back to Alta.

COTTONWOOD RIDGE (No. R-4)
Twin Lakes Pass To Superior

	Twin Lakes Pass to Days Fork	Days Fork to Cardiff Pass	Cardiff Pass to Superior
One-Way Miles:	1-1/2	1-1/2	3/4
Elevation Change:	-113	160	1000
Total Ascent:	1206	950	1280
Highest Point:	10,479	10,530	11,040
Hiking Time One Way:	1h 55m	1h 50m	1h 25m
Special Difficulties:		Scrambling	Scrambling, Exposure

Note: Measurements are for ridge segments only, and do not include the hike from the road to the ridge.

The ridge route over the Honeycomb Cliffs, Davenport Hill, Flagstaff Peak, and on to Mount Superior is a rewarding alpine hike requiring some scrambling. The area is full of abandoned mines, and this traverse is often done as the start of ski tours into Silver Fork or Days Fork. Snow and ice remain in sheltered areas well into the summer, and this route can be done as a spring snow climb. Later in the season, an unmaintained trail can be followed along much of the ridge.

The first mile from Twin Lakes Pass to Silver Fork offers views of Alta and a look down the steep cliffs at the head of Honeycomb Fork. There are three options along this section. One is to go directly over the top of the Honeycomb Cliffs along a fairly broad ridge crest. Another is to bushwhack and boulder-hop through brush and small cliffs along the Alta side, making a reasonably level traverse which takes about 20 minutes. The third choice is to drop 320 feet into Grizzly Gulch and reascend by the road which leads to the Prince of Wales Mine.

From the east pass of Silver Fork, a faint track provides an easy route, passing on the Alta side below Davenport Hill then following the ridge crest to join the trail that starts in Days Fork and crosses into the west bowl of Silver Fork. The route continues near the ridge crest for another 3/4 mile around the head of Days Fork and up Flagstaff Peak. The headwall of Days Fork is a steep scramble across slabs and scree. A grassy slope leads from the saddle west of Flagstaff down 200 feet to the road which continues to Alta.

The next 1/2 mile to Cardiff Pass is difficult, and may require 40 minutes to one hour. The ridge drops off steeply on both sides, and the crest is interrupted by two intermediate summits and an abrupt cliff. The cliff is bypassed by descending a moderate-angle couloir on the Alta side then traversing below the cliff. The alternative is to descend to the Flagstaff Mine and to reascend to Cardiff Pass.

The next section beyond Cardiff Pass is part of the standard route up Mount Superior from Alta. The Cottonwood Ridge beyond Monte Cristo to Twin Peaks is a mountaineering scramble.

BULLION DIVIDE (No. R-5)
Albion Basin To White Pine Ridge Run

Destination:	Hidden Peak (Tram)	Am. Fork Twin Peaks	Red Baldy	White Pine Trailhead
One-Way Miles:	3	4	5-1/4	9-3/4
Elevation Change:	1592	2033	2089	-1696
Total Ascent:	1952	2713	3689	3689
Highest Point:	10,992	11,489	11,171	11,489
Hiking Time One Way:	2h 40m	3h 55m	5h 10m	7h 45m
Special Difficulties:		Exposure, Scrambling		Boulder- fields

Note: All measurements are cumulative from Albion Basin.

The route passes over Mount Baldy and Hidden Peak (Snowbird tram), then crosses the knife-edged ridge to American Fork Twins and continues on to Red Baldy before descending a boulderfield to White Pine Lake. The normal start is from Albion Basin (Trail No. L-12) since this requires the least elevation gain to reach the summits along the ridge. The Collins Gulch and Peruvian Gulch roads provide alternative access but require more elevation gain.

The route follows the ridge crest and is above tree line all the way. The section from Germania Pass to Hidden Peak is moderate hiking on an unmaintained foot track and is popular with persons who ride the tram up. An alternative route from Germania Pass descends south to Mineral Flat then traverses to American Fork Twin Peaks, staying between 10,400 and 10,600 feet. Beyond Hidden Peak, the ridge becomes a knife-edge and exposed scrambling is encountered, followed by an intimidating ascent of Twin Peaks. From Twin Peaks to Red Baldy, the ridge crest gets wider and becomes moderate off-trail hiking. You can descend into White Pine Canyon from East Pass or can cross over Red Baldy and descend from West Pass. Both involve about 600 feet of boulder-hopping to the trail.

Hikers along the Bullion Divide (Hike R-5). The west summit of American Fork Twin Peaks is ahead.

THE BEATOUT HIKE (No. R-6)
Alpine Ridge from Red Pine to Bells Canyon

Trail Section:	White Pine Trailhead to Pfeifferhorn	Pfeifferhorn to South Thunder Mountain	South Thunder Mountain to Bells Canyon Trailhead
One-Way Miles:	4-1/2	2	5-1/4
Elevation Change:	3622	-172	-5854
Total Ascent:	3622	1000	0
Highest Point:	11,326	11,326	11,154
Hiking Time One Way:	4h 20m	2h	4h 30m
Special		Scrambling	No trail
Difficulties:		Exposure	at top.

Note: Hiking times are for individual trail segments under spring conditions on consolidated snow.

This long route crosses the most rugged glacier-carved terrain in the Wasatch as it climbs over the Pfeifferhorn, circles above the sheer headwall of Hogum Fork, climbs the seldom-visited south peak of Thunder Mountain,

192

makes a short detour to Chipman Peak, and descends the cirque at the head of Bells Canyon. The east and north sides of Lone Peak dominate the view for much of the trip.

The best time to do the route is late May or early June, when consolidated summer snow smooths over the boulderfields. This hike starts with the route previously described for hiking to the Pfeifferhorn from Red Pine Lake. There are no easy shortcuts to the road after you pass the Pfeifferhorn, so evaluate your progress before continuing. Although this is the highest point on the route, you have more summits to traverse on ridges similar to the Pfeifferhorn approach, seven more miles, and a 6000-foot descent ahead.

From the Pfeifferhorn, the route descends the boulder-covered west ridge, then either follows the ridge over the unnamed peak (elev. 11,137) just ahead, or alternatively makes a descending traverse across the south slope directly to the saddle beyond. Next comes a 1/4-mile moderately difficult boulder-scrambling ascent to the small saddle separating Chipman Peak (elev. 10,954) from the main ridge. The Chipman summit is a 20-minute side trip. From the Chipman saddle, the route follows the main ridge northwest above the 400-foot-high headwall of Hogum Fork. A final, steep boulderfield brings you to South Thunder Mountain (elev. 11,154) and the triple divide between Dry Creek, Hogum Fork, and Bells Canyon. Alternatively, traverse high in the broad south-facing bowl which continues down to Lake Hardy, then reascend to South Thunder Mountain.

The normal descent is to go west from South Thunder Mountain to the upper Bells Canyon reservoir, where the trail can be found. Pick out a few landmarks to the reservoir, which sits in a depression; it is visible from the ridge but is hard to see from lower down. One route is to drop from the summit and follow a small gully southeast until the slope becomes more gradual at about 10,000 feet. From here, proceed northeast along the base of the steep slope to a small tree-covered notch, then cross the ridge separating the reservoir from the main Bells Canyon drainage. A steep chute leads from the notch to the reservoir. Pass south of the reservoir and join the trail at the dam.

The next 3/4 mile is a steep 1400-foot descent through forested terrain to a meadow at 7900 feet. If the trail is snow-covered, work your way down, stay north of the stream draining the reservoir, and look for trail fragments on the small ridge separating the stream from the next gully north. From the meadow, the trail continues along the north side of the stream for about 1/2 mile before crossing back to the south side. From here on, follow the well-worn trail down Bells Canyon.

Thunder Bowl, a north-facing cirque overlooking the city, is often snow-filled late into the summer and provides a more difficult but exciting alternative descent into Bells Canyon. Scramble north along the ridge from South Thunder Mountain for 1/4 mile to the notch leading into Thunder Bowl. After descending the snow, work your way down to the meadow, avoiding the most difficult cliffs by picking your way down the steep west slope.

MOUNTAINEERING SCRAMBLES

Experienced hikers and mountaineers will be challenged by the strenuous off-trail alpine routes, spring snow routes, and mountaineering scrambles included in this section. These routes are intermediate in difficulty between the trail hikes and the routes included in technical rock climbing guidebooks. But difficulty depends on circumstances. Getting off-route, bad weather, and ice or snow can make the route far more dangerous and difficult.

A basic mountaineering course is highly recommended before attempting these routes. If the route involves steep snow and ice, everyone should know how to use an ice axe instinctively. Everyone should also be familiar with basic rock climbing techniques and should know their climbing limits. These are not roped climbs, but carrying a climbing rope can provide an extra margin of safety. Be prepared for 8 to 12 hours of steady travel across rough terrain. Several of the routes are difficult to exit, and once started, it is easiest to complete the route. Maintain a margin of safety and consider the terrain, the weather, and the group's skill.

Only a few of the more popular and worthwhile mountaineering routes are included here. They approach or even equal the experiences available in more popular areas, such as the Tetons, the Cascades, or foreign mountain ranges, yet they are within 20 miles of a major city.

In early June, the snow-covered Pfeifferhorn towers majestically above Maybird Gulch. A member of a group crossing the gulch, on the way to a climb in Hogum Cirque, once asked, "Why travel around the world when you have this near your home?" The party included experienced climbers who had visited the Alps, Alaska, Peru, and Nepal; yet everyone agreed that there are few places to live that match the opportunities available here in the Wasatch.

MT. OLYMPUS SCRAMBLING ROUTES
North Face (No. MS-1)

Starting from a suburban street, the route follows the crest of a ridge, climbs steep slabs, then crosses into the hidden couloir that runs diagonally up the north face to the crest. There are only a few sections where use of hands is required, yet you climb through some of the wildest and steepest terrain in the Wasatch.

The photo traces the main features of the route. Start from the water tanks and continue on a faint foot track onto the crest of the steep ridge. Follow the ridge until it runs into the north face of the mountain, then drop into the tree-filled couloir to the west. Scramble up the steep slabs, following the trees, until you reach the top of the face that is actually separated from the main mountain. Drop into the large, grassy couloir behind and follow it up. This couloir can also be reached by a bushwhack up Norths Fork from Neffs Canyon. The last section is a scramble along the crest of the ridge to the north summit of Olympus.

Descent options include scrambling over to the south summit or descending the west ridge of the north summit.

North face of Mount Olympus. Route MS-1, is a mountaineering scramble. The route follows the dashed line up the ridge crest, drops right onto the difficult tree-covered slabs, then crosses into the hidden couloir (dotted line) which is followed to the summit ridge.

West Ridge of North Summit (No. MS-5)

This is the ridge that forms the distinctive skyline of Mount Olympus. The scrambling is on solid rock with plenty of good holds. Start from the standard hiking trail and look for a game trail heading left up the ridge, about 200 yards before the stream crossing in Tolcat Canyon. Climb northeast, utilizing the game trails until you reach the forested saddle at 7400 feet. The route is moderate off-trail hiking to the saddle and becomes scrambling beyond. Follow the ridge, with occasional detours into the couloir to the south. As you pass above the west slabs, the ridge narrows to a knife-edge that continues past the north face scrambling route and on to the north summit.

From North Summit to South Summit

The scramble between the summits of Olympus is usually done in combination with one of the other mountaineering routes. The safest route is to drop on the west to bypass the buttresses between the summits, then reascend to the tree-filled saddle immediately north of the south summit. The scramble up the wall of the south summit is very steep, but there are plenty of ledges and handholds.

Other Routes on Mount Olympus

In addition to these routes, John Gottman's book *Wasatch Quartzite* lists four routes up Olympus that involve easy technical rock climbing and much scrambling. These climbing routes are the West Slabs, the Great Chimney, the East Ridge of the North Summit, and the West Ridge of the South Summit (Geurt's Ridge).

WILDCAT RIDGE (No. MS-3)
Mount Olympus to Raymond

The skyline ridge east from Mount Olympus travels through a seldom-visited part of the Mount Olympus Wilderness. It offers access to the upper reaches of Mule Hollow, Whipple Fork, and Mill B North Fork Basin. I have seen mountain goats in this area twice, and rattlesnakes are common among the boulders.

From the Olympus summit to the pass between Neffs Canyon and Mill B Gulch, the route is a mountaineering scramble across knife-edged ridges, around pinnacles, and through boulderfields. There is no trail and only occasional animal tracks. The continuation from the Neffs/Mill B saddle to Porter Fork is on an unmaintained trail (See No. B-11.1). Most parties will require 10 to 12 hours to complete the route. Starting from Olympus puts the most difficult part early in the day.

From the south summit of Olympus, follow the ridge east picking your way down through small cliffs. The knife-edge section ahead is the most difficult part of the route. Stay on the ridge crest or within 50 feet of it on the Heughs Canyon side until you reach the saddle above Norths Fork at 8600 feet. From here, drop well off the ridge and traverse until you reach a ramp, covered with gravel and boulders, leading up to the easy summit slabs of Peak 9400, called Triangle Peak for its distinctive north face. The distance from Mt. Olympus to Triangle Peak is less than a mile but can require three hours. A possible shortcut goes from the saddle south of Mt. Olympus and traverses down into Heughs Canyon before climbing back to Triangle Peak. This shortcut requires careful track finding.

From Triangle Peak to the head of Whipple Fork, stay generally near the ridge crest except for a short traverse on the north side of the ridge past Peak 9560. Next, continue on the forested ridge crest across the top of Peak 9773. Peak 9570 can be passed by ascending the short couloir on the north, then the ridge can be followed northeast for 1/4 mile to the second minor summit. Alternatively, you can drop into upper Whipple Fork and traverse below the couloirs splitting the red cliff face, then cross the ridge into Mill B and work back north to the main divide.

Follow the rounded, open ridge crest east, then northeast until you can drop down the brushy slope to the Neffs/Mill B saddle at 9200 feet. The Neffs Canyon Trail is below and the Porter Fork West Pass is reached by a foot track which traverses on the Big Cottonwood side. This track stays near the crest of the forested ridge but generally bypasses the minor summits.

Wildcat Ridge. The scrambling route along the ridge (Route MS-3) is the best access into this rugged area. The saddle on the right leads to Neffs Canyon and can be reached by hiking either route WF-1.1 or B-11.1.

TWIN PEAKS VIA STAIRS GULCH
(No. MS-4)

Stairs Gulch is walled by buttresses and steep slabs, with the magnificent east face of Storm Mountain towering high above. This route is best done in late spring or early summer, after the last avalanches have released from the slabs but before the melting snow exposes the boulders. Be alert to weak snow bridges with running water below. An ice axe is essential and crampons are recommended.

The Storm Mountain hiking trail ends in 1/2 mile. The mountaineering route continues, staying generally to the left side of the gulch, making detours as needed to avoid cliffs. About 1/2 mile beyond the trail, a spur ridge begins to divide the gulch and the terrain tends to draw you to the west (right), but the route stays on the left. The ascent of Stairs Gulch to the crest of the ridge overlooking Broads Fork is a climb of 4000 feet in 1-1/2 miles. From here, scramble along the ridge for 3/4 mile passing on the Broads Fork side of two unnamed peaks, and continue to Twin Peaks. This ridge can also be reached by routes from Broads Fork and from Ferguson Canyon.

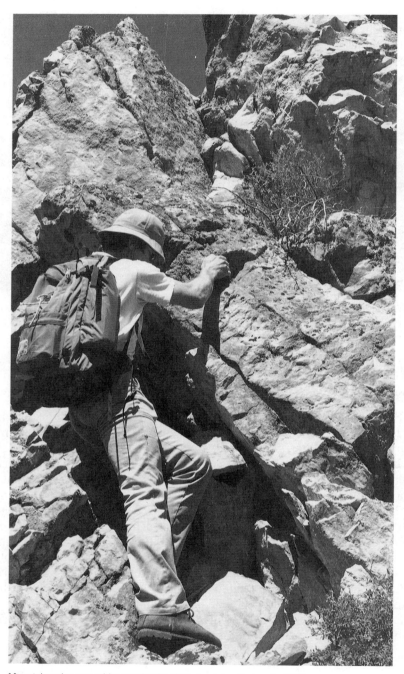

Mountaineering scrambles require the ability to make short rock climbing moves.

Glissading is a fast and exciting way to descend steep spring snow. This technique involves "skiing" the firm snow using your boots and should be attempted only after mastering use of an ice axe for self- arrest.

TANNERS GULCH–TRIPLE TRAVERSE
(No. MS-5)

This is the finest spring snow climb in the Wasatch. It ascends a steep couloir with several short rock bands, then climbs along the steep knife-edge connecting Dromedary, Sunrise, and Twin Peaks, followed by a choice of descent routes. The route offers a mix of snow, rock, and ice climbing problems.

This route must be done during a short time window, which normally occurs in late May or early June, after the last major avalanches have released and before the snow completely melts from Tanners Gulch. The best plan is to check snow conditions weekly and go when the route is safe. Once the snow melts, Tanners Gulch is full of falling rock and loose gravel. Since the route is long and exposed to avalanches and rockfall, a very early start is advisable. The entire party should be out of Tanners Gulch before 9 AM.

The route starts in Little Cottonwood Canyon and ascends Tanners Gulch, which is across the road from the Tanners Flat Campground. If the rock bands are exposed, some difficult scrambling up wet cracks will be required. The gulch forks near the top. The right branch leads to Dromedary Peak, while the left branch leads to the saddle between Dromedary and Sunrise. Follow the ridge crest from Dromedary over Sunrise Peak and over an unnamed peak, then scramble along the south side below the ridge crest to the saddle where this route joins the standard route from Broads Fork to Twin Peaks.

In spring, the fastest descent is down the snow fields in Broads Fork but the scramble down to Lisa Falls will avoid the need for a car shuttle, and the Deaf Smith Canyon descent is always spectacular.

SAM THOMAS GULCH

Sam Thomas Gulch is the gully immediately west of the very prominent waterfall located just west of Coalpit. The waterfall is very popular with ice climbers in winter, and Sam Thomas Gulch is often used as a climber descent route.

Hiking up the gulch is not difficult, but watch out for running water from the nearly permanent stream, some loose rock, and acres of stinging nettles. Start from the power plants on the road and bushwack into the gulch.

Getting out of the top is more challenging. You need to eventually travel east (left) and drop into Coalpit. Go onto the minor rocky ridge left of the stream as soon as it is easy to do so, and continue up the ridge until it's relatively easy to go left and down a short canyon which leads right to the base of the headwall of North Thunder. Dropping into Coalpit either too early or too late will result in an encounter with some difficult cliffs. The easiest ascent to the summit is along the left ridge.

The entire route up Sam Thomas Gulch, from the entry to the exit in Coalpit, is not more than a few thousand linear feet, but it seems a lot longer. It is an attractive, if somewhat unpleasant, route. It is a very good alternative to the lower part of Coalpit Gulch.

COTTONWOOD RIDGE (No. MS-7)
Mount Superior to Dromedary

This knife-edged ridge is a seldom-visited part of the Twin Peaks Wilderness. The south side drops steeply into Little Cottonwood Canyon, and the south approaches are limited to the Cardiff Pass route to Mount Superior, the South Ridge of Superior (a technical climb described in Gottman's *Wasatch Quartzite*, and Tanners Gulch. This ridge passes above the branches of Lake Blanche Fork and can be reached at several points from the Big Cottonwood side.

This section of the Cottonwood Ridge contains difficult scrambling over and around pinnacles and involves about 1300 feet of ascent and descent in 1-3/4 miles. Progress is agonizingly slow but the purpose of a mountaineering route is adventure.

COALPIT GULCH (No. MS-8)

North Thunder Mountain

This narrow and intimidating notch in lower Little Cottonwood Canyon leads through the cliffs into a beautiful hanging canyon, perched between Hogum Cirque and upper Bells Canyon and inaccessible to anyone but expert hikers and climbers. The north peak of Thunder Mountain lies at the head of the gulch.

Start from the power station, 1.9 miles up Little Cottonwood Canyon. Find your way to the stream draining northwest out of Coalpit Gulch, and follow the stream up between the granite buttresses. The scrambling route stays very near the stream and may be impassable during peak runoff. The sidewalls are treacherous, with loose handholds and false routes to trap the unwary. Pass the first two waterfalls on the left. The third waterfall is the crux of the route and is passed by climbing near the stream, starting about 5 feet to the right of the waterfall. Above the third waterfall, the route traverses a broken ledge back toward the stream. Beyond here, the angle eases and the gulch soon widens. The route to North Thunder Mountain stays in the drainage until nearly 10,000 feet, then approaches the summit from the northeast along the ridge.

The lower gulch is a dangerous place, with rockfall from the cliffs and much loose rock underfoot. Climbing helmets are recommended. The party should contain either someone who has done the route before or a few experienced rock climbers who are confident at routefinding.

BIBLIOGRAPHY

HIKING AND MOUNTAINEERING

Bottcher, Betty: *Wasatch Trails, Volume* 1, Wasatch Mountain Club, Salt Lake City, 1973. The first local trail guide, over 30,000 copies sold but now somewhat inaccurate due to changes over the years. (out of print)

Gerry, Daniel: *Wasatch Trails, Volume 2,* Wasatch Mountain Club, c/o Wasatch Publishers, Salt Lake City, 1976. Intermediate and advanced hikes. Includes some not described in this book. (out of print)

Hall, Dave: *Hiking Guide to Utah,* Falcon Press Publishing: Billings, Montana 1982. Best state-wide hiking guidebook. Includes very detailed descriptions of nine routes in central Wasatch plus excellent background material.

Kelner, Alexis & Hanscom, Dave: *Wasatch Tours,* Wasatch Publishers, Salt Lake City, 1976. A ski touring guidebook covering the central Wasatch. The perspective drawings, photographs, and background information complement this book. (out of print)

Ringholtz, Raye Carlson: *Park City Trails,* Wasatch Publishers, Salt Lake City, 1984. Covers areas immediately to the east of this guidebook.

Paxman & Taylor: *Utah Valley Trails,* Wasatch Publishers, Salt Lake City, 1978. Covers areas south of American Fork Canyon.

Seattle Mountaineers: *Mountaineering, The Freedom of the Hills,* The Mountaineers, Seattle, WA. This is the classic book on wilderness travel, safety, the mountain environment, and mountaineering technique. It is highly recommended for anyone who leaves the maintained trails.

Veranth, John: *Wasatch Winter Trails,* Wasatch Publishers: Salt Lake City, 1991 A ski touring and snowshoe guidebook to the central Wasatch and eastern Uintas.

GEOLOGY–GENERAL

Stokes, William Lee: *Geology of Utah,* Utah Museum of Natural History, Salt Lake City, 1986. Superb presentation of statewide geology for the college student and curious amateur. Many maps and illustrations. Highly recommended.

Utah Geological and Mineral Survey: Salt Lake City, *Geology of Salt Lake County,* 1964. Detailed, but written for the layman. Out of print, but can be found in libraries.

GEOLOGY–TECHNICAL

Granger & Sharp: *The Geology of the Wasatch Mountains East of Salt Lake City,* in *Utah Geological Society Guidebook to the Geology of Utah* No. 8, 1952. Out of print.

James, Laurence: *Geology, Ore Deposits and History of the Big Cottonwood Mining District,* Utah Geological and Mineral Survey, Salt Lake City, 1979.

NATIVE PLANTS–GENERAL

Anderson, B.A. & A.H. Holmgren: *Mountain Plants of Northeastern Utah,* Circular 319, Utah State University, Logan, UT. Available through Utah State Extension Service. The best and most complete field guide for the Wasatch and Uintas. Uses clear line drawings and well written text to identify most of the common trees, shrubs and flowers. Highly Recommended.

Anderson, B.A. & A.H. Holmgren: *A Guide to Mountain Flowers,* Utah State University Extension Services, Logan, UT. A little beginner book that costs only a dollar. Keys by habitat and color. Good illustrations of terms for plant parts.

Craighead, J.J. *et al.*: *Field Guide to Rocky Mountain Wildflowers,* Peterson Field Guide Series, Houghton Mifflin Company, Boston. Regional in scope, with color pictures and interesting text.

Johnson, Carl M: *Native Trees of the Intermountain Region,* Utah State University, Logan. Key, photographs, and distribution maps are used.

Shaw, Richard J.:*Wildflowers of the Wasatch and Uinta Mountains,* Wheelwright Press. Color pictures make this a good beginners' book but it leaves out many common plants.

NATIVE PLANTS–TECHNICAL

Arnow, L., B. Albee, & A. Wycoff: *Flora of the Central Wasatch Front, Utah,* University of Utah, Salt Lake City, 1980. All you will ever want to know and more. This is the professionals' reference.

Treshow, Michael: *Wildflowers of the Western Rockies,* Out-of-print. Comprehensive fieldbook-size taxonomic key with line drawings.

Welsh, Stanly, N. Duane Atwood, Sherel Goodrich, and Larry Higgins: *A Utah Flora,* Brigham Young University, Provo, UT. 1987. Most recent reference.

WILDLIFE–GENERAL

Baker, W., *et al.*: *Wildlife of the Northern Rocky Mountains,* Naturegraph Publishers: Happy Camp, CA. This field size book covers habitats, common plants, mammals, birds, reptiles, and amphibians with text and line drawings. Coverage includes the Wasatch.

Burt, W.H., & R.P. Grossenheider: *A Field Guide to the Mammals,* Peterson Field Guide Series, Houghton Mifflin Co., Boston, 1964. Has distribution maps and color plates. Covers all species found north of Mexico.

Chandler, R.S., B. Bruun, & H.S. Zim: *Birds of North America,* Golden Field Guide Series, Golden Press, New York, 1983. More up-to-date on taxonomy and easier to use than the Peterson Guide to Western Birds.

Murie, Olaus: *A Field Guide to Animal Tracks,* Peterson Field Guide Series, Houghton Mifflin Co., Boston. Tracks are the best way to locate rare and nocturnal mammals.

Peterson, Roger Tory: *A Field Guide to Western Birds,* Peterson Field Guide Series, Houghton Mifflin Co., Boston, 1961.

WILDLIFE–TECHNICAL

Behle, W.H., E.D. Sorensen, & C.M. White: *Utah Birds: A Revised Checklist,* Utah Museum of Natural History, Salt Lake City, 1985. Distribution and occurrence data and an extensive bibliography.

Crane, Harold: *The Mammals of Salt Lake County,* University of Utah Thesis, 1948. Documents extensive field work with live traps. More recent distribution and taxonomy studies exist for Davis, Summit, and Utah Counties.

HISTORY AND ENVIRONMENTAL ISSUES

Kelner, Alexis: *Skiing in Utah, A History,* Alexis Kelner, Salt Lake City, 1980. Extensive photographs, personal interviews and bibliography.

Hardy, Clyde: *The Historical Development of Wasatch Trails in Salt Lake County,* MS Thesis, Brigham Young University, Provo, UT, 1975.

Peterson, Charles: "Albert F. Potter's Wasatch Survey, 1902," in *Utah Historical Quarterly,* Volume 39 No. 3, 1971.

U.S. Department of Agriculture, Forest Service: *Salt Lake Planning Unit, Land Management Plan,* 1979.

COMMON HIKING AND MOUNTAINEERING TERMS

Boulder-hopping: Travel across large relatively stable rocks. This is very exhausting and slow since the hiker is constantly stepping up and jumping down.

Bushwhack: Off-trail travel through brush where no cleared path exists and hikers have to force their way through the branches.

Cairn: A small pile of stones used as a trail marker.

Cirque: The steep walled bowl carved by glacial action at the head of a side canyon.

Couloir: A steep, relatively narrow groove in a rock wall. Typically, couloirs are wider than "cracks" and smaller than "gullies," and are important as routes up the mountainside.

Crampons: A set of metal spikes which are strapped to the boots to provide secure footing on steep ice or consolidated snow.

Knife-edge: A very narrow ridge crest. In spots, the crest of a knife-edge is too angular to walk on, and travel requires scrambling over and around pinnacles, along ledges on the side of the ridge, or even straddling the ridge.

Massif: A compact mountain group consisting of several summits.

Scree: Loose rock, typically fist size or smaller that accumulates at the base of a rock wall. See Talus.

Side Canyons: In decreasing order of size, local usage is: Canyon, fork, gulch.

Switchback: A sharp turn, typically constructed on trails climbing steep slopes, to allow ascending in a series of more gradual segments.

Talus: The loose rock of all sizes that falls from a cliff and accumulates at the base. The distinction between scree and talus is generally that talus is large enough not to move underfoot.

Technical Climbing: Mountain climbing requiring use of ropes and fixed belay anchors on either rock or ice. Also includes any sustained climbing where the arms are used to pull upward rather than being used solely for balance.

Traverse: Horizontal travel across a mountainside or over a ridge. An ascending or descending traverse refers to a gradual elevation change while traveling across a much steeper slope.

MAMMAL CHECKLIST FOR THE CENTRAL WASATCH MOUNTAINS

Insectivors (Insectivora)

Masked Shrew	Sorex cinereus	
Vagrant Shrew	Sorex vagarans	Desert to Montane Streamside
Water Shrew	Sorex palustris	Foothill to Alpine Streamside

Bats (Chiroptera)

The source lists include a total of 10 species but there is poor agreement between studies as to which ones are present.

Rabbits, Hares, and Pikas (Lagomorpha)

Pika	Ochotona princeps	Rock, Montane Zone
White-Tailed Jackrabbit	Lepus townsendii	Foothill
Black-Tailed Jackrabbit	Lepus californicus	Valley
Snowshoe Hare	Lepus americanus	Montane Zone
Nuttals Cottontail	Sylvilagus nuttallii	Foothill

Rodents (Rodentia)

Least Chipmunk	Eutamias minimus	Foothill & Montane
Cliff Chipmunk	Eutamias dorsalis	Montane
Unita Chipmunk	Eutamias umbrinus	Foothill shrub
Yellow-bellied Marmot	Mormota flaviventris	Alpine Zone
Uinta Ground Squirrel	Citellus armatus	Foothill & Montane
Golden-manteled Squirrel	Citellus lateralis	Montane rock
Rock Squirrel	Citellus variegatus	Foothill
Red Squirrel	Tamiasciurus hudsonicus	Montane
Northern Flying Squirrel	Glaucomys sabrinus	Montane
Northern Pocket Gopher	Thomomys talpoides	Foothill & Montane
Beaver	Castor canadensis	Foothill & Montane streamside
Deer Mouse	Peromyscus maniculatus	Desert to Montane Zones
Pinion Mouse	Peromyscus truei	Foothill rock
Western Jumping Mouse	Zapus princeps	Montane streamside
Boreal Redback Vole	Clethrionomys gapperi	Montane
Longtail Vole	Microtus longicaudus	Foothill & Montane streamside
Bigfooted Vole	Microtus richardsoni	Montane streamside
Mountain Vole	Microtus montanus	Desert to Montane streamside
Bushytail Woodrat	Neotoma cinerea	Montane
Muskrat	Ondatra zibethica	Streamside
Porcupine	Erethizon dorsatum	Foothill & Montane

Carnivores (Carnivora)

Black Bear	*Ursus americanus*	Montane
Pine Martin	*Martes americana*	Montane
Long-tailed Weasel	*Mustela frenata*	Desert to Montane
Mink	*Mustela vison*	Foothill streamside
Spotted Skunk	*Spilogale putorius*	Desert & Foothill
Striped Skunk	*Mephitis mephitis*	Desert & Foothill
Badger	*Taxidea taxus*	Foothill & Montane
Coyote	*Canis latrans*	Desert to Montane
Red Fox	*Vulpes vulpes*	Hypothetical
Mountain Lion	*Felis concolor*	Montane
Bobcat	*Lynx rufus*	Foothill

Deer (Cervidae)

Mule Deer	*Odocoileus hemionus*	Foothill & Montane
Elk	*Cervus canadensis*	Foothill & Montane
Moose	*Alces alces*	Montane Streamside

Goats & Sheep (Bovidae)

Mountain Goat	*Oreamnos americanus*	Cliffs, Introduced 1967
Bighorn Sheep	*Ovis canadensis*	Native — No longer in area.

This list was compiled from the following studies:

Crane (1948)	*Mammals of Salt Lake County*	Univ. of Utah Thesis
Dearden (1967)	*Mammals of Summit County*	Univ. of Utah Thesis
Frost (1970)	*Mammals of Davis County*	Univ. of Utah Thesis
Bee (1947)	*Mammals of Utah County*	BYU Thesis

The Wasatch Mountains are within the historical or hypothetical range of additional species. Also, this list does not include reported species which are normally found in the Desert Shrub Zone unless they are also common at higher elevations.

HIKE MASTER LIST

WASATCH MOUNTAIN CLUB

Founded 1920

Article II of the WMC Constitution

The purpose shall be to promote the physical and spiritual well being of its members and others by outdoor activities: to unite the energy, interests and knowledge of students, explorers, and lovers of the mountains, deserts and rivers of Utah: to collect and disseminate information regarding the Rocky Mountains in behalf of science, literature, and art: to explore and picture the scenic wonders of this and surrounding states: to foster awareness of scenic beauties: and to encourage preservation of our natural areas including their plant, animal, and bird life.

Early Days of Wasatch Mountain Club.

The Wasatch Mountain Club schedules frequent hikes throughout the season. This *group is on a Thursday Night hike which started after work and climbed to Circle-All Peak. To keep the group size down, Thursday Night hikes are for members only, but most hikes are open to non-members.*

THE WASATCH MOUNTAIN CLUB

The Wasatch Mountain Club has introduced thousands of people to the local mountains since it was founded in 1920. It began as a small group of hikers who started their outings with a train ride from downtown Salt Lake City to the mountains, and it has grown into a large outdoor-activity social and conservation organization.

There are currently over 1200 members, ranging in age from teenagers to octogenarians. The club has a very active trip schedule including hiking, ski touring, bicycling, rock climbing, mountain and desert backpacking, rafting, kayaking, and canoeing. The club lodge at Brighton is used for scheduled activities and is also available for rental to members and to community groups. The lodge was built in the 1930's and is now a registered historic site. The conservation activites of the club include public education and active representatives on committees and study groups.

During the April through September hiking season, the Wasatch Mountain Club schedules four to eight hikes per weekend. Usually there are beginner, intermediate, and advanced hikes scheduled on both Saturday and Sunday. Most hikes are open to non-members and are an excellent way to meet people and see the mountains.

A membership application and two sample issues of the club's monthly newsletter, *The Rambler* **, can be obtained by sending a request and $3.00 to the Membership Director, Wasatch Mountain Club, 888 South 200 East, Salt Lake City. Prospective members need to participate in two scheduled outings and have the application form signed by the trip leaders.**

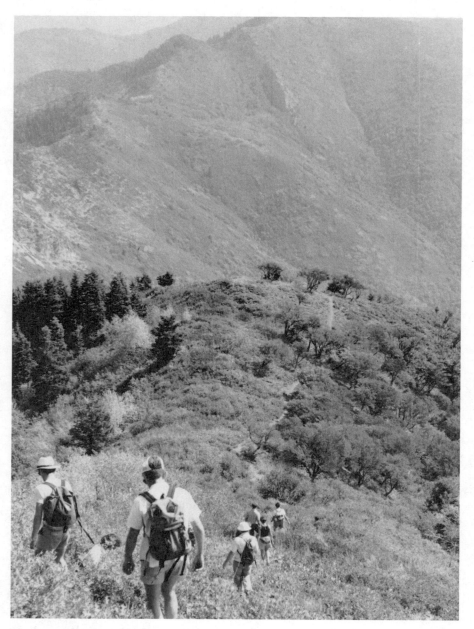

Hikers returning home from Grandeur Peak.

BIOGRAPHICAL NOTE

A first hike, like a first love, is a memorable and hopefully rewarding experience. My first real hike was with a group of college acquaintances ascending Mount Monadnock in New Hampshire in 1967. Before that, I had taken short walks through the woods in the flatlands of the Midwest, but this was different. This was a trail up a real mountain. My legs ached all the way up, but the changing views of New England rock and fall foliage were enough motivation. That experience started an interest that has grown into an obsession. Hikes became longer and more frequent until I was planning my time to take trips from Boston to the mountains every weekend.

I would listen to fellow members of the MIT Outing Club describe their trips to the mountains in the west. Right after graduation, I came to Salt Lake City for a job interview and managed to squeeze in only a short hike in the foothills. I did not get the job but I had fallen in love with the Wasatch.

Important affairs kept me east for a few more years, and I had to be satisfied with the low mountains of New Hampshire, Pennsylvania, and West Virginia, and with summer trips to the west. After I finished graduate school, my wife of four months and I headed west determined to find work near the mountains. I found an engineering job in Salt Lake and we quickly became active in the Wasatch Mountain Club.

From that original mountain hike, my interests have expanded to include desert hiking, snowshoeing, cross-country skiing, river running, technical rock climbing, and expedition mountaineering. Outings have included many of the most enjoyable days of my life and hiking has remained a favorite activity.

Writing this book was motivated by a desire to organize and record the information I had gained from other hikers over the years so it could be shared with those who are just discovering the marvels of the Wasatch.

John Veranth

OTHER LOCAL GUIDEBOOKS

Wasatch Quartzite by John Gottman, forward by Harold Goodrow. Wasatch Mountain Club, c/o Wasatch Publishers, 1979. A rock climbing guide to many moderate climbs and scrambles. Includes a history of the early days of climbing in the Wasatch. $3.00

Wasatch Trails, Volume 2 by Daniel Gerry. Wasatch Mountain Club, c/o Wasatch Publishers, 1976. Intermediate and advanced hikes, including some not described in **Hiking The Wasatch.** $2.50

Park City Trails by Raye Carlson Ringholtz. Wasatch Publishers, 1984. Covers areas on the east side of the Wasatch which are readily accesible from Park City. $6.50

High Uinta Trails by Mel Davis and John Veranth. Wasatch Publishers, 1992. Hiking, backpacking and fishing guide to the High Uintas Wilderness Area. $7.50

Wasatch Winter Trails by John Veranth. Wasatch Publishers, 1991. A ski touring and snowshoe guide to the central Wasatch and eastern Uintas. $7.00

Hiking the Wasatch—The Official Wasatch Mountain Club Trail Map for the Tri-Canyon Area by Dale Green and Connie Pixton. Wasatch Mountain Club and the University of Utah Press, 1994. A topographic map for Mill Creek, Big Cottonwood, and Little Cottonwood Canyons. $9.95

These books are available in local bookstores and outdoor shops and are available by mail order from the publisher:

Wasatch Publishers
4460 Ashford Drive
Salt Lake City, Utah 84124

Please include $2.00 per order for postage and handling.

Prices subject to change without notice.